Obstetrics/Gynecology and the Law

health administration press

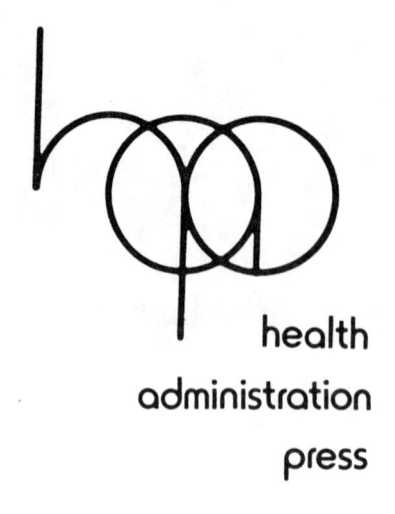

EDITORIAL BOARD

John R. Griffith
Chairman
The University of Michigan

Gary L. Filerman
Association of University Programs in Health Administration

Gordon D. Brown
University of Missouri-Columbia

R. Hopkins Holmberg
Boston University

Arnold D. Kaluzny
University of North Carolina

Carl Meilicke
University of Alberta

Stephen M. Shortell
Northwestern University

David G. Warren
Duke University

The Press was established in 1972 with the support of the W.K. Kellogg Foundation as a joint endeavor of the Association of University Programs in Health Administration (Washington, D.C.) and The University of Michigan Program and Bureau of Hospital Administration.

Obstetrics/Gynecology and the Law

Keith S. Fineberg, J.D.
J. Douglas Peters, J.D.
J. Robert Willson, M.D.
Donald A. Kroll, M.D., Ph.D.

Health Administration Press
1984

Copyright © 1984 by the Regents of The University of Michigan. Printed in the United States of America. All rights reserved. This book or parts thereof may not be reproduced in any form without written permission of the publisher.

Library of Congress Cataloging in Publication Data
Main entry under title:
Obstetrics/gynecology and the law.
  Bibliography: p.
  Includes index.
  1. Obstetricians—Malpractice—United States. 2. Obstetricians—Legal status, laws, etc.—United States. 3. Obstetrics—Law and legislation—United States. 4. Gynecologists—Malpractice—United States. 5. Gynecologists—Legal status, laws, etc.—United States.
I. Fineberg, Keith S., 1951-   . [DNLM: 1. Obstetrics—United States—Legislation.
2. Gynecology—United States—Legislation. 3. Malpractice—United States—Legislation.
4. Jurisprudence—United States. WP 33 AA1 014]
KF2910.G943O27   1983   344.73'0412   83-18409
ISBN 0-914904-93-0   347.304412

Health Administration Press
School of Public Health
The University of Michigan
1021 East Huron
Ann Arbor, Michigan 48109
(313) 764-1380

Contents

Abbreviations xi

Foreword xii

Preface xiv

LEGAL ASPECTS OF OBSTETRICAL
AND GYNECOLOGICAL CARE

PART I: LIABILITY

Chapter I: The Law of Malpractice 5

§ 1.10	Introduction 5
§ 1.20	Elements of Negligence 9
§ 1.30	Duty 10
	§ 1.31 The Physician-Patient Relationship 13
	§ 1.32 Standard of Care 21
	§ 1.33 Consent and Informed Consent 30
§ 1.40	Breach of Duty 39
§ 1.50	Causation 42
	§ 1.51 Legal Principles of Causation 43
	§ 1.52 Res Ipsa Loquitur 47
§ 1.60	Damages 56

Chapter II: Other Theories of Liability 76

§ 2.10	Introduction 76
§ 2.20	Contract Theory 76
§ 2.30	Vicarious Liability 83

		§ 2.31 Liability of the Surgeon 87
		§ 2.32 Liability of the Hospital 89
§	2.40	Birth-Related Causes of Action 92
		§ 2.41 Wrongful Conception 93
		§ 2.42 Wrongful Birth 98
		§ 2.43 Wrongful Life 102
§	2.50	Legal Status of the Fetus 105
§	2.60	Liability Arising from Medical Records 108
§	2.70	Products Liability 111
		§ 2.71 Theories of Recovery 111
		§ 2.72 Defective Products 122
		§ 2.73 Procedural Aspects 127

Chapter III: Defenses 140

§	3.10	Introduction 140
§	3.20	Contributory Negligence 140
§	3.30	Comparative Negligence 145
§	3.40	Assumption of Risk 147
§	3.50	Statute of Limitations 148
§	3.60	Res Judicata and Collateral Estoppel 158
§	3.70	Release from Liability Forms 160

Chapter IV: The Lawsuit in Court 164

§	4.10	Introduction 164
§	4.20	Pleadings 164
		§ 4.21 The Patient's Complaint 165
		§ 4.22 The Physician's Answer 165
§	4.30	Discovery 166
		§ 4.31 Depositions 166
		§ 4.32 Subpoena 168
		§ 4.33 Written Interrogatories 168
		§ 4.34 Production of Documents and Things 168
		§ 4.35 Physical Examinations 169
		§ 4.36 Protective Orders 169
§	4.40	Evidence and Witnesses 169
		§ 4.41 Expert Testimony 170
		§ 4.42 Court-Appointed Expert 174
		§ 4.43 Hypothetical Question and Opinion Testimony 174
		§ 4.44 Textbooks 176
		§ 4.45 Adverse Witness Provisions 176
		§ 4.46 Physician-Patient Privilege 177

		§ 4.47 Medical Records 178
§	4.50	Countersuits 181

PART II: REGULATION

Chapter V: Governmental Regulation 189

§	5.10	Introduction 189
§	5.20	State Licensure 190
		§ 5.21 Requirements 192
		§ 5.22 Relicensure and Continuing Medical Education 196
		§ 5.23 Disciplinary Proceedings 197
§	5.30	Professional Review Organizations 205
§	5.40	Other Regulation 209
		§ 5.41 Drugs 209
		§ 5.42 Human and Fetal Research 213
		§ 5.43 Reporting Requirements 215
		§ 5.44 Testing Requirements 218
		§ 5.45 Abortion 220
		§ 5.46 Contraception 228
		§ 5.47 Sterilization 230

Chapter VI: Professional Regulation 250

§	6.10	Specialty Certification 250
		§ 6.11 Obstetricians and Gynecologists 251
		§ 6.12 Professional Organizations 254
§	6.20	Midwives 256
		§ 6.21 American College of Nurse-Midwives 257
		§ 6.22 Nurse-Midwife Legislation 261
		§ 6.23 Lay Midwives 263

Chapter VII: Hospital Regulation 267

§	7.10	Introduction 267
§	7.20	Origin and Development 267
§	7.30	Types of Hospitals 268
§	7.40	Legal Bases for Hospital Operation 271
		§ 7.41 Corporations 271
		§ 7.42 Bylaws 272
§	7.50	Organization and Administration 274
		§ 7.51 Governing Board 274
		§ 7.52 Hospital Administrator 275

		§ 7.53 Medical and Other Staff	276
§	7.60	Services and Procedures	277
		§ 7.61 Admissions	277
		§ 7.62 Emergencies	277
		§ 7.63 Discharge.......................................	279
		§ 7.64 Utilization Review Committee	279
		§ 7.65 Abortion and Sterilization.......................	280
§	7.70	Regulation of the Hospital	282
		§ 7.71 Joint Commission on the Accreditation of Hospitals ..	282
		§ 7.72 Licensure	283
		§ 7.73 Certificate of Need	283
		§ 7.74 Professional Review Organizations	284
§	7.80	Obstetric and Gynecologic Services	284
		§ 7.81 JCAH Standards	284
		§ 7.82 State Regulation	286
§	7.90	Medical Staff Privileges	288
		§ 7.91 Substantive Due Process	288
		§ 7.92 Procedural Due Process	290
§	7.100	Exclusive Contracts	291

MEDICAL-LEGAL ASPECTS OF OBSTETRICAL AND GYNECOLOGICAL CARE

Introduction 301

PART III: CONTRACEPTION AND CONCEPTION

Chapter VIII: Contraception 305

§	8.10	Oral Contraceptives	305
§	8.20	Intrauterine Devices	311
§	8.30	Sterilization	319

Chapter IX: Genetic Counseling 329

§	9.10	Pre-conception Counseling	329
§	9.20	Genetic Screening	332
§	9.30	Amniocentesis	335

PART IV: PREGNANCY AND BIRTH

Chapter X: Pregnancy 347

§ 10.10	Diagnosis	347
	§ 10.11 Extrauterine Pregnancy	359
§ 10.20	Management	363
	§ 10.21 Rubella	364
	§ 10.22 Preeclampsia and Eclampsia	369
	§ 10.23 Fetal Condition	374
	§ 10.24 Spontaneous Abortion	378
	§ 10.25 Administration of Drugs	384
	§ 10.26 Substance Abuse	388
§ 10.30	Abortion	392
§ 10.40	Surrogate Parenting	398

Chapter XI: Parturition 403

§ 11.10	Labor	403
	§ 11.11 Induction of Labor	407
§ 11.20	Delivery	413
	§ 11.21 Breech Presentation	414
	§ 11.22 Dystocia	420
	§ 11.23 Placental Anomalies	427
	§ 11.24 Rupture of the Amnion	430
	§ 11.25 Forceps Delivery	433
	§ 11.26 Cesarean Section	438
	§ 11.27 Episiotomy	447
§ 11.30	Obstetrical Analgesia and Anesthesia	450
§ 11.40	Fathers in the Delivery Room	460

Chapter XII: Postpartum Complications 467

§ 12.10	Hemorrhage and Hypovolemic Shock	467
§ 12.20	Infection	471
§ 12.30	Injury to the Child	475

PART V: ASPECTS OF GYNECOLOGY

Chapter XIII: Diagnosis and Treatment 485

§ 13.10	Physical Examination and Evaluation	485
§ 13.20	Hysterectomy	497
§ 13.30	Dilation and Curettage	516

Chapter XIV: Diseases 524

§ 14.10   Cancer 524
§ 14.20   Endometriosis 538
§ 14.30   Infections of the Pelvis 542

Appendix A: Invalid Release Form 555

Appendix B: Sample Complaint (Fact Pleading) and Sample Answers ... 557

Appendix C: 1982 Joint Commission Utilization Review Requirements .. 569

Appendix D: Sample Obstetrics/Gynecology Department Protocol 571

Appendix E: Ethical Issues in Surrogate Motherhood 579

Appendix F: Sample Assault Victim Medical Report Form 583

Appendix G: Medical History of the Sexual Assualt Victim 590

Appendix H: General Office Procedures 591

Appendix I: Sample Patient Care Flow Chart 592

Glossary 593

Selected Bibliography 601

Index to Case Illustrations 603

Subject Index 606

Abbreviations

AAMC	Association of American Medical Colleges
ABMS	American Board of Medical Specialties
ABOG	American Board of Obstetrics and Gynecology, Inc.
ACNM	American College of Nurse-Midwives
ACOG	American College of Obstetricians and Gynecologists
AMA	American Medical Association
CAT	Computerized axial tomography
CIN	Cervical intraepithelial neoplasia
CME	Continuing medical education
D&C	Dilation and curettage
d.a.w.	Dispense as written
DES	Diethylstilbestrol
DHHS	Department of Health and Human Services
FCSA	Federal Controlled Substances Act
FDA	Food and Drug Administration
FMG	Foreign medical graduate
FTC	Federal Trade Commission
HCFA	Health Care Financing Administration
HCG	Human chorionic gonadotropin
IUD	Intrauterine device
IUGR	Intrauterine growth retarded
JCAH	Joint Commission on the Accreditation of Hospitals
LSD	Lysergic acid diethylamide
NAIC	National Association of Insurance Commissioners
OMB	Office of Management and Budget
PKU	Phenylketonuria
PRO	Professional Review Organization
PSRO	Professional Standards Review Organization
THC	Tetrahydrocannabinol
UCSA	Uniform Controlled Substances Act

Foreword

As an attorney who instructs health administration and other students and also interacts in the practice of law with hospital executives and medical personnel, my experience has been that comprehension of the law's relation to clinical activities is often poor. In *Obstetrics/Gynecology and the Law,* the authors, Keith S. Fineberg, J. Douglas Peters, J. Robert Willson, and Donald A. Kroll have achieved a synthesis of law and medicine oriented toward obstetrical-gynecological practice. However, the basic material in this book deals with a wide variety of matters, such as the function of the expert witness, the physician-patient privilege, and the principles of liability and thus constitutes a fund of information useful to all physicians, regardless of clinical specialty.

The authors have judiciously used case illustrations—summaries of actual decisions in litigation—to emphasize, dramatize, and clarify important elements of their text. Perhaps of greatest value in this book are the discussion of the scope of practice issues and the emphasis upon the cruciality of the factual questions in litigation. Matters of licensing, legislation definitions, customary medical delegation practices, and so on abound in the area of scope of practice issues, and these issues are not handled uniformly in the various states.

As for the importance of the facts in litigation, a frequent concern expressed by physicians, regardless of specialty, is that the jury or the court will be "wrong" on the basic medical issues in a particular case. Attorneys have difficulty in conveying to physicians that the jury and judge are bound by the evidence submitted at trial. When the events in a case—elapsed time, presence of signs of patient distress, and so on—are disputed, or when the standard of care applied to the provider is the subject of conflict, the result of litigation may offend physicians who read media accounts of such litigation or the court reports themselves.

In Parts III-V, the device of organizing both medical and legal authority respecting the standard of care for various aspects of obstetrical-gynecological services has many advantages. It works well for reference purposes and for readers with specific concerns about the currently recognized standard of care.

The authors frankly acknowledge that the device requires the reader to exercise caution, particularly with regard to legal authority. Because the trier of fact is bound by evidence of the standard of care specific to a given point in time, changes in practice standards reflecting new developments or questionable expert testimony occasionally make legal authority unreliable guidance respecting professionally appropriate medical services. On several occasions members of an audience have come up to me after a talk to inform me that, though the legal principles in the case I discussed were correct, the standard of medical practice reflected in the court's opinion no longer is, and perhaps never was, in conformity with recognized standards of practice.

The authors have also made it possible for providers of obstetrical-gynecological care to understand how changes in their performance can build a better fact situation and minimize the potential for liability in the event an untoward occurrence precipitates a claim, or even litigation. This may well reflect the experience of one of the authors, attorney J. Douglas Peters, a shareholder with Charfoos, Christensen, Gilbert & Archer, P.C., a Detroit law firm actively engaged in professional liability litigation. To the extent that the number and severity of incidents involving apparent or actual harm are reduced by greater awareness, the interests of providers and the public they serve are fostered.

The contribution made by the authors is an extremely valuable one, and the availability of this book as a source of information in this period of renewed attention to enhancing patient care and concern about liability should be welcomed by all involved in the health and medical services field. I will add in conclusion that this volume will most certainly be a welcome addition to the libraries of both plaintiff and defense attorneys who specialize in malpractice litigation.

Nathan Hershey
Professor of Health Law
Graduate School of
Public Health
University of Pittsburgh

Preface

This book is designed to serve as a reference and resource tool for obstetricians and gynecologists, attorneys with medical-legal practices, hospital administrators, and medical-legal educators and students. The underlying assumption is that well-informed physicians, like well-informed patients, are better able to choose courses of action consistent with their own best interests, as well as with those of society in general. The physician who is able to evaluate both the medical and the legal implications of a medical situation can avoid possible unexpected legal consequences that may follow a well-intentioned medical action. Seeing how and where liability has been imposed on obstetricians and gynecologists may also help the physician avoid medical malpractice suits.

The material presented in the text is based on reported obstetrical and gynecological cases, statutes, regulations, court rules, and rules of evidence from the 50 state jurisdictions, as well as on Supreme Court decisions and federal statutes and regulations applicable to the practice of obstetrics and gynecology.

In approaching the legal system, two thoughts should be kept in mind. First, the legal system is not a unity; rather, it is comprised of a multiplicity of federal and state jurisdictions, each with its own rules and case law. Second, not all questions of law, whether relevant to the practice of medicine or to private life in general, have been decided in any one particular jurisdiction. Therefore, gaps and uncertainties pervade the field. For instance, in response to the same question, Wisconsin may have answered in the affirmative, New York in the negative, and to complicate matters even more, Michigan may not have taken a position at all.

Where divergent doctrines exist, each is presented, because the law is subject to change: one jurisdiction may approve of and eventually adopt the law of another. Which doctrines apply to an individual obstetrician or gynecologist depends largely on the jurisdiction in which he or she practices.

This book is not intended as a substitute for competent legal counsel. Because the entire field of law and medicine is one of the most highly legislated, highly regulated, and highly litigated areas of law, it changes daily. And because the changes are often significant, competent legal counsel should always be consulted for definitive answers to questions of law. We have attempted to define and demonstrate the concept of standard of care, as articulated by legal decisions and medical authority. With this concept as a framework, specific obstetrical or gynecological standards governing diagnosis, treatment, and management of pregnancy have been identified. We realize both that these standards are never static and that leading authorities may differ on the validity of a particular treatment procedure. Accordingly, we intend to invite debate as to the validity and relevancy of the standards stated by offering this reference text to those who make life-and-death decisions daily. It is hoped that these written standards will stimulate discussion that will result in further clarification and accuracy, inuring to the benefit of both the practitioner and the patient.

An extensive staff was involved in the preparation of this text. Staff members include Elaine Brock, M.H.S.A., J.D., and John R. Gillespie, J.D., staff attorneys; Jody Aaron, Claire de Chazal, Paul Falon, Janice Fernette, Debbie Greenspan, Adrienne Gregory, James Kalyvas, Jacqueline Kuster, Steven Meador, Thomas Moga, Marcia Murray, David Parker, Martin Richards, James Seitz, Patricia A. Steele, research assistants; and Sherri Gorelick, Sharon LeGoullon, Alison Novick, Linda Pierce, Jill Taber, Julie Valentine, Carole Worthing, and Gail Zumstein, secretaries and materials coordinators. We wish to recognize and thank each of these individuals for the time and effort they have contributed to the production of this text.

Finally, we extend our special thanks to Charles Aldridge, M.D., for his review and critique of the manuscript in its final stages of completion.

    Keith S. Fineberg
    J. Douglas Peters
    J. Robert Willson
    Donald A. Kroll

Ann Arbor, Michigan
June 1983

LEGAL ASPECTS OF OBSTETRICAL AND GYNECOLOGICAL CARE

Part I
Liability

Chapter I

The Law of Malpractice

§1.10 INTRODUCTION

Patients have always been entitled to sue their physicians under the American legal system. Until the 1950s, however, malpractice lawsuits were relatively rare. From 1950 until the mid-1960s, malpractice lawsuits steadily increased at a rate of two to five percent per annum. Beginning in the mid-1960s, the rate of increase jumped suddenly to 15 percent per annum, a rate that has been more or less maintained since.[1]

The term "malpractice" refers to any professional misconduct that embodies an unreasonable lack of skill or fidelity in carrying out professional or fiduciary duties.[2] The purpose of the medical malpractice lawsuit is to afford recovery for damages sustained as a result of a physician's failure to exercise ordinary and reasonable care in the diagnosis and treatment of a patient.[3]

Currently, malpractice theory provides the predominant mode for imposing liability on physicians, although physicians may find themselves involved in suits brought on other legal theories. Thus, physicians may be sued for disclosing confidential medical information (see § 2.60, Liability Arising from Medical Records), for injury resulting from the use of a defective drug or medical product (see § 2.70, Products Liability), or for the negligent acts of health care personnel providing treatment under the direction of the physician (see § 2.30, Vicarious Liability). However, most suits brought against physicians on these other theories usually involve malpractice principles as well. The purpose of this chapter is to acquaint the physician with the legal concepts involved in the typical medical lawsuit, providing the necessary legal vocabulary to apply these principles to the practice of obstetrics and gynecology.

From its beginnings, the law has imposed liability on the physician if his or her conduct failed to reflect professional skill and care. As the law of contracts developed, courts increasingly analyzed the physician's liability in terms of emerging contract concepts[4] (see § 2.20, Contract Theory). The negligence action developed later: negligence as a separate tort has been recognized only for about one-and-a-half centuries. As this branch of law took shape, courts began adopting its principles for application to medical malpractice cases.[5] Currently, both contract and negligence theories may be used in a malpractice suit in most jurisdictions, and the outcome of the suit can often depend upon which theory the patient-plaintiff adopts. Contract as a basis of the malpractice suit has fallen into disfavor in many jurisdictions where the courts are disinclined to interpret a physician's words of reassurance as contractual obligations to achieve certain results.[6] Some states, such as Michigan, have gone so far as to legislate that, in order for a patient to recover against a physician on a breach of contract claim, the contract must be expressed rather than implied *and* it must be in writing.[7]

Limiting the legal theories under which a malpractice lawsuit may be brought has not, however, had much of an impact on the number of suits brought. The incidence of malpractice litigation increased to such an extent in the mid-1970s that many commentators saw fit to label the phenomenon a "malpractice crisis." Although this label suggests a deterioration of quality in medical care, it actually reflects a number of factors, including the increasing unavailability and high cost of malpractice insurance coverage, double-digit inflation, increasing health care costs, and a higher claims consciousness on the part of the public. One outgrowth of the malpractice crisis has been the efforts of various groups to develop statistical analyses of the phenomenon. With statistical data categorized according to specific medical procedures, medical specialties, and other such isolated contributing factors, some health care facilities have proposed so-called "risk management" programs to alleviate the problem, relying on subsequent data to validate their efforts. These data also provide another perspective: even if the incidence of malpractice is on the decline, as some observers currently maintain,[8] the data identify the relative "malpractice risk" associated with various medical procedures.

In June 1975, The National Association of Insurance Commissioners (NAIC), a voluntary, unincorporated association of the insurance commissioners from 54 states and territories, adopted a statistical program for medical malpractice and initiated the collection of comprehensive data on claims closed since July 1975 that were reported by insurers writing $1 million or more worth of malpractice insurance in any year since 1970.[9] The data consider 3,879 cases by specialty, of which 548 were generated by the practices of obstetricians or gynecologists. Of these cases, 94 percent were attributed to those who regularly perform major surgery, five percent to those performing minor surgery, and less than one percent to those who reported performing no surgery. The dollar amounts for these three subgroups, respectively, were $17,026,883 (97 percent), $498,562 (three percent), and $11,456 (less than one percent). Together these cases accounted for 14 percent of the total claims and 18 percent of the dollars paid.[10]

Of those cases where medical procedures caused an injury leading to lawsuit, obstetrical and gynecological procedures accounted for 14 percent of the total cases and 13 percent of the dollar amounts awarded. The average

§ 1.10   Introduction   7

indemnity per claim was $35,592, compared with an overall average of $37,558.[11]

The risk indices presented by the NAIC were developed by dividing the total indemnity by the reported overall frequency for each procedure. The indices for all procedures range from 0.00 (numerous procedures) to 725.99 (partial gastrectomy). For obstetrical and gynecological procedures the range is 0.02 (destruction of Bartholin cyst) to 204.89 (insertion of an IUD, intrauterine contraceptive device). Table 1.1 shows the ten procedures most commonly resulting in liability by risk index for obstetrics and for gynecology.[12]

In another study, Harold Hirsch and Edward White considered 1,566 malpractice claims reported from April 1971 through November 1977. Of these claims, 189 (12.1 percent) stemmed from gynecological treatment and 80 (5.1 percent) arose from obstetrical treatment. The authors of this study concluded, with regard to gynecology, that more than one-half of the cases involved claims of negligence in prescribing specific therapy or in the performance of an operative procedure. In the area of therapy, prescribing oral contraceptives and estrogens was the most common source of trouble. These prescriptions were frequently found to be ill-advised, indiscriminate, and prolonged, with inade-

TABLE 1.1   Risk Indexes and Average Indemnities for the Ten Obstetrical and Gynecological Procedures Most Commonly Resulting in Liability

Procedure	Risk Index	Average Indemnity ($)
Obstetrics		
Cesarean section, type unspecified	89.86	89,862
Cesarean section, internal and combined version	50.00	150,000
Cesarean section, NEC	46.20	115,503
Forceps to aftercoming head	44.67	116,150
Assisted delivery, NEC	22.50	22,500
Intra-amniotic injection	17.73	116,660
Partial breech extraction	16.21	141,875
Forceps rotation of fetal head	11.70	275,000
Medical induction of labor	7.45	121,086
Low forceps delivery without episiotomy	4.74	41,083
Gynecology		
Insertion of IUD	204.89 (1 claim)	32,597
Hysterotomy	64.50	16,125
Subtotal abdominal hysterectomy	39.84	53,126
Tubal repair	20.63	82,500
Trachelectomy	11.36	125,000
Total abdominal hysterectomy	10.86	34,944
Excision of uterine lesion	10.35	69,875
Salpingectomy	10.03	36,099
Radical abdominal hysterectomy	7.88	10,500
Unilateral oophorectomy	7.13	85,583

quate clinical and laboratory follow-up. In the area of surgery, complications of hysterectomies, dilation and curettage (D&C), abortion, and sterilization were common causes of lawsuits.[13]

About one-fourth of the gynecology cases arose out of the alleged failure to adequately monitor the progress of the patient. Most often, the gynecologist assigned the postoperative care to the house staff or the primary care physician. In essence, the postoperative visits were alleged to be either infrequent, brief, incidental, or a combination of the three. A significant number of cases involved the gynecologist's failure to test on a timely basis; these cases usually involved Pap smears for carcinoma of the cervix or studies for breast cancer.[14]

The malpractice claims against obstetricians primarily involved negligence during labor and delivery, negligent postoperative care, and failure to test in a timely fashion. The second most common cause of lawsuits was identified as delinquent attendance on the part of the obstetrician during labor and delivery, resulting in harm to the patient. In many cases, management of the patient during these stages was left to nurses and house officers or trainees. Allegations of lack of timely testing usually arose out of the failure to determine the adequacy of the pelvis by X ray so that a reasonably knowledgeable decision regarding whether to proceed with a vaginal delivery or to perform a cesarean section could be made. In general, the data disclosed the common complaint of the obstetrician's failure to assume adequate responsibility for the ongoing care of the patient.[15]

The fields of obstetrics and gynecology are concerned with the patient's prenatal period; her pregnancy and its complications, including care of the patient and the fetus; obstetric procedures during parturition; the postpartum period; and considerations of infertility, contraception, and avoidance of disease and injury to mother and child. It is safe to say that the reason obstetrical and gynecological care result in injury as often as they do is because every woman in the population receives treatment in at least one of these areas during her lifetime. Medically mandated treatment and care often require the use of invasive techniques, increasing the risk of injury. Furthermore, in obstetrics, a dual potential for liability exists because the physician is dealing with two lives.

To minimize the risk of lawsuit, the obstetrician or gynecologist should carry out his or her duties to the patient with proper care. One such duty includes accurate diagnosis. Cases indicate that the physician should never assume that a woman is not pregnant; verdicts have been delivered against physicians who have assumed tumors and obstructions were causing the patient's symptoms without checking the possibility of early or late pregnancy.[16]

More than one commentator has stressed that establishing good rapport with the patient does much to avoid litigation.[17] The field of obstetrics embraces complex, personal relationships in medical treatment and counseling, usually involving the patient's family. If the physician has not established good rapport, communication regarding these sensitive areas may not be properly received or acted upon; bad feelings may develop if injury results, and litigation may follow.

§ *1.20* *Elements of Negligence* 9

The malpractice crisis has generated various responses in both the medical and legal fields. Medicine has responded by imposing continuing medical education requirements in an attempt to ensure that medical care of high quality is provided by the profession and that the profession is kept abreast of new developments. Some physicians have begun to practice "defensive" medicine, whereby unnecessary tests and treatments are conducted in an effort (usually ineffectual) to avoid legal liability. Legal responses have included arbitration or mediation, an alternative to conventional litigation in which a conflict is resolved by an impartial third party selected by the contestants. Some state legislatures have limited malpractice attorneys' fees and the amount of damages that may be claimed in the malpractice complaint. At best, these "Band-Aid" measures only relieve the symptoms. As one study stated:

> Our conclusion, based on patient complaints, is that most of the cases could have been prevented if the health care providers had exercised greater vigilance, diligence, and attention to the details of patient care, particularly in communicating with the patient. Proper drug therapy and timely testing are also very important in preventing malpractice, and these can be accomplished relatively easily. . . . In conclusion, prophylaxis can beat malpractice.[18]

§ 1.20 ELEMENTS OF NEGLIGENCE

Generally, when a patient sues a physician for an injury stemming from the physician's treatment, the patient is suing for malpractice. Negligence is the legal theory most commonly used by malpractice plaintiffs. To succeed under a negligence theory, or, in legal jargon, to present a cause of action for negligence, a patient-plaintiff must prove four things:

1. DUTY—The patient-plaintiff must show that the obstetrician or gynecologist in question owed her a particular duty or obligation. This duty, recognized by law as created by the physician-patient relationship, requires the obstetrician or gynecologist to act in accordance with specific norms or standards established by the profession, commonly referred to as standards of care, for the protection of patients against unreasonable risks.

2. BREACH OF DUTY—The patient-plaintiff must show that the obstetrician or gynecologist failed to act in accordance with those norms by any commissive or omissive act violating the standard of care owed to the patient-plaintiff.

3. CAUSATION—The patient-plaintiff must show that a reasonable, close, causal connection exists between the acts of the obstetrician or gynecologist and the resulting injury. This is commonly known as "legal cause" or "proximate cause," which differs from medical causation in that it refers to *a* cause and not necessarily *the* cause or even the most immediate cause, as is the case with medical causation.

4. DAMAGES—The plaintiff must establish that, because of the physician's acts, actual loss or damage has been incurred. Damages may include physical, financial, or emotional injury to the patient or related others (such as spouse, heirs, and so on).[19]

In order to recover, the plaintiff must prove by a preponderance of the evidence that all four of these elements exist. "Preponderance of the evidence" means proof that leads the trier of fact (the judge or jury) to find that the existence of the fact at issue is more probable than not.

§ 1.30 DUTY

The definition of duty, stated above, refers to the duty component of negligence as it would be applied to an obstetrician or gynecologist. The *general* concept of duty, as an element of negligence, presupposes some uniform standard of behavior. Because of the infinite variety of situations that may give rise to negligent conduct, it is virtually impossible to prescribe specific standards for all aspects of human behavior. The law has responded to this difficulty with something in the nature of a formula that it leaves to the jury or the court to apply. Certain necessary qualities of such a formula have been recognized by the law: the standard applied must be objective and not left to the individual judgment of the actor; it must be uniform, to avoid any semblance in the law of favoritism; and it must allow for the risk apparent to the actor, his capacity to respond to it, and the circumstances under which he must act. In response to these considerations, the law has created the standard of the reasonable man of ordinary prudence who acts with reasonable and due care in a given situation. The actor has a duty to conform his behavior to that of this ideal individual—the reasonable man placed in the actor's shoes.[20]

Within the confines of malpractice, the courts have provided greater focus with respect to duty. The reasonable man becomes the reasonable physician. This legal fiction requires that every physician possess the requisite skill or exercise the requisite skill, care, and diligence the particular case demands.[21] The patient may show that the physician failed to exercise the required care either by commission or omission—in other words, by doing something that should not have been done (commission) or by failing to do or cause to be done something that should have been done (omission).[22] It may not suffice that the physician has performed at full potential and in the utmost good faith. Rather, the physician must have conformed to the standard of a "reasonable physician" under like circumstances.[23]

While such statements provide a general standard of care or duty, they do not define the duty of a particular physician in a particular case. Because most medical malpractice cases involve a highly technical evaluation of the propriety and skill of a physician in his or her treatment of a patient, it is necessary that witnesses with special medical or scientific qualifications provide guidance to a

§ 1.30   Duty   11

lay jury by furnishing them with the necessary knowledge to render a just verdict.[24] Consequently, the standard of medical care must be ascertained from expert testimony in nearly all instances;[25] in the case of a specialist, that standard of care is the care and skill commonly possessed and exercised by similar specialists in like circumstances[26] (see § 1.32, Standard of Care). This specialty standard may often be higher* than that required of general practitioners,[27] it is the standard against which various courts have measured the conduct of obstetricians[28] and gynecologic surgeons.[29]

While the standard of care defines the duty owed, it is often less clear, particularly in obstetrics, to *whom* that duty is owed. The courts recognize a duty to possess and use reasonable skill owed to the patient-plaintiff,[30] and this duty is applicable to diagnosis as well as treatment.[31] But the courts have also recognized a duty to a person whose existence may not have been apparent at the time of the physician's act: a child not yet conceived but foreseeably harmed by a breach of duty to its mother.[32] Originally, an action for injuries could not be maintained for the wrongful death of a child who did not survive premature birth,[33] because the child-plaintiff would have been a prenatal being at the time of the injury and the law did not recognize a prenatal being as having a separate legal existence.[34] Eventually, the courts recognized a right of action for prenatal injuries, arguing that an infant has a legal existence separate from the mother at such time as it is viable or capable of sustaining life separate from her.[35] At first, this recognized duty was limited to a case involving the wrongful death of a viable child, injured in utero, who is born alive but thereafter dies.[36] Later, this duty was extended to permit a wrongful death action for a viable child wrongfully injured in utero.[37] As medical science progressed, the courts took notice that a fetus is a separate entity prior to birth. Because it is by now commonly accepted that the egg and sperm unite at conception to jointly provide the genetic material required for human life, various courts have come to recognize that the embryo is a separate organism from the moment of conception and that it may be legally compensated for negligently inflicted prenatal harm. These considerations, coupled with the recognition that medical science has developed various techniques which can mitigate or, in some cases, totally alleviate a child's prenatal harm, have been held to extend the physician's duty: in one case, the infant-plaintiff was born approximately nine years after the physician's act complained of.[38] The case is set out below. While the defendants in this case were a hospital and its director of laboratories, rather than an obstetrician, the principles stated in the case indicate the extent of the physician's duty.

---

*While some courts characterize a national specialty standard as "higher" than that applied to a general practitioner, the specialist does not owe a *greater amount* of care than the general practitioner; rather, the specialist, like the general practitioner, owes the patient due care in the application of the skill actually possessed. Consequently, by virtue of the specialty, the specialist is thought to possess greater skill in his or her specialty than does the general practitioner.

CASE ILLUSTRATION

In October 1965, when the unborn child's mother was 13 years old, the defendants, a hospital and its director of laboratories, on two occasions negligently transfused the mother with 500 cubic centimeters of Rh-positive blood. The mother's Rh-negative blood was incompatible with, and was sensitized by, the Rh-positive blood. The mother had no knowledge of an adverse reaction from the transfusions and did not know she had been improperly transfused or that her blood had been sensitized. The mother first discovered her condition in December 1973, when a routine blood screening was ordered by her physician in the course of prenatal care. Prior to this, the defendants had discovered that they had administered the incompatible blood, but at no time did they notify the mother or the mother's family. The resulting desensitization of the mother's blood allegedly caused prenatal damage to the child's hematologic processes, which put her life in jeopardy and necessitated her induced premature birth. The child was born on March 25, 1974, jaundiced and suffering from hyperbilirubinemia. When born, she required an immediate, complete exchange transfusion of her blood and another such transfusion shortly thereafter. She suffered from permanent damage to various organs, her brain, and her nervous system. The child sued the hospital and its laboratory director, and the court held that, despite the fact that the child had not been conceived at the time of the negligent act, her ultimate existence was reasonably foreseeable, and the defendants were therefore held liable for her injuries (*Renslow v. Mennonite Hospital*, 1977).[39]

With respect to duties owed to the patient, the physician has a general duty to make a properly skillful and careful diagnosis of the patient's ailment; if the physician fails to bring to that diagnosis the proper degree of skill or care and makes an incorrect diagnosis, he or she may be held liable to the patient for the damage caused just as readily as he or she must answer for improper treatment.[40] The physician is not responsible for an error of judgment unless the error is so gross as to be inconsistent with the degree of skill the physician has a duty to possess. Where the symptoms are obscured, there is no liability for an error in diagnosis.[41] Failure to make use of a standard test to confirm or deny a possible pregnancy may indicate a lack of due care in arriving at a conclusion.[42] However, where the usual tests are made, accepted diagnostic means are followed, and a false negative result is obtained, the physician is not usually held liable for relying on test results.[43] While a specialist in obstetrics and gynecology is expected to have and use a higher standard of skill, care, and knowledge in diagnosis than a general practitioner,[44] the specialist may rely on the diagnosis of the general practitioner who refers the patient, where no symptoms exist which would indicate that a contrary conclusion should be reached.[45] Physicians have been held liable both for the failure to diagnose at all and for the failure to diagnose correctly. The courts have recognized that when the patient is a woman of childbearing age pregnancy should be considered a possibility if symptoms indicating such things as fibroid tumors,[46] gallbladder problems,[47] and kidney infections[48] are presented. This may even be the case when the patient denies having engaged in any sexual activity.[49] This duty is imposed to safeguard the health of the mother and the fetus[50] and has also been viewed as protecting the right of the mother to obtain a legal, first trimester abortion[51] (see § 5.45, Abortion).

§ 1.31 The Physician-Patient Relationship

Unless a physician-patient relationship can be found to exist, a physician cannot be held liable for medical malpractice.[52]

According to the American Medical Association's "Principles of Medical Ethics," a physician is free to choose whom to serve.[53] Consequently, the physician is not obligated to accept any patient, even one urgently in need of his or her services.[54] This is in line with the tenets of the Hippocratic Oath, which assumes a preexisting physician-patient relationship.[55] Unless such a relationship exists, a physician owes no legal duty to the would-be patient and cannot be held liable for medical malpractice.[56]

In certain situations, a physician may provide treatment or services to a patient without creating a physician-patient relationship. One such situation occurs when medical services are provided for the benefit of a third party rather than the patient, as is the case when a physician examines a patient for an insurer,[57] for a potential employer,[58] or for purposes of a worker's compensation claim.[59] Another such case is where a physician who is treating a patient discusses the patient's case with a second physician for advice or consultation and the patient receives no direct treatment or service from the second physician; there is no physician-patient relationship between the patient and the second physician.[60] It has also been held that there is no physician-patient relationship between members of a medical school staff working in a hospital and the hospital's patients, where the patients could not choose their physicians and were generally treated by several different physicians.[61]

The physician-patient relationship is formed when the professional services of the physician are accepted for the purpose of medical and surgical treatment.[62] The relationship is viewed by courts as contractual, created by an expressed or implied agreement between the parties. It is a fiduciary relationship,[63] meaning the patient may rely on the physician to safeguard his or her best interests. Courts have noted that the trust and confidence the patient may have in the physician are based on the physician's special skills and knowledge in an area of vital importance to the patient.[64]

An implied agreement to enter into the physician-patient relationship may be found where a patient seeks medical assistance and the physician offers treatment without any specific reference to an agreement or the relationship.[65]

While express agreements are rarely made between physicians and patients, they are generally enforceable, and the obstetrician or gynecologist has the right to impose certain conditions or create obligations additional to those inherent in the legal relationship[66] (see § 2.20, Contract Theory). However, an express agreement signed by the patient to absolve the physician of any liability for injury resulting from negligent treatment has been held to be contrary to public policy and does not protect a physician from liability.[67] Such an agreement differs from the duty to obtain the patient's informed consent to treatment; where informed consent has been obtained, it is recognized by the courts (see § 1.33, Consent and Informed Consent).

Mutual assent is not absolutely required to create a physician-patient relationship. An unconscious patient, for example, may have no opportunity to select a particular hospital or surgeon. Nonetheless, when a physician undertakes to render care to a patient, a professional relationship is created, along with the corresponding duty of care to the recipient.[68] Where there has been some overt conduct by the physician, courts have had little trouble in finding a sufficient undertaking to create a physician-patient relationship.[69]

The physician-patient relationship has been described as contractual and wholly voluntary, created by an agreement either expressed or implied.[70] Therefore, a physician may limit his or her obligation to treat the patient geographically as well as professionally by special agreement with the patient.[71]

CASE ILLUSTRATION

The patient, whose home was in a rural area, consulted the physician at his office in a small town during the early stages of her pregnancy and was checked by him several times at his office. Two weeks prior to the projected delivery date, the patient inquired whether the physician could deliver the child at her home and was informed that this could not be done, since the home lacked the facilities available at the town hospital for safe childbirth, particularly in the event of complications. Accordingly, the patient made arrangements for a midwife to attend during delivery. The midwife, when summoned upon the onset of labor, just after midnight, advised the patient to secure a physician, since she determined that the birth was going to be difficult and accompanied by complications. Calls were placed to two other physicians and eventually to the original physician; all three physicians advised that the patient be brought to a hospital, where necessary surgical and medical facilities were available. Finally, at 6:30 a.m. the patient was brought to the hospital, the unborn baby already dead. The patient's own life was saved by the medical intervention of her physician. The particular complication that occurred in this case, technically termed a "hand presentation" (where the hand is born first), neces-

§ 1.31   *Physician-Patient Relationship*   15

sitated the use of a procedure that could only be performed with the facilities of a hospital delivery room. The patient sued her physician. The court held that a physician is not required to accept professional employment on terms determined by the patient but may limit his obligation by undertaking to treat or care for the patient only in a hospital rather than in a patient's home. Consequently the court found that the actions of the physician-defendant instanced a full performance of any legal, ethical, or humanitarian duty to the patient, and no liability was imposed (*Vidrine v. Mayes*, 1961).[72]

Although a physician may arbitrarily refuse to treat a person who is not already his or her patient, hospitals with emergency rooms have been held to offer service to the public and therefore must admit and treat patients in need of emergency care[73] (see § 7.62, Emergencies). Consequently, the physician assigned to the emergency room must treat every emergency that presents itself. The duty extends to private as well as public hospitals[74] and protects all patients, regardless of where they live or their ability to pay.[75] Some states have codified this duty by statute.[76]

What constitutes an emergency is a jury question. It has been held that a broken arm is an emergency,[77] yet some Southern courts have held that a woman in labor,[78] even two months prematurely,[79] does not constitute an emergency.

CASE ILLUSTRATION

The patient, who lived in Illinois, was in Kentucky for a funeral when she went into premature labor. She was refused admittance at a local hospital. The baby was born at home and died before reaching a hospital. The patient sued the hospital, the two physicians at the hospital she was turned away from, and the nurse in the emergency room at the time. The court held that the hospital did not have to admit a patient who had no local physician, the physicians did not have to accept the plaintiff as a patient, and the nurse could not force the physicians to accept the plaintiff (*Hill v. Ohio County*, 1971).[80]

Cases that have found no duty on the part of emergency rooms to treat cannot be reconciled with the general trend in this area of law. *Hill v. Ohio County* may be viewed as a regional rule (Southern), but in light of the fact that courts are responding more readily to arguments concerning the public responsibility of hospitals vis-a-vis their emergency rooms, this rule will probably be discarded in time, even in the South.

In most states, the rendering of treatment outside the hospital room in an emergency situation by a physician who does not already have an ongoing physician-patient relationship with the emergency victim does not establish the physician-patient relationship. Except for acts or omissions amounting to gross negligence or willful and wanton misconduct, the physician is usually not liable for any civil damages resulting from acts or omissions in the rendering of emergency care. This is a general statement of the so-called Good Samaritan statute,[81] enacted in every state but Kentucky. The justification for such statutes is that without them a bystander who renders aid to a stranger in distress assumes a legally enforceable obligation to exercise a reasonable care and skill in the task voluntarily assumed; this has been viewed as a deterrent to voluntary assistance. Without a Good Samaritan statute, the volunteering physician would, in providing treatment, create a physician-patient relationship, with all its attendant obligations, whether the services rendered are gratuitous or compensated.[82]

State Good Samaritan statutes designed to alleviate this problem vary in their approach to the solution. Variations appear in what constitutes the scene of the emergency: some limit the statute's application to motor vehicle accidents,[83] but most states protect the Good Samaritan at the scene of an accident or emergency generally.[84] Some states provide immunity from liability only if the physician volunteer receives no compensation from the emergency victim.[85] A number of states extend immunity only to those licensed under their own laws,[86] while others immunize licensees of any state.[87] Most of the statutes restrict immunity to cases in which the actions of the physician volunteer do not amount to gross negligence or willful and wanton misconduct.[88]

The following Good Samaritan statute, adopted in Indiana, is a typical example of Good Samaritan legislation.

> From and after the effective date of this act, no civil action may be brought against a person licensed to practice the healing arts in the State of Indiana, who has gratuitously rendered first aid or emergency at the scene of an accident, casualty, or disaster to a person injured therein, for the recovery of civil damages as a result of any act or omission by the said person rendering such first aid or emergency care in the rendering of such first aid or emergency care. This immunity does not apply to acts or omissions constituting gross negligence or willful or wanton misconduct.[89]

In the usual nonemergency creation of the physician-patient relationship, the patient who engages a physician to treat her is considered to have implicitly engaged that physician to attend her throughout the illness or until the physician's services are dispensed with. Thus the physician is under a duty to continue treatment.[90] In the absence of special agreement, the physician must attend the case as long as it requires attention, unless he or she gives notice of the intent to terminate medical services; the physician must exercise care in determining when attendance may end.[91]

CASE ILLUSTRATION

The physician-defendant inserted an IUD of the type known as the Dalkon

Shield into the patient in 1972. Subsequently, the device was found to be unsafe and was removed from the market in 1974. The patient was later injured by the IUD and sued the physician for not notifying her when it was found to be unsafe. In reversing the judgment for the physician, the court held that the patient had stated a "malpractice action arising from the imposed continuing status of physician-patient where the danger arose from that relationship" (*Tresemer v. Barke*, 1979).[92]

Leaving the patient prematurely may give rise to an action for abandonment. Abandonment has been defined as the unilateral severance of the professional relationship with the patient without adequate notice and while the necessity of continuing medical attention still exists.[93] The physician is not at liberty to terminate the physician-patient relationship at will. The relationship continues until it is ended by either the patient's lack of need for further care or the withdrawing physician's replacement by an equally qualified physician. Withdrawal from the case under any other circumstance constitutes a wrongful abandonment of the patient; if the patient suffers any injury as a proximate result of such wrongful abandonment, the physician is liable for it.[94]

CASE ILLUSTRATION

The patient visited an obstetrician during her pregnancy. When 8½ months pregnant, she began to experience labor pains. The obstetrician was called, but he declined to come to the patient's home, stating it was probably false labor. The pains persisted, and the obstetrician was called again, whereupon he visited the patient, checked on her condition, and declared she would not deliver for two weeks. The pains persisted further, the obstetrician was again called, but he refused to return. After repeated calls, the obstetrician stated that he would have nothing further to do with the patient. The baby was subsequently born at home without medical attention. The patient sued the obstetrician for pain and suffering and mental distress due to abandonment. The court found the physician liable (*Norton v. Hamilton*, 1955).[95]

The physician who has abandoned a patient may not assert that there is no way to prove his or her efforts would have made any difference, because it is the conduct of the physician, not the patient, that makes such proof speculative. The patient is entitled to rely on the physician's best efforts, which might have reduced or eliminated the injury.[96] If abandonment can be proved, the patient may be entitled to an award of punitive damages in some jurisdictions[97] (see § 1.60, Damages).

To be found to have abandoned a patient, the physician need not commit an affirmative act. The failure to properly monitor or treat a patient as she recovers from surgery may be held to constitute abandonment.

CASE ILLUSTRATION

The patient suffered from a prolapse, or dropping, of the uterus and a protrusion of the walls of the rectum through the vaginal opening. The physician performed a hysterectomy in his clinic to correct these problems, and the patient remained under his care for nine days, after which she was allowed to return home. The site of the operation was not examined by the physician during this period. The patient returned for a postoperative checkup six weeks later, at which time the physician still did not examine her but gave her medication, telling her to return home and cleanse her female organs. When she returned home, she discovered that she could not use the medication because her organs had grown together. She returned to the physician's clinic reporting this condition, and the physician then examined her for the first time. After the examination, the physician admitted that if he had examined the patient sooner the problem would have been avoided. Although another physician testified that, in such a situation the physician must choose whether to risk infection by making a manual inspection, the court held that an operating surgeon must exercise the same skill and judgment in the subsequent treatment of the patient as in the performance of the operation itself. A physician who fails to do so may be held liable for the failure to exercise skill and sound judgment in the postoperative care and treatment of the patient (*Wooten v. Curry*, 1961).[98]

No abandonment will be found where treatment is delayed or not implemented because of some act by the patient. For example, a physician who did not check a patient's recovery from a hysterectomy because the patient continually failed to keep her appointments was not held liable for abandonment.[99] Where the physician-patient relationship is terminated by mutual consent, abandonment does not exist.[100]

Under normal circumstances, a physician does have a definite right to withdraw from a case, provided the physician gives the patient reasonable notice to secure other medical assistance[101] and all conditions for the physician's rightful withdrawal have been met, including a release signed by the patient that is sufficiently complete and formal to allow another physician to take the case.[102] A physician may furnish a substitute,[103] provided the substitute is acceptable to the patient.[104] The physician must provide his or her successor with all the relevant medical data available.[105] If a physician leaves town or is otherwise unable to attend hospitalized patients, the physician is not negligent as long as he or she has made arrangements to assure that competent medical help is available to patients during his or her absence.[106]

CASE ILLUSTRATION

The patient contacted an obstetrician to deliver her child. The obstetrician projected the delivery for May 16. On May 19, the obstetrician decided he needed a rest and left for a two-day fishing trip. The obstetrician did not notify the patient of his absence, but he did arrange with another physician to cover for him. The patient delivered during the obstetrician's absence, without complication. She sued him, however, on the grounds that she had suffered mental anguish from having a strange physician deliver her baby. The jury found for the patient, but on appeal the court reversed and ordered a new trial (*Miller v. Dore,* 1959).[107]

In obstetrical malpractice cases, abandonment might be alleged where the physician discontinues treatment of the patient immediately following childbirth (see Chapter XII, Postpartum Complications). The essence of this claim is that the physician has effectively severed the physician-patient relationship, at a time when it is necessary to continue medical attention, without reasonable notice and without providing an adequate medical attendant as a substitue.[108] The courts have recognized that a physician is liable if he or she improperly fails to respond to postpartum patient complaints that indicate a need for attendance.

CASE ILLUSTRATION

On January 11, the obstetrician delivered the 16-year-old patient of a normal 8-pound 11-ounce child. The patient's recovery period was uneventful except for some abdominal pain, which the obstetrician attributed to normal postpartum discomfort. Three days after delivery, the obstetrician discharged the patient, despite her continued complaints of pain. During the evening of the day of discharge, the patient's mother telephoned the obstetrician and reported that the patient was suffering from intense pain and that the patient's stomach was black and hard. The obstetrician attributed this to normal postpartum complaints of a young mother who had delivered a large child and prescribed sitz baths and additional medication. On January 15, the mother again called the obstetrician and reported that the patient's pain was worse. The obstetrician ordered continuation of medication and sitz baths. These same events occurred again on January 16. On January 17, the mother reported to the obstetrician that the patient had a fever. There was a dispute in the evidence as to whether the mother reported that the patient was suffering from chills. The obstetrician instructed the mother to take the patient's temperature and report back to him. When the mother responded that she did not have a thermometer and could not read one, the obstetrician suggested that she obtain one, have a friend or neighbor read it, and report back to him. The mother never took the patient's temperature. The mother asserted that she made further calls on January 18 and 19 to report that the patient's condition was worse. The obstetrician denied receiving the calls.

At 5:00 a.m. on January 20, the patient voluntarily readmitted herself to the hospital. The obstetrician arrived at 6:00 a.m. and found her to have a fever of 99.8 degrees, a distended abdomen, and considerable pain. Three days later, a surgeon performed a laparotomy, which revealed abscesses of the patient's fallopian tubes and ovaries on both sides. One side had ruptured and spread purulent material throughout the abdominal cavity. There were also two abscesses of the lower diaphragm. The surgeon removed both tubes and ovaries, drained the other abscesses, and cleaned out the abdomen. The patient remained hospitalized for almost one month. She sued the obstetrician, alleging that he had been negligent in not examining her after receiving recurrent complaints of pain and fever after her discharge. The lower court found for the patient-plaintiff and the higher court affirmed. The court ruled that the evidence supported a finding that the obstetrician-defendant had been negligent in failing to see a patient in need of his care and that this failure was the proximate cause of increased morbidity for the patient-plaintiff (*White v. Edison*, 1978).[109]

In a 1976 case, a patient went into shock shortly after giving birth at 9:25 a.m. She lapsed into unconsciousness at 1:45 p.m. and died at 5:00 p.m. The evidence showed that her obstetrician and internist were absent at several critical times during this period. The obstetrician left to treat six patients at his office. In upholding a jury finding that this absence constituted negligence, the Supreme Court of Connecticut adopted the following rule:[110]

> [In the absence of an emergency or special circumstances] a physician is under the duty to give his patient all necessary and continued attention as long as the case requires it, and . . . he should not leave his patient at a critical stage without giving reasonable notice or making suitable arrangements for the attendance of another physician.

A hospital-defendant may also be liable for postpartum abandonment. In one case, a patient-plaintiff sued a hospital after she fell from her bed and suffered head and chin injuries following the birth of her child. The court overruled a directed verdict for the hospital-defendant and stated that a jury should settle the question of whether the patient had been properly attended. The sedatives that had been administered to the patient were of a sufficient amount to support a finding that she was not oriented and alert and that she required greater assistance than she was in fact given.[111]

As can be seen, once the physician-patient relationship is formed, certain rules arise governing its existence and maintenance. If created out of a medical need precipitated by an emergency, most states protect physicians from liability for ordinary negligence, in order to encourage them to provide treatment. However it is created, the relationship may not be terminated prematurely; premature termination will constitute abandonment. The obstetrician must be particularly careful in his or her treatment of the postpartum patient to ensure that medical standards required by such a physician-patient relationship are met.

§ 1.32 Standard of Care

As physicians, obstetricians and gynecologists are not held to be insurers against harm nor guarantors of a favorable result.[112] The duty owed to the patient is to possess and exercise the knowledge and skill necessary to provide appropriate obstetrical or gynecological treatment. "Standard of care" is the legal term used to refer to this required expertise. The standard of care provides an objective standard against which to measure the conduct of the physician sued for malpractice. Because it must be objective, the standard does not depend upon the individual physician's own knowledge. The law cannot equate the mental ability of various individuals: it seeks to fix a uniform standard by which a jury may determine whether or not the practitioner has properly performed his or her duties toward the patient.[113]

The specialist in a branch of medicine is judged on a standard based on the skill and knowledge common to other physicians in that specialty.[114] Originally, a medical practitioner had the duty to possess and exercise only that degree of care and skill customarily possessed and exercised by other practitioners in the same or similar locality.[115] This legal doctrine is known as the "community standard" or "locality rule." The courts reasoned that medical sophistication is a function of community size and resources and that no physician should be held liable for the failure to meet more sophisticated standards. As a Texas court noted, "the community standard rule does not require a small office of rural medical practitioners to possess either the skills or equipment of a sophisticated clinic; but the standard demands, at least, that one exercise ordinary care commensurate with the equipment, skills, and time available."[116]

Through the years, the locality concept was broadened somewhat, principally to avoid the result of the patient failing to recover solely because of his or her inability to obtain an expert witness familiar with medical practice in the locality.[117] Consequently, the word "similar" in "similar locality" was given an elastic interpretation. While the traditional approach focused on the geographic proximity of the areas, some courts began to examine the socioeconomic similarities of the physician-defendant's and the expert's communities.[118] These courts applied the locality rule to such areas as a multistate region,[119] the general neighborhood,[120] and a community in close proximity.[121] Finally one court, faced with interpreting the rule, offered the perspective that the entire body of American physicians constituted one community.[122]

In a 1968 Massachusetts case, the locality rule was abandoned with respect to specialists.[123] In light of the rule's history, such a development may be seen as evolutionary rather than revolutionary. As justification for recognizing a national standard for specialists, the courts have noted: (1) the refusal of physicians in the medical community to testify against one another, a condition identified by the courts as a "conspiracy of silence";[124] (2) the fact that the various specialities of medicine have set up uniform requirements governing the certification of specialists, including rules regarding the length of residency training, subjects to be covered, and examination;[125] and (3) the existence of continuing medical education requirements, which compel specialists to continue to study, attend refresher courses, and acquire access to journals that expose them to the latest treatments and procedures.[126]

Currently, for a patient-plaintiff to recover in a medical malpractice case involving a specialist, the plaintiff must prove that the specialist-defendant's conduct failed to meet the standard of care required of other physicians in the same speciality.[127] Although there is no indication that it will be followed, at least one court has refused to hold a general practitioner accountable to a national speciality standard where the general practitioner provides medical treatment usually provided by a specialist.[128]

CASE ILLUSTRATION

An infant born 3½ months prematurely was placed immediately upon birth in an Isolette, where controlled oxygen was given to him for two months. He developed retrolental fibroplasia, a scarring of the eye tissue, resulting in total, permanent blindness. The infant's parents sued the general practitioner who attended the birth and treated the newborn, claiming the disease was caused by the infant's continued exposure to oxygen while in the Isolette. At trial, a pediatrician testified regarding the standard of treatment employed by pediatric physicians in such cases. The court held for the general practitioner, ruling that the standard for general practitioners continues to be the standard of such professional practice as that practiced in the community or similar communities and is not governed by the practice of pediatrics (*Siirila v. Barrios*, 1975).[129]

Of course, the applicable standard of care may require that the general practitioner consult with or refer a particular case to a specialist if he or she realizes that a condition is beyond his or her capacity to treat, and some courts have recognized this duty to refer.[130]

In order to establish a particular standard to apply to a particular injury, the courts have required the use of medical expert testimony in most malpractice cases.[131] Thus the legal system looks to the medical profession to set its own standards of care. One legal commentator has identified the reasons.[132]

This long-standing rule which permits the medical profession to set its own standards of care is supported by three sound considerations. First, courts presume that the medical profession will not adopt unreasonable standards of care. History has shown that the medical profession consistently strives to improve medical practice and has implemented advances into their recognized standards of conduct.

§ 1.32   Standard of Care   23

Second, the character of medical decision-making frequently requires physicians to balance competing considerations not amenable to being synthesized into strict, inflexible rules. Third, the complexity of medical science typically renders laymen, including judges, unable to determine the reasonableness of specific medical practices. Consequently, courts tend to defer to the profession's judgment concerning medical standards.*

Thus, the courts recognize that medical facts and practices are matters not usually within the realm of common knowledge. Without expert testimony, the finder of fact, which is the jury in most cases, could not determine whether these matters fail to measure up to the criteria used to determine medical malpractice.[133]

To qualify an expert to express an opinion on what the standard of care is for the speciality of the physician-defendant, the party offering the witness must establish the witness's knowledge of and familiarity with the standard of care and treatment commonly practiced by physicians engaged in the same specialty as the physician-defendant; it need not be a physician from the same specialty.[134] Furthermore, the expert witness need not possess actual occupational experience or practical knowledge of the subject; at least one court has held that a physician may testify to a standard of care in existence ten years before he began the practice of medicine, the degree of his knowledge affecting only the weight to be given his testimony.[135]

CASE ILLUSTRATION

In 1949, while the patient was in the hospital recovering from an operation performed by the physician, a nurse, in administering an enema, forced a hard rectal tube from the patient's rectum into her vagina. This created a rectovaginal fistula, a small hole in the wall between the vagina and the rectum. The next day, the physician, in attempting surgical repair, stitched the fistula with stainless steel sutures, which are not absorbable by the body. In the year following the operation, the patient experienced considerable physical and emotional difficulties. In 1968, another physician who treated the patient discovered that she had a rectovaginal fistula. He proceeded to repair this condition surgically, and in doing so discovered that the stainless steel sutures employed by the physician in 1949 had become distorted into a figure eight in the immediate area of the fistula. After the 1968 surgery, the patient's condition improved markedly.

---

*This commentator points out that the Washington and California Supreme Courts in three decisions appear to be departing from the practice of looking to the medical profession for standards of care. These courts have concluded that, where a physician could better protect the patient by following a more prudent course of conduct than that mandated by the medical standard of care, the law requires the physician to do so. *See* Peters, *The Application of Reasonable Prudence to Medical Malpractice Litigation: The Precursor to Strict Liability?* Law, Med. Health Care 21 (1981).

The patient sued the first physician, and, at the trial, attempted to elicit testimony from the second physician as to the standard of care which prevailed in 1949 regarding the use of stainless steel sutures in the repair of rectovaginal fistulas. She offered to make this showing on the basis of evidence as to the standard after 1959, when the second physician was engaged in active medical practice, arguing that the same standard prevailed in 1949, when the original operation was performed. According to the patient, the second physician, in preparation for his testimony regarding the standard of care applicable in 1949 and thereafter, had made an exhaustive study of virtually all the available medical literature on the subject. The physician-defendant objected to this testimony on the ground that the witness's opinion as to the 1949 standard of care was not based on his actual practice of medicine during the time in question.

The court held that, while a layman may not testify to a fact that he or she has learned only by reading a medical book, there is no question that the professional physician may rely upon medical texts as the basis for testimony. Since a physician possesses professional experience that gives him or her a knowledge of trustworthy authorities and proper sources of information, as well as a degree of personal familiarity with the general subject, the physician is qualified to estimate the validity of the views expressed. Furthermore, it may be impossible to obtain information on the particular matter except through reported data. This consideration, coupled with the fact that there was little likelihood that the patient-plaintiff could have secured any expert witness qualified to testify as to the standard of care prevalent for a particular operation, notably uncommon in nature, performed 23 years prior to the trial, supported the admissibility of the second physician's testimony and a consequent finding in favor of the patient-plaintiff (*Brown v. Colm,* 1974).[136]

Exceptions to the expert testimony requirement have been recognized. Expert testimony is not needed where the patient presents evidence showing the physician's lack of care to be so obvious as to be within the comprehension of a layperson.[137] This common knowledge exception to the expert testimony requirement has been applied generally in cases where injury results to a part of the body not involved in treatment[138] or from failure to remove a sponge from a surgical incision before closing it.[139] Other situations regarded by the courts as negligence within the common knowledge of laypersons have included injuries resulting from a surgeon's failure to sterilize his instruments[140] and injuries sustained by a newborn when the attending physician cut too deeply during a cesarean section.[141] The most common application of the exception is where the physician injures a part of the body not involved in the treatment.[142]

§ 1.32 *Standard of Care* 25

CASE ILLUSTRATION

The patient underwent surgery for the removal of a cyst from her right ovary. The condition was diagnosed and the surgery performed by the physician. In the course of the surgery, the complete removal of the right ovary was found to be necessary. Since the patient's uterus had been removed in previous surgery and her ovaries were no longer of use as reproductive organs, the physician concluded that the left ovary should be removed also. In the process of removing the left ovary, the left ureter was severed. The patient sued the operating physician.

At trial, the evidence indicated no medical urgency that might have required speed or an unusual procedure that might have justified the inadvertent severing of the ureter in the surgical removal of the left ovary. The evidence further indicated that the physician-defendant proceeded to remove the left ovary without first identifying the left ureter and only found the left ureter when he noticed the severed end of it in the severed pedicle of the ovary. In response to the physician-defendant's assertion that expert medical testimony was necessary as a matter of law to establish the defendant's negligence, the court held that expert testimony from third-party medical witnesses is not essential in every malpractice case and that it is not required when the asserted negligence lies within the common knowledge of laypersons. The court ruled in favor of the patient-plaintiff (*Pry v. Jones,* 1973).[143]

In addition, expert testimony may not be required in cases to which the doctrine of res ipsa loquitur applies (see § 1.52, Res Ipsa Loquitur) and in cases involving the issue of informed consent (see § 1.33, Consent and Informed Consent).

Proof of the standard of care may sometimes be obtained through sources other than an independent medical expert. Evidence of the standard of care may be found in the testimony in court of the physician-defendant[144] or in an out-of-court admission of negligence by the physician.[145]

CASE ILLUSTRATION

The patient consulted the physician to determine whether she was pregnant. The physician ran tests and advised the patient that she was not pregnant but was afflicted with an internal tumor that should be surgically removed immediately. The patient underwent an operation, performed by the physician, which disclosed that she did not have a tumor but was in fact pregnant. The physician closed the surgical wound and reported to the patient's husband, "Your wife is approximately 3½ months pregnant. This is a terrible thing I have done—I wasn't satisfied with the lab report, she did have signs of being pregnant. I should have had tests run again, I should have made some other tests." The patient and her husband sued the physician. The court relied on the statement as an admission that the faulty diagnosis had been made due to the failure of the physician-defendant to use and apply the customary and usual degree of skill exercised by like physicians (*Greenwood v. Harris,* 1961).[146]

While a statement or admission by the physician may establish the standard of care, it does not necessarily establish negligence. Where the statement concerns only the explanation of a bad result without an admission of fault or error, the standard of care may not be established.[147]

CASE ILLUSTRATION

The physician determined that the patient had a growth in the left ovary, that her vagina was filled with blood, and that her uterus was retrocessed, tender, firm, and enlarged. On the advice of the physician, the patient underwent surgery for the removal of her uterus and left ovary; the surgery was performed by the physician. Approximately one hour after the patient was removed to the recovery room, it was noticed that she had excessive vaginal bleeding. She was taken back into the operating room, where the physician identified a "bleeder" near the left side of the vaginal cuff. The physician placed a clamp on this bleeder and then placed a suture in the shape of a figure eight in the left side of the vaginal wall close to the bladder wall; the physician thereafter removed the clamp. This procedure resulted in a cessation of the vaginal bleeding.

On the second day after she returned home, and approximately nine days after the operation, the patient experienced a sudden gushing of urine from her vagina. She returned to the physician's office approximately one month after the operation. On examination of the patient, the physician found water in her vagina but was unable to locate any hole or perforation between the vagina and the bladder. After prescribing medication and the insertion of an in-dwelling catheter to take pressure off the bladder and allow the opening to heal properly, the patient's problem remained. The physician referred the patient to a urologist, who concluded that the cause of the patient's trouble was a small vesicovaginal fistula that stretched sufficiently when the bladder was full to allow urine to leak from the bladder into the vagina. In order to correct this problem, the urologist suggested that the patient enter the hospital once again so that he could cauterize her vaginal tract. This procedure was performed, and the patient recovered. The physician, in discussing with the patient the likely causes of her postoperative trouble, stated that he had placed a suture in the bladder and that, upon dissolution, it had left a hole. The patient sued the physician. At trial, this statement was brought out in addition to the physician-defendant's testimony that the fistula could have resulted from the operation he performed. The court held in favor of the physician, stating that, upon viewing the evidence in the light most favorable to the patient, the most that the patient had proved was that an undesired and bad result followed the operation. Despite the statements made by the physician, the court held that negligence can not be shown in this type of case without medical testimony that the physician-defendant failed in some particular respect to use ordinary skill and care, unless the matter at issue is within the common knowledge of laypeople. This case was held to be of the type involving a highly complex operation about which laypeople have no common knowledge (*Dazet v. Bass*, 1971).[148]

Another source of the standard of care is the medical textbook. The admissibility of such evidence as proof of the standard, however, varies among jurisdictions. The traditional rule is that medical texts may be used in a malpractice lawsuit only to cross-examine a medical expert.[149] This is accomplished by framing a proposition in the exact language used by the author of the medical text, and then asking the witness whether he or she agrees. The expert witness being cross-examined need not initially agree that the text is standard or authoritative, otherwise the witness would have complete control of the cross-examination and could conceivably preclude the use of any text.[150] Even in those jurisdictions that adhere to this old rule, there is growing recognition of the emerging trend toward allowing such evidence to play a greater role at trial. The Supreme Court of Michigan, a state that maintains the old rule, has stated that the testimony of an expert witness is probably less reliable than testimony derived from textbooks since ordinary expert witnesses derive their knowledge not from personal experience but from studying scientific literature. The Court also pointed to the circumstances attending the publication of learned treatises and concluded that there is a fair probability that the work is trustworthy. The Court rejected the dangers of using passages that are explained away or contradicted in other parts of the book and noted that opposing attorneys, with the aid of the expert witness, may ask questions to point out the inaccuracy of the questionable text or to explain the meaning of technical passages. However, despite its recognition of the validity of these arguments, the Supreme Court of Michigan has refused to extend the permissible role of medical texts beyond the area of cross-examination.[151]

The Supreme Court of Wisconsin, in abolishing the old rule for that jurisdiction, made the following observation:

> The rule that medical and scientific textbooks are inadmissible as independent, substantive evidence has worked hardship in many cases, particularly because of the difficulty of obtaining medical testimony. Where the foundation is laid that the

work is authoritative, recognized by the medical profession, and one which has influence upon medical opinions, such works have now been admitted as independent evidence. . . . The Uniform Rules of Evidence . . . provide that "[a] published treatise, periodical or pamphlet on a subject of history, science or art" should be admitted in evidence as an exception to the hearsay rule "to prove the truth of a matter stated therein if the judge takes judicial notice or if a witness expert in the subject testifies, that the treatise, periodical, or pamphlet is a reliable authority on the subject" . . . we consider this to be the better rule and adopt it for future cases. This is but another example of accepting the scientific process in the search for truth instead of reliance upon the efficacy of an oath as a guarantee of trustworthiness.[152]

If a malpractice case is tried in a federal court, the Federal Rules of Evidence will apply; these allow statements from texts to be read directly into evidence[153] (see § 4.44, Textbooks).

In some jurisdictions, the recommendations of a drug or equipment manufacturer contained in the manufacturer's brochure or package insert have been used to establish the standard of care applicable to the use of that drug or device.[154] In other jurisdictions, however, manufacturers' recommendations have either been directly rejected as proof of the standard of care[155] or have been used to prove only that a physician had notice and should have been aware of the risks involved in the use of a drug or other medical product but have not been used by themselves to prove a specific standard of care.[156] The Minnesota Supreme Court has stated that, where a drug manufacturer recommends to the medical profession (1) the conditions under which its drug should be prescribed; (2) the disorders it is designed to relieve; (3) the precautionary measures that should be observed; and (4) warnings of the dangers inherent in its use, a physician's deviation from such recommendations is direct evidence of negligence if there is competent medical testimony that his or her patient's injury or death resulted from failure to adhere to the recommendations.[157]

The physician-defendant is not necessarily bound by the standard of care proved by the patient-plaintiff. If a choice may be made among various methods of medical treatment, the physician is not guilty of negligence for using a method recognized as good practice, even though a different physician might have employed another method.[158]

CASE ILLUSTRATION

The patient was pregnant for the third time. The physician determined late in the pregnancy that the patient's uterus may have been developing larger than normal. Within two hours of the onset of labor, the baby's head was engaged; within three hours, the cervix was fully dilated and completely effaced, and the membrane ruptured. At this time, fetal distress was noted. (On delivery, the umbilical cord was found wrapped around the infant's

§ *1.32* Standard of Care 29

neck.) The fetus was low down in the pelvis, in a face-up rather than in the more common face-down position. Several unsuccessful attempts were made to rotate the head manually. The physician decided to use forceps; the head was delivered and the wrapped cord discovered. However, the shoulders were not then delivered. The right shoulder had overriden the mother's pubic bone and was obstructed by it, preventing delivery. The baby suffered shoulder dystocia and resultant brachial plexus palsy.

The patient sued the physician. At trial, the patient-plaintiff asserted that the physician's failure to perform an X-ray pelvimetry in order to ascertain the necessity of a cesarean section delivery was negligent. The court stated that the failure to do an X-ray pelvimetry was not a departure from accepted medical practice, because the record revealed that the patient had undergone clinical pelvimetry which had disclosed an intertuberous diameter of 8.0 centimeters. Such a dimension does not indicate a need for X-ray pelvimetry. X-ray studies ruled out any congenital abnormality or multiple birth, and the intertuberous measurement indicated that the patient had an adequate pelvis for the delivery of a child. She had already given birth to an average-sized baby without difficulty. The court recognized that X-ray pelvimetry could be reasonably rejected in light of the fact that shoulder dystocia, a condition attendant at birth, could not be forecast by X-ray pelvimetry or any other diagnostic test. The court concluded that it could not be said that excessive force was used to deliver the shoulder merely because the child was delivered with palsy, a known complication of dystocia. The presence of an injury does not necessarily mean there was negligence. The court accepted the physician's use of his own judgment in choosing a vaginal delivery rather than a cesarean section in this case and exonerated him from liability (*Henry v. Bronx Lebanon Medical Center*, 1976).[159]

Where there is an honest difference of opinion between competent physicians, a physician who uses his or her own best judgment cannot be found negligent, even though it may afterwards develop that the physician was mistaken, unless it is shown that the course pursued was clearly against the course recognized as correct by the profession generally.[160] This is referred to as the "best judgment rule."* However, if the physician fails to assess the circumstances (for example, failing to make an adequate physical examination, failing to order necessary tests, and so on) with the requisite degree of skill, liability may be found.[161] In certain circumstances, a physician's departure from his or her own

---

*The best judgment rule does not usually serve as a successful defense in exonerating the physician. To invoke the rule as a defense, the physician must introduce evidence that all necessary tests and examinations were performed and followed up on; this then allows the court only to instruct the jury as to the existence of the best judgment rule.

best judgment may result in liability, even though in failing to reach this best judgment standard the physician complies with conventional good practice. This was the result in a New York case decided in 1968, where premature babies were blinded by retrolental fibroplasia as a result of the physician's excessive use of oxygen over an extended period of time in the incubator.[162]

The course of action followed by the physician in the exercise of his or her best judgment must be recognized as a proper course by at least a respectable minority of physicians. Showing that "some" obstetricians and gynecologists would have followed the physician-defendant's course of action does not rise to the level of a respectable minority.[163]

Where different schools of medical thought exist (for example, osteopathy versus allopathy), the law does not attempt to settle the debate; rather, the physician is held to the tenets of the school he or she professes to follow; this rule is also applied in the case of specialists.[164] Thus the osteopathic gynecologist may conduct his or her practice differently than the allopathic gynecologist, as long as the divergent practice conforms to principles governing the practice of osteopathic gynecology. Generally, the patient seeking treatment from an osteopath is assumed to know that the osteopath will follow the methods and practices observed by that school of medicine; the courts will not entertain the complaint that the osteopath failed to adhere to the standards of practice of another school.[165] Where procedures in different schools of medicine are similar, however, members of the different schools of medicine may be held to the same standard of care; a member of one school may testify to the standard observed by the other where he or she is shown to be familiar with the medical treatment procedure in question.[166] The Texas Court of Civil Appeals has stated that physicians of different schools may testify as to the applicable standard in malpractice cases where the particular subject of inquiry is common to and equally recognized and developed in both schools of practice and where the subject of inquiry relates to the manner of use of mechanical or electrical apparatus commonly used in both schools.[167]

§ 1.33 Consent and Informed Consent

Consent and *informed consent* are separate and distinct entities. When patients give or refuse to give consent, they are saying "yes" or "no." The quality and amount of information physicians give to secure the "yes" or "no" determines whether or not the patients gave consents based on sufficient information to make a decision—that is, informed consent.

Before a physician may treat or operate on a patient, the physician must obtain the patient's consent, if the patient is competent to give it; if the patient is not competent, the physician must obtain consent from someone legally authorized to give it on the patient's behalf.[168] The requirement for consent has been said to arise from the contractual nature of the physician-patient relationship; consent specifies what the parties understand is to be done.[169] The law imposes this requirement because it acknowledges that every human being of adult years and sound mind has a right to determine what shall be done with his or her own body.[170] For example, when an obstetrician/gynecologist prescribes contraceptives, the American College of Obstetricians and Gynecologists specifies (in *Technical Bulletin No. 46*) that "information should be provided regarding the relative effectiveness of various methods as well as their benefits and risks. Patients should be informed about potential minor and major side effects. They should be advised of possible symptoms, the occurence of which may necessitate a problem visit or discontinuation of the method."

Liability for failure to obtain the consent of the patient may be imposed under one of two different legal doctrines, depending upon the nature of the consent actually obtained. If the patient gives no consent to medical treatment, the physician who nevertheless renders such treatment may be legally liable for assault and battery. If the patient consents to medical treatment but does so without a fully informed understanding of the risks and hazards of the proposed treatment, the physician who fails to provide such information may be liable for breach of the duty to obtain the patient's informed consent.

Consent: Assault is defined as the act of placing a person in apprehension of a harmful contact;[171] battery is the actual contact. In other words, battery is the offensive touching of another without the consent or authorization of that person.[172] In most jurisdictions, the distinction is blurred and the legal action is for assault and battery under either definition.

In order to be held liable for assault and battery, a defendant must have commited some affirmative act that is intended to cause an unpermitted contact.[173] Assault and battery is an *intentional* tort (as opposed to negligence, which is an *unintentional* tort) in that it involves the planned and conscious touching of the patient-plaintiff's person. It is enough that the physician-defendant sets in motion a force that ultimately produces the result. The gist of the action for assault and battery is not the hostile intent of the defendant, but rather the absence of consent to the contact on the part of the plaintiff.[174] Thus, a plaintiff's cause of action for assault and battery must allege: (1) the defendant's intentional act, which resulted in (2) the offensive contact with the plaintiff's person and (3) the plaintiff's lack of consent thereto.[175]

In medical malpractice actions, a claim for assault and battery is most often based on an allegation that the physician operated or provided treatment without first obtaining the patient's authorization for the operation or procedure performed. If the patient can prove that the operation was performed without consent of any kind, liability will result. But the fact that a patient has manifested no express oral or written consent will not necessarily create liability for assault and battery. Instead, the circumstances surrounding the operation may well be such that *implied consent* can be found.

Courts have typically found implied consent in (1) discussions and conduct of the physician and patient in the course of their relationship; (2) an emergency requiring immediate treatment when the patient is unable to consent; or (3) a necessary extension of treatment during a procedure to which the patient has consented.

Discussions and conduct of the parties during the physician-patient relationship may modify the terms of a patient's previously expressed consent or may establish authority by implication for a treatment never expressly considered. Although the court found consent in the actions of the parties in the following case, such an outcome is rare, and most physicians should exercise great care to obtain express patient authorization for proposed treatment.

CASE ILLUSTRATION

The patient sued her physician, claiming that he had tied her fallopian tubes without her consent during the course of a cesarean section. Prior to the operation, the physician, the patient, and the patient's husband had discussed the cesarean section and the tubal ligation as a "package deal"; they had a tacit understanding that the physician would perform the ligation during the cesarean section unless the patient informed the physician that she did not want the ligation. The court stated that she had given implied consent to both operations. The court also noted as corroborative of this implied consent that the patient did not protest when the physician first informed her of having performed the ligation and that she continued under the physician's care without complaint. The court held in favor of the physician (*Haywood v. Allen*, 1966).[176]

An operation is not actionable on grounds that it was not described in the written consent form if there is sufficient evidence that the patient was given an oral explanation of the procedure and that she did not object.[177] The patient's silence at the beginning of treatment, however, does not give the physician free rein. Thus, a patient who periodically undergoes nonsurgical treatment for a condition does not by silence consent to surgical treatment.[178] Consent to a minor operation is not consent to a major one. If a patient signs a consent form for exploratory surgery and a consulting surgeon later performs remedial surgery without obtaining additional consent, the consulting surgeon may be held liable.[179]

It has been recognized that a physician is free to render *some* measure of medical or surgical assistance in *some emergency situations* without first obtaining the consent of the patient. Most courts in such cases imply consent from the circumstances, holding that the patient would have consented to the operation had she been able to do so. Some legal commentators explain that the physician may treat under these circumstances because the physician may reasonably assume that, if the patient were competent and able to understand the situation, she would consent. Therefore it is permissible to act as though consent had been given.[180]

The circumstances surrounding the injury and treatment dictate whether a court will acknowledge an emergency to exist. In general, an emergency exists if a patient is threatened with death or serious bodily injury[181] unless she receives immediate medical attention[182] but is incapable of consenting to the necessary treatment because of unconsciousness or some other incapacity. If the operation or procedure would benefit the patient but is not immediately necessary to preserve her life or health, an emergency does not exist.[183] In a Kentucky decision where a physician discovered during an operation that the patient's fallopian tubes were swollen and sealed and removed them on the grounds that they would have to be removed within six months anyway, the court held that liability would be imposed unless it was shown that the diseased tubes posed an immediate danger to the patient's life.[184] In cases where expert testimony established that removal of parts of a patient's fallopian tubes during an operation for appendicitis and salpingitis[185] and removal of an acutely inflamed appendix during an operation for a tubal pregnancy[186] were necessary to save the patient's life, courts have found emergencies to exist. The unplanned medical procedure must be shown to constitute treatment of a life-threatening condition.

Whether a necessary extension of treatment beyond that originally contemplated may be made without obtaining further consent from the patient is a question closely related to the emergency doctrine discussed above. If an emergency exists, the operation may be extended; if there is no emergency, an extension may give rise to liability. Some courts go beyond the emergency exception and hold that, at least in the case of internal operations, a physician may lawfully perform an operation consistent with good surgical practice even when to do so requires an extension of the originally planned operation.[187] These courts generally state that only necessary extensions may be undertaken,[188] but it is unclear whether "necessary" refers only to operations needed to preserve the patient's life or health or whether it includes those that will forestall future health problems. The latter interpretation would permit physicians to undertake unplanned operations even in the absence of a medical emergency.

The nature of the unplanned procedure may bear upon the question of liability. Some courts hold that the rule prohibiting an operation without consent applies only to operations *different in nature* from that for which consent was given.[189]

CASE ILLUSTRATION

The patient developed a vesicovaginal fistula after undergoing a trachelotomy and oophorectomy. She gave her written consent to a subsequent operation to repair the fistula. During this second operation, the physician noticed a small mole on the patient's leg and removed it. The patient brought suit, contending, among other things, that the removal of the mole constituted assault and battery. In upholding a jury award of $500 for the removal of the mole, the court rejected the physician's argument that removal was authorized by the patient when she gave written consent to the fistula operation. In fact, said the court, "Such written consent does not constitute consent to an operation other than the one to be performed when there is no evidence that a necessity arose during the authorized operation" (*Lloyd v. Kull,* 1964).[190]

This rule has also worked to the advantage of plaintiffs in cases where a hysterectomy was performed during an appendectomy[191] and an unnecessary appendectomy was performed during a hysterectomy.[192] Other courts, however, have shown greater willingness to allow physicians to exercise discretion, so long as the unplanned procedure concerned abnormal or diseased conditions found in the area of the original incision.[193]

In many situations the physician may justify an extension of the operation, not on the grounds that an emergency existed, but on the authority given the physician in a broadly worded consent form signed by the patient. Such a form may authorize the physician to perform any operations or procedures that he or she may consider necessary or advisable in the course of the operation.[194] In the absence of a showing that the patient's signature was obtained through fraudulent misrepresentation, such forms are presumed to establish a valid consent.[195] Thus, physicians who performed a complete hysterectomy during exploratory surgery[196] and a bilateral salpingectomy during pelvic surgery[197] were held not liable where the patients, prior to surgery, had signed consent forms broad enough in scope to include the unplanned operations.

Informed Consent: A patient who alleges lack of informed consent as the basis of a lawsuit does not deny that she consented to the operation actually performed but argues that her consent should be held ineffective because it was made on the basis of inadequate information. An operation performed on the basis of ineffective consent is tantamount to operating with no consent at all, and liability may result. It is important therefore to know what standard of disclosure must be met to obtain an informed consent.

In general, the physician has a duty to inform the patient of risks and expected results of the proposed treatment. Except in emergencies, this information should include the nature of the specific procedure or treatment, the medically significant risks involved, and the probable duration of incapacitation, if any. The physician must also discuss medically significant alternatives for care and treatment with the patient. Furthermore, the American Hospital Association's Patient's Bill of Rights states that the patient has the right to know the name of the person responsible for the procedures involved in the treatment.[198]

In a majority of states, the courts measure the physician's duty to disclose and the amount of information the physician must impart to the patient by the standards of the medical community.[199] Courts in these states have reasoned that the medical community can best determine which risks warrant disclosure;[200] in other words, whether disclosure of certain risks is necessary in a given case is determined by what other physicians in the same circumstances would have disclosed. Under this professional standard, some courts require the physician to prove compliance with the professional standard once the patient has proved nondisclosure of a specific risk.[201]

Some states have rejected the idea that the medical community should determine the standard of disclosure. These states have adopted a standard based on what a reasonable person in the patient's position would think and do. If a reasonable person would be likely to attach significance to the risk or risks in question, then the risk is material, and the physician must disclose any material risk to the patient. This standard emphasizes both the patient's right of self-determination and the idea that materiality of risk is often a nonmedical judgment.[202] Many courts have supported this standard.[203]

Even under this stricter standard, the patient must convince the jury that a reasonable person would not have consented to the operation.

CASE ILLUSTRATION

Having experienced recurrent vaginal bleeding since the birth of her fourth and last child, the patient consented to the physician's recommendation of a hysterectomy. The physician did not tell the patient that a vesicovaginal fistula might result. When a fistula did develop following the operation, the patient brought suit, contending that her consent had not been an informed consent. The jury returned a verdict for the physician, finding that a reasonable woman would not have been deterred from a hysterectomy by the remote possibility that a fistula would occur. The patient appealed, arguing that the standard should not be what a hypothetical reasonable woman would have done. The court rejected this argument and affirmed the verdict for the physician, stating: "The physician is bound to disclose only those risks which a reasonable [woman] would consider material to [her] decision whether or not to undergo treatment." If a reasonable woman informed of the risks would not have refused treatment, said the court, a failure to disclose will not create liability (*Bowers v. Garfield*, 1974).[204]

Regardless of which standard is applicable, the physician should always disclose risks unless he or she has a sound reason not to. A physician must be particularly careful to disclose risks of death or serious bodily injury before employing an uncommon treatment or procedure.[205]

Exclusions and Exceptions: Inverting the general rule, physicians have no duty to disclose risks that are not generally disclosed as a matter of accepted professional practice in their locality or within their specialty.

Foremost among the list of generally recognized exceptions to the physician's duty of disclosure are those risks that are minor or remote.[206]
Other exceptions arise where:

1. The patient is already aware of risk
2. Existence of the risk is a matter of common knowledge (the patient's knowledge of that risk may be inferred)
3. The risk was not generally known to the medical community at the time the procedure was carried out
4. Risk exists only when the procedure is negligently or improperly performed
5. Patient expressly requests that he or she not be informed*[207]

CASE ILLUSTRATION

For the convenience of the patient, the physician agreed to perform an amniotomy for the purpose of inducing labor. Although the induced birth was itself normal, the patient bled excessively from the vagina following the expulsion of the afterbirth. Massage of the uterus and administration of Pitocin failed to stop the bleeding. The physician then performed an emergency hysterectomy to prevent the patient from bleeding to death. The patient brought suit, contending that her consent to the amniotomy was not an informed consent because she was not told of the possibility that a postpartum hemorrhage might result. The court rejected this argument, holding that, because the procedure employed did not increase the risks already faced by the patient, the physician was under no duty of disclosure. "Postpartum hemorrhage," said the court, "is a risk or possibility in the delivery of a baby under any circumstances. Inducing labor by amniotomy under the circumstances present in this case created no additional risk, and there was no duty on the part of [the physician] to discuss the possibility with his patient" (*Parker v. St. Paul Fire & Marine Insurance Co.*, 1976).[208]

As with general consent requirements, medical *emergencies* constitute an exception to the informed consent requirement. An emergency exists when the patient is unconscious or otherwise incapable of consenting and failure to treat will result in harm outweighing any potential harm from the proposed treatment. In such situations the courts recognize an implied consent.[209]

One recognized limitation to the duty to disclose is referred to as *therapeutic privilege*. The courts recognize that complete disclosure may harm a pa-

---

*If the patient makes such a request, it must be noted in the patient's record. Otherwise, the physician will be unable to *show* that such a request was made, and it will be the patient's word against the physician's (see § 4.47, Medical Records).

tient.[210] Medical judgment must be used in determining whether disclosure of possible risks may so adversely affect the patient as to jeopardize success of the proposed therapy, no matter how expertly performed.[211] Because this is recognized as a medical decision, expert testimony may be required to prove that the therapeutic privilege has been properly exercised. In any event, it is generally the physician-defendant's burden to prove that the exercise of therapeutic privilege was justified.

In order to recover for a physician's failure to obtain an informed consent, the patient must prove the following: (1) that the physician failed to inform the patient of alternative treatments, of the reasonably foreseeable material risks of each alternative, and of the risks of no treatment at all; (2) that the patient (under the professional standard) or a reasonable patient (under the reasonable patient standard) would have chosen no treatment or a different course of treatment had the alternatives and the material risks been revealed; and (3) that the patient has been injured as a result of submitting to the treatment.[212] The patient will also have to produce expert testimony to show the existence and significance of the risk, the existence of alternative methods, and the fact that the patient's injury was caused by the occurrence of an undisclosed risk.[213]

Consent of Spouse: If a woman is mentally competent, her consent to an abortion or to the treatment of her own body is sufficient. The physician does not need to obtain her husband's consent, even if the operation will terminate pregnancy,[214] cause a possible miscarriage,[215] or render her infertile.[216]

CASE ILLUSTRATION

A physician performed a hysterectomy on a patient with her consent but without the consent of her husband. The husband brought suit against the physician and claimed damage to his right of consortium and to his right to have another child. The court upheld a judgment for the physician, declaring that a married woman in full possession of her faculties may submit to a surgical operation that will render her infertile, even though her husband has not consented to the operation. The court stated that a married woman has a natural right to her health and is not required to have the consent of her husband in order to receive surgical care from a physician (*Murray v. Vandevander*, 1974).[217]

In cases where the patient is unable to give consent, the physician may obtain the spouse's informed consent to proposed treatment.[218] If the patient is competent, however, her husband's consent may not be substituted for her own. For example, a Louisiana court held in 1978 that, in the absence of an emergency, a husband has no authority to approve the performance of a tubal ligation upon his wife in connection with childbirth.[219]

It is uncertain whether a woman may constitutionally be required to *consult* with her spouse before obtaining an abortion. In a 1979 case,[220] a federal court ruled that a statute providing for mandatory notification of the husband imposed an undue burden on a woman's right to terminate her pregnancy. The court indicated that, while such a statute might nonetheless be constitutional if it served a compelling state interest, the particular statute considered was overinclusive and therefore could not be upheld. In particular, the court objected to the statute's failure to make an exception for a married woman carrying the child of someone other than her husband. Instead, the court suggested a valid notification statute must be based upon fatherhood, not spousal status. In any event, giving the father of the unborn child a right to be notified or consulted is not equivalent to giving him veto power over the woman's decision to abort.

Capacity of Minor to Consent: Generally a minor cannot give consent, and a physician must obtain consent from a parent or guardian.[221] The U.S. Supreme Court, however, has consistently struck down state statutes requiring the consent of a parent, guardian, or person in loco parentis before performing a first trimester abortion on a pregnant woman under 18 years of age.[222] Special statutes in most states also permit a minor to give effective consent to medical examination for and treatment of venereal disease without parental consent.[223]

Although a state cannot constitutionally require parental *consent* to the provision of contraceptive services or abortions,[224] many states require parental *notification* prior to the provision of such services.[225] Such statutes, and parental notification in general, have been both criticized as imposing an undue burden upon the minor's decision to seek needed contraception[226] and extolled as a necessary safeguard of family integrity and stability.[227] The U.S. Supreme Court has recently resolved the notification issue by holding constitutional a state statute that requires the parents of an unemancipated minor to be notified before the performance of an abortion.[228]

Aside from special statutes and concerns of procreative rights, four other generally recognized exceptions to the parental consent requirement exist.

1. The minor requires emergency treatment: the courts generally construe the term "emergency" narrowly and apply it only where there is a danger to the minor's life requiring immediate attention.[229]
2. The minor is emancipated: an emancipated minor is a person under the age of majority who is no longer under the care or custody of his or her parents or other guardian.[230] A minor may be emancipated by marriage, by judicial decree, by consent of the parents, or by failure of the parents to meet their legal responsibilities of support to the minor. A minor will also generally be deemed emancipated if he or she lives apart from the parents, is self-supporting, and exercises general control over his or her own life. An emancipated minor may effectively consent to medical treatment provided he or she understands the nature and consequences of the treatment in question.[231]

3. The parents are so far away that it would be impractical to obtain consent in time: this exception, like the emergency exception above, is likely to be construed narrowly by the courts. The exception may justify treatment of the minor in the absence of parental consent only if the delay created by obtaining such consent would result in a serious deterioration in the minor's condition.
4. The child is close to maturity and knowingly gives an informed consent: some courts have held that "mature," unemancipated minors can give effective consent to medical treatment where the procedure is for the benefit of the minor and where the minor can understand its nature and consequences.[232]

§ 1.40 BREACH OF DUTY

A duty is an obligation recognized by the law (see § 1.30, Duty). The physician's duty to the patient is to provide the degree of care ordinarily exercised by physicians practicing in the same community or area of specialization (see § 1.32, Standard of Care). A breach of duty occurs when the physician's care fails to meet this standard.

The law holds a party who has committed a breach of duty responsible for all the consequences that a prudent, experienced person, fully acquainted with all the circumstances, would have thought at the time of the breach to be reasonably possible to follow.[233]

The legal inquiry as to breach of duty was expressed by one court, deciding a case involving misdiagnosis, in the following manner: "where . . . there is admittedly a misdiagnosis, the question remains as to whether such misdiagnosis was the exercise of a reasonable medical judgment or a judgment arrived at without the exercise of appropriate care," the implication is that a breach exists in the latter situation. The courts recognize that a physician cannot ensure satisfactory results and that unsuccessful results are not necessarily evidence of negligence.[234] This is generally an evidentiary task, accomplished through an examination of the facts of the case that gave rise to the malpractice lawsuit.

CASE ILLUSTRATION

The specialist in obstetrics and gynecology (hereinafter referred to as "gynecologist") delivered the patient's child by cesarean section. Some 20 months later, the patient returned to the gynecologist, complaining of pain in the lower right side of her abdomen. The gynecologist diagnosed an ovarian cyst. He administered an injection to suppress the cyst and prescribed further medication. A week later the patient returned, still complaining of abdominal pain. The gynecologist's examination confirmed that the cyst was still present, and he prescribed penicillin as well as pain tablets. On examination a week later, the gynecologist concluded that the size of the cyst had decreased; at this time, he learned that the patient had not menstruated, although menstruation had been due several weeks earlier. The gynecologist performed a D&C on the patient at the hospital, after which he concluded that the patient had neither ovulated nor miscarried. At the postoperative examination, the gynecologist felt no cysts in the patient's ovary.

A month later, the patient reported to the gynecologist that she had not yet menstruated, and the gynecologist prescribed medication which brought on menstruation. Three months later, the patient called the gynecologist's office complaining of pain in her left side. She was instructed to visit the office but never did. Four months after this, the gynecologist fitted the patient for an IUD, at her request. Six months later, at her regular checkup, the patient was examined, and the gynecologist found no problems. One month later, however, the patient returned, complaining of pain in her lower right abdomen. The gynecologist concluded that she had a tender right ovary and prescribed ampicillin. Four days later, the patient returned, still complaining of abdominal pain. Because of fever and an elevated white blood count, the gynecologist diagnosed appendicitis, along with the tender right ovary, which he classified as the same thing treated over a year earlier. In view of the diagnosis of appendicitis, the gynecologist referred the patient to a general surgeon.

The general surgeon saw the patient and initially diagnosed ovarian disease; however, based on conversations with the gynecologist, who stated that the patient's symptoms did not stem from gynecological problems, the general surgeon concluded that the patient's primary problem was appendicitis. The general surgeon performed exploratory surgery in the area of the patient's abdomen. He discovered appendicitis, which the pathological report classified as acute appendicitis. He also noted an oozing surface on the patient's right ovary, indicating a ruptured corpus luteum cyst, and he sutured the site of the oozing. During the operation, the general surgeon was able to see and examine the patient's reproductive organs, including both ovaries, her fallopian tubes, and her uterus. He concluded that there was no evidence of gynecological or ovarian disease, despite the presence of the ruptured corpus luteum cyst, which the surgeon regarded as a very common sight during an appendectomy.

Because of her complaint one month later of abdominal and chest pain and a burning sensation when she urinated, the patient was examined by an associate of the general surgeon. The general surgeon reexamined the patient the next day and conducted additional tests. Her symptoms included pain in the area of her incision and in her chest, tarry stools, and epigastric pain. Because of these symptoms and the patient's report of stress, the surgeon suspected an ulcer. The patient was admitted to the hospital because of continued abdominal pain, as well as a 40-pound weight loss. After extensive tests and numerous consultations, the diagnosis was recorded as "abdominal pain of unknown etiology."

Four months later, the patient experienced bleeding for 31 days. She consulted a second gynecologist. He examined the patient, observed that she experienced minimal tenderness in her uterus and ovaries, and suspected endometritis. A week later, he reexamined the patient. She was then experiencing pain in her right fallopian tube and ovary, along with vaginal bleeding. The second gynecologist removed the IUD at this time because the device often causes endometritis. Within a week, the patient again consulted the second gynecologist, complaining of pain on both the left and right sides of her abdomen. The gynecologist hospitalized her and performed a D&C. Approximately one week after the D&C, the patient again saw the second gynecologist, complaining of moderate to severe pain in her sides and abdomen; he found her to be suffering a prolapsed uterus. The second gynecologist recommended and subsequently performed a total hysterectomy.

The patient sued her original gynecologist and the general surgeon, alleging that their negligent treatment necessitated the hysterectomy. At trial, the second gynecologist testified as to his observations (made during surgery) of the patient's physical condition: the uterus was deeply recessed in the cul-de-sac and larger and softer than usual; the fallopian tubes appeared grossly abnormal; both ovaries were enlarged and cystic; the left ovary was twice the normal size and had a bleeding cyst; blood was present in the peritoneal cavity; both tubes and ovaries were adhered to by some fine tubo-ovarian adhesions; the veins in the infundibulopelvic ligament were larger than normal, and a few of them were tortuous, suggesting a pelvic congestion syndrome. The second gynecologist estimated that the condition had developed over a period of approximately two years but that the signs or symptoms may not have been apparent at the outset of the problem.

With respect to the breach of any duty owed the patient by the first gynecologist, the court stated:

> There is no suggestion that [the gynecologist's] treatment of [the patient's] complaints of a tender ovary . . . was not proper. [The gynecologist] testified that 15% of his patients each month have this complaint and that the condition almost always subsides with conservative treatment, as [the patient's] did.
>
> Nor is there any suggestion that the [first] "D&C" procedure . . . was improperly undertaken or yielded untoward results.
>
> [The patient's] next complaint was 14 months later and one month after a completely normal periodic checkup. [The gynecologist] began conservative treatment with antibiotics, but when a serious situation with possible appendicitis presented itself four days later, he immediately referred her to the proper specialist.

With respect to the breach of any duty owed the patient by the general surgeon, regarding his failure to discover the diseased organs during the appendectomy and his failure to seek gynecological consultation during the period in which he was unable to explain the patient's complaints of abdominal pain, the court stated:

> [The second gynecologist] carefully explained that [the patient] may have had normal looking organs at the time of surgery even if she complained of pain. . . .
>
> As to the failure to seek consultation by a gynecologist, [the general surgeon] explained that . . . [the patient] never stated any history of menstrual complaints or vaginal bleeding or discharge, or any other symptoms which would call for consultation with a gynecologist. There is absolutely no evidence in this record that she described any of these symptoms. More importantly, there is absolutely no expert testimony that because of the symptoms [the patient] did describe, [the general surgeon] should have called a gynecologist in consultation. In fact, the only expert evidence is directly to the contrary.

Accordingly, the court held that the physicians' conduct did not fall below accepted standards of proper medical care and thus did not constitute a breach of any duty owed the patient. The court exonerated both physicians (*Baker v. Beebe,* 1979).[235]

Courts often fail to distinguish between the duty and its breach in malpractice cases. The focus is generally on what duty is owed, and this may be defined by the standard of care. The parties to a case usually agree on the facts of the case but disagree on the appropriate standard of care. For example, in a case where the patient-plaintiff claims she was given an overdose of a drug, the medical record may disclose that the patient, suffering from X, was treated by the defendant-physician, who ordered a certain dosage of Y to be administered a certain number of times per day. Expert witnesses will then attempt to establish the standard of care—that is, the proper dosage for treating a patient with medical problem X with drug Y (see § 4.41, Expert Testimony). The standard is closely tailored to the facts of the case, and, once the court or jury decides on the proper standard of care, it is often obvious whether it has been breached. Thus, the question of the proper standard of care can "swallow up" the question of whether the standard has been breached. However, a finding a negligence requires both the determination of the standard of care and a determination that the acts of the defendant-physician have fallen below that standard.

§ 1.50 CAUSATION

Another of the essential elements for any claim of negligence is proof of causation—that is, that there be some reasonable connection between the act or omission of the defendant-physician and the injury the plaintiff has suffered. In fact, it has been held that if causation cannot be shown it is immaterial whether the patient-plaintiff sustained any damage[236] (see § 1.60, Damages).

It is important for a physician to realize that judges and attorneys view causation differently from physicians. A physician, in viewing a patient's current medical problems, usually searches for the basic or most immediate cause or causes of the disorder that underlies those problems. Also, the physician strives to identify and understand all aspects of the patient's condition. In contrast, the goal of judges and attorneys involved in a malpractice suit is to determine whether *a* particular occurrence has caused a specific condition suffered by the patient; they limit their concern to whether or not the event in question has caused the condition. Another difference is that the legal requirement of establishing proximate cause is generally "probability," "50.1 percent," "more likely than not," or "reasonable medical certainty"—none of which is as demanding as the scientific proof sought by physicians.[237] Consequently, causation means one thing to most physicians and quite another thing to judges and attorneys.

§ 1.51 Legal Principles of Causation

The legal issue of causation may be broken down into two inquiries: cause in fact and proximate cause. The cause-in-fact inquiry asks whether the conduct of the defendant caused the plaintiff's harm. The proximate cause inquiry attempts to limit legal responsibility to those causes so closely connected with the result in time and space and of such significance that the law is justified in imposing liability. This often involves a question of policy: some boundary must be set to limit liability for the consequences of any act, based upon some social concept of justice or policy;[238] this boundary is set by factual proximity.

Two formulas have evolved for dealing with questions of cause in fact. First is the "but for" formula, which directs that the defendant's conduct is not a cause of the event which resulted in the plaintiff's injury if the event would have occurred without it. In other words, the plaintiff's injuries would not have occurred *but for* the defendant's conduct. The formula works only to exclude certain defendants from liability. Even if the event would not have occurred but for the defendant's negligence, it does not necessarily follow that the defendant will be held liable. Thus, in a sense, this formula cannot by itself single out those defendants who should be held legally responsible.[239]

The second formula used by the courts in determining cause in fact is whether the defendant's conduct is a substantial factor in bringing about the harm.[240] The "substantial factor" formula may work to answer the question of causation in situations where the "but for" rule fails. For example, when there exist two causes, either of which operating alone would have been sufficient to cause a given result, the "but for" rule fails. However, each of the causes may be found to have been substantial factors in bringing about the event, and therefore liability may be found.[241] Although these formulas are not hard and fast rules used by the courts, they do provide a general sense of the content of the causation inquiry.

Proof of Causation: An important consideration in proving the existence of cause in fact is upon which party the burden of proof is placed. Generally, the burden of proof that the tortious conduct of the defendant has caused harm to the plaintiff is upon the plaintiff.[242] This means that, in most suits for malpractice, the plaintiff must introduce evidence showing that, more likely than not, the conduct of the physician was a substantial factor in bringing about the plaintiff's injury.[243] Thus, evidence must be presented that the patient's injury was more probably caused by the physician's conduct than not; proving that it was *possibly* caused by the physician's conduct is not sufficient.[244] A plaintiff has successfully proved causation when the evidence, taken as a whole, indicates that the defendant's negligence was the most plausible or likely cause of the occurrence and that no other factor can as reasonably be ascribed as the cause.[245]

In certain circumstances the burden of proof may be placed on the defendant. For example, when the conduct of two or more parties combines to bring about harm to the plaintiff, and one or more of the parties seeks to limit his liability on the grounds that harm is apportionable among them, the burden of proof as to the apportionment is upon each party. Also, when the conduct of two or more parties has been found to be negligent and it is proved that the injury to the plaintiff has been caused by only one of them, where there is uncertainty as to which one has caused it, the burden is upon each to prove that he or she has not caused the harm.[246] Thus, when two or more physicians may have injured a patient through negligent behavior, the burden of proof may be placed on them as to (1) what portion of the harm may have been caused by each and (2) whether or not the harm may have been caused solely by the other physician.

The question of which party has the burden of proof becomes important when the evidence shows only that it is as equally probable that the defendant's conduct caused the plaintiff's harm as it is that his or her conduct did not. In this situation, the court must direct a verdict for the party that did not have the burden of proof, since the party with the burden has failed to meet it.[247] Therefore, when a patient alleges negligence on the part of a physician but can only introduce evidence that there is an equal chance that the physician did or did not cause the patient's injury, the court must decide in favor of the physician-defendant.

CASE ILLUSTRATION

The patient underwent a hysterectomy and afterwards sustained a loss of feeling and mobility in her left arm. The patient sued her gynecologist, the nurse-anesthetist and the hospital. At trial, she offered medical testimony suggesting that she had suffered a brachial plexus injury to her left arm as a result of improper positioning of her arms during surgery. The physician-defendant showed at trial that the positioning of the patient was in accordance with the standard procedures for positioning and offered testimony showing that her symptoms were also compatible with the diagnosis of a small artery occlusion in the brain. About two years after the hysterectomy, the patient suffered additional cardiovascular problems. A transfemoral aortic angiogram showed significant blockage of the artery supplying her left arm in the left side of her brain. The jury found the defendant's theory of causation more persuasive and therefore exonerated the physician. The appellate court affirmed this conclusion, stating that ample evidence was submitted to permit the jury to find that the patient had not suffered a brachial plexus injury or that, if she had, it was not the fault of the physician (*Bertrand v. Aetna Casualty and Surety Co.*, 1975).[248]

Causation in fact is a question of fact and is appropriately left for the laypersons of the jury. The jury, or the judge in a nonjury trial, assesses this causal link by considering relevant evidence. Causation, like any other fact, may be proved by direct or circumstantial evidence.[249] However, expert medical testimony is generally required to supply evidence of causation. The jury is not permitted in the absence of such testimony to speculate whether different treatment would have yielded a different result.[250]

CASE ILLUSTRATION

A physician diagnosed that the patient, a 33-year-old woman, was suffering from a uterine tumor. Pursuant to that diagnosis, he performed an operation, during which no tumor was found, but the patient was discovered to be six to eight weeks pregnant. Twenty-two days after the operation, the patient miscarried. She subsequently sued the physician for negligence, alleging that the physician's actions had caused her miscarriage. The evidence of proximate cause at the trial consisted only of the fact that miscarriage occurred 22 days after the operation and the statement of the physician that the operation "could have" caused the miscarriage, although in his opinion it did not. The patient introduced no expert medical testimony that the operation probably did cause the miscarriage, nor was there any evidence of any signs or symptoms of impending spontaneous abortion between the time of the operation and the occurrence of the miscarriage. The court acknowledged the rule that ordinarily expert evidence is necessary to support the conclusion of causation. The court also acknowledged that there may be situations in which causation is so apparent that laypersons with a general knowledge would have no difficulty in recognizing it. But the court adhered to the rule that the causal connection between an accident and an injury must be shown by medical testimony and that testimony must reveal that causation is probable and not merely possible. On this question, the court stated that it is general knowledge that miscarriages may result from a myriad of causes. The court found nothing in the circumstances of the case to establish the probability, rather than merely the possibility, that the operation was the cause in this particular instance. Therefore, the court concluded that there was insufficient evidence of causation and held in favor of the physician (*Jarboe v. Harting*, 1965).[251]

In situations where causation is so apparent that laypersons with general knowledge would have no difficulty in recognizing it, expert testimony may not be required[252] (see § 1.32, Standard of Care).

Proximate Cause: Once the issue of cause in fact has been settled in favor of the plaintiff, the question remains whether the defendant-physician should be held legally responsible for the harm he or she has caused. This inquiry becomes essentially a question of whether the policy of the law will extend the responsibility for the conduct to the consequences that resulted. This issue can be stated as whether the defendant has a duty to protect the plaintiff against such consequences.[253] In other words, the foreseeability of the actual injury suffered is considered. A party charged with negligence is responsible for those consequences of the negligent act that a prudent person, fully acquainted with all the circumstances that exist, whether ascertainable by reasonable diligence or not, would have thought at the time of the negligent act to be reasonably possible to follow.[254] Thus, responsibility will only be imposed where the conduct is the proximate cause of those consequences. The word "proximate" is used in the sense of nearness and refers to the fact that the conduct must be sufficiently close to the injury to justify holding the actor liable. Some confusion has resulted from labeling this inquiry "proximate" cause. The suggestion has been raised that the terms "legal cause" or "responsible cause" would be more appropriate. However, it is unlikely that the courts will substitute either term.[255]

An Oklahoma court has stated that, since a proximate contributing cause is not required to be the only cause of the injury, a defendant should be held responsible for setting in motion a chain of circumstances that resulted in the ultimate injury, even though other circumstances also contributed to the injury. The court also stated that the proximate cause of any injury must be the efficient cause of what sets in motion the chain of circumstances leading to the injury; if the negligence complained of merely furnishes a condition by which the injury was possible and a subsequent independent act caused the injury, the existence of such a condition is not the proximate cause of the injury.[256]

The causal effect of a physician's conduct may not be limited, however, by a speculative assertion that the patient *might* have refused treatment to correct the injury. If it can be proved, such an argument is viewed as one in mitigation of damages only[257] (see § 1.60, Damages).

CASE ILLUSTRATION

After the physician delivered the patient's third child, he inserted a Dalkon Shield, a type of IUD. Two months later, the patient returned to the physician for an examination, at which time the physician was unable to manually locate the IUD. He ordered X rays to be taken, and, based on the X-ray reports, he informed the patient that the IUD was properly located. Seven months later, the patient became pregnant and agreed to an abortion and a tubal ligation to be performed by the physician. During surgery, the physician was unable to locate the IUD, and he ordered X rays immediately after surgery; these were taken by the hospital radiologist. Later that day, the patient spoke to the physician, asking about the location of the IUD. He told her it was gone and not to worry. Shortly thereafter, the patient was released from the hospital. The following month, the patient called the physician, complaining of pain and discomfort, for which he prescribed medication. During the next two years, the pain and discomfort increased to the point where the patient was forced to quit her job. Finally, the pain was so extreme that the patient was again admitted to the hospital. X rays were ordered and taken immediately. The X rays revealed the IUD to be located in the patient's peritoneal cavity. The physician operated the next day, successfully removing the IUD. Afterwards, the patient healed and progressed well.

The patient sued the physician, alleging that he failed to use due care by neglecting to inform himself of the results of the original X rays he ordered to determine the location of the IUD and that such failure caused the patient compensable pain and suffering. On the issue of causation, the physician asserted that there was no evidence that the patient would have consented to the removal of the IUD if she had been informed of its location earlier. In other words, the physician claimed that the patient's pain and suffering was caused by the patient's refusal or failure to submit to an operation to remove the IUD. The court held, based on expert testimony, that the jury could determine that the patient's pain of two years' duration was caused by the presence of the IUD in the peritoneal cavity. Furthermore, the court noted that, because the patient consented to the removal of the IUD at the time of the abortion and tubal ligation and immediately consented to its removal two years later when its location was discovered, strong and convincing evidence existed that she would have undergone an earlier operation if given the chance. Consequently, the court reversed a judgment favoring the physician and ordered a new trial (*Killebrew v. Johnson*, 1980).[258]

§ 1.52 Res Ipsa Loquitur

If a patient suffers an injury under circumstances making it difficult to identify the cause, and if the injury is one that would not ordinarily have occurred without negligence, the law affords the patient a possible means of recovery: the doctrine of res ipsa loquitur. "Res ipsa loquitur" is a Latin phrase that means "the thing speaks for itself."[259] Res ipsa loquitur permits the jury to draw logical conclusions from circumstantial evidence,[260] and negligence, like any other fact, may be proved by circumstantial evidence.[261]

The basic premise of res ipsa loquitur is that in certain factual situations the probability that the defendant was negligent "speaks for itself." In these cases the patient-plaintiff is relieved of the usual burden to prove a specific act or omission constituting negligence. The 1863 English case in which the doctrine was first applied provides an example of a situation where, in the absence of contrary evidence, common sense says there *must* have been negligence.

CASE ILLUSTRATION

The plaintiff was walking down a street when he was hit and injured by a barrel of flour that rolled out of a warehouse window. The plaintiff sued the owner of the warehouse but could not identify the specific negligent act that allowed the barrel to fall. In prior lawsuits, a plaintiff's inability to produce such evidence would have required dismissal of his suit. The court, however, applied the doctrine of "res ipsa loquitur," holding that a barrel is so unlikely to fall out of a warehouse window in the absence of negligence that proof of a specific act of negligence is unnecessary. Instead, said the court, the facts surrounding the injury by themselves create an inference of negligence sufficient to allow recovery by the plaintiff (*Byrne v. Boadle*, 1863).[262]

A small number of jurisdictions have expressly excluded the application of res ipsa loquitur to malpractice cases.[263] Where the doctrine has been applied, courts and legal commentators have provided policy arguments supporting the use of res ipsa loquitur in appropriate cases. The doctrine has been described as providing an otherwise unavailable remedy for the person who is unexplainedly injured so that he or she will not have to bear the full burden of the injury.[264] In the context of medical malpractice, it is argued that placing the risk of unexplained injuries on the physician-defendant could possibly result in better procedures and greater protection for the unconscious patient.[265]

The reluctance of physicians to testify against one another has given impetus to the application of res ipsa loquitur to medical malpractice cases.[266] No matter how lacking in skill or how negligent the physician-defendant might be, it has often been almost impossible to find physicians willing to provide adverse testimony in litigation based on the defendant's alleged negligence. Not only would the guilty person thereby escape civil liability for the wrong committed, but his or her colleagues would have failed to ensure that the same results would not occur again at the same hands. To overcome this difficulty, and to aid patients who, because of their lack of medical knowledge, cannot identify the source of their injury, the courts place the burden of explaining what occurred on the physician.[267] Thus, res ipsa loquitur has been applied in medical malpractice the result was unusual and unexpected,[283] or even fatal, because without an abnormal consequence no legal action in damages could be brought in the first place. For res ipsa loquitur to apply, the patient-plaintiff must show that some extraordinary or unusual event outside the routine of the medical treatment procedure occurred and that this event, if unexplained, would reasonably speak to the average person as negligence.[284] If no reason exists to suspect negligence, res ipsa loquitur cannot be applied.

CASE ILLUSTRATION

One-and-one-half years after the physician performed a bilateral tubal ligation upon her, the patient became pregnant. After the birth of the child, the patient and her husband brought suit against the physician to recover medical expenses and the expenses they expected to incur in raising the child. Expert testimony at trial indicated that 1½ to 2 percent of properly performed tubal ligations are unsuccessful and do not result in sterility. There was no evidence that any specific act of negligence had occurred during the operation. The court refused to apply res ipsa loquitur, stating that, "since ensuing pregnancy does not necessarily indicate improper performance of the operation, res ipsa loquitur is not applicable" (*Coleman v. Garrison*, 1975).[285]

The patient's inability to demonstrate that her unexplained injury was probably the result of negligence has prevented application of res ipsa loquitur in a number of cases. As stated above, the doctrine is particularly inapplicable if the injury might ordinarily happen in the absence of negligence. Courts have refused to apply the doctrine where the patient developed a partial bowel obstruction following a cesarean section;[286] where the patient suffered severe pain in the pubic area after surgery on an enlarged ovary;[287] and where the patient developed a ureterovaginal[288] or vesicovaginal fistula following a hysterectomy.[289] On the other hand, if the most apparent explanation for the injury complained of is negligence on the part of the defendant, the doctrine may be applied. Thus res ipsa loquitur has been held to apply in cases where the patient's ureter was severed during performance of a modified radical hysterectomy;[290] where the patient's baby suffered blindness in one eye following a forceps delivery;[291] and where a sponge was left in the patient's vaginal tract following childbirth.[292] Negligence is particularly likely to be inferred if the injury is to a part of the body not within the operative field, as where the patient suffers burns on her buttocks during a vaginal operation[293] or emerges from a hysterectomy with a paralyzed right arm.[294] The courts assert that, if surgery to or manipulation of a part of the body normally *will* produce drastic symptoms in parts of the body unrelated to the site of the surgery or manipulation, the physician should be able to rebut the inference of negligence by simply proving that fact.[295]

Some courts require the evidence to support a finding that injuries such as the patient's are more likely the result of negligence than some other cause.[296] Other courts have stated that all possible explanations of the injury other than the defendant's negligence must be excluded.[297] It has also been held that, when the record is abundantly clear that what occurred in the case could not have been prevented by any technique known to and recognized by the medical profession, the doctrine of res ipsa loquitur will not be applied.[298] The evidence must demonstrate at least a probability that the patient's mishap could not have occurred without negligence by the physician.[299] Some courts have also imposed a corollary requirement that no direct evidence should exist establishing that some specific act of negligence could be the only likely cause of the harm. If such a specific act is the only explanation, it must be proved without the aid of the doctrine.[300]

Where a patient alleges negligence on the part of a physician-defendant, it generally must be proven by a preponderance or greater weight of the evidence. Res ipsa loquitur does not eliminate this burden,[301] it only modifies it to require a showing that the injury would not have occurred unless the defendant was negligent. Requirements vary among the jurisdictions regarding the sort of evidence necessary to prove the patient's injury was caused by negligence. Some require that there be definite medical expert testimony to that effect[302] unless it is so apparent that a layperson would have no difficulty recognizing it.[303] In some situations, expert testimony may be required to invoke the doctrine of res ipsa loquitur at all, because medical expertise may be needed to assist the lay members of the jury when the medical cause of the injury is not grossly apparent.[304] Some jurisdictions allow expert medical testimony, seemingly at the patient-plaintiff's option in appropriate cases, where such testimony merely strengthens the inference that accidents of the kind in question do not commonly happen in the absence of negligence.[305] In situations where expert testimony is required, the plaintiff's failure to provide expert testimony linking the physician's negligence with the patient's injuries would prevent the doctrine from being applied.[306] The expert opinion requirement has been held to apply only to such matters as are within the domain of medical science; matters within the common knowledge of mankind may be testified to by anyone familiar with the facts.[307]

Some jurisdictions require that, in order for res ipsa loquitur to apply, it must be a matter of common knowledge among laypeople or medical practitioners, or both, that the patient's injury would not have occurred without negligence.[308] It is the general rule in Texas[309] and some other jurisdictions[310] that res ipsa loquitur never applies in medical malpractice cases except where the nature of the alleged malpractice and injuries are plainly within the common knowledge of laypeople.[311] General examples of common knowledge situations indicating negligence include surgical instruments or foreign objects left inside the body or an injury to a part of the body not involved in the operation.[312] On the other hand, injuries such as a ureterovaginal[313] or vesicovaginal[314] fistula resulting from a hysterectomy and secondary anemia due to an alleged misdiagnosis of complete abortion[315] have been held to be not the type that a layperson could determine by common knowledge were caused by negligence. Determinations of negligence have been said to be within common knowledge when they could be made in the light of past experience[316] or on the basis of common sense.[317]

Where evidence is offered that the injury could have resulted from other causes, the use of res ipsa loquitur has been questioned by the courts. Those jurisdictions that do not require the plaintiff to exclude every possibility that the injury was caused by something other than the defendant's negligence let the jury draw an inference of the defendant's negligence if the plaintiff produces sufficient evidence. This approach is supported by the concept that, where reasonable parties differ as to the balance of probabilities at fault, the court must leave the question to the jury.[318] This approach to the application of the doctrine has been referred to as "conditional res ipsa loquitur" by some courts.[319] Some jurisdictions have further refined this requirement by holding that, where two or more possible causes of the injury exist and the physician was only responsible for one of them, the several causes of the injury must be equally probable to preclude the jury from applying res ipsa loquitur.[320] In jurisdictions that apply the doctrine, the plaintiff is allowed to offer proof that specific acts of the defendant caused the injury and still rely on res ipsa loquitur, unless the evidence of the specific acts fully explains the cause of the injury. If the specific proof is unpersuasive, however, the plaintiff may rely on res ipsa loquitur.[321]

In practice, the fact that there may be multiple causes of a particular injury often results in the nonapplication of res ipsa loquitur.

CASE ILLUSTRATION

Fourteen days after undergoing an abdominal hysterectomy, the patient developed a vesicovaginal fistula. A second operation corrected the condition. The patient sought to apply res ipsa loquitur in a suit brought against the gynecologist who performed the hysterectomy, contending that the operation was under his exclusive control and that the patient's injury was of a type that does not ordinarily occur in the absence of negligence. Evidence at trial established that the patient's fistula could have been caused by clamping, stitching, or suturing the bladder and vagina together or by an abscess that ruptured into the vagina. Holding that under these circumstances res ipsa loquitur could not be applied, the court stated: "In view of the alternative possible causes of the fistula established by the evidence, one of which was an abscess not stemming from negligence, it cannot be said the occurrence of that injury, in itself, establishes negligence on the part of the defendant" (*Tatro v. Lueken*, 1973).[322]

As noted above, however, the mere *possibility* that the patient's injury had a nonnegligent cause will not preclude use of res ipsa loquitur as long as negligence remains the most likely explanation. Thus, a patient who suffered burns on her buttocks during a vaginal operation was permitted to use res ipsa loquitur, even though the physician-defendant suggested that the burns might have resulted from an allergy.[323] The doctrine is also likely to be applied in a case where the injury could have had a nonnegligent cause if it is shown that actual negligence did occur, *increasing the risk* of such an injury.[324]

To summarize, where the plaintiff can show that her injury was of the type that would only occur as the result of the defendant's negligence, she has proved the first element required by the doctrine of res ipsa loquitur. In some jurisdictions this element is not satisfied if common knowledge would not permit an inference of negligence; in others, if expert testimony will not support it. Where causes other than negligence may explain the injury, the first element of res ipsa loquitur is not proven unless the plaintiff's evidence permits an inference of negligence despite the existence of other explanations. In all cases, res ipsa loquitur is merely an evidentiary doctrine; it is the jury or court that makes the final decision of fact.

Defendant-Controlled Instrumentality: Once the requirements of the first element of res ipsa loquitur are met, the plaintiff must address the second element and show that the injury was caused by an agency or instrumentality within the exclusive control of the defendant.[325]

A minority of courts have employed this requirement to limit the applicability of the doctrine. Where a number of people have control or partial control of the patient during surgery and thereafter, and where the patient's injury may have occurred by the act or omission of any of them, res ipsa loquitur has not been applied due to failure on the part of the patient to show the actual thing, instrument, or occurrence causing the disability.[326]

An increasing number of jurisdictions follow the rule established in the case of *Ybarra v. Spangard*. In that case, the plaintiff sought recovery from the owner of the hospital and from multiple physicians and nurses for an arm injury apparently suffered during the course of an appendectomy. The defendants stated their defense in two propositions: (1) that, where there are several defendants and a division of responsibility in the use of the instrumentality that caused injury and where the injury might have resulted from the separate acts of one of two or more persons, res ipsa loquitur should not be used; and (2) that, where there are several instrumentalities and no showing is made as to which caused the injury or as to the particular defendant in control of it, the doctrine should not be applied. The court responded that every defendant who had custody of the plaintiff for any period concomitantly had control of the instrumentality causing the injury. This test, one of right of control rather than actual control, placed the burden of explanation upon the defendants. Since the plaintiff was rendered unconscious, said the court, it was unreasonable to insist that he identify the particular defendant who committed the negligent act. The court also rejected the defendant's second argument, holding that the unconscious patient does not have to identify the specific instrumentality which injured him, but must show only that he suffered an injury resulting from an external force applied while he lay unconscious, since this is as clear a case of identification of the instrumentality as the plaintiff might ever be able to make.[327]

Most courts do not give this control requirement a strict literal interpretation, and the phrase "exclusive control" has been criticized as not being in all cases an accurate statement of the principle. The principle requires that other responsible causes, including the conduct of the plaintiff and third persons, be sufficiently eliminated by the evidence. "Control" is afforded substantial flexibility by the courts. It has been held to be sufficient that the defendant has the right or power of control, that he or she has the opportunity to exercise it, and that he or she shares the duty and the responsibility of such control. A Colorado court has stated that it is sufficient to show that at the relevant time the instrumentality was under the control of no person who was not a defendant or an employee of a defendant.[328] Certain courts have commented that it would be far better, and avoid much confusion, if the idea of control were discarded altogether in favor of a statement that the apparent cause of the accident must be such that the defendant should be held responsible for any negligence connected with it.[329]

Absence of Patient's Contributory Negligence and Accessibility of Evidence: The third factual requirement of res ipsa loquitur, that the patient's injury must not have been due to any voluntary action or contribution on the part of the patient,[330] has not often been an issue in cases involving gynecological or obstetrical treatment. Particularly when the patient is anesthestized or restrained, it would be difficult for her to act in a manner that would contribute to her injury.[331] However, where a patient knowingly fails to disclose to the physician a condition or symptom germane to a proposed course of treatment or fails to follow the physician's instructions on self-care, the court may find contributory negligence on the part of the patient. Such a finding would bar use of res ipsa loquitur.

The fourth factual requirement that the evidence as to the cause of the injury be more accessible to the physician than to the patient,[332] has been given minimal elucidation by the courts. The courts recognize that the patient's lack of knowledge as to the facts causing the injury might exist not only where she is totally unconcious but also where she is partially unconscious and largely, if not entirely, unaware of what the medical personnel are doing.[333] However, it is not uncommon for the courts, when listing the elements of res ipsa loquitur, to omit all mention of this fourth element.[334] Even the third element (absence of contributory negligence) is sometimes omitted from the definition.[335] It is thus apparent that the third and fourth elements of res ipsa loquitur generally are not as important as the first two.[336] The fourth is often referred to as "another factor which some of the cases have considered in applying the doctrine."[337] Some commentators have stated that the situation should be otherwise, recognizing that:

> [S]ince res ipsa loquitur alters what a physician-defendant would ordinarily be required to do in defending against a malpractice claim, equity requires that the *lack* of greater accessibility to evidence by the physician-defendant be considered. One need not be a physician to know that operative procedures, for example, are becoming more sophisticated and complicated, and there is necessarily greater reliance by physicians on the expertise of a growing number of fellow professionals. Consequently, a physician may well have no more personal knowledge of the circumstances immediately surrounding the injury than the plaintiff, and it may be unreasonable to assume that he has superior knowledge or access thereto in every situation. The physician may have superior knowledge in medical matters generally, and he may have voluntarily assumed the position of special trust and confidence to his patient; but it does not necessarily follow that the physician be prevented from effectively asserting good faith objection to the application of res ipsa loquitur where he has no greater access to explanatory evidence than does the patient.[338]

§ 1.60 DAMAGES

Damages must be proved by the patient-plaintiff in order to succeed in a negligence cause of action against a physician for malpractice.[339] Generally, the concept of damages encompasses actual loss or damage resulting to the interests of another.[340] Where such damages can be proved, they may encompass a wide range of financial, physical, or emotional injuries. The law has identified these various injuries by recognizing certain categories of damages. This categorization is often imprecise and inconsistent because some of the categories tend to overlap or are not strictly adhered to by the courts. Furthermore, myriad variations exist among the jurisdictions. The more common categories include:

1. *General damages*—those that the law presumes to have accrued from the wrong complained of, in that they are the immediate, direct, and proximate result, or those that necessarily result from the injury without reference to any special circumstance of the plaintiff,[341] such as generalized pain and suffering.

2. *Special damages*—those that are the actual but not the necessary or inevitable result of the injury complained of and that follow the injury as a natural and proximate consequence in the particular case,[342] such as the cost the plaintiff might incur in hiring a visiting nurse as a result of her injury. Typical items of special damage that the law regards as compensable include (1) past and future medical, surgical, hospital, and related costs, (2) past and future loss of income (wages, salary, profits), (3) the necessary hiring of a substitute, (4) in a death case, funeral expenses, and (5) unusual physical or mental consequences of the injury alleged, such as aggravation of a preexisting condition, miscarriage or disturbance of menstruation, and neurosis or psychosis.[343]

§ 1.60 Damages 57

3. *Punitive/Exemplary damages*—those awarded to the plaintiff over and above his or her actual losses, when the wrong done was aggravated by circumstances of violence, oppression, malice, fraud, or wanton and intentional conduct on the part of the defendant. Such damages are intended by some courts to make an example of the defendant or to punish negative behavior.[344] Other courts, however, assert that the idea of punishment does not enter into the definition, the term being employed to mean an increased award in view of the supposed aggravation of the injury to the plaintiff by the wanton or reckless act of the defendant.

With the possible exception of exemplary damages, the purpose of a damage award is to compensate the plaintiff for the injury suffered in the only manner open to the law—payment of money damages. The goal is to do substantial justice between the parties to the suit,[345] pursuant to the recognition that, but for the negligence of the defendant, the plaintiff would be in a better position than she currently is in.[346] Damages are measured by comparing the condition the plaintiff would have been in had the defendant not been negligent, with the plaintiff's impaired condition resulting from such negligence;[347] they are awarded to the extent that a plaintiff can be restored to the position he or she would have occupied had the injury not occurred.[348] Some courts hold that the person responsible must respond for all damages resulting directly from and as a natural consequence of the wrongful act, according to common experience and in the usual course of events, whether the damages could or could not have been foreseen by the defendant.[349]

As items of general damages, the injured party may recover both for the actual physical injury sustained and for the mental and emotional suffering that flow as a natural consequence of the wrongful act.[350] In a discussion of possible damages that might result in a case where a sterilization operation fails, a California court cited the following examples:[351]

> The mental suffering attendant to the unexpected pregnancy because of the complications which may or may not result, the complications that do result, and the delivery of a child are all foreseeable consequences of the failure of the [sterilization] operation. If the mother dies in childbirth from foreseeable complications of the proscribed pregnancy, the defendants may be chargeable therewith. . . . Presumably the . . . surviving children and the husband would be compensated in an action for wrongful death for the value of her society, comfort, care, protection and right to receive support which they lost.
>
> If she survives but is crippled from the same causes and is no longer able to perform her maternal and conjugal duties, the physicians would have to compensate her for her injuries, and her husband for loss of her services and for medical expenses.
>
> Where the mother survives without casualty there is still some loss. She must spread her society, comfort, care, protection and support over a larger group. If

this change in the family status can be measured economically it should be as compensable as the former losses.[352]

The courts recognize the difficulty in objectively evaluating and presenting evidence of subjective pain. In some jurisdictions, in order to prevent self-serving testimony, no lay witness may express an opinion on the matter;[353] other jurisdictions allow the injured party to testify to his or her own pain.[354] This problem of objectivity has not prevented recovery, however, and damages for physical pain have been awarded for a mother's pain and suffering during a normal pregnancy and delivery where a child was born subsequent to a negligently performed sterilization[355] and for pain suffered when a physician and hospital staff failed to attend a delivery and the mother suffered an abruptio placenta.[356] In some cases the newborn infant, injured as a result of proven physician negligence, may seek damages for pain, if such can be proven, during a lengthy hospitalization subsequent to its birth. The courts recognize that, although pain is a subjective reality, the infant may be too young to testify to it. However, a jury can determine from the infant's, parents', and physicians' testimony of its injuries and responses what is fair and reasonable compensation for such suffering.[357] In addition, the likelihood of future pain may be compensated, if proven; such proof is generally required to come from expert testimony.[358]

The courts have also wrestled with the subjective aspect of general damages for emotional suffering and anguish, leaving the issue largely unsettled. Emotional damages such as anxiety and mental distress are usually recoverable where they can be shown to be a direct injury flowing from the physician-defendant's breach of duty. Emotional distress has been found to be a direct result of a physician's negligence where a patient-plaintiff gave birth to a child with Down's syndrome after having been advised by her physician that the child would be normal despite the patient's medical history (she was 37 years old, had a thyroid condition, and had previously given birth to a deformed child) and without having been advised of the availability of an amniocentesis test.[359] The courts have recognized that mental and emotional distress are just as real as physical pain, and just as compensable.[360]

The courts note that medical knowledge about the relationship between emotional disturbance and physical injury has expanded and that the existence of the relationship no longer seems open to serious challenge.[361] Moreover, not only justice, but logic, compels the conclusion that, if the claimant is entitled to recover pecuniary losses for physical injury, she is also entitled to recover for the emotional harm caused by the same tortious act.[362] While this recognition allows some courts to award damages for emotional suffering where physical injury is also shown, it can preclude recovery for negligent infliction of emotional distress in the absence of physical injury.[363]

Often a plaintiff will seek damages for emotional trauma resulting from physical injury to someone with whom they have a close personal relationship, such as parents who witness injuries to their children.[364] In the context of obstetrics, some jurisdictions recognize a cause of action seeking damages for emotional distress where the pregnant patient seeks genetic counseling and is told that her fetus is normal[365] or where the physician fails to properly attend delivery[366] and the patient subsequently gives birth to a defective child. Those courts view the parent's mental anguish resulting from the birth of a defective child as the type of direct injury flowing from the physician-defendant's alleged breach of duty that may be compensated[367] and acknowledge that the shock to a mother resulting from danger or harm to her child may be both a real and a serious injury.[368]

Other jurisdictions reject this analysis and require that such an injury must be a reasonably foreseeable consequence of the defendant's negligence,[369] in order to limit what has been characterized as "the otherwise potentially infinite liability which would follow every negligent act."[370] The current test of foreseeability of emotional damages requires that such factors as the following be taken into account:

1. Whether the plaintiff was located near the scene of the accident
2. Whether the shock resulted from a direct emotional impact upon the plaintiff from the sensory and contemporaneous observance of the accident
3. Whether the plaintiff and the victim were closely related[371]

Those jurisdictions that require foreseeability for recovery of emotional damages recognize that this is not the only test that should be applied. They fear that, if foreseeability were the sole test, then liability, once established, could potentially be applied almost limitlessly: it would extend to other children, fathers, grandparents, relatives or others in loco parentis, and even to sensitive caretakers or affected bystanders. Moreover, in any one incident, there might well be more than one person indirectly but seriously affected by the shock of injury or death to the child.[372] A New York court has sought to limit such damages by awarding them to the mother but not the father.[373] Despite these obstacles, many courts have held that emotional distress of the parents is a foreseeable consequence of injuries negligently inflicted on a child prenatally or at birth[374] and is a recoverable item of general damages.

Special damages recoverable by the plaintiff include such medical expenses as have been reasonably or necessarily incurred or will, to a reasonably medical certainty, be incurred in the future by reason of the additional medical, hospital, or supportive expense occasioned by the injury.[375] Some jurisdictions have characterized this expense as economic injury that flows from negligent conduct.[376] In a reported case where a patient underwent a negligently performed tubal ligation and subsequently gave birth to a normal child, the court awarded special damages of the medical expenses incurred due to the patient's hospital confinement as well as the expenses of an additional sterilization operation.[377] Cases with facts such as these are referred to as "wrongful conception" cases (see

§ 2.41, Wrongful Conception). In such cases, plaintiffs have sought special damages for the expense of raising and educating the unwanted child. Most courts have rejected this approach as against public policy in that it would mean the physician would have to pay for the joy and affection that the parents will derive from rearing and educating the newborn.[378] Those courts that do award the cost of raising the child argue that the notion that individuals should be compensated for an unwanted child no more offends the belief that birth or life in any form is an ultimate good than does the concept of birth control. It is no answer to say that a result which a patient specifically sought to avoid might be regarded as a blessing by someone else. Furthermore, these courts have found it unsatisfactory to, in effect, grant immunity to physicians who negligently perform sterilization procedures by denying such damages to the plaintiff.[379]

In "wrongful birth" cases, which involve the birth of a defective child resulting from the physician's negligent genetic counseling or treatment (see § 2.42, Wrongful Birth), the same special damages are often sought.[380] Recovery appears to depend upon the extent of the defect as well as certain accepted policy considerations. Where expenses of raising a child with Down's syndrome were alleged as damages in a 1979 New Jersey case, the court stated:

> Although these costs were "caused" by defendants' negligence in the sense that but for the failure to inform, the child would not have come into existence, we conclude that this item of damage should not be recoverable. In essence . . . [the plaintiffs'] desire to retain all the benefits inuring in the birth of the child—i.e., the love and joy they will experience as parents—while saddling defendants with the enormous expenses attendant upon her rearing. Under the facts and circumstances here alleged, we find that such an award would be wholly disproportionate to the culpability involved, in that allowance of such a recovery would both constitute a windfall to the parents and place too unreasonable a financial burden upon physicians.[381]

In a 1977 New York case, in which the parent-plaintiffs were advised after one of their children was born with polycystic kidney disease that their future children would not have the disease and a subsequent child was born suffering from the disease, the court awarded damages for support expenses incurred during the lifetime of the child, arguing that such expenses were damages flowing directly from the physician's negligence.[382]

Other special damages often sought in cases involving obstetrics and gynecology are those for the loss of services of the injured party by family members. When a spouse seeks such damages they are referred to as loss of consortium,* and they are awarded if they can be shown to "flow from the tort."[383] Each spouse has a cause of action for loss of consortium caused by negligent or intentional injury to the other spouse by a third party. Some courts hold that

---

*Consortium refers to the conjugal fellowship of husband and wife and the right of each to the company, cooperation, affection, and aid of the other in every conjugal relation.

special damages for loss of consortium may only be awarded if a physical injury is suffered by the nonplaintiff spouse.[384] Where a wife is debilitated as the result of negligently performed treatment, any resulting injuries she sustains constitute a direct tort on her but not her husband. The actionable wrong against the husband is seen to be the interference with his marital rights, depriving him of his wife's services, society, and companionship and requiring expenditures by him for her medical treatment and care.[385] Where a father seeks damages for the loss of services of a child born deformed, courts will not award such damages where the infant's cause of action will not be recognized.[386] Where the infant sues for negligence in the genetic counseling of his parents resulting in his birth with deformity, such a cause of action is referred to as "wrongful life" (see § 2.43, Wrongful Life). Wrongful life actions have generally not been recognized by the courts.

Children have been prevented from recovering for the loss of services of their mother. This issue was raised in a 1979 Washington case where a mother suffered a stroke as the result of an oral contraceptive prescription. She suffered significant permanent impairment, including loss of mobility and inability to speak and converse in a normal manner. The court noted numerous considerations that weighed against granting children a right of action, including (1) the absence of any legally enforceable claim by a child to his parent's services, (2) the absence of precedent for such a holding, (3) the uncertainty and remoteness of the damages involved, (4) the possible overlap with the other parent's recovery for loss of consortium, (5) the potential multiplication of litigation if such damages were allowed, (6) the possibility of settlements made with parents in the same suit being disrupted, (7) the danger of fabricated actions, and (8) the predicted resulting increase in insurance costs.[387]

On the other hand, in a 1980 Texas case involving a mother who died during an elective operation to remove her gallbladder, the court held that children may recover damages for the loss of their mother's services. In such cases, the court stated, juries may consider the care, maintenance, support, services, education, and advice that the children would in reasonable probability have received from their mother.[388]

While punitive or exemplary damages are rarely awarded in malpractice actions,[389] courts have noted that there is no rational justification for a separate rule or language applicable to the medical profession.[390] Exemplary damages may only be assessed when the actions of the physician-defendant constitute gross negligence or intentional or malicious conduct.[391] A leading authority defines punitive damages as "damages, other than compensatory or nominal damages, awarded against a person to punish him for his outrageous conduct." Outrageous conduct is further defined to include "acts done with a bad motive or with a reckless indifference to the interests of others."[392] Conduct supporting a punitive damage award must possess the outrageous character frequently associated with actual crime: it must be willful or wanton.[393] Ordinary negligence alone is insufficient to support punitive damages, however culpable that negligence may be.[394]

Attaching a monetary valuation to such subjective concepts as physical pain, emotional pain, suffering, or loss of conjugal relations is a task generally left to the jury.[395] While it has been stated by the courts that the damages may not be determined by mere speculation or guess,[396] calculations described as "a reasoned estimate of the damages sustained"[397] or "the best estimate that can be made under the circumstances"[398] have been held acceptable. The courts assert that calculations of this nature are not alien to the American judicial system; jurors are called upon to make similar determinations quite often.[399] Furthermore, such calculations are made by estate planners, insurance companies, and sometimes by private parties incident to support proceedings or matrimonial settlements.[400]

Imprecision in the estimation of monetary value has not been allowed to constitute a barrier to the plaintiff's recovery.[401] There need only be a reasonable basis for ascertaining the amount of damages.[402] A New Jersey court has expressed this consideration in the following strong language:

> [W]here a wrong itself is of such a nature as to preclude the computation of damages with precise exactitude, it would be a perversion of fundamental principles of justice to deny all relief to the injured party and thereby relieve the wrongdoer from making any amend for his act.[403]

The actual amount to be awarded in damages is generally determined by the jury in a malpractice case.[404] Once a jury makes a damage award, it is highly unlikely that its award will be altered by either the trial judge or a reviewing appellate court[405] unless it shocks the court's conscience or is clearly erroneous.[406]

A plaintiff is generally required to offset or mitigate the damages he or she suffers by any benefit coincidentally derived from the defendant's conduct. For example, in a California case where the failure of a sterilization operation and the ensuing pregnancy benefited the patient's emotional and nervous makeup and infirmities in her kidney and bladder, the physician-defendant was allowed to offset those benefits against the patient's recovery.[407] Other examples of mitigating factors in failed sterilization cases are the satisfaction, joy, and companionship that parents receive in the rearing of a child.[408] Furthermore, any conduct by the patient that contributes to her damages lessens the physician-defendant's liability[409] (see § 3.20, Contributory Negligence).

Sometimes courts identify an affirmative duty on the part of the patient to take steps to lessen the degree of damage she has suffered: she cannot recover for damage that she could readily avoid without undue risk or expense, such as undergoing safe and simple treatment to correct the injury complained of.[410] Nor may the patient aggravate or increase her injury by her own negligence,[411] for example by failing to follow her physician's advice. On the other hand, a patient need not undergo a dangerous or serious operation that poses a threat to her life or that represents one choice among several less radical treatments.[412] Thus a patient who becomes pregnant subsequent to a negligently performed sterilization operation is not necessarily required to undergo an abortion to mitigate her damages. This is because courts see abortion as a right, not an obligation, and because imposing a legal requirement to abort a fetus is an invasion of the patient's privacy and is in violation of the law. The courts also recognize that a number of factors must be considered in the abortion decision, including the stage of pregnancy when the abortion is sought, the health and physical condition of the mother, and the medical judgment of a physician as to the advisability of such a procedure.[413] A Minnesota court has summarized the appropriate measure of damage for the birth of a normal, healthy child caused by a negligently performed sterilization operation as follows:

> Computation of rearing costs must begin with an assessment of the reasonably foreseeable expenses that will be incurred by the parents to maintain, support, and educate their child. In the case of a normal, healthy child, we would anticipate that these expenses could not ordinarily be projected beyond the age of his majority, for it is at that age that the parental duty to support ceases. . . . [In order] to prevent unjust enrichment, the [jury] will then be required to reduce these costs by the value of the child's aid, comfort, and society which will benefit the parents for the duration of their lives. While we recognize that the dollar value of the benefits to be offset is difficult to assess, we have routinely allowed recovery for the loss of aid, comfort, and society in wrongful death actions where similar problems of proof are presented.
>
> To assist the jury in measuring the various and complex elements of damage, we finally require that all future actions for wrongful conception be submitted to the jury with a special verdict* form along with explanatory instructions. Coupled with these precautions should be a strict judicial scrutiny of verdicts to prevent excessive awards.[414]

NOTES

1. Continuing Medical Malpractice Insurance Crisis: Hearings before the Subcommittee on Health of the Committee on Labor and Public Welfare, 94th Cong., 1st Sess. 154, 220 (1975–76).
2. Black's Law Dictionary 1111 (4th ed. 1968).
3. Ziemba v. Sternberg, 45 A.D.2d 230, 357 N.Y.S.2d 265 (1974).
4. Leighton v. Sargent, 27 N.H. 460, 59 Am. Dec. 388 (1853).
5. W. Prosser, Handbook of the Law of Torts 139 (4th ed. 1971).
6. Stewart v. Rudner, 349 Mich. 459, 84 N.W.2d 816 (1957).
7. Mich. Comp. Laws Ann. § 556.132 (1967 & Supp. 1981–82).
8. National Association of Insurance Commissioners, 2 NAIC Malpractice Claims 3 (1978).
9. *Id.* at 1.
10. *Id.* at 26–29.

---

*A special verdict is a special finding of the facts of a case by a jury on each material issue of the case, as opposed to a general verdict, whereby the jury finds either for the plaintiff or for the defendant in general terms.

11. *Id.* at 68.
12. *Id.* at 71–72.
13. Hirsch & White, *The Pathologic Anatomy of Medical Malpractice Claims,* 6 Legal Aspects Med. Prac. 28–29 (1978).
14. *Id.*
15. *Id.*
16. *See, e.g.,* Bir v. Foster, 123 So.2d 279 (Fla. App. 1960); Burks v. Baumgartner, 72 N.M. 123, P.2d 57 (1963).
17. *See* Hirsch & White, *supra* note 13, at 32; R. Dripps, S. Eckenhoff & L. Vandam, Introduction to Anesthesia 53 (5th ed. 1977).
18. Hirsh & White, *supra* note 13, at 32.
19. W. Prosser, *supra* note 5, at 143.
20. *Id.* at 149–50.
21. Yoshizawa v. Hewitt, 52 F.2d 411 (9th Cir. 1931); Boyce v. Brown, 51 Ariz. 416, 77 P.2d 455 (1938); Ales v. Ryan, 8 Cal.2d 82, 64 P.2d 409 (1936); Rierce v. Patterson, 50 Cal. App.2d 486, 123 P.2d 544 (1942); Froid v. Knowles, 95 Colo. 223, 36 P.2d 156 (1934); Hudson v. Weiland, 150 Fla. 523, 8 So.2d 37 (1942); Merker v. Wood, 307 Ky. 331, 210 S.W.2d 946 (1948).
22. Childs v. Weis, 440 S.W.2d 104 (Tex. Civ. App. 1969); Kreisman v. Thomas, 12 Ariz. App. 215, 469 P.2d 107 (1970); Clark v. Smith, 494 S.W.2d 192 (Tex. 1973).
23. Restatement (Second) of Torts § 283 (1965).
24. Robinson v. Wirts, 387 Pa. 291, 127 A.2d 706 (1956).
25. Lince v. Monson, 363 Mich. 135, 108 N.W.2d 845 (1961).
26. Alexandridis v. Jewett, 388 F.2d 829 (1st Cir. 1968).
27. Koury v. Follo, 272 N.C. 366, 158 S.E.2d 548 (1968).
28. Alexandridis v. Jewett, *supra* note 26.
29. Hart v. Steele, 416 S.W.2d 927 (Mo. 1967).
30. Pugh v. Swiontek, 115 Ill. App.2d 26, 253 N.E.2d 3 (1969); *See also* Renslow v. Mennonite Hosp., 67 Ill.2d 348, 10 Ill. Dec. 484, 367 N.E.2d 1250 (1977).
31. Pugh v. Swiontek, *supra* note 30.
32. Renslow v. Mennonite Hosp., *supra* note 30.
33. Dietrick v. Inhabitants of Northampton, 138 Mass. 14, 52 Am. Rep. 242 (1884).
34. Allaire v. St. Luke's Hosp., 184 Ill. 359, 56 N.E. 638 (1900).
35. Bonbrest v. Kotz, 65 F. Supp. 138 (D. D.C. 1946).
36. Amann v. Faidy, 415 Ill. 422, 114 N.E.2d 412 (1953).
37. Chrisafogeorgis v. Brandenberg, 55 Ill.2d 368, 304 N.E.2d 88 (1973).
38. Renslow v. Mennonite Hosp., *supra* note 30.
39. *Id.*
40. Bounet v. Foote, 47 Colo. 282, 107 P. 252 (1910); Paulson v. Stocker, 53 Ohio App. 229, 4 N.E.2d 609 (1935); Lagerpusch v. Lindley, 253 Iowa 1033, 115 N.W.2d 207 (1962); Ziemba v. Sternberg, *supra* note 3; Greenwood v. Harris, 362 P.2d 85 (Okla. 1961); Pugh v. Swiontek, *supra* note 30.
41. McHugh v. Audet, 72 F. Supp. 394 (M.D. Pa. 1947).
42. Jarboe v. Harting, 397 S.W.2d 775 (Ky. 1965); Just v. Littlefield, 151 P. 780 (Wash. 1915).
43. Crovella v. Cochrane, 102 So.2d 307 (Fla. App. 1958).
44. Bilk v. Schweizer, 149 S.E.2d 565 (N.C. 1966).
45. Pilgrim v. Landham, 63 Ga. App. 451, 11 S.E.2d 420 (1940).
46. Gridley v. Johnson, 476 S.W.2d 475 (Mo. 1972).
47. Paulson v. Stocker, 53 Ohio App. 229, 4 N.E.2d 609 (1935).
48. Stevenson v. Yates, 208 S.W. 820 (Ky. 1919).
49. Robinson v. Amick, 24 S.E.2d 461 (W. Va. 1943).

50. Gridley v. Johnson, *supra* note 46.
51. Ziemba v. Sternberg, *supra* note 3.
52. Childs v. Weiss, *supra* note 22.
53. American Medical Association, *Principles of Medical Ethics,* VI in Current Opinions of the Judicial Council of the American Medical Association ix (1981) [hereinafter cited as AMA].
54. Hill v. Ohio County, 468 S.W.2d 306 (Ky. 1971).
55. Childs v. Weiss, *supra* note 22.
56. Kilbane v. County of Ramsey, 193 N.W.2d 301 (Minn. 1971).
57. Keene v. Wiggins, 69 Cal. App. 3d 308, 138 Cal. Rptr. 3 (1977).
58. Wilcox v. Salt Lake City Corp., 26 Utah 2d 78, 484 P.2d 1200 (1971); Rogers v. Horvath, 65 Mich. App. 644, 237 N.W.2d 595 (1976).
59. Johnston v. Sibley, 558 S.W.2d 135 (Tex. 1977).
60. Rainer v. Grossman, 31 Cal. App.3d 539, 107 Cal. Rptr. 469 (1973); Oliver v. Brock, 342 So.2d 1 (Ala. 1977).
61. Shapira v. United Medical Services, Inc., 15 N.Y.2d 200, 205 N.E.2d 293 (1965).
62. Travelers Ins. Co. v. Bergeron, 25 F.2d 680 (8th Cir. 1928), *cert. denied,* 278 U.S. 638 (1928); Findlay v. Board of Supervisors, 72 Ariz. 58, 230 P.2d 526 (1951); Kennedy v. Parrott, 243 N.C. 355, 90 S.E.2d 754 (1956); Hull v. Enid Gen. Hosp. Found., 194 Okla. 446, 152 P.2d 693 (1944).
63. Hammonds v. Aetna Cas. & Sur. Co., 237 F. Supp. 96 (N.D. Ohio 1965); Berkey v. Anderson, 1 Cal. App. 3d 790, 82 Cal. Rptr. 67 (1969); Adams v. Ison, 249 S.W.2d 791 (Ky. App. 1952).
64. Stacey v. Pantano, 177 Neb. 694, 131 N.W.2d 163 (1964).
65. Hankerson v. Thomas, 148 A.2d 583 (D.C. 1959).
66. McNamara v. Emmons, 36 Cal. App.2d 199, 97 P.2d 503 (1939); Stewart v. Rudner, *supra* note 6.
67. Tunkl v. Regents of the University of California, 60 Cal.2d 92, 383 P.2d 441, 32 Cal. Reptr. 33, (1963); Olson v. Molzen, 558 S.W.2d 429 (Tenn. 1977).
68. Restatement (Second) of Torts § 323 (1965).
69. *See generally* W. Prosser, *supra* note 5, at 344.
70. Childs v. Weiss, *supra* note 22.
71. Granger v. Craven, 159 Minn. 296, 199 N.W. 10 (1924).
72. Vidrine v. Mayes, 127 So.2d 809 (La. App. 1961).
73. Williams v. Hosp. Auth., 119 Ga. App. 626, 168 S.E.2d 336 (1969); Wilmington Gen. Hosp. v. Manlove, 174 A.2d 135 (Del. 1961).
74. Manlove v. Wilmington Gen. Hosp., 169 A.2d 18 (Del. 1961).
75. Guerrero v. Copper Queen Hosp., 112 Ariz. 104, 537 P.2d 1329 (1976).
76. Cal. Health & Safety Code, § 1407.5.
77. Williams v. Hosp. Auth., *supra* note 73.
78. Campbell v. Mincey, 413 F. Supp. 16 (D. Miss. 1975); Hill v. Ohio County, *supra* note 54.
79. Childs v. Weiss, *supra* note 22.
80. Hill v. Ohio County, *supra* note 54.
81. Ala. Code § 7-121(1) (1975 & Supp. 1980); Alaska Stat. § 08.64.365 (1977); Ariz. Rev. Stat. Ann. § 32-1471 (1976 & Supp. 1980-81); Ark. Stat. Ann. § 72-624 (1979); Cal. Bus. & Prof. Code § 2144 (West 1974 & Supp. 1981); Colo. Rev. Stat. § 13-21-108 (Supp. 1982); Conn. Gen. Stat. Ann. § 52-557b (West Supp. 1981); Del. Code Ann. tit. 24, § 1767 (Supp. 1980); D.C. Code Encycl. § 2-142 (West Supp. 1978-79); Fla. Stat. § 768.13 (West 1976 & Supp. 1980); Ga. Code Ann. § 84-930 (Harrison 1979 & Supp. 1980); Hawaii Rev. Stat. § 663-1.5 (1976); Idaho Code § 5-330 (1979 & Supp. 1981); Ill. Ann. Stat. ch. 91, § 2a (Smith-Hurd 1978

& Supp. 1980–81); Ind. Code Ann. § 34-4-12-1 (Burns 1976); Iowa Code Ann. § 613.17 (West Supp. 1981–82); Kan. Stat. Ann. § 65-2891 (1980); La. Rev. Stat. Ann. § 9:2793 (West 1977 & Supp. 1981); Me. Rev. Stat. Ann. tit. 32, § 3151 (1980); Md. Health Code Ann. art. 43, § 149A (Supp. 1980); Mass Gen. Laws Ann. ch. 112, § 12B (1980); Mich. Comp. Laws Ann. § 691.1501 (Supp. 1981–82); Minn. Stat. § 604.05 (Supp. 1983); Miss. Code Ann. § 88-93-5 (1972); Mo. Rev. Stat. § 6190.195 (1983); Mont. Rev. Codes Ann. § 17-410 (1970 & Supp. 1977); Neb. Rev. Stat. § 25-1152 (1965); Nev. Rev. Stat. § 41.500 (1979); N.H. Rev. Stat. Ann. § 329:25 (1966 & Supp. 1979); N.J. Stat. Ann. § 2A:62A-1 (West Supp. 1981–82); N.M. Stat. Ann. § 12-12-3 (Supp. 1975); N.Y. Educ. Law § 6513 (McKinney 1972 & Supp. 1980–81); N.C. Gen. Stat. §§ 20-166, 8-95 (1975 & Supp. 1979); N.D. Cent. Code § 43-17.37 (1960 & Supp. 1977); Ohio Rev. Code Ann. § 2305.23 (Page 1980); Okla. Stat. Ann. tit. 76, § 5 (Supp. 1980–81); Or. Rev. Stat. § 30.800 (1979); 12 Pa. Cons. Stat. Ann. §§ 1641, 1642 (Purdon Supp. 1981–82); R.I. Gen. Laws § 5-37-14 (Supp. 1980); S.C. Code § 46-803 (Supp. 1980); S.D. Codified Laws Ann. §§ 20-9-3, -4, -4.1 (1979); Tenn. Code Ann. § 63-622 (1976); Tex. Rev. Civ. Stat. Ann. art. la (Vernon Supp. 1980–81): Utah Code Ann. § 58-12-23 (1974 & Supp. 1979); Vt. Stat. Ann. tit. 12, § 519 (Supp. 1980); Va. Code § 54-276.9 (1978); Wash. Rev. Code §§ 4.24.300, .310 (Supp. 1981); W. Va. Code § 55-7-15 (1981); Wis. Stat. Ann. § 147.17(7) (West Supp. 1980–81); Wyo. Stat. Ann. § 33.343 (1977).

82. D. Louisell & H. Williams, Medical Malpractice § 21.35 (1980).
83. *See, e.g.*, Va. Code § 54-276.9 (1978).
84. *See, e.g.*, Ga. Code Ann. § 84-930 (Harrison 1979 & Supp. 1980); Md. Health Code Ann. art. 43, § 142A (Supp. 1980); Mich. Comp. Laws Ann. § 691.1501 (Supp. 1981–82).
85. *See, e.g.*, Ariz. Rev. Stat. Ann. § 32-1471 (1976); Conn. Gen. Stat. Ann. § 52-557b (West Supp. 1981); Mass. Gen. Laws Ann. ch. 112, § 12B (1980); N.Y. Educ. Law § 6527 (McKinney 1972 & Supp. 1980–81); Ohio Rev. Code Ann. § 2305.23 (Page 1980).
86. *See, e.g.*, Cal. Bus. & Prof. Code § 2144 (West 1974 & Supp. 1981); Conn. Gen. Stat. Ann. § 52-557b (West Supp. 1981); Mass Gen. Laws Ann. ch. 112, § 12B (1980).
87. *See, e.g.*, N.D. Cent. Code § 43-17.37 (1975 & Supp. 1977); N.H. Rev. Stat. Ann. § 329:25 (1966 & Supp. 1979); S.D. Comp. Laws Ann. § 20-9-3 (1979); Mass. Gen. Laws Ann. ch. 112, § 12B (1980).
88. *See, e.g.*, Mich. Comp. Laws Ann. § 691.1501 (Supp. 1981–82); N.Y. Educ. Law § 6527(10) (McKinney 1972 & Supp. 1980–81); 42 Pa. Cons. Stat. Ann. §§ 8331 (a), (b) (Purdon Supp. 1981–82).
89. Ind. Code Ann. § 34-4-12-1 (Burns 1976).
90. Dale v. Donaldson Lumber Co., 48 Ark. 188, 2 S.W. 703 (1887); Miller v. Dore, 154 Me. 363, 148 A.2d 692 (1959); Schmit v. Esser, 183 Minn. 354, 236 N.W. 622 (1931); Boyd v. Andrae, 44 S.W.2d 891 (Mo. 1932); Welch v. Frisbie Memorial Hosp., 90 N.H. 337, 9 A.2d 761 (1939); Halverson v. Zimmerman, 60 N.D. 113, 232 N.W. 754 (1930); Ricks v. Budge, 91 Utah 307, 64 P.2d 208 (1937); McManus v. Donlin, 23 Wis.2d 289, 127 N.W.2d 22 (1964).
91. Lawson v. Conaway, 37 W. Va. 159, 16 S.E. 564 (1892); Ricks v. Budge, *supra* note 90.
92. Tresemer v. Barke, 86 Cal. App.3d 656, 150 Cal. Rptr. 384 (1979).
93. Lee v. Dewbre, 362 S.W.2d 900 (Tex. Civ. App. 1962).
94. Ascher v. Gutierrez, 533 F.2d 1235 (D.C. Cir. 1976).

Notes: Chapter I

95. Norton v. Hamilton, 92 Ga. App. 727, 89 S.E.2d 809 (1955).
96. *Id.*
97. Medvecz v. Choi, 569 F.2d 1221 (3d Cir. 1977).
98. Wooten v. Curry, 362 S.W.2d 820 (Tenn. App. 1961).
99. Williams v. Bennet, 582 S.W.2d 577 (Tex. App. 1979).
100. Roberts v. Wood, 206 F. Supp. 579 (S.D. Ala. 1962).
101. Lee v. Dewbre, *supra* note 93; *see also,* AMA *supra* note 53, at § 5.50.
102. Johnson v. Vaughn, 370 S.W.2d 591 (Ky. App. 1963).
103. Kenney v. Piedmont Hosp., 136 Ga. App. 660, 222 S.E.2d 162 (1975).
104. Howell v. Carpenter, 19 Mich. App. 233, 172 N.W.2d 549 (1969).
105. *In re* Culbertson's Will, 57 Misc.2d 391, 292 N.Y.S.2d 806 (1968).
106. Sendjar v. Gonzales, 520 S.W.2d 478 (Tex. App. 1975).
107. Miller v. Dore, 148 A.2d 692 (Me. 1959).
108. Lee v. Dewbre, *supra* note 93.
109. White v. Edison, 361 So.2d 1292 (La. App. 1978), *cert. denied,* 363 So.2d 915 (La. 1978).
110. Katsetos v. Nolan, 368 A.2d 172 (Conn. 1976).
111. Vick v. Methodist Evangelical Hosp., Inc., 408 S.W.2d 428 (Ky. 1966).
112. Prosser, *supra* note 5, at 162.
113. Eckleberry v. Kaiser Found. Northern Hosp., 226 Or. 616, 359 P.2d 1090 (1961).
114. Kronke v. Danielson, 108 Ariz. 400, 499 P.2d 156 (1972).
115. Small v. Howard, 128 Mass. 131, 35 Am. Rep. 363 (1880).
116. Webb v. Jorns, 488 S.W.2d 407 (Tex. 1972).
117. *See* Sampson v. Veenboer, 252 Mich. 660, 234 N.W. 170 (1931); McGulpin v. Bessmer, 241 Iowa 1119, 43 N.W.2d 121 (1950).
118. *Id.*
119. Vita v. Dolan, 132 Minn. 128, 155 N.W. 1077 (1916).
120. Ardoline v. Keegan, 140 Conn. 552, 102 A.2d 352 (1954).
121. Sales v. Bacigalupi, 47 Cal. Rptr. 2d 82, 117 P.2d 399 (1941).
122. Gist v. French Hosp. & Clinic, 136 Cal. App.2d 247, 288 P.2d 1003 (1955).
123. Brune v. Belinkoff, 354 Mass. 102, 235 N.E.2d 793 (1968).
124. Christy v. Saliterman, 288 Minn. 144, 179 N.W.2d 288 (1970).
125. Kronke v. Danielson, *supra* note 114.
126. Wiggins v. Piver, 276 N.C. 134, 171 S.E.2d 393 (1970); Naccarato v. Grob, 384 Mich. 248, 180 N.W.2d 788 (1970).
127. Kronke v. Danielson, *supra* note 114; Roberts v. Tardif, 417 A.2d 444 (Me. 1980).
128. Siirila v. Barrios, 58 Mich. App. 721, 228 N.W.2d 801 (1975).
129. *Id.*
130. Sinz v. Owens, 33 Cal.2d 749, 205 P.2d 3 (1949); Baldor v. Rodgers, 81 So.2d 658 (Fla. 1955); Osborne v. Frazor, 58 Tenn. App. 15, 425 S.W.2d 768 (1968).
131. Voegeli v. Lewis, 568 F.2d 89 (8th Cir. 1977); Hamilton v. Hardy, 549 P.2d 1099 (Colo. App. 1976).
132. Peters, *The Application of Reasonable Prudence to Medical Malpractice Litigation: The Precursor to Strict Liability?* 9 Law, Med. & Health Care 21 (1981).
133. Carmichael v. Reitz, 95 Cal. Rptr. 381, 17 Cal. App.3d 958 (1971); Dazet v. Bass, 254 So.2d 183 (Miss. 1971).
134. Kronke v. Danielson, *supra* note 114; Croda v. Sarnacki, 414 Mich. 882, 322 N.W.2d 712 (1982).
135. Brown v. Colm, 11 Cal.3d 639, 114 Cal. Rptr. 128, 522 P.2d 688 (1974).
136. *Id.*
137. Perin v. Hayne, 210 N.W.2d 609 (Iowa 1973); Tomei v. Henning, 67 Cal.2d 319,

62 Cal. Rptr. 9, 431 P.2d 633 (1967); Halligan v. Cotton, 193 Neb. 331, 227 N.W.2d 10 (1975); Pry v. Jones, 253 Ark. 534, 487 S.W.2d 606 (1973).
138. Pry v. Jones, *supra* note 137.
139. Graham v. Sisco, 248 Ark. 6, 449 S.W.2d 949 (1970).
140. Lanier v. Trammel, 207 Ark. 372, 180 S.W.2d 818 (1944).
141. Davis v. Kemp, 252 Ark. 925, 481 S.W.2d 712 (1972).
142. Pry v. Jones, *supra* note 137.
143. *Id.*
144. Pry v. Jones, *supra* note 137; Rolentson v. La Croix, 534 P.2d 17 (Okla. 1975).
145. Greenwood v. Harris, 362 P.2d 85 (Okla. 1961).
146. *Id.*
147. Halligan v. Cotton, *supra* note 137.
148. Dazet v. Bass, *supra* note 133.
149. Gridley v. Johnson, 476 S.W.2d 475 (Mo. 1972); Bivens v. Detroit Osteopathic Hosp., 77 Mich. App. 478, 268 N.W.2d 527 (1977).
150. Gridley v. Johnson, *supra* note 149.
151. Jones v. Bloom, 388 Mich. 98, 200 N.W.2d 196 (1972).
152. Lewandowski v. Preferred Risk Mut. Ins. Co., 33 Wis.2d 69, 149 N.W.2d 69 (1966).
153. Fed. R. Evid. 803(18).
154. Lhotka v. Larson, 307 Minn. 121, 238 N.W.2d 870 (1976); Mueller v. Mueller, 221 N.W.2d 39 (S.D. 1974).
155. Hamilton v. Hardy, 549 P.2d 1099 (Colo. 1976); Sanzari v. Rosenfeld, 34 N.J. 128, 167 A.2d 625 (1961).
156. Sanzari v. Rosenfeld, *supra* note 155.
157. Mulder v. Parke-Davis & Co., 288 Minn. 332, 181 N.W.2d 882 (1970).
158. Rogers v. Kee, 171 Mich. 551, 137 N.W. 260 (1912); Rostrow v. Klein, 23 Mich. App. 288, 178 N.W.2d 675 (1970); Henry v. Bronx Lebanon Medical Center, 385 N.Y.S.2d 772, 53 A.D.2d 476 (1976); Roberts v. Tardif, *supra* note 127.
159. Henry v. Bronx Lebanon Medical Center, *supra* note 158.
160. Haase v. Garfinkel, 418 S.W.2d 108 (Mo. 1967); Snyder v. St. Louis Southwestern R.R. Co., 228 Mo. App. 626, 72 S.W.2d 504 (1934); Rickett v. Hayes, 251 Ark. 395, 511 S.W.2d 187 (1971).
161. Luka v. Lowrie, 171 Mich. 122, 136 N.W. 168 (1928).
162. Toth v. Community Hosp. at Glen Cove, 22 N.Y.2d 255, 239 N.E.2d 368 (1968).
163. Hamilton v. Hardy, *supra* note 155.
164. W. Prosser, *supra* note 5, at 163; *see also* Eastin v. Broomfield, 116 Ariz. 576, 570 P.2d 744 (1977); Rickett v. Hayes, *supra* note 160.
165. Bryant v. Biggs, 331 Mich. 64, 49 N.W.2d 63 (1951).
166. Ferguson v. Gonyaw, 64 Mich. App. 685, 236 N.W.2d 543 (1975); Harris v. Bales, 459 S.W.2d 742 (Mo. App. 1970).
167. Drummond v. Hodges, 417 S.W.2d 740 (Tex. Civ. App. 1967).
168. Hundley v. St. Francis Hosp., 161 Cal. App.2d 800, 327 P.2d 131 (1958); Beck v. Lovell, 361 So.2d 245 (La. App. 1978).
169. Gray v. Gunnagle, 423 Pa. 144, 223 A.2d 663 (1966).
170. Schloendorff v. Society of N.Y. Hosp., 211 N.Y. 125, 105 N.E. 92 (1914).
171. Black's Law Dictionary, *supra* note 2, at 147.
172. *Id.* at 143.
173. Mink v. University of Chicago, 460 F. Supp. 713 (N.D. Ill. 1978).
174. W. Prosser, *supra* note 5, at 35–36.
175. Mink v. Univ. of Chicago, *supra* note 173.
176. Haywood v. Allen, 406 S.W.2d 721 (Ky. 1966).

177. Kritzer v. Citron, 101 Cal. App.2d 33, 224 P.2d 808 (1950); Charley v. Cameron, 215 Kan. 750, 528 P.2d 1205 (1974).
178. Shulman v. Lerner, 2 Mich. App. 705, 141 N.W.2d 348 (1966).
179. Gray v. Gunnagle, *supra* note 169.
180. W. Prosser, *supra* note 5, at 103.
181. *Id.*
182. Tabor v. Scobee, 254 S.W.2d 474 (Ky. 1951).
183. Rogers v. Lumbermen's Mut. Cas. Co., 119 So.2d 649 (La. App. 1960).
184. Tabor v. Scobee, *supra* note 182.
185. Danielson v. Roche, 109 Cal. App.2d 832, 241 P.2d 1028 (1952).
186. Barnett v. Bachrach, 34 A.2d 626 (Mun. Ct. App. D.C. 1943).
187. Kennedy v. Parrott, 243 N.C. 355, 90 S.E.2d 754 (1956).
188. *E.g.*, Hundley v. St. Francis Hosp. *supra* note 168.
189. Rogers v. Lumbermen's Mut. Cas. Co., *supra* note 183.
190. Lloyd v. Kull, 329 F.2d 168 (7th Cir. 1964).
191. Rogers v. Lumbermen's Mut. Cas. Co., *supra* note. 183.
192. Church v. Adler, 350 Ill. App. 471, 13 N.E.2d 327 (1953).
193. *See, e.g.*, Kennedy v. Parrott, *supra* note 187; Rothe v. Hull, 352 Mo. 926, 180 S.W.2d 7 (1944).
194. Winfrey v. Citizens & Southern Nat'l Bank, 149 Ga. App. 488, 254 S.E.2d 725 (1979).
195. *Id.*; Watson v. Worthy, 151 Ga. App. 131, 259 S.E.2d 138 (1979).
196. Winfrey v. Citizens & Southern Nat'l Bank, *supra* note 194.
197. Watson v. Worthy, *supra* note 195.
198. The American Hospital Association, A Patient's Bill of Rights (1972).
199. W. Prosser, *supra* note 5, at 165.
200. Pegram v. Sisco, 406 F. Supp. 776 (D. Ark, 1976); Riedisser v. Nelson, 111 Ariz. 552, 534 P.2d 1052 (1975); Bly v. Rhoads, 216 Va. 645, 222 S.E.2d 783 (1976).
201. Stauffer v. Karabin, 30 Colo. App. 357, 492 P.2d 862 (1971).
202. Sard v. Hardy, 281 Md. 432, 379 A.2d 1014 (1977).
203. Parker v. St. Paul Fire & Marine Ins. Co., 335 So.2d 725 (La. App. 1976); Holland v. Sisters of St. Joseph of Peace, 270 Or. 129, 522 P.2d 208 (1974); Bowers v. Garfield, 382 F. Supp. 503 (E.D. Pa. 1974), *aff'd.*, 503 F.2d 1398 (3d Cir. 1974); Thimatariga v. Chambers, 416 A.2d 1326 (Md. App. 1980); Harnish v. Children's Hosp. Med. Center, 439 N.E.2d 240 (Mass. 1982).
204. Bowers v. Garfield, *supra* note 203; Holder, *Informed Consent,* 215 J.A.M.A. 611 (1971).
205. Cobbs v. Grant, 8 Cal.3d 229, 104 Cal. Rptr. 505, 502 P.2d 1 (1972).
206. Sard v. Hardy, *supra* note 202; Longmire v. Hoey, 512 S.W.2d 307 (Tenn. App. 1974).
207. Sard v. Hardy, *supra* note 202; Canterbury v. Spence, 464 F.2d 772 (D.C. Cir. 1972); Mallett v. Pirkey, 171 Colo. 271, 466 P.2d 466 (1970); *see also* Comment *A Doctor's Duty to Inform—Holland v. Sisters of St. Joseph of Peace, and Decisions in Complying with the Legal Doctrine of Informed Consent,* 114 Radiology 231, 233–34 (1975).
208. Parker v. St. Paul Fire & Marine Ins. Co., *supra* note 203.
209. Beck v. Lovell, *supra* note 168; Rogers v. Lumbermen's Mut. Cas. Co., *supra* note 183; Tabor v. Scobee, *supra* note 182.
210. Sard v. Hardy, *supra* note 202.
211. *See, e.g.*, Dunham v. Wright, 302 F. Supp. 1108 (M.D. Pa. 1969); Nishi v. Hartwell, 52 Hawaii 188, 473 P.2d 116 (1970); Carman v. Dippold, 63 Ill. App. 3d 419, 379 N.E.2d 1365 (1978); Sard v. Hardy, *supra* note 202.

212. Holt v. Nelson, 11 Wash. App. 230, 523 P.2d 211 (1974); Reynier v. Delta Women's Clinic, Inc., 359 So.2d 733 (La. App. 1978).
213. Sard v. Hardy, *supra* note 202; Carman v. Dippold, 63 Ill. App.3d 419, 379 N.E.2d 1365 (1978).
214. Planned Parenthood v. Danforth, 428 U.S.52 (1976).
215. Rosenberg v. Feigin, 119 Cal. App.2d 783, 260 P.2d 143 (1953).
216. Porter v. Porter, 135 N.J. Super. 50, 342 A.2d 574 (1975); Murray v. Vandevander, 522 P.2d 302 (Okla. App. 1974).
217. Murray v. Vandevander, *supra* note 216.
218. Haywood v. Allen, *supra* note 175; Rothe v. Hull, *supra* note 193.
219. Beck v. Lovell, *supra* note 168.
220. Scheinberg v. Smith, 482 F. Supp. 529 (S.D. Fla. 1979).
221. Darrah v. Kite, 32 App. Div.2d 208, 301 N.Y.S.2d 286 (1969).
222. Planned Parenthood v. Danforth, *supra* note 214; Bellotti v. Baird, 428 U.S. 132 (1976); *see also* State v. Koome, 84 Wash.2d 901, 530 P.2d 260 (1975).
223. Pilpel, *Minor's Right to Medical Care*, 36 Alb. L. Rev. 462, 467 (1972).
224. Bellotti v. Baird, 443 U.S. 622 (1979); Planned Parenthood v. Danforth, *supra* note 214.
225. *See, e.g.,* La. Rev. Stat. Ann. § 40: 1299, 24.4; Mass. Gen. Laws Ann. ch. 112 § 12S (1980); Me. Rev. Stat. Ann. tit. 22 § 1597; N.D. Cent. Code § 14-02.1-03; Tenn. Code Ann. § 39-302 (1976); Utah Code Ann. § 76-7-304.
226. *To Be Young, Poor, Sexually Active, and in Need of Birth Control: Indigent Minors' Access to Contraceptives*, 1 W. New Eng. L. Rev. 711 (1979).
227. Doe v. Irwin, 428 F. Supp. 1198 (W.D. Mich. 1977), opinion after remand, 441 F. Supp. 1247 (W.D. Mich. 1977), *rev'd*, 615 F.2d 1162 (5th Cir. 1980).
228. H.L. v. Matheson, 450 U.S. 398 (1981).
229. Pilpel, *supra* note 223, at 464.
230. Black's Law Dictionary, *supra* note 2, at 468.
231. Pilpel, *supra* note 223, at 464–65.
232. *See, e.g.,* Younts v. St. Francis Hosp. & School of Nursing, 205 Kan. 292, 469 P.2d 330 (1970).
233. Sturm v. Green, 398 P.2d 799 (Okla. 1965).
234. Pugh v. Swiontek, *supra* note 30.
235. Baker v. Beebe, 367 So.2d 102 (La. 1979).
236. Hunter v. Robison, 488 S.W.2d 555 (Tex. 1972).
237. Danner & Sagall, *Medicolegal Causation: A Source of Professional Misunderstanding*, 3 Am. J. L. & Med. 303 (1977).
238. W. Prosser, *supra* note 5, at 237.
239. *Id.* at 239.
240. Restatement (Second) of Torts, § 431 (1964).
241. *See* W. Prosser, *supra* note 5, at 239; *see also* Killebrew v. Johnson, 404 N.E.2d 1194 (Ind. 1980).
242. Restatement (Second) of Torts, § 433B(1) (1964).
243. W. Prosser, *supra* note 5, at 241.
244. Beauvais v. Notre Dame Hosp., 387 A.2d 689 (R.I. 1978); Aubert v. Charity Hosp. of La., 363 So.2d 1223 (La. 1978).
245. Aubert v. Charity Hosp. of La., *supra* note 244.
246. Restatement (Second) of Torts, § 433B(2)-(3) (1964).
247. W. Prosser, *supra* note 5, at 241.
248. Bertrand v. Aetna Casualty & Surety Co., 306 So.2d 343 (La. 1975).
249. Aubert v. Charity Hosp. of La., *supra* note 244.
250. Cornfeldt v. Tongen, 295 N.W.2d 638 (Minn. 1980).

Notes: Chapter I

251. Jarboe v. Harting, 397 S.W.2d 775 (Ky. 1965).
252. *Id.*
253. W. Prosser, *supra* note 5, at 244.
254. Sturm v. Green, *supra* note 233.
255. W. Prosser, *supra* note 5, at 244.
256. Sturm v. Green, *supra* note 233; Killebrew v. Johnson, *supra* note 241.
257. Killebrew v. Johnson, *supra* note 241.
258. *Id.*
259. Black's Law Dictionary, *supra* note 2, at 1471.
260. Weeks v. Latter-Day Saints Hosp., 418 F.2d 1035 (10th Cir. 1969); Ewen v. Baton Rouge Gen. Hosp., 378 So.2d 172 (La. App. 1979); Haas v. United States, 492 F. Supp. 755 (D. Mass. 1980).
261. W. Prosser, *supra* note 5, at 212.
262. Byrne v. Boadle, 2 H. & C. 722, 159 Eng. Rep. 299 (1863).
263. *See, e.g.,* Riedisser v. Nelson, 111 Ariz. 542, 534 P.2d 1052 (1975); Starr v. Fregosi, 370 F.2d 15 (5th Cir. 1966); Hayes v. Brown, 108 Ga. App. 360, 133 S.E.2d 102 (1963); Hans v. Franklin Square Hosp., 29 Md. App. 329, 347 A.2d 905 (1976); Sagmiller v. Carlsen, 219 N.W.2d 885 (N.D. 1974); Harle v. Krchnak, 422 S.W.2d 810 (Tex. Civ. App. 1967); Louis v. Parchman, 493 S.W.2d 310 (Tex. Civ. App. 1973).
264. Meisel, *The Expansion of Liability for Medical Accidents: From Negligence to Strict Liability by Way of Informed Consent,* 56 Neb. L. Rev. 51 (1979).
265. Thode, *The Unconscious Patient: Who Should Bear the Risk of Unexplained Injuries to a Healthy Part of His Body?* 1969 Utah L. Rev. 1.
266. W. Prosser, *supra* note 5, at 223.
267. Salgo v. Leland Stanford Jr. Univ. Bd. of Trustees, 154 Cal. App.2d 560, 317 P.2d 170 (1957).
268. Mayor v. Dowsett, 240 Or. 196, 400 P.2d 234 (1965); Seneris v. Haas, 45 Cal.2d 811, 291 P.2d 915 (1955).
269. Fogal v. Genesee Hosp., 41 A.D.2d 468, 344 N.Y.S.2d 552 (1973); Wiles v. Myerly, 210 N.W.2d 619 (Iowa 1973).
270. Faris v. Doctor's Hosp., Inc., 18 Ariz. App. 264, 501 P.2d 440 (1972); Haas v. United States, *supra* note 260.
271. Ybarra v. Spangard, 25 Cal.2d 486, 146 P.2d 983 (1944).
272. Salgo v. Leland Stanford Jr. Univ. Bd. of Trustees, *supra* note 267.
273. Stephenson v. Kaiser Found. Hosp., 203 Cal. App. 631, 21 Cal. Rptr. 646 (1962).
274. Voss v. Bridwell, 188 Kan. 643, 364 P.2d 955 (1961); Funke v. Fieldman, 212 Kan. 524, 512 P.2d 539 (1973).
275. Ewen v. Baton Rouge Gen. Hosp., *supra* note 260.
276. *See, e.g.,* Cronin v. Hagan, 221 N.W.2d 748 (Iowa 1974); Beaudoin v. Watertown Mem. Hosp., 32 Wis.2d 132, 145 N.W.2d 166 (1966).
277. Spidle v. Steward, 68 Ill. App.2d 134, 24 Ill. Dec. 489, 385 N.E.2d 401 (1979); Bryant v. St. Paul Fire & Marine Ins. Co., 272 So.2d 448 (La. App. 1973).
278. Haas v. United States, *supra* note 260.
279. Haas v. United States, *supra* note 260; Kitto v. Gilbert, 39 Colo. App. 374, 570 P.2d 544 (1977); Warrick v. Giron, 290 N.W.2d 166 (Minn. 1980); Spannaus v. Otolaryngology Clinic, 308 Minn. 334, 242 N.W.2d 597 (1976); Reidisser v. Nelson, *supra* note 263.
280. Roberson v. Factor, 583 S.W.2d 818 (Tex. Civ. App. 1979); Spidle v. Steward, *supra* note 277; Cronin v. Hagan, *supra* note 276; Carpenter v. Campbell, 271 N.E.2d 163 (Ind. App. 1971).
281. Louis v. Parchman, *supra* note 263.

282. Roberson v. Factor, *supra* note 280; Beaudoin v. Watertown Mem. Hosp., *supra* note 276.
283. Warrick v. Giron, *supra* note 279; Mayor v. Dowsett, *supra* note 268.
284. Spidle v. Steward, *supra* note 277.
285. Coleman v. Garrison, 327 A.2d 757 (Del. Super. Ct. 1974), *aff'd.*, 349 A.2d 8 (Del. 1975).
286. Carpenter v. Campell, *supra* note 280.
287. Roberson v. Factor, *supra* note 280.
288. Cronin v. Hagan, *supra* note 276.
289. Tatro v. Lueken, 212 Kan. 606, 512 P.2d 529 (1973).
290. Bryant v. St. Paul Fire & Marine Ins. Co., *supra* note 277.
291. Larrabee v. United States, 254 F. Supp. 613 (S.D. Cal. 1966).
292. Druilhet v. Comeaux, 317 So.2d 270 (La. App. 1975).
293. Beaudoin v. Watertown Mem. Hosp., *supra* note 276.
294. Horner v. Northern Pacific Beneficial Ass'n Hosps., Inc., 62 Wash.2d 351, 382 P.2d 518 (1963).
295. *Id.*
296. Martin v. Stratton, 515 P.2d 1366 (Okla. 1973).
297. Haas v. United States, *supra* note 260.
298. Hughes v. Hastings, 469 S.W.2d 378 (Tenn. 1971).
299. Galbraith v. Busch, 267 N.Y. 230, 196 N.E. 36 (1935).
300. Kitto v. Gilbert, *supra* note 279.
301. Wiles v. Myerly, *supra* note 269.
302. Pederson v. Dumochel, 72 Wash.2d 73, 431 P.2d 973 (1967).
303. Faris v. Doctor's Hosp., Inc., *supra* note 270.
304. Haas v. United States, *supra* note 260; Merritt v. Deaconess Hosp., 43 Ohio Misc. 7, 357 N.E.2d 65 (1975).
305. Mayor v. Dowsett, *supra* note 268.
306. Haas v. United States, *supra* note 260; Kitto v. Gilbert, *supra* note 279.
307. Voss v. Bridwell, *supra* note 274.
308. Salgo v. Leland Stanford Jr. Univ. Bd. of Trustees, *supra* note 267.
309. *See, e.g.,* Harle v. Krchnak, *supra* note 263; Louis v. Parchman, *supra* note 263; Goodnight v. Phillips, 418 S.W.2d 862 (Tex. Civ. App. 1967); Bell v. Umstattd, 401 S.W.2d 306 (Tex. Civ. App. 1966).
310. *See, e.g.,* Reidisser v. Nelson, *supra* note 263; Hayes v. Brown, *supra* note 263; Hans v. Franklin Square Hosp., *supra* note 263; Sagmiller v. Carlsen, *supra* note 263.
311. Miller v. Hardy, 564 S.W.2d 102 (Tex. 1978); Forney v. Memorial Hosp., 543 S.W.2d 705 (Tex. 1976).
312. Horner v. Northern Pacific Beneficial Ass'n Hosp., Inc., *supra* note 294.
313. Riedisser v. Nelson, *supra* note 263; Sagmiller v. Carlsen, *supra* note 263.
314. Tatro v. Lueken, *supra* note 289.
315. Acosta v. City of New York, 67 Misc.2d 756, 324 N.Y.S.2d 137 (1971).
316. Tatro v. Lueken, *supra* note 289.
317. Acosta v. City of New York, *supra* note 315.
318. Younger v. Webster, 9 Wash. App. 87, 510 P.2d 1182 (1975).
319. Crawford v. County of Sacramento, 239 Cal. App.2d 791, 49 Cal. Rptr. 115 (1966).
320. Cowlthorp v. Branford, 279 Or. 273, 567 P.2d 536 (1977).
321. Voss v. Bridwell, *supra* note 274.
322. Tatro v. Lueken, *supra* note 289.
323. Beaudoin v. Watertown Mem. Hosp., *supra* note 276.
324. Quintal v. Laurel Grove Hosp., 62 Cal.2d 154, 41 Cal. Rptr. 577, 397 P.2d 161 (1964).

Notes: Chapter I

325. McAdams v. Holden, 349 So.2d 900 (La. App. 1977); Hoven v. Kelble, 79 Wis.2d 444, 256 N.W.2d 379 (1977).
326. Talbot v. Dr. W. H. Groves' Latter-Day Saints Hosp., Inc., 21 Utah 2d 73, 440 P.2d 872 (1968).
327. Ybarra v. Spangard, *supra* note 271.
328. Kitto v. Gilbert, *supra* note 279.
329. Hoven v. Kelble, *supra* note 325.
330. Spidle v. Steward, *supra* note 277; Riedisser v. Nelson, *supra* note 263.
331. Spidle v. Steward, *supra* note 277.
332. Riedisser v. Nelson, *supra* note 263; McCann v. Baton Rouge Hosp., 276 So.2d 259 (La. 1973).
333. Clark v. Gibbon, 66 Cal.2d 399, 58 Cal. Rptr. 125, 426 P.2d 525 (1967).
334. Spidle v. Steward, *supra* note 277; Roberson v. Factor, *supra* note 280; Carpenter v. Campbell, *supra* note 280.
335. Cronin v. Hagan, *supra* note 276.
336. *See, e.g.,* Hoven v. Kelble, *supra* note 325.
337. Seneris v. Haas, *supra* note 268.
338. Note, *Res Ipsa Loquitur: A Case for Flexibility in Medical Malpractice,* 16 Wayne L. Rev. 1136, 1144 (1970).
339. Karlsons v. Guerinot, 57 A.D.2d 73, 394 N.Y.S.2d 933 (1977).
340. W. Prosser, *supra* note 5, at 143.
341. Black's Law Dictionary, *supra* note 2, at 468.
342. *Id.* at 469.
343. J. Waltz & F. Inbau, Medical Jurisprudence 284 (1971).
344. Black's Law Dictionary, *supra* note 2, at 467.
345. *See* Beck v. Lovell, *supra* note 168.
346. Karlsons v. Guerinot, *supra* note 339.
347. Betancourt v. Gaylor, 136 N.J.Super. 69, 344 A.2d 336 (1975).
348. Stills v. Gratton, 55 Cal. App. 3d 698, 127 Cal. Rptr. 652 (1976).
349. *Id.*; Betancourt v. Gaylor, *supra* note 347; Ziemba v. Sternberg, *supra* note 3; Park v. Chessin, 60 A.D.2d 80, 400 N.Y.S.2d 110 (1977).
350. Park v. Chessen, *supra* note 349.
351. Custodio v. Bauer, 251 Cal. App. 2d 303, 59 Cal. Rptr. 463 (1967).
352. *Id.*
353. Beagle v. Vasold, 65 Cal.2d 166, 53 Cal. Rptr. 129, 417 P.2d 673 (1966).
354. *E.g.,* Judd v. Rudolph, 222 N.W. 416 (Iowa 1928); Happy v. Waltz, 244 S.W.2d 380 (Mo. App. 1951).
355. Sherlock v. Stillwater Clinic, 260 N.W.2d 169 (Minn. 1977).
356. Friel v. Vineland Obstetrical and Gynecological Professional Ass'n, 166 N.J. 579, 400 A.2d 147 (1979).
357. *Id.*
358. *E.g.,* Neinez v. Wilson, 211 Kan. 443, 507 P.2d 329 (1973).
359. Karlsons v. Guerinot, *supra* note 339.
360. Berman v. Allan, 80 N.J. 421, 404 A.2d 8 (1979).
361. Friel v. Vineland Obstetrical Gynecological Professional Ass'n., *supra* note 356.
362. Johnson v. State, 37 N.Y.2d 378, 372 N.Y.S.2d 638, 334 N.E.2d 590 (1975).
363. Molien v. Kaiser Found. Hosp., 96 Cal. App. 3d 468, 158 Cal. Rptr. 107 (1979); Bishop v. Bryne, 265 F. Supp. 460 (S.D. W.Va. 1967)
364. *See* Friel v. Vineland Obstetrical and Gynecological Professional Ass'n., *supra* note 356.
365. Karlsons v. Guerinot, *supra* note 339; Berman v. Allan, *supra* note 360.
366. Friel v. Vineland Obstetrical and Gynecological Professional Ass'n., *supra* note 356.

367. Karlsons v. Guerinot, *supra* note 339; Haught v. Maceluch, 681 F.2d 291 (5th Cir. 1982).
368. Friel v. Vineland Obstetrical and Gynecological Professional Ass'n., *supra* note 356.
369. Molien v. Kaiser Found. Hosp., *supra* note 363.
370. Dillon v. Legg, 68 Cal.2d 728, 69 Cal. Rptr. 72, 441 P.2d 912 (1968).
371. *Id.*
372. Tobin v. Grossman, 24 N.Y.2d 609, 301 N.Y.S.2d 554, 249 N.E.2d 419 (1969); *see also* Karlsons v. Guerinot, *supra* note 339.
373. Vaccaro v. Squibb Corp., 71 A.D.2d 270, 422 N.Y.S.2d 679 (1979).
374. Friel v. Vineland Obstetrical and Gynecological Professional Ass'n., *supra* note 356.
375. Dumer v. St. Michael's Hosp., 69 Wis.2d 766, 233 N.W.2d 372 (1975).
376. Park v. Chessin, *supra* note 349.
377. Custodio v. Bauer, *supra* note 351.
378. Wilczynski v. Goodman, 73 Ill. App. 3d 51, 29 Ill. Dec. 216, 391 N.E.2d 479 (1979); Sala v. Tomlinson, 73 A.D.2d 724, 422 N.Y.S.2d 506 (1979).
379. Rivera v. State, 404 N.Y.S.2d 950, 94 Misc.2d 157 (1978); Sherlock v. Stillwater Clinic, *supra* note 355.
380. *See generally* Jacobs v. Theimer, 519 S.W.2d 846 (Tex. 1975); Berman v. Allan, *supra* note 360; Park v. Chessin, *supra* note 349.
381. Berman v. Allan, *supra* note 360.
382. Park v. Chessin, *supra* note 349.
383. *Id.*
384. Molien v. Kaiser Found. Hosp., *supra* note 363.
385. Custodio v. Bauer, *supra* note 351.
386. Karlsons v. Guerinot, *supra* note 339.
387. Roth v. Bell, 24 Wash. App. 92, 600 P.2d 602 (1979).
388. Garza v. Berlanga, 598 S.W.2d 377 (Tex. Civ. App. 1980).
389. *See generally* Kelly v. Chillag, 381 F.2d 344 (4th Cir. 1967); Karlsons v. Guerinot, *supra* note 339.
390. Noe v. Kaiser Found. Hosp., 248 Or. 420, 435 P.2d 306 (1967).
391. Karlsons v. Guerinot, *supra* note 339.
392. Restatement (Second) of Torts § 908(i) (2d ed. 1964).
393. *See* Roginsky v. Richardson-Merrill, Inc., 378 F.2d 382 (2d Cir. 1967).
394. Moore v. Wilson, 20 S.W.2d 310 (Ark. 1929).
395. Kitto v. Gilbert, *supra* note 279; Frisnegger v. Gibson, 598 P.2d 574 (Mont. 1979).
396. Berman v. Allan, *supra* note 360.
397. Karlsons v. Guerinot, *supra* note 339.
398. Betancourt v. Gaylor, *supra* note 347.
399. Karlsons v. Guerinot, *supra* note 339.
400. Rivera v. State, *supra* note 379.
401. Green v. Sudakin, 81 Mich. App. 545, 265 N.W.2d 411 (1978); Karlsons v. Guerinot, *supra* note 339; Betancourt v. Gaylor, *supra* note 347.
402. Green v. Sudakin, *supra* note 401.
403. Berman v. Allan, *supra* note 360.
404. Bishop v. Byrne, *supra* note 363; Betancourt v. Gaylor, *supra* note 347.
405. Thimatariga v. Chambers, *supra* note 203; Montgomery v. Stephan, 395 Mich. 33, 101 N.W.2d 227 (1960).
406. Penetrante v. United States, 604 F.2d 1248 (9th Cir. 1979).
407. Custodio v. Bauer, *supra* note 351.
408. Anonymous v. Hospital, 366 A.2d 204 (Conn. Super. 1976).
409. Killebrew v. Johnson, *supra* note 241.
410. King v. St. Louis, 155 S.W.2d 557 (Mo. App. 1941).

411. Blair v. Eblen, 461 S.W.2d 370 (Tex. Civ. App. 1970).
412. Dodds v. Stellar, 77 Cal. App.2d 411, 175 P.2d 607 (1946).
413. Rivera v. State, *supra* note 379.
414. Sherlock v. Stillwater Clinic, *supra* note 355.

Chapter II

Other Theories of Liability

§ 2.10 INTRODUCTION

Legal theories other than negligence may expose a physician to liability for injuries arising from his or her practice. In some jurisdictions, depending upon the facts of the case, the courts may view the physician's conduct not as a breach of duty, but as the breach of a contract with the patient (see § 2.20, Contract Theory). Such a resolution by the courts, while rare, still occurs.

The physician may also be held legally responsible for the acts of health care personnel whom he or she directs or supervises (see § 2.30, Vicarious Liability). The specific nature of the relationship between the physician and these individuals has far-reaching legal consequences. The medical record prepared by the physician in treating the patient presents the potential for legal dispute over such questions as property and privacy rights with respect to the contents of the records (see § 2.60, Liability Arising From Medical Records). Finally, in rendering treatment, physicians typically prescribe drugs and use devices ranging from simple hypodermics to sophisticated CAT (computerized axial tomography) scanners. These drugs and devices are governed by a complex body of law known as "products liability" (see § 2.70, Products Liability).

The obstetrician-gynecologist who engages in genetic counseling or performs a tubal ligation may be held liable for negligence under certain birth-related causes of action (see § 2.40, Birth-Related Causes of Action).

To gain a full understanding of his or her liability potential, the physician should be familiar with these legal principles, as well as with those governing the malpractice cause of action based on negligence theory. The following chapter discusses these concepts.

§ 2.20 CONTRACT THEORY

Under early English law, the liability of a physician for failure to exercise professional skill and care was based on the notion that the physician's profession was a public, or common, calling, somewhat like that of an innkeeper or common carrier (trolley or train operators). Because of this common calling and because the public was served, special duties were imposed by law. The physician was answerable for mistakes because he or she undertook the care of the patient in the course of a public calling.[1]

Early American courts looked to English court decisions and legal values for precedential guidance and at first applied the same analysis. However, as the American law of contracts developed, American courts increasingly chose to analyze the physician's liability in terms of contract concepts.* Approximately a century and a half ago, negligence received judicial recognition as a separate tort[2] (see § 1.20, Elements of Negligence). Today, most malpractice actions are based on the legal theory of negligence; however, the status of the contract action as the basis for a malpractice suit remains unsettled, despite the arguments of its critics and various legislative attempts to limit its availability.

The law recognizes two types of contracts: express and implied.

A contract is express when the parties reach a specific agreement by written or spoken words. Thus, there are two kinds of express contracts: written and oral.

A contract is implied when parties (such as a physician and a patient) engage in activities creating mutual obligations (the physician accepts and treats the patient and the patient agrees to pay the physician) but no words of agreement are spoken or written. Accordingly, although an implied contract is not a true contract, it is an obligation imposed by law to do justice because of activities engaged in by the parties. The jury, after examining the circumstances of each case, determines whether or not an implied contract exists.[3]

The distinction between contract and negligence is important to understand, because the legal theory pursued by the patient-plaintiff affects various aspects of the suit, often including the outcome. The basic theoretical difference between contract and negligence lies in the nature of the interest protected: negligence actions are intended to protect members of society from various kinds of harm, whereas contracts are intended to protect the interests of specific individuals by having specific promises made between them enforced and performed.

In negligence actions, the duties of conduct between individuals are imposed by law and are based primarily upon social policy, not necessarily the will, intention, or promises made between the parties. Further, the duties involved may be owed to all individuals within the range of harm.

Contract actions are designed to protect the agreements made between limited and specifically identifiable parties, and the duties are imposed because the parties to the contract have agreed to assume them.

Contract theory provides certain advantages to patient-plaintiffs. Negligence theory is based on fault concepts in that it identifies a standard of conduct the physician failed to meet, whereas contract theory asserts only that the phy-

---

*A contract is a promissory agreement between two or more persons which creates a relation between the parties and entails certain agreed-upon rights and duties which are enforceable by law.

sician failed to live up to his or her part of the bargain. The result is that the patient has a less burdensome requirement of proof at trial under a contract theory than under negligence.

Also, in many jurisdictions, there is a longer statute of limitations (see § 3.50, Statute of Limitations) for contract actions than for tort actions, and patients will sometimes attempt to recover under a breach of contract theory after the statute of limitations for tort actions has run.[4] For example, in Michigan the patient has two years to bring an action charging malpractice through negligence,[5] but a general statute governing contract actions allows the patient six years to bring a contract action.[6] However, Michigan courts have rejected the general contract statute of limitations in certain malpractice cases in favor of a statute allowing only three years for actions to recover damages for injuries to persons and property.[7] At present, where an action is brought to recover damages for injury to persons or property on a claim arising out of an implied contract to treat, the three-year statute applies. If an action is brought on an express contract, the six-year statute applies.[8] In either case, the patient (in Michigan) has a greater period of time in which to sue under a contract theory than under a negligence theory.

Courts tend to take a strict view of actions in contract, probably because of the availability to the patient of the more commonly used action in tort of malpractice. Some of the disadvantages of contract theories for patients are that there are generally more limits on the amount and type of damages that may be recovered (see § 1.60, Damages). The traditional rule in contract law has been that punitive damages and damages for mental suffering or anguish are seldom awarded.[9] Such damages have been held to be recoverable where the contract is closely related to the human body or human life and mental or emotional damages are inevitable or foreseeable if the contract is breached.[10]

CASE ILLUSTRATION

The patient had a history of two stillbirths and was concerned that she could not deliver normally. When she became pregnant again, she consulted her physician and demanded that he perform a cesarean section at the appropriate time. This demand was repeated on every occasion that the patient visited the physician, and the physician apparently agreed to perform the operation. When the patient first felt labor pains, she was examined by the physician, who told her that all was normal and she should return home. At this time, fetal heart tones were audible and "quite strong." When the patient was admitted to the hospital early the next morning, however, the fetal heart tones could no longer be heard. The patient was delivered of a stillborn child later that day.

The patient sued the physician. In affirming a judgment for the patient, the court held that the jury could reasonably have found that the physician breached his contract by failing to perform a cesarean section when the patient first experienced her pains. Had the operation been performed at that time, said the court, it is conceivable, though not certain, that the child would have survived. The court also held that the patient could recover damages for the mental anguish and suffering incident to the death of her baby. Although noting that such damages are not ordinarily recoverable in contract actions, the court stated that, "when we have a contract concerned not with trading and commerce but with life and death . . . not with pecuniary aggrandizement but with matters of mental concern and solicitude, then a breach of duty with respect to such contracts will inevitably and necessarily result in mental anguish, pain, and suffering. In such cases the parties may reasonably be said to have contracted with reference to the payment of damages therefor in the event of breach" (*Stewart v. Rudner*, 1957).[11]

Courts generally permit contract actions only if there is an express written or oral agreement between the parties.[12] Some examples of statements that have been construed as express promises include assertions that an operation is a "foolproof thing" or "perfectly safe."[13] Failure to achieve the promised result or to perform the promised service may give rise to liability. Thus, in a Connecticut case where a physician failed to perform an agreed-upon hysterectomy and the patient subsequently became pregnant and died during childbirth, the court permitted the patient's husband to recover certain elements of damages suffered as a consequence of the physician's breach.[14] Liability may also arise if the physician delegates performance of a contractual duty to some person less skilled or experienced than himself or herself.[15]

CASE ILLUSTRATION

The patient contracted with two obstetricians, members of a partnership, for the delivery of her baby. When the patient gave birth, however, she was delivered by a first-year obstetrics resident because the partner who was on call had not yet arrived at the hospital. (There was a conflict in testimony regarding how long the patient and her husband had been in the hospital before she was delivered.) The resident performed an episiotomy; the patient suffered a third-degree tear (that is, down to the rectal sphincter muscles). (The patient alleged this was caused by the resident's cutting too deeply during his episiotomy incision. The obstetricians insisted that the baby's head caused the tear into the sphincter muscles as the head emerged through the birth canal.) An infection developed several days later at the site of the sutures, and the patient was left with rectal incontinence that was not corrected by two subsequent operations.

The patient sued the obstetricians. In determining the liability of the two obstetrics-gynecology specialists, the issue was whether the conduct of the resident would be compared to the standard of care for physicians with similar training and experience in that community or to the higher standard applied to specialists like the partners. It was held that, since the patient had contracted to receive the care of specialists, the partners could delegate their duties under the contract only to someone who possessed skills equal to their own. The specialists could not lower the standard of care by assigning the responsibility to someone else. Therefore, said the court, if it was shown that the patient's injury would not have occurred had she been delivered by someone with the skills of a specialist rather than those of a resident, the obstetricians should be held liable (*Alexandridis v. Jewett*, 1968).[16]

In order to succeed under a contract action, the patient must usually prove a special contract or promise. This must be an express promise or warranty of a specific result; an implied warranty would be insufficient.[17] Such an express promise may be distinguished from therapeutic assurances of recovery, which the courts recognize physicians must make to patients on occasion. The need to provide therapeutic reassurance to the patient and the right of individuals to enter into and enforce contracts represent competing considerations that the courts must balance.[18]

In many cases, however, the courts will hold that the parties have not reached an express agreement. In these cases a patient may attempt to recover on the basis of an implied contract. For example, a patient may allege the breach of an implied contract to provide medical services in a professional manner or of an implied contract to meet the standard of care of the profession. But the courts have held that this is really a restatement of an action for negligence (a breach of duty or a failure to meet the standard of care); the courts usually hold that the standard for recovery for breach of an implied contract would therefore be that of recovery for breach of duty for negligence, and they apply to the action the rules for tort rather than contract action.[19]

Statutes in 25 states require actions for medical malpractice to be in tort and not in contract, and courts in most states do not permit malpractice actions to be brought on an implied contract theory.[20] Some courts still feel there is a need to maintain the availability of the contract action; for example as a control against the unprincipled promises of medical charlatans.[21]

Some jurisdictions may not permit the patient to bring an action on a physician's expressed promise unless she has relied on that promise to her detriment. Proof of such reliance is usually not difficult to make.

An additional doctrine in contract law, and one that may be critical in a contract action, is the doctrine of consideration. The doctrine of consideration recognizes that, before a promise can be enforced, something of value, such as a money payment, must be given in exchange for that promise. Promises that are made without any exchange by the other party may not be enforced if they are broken. Therefore, the law in a jurisdiction might require that a patient give or pay something specifically in exchange for a physician's promise to her.[22] The doctrine of consideration, however, is a malleable one and is sometimes used to reach whatever result is desired. One court might hold that the fee paid by a patient to a physician was only for medical services and could not support a separate contract of a perfect result. Another court might hold that a single consideration could support several promises and reach a result favorable to the plaintiff.

Many cases of attempted recovery under a breach of contract theory in obstetrics and gynecology have involved failure of a sterilization procedure such as tubal ligation.[23] In general, patients have alleged a failure of physicians to perform their promise to render them infertile. Here, the physician who is performing the procedure must consider providing the patient with contradictory information. On the one hand, the physician must inform the patient and the spouse that such a procedure is irreversible and will result in permanent infertility. On the other hand, the prudent physician should also inform the patient that she might remain fertile, even if the operation is performed properly and with due care. Patients who have received only the former information may construe as a promise or express contract that a certain result will be achieved. Generally, courts have held that this statement by itself is not sufficient to constitute an express promise.

CASE ILLUSTRATION

Before performing a tubal ligation upon the patient, the physician told her that the operation would be irreversible and that she would not be able to have any more children. He also told her that she would be able to engage in sexual intercourse with her husband without becoming pregnant. The patient said that this was what she wanted. Later, the patient became pregnant with another child. The patient brought suit, contending that the physician had expressly warranted and contracted that the operation would sterilize her. She did not allege that the operation itself had been performed negligently. The court held that the physician's statement did not create a contract and would not support an action against him. Instead, stating that his comments regarding the operation only "expressed an opinion as to its probable outcome," the court found that "such admonitions were both necessary and proper under the circumstances and should not, in the absence of an express undertaking, be elevated to the stature of a warranty." The court also distinguished express promises to achieve a specific result from "so-called therapeutic reassurances," concluding that it is doubtful "that an action for breach of warranty can ever result from a physician's expression of opinion" (*Rogala v. Silva*, 1973).[24]

Assurances of sterility made *after* the operation have also been held insufficient to establish an express warranty on the part of the physician.[25] In deciding these cases, the courts are often guided by the general maxim that a physician does not warrant or insure that treatment will be successful in the absence of a special contract to that effect.[26] The patient's failure to provide additional consideration for the alleged "warranty" of sterility has also been cited as an argument against the existence of a contract.[27] The patient's signature on a consent form in which she acknowledged her awareness that she "may not be completely or permanently sterile after the operation" has been held to rebut, at lease in part, an argument that the physician expressly warranted the success of the operation.[28] Finally, some courts raise a further barrier to recovery by placing a special burden of proof upon the patient who alleges breach of a medical contract. These courts hold that there can be no recovery for breach of an alleged expressed warranty unless the existence of the warranty is shown by "clear proof," that is by "clear and convincing evidence."[29] According to one court, the "clear proof" rule requires the judge or jury to specifically consider whether the physician made a statement which could have been reasonably interpreted by the patient as a promise that a given result or cure would be achieved.[30] If, under the circumstances of the case and the context of the particular physician-patient relationship, no such statement can be found, there can be no liability for breach of warranty.

This is not to say, however, that a patient can never recover on a breach of contract theory for the failure of a sterilization operation. In a Michigan case decided in 1978, the physician did not perform an agreed-upon tubal ligation and failed to inform the patient of that fact. The patient promptly became pregnant. The court permitted her to recover in her suit for breach of contract both the expenses of rearing the child and damages for mental anguish.[31]

If a contract cause of action does exist in a given case, the physician may be able to raise as a defense any provisions of the consent or authorization form that purport to reduce the physician's liability for malpractice or breach. The courts, however, often refuse to enforce purely exculpatory contracts, holding them to be void as contrary to public policy (see § 3.70, Release from Liability Forms). Thus, the courts have refused to enforce forms which attempted, in advance of treatment, to release an osteopath and his staff from any and all liability resulting from an abortion[32] or to limit a patient's maximum recovery to $15,000 while further requiring her to give the physician immediate notification of any claim against him as a condition of bringing suit.[33]

In conclusion, patients will usually recover in contract actions only if they can prove clearly that there was an express agreement between the parties. Courts will not extract an implied contract from physician-patient communications unless a specific promise has been made. To avoid liability for breach of contract, the physician should provide realistic and reasonably accurate assessments of what should be anticipated from a particular course of treatment.

§ 2.30 VICARIOUS LIABILITY

As the term implies, vicarious liability is a theory of law that imposes liability on a party who may not have committed any negligent act but is held responsible for the actions of the party who did. Responsibility for the actions of others can arise out of an agency relationship. A person becomes the agent of a second party when that person has been authorized to act for or represent the second party. The parties to an agency relationship are referred to as the principal and agent or the master and servant. In legal jargon, the doctrine is known as respondeat superior, a Latin phrase meaning "let the master answer."[34]

The essential elements of vicarious liability are well established. The agent is the individual who commits the allegedly negligent act. The principal is the person or organization allegedly responsible for the acts of the agent. Before a principal may be held liable for the acts of an agent, certain facts must be established. First, the existence of an agency relationship must be proven.[35] This usually hinges upon the question of whether one party is subject to the control or right of control of the other. The law recognizes the existence of the agency relationship in certain other situations, based on the borrowed servant doctrine or the captain of the ship doctrine, legal concepts that are discussed below. Further, it must be shown that the agent was acting on the business of the principal, or at least for the principal's benefit, and within the scope of the agent's duties.[36] If these facts can be proven, a principal may be held liable for the negligent act of his or her agent. Liability may be imposed even though the principal has in no way aided or encouraged the negligent act and may even have attempted to prevent it.[37]

Justification for applying vicarious liability in a given case is derived from the point of view of the victim of the agent's negligent act. Consider an agent engaged in work for his or her principal, the profits of the work going to the principal. If an individual harmed by the agent is limited to suing the agent, he or she may be effectively barred from recovery. To compensate the individual, a "deep pocket" must be found. Generally, the law recognizes that principals are able to compensate victims more fully, are better able to absorb the costs, and can insure themselves more easily. The cost of indemnifying can be included in the principal's costs of doing business, and the principal will thus be motivated to select his or her agents with care. Vicarious liability serves to assure full recovery for injured persons and seeks to deter future acts of negligence.[38]

Historically, the search for a deep pocket to compensate for injuries related to medical care had to go beyond the hospital because of the concepts of governmental and charitable immunity. In many jurisdictions hospitals, which were either governmental or charitable institutions, were legally immune from lawsuits. Thus, vicarious liability could not have been imposed on the hospital for the negligence of its employees. The physician working with the hospital employee was the only logical party left upon whom to impose liability.[39] Immunity for hospitals is currently being abandoned in many states,[40] thus some of the original impetus for imputing the liability of the hospital employee to the physician is disappearing. However, changes in the various rules of law do not occur concurrently, and an absolute statement of law with regard to vicarious liability in the medical care setting cannot be made.

In any event, the proof of the principal-agent relationship is a complex problem in medical malpractice cases because there are several ways in which the principal-agent relationship can arise in the health care setting. Part of the complexity arises from the concept of control as it applies to the interactions of the various medical personnel in providing health care. A scrub nurse, for example, is frequently under the control of the surgeon. An anesthesiologist, however, may not be under the surgeon's control.

In some situations the lack of control is so obvious that the court will find no principal-agent relationship. Referrals by one physician to another illustrate such a situation. The referring physician is not subject to liability for any negligent acts of the physician to whom he or she referred the patient unless the two physicians are partners or engaged in some other type of employment relationship. The recommended physician is independent and liable only for his or her own negligence.[41] It is important to note, however, that in some jurisdictions physicians have been held responsible for "negligent referrals"; and this may be an emerging trend. Accordingly, physicians should use due care in making referrals.

An employer is frequently held vicariously liable for the negligence of an employee. The employee in the work setting almost always acts on the business of the employer; equally common is the employer's right to control the employee. Thus, physicians in a professional service corporation are liable for the negligence of corporation employees who fail to perform the duties owed by a physician to a patient, including clerical details necessary for competent medical treatment.[42]

Vicarious liability of the principal does not negate the liability of the agent. Rather, both parties to the agency relationship are jointly liable for the negligence of the agent. Vicarious liability, therefore, broadens rather than shifts liability.

CASE ILLUSTRATION

The patient fell on a piece of soap left on the bathroom floor in her hospital room, sustaining a herniated disk that required two subsequent hospitalizations and a laminectomy. The patient sued the hospital on a respondeat superior theory and settled out of court for $10,000, the maximum the hospital could be held liable for by statute in the state where the incident took place. The patient then sued the three floor nurses allegedly responsible for the unsafe condition. The nurses claimed the settlement with the hospital barred the plaintiff from suing them.

In rejecting the nurses' argument, the court stated, "[This] case presents the question as to whether [plaintiff is barred from bringing] separate suits against a master on the theory of respondeat superior and its [sic] servants based upon identical negligent acts . . . [A]lthough the act of negligence complained of is the same in each action, there are nevertheless two distinct and separate persons responsible to the plaintiff, the actual tortfeasor himself and the person vicariously liable for the tort." The court held that, if the jury found the patient's damages to be in excess of $10,000, the nurses could be held responsible for the balance (*McFadden v. Turner*, 1978).[43]

Vicarious liability may be imposed beyond the employee-employer setting. Under the borrowed servant doctrine, one party may be liable for the acts of an employee of another party if the negligent act occurs while the employee is under the first party's direction or control. Thus, a surgeon may be held liable for the negligence of a member of his surgical team, even though that member is employed by the hospital and not by the surgeon.[44]

There are two interpretations of the borrowed servant doctrine. The narrower of the two requires that the master actually exercise control over the borrowed servant at the time of the negligent act in order for the master to be vicariously liable.[45] It has been calculated that, as of 1974, 21 jurisdictions follow this interpretation of the borrowed servant doctrine. Where the master has actual control over the borrowed servant, it is necessary that such control be exercised with reasonable care.[46]

CASE ILLUSTRATION

The physician's patient was admitted to the hospital for delivery of her baby. Prior to the actual delivery of the child, an anesthetic was administered by a certified, registered nurse-anesthetist, an employee of the hospital. Anesthesia was accomplished by means of an airway and catheter inserted into the patient's mouth. During the course of the delivery, the patient suffered damage to her teeth and mouth as a result of the administration of the anesthetic. The physician was present during delivery. The patient brought a lawsuit alleging that the physician should be held liable for the negligence of the nurse-anesthetist. The court held that the nurse-anesthetist did *not* become the legal servant of the physician merely because she received instructions from him as to the work to be performed. Furthermore, there was no evidence that the physician undertook to exercise any control over the nurse-anesthetist. Consequently, the court held that the physician could not be held vicariously liable for the conduct of the nurse-anesthetist (*Sesselman v. Muhlenberg Hospital*, 1973).[47]

A majority of states adhere to a broader interpretation of the borrowed servant doctrine: the principal need have only the *right* to direct or control the agent.[48] Under the broader interpretation, the courts distinguish between the right to supervise a person and the right to control him or her. A supervisor may have considerable power over an agent, but a supervisor is not ultimately responsible[49] for the acts of the agent. Whether the test used is actual control or the right to control, the issue of control is a question of fact to be decided by the jury.[50]

It is not clear whether the borrowed servant doctrine broadens liability (by making three parties—the agent, the primary principal, and the borrowing principal—all liable) or merely shifts vicarious liability from the primary principal to the borrowing principal. At least one court has held that, before a nurse-anesthetist may become a borrowed servant, he or she must become wholly subject to the control and direction of the physician and free from the control of the hospital.[51] Under this theory of the borrowed servant doctrine, an agent can have only one principal at a time. Thus, either the hospital or the physician, but not both, may be vicariously liable for the negligence of a hospital employee. Other courts, ruling that a nurse-anesthetist employed by a hospital may be acting as the agent of a physician and the hospital simultaneously, have held both physician and hospital vicariously liable for the negligence of the nurse anesthetist.[52]

Some courts have followed this principle of simultaneous agency under the theory that it would be unrealistic to hold that the loan of a nurse or other hospital employee to a physician, so as to render the physician liable under the borrowed servant theory for the employee's negligence, would necessarily free the hospital from any vicarious liability for the employee's acts.[53] In fact, most often a hospital employee who is temporarily lent to a physician continues to carry out hospital duties. The employee's work is then of mutual interest to the physician and the hospital and is performed to effect their common purpose. In determining the question of agency, the jury must consider whose work was being done, who had the right to control the work and the manner of doing it, and who received the benefit from the performance of the work.[54]

A hospital resident who is an employee of the hospital but who performs his or her services under the supervision of an independent physician is in a similar situation. It has been consistently held that a hospital resident may be simultaneously the agent of the hospital and of another physician even though his or her employment is not joint.[55]

Respondeat superior and the borrowed servant doctrine are aspects of general agency law. Some jurisdictions have fashioned a very broad form of vicarious liability for medical malpractice cases only. Known as the captain of the ship doctrine, the surgeon or head of an operating team is seen as analogous to the captain of a ship, and the operating team is analogous to the ship's crew. As originally used in Pennsylvania, the phrase was merely meant to explain the operation of the borrowed servant doctrine in the hospital setting.[56] However, as the phrase was used in subsequent cases it emerged as an independent doctrine, whereby the issue of whether an agent had become a borrowed servant changed from a question of fact for the jury to decide to a question of law, allowing the court to impose liability.[57]

In one case, a surgeon was held liable for a negligent act of the operating room team that occurred outside the operating room and without the surgeon present.[58] A later case held a surgeon responsible for the negligence of a chief anesthesiologist which occurred prior to surgery and which the surgeon was not made aware of; in other words, he was made vicariously liable for the negligence of an agent he had no right to control.[59] Thus, the doctrine imposed a form of strict liability on the surgeon for whatever negligence might occur in the course of the operation.

Many other courts have borrowed the phrase, "captain of the ship." Some borrowed it soon after it was coined, when it was intended as a mere analogy.[60] Other courts adopted it later as a doctrine of strict liability.[61] Still other courts expressly rejected this form of the doctrine.[62]

The doctrine's use has been continually criticized. It has been observed that what originated as an illustrative expression has led, because of "its felicity[,] . . . to its lazy repetition; and repetition soon establishes it as a legal formula, undiscriminatingly used to express different and sometimes contradictory ideas."[63]

In a 1971 decision, Pennsylvania, the jurisdiction in which the doctrine originated, limited its strict liability construction. The Pennsylvania Supreme Court held that the term "captain of the ship" constitutes a simple analogy and that the jury must decide whether a master-servant relationship exists at the time of the negligent act.[64] However, other jurisdictions are not restricted to Pennsylvania's revised interpretation, and those that have adopted it may continue to apply the doctrine in its strictest sense.

§ 2.31 Liability of the Surgeon

The surgeon's vicarious liability occurs most often in the operating room. The sheer number of persons involved in a surgical procedure increases the chances of a negligent act, even among competent and well-trained professionals.

The general principles discussed above apply to a surgeon's vicarious liability for negligent acts of other operating room personnel. Some courts hold that the surgeon is the master when the hospital yields control of its employees to the surgeon in the operating room and he or she exercises immediate personal supervision over them. Any negligent acts occurring during the course of this master-servant relationship are imputable to the surgeon.[65] However, at least one court has held that, when the surgeon leaves the operating room after having instructed the hospital employees in what to do, the hospital will be liable for any negligent acts performed in the surgeon's absence.[66] The Texas Supreme

Court has stated that a surgeon's mere presence in the operating room does not make him or her automatically liable for the negligence of others. The court found that a scrub nurse who had miscounted sponges was a hospital employee and not the surgeon's "servant"; the hospital was held liable for the nurse's negligence.[67]

CASE ILLUSTRATION

After delivery of her third child, the patient experienced uterine atony and began to bleed excessively. The physician performed manual massage and administered Pitocin, but these measures were ineffective in stopping the bleeding. To prevent death from hemorrhage, the defendant decided to perform an emergency hysterectomy. During the course of the operation, the physician ordered blood transfusions to replace the patient's excessive blood loss. The patient's blood was O-positive, but the hospital personnel inadvertently administered A-positive blood intended for another patient. When notified of the error, the physician treated the patient properly for transfusion reaction, and the patient appeared to suffer no renal or other permanent damage. In the patient's suit against the physician and the hospital, the court stated that, although the general rule holds the surgeon in charge of all personnel during the performance of an operation, the master-servant relationship does not necessarily apply in the instance of operations performed under modern techniques. The court noted that present operating procedure requires team performance and that the nurses and other personnel assisting in the operating room are not at all times under the immediate supervision and control of the operating surgeon. Because the hospital personnel responsible for administering the blood were not under the immediate control of the surgeon, he was not liable for their negligence in checking the unit before beginning the transfusion (*Parker v. St. Paul Fire and Marine Insurance Co.*, 1976).[68]

A surgeon may be liable for negligent surgery performed by a resident under his or her supervision. A Michigan court held that the obstetrics-gynecology specialists responsible for supervising a tubal ligation were liable for the negligent failure of the resident to perform the procedure properly. The court held the specialists and the resident to a national standard of care applicable to specialists in their field; although they did not perform the operation, they were under a duty to see that it was performed properly. The court reasoned that the defendants' advanced skill and learning enabled them to judge the competence of the resident's performance. Because they failed to take reasonable care in ascertaining that the surgery was competently performed, they were liable for the resulting damages.[69]

§ 2.32 Liability of the Hospital

Vicarious liability for patient injuries may be imposed on hospitals under agency principles. This means that any finding of negligence on the part of an agent of the hospital imputes that negligence to the hospital itself.

Although patients have been more successful in recovering against hospitals when their injury was the result of a failure on the part of hospital personnel to provide treatment or care on a par with accepted medical standards, cases have also been brought under the legal theory of informed consent in an attempt to recover from the hospital. Generally, obtaining the informed consent of the patient is the function of the physician, and such suits against hospitals have been unsuccessful.

CASE ILLUSTRATION

The patient entered the hospital in premature labor for the birth of her third child. With her consent, she had been scheduled for delivery-possible cesarean section. Although there was a known blood incompatibility between the patient and her husband, which poses a greater threat to each conceived child in succession, the patient's first two children were born normal. The patient was fully aware of the problem, having been informed by the physician. Prenatal tests disclosed that the third child would be affected. During either the first or second pregnancy, the physician suggested a hysterectomy, which the patient rejected as "too final." There was disagreement between the patient and the physician as to whether or not the patient finally consented to a tubal ligation. Upon admission to the hospital, the patient was requested by the admitting nurse to sign a "Consent To Operation, Anesthetics, and Other Medical Services" form provided by the hospital. The form contained the following provision: "I am aware that sterility may result from this operation. I know that a sterile person is incapable of becoming a parent." This provision, at the patient's insistence, was stricken from the form. As altered, the form accompanied the patient's chart into the operating room and was present there during the surgical procedure. After delivery, the assisting physician asked the physician whether the patient's tubes were to be tied. The question of consent arose and was discussed by the two physicians. Because the patient was under anesthesia and no hospital tubal ligation consent form was found on the patient's chart, the physician sent one of the attending nurses into the hall, where the form was presented to and signed by the patient's husband.* The nurse presented the signed form to the physician, who then performed the ligation, accompanied by the assisting physician. The patient

---

*Consent by a patient's spouse is generally legally inadequate (see § 1.33 for a discussion of consent).

sued the hospital (among other defendants) for failure to obtain her informed consent. The court held that there was no negligence on the part of the attending nurse who obtained the consent of the patient's husband because the nurse was acting on the orders of the physician; nor was there any negligence on the part of the admitting nurse, since she attached the form as signed by the patient to the patient's chart, which accompanied her into the operating room. In so doing, the nurse followed hospital regulations and discharged her duty toward the patient. Therefore, the hospital was held not liable (*Beck v. Lovell,* 1978).[70]

Hospitals generally will escape vicarious liability for the conduct or orders of a physician. The law is clear that a hospital is protected from liability when its staff follows the direct and explicit orders of the attending physician unless its staff knows that the physician's orders are so clearly contraindicated by normal practice that ordinary prudence requires inquiry into their correctness.[71] Generally, where there is no evidence that the hospital has any control over the physician, which is true in most cases, the hospital will not be liable for the physician's conduct, treatment, or manner of performing surgery.[72]

The hospital is often liable when the injury that the patient suffers is the result of the negligent conduct of hospital nurses or other hospital personnel. Where the sum total of treatment and care provided by the hospital staff exposes a patient to danger involving an unreasonable risk of harm, the hospital will be held liable.[73]

CASE ILLUSTRATION

The patient entered the hospital in labor, and a normal delivery was anticipated, although the head of the fetus was not "fixed" at that time. After almost seven hours of labor, the patient's dilation had not progressed, and her contractions intensified in severity and duration. She was in great discomfort and was vomiting. The fetal heartbeat was difficult to find, and it was fluctuating. A fetal monitor was available, but the labor room nurse was not educated in its use; the resident on duty, however, knew how to use the monitor. When sometime later the nurses could not detect a fetal heartbeat, they called the resident, who examined the patient and saw indications of fetal distress and possible asphyxiation. He performed an emergency cesarean section before the administered anesthetic took effect on the patient, but the baby was stillborn. The patient brought suit. At trial there was evidence which indicated that, if the baby had been delivered by cesarean section about an hour earlier or when there was a normal heartbeat, it would have survived. The court held that the hospital staff was negligent in allowing the patient to remain unattended without an

§ 2.32   *Liability of Hospital*   91

examination by a physician or a resident and was liable for the injury she suffered (*Samii v. Baystate Medical Center, Inc.*, 1979).[74]

The courts have recognized that the primary duty of a hospital's nursing staff is to follow the physician's orders, and a hospital is normally protected from tort liability if its staff follows those orders. If a physician's orders are to be a hospital's shield from liability, the hospital must see to it that those orders are followed; staff deviation from those orders cannot be defended on the grounds that other physicians or hospitals might consider the treatment acceptable. More important than the question of logical consistency is the issue of social policy. There is every reason to encourage the hospital staff to carry out diligently the physician's orders, and there is no reason to relieve the hospital from liability for failing to do so.[75] Thus, where a physician orders treatment properly indicated by the patient's condition and the treatment is negligently administered or otherwise improperly provided by a hospital nurse, the hospital and not the physician will be held liable.[76]

CASE ILLUSTRATION

Early one morning, the physician learned that his patient was in labor. He telephoned the hospital and gave instructions to a nurse there concerning the patient, who was en route to the hospital. One instruction was to inject the patient with 50 milligrams of Phenergan, commonly used to relieve anxiety and dispel nausea. The patient was admitted to the hospital, and a registered nurse with six months' experience injected the Phenergan into the patient's right buttock using a 22-caliber gauge needle 1½ inches long. The nurse knew that an injection into or near the sciatic nerve (located in the lower back) would cause immediate and irreparable damage to the nerve. She knew that care must be taken to inject the needle perpendicularly to the point of entry. The nurse did not record in the labor room records the time at which the injection was given, as standard nursing practice required. Upon receiving the injection, the patient immediately experienced a severe burning pain radiating downward from her right buttock to her right leg and foot and she so informed the nurse. The hospital records contain no entry of the patient's complaint of pain. Throughout the day, the patient complained of right leg pain to the nursing staff and to her relatives who were present. However, no recording of her complaints was made by the nursing staff. The patient stated that the pain was so severe that she attempted to carefully position herself during labor to try to lessen the pressure. The physician was never informed, nor could he ascertain by the patient's records that the patient was experiencing pain in her right leg. The next day, after receiving other injections and a spinal anesthetic, the patient delivered a healthy baby girl.

The patient brought suit. At trial, she testified that her right leg pain continued to be so severe that she could not nurse the baby; she had difficulty caring for the child and doing ordinary housework; she could not stand, sit, or lie down for any length of time. The court held that, although there was no evidence establishing a reasonable causal connection between the act of the physician and the patient's injury, the evidence was sufficient to support the judgment against the hospital. Consequently, the court held the hospital liable for the acts of its nurse (*Frantz v. San Luis Medical Clinic*, 1978).[77]

§ 2.40 BIRTH-RELATED CAUSES OF ACTION

Modern developments, both medical and legal, have given rise to causes of action* that were unheard of as recently as 20 years ago.[78] In the field of genetic counseling, the development of more sophisticated biochemical and cytogenetic tests has enhanced the efficacy of predictive counseling. Indeed, there is increasing evidence that genetic counseling is an important technique that can be used to prevent birth defects.[79] The law has responded by generally recognizing suits brought by persons who have been injured by failures in the process of genetic counseling.

At present, certain chromosomal disorders and about 50 inherited diseases associated with enzyme deficiencies, which constitute between three and five percent of all known birth defects, can be diagnosed prenatally.[80] Amniocentesis, a relatively new diagnostic technique, can identify various genetic defects and chromosomal anomalies, as well as the sex and blood type of the fetus.[81] These services are becoming available to a larger segment of the population, and improving techniques and new knowledge are expanding their efficacy and application.

The legal system acts to monitor and regulate professional activities in both the private and public sectors. This includes the entire medical profession, as well as the subfield of genetic counseling. The conduct of the genetic counselor is subject to the same legal scrutiny from the private sector as the rest of the medical profession with regard to standards of duty and care and particularly informed consent (see Chapter IX, Genetic Counseling).

Recent case law has added and somewhat modified many "traditional" legal strictures. In 1973, in the case of *Roe v. Wade*,[82] the U.S. Supreme Court effectively abolished state legislation prohibiting the performance of an abortion during the first trimester of pregnancy. The court affirmed the pregnant woman's Constitutional right to privacy as a compelling factor in allowing her to obtain

---

*The term "cause of action" refers to a theory recognized by law under which a plaintiff is entitled to bring a lawsuit. For example, a plaintiff may bring a suit under a contract or a negligence cause of action; in legal parlance, he or she may bring a cause of action sounding in contract or negligence.

an abortion without legal sanction. Subsequent to this decision, case law has underscored the recognition of the legal right of a woman to a first trimester abortion[83] (see §§ 5.45, 7.65, and 10.30 for discussion of the legal issues involved in abortion).

Abortion of a fetus found defective through amniocentesis will most likely take place in the second or third trimester of pregnancy, because the sixteenth week of gestation is believed to be the most fruitful time for amniocentesis[84] and because analysis of amniotic fluid requires an additional three to five weeks.[85] The *Roe* decision only allows second and third trimester abortions if, in the words of the court, termination of the pregnancy is necessary to preserve "the life or health of the mother."[86] Some courts have interpreted the term "health" to include mental health,[87] which should allow the pregnant woman to obtain a later abortion if she is distressed by a diagnosis of genetic disease. Some states have enacted statutes adopting this interpretation.[88]

The woman's right to privacy recognized by the *Roe* decision[89] arose against a backdrop of legal policy arguments in earlier cases recognizing that family planning which is motivated solely by personal or socioeconomic considerations is not antithetical to public policy.[90] It has been noted that, if the public policy is not violated by the termination of pregnancy, then a fortiori public policy is not violated by purposeful acts of birth control.[91]

The impact of these legal and medical developments is to provide the individual with more choices involving procreation. To the extent that the law recognizes the individual's right to make such decisions and see them implemented, they will be enforced in a court of law. The new causes of action alluded to above include wrongful conception, wrongful birth, and wrongful life. Although all three originally met with resistance in the courts, wrongful conception and wrongful birth are increasingly being recognized by courts across the country. Today, the obstetrician-gynecologist who engages in genetic counseling and implementing procreative controls is subject to specific legal liability for substandard treatment or conduct in this area.

§ 2.41 Wrongful Conception

Wrongful conception suits are brought against a physician by the parents of a healthy newborn to recover for the physical and financial injury resulting from an improperly or negligently performed sterilization procedure undergone for the purpose of preventing conception and birth.[92] In these suits, the birth of the child is the principal injury claimed, not because the child is unwanted or unloved or because it was born defective, but because it was unplanned.[93]

That public policy allows patients to enforce their choice in matters of birth control is reflected in state statutes that encourage family planning and birth control,[94] even to the point of subsidizing contraceptives as part of state welfare programs.[95] Case decisions recognizing that elective sterilization is compatible with public policy also form a foundation supporting wrongful conception suits.[96] Thus, in response to these values, many courts have recognized that, where the fundamental right not to procreate has been violated, the law will provide a remedy.[97]

Although wrongful conception causes of action are generally recognized across the United States, two controversies persist: first, what damages may be recovered in a wrongful conception case[98] and second, what term will be used to describe causes of action brought by parents with an unwanted pregnancy after a failed sterilization—wrongful conception or wrongful birth?[99]

Although a negligently performed sterilization or abortion generally gives rise to a wrongful conception case, courts have referred to these cases variously as wrongful sterilization, wrongful pregnancy, wrongful birth, and wrongful life cases. The first two labels, wrongful sterilization and wrongful pregnancy, are interchangeable with the concept of wrongful conception. The latter two classifications, however, are misleading, as they have precise meanings (see §§ 2.42, Wrongful Birth and 2.43, Wrongful Life).

The question of what damages may be recovered in a wrongful conception case is a more complex problem. The idea that the birth of a healthy child is an ultimate good holds a place of importance in many people's religious and philosophical beliefs.[100] In response to these values, at least one court has declared that it is not within the province of the courts to decide that the existence of life is a wrong for which damages can be recovered.[101] Several older decisions suggest that the birth of a healthy child, even if unplanned, cannot be considered an injury.[102] Another court even expressed a concern for the potential emotional harm to the child if he or she later learns of the wrongful conception court action.[103] Indeed, until a 1967 California decision,[104] there had been a marked tendency on the part of the courts to reject wrongful conception causes of action.

Although wrongful conception causes of action are now generally recognized, the problem with computing damages has become even more confused as courts in different states reach different conclusions. On one hand, parent-plaintiffs argue that the costs associated with raising a healthy child are greater than the costs of not having to raise that child. On the other hand, from the physician's point of view, the burdens of an unplanned, healthy child should be offset by the benefits the parents receive from that child. This dichotomy has prompted several courts to adopt the "benefits rule," which balances these competing values.

Michigan was one of the first states to adopt the benefits rule.[105]

CASE ILLUSTRATION

After visiting with her physician, the patient took a prescription for birth control pills to her pharmacist. The prescription was filled with a mild tranquilizer. The patient became pregnant and delivered a healthy child. Subsequently, she sued for the costs associated with the unplanned preg-

§ 2.41 Wrongful Conception

nancy as well as the costs associated with raising a healthy child. The pharmacist argued that public policy militated against awarding damages when the result of the wrongful act was the birth of a normal, healthy child. In response to this assertion, the court determined that it is in the interest of the public to encourage pharmacists to exercise great care in filling prescriptions. Recognizing that contraceptives are intended to prevent the birth of healthy children, the court ruled that the costs of raising a child born as a result of the negligent act of the pharmacist were recoverable. However, the court also ruled that the benefits rule should be applied in balancing the benefits conferred by the birth of a healthy child against the damages of the cost of raising the child. This appellate court returned the case to the trial court, where a jury assessed damages (*Scarf v. Troppi*, 1971).[106]

In states where the benefits rule is applied, it is left to the trier of fact, usually a jury, to balance these competing values and to determine the awarding of damages.[107]

Three recent decisions in three different states have rejected the benefits rule. Two of these decisions benefit physician-defendants, the third does not.

In the first,[108] the parents requested damages for the cost of raising the unplanned but otherwise healthy child. The court said no. It ruled that the mother could claim damages for the difficulty she experienced incident to the unexpected pregnancy. The parents could not, however, recover the costs associated with raising the unplanned child, because this would constitute a windfall to the parents while at the same time imposing an excessive burden on the physician.

In the second case,[109] a New Jersey court found that a healthy child was born after the physician-defendant performed a tubal ligation on the plaintiff. The parents' claim for the costs of raising, educating, and supervising the unplanned child were rejected by the court. No recovery was allowed.

As the preceeding case demonstrates, one of the reasons courts have been reluctant to allow unbridled damage recovery in wrongful conception cases is the negative impact such a finding would have on physician-defendants. As one court held:

> To permit the parents to keep their child and shift the entire cost of its upbringing to a physician who failed to . . . [sterilize the mother] would create a new category of surrogate parent. Every child's smile, every bond of love and affection, every reason for parental pride in a child's achievements, every contribution by the child to the welfare and well-being of the family and parents is to remain with the mother and father. For the most part, these are intangible benefits, but they are nonetheless real. On the other hand, every financial cost or detriment . . . including the cost of food, clothing, and education would be shifted to the physician . . . [S]uch a result would be wholly out of proportion to the culpability involved.[110]

In the third case, an Illinois intermediate appellate court rejected the benefits rule, to the detriment of the physician. The court found that, although the emotional benefits of rearing a child may be great, these benefits do not offset the financial costs associated with raising the unplanned child. In other words, even if the parents derive benefits from an unplanned child, these benefits do not relieve them of unplanned costs. The Illinois Supreme Court reviewed and reversed the lower appellate court finding.[111]

In sum, the benefits rule has been used to deny any recovery; to allow for a balanced recovery whereby the amount of damages owed by the physician-defendant is determined by balancing the parents' loss against their gain and holding the physician liable for the difference; and, finally, to hold the physician liable for all costs associated with the unplanned child, because physicians should not be able to lessen their responsibility just because their wrongful act provided an alleged benefit to parents who expressly chose not to seek such a benefit.

Courts that recognize and enforce wrongful conception causes of action regardless of the benefits rule note that allowing recovery for the negligence of a physician in facilitating the birth of an unwanted child is no more offensive than the concept of birth control itself.[112] Consequently, an operation for the purposes of family limitation motivated solely by personal or socioeconomic considerations is acknowledged as being consistent with public policy and a matter of individual conscience.[113] It has also been argued that for the courts to endorse a policy that makes physicians liable for the forseeable consequences of all negligently performed operations except those involving sterilization would constitute an impermissible infringement of a fundamental right.[114]

Where the wrongful conception cause of action is recognized, the facts of the case will dictate the appropriate theory of recovery. If the plaintiff pursues his or her suit on a negligence theory, the breach of some duty must be alleged and proved (see § 1.30, Duty). Negligence may be alleged in the improper performance of the sterilization operation[115] or in postoperative failure to ascertain whether the operation was successful or to advise or properly prescribe for the patient so that she might be properly guided in preventing conception.[116] In the area of negligent performance of an operation, proof of negligence may be difficult. First, because operations are performed on internal organs, misfeasance is often not readily apparent.[117] Second, the possibility that the pregnancy and birth are a result of the recanalization of the patient's fallopian tubes exists and must be overcome. Any tubal ligation carries a small statistical risk that it will not be successful.[118] Finally, the physician may show by expert testimony that the procedure performed comported with the applicable medical standards of care[119] (see § 1.32, Standard of Care).

These problems of proof can be surmounted, however. Testimony may be given by a physician who either performed a cesarean delivery of the wrongfully conceived child or who performed a second sterilization and was actually able to view the nonligated tubes.[120] The patient may undergo a radiologic examination of her fallopian tubes and offer the results as proof of negligence.[121] Furthermore, a pathology report evaluating removed structures will reveal whether they were in fact segments of fallopian tube.[122] Some courts have held that the mere fact of subsequent pregnancy presents a sufficient question of negligence for a jury to resolve.[123] Finally, some courts have even disregarded the possibility of recanalization as a probable explanation for the failed sterilization because of the low rate at which this phenomenon occurs.[124]

Under a negligence theory, the wrongful conception cause of action must address the issue of causation (see § 1.50, Causation). Thus, in order for the patient to recover, the improperly performed sterilization must be the proximate cause of the patient's injury (the birth of the unplanned child), and the injury must be a reasonably foreseeable consequence of the negligence.[125] Those courts which recognize the wrongful conception cause of action have had no trouble in applying the above analysis to cases before them.[126] Some physician-defendants in wrongful conception actions have argued that the cause of the patient's pregnancy is the sexual intercourse engaged in subsequent to the sterilization procedure and therefore the direct cause of the pregnancy is sexual intercourse, not the failure of the sterilization. This argument has been rejected by most courts because the purpose of the operation is to allow the woman to engage in intercourse without fear of pregnancy. Consequently, sexual relations are naturally foreseeable to both the physician and the patient and are not a separate, intervening cause sufficient to relieve the physician of his or her responsibility.[127] Thus, to recover on a negligence theory the patient-plaintiff must show that the physician had a duty, that he or she breached it, and that the breach caused a damage. As demonstrated earlier in this section, however, the problem of determining damages is a hurdle several courts have refused to leap.

Wrongful conception cases have also been brought under a breach of warranty theory. Breach of warranty is tied to contract law and refers to the failure of a promisor to keep his or her promise or otherwise comply with assurances or representations made to the patient. Patients who have undergone unsuccessful sterilizations have alleged that representations by the physician that the sterilization would be irreversible,[128] or that the patient would have no more children,[129] or that the sterilization would be 100 percent successful[130] constituted warranties. In most cases, the courts have rejected such claims as grounds for recovery.[131] The courts have generally required a patient to prove the making of the warranty, reliance on the warranty, and a consideration separate from the physician's fees for the performance of the sterilization[132] (see § 2.20, Contract Theory).

Somewhat related to breach of warranty in the context of wrongful conception is the doctrine of informed consent (see § 1.33, Consent and Informed Consent). Patients have alleged that they were not informed that the sterilization procedure was not absolutely foolproof in preventing pregnancy.[133] While this theory of liability has met with mixed success, the cases indicate that the physician should inform his or her patient of the various methods available for performing a tubal ligation, the possibility of natural failure, and, if the operation is performed in connection with a cesarean delivery, of the higher rate of failure of any method of tubal ligation performed at that time.[134]

In sum, although the present legal trend is to allow for the recovery of some amount of damages against physician-defendants for doing or failing to do something to prevent pregnancy and birth, a review of these cases suggests that some courts are still troubled by the concept of awarding money to parents for the birth of a healthy child. Indeed, the benefits rule is probably the best evidence of this dilemma and of how the courts have strained to achieve a balanced position.

§ 2.42 Wrongful Birth

Wrongful birth suits are brought against physicians by the parents of defective newborns. This cause of action is generally recognized across the United States.[135]

In wrongful birth suits, the parents claim that, if it had not been for the physician-defendant's negligence, they would have been advised not to conceive (see § 9.10, Pre-conception Counseling) or that, if the woman is already pregnant, the physician-defendant failed to perform required tests or to give advice that would have shown the fetus to be defective, thereby denying the parents the choice of an abortion (see §§ 9.30, Amniocentesis and 10.21, Rubella).

Although wrongful birth suits are sometimes referred to as wrongful conception or wrongful life suits (see §§ 2.41, Wrongful Conception and 2.43, Wrongful Life), there is general agreement that when parents sue, claiming money damages as a consequence of giving birth to a defective child, that suit is properly called a wrongful birth suit.

CASE ILLUSTRATION

Parents of Jewish descent went to the physician-defendant for testing to determine whether they were Tay-Sachs carriers. Blood samples were withdrawn and mislabeled; when the negative results came in, the parents proceeded with the pregnancy. Their child was born with Tay-Sachs, and a wrongful birth suit was filed against the physician. The jury returned a verdict for the parents, and the physician appealed. The appellate court held that (1) the parents had a cause of action for the wrongful birth of their child since they were owed a duty of reasonable care in the handling of the blood withdrawn for the test, there was a breach of duty due to negligence in the mislabeling of the father's blood, there was a causal connection between the breach of duty and the decision of the parents to continue pregnancy rather than abort the fetus, and there was direct injury in depriving the parents of an opportunity to accept or reject continuance of the mother's pregnancy; (2) the parents were entitled to recover damages

§ 2.42 Wrongful Birth

for expenses incurred in the care and treatment of their child; and (3) the parents were entitled to damages for emotional distress (*Naccash v. Burger*, 1982).[136]

The decided cases indicate that physicians may face wrongful birth suits in connection with four distinct factual situations (all of which are treated in detail elsewhere).

1. A failure to diagnose or advise of the effects of a medical condition of the mother's that may bear significantly on fetal health. Litigation in this area has been principally concerned with negligence in the diagnosis or treatment of rubella[137] (see § 10.21, Rubella).
2. A failure to diagnose pregnancy promptly enough to permit elective abortion, in consequence of which a normal, not deformed, child is born. Since many courts still believe that "the existence of a normal healthy life is an esteemed right . . . rather than a compensable wrong,"[138] the plaintiffs in this situation may be held ineligible for substantial damages (see § 2.40, Birth-Related Causes of Action).
3. Negligence in the performance of an abortion. The birth of a deformed child may lead to a higher measure of damages,[139] but some courts permit recovery of the full costs of child rearing even if the child is normal[140] (see §§ 10.30, Abortion and 2.41, Wrongful Conception).
4. Negligence in genetic counseling. This may involve failure to take a proper history that would alert the physician to the possibility of birth defects,[141] failure to advise the mother of the availability of an amniocentesis test[142] or of the risk of bearing a deformed child,[143] or failure to recognize the presence of a genetic disease[144] (see §§ 9.10, Preconception Counseling and 9.30, Amniocentesis).

In a wrongful birth action, as in any other action for malpractice, the parents must prove that the physician's negligent breach of a duty owed them caused the injury of which they complain.[145] This established rule of tort law often poses no special difficulty for patient-plaintiffs in wrongful birth actions. If, for example, the physician's negligent failure to diagnose rubella or to detect a genetic defect results in the birth of a deformed child that would otherwise have been aborted, it cannot accurately be said that the physician's negligence caused the defects. However, the courts have found the requisite causal connection in the breach of the physician's duty to diagnose conditions relevant to the patient's pregnancy[146] or to inform the patient of the facts she needs to make intelligent use of her prerogative to abort.[147] The physician's negligence, in other words, is seen not as the cause of the child's defects, but as the cause of its birth. To show a causal connection, the patient must prove that, if the physician had not been negligent and if she had been properly diagnosed or advised, she would have aborted her unborn child.[148]

The few courts that have rejected or limited the wrongful birth cause of action have often done so on grounds of public policy. In some of these cases, particularly in those decided before the landmark Supreme Court abortion decision of *Roe v. Wade*,[149] a strong antiabortion stance on the part of the judges is apparent. Thus one court, holding that the parents of a deformed child had no cause of action for the physician's alleged negligence in failing to advise the mother of the possible effects of her rubella, asserted that "the right of [the] child to live is greater than and precludes [the parents'] right not to endure emotional and financial injury."[150] The court reached this conclusion even though, for purposes of the case, it assumed the mother could legally have obtained a therapeutic abortion. *Roe v. Wade*, however, clearly established a woman's constitutional right to procure an abortion during the first trimester. It has been asserted that the public policy behind *Roe v. Wade* supports recognition of the wrongful birth cause of action.[151] State statutes have been revised to reflect the sweeping changes in abortion law mandated by *Roe v. Wade*. Accordingly, the antiabortion beliefs of individual judges should not play a significant role in future decisions concerning wrongful birth cases.

The public policy issues raised by wrongful birth actions extend beyond the profound moral and religious dilemmas raised by abortion. Public policy, as implemented through tort law, is largely intended to discourage asocial, destructive, or injurious behavior, while compensating persons injured through the negligence or intentional acts of others. To this end, tort-feasors are held liable for damages to injured parties for the effects of their negligence insofar as this can be done without assessing liability disproportionate to the harm inflicted.

Damages in tort law are primarily restorative in nature. They are designed to compensate the aggrieved party for any harm suffered in consequence of the wrongdoer's negligent act.[152] The wrongdoer is accordingly held liable for all injuries directly resulting from the negligent act, whether foreseen by the wrongdoer or not, provided they are the legal and natural consequences of the natural act and, according to common experience, might reasonably have been anticipated[153] (see § 1.60, Damages). The law recognizes, however, that a negligent act may confer benefit as well as cause injury. Because the object of tort law is not to better the injured party's position, but merely to return it to where it was before the injury, the value of a benefit conferred is considered in mitigation of damages.[154]

Courts in the United States, however, have not been prepared to say that the benefits of raising a child born with deformities or a terminal illness outweigh the burdens of extremely high emotional and economic costs associated with a defective or seriously ill child. Thus, courts that might otherwise deny the wrongful birth cause of action have demonstrated a willingness to allow an expanded measure of damages in such cases. In one such case, the patient gave birth to a deformed child after the physician diagnosed her rubella as a skin rash.[155] The court held that, if the misdiagnosis was the result of negligence, the patient and her husband could recover the additional medical and support expenses incurred as a result of their child's deformities. There is some measure of logic in this resolution of the damages problem. Unlike the parents of an unplanned child born in wrongful conception cases, the parents of the defective child generally wanted a child and intended to support it. It is probably appropriate, therefore, to award such parents the extra expenses necessitated by their child's deformities, not the ordinary expenses they would have incurred in raising the healthy, normal child they desired.[156]

A third group of cases recognizes the parents' cause of action for child support and awards damages according to normal tort principles, without limitations based on public policy. Although the jury may be asked to weigh the benefits of parenthood against the parents' claimed damages,[157] the effect is to extend full judicial recognition to the wrongful birth claim for damages. The physician may be held liable not only for medical expenses, loss of income, loss of services, pain, emotional suffering,[158] or other injury to the parents associated with the unwanted pregnancy, but also for the full costs of raising and educating the child.[159] Child-rearing costs, it has been asserted, "are a direct financial injury to the parents, no different in immediate effect than the medical expenses" incurred by the mother in consequence of the physician's negligence.[160] Also, if the parents must spread their "society, comfort, care, protection, and support" over a larger group, the change in family status may constitute a compensable item of damages.[161] In the case of a healthy, normal child, the physician's liability for child-rearing costs will not ordinarily be projected beyond the age of majority, since at that time parental duty to support terminates. If, however, the unplanned child is born with congenital deformities rendering him or her permanently incapable of support, the physician's liability for support might extend indefinitely.[162]

Established principles of tort law require a party injured by the negligence of another to mitigate his or her damages, and they preclude recovery of such damages if they could have been avoided through reasonable mitigation.[163] Nonetheless, a woman's refusal to abort a "wrongfully" conceived child or to put her defective child up for adoption following its birth will not be construed by the court as a failure to mitigate damages.[164] Although such actions would undeniably reduce the economic burden associated with a defective child, to require them as a prerequisite to recovery would probably constitute an unreasonable, even unconstitutional, invasion of familial privacy.[165] Accordingly, courts that recognize a parental action for child support are unlikely to place limits on the recoverable damages simply because the parents were not obligated to keep the child.

Courts are also divided on the question of whether a parent may recover damages for emotional suffering incurred incident to the birth of a defective child. Such suffering is particularly acute in cases involving children afflicted with substantial birth defects or a terminal illness.[166] The reaction of a particular court to this issue can be surprising. In one case, the court barred the parents from recovering child support for reasons of public policy, yet permitted recovery of emotional damages.[167] Child support, said the court, would disproportionately burden the negligent physician, but liability for emotional suffering would not. On the other hand, courts that recognize a physician's liability for the pecuniary expenses of raising a child have sometimes denied the recovery of emotional damages.[168] Courts denying recovery have asserted that the damages for emotional suffering are too speculative to be computed in a court of law[169] or that emotional damages, while recoverable in some instances, are generally unavailable to persons who have not themselves suffered a physical injury.[170] The latter rationale precludes recovery of emotional damages by the parents of a defective child, for their injuries are exclusively psychological. It is unlikely that the courts will soon reach a uniform conclusion as to the desirability of compensating parents for emotional damages in wrongful birth actions.

In sum, although wrongful birth suits are generally allowed where a physician's negligence denies parents the choice of avoiding the birth of a defective child, significant disparity as to what damages will be allowed exists among the various states. There is even some disparity as to what label will be placed on this cause of action.

§ 2.43 Wrongful Life

Wrongful life suits are the child of wrongful birth suits (see § 2.42, Wrongful Birth). When parents give birth to a defective child due to genetic counseling failures, testing failures, or other negligent acts that deny them the choice of not conceiving or of abortion after conception, the parents' suit is for wrongful birth. The defective child born to such parents has, in at least two jurisdictions,[171] a lawsuit of his or her own—wrongful life. Prior to these California and Washington decisions, however, the general trend in states where the question was considered has been to reject the child's cause of action for wrongful life, while recognizing the parents' claim for wrongful birth.[172] Thus, although the physician-defendant ends up having to pay someone, that someone is usually the parents, not their defective child.

The wrongful life cause of action, virtually unheard of as recently as 15 years ago, is an outgrowth of recent advances in the fields of genetic counseling and fetal diagnosis. New techniques and technologies have made it possible in many cases to estimate the risk of genetic disease prior to conception and to detect the actual or probable presence of birth defects prior to delivery. These procedures have enabled physicians to counsel their patients better on the risks of conceiving or giving birth to defective children. In turn, prospective parents informed of these risks may choose to use contraception or to abort. The wrongful life cause of action arises when this counseling process breaks down, that is,

§ 2.43

when the physician negligently fails to detect or disclose the possibility that an unconceived or unborn child will suffer from genetic or other defects.

Wrongful life actions have been brought in connection with three factual situations. Most often the action arises from alleged negligence in genetic counseling. This may involve a failure to recognize the presence of genetic disease in the parents[173] or a failure to advise parents of the risk of conceiving a deformed child.[174] Failure to inform the mother of the availability or advisability, or both, of tests (for example, amniocentesis) that would have detected fetal defects has also been alleged as negligence.[175]

Another factual situation concerns the physician's negligent failure to diagnose or advise of the effects of a maternal medical condition on fetal health. Specifically, wrongful life actions have been brought where a deformed child was born in consequence of a physician's negligence in the diagnosis or evaluation of rubella.[176] Wrongful life actions have also been brought on behalf of children born alive following a negligently performed abortion or sterilization operation.[177]

In a 1982 California decision, a wrongful life suit was allowed where there was a failure to diagnose hereditary deafness in the older sister of the child-plaintiff.

CASE ILLUSTRATION

Parents took their baby girl, Hope, for a hearing evaluation. The test results showed that Hope had normal hearing. Over a year later, however, it turned out that the test had been negligently performed and that Hope was completely deaf as a result of a hereditary ailment. In the interim, relying on the defendants' diagnosis of Hope, the parents conceived a second child, Joy. Joy was born totally deaf. A lawsuit was filed against the defendants. The parents sued for their own damages on a wrongful birth theory (see § 2.42, Wrongful Birth), and they sued on behalf of Joy on a wrongful life theory. In the wrongful life suit they alleged that, if the defendants had not been negligent in testing Hope, they would have discovered Hope's hereditary defect; further, if they had known of this defect they would not have conceived Joy. They also alleged that the defendants' negligence deprived Joy of the fundamental right of a child to be born as a whole, functional human being, without total deafness. In other words, if the defendants had performed their jobs properly, Joy would not have been born with her hearing intact, but rather would not have been born at all. The trial court dismissed Joy's wrongful life claim. An appeal was filed. The appellate court rejected the defendants' argument that an impaired life was necessarily preferable to no life. Before reversing the trial court's dismissal of Joy's wrongful life suit, however, the appellate court outlined the damages Joy was entitled to claim. Joy, as the child-plaintiff in a wrongful life suit, could not recover *general damages* for being born impaired as opposed to not being born at all, however she was allowed to recover *special damages* for the extraordinary expenses necessary to treat her hereditary ailment and impairment (*Turpin v. Sortini*, 1982).[178]

As in any malpractice action, the child-plaintiff in a wrongful life case must prove that the physician's negligent breach of a duty owed the plaintiff caused the injury of which the child-plaintiff complains.[179] Proof of some of these constituent elements is not difficult in the wrongful life context. Since the 1946 case of *Bonbrest v. Kotz*,[180] it has been recognized that a child born alive has a cause of action for prenatal injuries. Subsequent cases have established that a physician may be held liable for pre-conception negligence resulting in prenatal injuries to a subsequently conceived child.[181] Accordingly, the courts no longer have difficulty finding that a physician owes a duty to an unborn child. Likewise, proof of proximate causation poses no special difficulty to the wrongful life plaintiff. While it cannot accurately be said that the physician caused the child's defects, since these are the unavoidable outcome of medical or genetic conditions that could not have been treated in the exercise of reasonable care,[182] the defects are not the injury of which the child complains.[183] Instead, the child seeks recovery for his or her existence. The child must therefore prove that its existence is a consequence of the physician's negligence. This proof is satisfied by a demonstration that the child's mother would not have conceived or would have aborted her unborn child had the physician not been negligent. Proof of either of these contingencies satisfies the requirement of proximate cause.[184] Nonetheless, courts that have considered the action have consistently held that the plaintiff did not prove one or both of the final two elements of a negligence cause of action: the existence of an injury and legally cognizable damages (see § 1.20, Elements of Negligence).

Although recognizing the suffering that a deformed child must experience, a number of courts have concluded that the wrongful life plaintiff has not suffered an injury compensable at law. Courts have stated that there is no fundamental right of a child to be born as a whole, functional human being.[185] In addition, courts have been reluctant to find that a child has suffered an injury simply by being born alive. One court stated that resolution of this question is a matter outside judicial competence. Refusing to recognize the action, the court stated, "Whether it is better never to have been born at all than to have been born with . . . gross deficiencies is a mystery more properly to be left to the philosophers and the theologians."[186]

It has also been argued that the ability of a deformed child to feel love, happiness, and pleasure makes questionable any assertion that the child would have been better off not having been born.[187] Finally, some courts have concluded that a public policy "supporting the preciousness of human life"[188] compels rejection of the wrongful life cause of action.[189] As an Alabama court stated:

"[A] legal right not to be born alive is alien to the public policy of this state to protect and preserve human life."[190]

The other reason commonly cited by the courts as grounds for rejection of the action is the difficulty of computing damages. The remedy afforded an injured party in negligence is designed to place that party in the position he or she would have occupied but for the defendant's negligence. The damages recoverable by a wrongful life plaintiff would, according to this established rule of tort law, be limited to those necessary to restore the infant to the position it would have occupied had the defendant not been negligent.[191] Yet if the defendant had not been negligent, the plaintiff would never have been born. Thus, the wrongful life plaintiff seeks as damages the difference in value between nonexistence and existence in an impaired state. Concluding that it is "logically impossible" to measure such damages,[192] some courts have held that the difficulty of computing damages precludes recognition of the action.[193] Although one court has stated that an otherwise valid cause of action should not be rejected solely because damages are difficult to ascertain, the court nonetheless rejected the action on grounds that a wrongful life plaintiff has not suffered a legally cognizable injury.[194]

A 1982 decision considering this aspect of wrongful life actions, however, states that:

> . . . while our society and our legal system unquestionably place the highest value on all human life, we do not think that it is accurate to suggest that this state's public policy establishes—as a matter of law—that under all circumstances "impaired life" is "preferable" to "nonlife."[195]

In sum, although most courts have rejected the child's claim for wrongful life, preferring to allow the parents' claim for wrongful birth, current California and Washington decisions may represent the beginning of a new trend. Indeed, several commentators have suggested that the wrongful life cause of action will receive judicial recognition as soon as the courts emerge from a "cultural lag" and adjust themselves to recent advances in medical science.[196]

From a clinical perspective, the "wrongful" causes of action suggest that physicians unfamiliar with genetic counseling and the state of the art in testing for hereditary defects should consider referrals whenever a patient needs or requests this type of service. Indeed, advances in medical technology and the "wrongful" causes of action are stimulating the growth of genetic counseling as a specialty.

§ 2.50 LEGAL STATUS OF THE FETUS

Many of the legal issues surrounding pregnancy converge on the question of the legal status of the human fetus. Legal commentators have noted that a determination of what legal right a fetus may claim is particularly important in light of contemporary medical advances: fetal research, in vitro fertilization, and an increasing awareness of the effect of a mother's activities during pregnancy on the health of her fetus.[197] However, the nation's courts have not yet clearly articulated the legal status of the fetus.

The decision of the U.S. Supreme Court in *Roe v. Wade*[198]—that a woman has a right to obtain an abortion under certain circumstances—necessarily limits legal protection of fetal interests. The Court held that "the word 'person,' as used in the Fourteenth Amendment, does not include the unborn."[199] The Court further held that the state's interest in the potential human life of a fetus does not become compelling until the fetus becomes viable—"potentially able to live outside the mother's womb, albeit with artificial aid"[200] (see § 5.45, Abortion). Because the *Roe* decision does not address the issue of fetal rights directly, it may not be directly applicable to a determination of fetal legal status.

Other courts have dealt specifically with this issue. Some courts have held that a subsequently born fetus can recover for damages caused by a tort committed before its conception.[201] Other courts have refused to recognize this action.[202] Thus, in a case decided in federal court in 1978,[203] a child alleged that the physician-defendants had negligently performed a cesarean section on his mother in 1972. He alleged that this negligence caused an occult rupture of the uterus while he was in gestation in 1974 and that the rupture resulted in hypoxia or anoxia, or both, with resultant brain damage. The court held that the complaint stated a cause of action for a "pre-conception tort." However, in a case decided in New York in 1981,[204] the court refused to recognize a cause of action with similar facts. The dissent in this case argued that the recent trend is in favor of relief for injury to an infant caused by a pre-conception tort against the mother.[205]

Most courts will allow an action when the fetus is negligently injured, is subsequently stillborn, and its representative attempts to recover for wrongful death.[206] Thus, in a case decided in Vermont in 1980,[207] the parents sued a hospital and physician for the wrongful death of their fetus. They alleged that the death was due to the failure of the defendants to adequately attend to and monitor the mother during labor and delivery. The Supreme Court of Vermont held that a viable fetus, later stillborn, is a "person" under the Vermont Wrongful Death Act. In support of its decision, the court discussed the reasoning of an earlier case decided by the Supreme Court of Nevada,[208] which had propounded two rules: (1) a wrongful death action can be maintained if an infant is injured, born alive, and dies just after death; and (2) a tort action can be brought by an infant who is injured during gestation, born alive, and who subsequently survives. The Supreme Court of Vermont engaged in the following analysis, based on these rules:

1. If a child, injured when it was a viable fetus as a result of another's negligence, has a cause of action when born, then it can make no difference in liability whether death occurs just prior to or just after birth.

2. A viable unborn child is, in fact, biologically speaking, a presently existing person and a living human being, because it has reached such a state of development that it can presently live outside the female body as well as within it.
3. If no right of action is allowed, there is a wrong inflicted for which there is no remedy. Where negligent acts produce a stillbirth and a right of action is denied, an incongruous result is produced. For example, if a physician acted negligently while delivering a baby and the baby died, the physician would be immune from lawsuit. However, if he or she badly injured the child, he or she would be exposed to liability. Under such a rule, there is the absurd result that the greater the harm, the better the chance of immunity, and the tort-feasor could foreclose his or her own liability.[209]

A smaller number of courts has held that a wrongful death action cannot be maintained for the death of a viable fetus.[210] On the other hand, most courts agree that a wrongful death action cannot be maintained when a nonviable fetus is injured and born dead.[211] In so holding, the Supreme Court of New Hampshire argued that its decision was at least consistent with, if not required by, *Roe v. Wade*:

> We remark also in passing that it would be incongruous for a mother to have a federal constitutional right to deliberately destroy a nonviable fetus . . . and at the same time for a third person to be subject to liability to the fetus for his unintended but merely negligent acts.[212]

Further support for this conclusion appears in *Planned Parenthood of Missouri v. Danforth*,[213] in which the U.S. Supreme Court invalidated a statute that required a physician who performed an abortion to attempt to preserve the life and health of the fetus, under penalty of conviction for manslaughter, even if viability had not been reached.[214] However, at least one case decided after *Roe v. Wade* ruled that recovery for injuries resulting in stillbirth is allowable, even if the fetus is not viable at the time of injury.[215] A persuasive dissenting opinion in a 1975 Michigan case[216] supports this decision by arguing that *Roe v. Wade* is simply not applicable to tort cases:

> In *Roe*, the Supreme Court considered how "important interests in safeguarding health, in maintaining medical standards, and in protecting potential life" restricted the privacy rights of a pregnant woman. . . . The balancing of the state's interest in regulating abortion with the right of privacy led to the Court's decision that the state interference in the abortion decision is sometimes impermissible. But the case at hand presents none of the interests found crucial in *Roe*. We are not concerned with the right of a mother to freely terminate her pregnancy at a certain stage. Rather we have the case of a wrongful and unwanted termination. Certainly a tortfeasor cannot invoke the mother's privacy rights to defend his wrongdoing. Nor is the issue of whether a fetus is a person within the meaning of the Fourteenth

Amendment presented. If it were, *Roe* would settle the issue. But nothing in *Roe* precludes this Court from ruling that a fetus, viable or not, is a person within the meaning of our state's wrongful death act.[217]

The courts have also considered whether a child born alive can maintain an action for injuries negligently inflicted before birth. The courts have ruled that such an action can be maintained without regard to fetal viability at the time of injury. In a 1980 decision,[218] the Supreme Court of New Hampshire explained this rule in the context of holding that viability at the time of injury is required in wrongful death actions:

> In *Bennett v. Hymers* . . . we held that a child born alive could maintain an action for injuries received before birth without regard to viability at the time of the injury. The plaintiff infers from this that because both nonviable and viable fetuses have causes of action following live birth for injuries prior thereto, there should be no distinction based on viability governing the applicability of [the wrongful death statute]. She concludes that an action for death should be maintainable regardless of the fetus' viability.
>
> In *Bennett,* the court considered not the cause of action of an unborn fetus, but that of a live person maintaining an action in his own behalf for injuries from which he then suffered. In that context, viability at the time of injury was irrelevant, because the live person was presently suffering from the injuries. *Bennett* allowed a cause of action for injuries inflicted before birth which resulted in suffering to the living being after birth; it recognized no such action on behalf of a nonviable fetus never born alive.[219]

The rule expressed in the *Bennett* case is accepted by almost all of the states. It nevertheless presents an incongruous result when considered with the majority rule that a wrongful death action cannot be maintained for a nonviable fetus: together, they mandate holding a tort-feasor liable for injuring a nonviable fetus but not for killing one.

An equally interesting question, which no court has yet answered, is that of whether a child born with injuries due to fetal alcohol syndrome can sue his or her mother or treating physician, or both, for negligence. The answer is probably yes, especially if the mother or the physician or both are aware that the mother is pregnant and abusing alcohol or other drugs and if the physician does not instruct the mother (and record the instruction) to discontinue alcohol or other drug intake. Whether state child abuse statutes could also be enforced in such cases is another unanswered question (see § 10.26, Substance Abuse).

§ 2.60 LIABILITY ARISING FROM MEDICAL RECORDS

It has long been the law that the health care provider is the owner of the patient's medical record and has absolute rights to its possession. Judicial decisions involving ownership of medical records have decided the issue almost universally on the basis of strict and narrow interpretations of the rules of personal property.

Ownership resides in the health care provider who owns and possesses the physical material on which the information is written.[220] The fact that the patient has paid fees for service does not constitute an entitlement to any rights of ownership in, or possession of, the medical records. In arriving at this conclusion, the courts have noted that, generally speaking, a patient does not seek out a physician for the purpose of obtaining records for his or her personal use but rather to acquire the physician's services. Although the patient may pay the costs involved in producing records, such as lab fees required for tests or X rays, the records are supplied to the physician for use in connection with the treatment of the patient.[221]

When a physician acts as the employee of another, such as a hospital or clinic, in examining or treating patients or in making records, records usually become the property of the employer unless there is an agreement to the contrary.[222] However, the patient can acquire ownership or control by contractual agreement with the health care provider. Courts would enforce such an agreement.[223]

While the courts recognize that records are primarily the physician's own notes for purposes of review and study during the course of illness and treatment,[224] the physician has the duty to permit inspection of medical records. Although information must be given, physicians' records themselves need not be turned over to the patient. The fiduciary nature of the physician-patient relationship places a duty on physicians to reveal to patients that which in their best interests they should know, and that duty also extends to the hospital, which is the repository of such information.[225] The physician or hospital may refuse to release information deemed harmful, forcing patients to institute legal proceedings.[226]

The hospital's property right is qualified by the patient's right to access. This qualification has been characterized as the splitting of the property interest between the hospital and the patient. The hospital has a right to the paper, tape, or film on which the record is stored. The patient's right is to the information contained thereon.[227]

The patient's right to know the contents of his or her record and his or her right to control who may have access to it are rights within the state's discretion to create and define.[228] State laws tend to vary in the extent to which the property rights of physicians or hospitals are qualified for the patient's benefit; Connecticut, Massachusetts, and Wisconsin have granted the patient or his authorized representative a direct right of access to the record.[229] The Connecticut statute allows access under any circumstances—that is, the patient has a right to see the record merely to satisfy his or her curiosity.

Other states place limitations on the patient's right to access. California explicitly allows access to the attorney only, not the patient, prior to the filing of a lawsuit.[230] New Jersey allows access to parties involved in personal injury litigation.[231] Under Mississippi law, the patient must show "good cause" in order to see his or her records.[232] Louisiana provides only that the patient or the attorney is entitled to a "full report from the hospital," implying that the patient has no right to see the actual, physical documents that comprise the record.[233] Illinois grants the patient's physician or attorney the right to examine the patient's hospital records.[234] Although the existing statutes vary with the jurisdiction, those cited above are representative of the legislative patterns governing the subject.

The statutes generally make no distinction as to the nature of the medical records, with one exception: psychiatric records are generally not open to patients, even in states that give a patient otherwise unrestricted access.[235]

Where the right of access is not statutory, courts granting access to medical records have generally recognized that, although the hospital clearly has a property right, the patient also clearly has an interest in certain information contained in the record.[236] One court has emphasized that the physician is required to disclose medical data to the patient or his representative on request, and the patient need not obtain a court order to compel disclosure. In the court's words, "the patient need not engage in legal proceedings to attain a loftier status in his quest for information."[237] Even in states where courts have granted access, hospital policies may present a further barrier to the patient. In the absence of specific legislation, a patient may be forced to take court action to obtain access to his or her record.[238]

Legal commentators have advocated a broadening of the patient's right of access.[239] A patient's attorney may request access to the patient's record in preparation for trial. Such a request is subject to state laws governing discovery (see § 4.32, Subpoena) and the physician-patient privilege (see § 4.46, Physician-Patient Privilege).

Legal interests tangentially related to property may also be involved in a consideration of medical records. Because of the confidential nature of the contents, the improper release of such information may subject the physician to liability for defamation or invasion of privacy.

Defamation constitutes an oral or written communication to a third party of information respecting a living person that injures his or her reputation by diminishing the esteem, respect, or confidence in which the person is held or by exciting adverse or derogatory feelings against the person. Such a communication made orally constitutes slander; if written, such a communication constitutes libel.[240] Defamation suits brought against physicians for the release of medical information have been largely unsuccessful,[241] generally because of the available defenses. The truth of the information disseminated, when disseminated pursuant to a good motive or justifiable end, will absolve a defamation defendant from liability. Also, statements published in judicial proceedings are protected.[242]

A suit for invasion of privacy may be brought where information is published or disseminated to a recipient with no legitimate interest in the information and where the publication constitutes an unreasonable and serious interference in the subject's personal affairs, exceeding the limits of decent conduct and offending persons of ordinary sensibilities. The truth of the publication does not provide a defense in a privacy case.[243] For example, a 1930 decision enjoined a hospital from publishing photographs of a malformed, deceased child to protect the privacy of the parents.[244] If the information disclosed advances the legitimate interests of the disclosing party or others, a privacy suit will fail. A New York court has held that a physician's disclosure of a patient's condition to the patient's spouse does not violate the patient's privacy.[245] Others who might have legitimate interest in such information include insurance carriers, the patient's attorney, various governmental agencies such as state health departments, and bona fide research personnel.[246] Signed authorizations may be a prerequisite to disclosure, however.

Cases for defamation and invasion of privacy may only be brought where information is released without the patient's consent. If consent is obtained, this generally constitutes a defense. Although defamation and privacy suits are rarely successful, the physician is well advised to confer with the patient and obtain consent before disclosing such information to third parties.

§ 2.70 PRODUCTS LIABILITY

Products liability law deals with the liability imposed on manufacturers and suppliers of products for harm caused by defects in their products.[247] It is a complex, rapidly changing area of law. Although there have been some efforts to enact nationwide legislation,[248] for the most part the laws of the various states prevail. Substantial diversity exists among them.

Products liability law has tremendous significance for the medical profession. Medical products comprise a huge and diverse class of items, many of which are capable of causing great harm if they are defective. In the field of obstetrics and gynecology, products liability cases usually involve drugs and their side effects, but in other areas litigation also focuses on defective medical devices, instruments, and equipment.[249] Indeed, with more than 10,000 types of medical devices and myriad drugs in use,[250] the potential number of medical products liability suits is enormous.

Generally, products liability theories of recovery apply only to the various manufacturers, suppliers, assemblers, packagers, and sellers of medical products. Physician and hospital liability is usually predicated on malpractice negligence principles.

§ 2.71 Theories of Recovery

A person injured by a defective product who decides to sue the manufacturer or seller may do so under three products liability theories, listed in order of their chronological development:

1. Negligence, in which an injured party must show that a specific manufacturer or seller failed to exercise proper care in making or marketing the allegedly defective product
2. Warranty, in which an injured party need not prove negligence, but instead must show that the manufacturer or seller breached an express or implied promise that the product was free from defects and was fit for the ordinary purposes for which such products are used
3. Strict liability in tort, in which an injured party need not prove negligence or breach of warranty but must show only that the product causing the injury was defective when it left the hands of the manufacturer or seller

In many ways, each developing theory made it easier for the plaintiff to recover against the defendant. Yet each successive one merely supplemented, rather than supplanted, its precursors.

Multiple products liability theories continue to exist for several reasons. Some lawyers are more comfortable with the conventional negligence cause of action and continue to plead it for that reason alone[251] (see § 1.20, Elements of Negligence). Furthermore, the strict liability theory may not always be available to a plaintiff. A small number of states have not yet recognized the theory,[252] and even in those that have the statute of limitations for bringing suits based on tort law, which applies to this theory, is frequently shorter than that for suits based on contract law (see § 3.50, Statute of Limitations). As a result, the warranty cause of action, which is based upon contract law, is useful to the plaintiff who has been barred by time from asserting a strict liability claim. These theories also coexist because, as the different state courts have interpreted them, there is considerable overlapping of terminology and criteria. Thus the liability imposed upon manufacturers and sellers in some jurisdictions may be called "strict," yet what the plaintiff is required to prove comes closer to traditional allegations of negligence. Finally, juries tends to award greater damages when the defendant is shown to have been negligent, and damages for mental and emotional suffering are usually not allowed under the strict liability theory. Consequently, most attorneys will bring products liability suits under a combination of the theories.

Negligence: A defendant is liable for negligence in the manufacture or sale of any product which may reasonably be expected to be capable of inflicting substantial harm if it is defective and which in fact causes such harm.[253] This means the defendant is held to an appropriate standard of care throughout the manufacturing and marketing process, and owes the consumer a corresponding series of duties: to design, assemble, and prepare the product so that it is free from hidden defect; to test and inspect the product adequately during the manufacturing stage and afterward to ensure its safety; and to inform purchasers and other contemplated users of the product's dangerous propensities and latent limitations by means of warnings, labels, and instructions. As in any other negligence action, the plaintiff must show the existence and breach of a duty, causation, and damages (see § 1.20, Elements of Negligence).

Originally, a plaintiff injured by a defective product could sue *only* under the negligence theory and faced a number of obstacles to recovery. The plaintiff had to establish that the defendant breached a duty of care at some stage of production or distribution, but he or she often had no idea at which stage the defect occurred. Witnesses to any act of negligence would generally be employees of the manufacturer, unwilling to admit they did not perform their job properly. Furthermore, to defend such a suit, the manufacturer could produce as evidence an impressive array of production-line safeguards and the like. Even though the plaintiff could invoke the doctrine of res ipsa loquitur to infer some act of negligence in cases where the accident ordinarily would not have occurred except through the fault of those in control of the product, a stringent set of requirements has to be met to bring the doctrine into the case (see § 1.52, Res Ipsa Loquitur). In drug products litigation the defendant frequently could exclude res ipsa loquitur on any of several grounds: the patient's conditions and reactions were beyond the manufacturer's control, and the drug may have been only one of a number of possible causes of the injury sustained; the patient had equal or superior access to knowledge of the cause of the accident and may have been contributorily negligent; the drug itself was not exclusively under the manufacturer's control and may have been altered from its original state at any point in the distributive chain.

The patient is faced with other problems under the negligence theory when the lawsuit involves drugs, as it usually does in the field of obstetrics and gynecology. Although the drug manufacturer is held to an extremely high standard of care in the preparation of the product, commensurate with the great risk of harm should that product be defective, suits for the negligent manufacture of drugs are uncommon. For one thing, the product is consumed during its use, so it is rarely available for analysis to determine whether it was safely manufactured, made in the right quantities, or was even the right drug. Furthermore, knowledge of how the drug could be prepared more safely may be lacking— even within the industry itself. Thus some act of negligence, some departure from the level of care exercised by the manufacturer, may be impossible to establish. Each manufacturer must comply with regulations promulgated by the Food and Drug Administration (FDA). The FDA controls manufacturing procedures, drug advertising, and drug labeling; monitors drug research and experimentation and the introduction of new drugs into the marketplace; and evalutes the effectiveness of the drugs it approves.[254] Approval by the FDA suggests that the drug's utility has been found to outweigh its potential hazards and that there is no negligence merely in selling it.

Despite FDA approval, the manufacturer may be negligent for marketing a drug that it has reason to know may be harmful and fails to inform of the facts which make it likely to be dangerous. That is, the manufacturer still must satisfy common-law duties to test the product adequately and to warn effectively of any known or foreseeable risks; compliance with FDA regulations is not conclusive on the issue of due care.

CASE ILLUSTRATION

Soon after the patient began using Norinyl, an oral contraceptive, she experienced headaches, nausea, falling hair, swollen extremities, and backache. When she discontinued using it, some six months later, the symptoms subsided. She resumed using Norinyl after a few months and within a short time began experiencing difficulty with her vision. About a month after that, she began to cough up blood. She went to a hospital, where a physician changed her prescription to Ortho-Novum, another oral contraceptive. A hospital ophthalmologist examined the patient and diagnosed her problem as nearsightedness. About 11 months afterwards, various lines and dots began to fill the patient's vision. A different ophthalmologist observed the growth of abnormal blood vessels in the patient's right eye. This was confirmed by the hospital ophthalmologist, who found retinal hemorrhages. Two weeks later, the sight in the patient's left eye began to deteriorate. A medical school physician advised the patient to stop taking oral contraceptives, which she did. Several photocoagulation operations were performed to stop the hemorrhaging. Nonetheless, the patient lost the use of her right eye altogether, and her left eye was scarred and tired easily. The patient sued the two drug manufacturers to recover damages for blindness in one eye and injuries to the other allegedly caused by their negligent failure to warn physicians about the dangerous propensities of their oral contraceptives to cause circulatory and visual damage. Both defendants appealed from a jury verdict for the plaintiff.

The Supreme Court of Oregon held: (1) a prescription drug manufacturer has a duty to warn the medical profession of the hazards it knows, or as an expert in the field should know, are inherent in the use of its drug, including hazards to a known, though statistically small, percentage of users; for the breach of this duty, the manufacturer is directly liable to the patient. (2) The warnings required for approval by such an agency as the FDA may be only minimal in nature; when the manufacturer knows or should know of greater dangers not included in the required warning, its duty to warn may not be fulfilled. There was substantial evidence in the case tending to prove that both manufacturers were negligent in failing to make warnings to the medical profession which were reasonable in light of each defendant's respective knowledge that its oral contraceptive had a dangerous propensity to cause the kind of harm suffered by the plaintiff.

§ 2.71   Theories of Recovery   115

(3) Substantial evidence existed to support the jury's finding that, if adequate and timely warnings had been given to the plaintiff's treating physicians by either defendant, the plaintiff's use of oral contraceptives would have been discontinued before her eye injuries became irreversible. Thus, each defendant's negligent failure to warn was a substantial cause of the plaintiff's ingestion of the drug. Further, because the negligence of both defendants combined to produce the plaintiff's injuries, the negligence of one is concurrent with that of the other and does not insulate the other from liability. This is true even though the negligent omission of each defendant occurred at different times and not pursuant to a joint plan and even though the negligence of the first defendant only contributed, but was not in itself sufficient, to bring about the plaintiff's harm. The court therefore affirmed the judgment of the trial court (*McEwen v. Ortho Pharmaceutical Corp.*, 1974).[255]

Similarly, one court has held that FDA approval of diethylstilbestrol (DES), a synthetic estrogen, does not prevent the presentation at trial of evidence of inadequate testing, nor does it preclude the verdict of liability.[256] Others have upheld on this same ground findings of negligence against the manufacturer of Quadrigen vaccine.[257] On the other hand, courts have not found negligence when the state of medical knowledge at the time in question made it impossible to detect hidden risks or when the manufacturer generally exercised due care in warning the medical community of those risks known at the time.[258]

The usefulness of the negligence cause of action in all fields of products liability is inevitably limited by the problems inherent in showing the existence and breach of a duty. More recently developed theories of recovery have attempted to circumvent these problems. Nevertheless, the conceptual underpinnings of the negligence theory—foreseeability, reasonableness, adequacy, even fault—do not entirely disappear from the products liability picture.

Warranty: Under this theory, a seller or manufacturer is liable for damages caused by a product's failure to conform to the representations made about its quality or character. Such representations are called warranties, and they may be either express or implied. An express warranty is a positive statement of fact about some feature of the product, typically made on a label or in an advertisement. It must be made by the defendant or his or her agent with the intention or expectation that it will reach the plaintiff or a class of persons that includes the plaintiff. If the particular feature proves to be defective, the warranty is false as to that product, and the plaintiff can sue on that basis if the defect caused some harm. An implied warranty, in contrast, is read into the very act of marketing a product in the first place. The seller or manufacturer is held to warrant implicitly that the product is free from defects and is fit for the ordinary purposes for which such products are sold. Again, if the particular product is defective or unfit and causes the plaintiff harm, a suit may be brought for breach of implied warranty.

Breach of either type of warranty is a species of contract law, since parties to a contract for the sale of merchandise must live up to the terms of their agreement. Accordingly, patients who sue under this theory derive certain benefits not available when the cause of action is in tort only (that is, for negligence or strict liability). Because warranty is a contract action, in most states the injured patient may have a longer period within which to bring her suit.

CASE ILLUSTRATION

A patient was prescribed and sold Enovid, an oral contraceptive, by the Planned Parenthood Association of Chicago. On or about May 30, 1965, the patient suffered a stroke and paralysis of portions of her body. She did not learn that the drug had caused her injury until June 1, 1967.

On May 29, 1969, the patient sued the manufacturer of Enovid and the Planned Parenthood Association to recover damages for her injuries, which were allegedly caused by the drug's dangerous side effects. The lower court held that both the implied warranty and strict liability counts were barred by Illinois' two-year statute of limitations for personal injury suits. The plaintiff appealed. The Illinois Supreme Court upheld dismissal of the strict liability claim, since the plaintiff filed her action more than two years after sustaining her injury. However, the court ruled that the Illinois four-year statute of limitations for actions on contracts of sale applied to the count in implied warranty and sent back that part of the case to be retried. In so doing, the court rejected the defendants' argument that an implied warranty provides only that the product be fit for its intended purpose, not that it be generally safe or fit for all purposes. That the pill successfully prevented conception, the court said, did not preclude a cause of action for breach of implied warranty by virtue of the pill's alleged injurious side effects (*Berry v. G.D. Searle & Co.*, 1974).[259]

The patient-plaintiff in an implied warranty action need not show the defendant was negligent, only that the product was defective or unsafe as marketed. In addition, a warranty action may be available where a tort claim is not. Both factors ease the plaintiff's burden in products liability litigation.

The warranty theory has been justified on several grounds.[260] Manufacturers of products that consumers buy and rely upon to be safe should have a greater incentive to guard against defects than the negligence theory provides. The manufacturers themselves are better able to bear the burden of inevitable accidents than the injured individual, since they can purchase insurance and distribute the costs to the general public by means of minimal price increases.

§ 2.71   *Theories of Recovery*   117

The manufacturers, by packaging, advertising, or otherwise, invite and solicit the public's use of their products; when a product proves defective, they should not be able to avoid responsibility by claiming that some middleman was the actual seller and that they made no contract with the consumer. Historically, such an argument barred recovery in early products liability cases under both the negligence and warranty theories. The producer would not be liable because he was not in "privity of contract"* with the ultimate user. The privity requirement has been gradually eliminated,[261] and today even innocent bystanders injured by the use of a defective product can sue the manufacturer directly.

Other contract defenses remain and diminish the utility of the warranty cause of action. A purchaser must rely on a warranty—that is, must buy the product because of some representation about its quality made by the seller or manufacturer and must be able to prove it—in order to enforce that representation against the warrantor. A plaintiff who fails to notify the manufacturer within a reasonable time that the product is defective may be barred by statute from bringing suit. Manufacturers can place disclaimers on their products to avoid liability from breach of warranty. A disclaimer may be as simple as the statement: "This product is sold without warranty, express or implied."

When applied to knowledgeable commercial parties of equal bargaining strengths, these rules of contract law make sense; they make less sense when applied to consumers ignorant of commercial law, to whom products are offered on a take it or leave it basis. Some courts have used a great deal of imagination to prevent these rules from barring injured consumers' suits. Extensive lengths of time between injury and notice have been found to be reasonable. The notice requirement itself has been held to apply differently in retail as opposed to commercial sales situations.[262] Disclaimers have been attacked on the grounds of affording insufficient notice themselves to the purchaser or of amounting to unconscionable "adhesion" contracts (contracts whereby one party is deprived of a bargaining position equal to the other and which are not enforced as a matter of public policy).

The warranty theory does not make the defendant an *insurer* of the product's safety, as other oral contraceptive cases demonstrate. One case has held that there is no cause of action for breach of implied warranty when the manufacturer warns the medical community of possible side effects in some users and the patient suffers the effect warned of.[263] Another case has maintained that there is no breach of either implied or express warranty where the manufacturer's documents do not claim that the pill is 100 percent effective in preventing pregnancy.[264] For the vast majority of users, the court said, the pill remains reason-

---

*Privity refers to the relationship between the actual, immediate parties to a contract. Thus the manufacturer and the retail seller are said to be in privity, but the manufacturer and consumer are not.

ably safe and fit as an oral contraceptive: the manufacturer cannot be required to insure against the plaintiff's "physiological idiosyncracy."[265]

On the whole, then, the warranty theory increases the plaintiff's chance for recovery, but it is cumbersome to use. Consequently, many jurisdictions have been drawn to the apparently simpler rule of strict liability in tort.

Strict Liability in Tort: According to the strict liability theory, which has been adopted by a vast majority of state jurisdictions:

1. One who sells any product in a defective condition unreasonably dangerous to the user or consumer or to his property is subject to liability for physical harm thereby caused to the ultimate user or consumer or to his property if
   a. the seller is engaged in the business of selling such a product, and
   b. it is expected to and does reach the user or consumer without substantial change in the condition in which it is sold.
2. The rule stated above applies although
   a. the seller has exercised all possible care in the preparation and sale of his product, and
   b. the user or consumer has not bought the product from or entered into any contractual relation with the seller.[266]

This rule was promulgated to hold the seller or manufacturer of a product liable for product-related injuries that would be difficult or impossible to prove under a negligence or warranty theory.[267] Thus, the rule dispenses with the key requirement of the negligence cause of action—that the plaintiff show the defendant failed to exercise proper care in manufacturing or marketing the product. Similarly, it rejects as a theory for recovery any contractual obligations between the seller and the injured party. It eliminates, therefore, the necessity of proving reliance and notice, which complicates a claim for breach of warranty. In short, because it gets rid of such impediments to the plaintiff's recovery, the rule is said to be one of strict liability in tort.

As the strict liability rule applies to the field of obstetrics and gynecology, a product may be in a defective condition unreasonably dangerous to the user because the product is contaminated by an impurity, because the product is unaccompanied by a warning of its dangerous propensities, or because, although the product is accompanied by a warning, the risk of danger outweighs the benefit attendant on its use. Where the benefit outweighs the risk, however, the product is deemed to be "unavoidably unsafe," and strict liability does not apply—provided that a proper warning is given.[268] Of course, another category is possible—where the injury is caused by some sort of instrument or equipment. There, the product may be unreasonably dangerous because of a design defect as well.

§ 2.71   *Theories of Recovery*   119

As the preceding paragraph suggests, failure-to-warn cases arise under the strict liability theory as well as under the negligence theory. In the strict liability context, the cases hinge on the meaning of "unreasonably dangerous." The term is difficult to interpret, and the state courts interpret it quite differently. For some, a product is unreasonably dangerous if it is unaccompanied by a warning of the particular injury that the user happens to suffer. For others, a product is unreasonably dangerous in the absence of a warning only if the manufacturer knew or had reason to know of the danger. Often the controversy is carried on within the same jurisdiction. In the following example, the two different positions and the arguments advanced in support of each are well represented.

CASE ILLUSTRATION

The patient entered the hospital when the fetus was in high station. Her physician ordered that she be infused intravenously with Pitocin to induce uterine contractions. The child was born vaginally with brain damage, permanent blindness, and quadriplegia. The patient and her husband brought suit against the manufacturer of Pitocin, alleging that the drug caused the infant's injuries. In the strict liability portion of their suit, the parents claimed that the manufacturer's failure to warn physicians and patients of the danger in using Pitocin while a fetus is in high station rendered the drug "not reasonably safe." The primary issue before the Illinois Supreme Court was whether, in such a failure-to-warn case, a plaintiff must allege and prove that the defendant knew or should have known of the danger.

Although the court acknowledged one line of decisions from other jurisdictions in which a defendant's knowledge of the danger is assumed under the strict liability theory, in accordance with another line of decisions it held that knowledge is an essential element that the plaintiff must prove. A product will be "unreasonably dangerous," the court said, and the manufacturer will be held strictly liable only if the manufacturer had knowledge, or by the application of reason, developed human skill, and foresight should have had knowledge, of the danger. Otherwise, to impose liability would make the manufacturer the virtual insurer of the product. The court gave the plaintiffs leave to amend their complaint to include the knowledge requirement.

In a dissenting opinion, three of the Illinois justices argued that it is the unreasonableness of the condition of the product, not of the conduct of the defendant, that creates liability. Under the strict liability theory, they reasoned, it is not necessary for the plaintiff to prove either that the defendant negligently created the unsafe condition of the product or was aware of it; such a standard is at odds with the language of the strict liability rule, that the seller is liable even though he has "exercised all possible care in the preparation and sale of his product." Rather, when a plaintiff simply proves there was a defect in the product and that the defect caused her injury, she will have proved the product unreasonably dangerous. In the view of the dissenters, the manufacturer is not made an insurer when it is held answerable for injuries to someone for whom its product was intended, who used it in the manner in which it was intended to be used, and whose injuries were proximately caused by an inherent danger in the product of which the user was unaware (*Woodill v. Parke-Davis & Co.*, 1980).[269]

Most of the strict liability failure-to-warn cases arising in obstetrics and gynecology have taken the position expressed by the majority in *Woodill*.[270] Yet the problems inherent in the use of the term "unreasonably dangerous" remain. On the one hand it represents a potentially confusing reversion to principles of negligence. For this reason a number of states, including California, Pennsylvania, New Jersey, Alaska, and West Virginia, have removed the unreasonably dangerous requirement from their strict liability statutes.[271] On the other hand, it can lead to the extension of strict liability into absolute liability. Citing this reason, Michigan courts do not recognize the strict liability doctrine at all. Instead, they maintain that breach of implied warranty wihout proof of privity offers sufficient protection for an injured party.[272]

Similar problems arise in those cases where the issue is whether it was unreasonably dangerous to market the product at all. A product is not defective merely because it is dangerous. Chain saws, explosives, and many other useful products are necessarily dangerous, but in most instances are not unreasonably so. Only if the product is unreasonably dangerous for its intended use will the manufacturer or seller be subject to strict liability. Failure to provide adequate warning can make a product that is perfectly free of manufacturing and design defects unreasonably dangerous under the strict liability theory. In other cases, however, even adequate warning may not be enough to prevent a finding of "unreasonably dangerous" if the risks inevitably associated with the product outweigh its potential benefits in the marketplace.

The courts have had to face this issue in the recent barrage of lawsuits involving synthetic estrogens—namely, DES and its generic variants. Pursuant to the manufacturers' recommendations, physicians in the late 1940s and for more than 20 years thereafter prescribed the drug for pregnant women to prevent miscarriages. After a latent period, vaginal and cervical cancer often developed in the users' daughters, who had been exposed to the drug in utero. As the ensuing litigation revealed, serious questions concerning the drug's potential carcinogenic effect existed in the medical community prior to and during the time DES was being marketed.

The courts have had to grapple with a standard for imposing strict liability in this situation, but, as in the failure-to-warn cases, their conclusions have been divergent. An Illinois court, for example, has applied the following analysis:[273]

if, in the state of human knowledge at the time, the product was incapable of being made safe for its intended and ordinary use and if it was accompanied by proper directions and warnings,[274] then it must be determined whether the product was so unsafe that marketing it at all was "unreasonably dangerous per se." To decide that, the court must balance the utility of the product against its dangers. A New York court, by contrast, has focused on the single question of whether a reasonable manufacturer would have marketed the drug if present knowledge of the drug's effect had been known at the time the plaintiff's mother was treated with it.[275] If not, a jury could find that DES was unreasonably dangerous. In New Jersey, where the "unreasonably dangerous" requirement has been eliminated by the legislature as a source of confusion, a superior court has flatly declared that rules which define whether a product was safe when marketed are really just rules of negligence, and it has formulated it own test accordingly. In prescription drug cases, strict liability is applicable only where the drug could not reasonably have appeared to be useful and desirable at the time of manufacture or where, despite some apparent efficacy, the medically recognizable risk foreseeably outweighed its utility.[276]

Whatever standard of strict liability a jurisdiction adopts, a product may be found defective for some purposes but not for others. It is not the overall safety of DES that is being challenged in the current litigation, only its safety when ingested by pregnant women. The drug continues to be prescribed and approved for estrogen replacement, menopausal therapy, treatment of some cancer cases, suppression of lactation, and as the major ingredient in a postcoital contraceptive.[277] Furthermore, the risk associated with a particular product may be offset by a finding that that product is "unavoidably unsafe."* Oral contraceptives, for example, are almost always regarded as "unavoidably unsafe."[278] In the cases brought to trial, therefore, the issue is whether they were accompanied by proper directions and adequate warnings. Drugs used for diagnostic purposes usually fall within the designation as well.[279] Intrauterine devices, however, have not received the same treatment by the courts. An Alabama court has denied the "unavoidably unsafe" defense to a manufacturer on the grounds that an IUD is closer to a device than a drug, that suitable alternatives exist, and that it lacks a high degree of social utility.[280] Other cases, though, treat an IUD as an oral contraceptive and automatically inquire about adequate warning.[281]

In sum, the strict liability theory eases the way to recovery by eliminating the contract defenses to a warranty claim and, in theory, by making it unnecessary to prove the seller or manufacturer was at fault somewhere along the production or distribution line. In practice, however, there is a great deal of overlap between negligence and strict liability as the state courts variously in-

---

*An unavoidably unsafe product is one whose benefit outweighs its risk of danger. A manufacturer of such a product will not be held liable under strict liability principles unless a proper warning of the dangers is not given.

terpret these theories. If only for this reason, strict liability does not really impose liability without fault. Furthermore, many state legislatures have succeeded in limiting the force of strict liability by enacting seller defenses, such as alteration and modification of the product after sale and a shorter statute of limitations period.[282]

§ 2.72 Defective Products

A product may be defective because of improper design, testing, manufacture, or packaging or because of faulty instructions for use or inadequate warnings of the product's dangerous propensities. In some cases, the type or extent of the defect may determine the appropriate products liability theory under which to bring suit, since the theories differ in their scope and coverage. Thus, if a product is simply ineffective, a plaintiff might only be able to sue for breach of warranty, because under the strict liability theory a simply ineffective product is not an unreasonably dangerous defective product.[283] A product, too, is universally recognized to include the container or package in which it is sold; if a bottle of soda explodes and causes injury, the plaintiff need not worry whether the glass or the liquid was defective.[284] As this example suggests, such cases are more common when the product is food rather than some kind of drug or medical device.

The classification of something as a medical product often proceeds not on the basis of physical characteristics, but, with a view toward the several products liability theories, on the basis of the likely sources of and control over potential defects. X rays have been found to be products.[285] X-ray machines are controllable, and their short-term effects on human beings are well understood. On the other hand, because blood banks and hospitals have an uncertain source of blood and no efficient way to detect blood-borne hepatitis, blood used for transfusions has been classified as a service by courts[286] and legislatures.[287] The distinction is significant: sellers of products can be subject to strict liability, whereas those who perform services cannot.

For the purposes of products liability actions, patients have been held to be the consumers of the medical devices used by health care providers in treating them. Patients may therefore sue the manufacturers, even if they did not purchase, use, or consume the product.[288] One who uses a prescription or over-the-counter drug qualifies as a consumer, too. A patient or drug user, however, cannot ordinarily sue his or her physician or hospital in a products liability action as the retailers of the product. Courts typically regard them as providing services instead.[289] Yet an Illinois court has recently held that a Planned Parenthood Association which dispensed birth control pills was engaged in a sale to which implied warranty attached, despite the clinic's contention that it was primarily a service organization.[290] Similarly, a New Jersey court has recently construed the merchandise-for-sale provision of the state's Consumer Fraud Act to apply to an IUD available only through a doctor's prescription.[291] Thus a trend toward expanding the potential defendants in a products liability action may be under way (see § 2.73, Procedural Aspects).

Drugs—The Manufacturer's Responsibilities: The manufacturer must test a drug product adequately before marketing it. As the cases indicate, FDA approval is not conclusive of adequate testing,[292] and a number of drugs initially determined to be safe have later been withdrawn from the market after dangerous side effects were discovered.[293] Thus if dangerous side effects surface only after the drug has been in use by the public, or if subsequent medical studies point to the existence of risks previously unforeseen, the manufacturer must resume testing.[294] That the drug turns out to be less effective than the original tests seemed to suggest, however, may not subject the manufacturer to liability if marketing the drug was justified at the time.[295] Further, if the manufacturer conducted adequate tests to isolate particular side effects and properly warned the medical community of them, a user who suffers such a side effect cannot sue the manufacturer for marketing an inadequately tested product.[296]

Even more important, the drug manufacturer must provide adequate instructions for a product's use and must warn effectively of its possible hazards. This cannot be overemphasized. Failure to provide such instructions and warnings gives rise to most products liability claims in this area. In general, a patient injured by a drug will sue both her physician and the drug manufacturer. A major issue will be whether the manufacturer has successfully informed the medical community of the dangers associated with the drug.

CASE ILLUSTRATION

The patient was hospitalized in October 1972, suffering from phlebitis. Her physician, who had earlier confirmed the patient's suspicions that she was pregnant, prescribed dicumarol, an anticoagulant that crosses the placental barrier. The patient received dicumarol while in the hospital and later as an outpatient. Her child was born in April 1973 with severe and irreparable birth defects, including brain damage and partial paralysis.

The patient sued two hospitals and four physicians for medical malpractice and three pharmaceutical companies on theories of products liability, alleging that the birth defects resulted from bleeding in the fetal brain caused by her ingestion of dicumarol. The physicians claimed that they had not been adequately warned by the drug manufacturers of the dangers of dicumarol to pregnant women. The drug manufacturers claimed their package inserts provided adequate warning and that the physicians caused the harm to the plaintiff's child by disregarding the inserts and failing to consult available reference material on dicumarol before prescribing it.

The court, noting that the *Physician's Desk Reference* for 1972 contained no warning and that pharmacists often discard package inserts before physicians can read them, held that the drug manufacturers had not adequately warned the medical profession of the dangers of dicumarol. They had sent no "Dear Doctor" letters, had published no notices in medical journals, had used no "detail men" to inform physicians in person about the drug. Furthermore, the physicians' failure to search the literature for warnings was not an intervening cause of the harm, because it was foreseeable to the manufacturers (*Baker v. St. Agnes Hospital*, 1979).[297]

A manufacturer's failure to provide adequate warnings establishes a prima facie case of product defect in every jurisdiction.[298] The rationale, as expressed by a New York court, is uniformly agreed upon:

> In today's world, it is often only the manufacturer who can fairly be said to know and to understand when an article is . . . safely made for its intended purpose. Once floated on the market, many articles . . . defy detection of defect . . . the manufacturer . . . alone . . . has the practical opportunity . . . to turn out useful . . . but safe products.[299]

These remarks are especially appropriate to the drug field. The FDA requires drug manufacturers to include inserts with their products listing uses, doses, contraindications, side effects, and hazards.[300] As *Baker* and the other cases demonstrate, however, that is only the beginning of the manufacturer's responsibilities.

The manufacturer must update its warnings. First, it must keep abreast of knowledge of its products as gained through research, adverse reaction reports, scientific literature, and other available methods. Second, it must take such steps as are reasonably necessary to bring that knowledge to the attention of the medical profession. The greater the potential hazard of the drug, the more extensive must be the manufacturer's efforts to make that hazard known.[301] In short, the manufacturer has a continuing duty to warn.[302] A change in warning, however, does not necessarily constitute evidence that the prior warning was inadequate.[303] Rather, the warning is judged on the basis of information the manufacturer knew or should have known at the time it was given[304]—in other words, on the standards applied to an expert in the field.[305] Furthermore, a manufacturer does not fulfill the duties of an expert by waiting for what it considers to be sufficient proof of a causal relationship before supplying the medical profession with an appropriate alert to the possibility of risk involved in the use of one of its products.[306]

The adequacy of a manufacturer's warning is measured by its form, content, and intensity—and not just those in a single document, but in all the information provided by the manufacturer and in all that it was reasonably possible to provide.[307] A warning may be inadequate if it is contrary to the evidence of potential dangers.[308] It may also be inadequate in not communicating a clear indication of risk.[309] The aggressiveness of a manufacturer's promotional campaign can significantly weaken or negate its warnings and will be considered in the overall balancing of factors.[310]

In the case of prescription drugs, courts have generally held that the manufacturer's duty to warn extends to the medical community only, including treating as well as prescribing physicians.[311] Physicians are the "learned intermediaries" between the manufacturer and the patient. Consistent with their own duty to inform, physicians must exercise discretion in conveying to each particular patient the information they believe that patient should have. Thus, although the manufacturer is not usually required to supplement the physician's warnings, one recent case has held otherwise.[312] According to a district court in Wisconsin, the federal administrative regulations[313] adopted under the Food, Drug, and Cosmetic Act[314] were intended to protect persons like the plaintiff from the harmful side effects associated with oral contraceptives by warning them of such effects so as to enable them to recognize them and to seek qualified medical assistance.[315] (The regulations require that users of birth control pills receive a warning by way of a patient package insert. Similar requirements exist for morning-after pills, IUDs, products containing estrogens, and progestational drugs.) Wisconsin holds that the violation of such a regulation by one on whom it imposes a duty, resulting in the harm which the regulation was designed to prevent, constitutes negligence per se. In consequence, the court concluded that the defendant-manufacturer had a duty to warn the plaintiff of the possible side effects of Ortho-Novum. The court went on to note that, although several other courts discussing the duty to warn imposed on a manufacturer of oral contraceptives have obviously been aware of the federal regulations requiring provision of information to the plaintiff, none of them has used the regulations to impose on the manufacturer a duty to warn the patient as well as the doctor. The Wisconsin district court's decision therefore may signal an important new trend in the area of products liability litigation in obstetrics and gynecology. Almost certainly its validity will be tested at higher judicial levels.

It is already recognized that the manufacturer must warn the patient directly in special circumstances. The manufacturer must do so, for example, when the drug is sold over the counter[316] or is dispensed in a mass immunization campaign.[317] In addition, the drug manufacturer must warn those consumers who are susceptible to rare adverse reactions due to allergy, hypersensitivity, or the idiosyncrasy of a known population group.[318] One drug company has been held liable for failing to warn that their oral polio vaccine may induce polio in as few as 1 in 3 million persons.[319]

Drugs—The Physician's Responsibilities: As one who is generally regarded as providing a service rather than selling a product, the physician ordinarily cannot be sued under a products liability theory of recovery. Nevertheless, because the physician often does serve, either in a prescribing or a treating capacity, or both, as an intermediary between the drug manufacturer and the consumer, the physician usually is joined as a defendant in a products liability action. Inevitably, the physician's own responsibilities are closely tied to those governing the manufacturer of the product in question.

The physician must be aware of the drug manufacturer's instructions and warnings, not only to avoid misusing the product, but also to be able to disclose possible hazards to patients and to avoid charges of failing to obtain the patient's informed consent[320] (see § 1.33, Consent and Informed Consent). In fact, some courts have held that if the manufacturer's warnings are unambiguous, the physician's deviation from them amounts to prima facie negligence.[321] The courts presume, however, that the physician relied on the manufacturer's warning, which requires the patient-plaintiff to provide proof to the contrary.[322]

Devices: Medical devices may inflict great harm if they are defective. With literally thousands of such devices in use, ranging from the simple forceps to the very complex incubator, the preventive obligations imposed upon manufacturers, hospitals, and physicians cannot be ignored. Whereas some of these obligations correspond to duties arising under drug liability, others are unique.

Like the drug manufacturer, the manufacturer of a medical device must warn of the dangers or limitations involved in the use of its product. The manufacturer of an incubator, for instance, will be liable if it does not furnish warnings relative to the risks of giving supplemental oxygen to premature infants and its failure to do so results in injury.[323] On the other hand, when a patient is injured by a relatively simple piece of equipment, the fault may lie in its misuse by a member of the hospital staff and not with any defect in the device as received from the manufacturer.[324]

A finding that the medical device was defective does not always exculpate the hospital and physician. The duty to select an appropriate device includes the duty to inspect the device for defects before it is used.[325] Physicians need only discover patent defects, while hospitals must discover less obvious ones, especially if the hospital is maintaining and servicing the device.[326] When a physician knows or suspects that a piece of equipment is defective, he or she should notify the appropriate department head in writing and recommend the necessary maintenance or replacement.[327] Once the device is known or suspected to be defective, the physician or hospital may not continue to use it without risking liability.[328]

Complex medical machines may injure a patient because of improper maintenance as well as defective design or manufacture, inadequate warnings, or improper use. Courts have recognized the physician's limited time and ability to check out the machines he or she uses in hospitals, so they have held the hospitals responsible instead. Hospitals can protect themselves from charges of negligent maintenance by contracting with the equipment manufacturer to service and maintain the equipment. When neither the hospital nor the manufacturer undertakes to ensure that the equipment is functioning properly, both may be held liable.[329]

§ 2.73 Procedural Aspects

Plaintiffs: Anyone who has been foreseeably harmed by a defective product may be a plaintiff in a products liability lawsuit.[330] In the field of medicine this usually means the patient or drug consumer herself, though in other areas liability may extend, for example, to an innocent bystander. Other medical products liability plaintiffs have included a deformed child, born alive, suing because of prenatal injury[331] and parents suing on behalf of their injured minor child or suing for the loss of their child. Children, however, have not been allowed to recover for the loss of parental consortium where the parent has suffered injury but not death.[332] Damages for mental suffering may be awarded to the plaintiff under a negligence theory,[333] but they are not recoverable when the cause of action is in strict liability.[334] In one case involving the violation of a state consumer fraud act, the statutory treble damages were awarded for the cost of the purchase and insertion of an IUD and for the cost of medical services needed to correct the physical injury caused thereby. Recovery was denied, however, for pain and suffering caused by the plaintiff's loss of good health and loss of consortium.[335] In rare cases, punitive damages are possible, but only upon the plaintiff's showing of malice in fact,[336] such as a deliberate misrepresentation in warnings (see § 1.60, Damages).

In all cases, the plaintiff must have suffered physical harm. Women who were given DES have had their actions dismissed when they relied upon only the unmaterialized risk of injury to themselves and their daughters to state a claim for relief.[337] A father has been denied recovery for mental and emotional harm sustained upon the birth of his deformed child, whose deformities were allegedly the result of the mother's ingestion of Delalutin to prevent miscarriage; even the mother was deemed to have failed to set forth a cause of action for independent physical injuries and was held not to be entitled to recovery for emotional and psychic harm.[338]

Drug liability plaintiffs sometimes face a special procedural obstacle—the statute of limitations that cuts off their claim before they know they have one (see § 3.50, Statute of Limitations). The injurious side effects of a drug may not surface until months or years after the patient first ingested it, and by then neither she nor her physician may be able to trace her symptoms back to that particular product. Thus a statute of limitations can work substantial hardship if it defines the time of ingestion as that time when a plaintiff's cause of action accrues.[339] Under more liberal interpretations, a plaintiff's cause of action is said to accrue when she discovers or should have discovered her injury.[340] The trend in this area may be toward allowing the cause of action to accrue once the plaintiff knows of her injury and that someone is or may be responsible for it.[341]

To date, plaintiffs seeking certification as a class in various lawsuits growing out of the DES controversy have had little success, mostly because as a group they do not satisfy the technical requirements courts impose upon such plaintiffs.[342]

Defendants: Potential defendants in a medical products liability action include the manufacturer and supplier of the product, the physician, and the hospital, as well as the assembler of the product, the maker of any defective part, and the packager, wholesaler, and retailer.[343] A drug brokerage firm, however, that merely arranged for the sale of a synthetic estrogen from its manufacturer to a drug company that incorporated it into 25-milligram pills has been held not liable, on grounds that the firm never had physical control over the drug and had no active role in the manufacturer's decision either to purchase the drug or to market it for use by pregnant women.[344] Similarly, a pharmacist who neither was negligent nor made any express warranty as to the safety of the DES prescription he filled has been dismissed as a defendant in the subsequent litigation arising from the injurious side effects of the drug.[345] Nor has the purchaser of a drug store been held liable for the sale of DES at the store 16 years earlier.[346] On the other hand, a university that as part of an experimental study administered DES to the subjects without informing them of the potential risks involved has been found liable for battery.[347] Whereas compliance with FDA regulations has been rejected as a defense for manufacturers in products liability actions,[348] the FDA itself has been declared immune from tort claims where it exercised its discretion in issuing a new drug application for a product that subsequently proved defective.[349]

When multiple defendants are joined in the same lawsuit, as they frequently are, each (necessarily represented by independent legal counsel) may try to shift the onus of liability to another. A manufacturer may defend a products liability claim by asserting that the patient's harm was caused by negligent storage or maintenance on the part of the hospital or negligent use or failure to warn by the physician. The physician and the hospital may attempt to exculpate themselves from the charge of negligence by establishing that the medical product was defective when it arrived from the manufacturer. Cross-defenses between several manufacturers or several physicians may also be asserted. In general, the decision as to whether one defendant's liability cuts off the liability of others is made on a case-by-case basis.

Special multiple-defendant problems have arisen in the ongoing DES litigation. In the ordinary case, the plaintiff knows or can easily determine the identities of the physicians, hospital staff members, and manufacturers whose services or products resulted in the harm she sustained; the issue is which of them will be liable. In the DES cases, however, the plaintiff has been injured by the side effects of a generic drug and cannot, because of the passage of time and absence of records, identify the manufacturer of the drug actually ingested. Thus, although the plaintiff has been injured through no fault of her own, if she brings a products liability action against a number of manufacturers, she faces the traditional reluctance of courts to award damages when the identity of the tort-feasor is in doubt. The issue in the DES cases, then, is whether any of the multiple defendants will be held liable at all or whether, because of the unique circumstances surrounding the marketing of the drug, the plaintiff will go uncompensated for her injuries.

The courts have considered a variety of different legal arguments in the DES cases, including:

1. *Alternative liability*—where the testing and marketing of DES by each of the defendants can be viewed as independent wrongful acts, one of which caused the plaintiff's injury, the burden should be upon each manufacturer to prove that it has not caused the harm.[350]

2. *Concerted action*—where the testing and marketing of DES constitutes a single wrongful act, in which each defendant has intentionally or by tacit understanding engaged, liability should be imposed upon any one of the defendants, who would then be entitled to a contribution from his fellow tort-feasors for their part of the overall damages awarded.[351]

3. *Market-share liability*—where all the defendants produced the drug from an identical formula and the manufacturer of the DES that caused the plaintiff's injuries cannot be identified, through no fault of the plaintiff, each defendant should be liable for that percentage of the plaintiff's injuries which corresponds to its share of the DES market at the time and place the plaintiff's mother took the drug.[352]

4. *Enterprise liability*—where each defendant's adherence to an industry-wide standard for testing and marketing DES perpetuates that standard, which results in the manufacture of the particular, unidentifiable injury-producing product, each industry member should be regarded as contributing to the plaintiff's injury, and the burden should be upon each defendant to show that its product could not have caused the injury.[353]

The enterprise liability theory has yet to be adopted by any jurisdiction;[354] the other arguments have been neither accepted nor rejected uniformly.[355] In addition, many of the DES cases are still in the intermediate stages of litigation and further alterations in the state of the law can be expected. As in so many other areas of products liability, a final verdict has not come in.

NOTES

1. Leighton v. Sargent, 27 N.H. 460, 59 Am. Dec. 388 (1853).
2. W. Prosser, Handbook of the Law of Torts 139, (4th ed. 1971).
3. Guilmet v. Campbell, 385 Mich. 57, 188 N.W.2d 601 (1971); Tschirhart V. Pethtel, 61 Mich. App. 581, 233 N.W.2d 93 (1975), *appeal denied*, 395 Mich. 774 (1976).
4. Woodbury, *Physicians and Surgeons—Sullivan v. O'Connor, A Liberal View of the Contractual Liability of Physicians and Surgeons*, 54 N.C. L. Rev. 885, 887 (1976).
5. Mich. Comp. Laws Ann. § 600.5805(3) (1968 & Supp. 1981–82).

6. Mich. Comp. Laws Ann. § 600.5807(8) (1968).
7. Mich. Comp. Laws Ann. § 600.5805(7) (1968).
8. Rach v. Wise, 46 Mich. App. 729, 208 N.W.2d 570, *appeal denied*, 390 Mich. 778 (1973); Kelleher v. Mills, 70 Mich. App. 360, 245 N.W.2d 749 (1976).
9. Karlsons v. Guerinot 57 A.D.2d 73, 394 N.Y.S.2d 933 (1977).
10. Green v. Sudakin, 81 Mich. App. 545, 265 N.W.2d 411 (1978); Stewart v. Rudner, 349 Mich. 459, 84 N.W.2d 816 (1957).
11. Stewart v. Rudner, *supra* note 10.
12. Liebler v. Our Lady of Victory Hosp., 43 A.D.2d 878, 351 N.Y.S.2d 480 (1974); Bishop v. Byrne, 265 F. Supp. 460 (S.D. W.Va. 1967).
13. Hockworth v. Hart, 474 S.W.2d 377 (Ky. App. 1971); Johnston v. Rodis, 251 F.2d 917, 918 (D.C. Cir. 1958).
14. Foran v. Carangelo, 153 Conn. 356, 216 A.2d 638 (1966).
15. Alexandridis v. Jewett, 388 F.2d 839 (1st Cir. 1968).
16. *Id.*
17. Sard v. Hardy, 281 Md. 432, 379 A.2d 1014 (1977); Coleman v. Garrison, 349 A.2d 8 (Del. 1975); Garcia v. VonMicsky, 602 F.2d 51 (2d Cir. 1979).
18. Woodbury, *supra* note 4, at 889.
19. Grewe v. Mount Clemens Gen. Hosp., 47 Mich. App. 111, 209 N.W.2d 309 (1973).
20. Woodbury, *supra* note 4, at 890.
21. Sullivan v. O'Connor, 363 Mass. 579, 583, 296 N.E.2d 183, 186 (1973).
22. Clegg v. Chase, 88 Misc.2d 1047, 391 N.Y.S.2d 966 (1977).
23. Garcia v. VonMicsky, *supra* note 17; Herrera v. Roessing, 533 P.2d 60 (Colo. App. 1975); Stephens v. Spivak, 61 Mich. App. 647, 233 N.W.2d 124 (1975).
24. Rogala v. Silva, 16 Ill. App. 3d 63, 305 N.E.2d 571 (1973).
25. Garcia v. VonMicsky, *supra* note 17; Clevenger v. Haling, 394 N.E.2d 1119 (Mass. 1979); Herrera v. Roessing, *supra* note 23.
26. Coleman v. Garrison, *supra* note 17.
27. Sard v. Hardy, *supra* note 17; Rogala v. Silva, *supra* note 24.
28. Garcia v. VonMicsky, *supra* note 17.
29. Clevenger v. Haling, *supra* note 25; Sard v. Hardy, *supra* note 17.
30. Clevenger v. Haling, *supra* note 25.
31. Green v. Sudakin, *supra* note 10.
32. Olson v. Molzen, 558 S.W.2d 429 (Tenn. 1977).
33. Tatham v. Hohe, 469 F. Supp. 914 (W.D. N.C. 1979).
34. Black's Law Dictionary 1475 (4th ed. 1968).
35. Sturm v. Green, 398 P.2d 799 (Okla. 1965).
36. Whitfield v. Whittaker Mem. Hosp., 210 Va. 176, 169 S.E.2d 563 (1969); Voss v. Bridwell, 188 Kan. 643, 364 P.2d 955 (1961); Restatement, Agency 2d § 220(1) (1958).
37. W. Prosser, *supra* note 2, at 568.
38. Leeper, *Torts—Texas Labels Captain of the Ship Doctrine: "False Rule of Agency,"* 14 Wake Forest L. Rev. 319 (1978); Young, *Separation of Responsibility in the Operating Room: The Borrowed Servant, The Captain of the Ship and the Scope of Surgeon's Vicarious Liability,* 49 Notre Dame L. Rev. 933(1974).
39. Leeper, *supra* note 38; *The Hospital's Responsibility for Its Medical Staff: Prospects for Corporate Negligence in California,* 8 Pacific L. J. 141 (1977).
40. R. Goodman and L. Goldsmith, Modern Hospital Liability: Law and Tactics 368, 371 (1972).
41. Llera v. Wisner, 171 Mont. 254, 557 P.2d 805 (1976).
42. Boyd v. Badenhauser, 556 S.W.2d 896 (Ky. 1977).
43. McFadden v. Turner, 159 N.J. Super. 360, 388 A.2d 244 (1978).

44. Whitfield v. Whittaker Mem. Hosp., *supra* note 36.
45. Synnott v. Midway Hosp., 287 Minn. 270, 178 N.W.2d 211 (1970); Sesselman v. Muhlenberg Hosp., 124 N.J. Super. 285, 306 A.2d 474 (1973); Martin v. Perth Amboy Gen. Hosp., 104 N.J. Super. 335, 250 A.2d 40 (1969).
46. Foster v. Englewood Hosp. Ass'n, 313 N.E.2d 255 (Ill. 1974).
47. Sesselman v. Muhlenberg Hosp., *supra* note 45.
48. Voss v. Bridwell, *supra* note 36; Whitfield v. Whittaker Mem. Hosp., *supra* note 36; Wiles v. Myerly, 210 N.W.2d 619 (Iowa 1973).
49. Voss v. Bridwell, *supra* note 36.
50. Whitfield v. Whittaker Mem. Hosp., *supra* note 36; Grubb v. Albert Einstein Med. Center, 387 A.2d 480 (Pa. 1978).
51. Foster v. Englewood Hosp. Ass'n, *supra* note 46.
52. Willinger v. Mercy Catholic Med. Center, 362 A.2d 280 (Pa. 1976).
53. Dickerson v. American Sugar Refining Co., 211 F.2d 200 (3d Cir. 1954).
54. Grubb v. Albert Einstein Med. Center, *supra* note 50; Collins v. Hand, 431 Pa. 378, 246 A.2d 398 (1968).
55. Tonsic v. Wagner, 458 Pa. 246, 329 A.2d 497 (1974); Yorston v. Pennel, 397 Pa. 28, 153 A.2d 255 (1959).
56. McConnell v. Williams, 65 A.2d 243 (Pa. 1949).
57. Young, *supra* note 38.
58. Yorston v. Pennell, 153 A.2d 255 (Pa. 1959).
59. Rockwell v. Stone, 173 A.2d 54 (Pa. 1961).
60. Minogue v. Rutland Hosp., 125 A.2d 798 (Vt. 1956).
61. Harle v. Krchnak, 422 S.W.2d 810 (Tex. 1967).
62. Foster v. Englewood Hosp. Ass'n, *supra* note 46; Sesselman v. Muhlenberg Hosp., *supra* note 45; Sparger v. Worley Hosp., Inc., 547 S.W.2d 582 (Tex. 1977).
63. Sparger v. Worley Hosp., Inc., *supra* note 62.
64. Thomas v. Hutchinson, 442 Pa. 118, 275 A.2d 23 (1971).
65. Miller v. Atkins, 142 Ga. App. 618, 236 S.E.2d 838 (1977).
66. *Id.*
67. Sparger v. Worley Hosp., Inc., *supra* note 62.
68. Parker v. St. Paul Fire & Marine Ins. Co., 335 So.2d 725 (La. App. 1976).
69. McCullough v. Hutzel Hosp., 88 Mich. App. 235, 276 N.W.2d 569 (1979).
70. Beck v. Lovell, 361 So.2d 245 (La. App. 1978).
71. Killeen v. Reinhardt, 419 N.Y.S.2d 175 (1979); Toth v. Community Hosp., 22 N.Y.2d 255, 292 N.Y.S.2d 440, 239 N.E.2d 368 (1968).
72. Beck v. Lovell, *supra* note 70.
73. Samii v. Baystate Med. Center, Inc., 395 N.E.2d 455 (Mass. App. 1979).
74. *Id.*
75. Toth v. Community Hosp., *supra* note 71.
76. Frantz v. San Luis Med. Clinic, 81 Cal. App. 3d 34, 146 Cal. Rptr. 146 (1978).
77. *Id.*
78. *See, e.g.,* Zepeda v. Zepeda, 41 Ill. App. 2d 240, 190 N.E.2d 849 (1963), *cert. denied,* 379 U.S. 945 (1964).
79. Golbus et al., *Prenatal Genetic Diagnosis in 3000 Amniocenteses,* 300 New Eng. J. Med. 157 (1979); Council Report, *Genetic Counseling and Prevention of Birth Defects,* 248 J.A.M.A. 221 (1982).
80. Howell & Moore, *Prenatal Diagnosis in the Prevention of Genetic Disease,* 70 Tex. Med. 61 (1974).
81. Carter, *Practical Aspects of Early Diagnosis,* in Early Diagnosis of Human Genetic Defects: Scientific and Ethical Considerations 17 (Fogarty Int'l Center Proceedings No. 6, 1971).

82. Roe v. Wade, 410 U.S. 113 (1973).
83. *See, e.g.*, Ziemba v. Sternberg, 45 A.D.2d 230, 357 N.Y.S.2d 265 (1974); Karlsons v. Guerinot, *supra* note 9.
84. Friedmann, *Prenatal Diagnosis of Genetic Disease*, 225 Sci. Am. 36 (Nov. 1971).
85. Nadler, *Prenatal Detection of Genetic Disorders*, in 3 Advances in Human Genetics, 1, 10 (Harris and Hirschhorn, eds., 1972).
86. Roe v. Wade, *supra* note 82, at 164–65.
87. *See* United States v. Vuitch, 402 U.S. 62 (1971).
88. *See. e.g.*, Ill. Ann. Stat. ch. 38, § 81-14(c).
89. Roe v. Wade, *supra* note 82.
90. Custodio v. Bauer, 561 Cal. App. 2d 303, 59 Cal. Rptr. 463 (1967).
91. Kashi, *The Case of the Unwanted Blessing: Wrongful Life*, 31 U. Miami L. Rev. 1409 (Nov. 1977).
92. Sherlock v. Stillwater Clinic, 260 N.W.2d 169 (Minn. 1977); *see also* Note, *Wrongful Conception: Who Pays for Bringing up Baby?* 47 Fordham L. Rev. 418 (1978).
93. Jackson v. Anderson, 230 So.2d 503 (Fla. App. 1970).
94. *See, e.g.*, Minn. Stat. Ann. §§ 145.911–22 (subsidies for family planning services), 617.25 (legalization of the sale, distribution, or advertisement of contraceptives); N.J. Stat. Ann. § 2A:170–76 (allowing sale of contraceptives).
95. *See, e.g.*, Or. Rev. Stat. § 435.205; Iowa Code Ann. §§ 234.21–.22; Mich. Comp. Laws Ann. § 400.14(b).
96. Christensen v. Thornby, 192 Minn. 123, 255 N.W. 620 (1934); *see also* Anonymous v. Hospital, 33 Conn. Supp. 126, 366 A.2d 204 (1976); Custodio v. Bauer, *supra* note 90; Jackson v. Anderson, *supra* note 93.
97. Scarf v. Troppi, 31 Mich. App. 240, 187 N.W.2d 511 (1971); Betancourt v. Gaylord, 136 N.J. Super. 69, 344 A.2d 336, (1975); Rivera v. State, 94 Misc.2d 157, 404 N.Y.S.2d 950 (1978); Mason v. Western Pennsylvania Hosp., 428 A.2d 1366 (1981); White v. United States, 510 F. Supp. 146 (D. Kan. 1981); Boone v. Mullendore, No. 80-423 Ala. Sup. Ct., June 30, 1982.
98. Greenfield, *Wrongful Birth [Conception]: What Is the Damage?*, 248 J.A.M.A. 926 (1982).
99. *Id.*
100. Rivera v. State, *supra* note 97.
101. Clegg v. Chase, *supra* note 22.
102. Christensen v. Thornby, *supra* note 96; Terrell v. Garcia, 496 S.W.2d 124 (Tex. 1973).
103. Coleman v. Garrison, *supra* note 17.
104. Custodio v. Bauer, *supra* note 90.
105. Scarf v. Troppi, *supra* note 97.
106. *Id.*
107. Mason v. Western Pennsylvania Hosp. and Scarf v. Troppi, *supra* note 97.
108. White v. United States, *supra* note 97; Wilber v. Kerr, 628 S.W.2d 568 (Ark. 1982); Sutkin v. Beck, 629 S.W.2d 131 (Tex. App. 1982); Boone v. Mullendore, 416 So.2d 718 (Ala. 1982).
109. P. v. Portadin, 179 N.J. Super. 465, 432 A.2d 556 (1981).
110. *Id.*
111. Cockrum v. Baumgartner, 99 Ill. App.3d 271, 425 N.E.2d 968 (1981) and No. 55733 Ill. S. Ct. (Feb. 1983), where a lower court finding for damages was reversed.
112. Rivera v. State, *supra* note 97; *see also supra* notes 96–97.
113. Anonymous v. Hospital, *supra* note 96.

Notes: Chapter II

114. Bowman v. Davis, 48 Ohio St.2d 41, 356 N.E.2d 496 (1976); Rivera v. State, *supra* note 97; Custodio v. Bauer, *supra* note 90.
115. *See* Clegg v. Chase, *supra* note 22; La Point v. Shirley, 409 F. Supp. 118 (W.D. Tex. 1976); Pritchard v. Neal, 139 Ga. App. 512, 229 S.E.2d 18 (1976); Custodio v. Bauer, *supra* note 90.
116. Custodio v. Bauer, *supra* note 90.
117. *See* Sherlock v. Stillwater Clinic, *supra* note 92.
118. *See* Sard v. Hardy, *supra* note 17; Custodio v. Bauer, *supra* note 90.
119. Coleman v. Garrison, *supra* note 17.
120. Bishop v. Byrne, *supra* note 12.
121. Pritchard v. Neal, *supra* note 115.
122. Coleman v. Garrison, *supra* note 17.
123. *See* Custodio v. Bauer, *supra* note 90; Jackson v. Anderson, *supra* note 93; Vaughn v. Shelton, 514 S.W.2d 870 (Tenn. Ct. App. 1974).
124. Custodio v. Bauer, *supra* note 90.
125. La Point v. Shirley, *supra* note 115.
126. *See* Custodio v. Bauer, *supra* note 90; Bishop v. Byrne, *supra* note 12.
127. *Id.*
128. Rogala v. Silva, 16 Ill. App. 3d 63, 305 N.E.2d 571 (1973).
129. Sard v. Hardy, *supra* note 17.
130. Coleman v. Garrison, *supra* note 17.
131. *See, e.g.,* Clegg v. Chase, *supra* note 22; Sard v. Hardy, *supra* note 17; Rogala v. Silva, *supra* note 128; Coleman v. Garrison, *supra* note 17; Bishop v. Byrne, *supra* note 12.
132. Rogala v. Silva, *supra* note 128.
133. Bennet v. Graves, 557 S.W.2d 893 (Ky. App. 1977); Garwood v. Locke, 552 S.W.2d 892 (Tex. Civ. App. 1977).
134. Sard v. Hardy, *supra* note 17.
135. *See* Gildiner v. Thomas Jefferson Univ. Hosp., 451 F. Supp. 692 (E.D. Pa. 1978); Naccash v. Burger, 223 Va. 491, 290 S.E. 2d 825 (1982); Eisbrenner v. Stanley, 106 Mich. App. 357, 308 N.W.2d 209 (1981); Robak v. United States, 658 F.2d 471 (7th Cir. 1981); Philips v. United States, 508 F. Supp. 537 (D.S.C. 1980); Berman v. Allan, 80 N.J. 421, 404 A.2d 8 (1979); Becker v. Schwartz, 413 N.Y.S. 2d 895, 386 N.E. 2d 807 (1978); Speck v. Finegold, 408 A.2d 496 (Pa. 1979); Jacobs v. Theimer, 519 S.W.2d 846 (Tex. 1975); Dumer v. St. Michael's Hosp., 69 Wis. 2d 766, 233 N.W.2d 372 (1975).
136. Naccash v. Burger, *supra* note 135.
137. Robak v. United States, Dumer v. St. Michael's Hosp., and Jacobs v. Theimer, *supra* note 135; Gleitman v. Cosgrove, 49 N.J. 22, 227 A.2d 689 (1967).
138. Wilczynski v. Goodman, 73 Ill. App. 3d 51, 29 Ill. Dec. 216, 391 N.E.2d 479, 487 (1979).
139. *Compare* Speck v. Finegold, *supra* note 135, with Wilczynski v. Goodman, *Id.*
140. Stills v. Gratton, 55 Cal. App. 3d 698, 127 Cal. Rptr. 652 (1976).
141. Howard v. Lecher, 46 N.Y.2d 109, 397 N.Y.S.2d 363, 366 N.E. 2d 64 (1977).
142. Berman v. Allan and Becker v. Schwartz, *supra* note 135; Howard v. Lecher, *id.*; Karlsons v. Guerinot, *supra* note 9.
143. Karlsons v. Guerinot, *supra* note 9.
144. Park v. Chessin *sub. nom.* Becker v. Schwartz, *supra* note 135. *See also* Turpin v. Sortini, 31 Cal. 3d 220, 182 Cal. Rptr. 337, 643 P.2d 954 (1982).
145. Speck v. Finegold, *supra* note 135.
146. Dumer v. St. Michael's Hosp., *supra* note 135.

147. Becker v. Schwartz, *supra* note 135.
148. Rieck v. Medical Protective Co., 64 Wis. 2d 514, 219 N.W.2d 242 (1974).
149. Roe v. Wade, *supra* note 82.
150. Gleitman v. Cosgrove, *supra* note 137.
151. Berman v. Allan, *supra* note 135.
152. W. Prosser, *supra* note 2, at 16.
153. Scarf v. Troppi, *supra* note 97.
154. *Id.*
155. Dumer v. St. Michael's Hosp., *supra* note 135.
156. Capron, *Tort Liability in Genetic Counseling,* 79 Colum. L. Rev. 618 (1979).
157. Sherlock v. Stillwater Clinic, *supra* note 92.
158. Naccash v. Burger, *supra* note 135.
159. Custodio v. Bauer, *supra* note 90.
160. Sherlock v. Stillwater Clinic, *supra* note 92.
161. Custodio v. Bauer, *supra* note 90.
162. Sherlock v. Stillwater Clinic, *supra* note 92.
163. W. Prosser, *supra* note 2, at 423.
164. Ziemba v. Sternberg, *supra* note 83; Terrell v. Garcia, *supra* note 102; Stills v. Gratton, *supra* note 140.
165. Capron, *supra* note 156.
166. *See, e.g.,* Berman v. Allan, *supra* note 135; Becker v. Schwartz, *supra* note 135; Howard v. Lecher, *supra* note 141.
167. Becker v. Schwartz, *supra* note 135. *See also* Naccash v. Burger, *supra* note 135.
168. Becker v. Schwartz, *supra* note 135.
169. Howard v. Lecher, *supra* note 141; Gleitman v. Cosgrove, *supra* note 137.
170. Howard v. Lecher, *supra* note 141. *See* Naccash v. Burger, *supra* note 135, for a contrary view.
171. Call v. Kezirian, 135 Cal. App. 3d 189, 185 Cal. Rptr. 103 (1982); Turpin v. Sortini, *supra* note 144; Harbeson v. Parke-Davis Inc.,___Wash.___(1983). *See also* Curlender v. Bio-Science Labs, 106 Cal. App. 3d 811, 165 Cal. Rptr. 477 (1980).
172. Philips v. United States, Becker v. Schwartz, Berman v. Allan, Speck v. Finegold, and Eisbrenner v. Stanley, *supra* note 135; Elliott v. Brown, 361 So. 2d 546 (Ala. 1978).
173. Park v. Chessin *sub nom.* Becker v. Schwartz, *supra* note 135.
174. Karlsons v. Guerinot, *supra* note 9.
175. Berman v. Allan and Becker v. Schwartz, *supra* note 135.
176. Dumer v. St. Michael's Hosp., *supra* note 135; Gleitman v. Cosgrove, *supra* note 137.
177. Speck v. Finegold, *supra* note 135; Elliott v. Brown, *supra* note 172; Stills v. Gratton, *supra* note 140.
178. Turpin v. Sortini, *supra* note 171.
179. Speck v. Finegold, *supra* note 135.
180. Bonbrest v. Kotz, 65 F. Supp. 138 (D. D.C. 1946).
181. Renslow v. Mennonite Hosp., 67 Ill. App. 2d 348, 367 N.E.2d 1250 (1977); Zepeda v. Zepeda, *supra* note 78.
182. Dumer v. St. Michael's Hosp., *supra* note 135.
183. *See* Sylvia v. Gobeille, 101 R.I. 76, 220 A.2d 222 (1966).
184. Becker v. Schwartz, *supra* note 135.
185. Speck v. Finegold and Becker v. Schwartz, *supra* note 135.
186. Becker v. Schwartz, *supra* note 135.
187. Berman v. Allan, *supra* note 135.

Notes: Chapter II

188. Gleitman v. Cosgrove, *supra* note 137.
189. Berman v. Allan and Becker v. Schwartz, *supra* note 135; Elliott v. Brown, *supra* note 172.
190. Elliott v. Brown, *supra* note 172.
191. Becker v. Schwartz, *supra* note 135.
192. Gleitman v. Cosgrove, *supra* note 137.
193. Elliott v. Brown, *supra* note 172.
194. Berman v. Allan, *supra* note 135.
195. Turpin v. Sortini, *supra* note 171, at 345.
196. Peters and Peters, *Wrongful Life: Recognizing the Defective Child's Right to a Cause of Action*, 18 Duq. L. Rev. 857 (1980); Furrow, *Diminished Lives and Malpractice: Courts Stalled in Transition*, 10 Law, Med. & Health Care 100 (1982).
197. King, *The Juridical Status of the Fetus: A Proposal for Legal Protection of the Unborn*, 77 Mich. L. Rev. 1647–87, 1647 (1979).
198. Roe v. Wade, *supra* note 82.
199. *Id.* at 158.
200. *Id.* at 160.
201. Renslow v. Mennonite Hosp., *supra* note 181; Bergstreser v. Mitchell, 577 F.2d 22 (8th Cir. 1978).
202. Albala v. City of New York, 78 A.D.2d 389, 434 N.Y.S.2d 400 (1981).
203. Bergstresser v. Mitchell, *supra* note 201.
204. Albala v. City of New York, *supra* note 202.
205. *Id.* at 404.
206. Vaillancourt v. Medical Center Hosp., 425 A.2d 92 (Vt. 1980).
207. *Id.*
208. White v. Yup, 85 Nev. 527, 458 P.2d 617 (1969).
209. Vaillancourt v. Medical Center Hosp., *supra* note 206, at 94–95.
210. *See, e.g.,* Justus v. Atchison, 19 Cal. 3d 564, 139 Cal. Rptr. 97, 565 P.2d 122 (1977); Duncan v. Flynn, 358 So.2d 178 (Fla. 1978).
211. *See, e.g.,* Wallace v. Wallace, 421 A.2d 134 (N.H. 1980).
212. *Id.* at 137.
213. Planned Parenthood v. Danforth, 428 U.S. 52 (1976).
214. *Id.* at 83.
215. Presley v. Newport Hosp., 117 R.I. 177, 365 A.2d 748 (1976).
216. Toth v. Goree, 65 Mich. App. 296, 237 N.W.2d 297 (1975).
217. *Id.* at 305.
218. Wallace v. Wallace, *supra* note 211.
219. *Id.* at 135.
220. Hirsch, *Difficulties the Attorney Encounters in Procuring Medical Documents*, 10 Forum 361 (Fall 1974).
221. *In re* Culbertson's Will, 292 N.Y.S.2d 806 (1968).
222. Hirsch, *supra* note 220, at 362.
223. *Id.* at 363.
224. Gotkin v. Miller, 514 F.2d 125 (2d Cir. 1975); Cannell v. Medical & Surg. Clinic, 21 Ill. App. 3d 383, 315 N.E.2d 278 (1974); *In re* Culbertson's Will, *supra* note 221.
225. Emmett v. Eastern Dispensary & Cas. Hosp., 396 F.2d 931 (D.C. Cir. 1967); Cannell v. Medical & Surg. Clinic, *supra* note 224.
226. Pyramid Life Ins. Co. v. Masonic Hosp. Ass'n, 191 F. Supp. 51 (W.D. Okla. 1961).
227. Rabens v. Jackson Park Hosp., 41 Ill. App. 3d 113, 351 N.E.2d 276 (1976); Gaertner v. State, 385 Mich. 49, 187 N.W.2d 429 (1971).
228. Felch, *Access to Medical and Psychiatric Records: Proposed Legislation*, 40 Alb. L. Rev. 580, 597 (1976).

229. Conn. Gen. Stat. Ann. §§ 4-104, 4-105 (West 1969); Mass. Gen. Laws Ann. C 111, § 70 (1971); Wis. Stat. Ann. § 269.57 (West Supp. 1975–76).
230. Cal. Evid. Code § 1158 (West Supp. 1976).
231. N.J. Rev. Stat. §§ 2A: 82-41–2A: 82-45 (West 1976 & Supp. 1981–82).
232. Miss. Code Ann. § 41-9-65 (1977).
233. La. Rev. Stat. Ann. § 40: 2014.1 (West 1977).
234. Ill. Ann. Stat. ch. 51, § 71 (Smith-Hurd 1977).
235. Hayes, *The Patient's Right of Access to His Hospital and Medical Records*, 10 Scalpel & Quill, No. 4, December, 1976; *reprinted in* 24 Med. Trial Technique Q. 295 (Winter, 1978).
236. *Id.*
237. Emmett v. Eastern Dispensary & Cas. Hosp., *supra* note 225; Cannell v. Medical & Surg. Clinic, *supra* note 224.
238. Hayes, *supra* note 235.
239. Grayson, *How State Medical Access Laws Are Working*, 8 Hosp. Med. Staff 10 (Sept. 1979).
240. W. Prosser, *supra* note 2, at 737–51.
241. *See, e.g.*, Klinge v. Lutheran Med. Center, 518 S.W.2d 157 (Mo. App. 1974); Quarles v. Sutherland, 215 Tenn. 651, 389 S.W.2d 249 (1965).
242. A. Southwick, The Law of Hospital and Health Care Administration, 317–21 (1978).
243. *Id.* at 321–31.
244. Bazemore v. Savannah Hosp., 171 Ga. 257, 155 S.E. 194 (1930).
245. Curry v. Corn, 52 Misc. 2d 1035, 277 N.Y.S.2d 470 (1966).
246. A. Southwick, *supra* note 242, at 327.
247. *See* W. Prosser, *supra* note 2, at 641 *et seq.*
248. *See* L. Frumer & M. Friedman, Products Liability § 4 (1960).
249. *E.g.*, Vergott v. Deseret Pharm. Co., 463 F.2d 12 (5th Cir. 1972) (catheter); Rose v. Hakim, 335 F. Supp. 1221 (D. D.C. 1971) (thermometer); Mattair v. St. Joseph's Hosp., 141 Ga. App. 597, 234 S.E.2d 537, *aff'd*, 239 Ga. 674, 238 S.E.2d 366 (1977) (hospital bed); Ardoin v. Hartford Accident & Indemnity Co., 350 So.2d 205 (La. App. 1977), *rev'd on other grounds*, 360 So.2d 1331 (La. 1978) (heart-lung machine); May v. Broun, 492 P.2d 776 (Or. 1972) (cauterizer); Ethicon, Inc. v. Parten, 520 S.W.2d 527 (Tex. App. 1975) (surgical needle).
250. Morris, *Defective Devices—Who's Liable?*, 8 Hosp. Med. Staff 2 (May 1979).
251. W. Prosser, *supra* note 2, at 644 n. 39.
252. *See* Frumer and Friedman, *supra* note 248, at § 2; 1 Prod. Liab. Rep. (CCH) ¶ 4015.
253. *E.g.*, Pitts v. Basile, 55 Ill. App. 2d 37, 204 N.E.2d 43 (1965); *rev'd on other grounds*, 35 Ill. 2d 49, 219 N.E.2d 472 (1966).
254. *See* M. Dixon, Drug Product Liability §§ 9.01, 9.06 (1974).
255. McEwen v. Ortho Pharm. Corp., 528 P.2d 522 (Or. 1974); *see also* Mahr v. G.D. Searle & Co., 72 Ill. App. 3d 540, 390 N.E.2d 1214 (1979).
256. Ferrigno v. Eli Lilly & Co., 175 N.J. Super. 551, 420 A.2d 1305 (1980).
257. Tinnerholm v. Parke-Davis & Co., 411 F.2d 48 (2d Cir. 1969); Stromsodt v. Parke-Davis & Co., 411 F.2d 1390 (8th Cir. 1969).
258. *E.g.*, Dunkin v. Syntex Laboratories, Inc., 443 F. Supp. 121 (W.D. Tenn. 1977).
259. Berry v. G.D. Searle & Co., 56 Ill. 2d 548, 309 N.E.2d 550 (1974).
260. *See* W. Prosser, *supra* note 2, at 650–51.
261. *See* MacPherson v. Buick Motor Co., 217 N.Y. 382, 111 N.E. 1050 (1916).
262. Fisher v. Mead Johnson Laboratories, Inc., 41 A.D.2d 737, 341 N.Y.S.2d 257

Notes: Chapter II 137

(1973); *but see* Wagmeister v. A.H. Robins Co., 64 Ill. App. 3d 964, 382 N.E.2d 23 (1978).
263. Dunkin v. Syntex Laboratories, Inc., *supra* note 258.
264. Whittington v. Eli Lilly & Co., 333 F. Supp. 98 (S.D. W.Va. 1971).
265. *Id.*
266. Restatement (Second) of Torts § 402A (1965).
267. 1 Prod. Liab. Rep. (CCH) ¶ 4030.
268. *See, e.g.,* Ortho Pharm. Corp. v. Chapman, 388 N.E.2d 541 (Ind. App. 1979).
269. Woodill v. Parke-Davis & Co., 79 Ill. 2d 26, 402 N.E.2d 194 (1980).
270. *See, e.g.,* Needham v. White Laboratories, Inc., 639 F.2d 394 (7th Cir. 1981) (Dienestrol); Lindsay v. Ortho Pharm. Corp., 637 F.2d 87 (2d Cir. 1980) (Ortho-Novum); Dunkin v. Syntex Laboratories, Inc., *supra* note 258 (Norinyl); Carmichael v. Reitz. 17 Cal. App. 3d 958, 95 Cal. Rptr. 381 (1971) (Enovid); Mahr v. G.D. Searle & Co., *supra* note 255 (Enovid); Ortho Pharm. Corp. v. Chapman, *supra* note 268 (Ortho-Novum); Leibowitz v. Ortho Pharm. Corp., 224 Pa. Super. 418, 307 A.2d 449 (1973) (Ortho-Novum); *but see* Hamilton v. Hardy, 37 Colo. App. 375, 549 P.2d 1099 (1976) (Ovulen).
271. 1 Prod. Liab. Rep. (CCH) ¶ 4065.
272. *Id.*, at ¶ 4007.
273. Needham v. White Laboratories, Inc., *supra* note 270 at 401.
274. *See* Restatement (Second) of Torts § 402A, Comment K (1965).
275. Bichler v. Eli Lilly & Co., 79 A.D.2d 317, 436 N.Y.S.2d 625 (1981).
276. Ferrigno v. Eli Lilly & Co., *supra* note 256.
277. Lyons v. Premo Pharm. Labs, Inc., 170 N.J. Super. 183, 406 A.2d 185 (1979).
278. *See, e.g.,* Lindsay v. Ortho Pharm. Corp., *supra* note 270; Ortho Pharm. Corp. v. Chapman, *supra* note 268.
279. *See* Restatement (Second) of Torts § 402A, Comment K (1965); *see, e.g.,* Gaston v. Hunter, 121 Ariz. App. 33, 588 P.2d 326 (1978).
280. Weaver v. Searle, Prod. Liab. Rep. (CCH) ¶ 8690 (N.D. Ala. 1980).
281. *E.g.,* Terhune v. A.H. Robins Co., 90 Wash. 2d 9, 577 P.2d 975 (1978).
282. *See* 1 Prod. Liab. Rep. (CCH) ¶¶ 4300-80.
283. Needham v. White Laboratories, Inc., *supra* note 270, at 402–403; *see also* Gaston v. Hunter, *supra* note 279.
284. Mead v. Coca-Cola Bottling Co., 108 N.E.2d 757 (Mass. 1952).
285. Dubin v. Michael Reese Hosp. and Med. Center, 74 Ill. App. 3d 932, 393 N.E.2d 588 (1979).
286. McDonald v. Sacramento Med. Found. Blood Bank, 62 Cal. App. 3d 866, 133 Cal. Rptr. 444 (1976); Perlmutter v. Beth David Hosp., 308 N.Y. 100, 123 N.E.2d 792 (1954).
287. *See, e.g.,* Idaho Code § 39-3702 (1977).
288. Carmichael v. Reitz, *supra* note 270; Ethicon, Inc. v. Parten, *supra* note 249.
289. *E.g.,* Carmichael v. Reitz, *supra* note 270; Vergott v. Deseret Pharm. Co., *supra* note 249.
290. Berry v. G.D. Searle & Co., *supra* note 259.
291. Jones v. Sportelli, 166 N.J. Super. 383, 399 A.2d 1047 (1979).
292. *E.g.,* Ferrigno v. Eli Lilly & Co., *supra* note 256.
293. *See, e.g.,* Stromsodt v. Parke-Davis & Co., *supra* note 257 (Quadrigen); Roginsky v. Richardson-Merrel, Inc., 378 F.2d 832 (8th Cir. 1969) (MER/29).
294. *E.g.,* Bichler v. Eli Lilly & Co., *supra* note 275.
295. Gaston v. Hunter, *supra* note 279.
296. Dunkin v. Syntex Laboratories, Inc., *supra* note 258 (Norinyl).

297. Baker v. St. Agnes Hosp., 70 A.D.2d 400, 421 N.Y.S.2d 81 (1979).
298. *See, e.g.,* Ezaqui v. Dow Chem. Corp., 598 F.2d 727 (2d Cir. 1979).
299. Bichler v. Eli Lilly & Co., *supra* note 275, *quoting* Codling v. Paglia, 32 N.Y.2d 880, 298 N.E.2d 622 (1973).
300. Comment, *Package Inserts for Prescription Drugs as Evidence in Medical Malpractice Suits,* 44 U. Chi. L. Rev. 398 (Winter 1977).
301. Baker v. St. Agnes Hosp. *supra* note 297.
302. Mink v. University of Chicago, 460 F. Supp. 713 (N.D. Ill. 1978); *accord* McEwen v. Ortho Pharm. Corp., *supra* note 255.
303. *E.g.,* Werner v. Upjohn Co., Inc., 628 F.2d 848 (4th Cir. 1980); *cert. denied,* 449 U.S. 1082 (1981); Leibowitz v. Ortho Pharm. Corp., *supra* note 270.
304. *E.g.,* Woodill v. Parke-Davis & Co., *supra* note 269 (Pitocin); Ortho Pharm. Corp. v. Chapman, *supra* note 268.
305. *E.g.,* Mahr v. G.D. Searle & Co. and McEwen v. Ortho Pharm. Corp., *supra* note 255.
306. Hamilton v. Hardy, *supra* note 270; *accord* Mahr v. G.D. Searle & Co., *supra* note 255.
307. Mahr v. G.D. Searle & Co., *supra* note 255; *see also,* Lawson v. G.D. Searle & Co., 46 Ill. 2d 543, 356 N.E.2d 779 (1976).
308. Stromsodt v. Parke-Davis & Co., *supra* note 257.
309. Ortho Pharm. Corp. v. Chapman, *supra* note 268.
310. Mahr v. G.D. Searle & Co., *supra* note 255; *see also,* Carmichael v. Reitz, *supra* note 270; Formella v. Ciba-Geigy Corp., 100 Mich. App. 649, 300 N.W.2d 356 (1980).
311. Lindsay v. Ortho Pharm. Corp., *supra* note 270; Mahr v. G.D. Searle & Co., *supra* note 255.
312. Lukaszewicz v. Ortho Pharm. Corp., 510 F. Supp. 961 (E.D. Wis. 1981).
313. 21 C.F.R. § 310.501 (1980).
314. 21 U.S.C. § 301 *et seq.* (1980).
315. *See* Pharmaceutical Mfrs. Ass'n v. Food & Drug Administration, 484 F. Supp. 1179 (D. Del. 1980) (holding that, although 21 U.S.C. §§ 352 and 353, regarding misbranding of drugs, were intended to make the prescribing physician the primary source of information available to a consumer of a prescription drug, 21 U.S.C. § 371(a) authorizes the Food and Drug Administration to require disclosure on the labeling of the drug of those possible side effects that are sufficiently serious as to be material to the patient's decision whether or not to use the drug).
316. *E.g.,* Torsiello v. Whitehall Laboratories, 165 N.J.Super. 311, 398 A.2d 132 (1979).
317. Reyes v. Wyeth Laboratories, 498 F.2d 1264 (5th Cir. 1974).
318. *See* M. Dixon, *supra* note 254, at § 9.05.
319. Givens v. Lederle, 556 F.2d 1341 (5th Cir. 1977).
320. *See, e.g.,* Klink v. G.D. Searle & Co., 26 Wash. App. 951, 614 P.2d 701 (1980).
321. Mueller v. Mueller, 221 N.W.2d 39 (S.D. 1974). *See also, e.g.,* Lhotka v. Larson, 238 N.W.2d 870 (Minn. 1976).
322. Ferrigno v. Eli Lilly & Co., *supra* note 256.
323. Air Shields, Inc. v. Spears, 590 S.W.2d 574 (Tex. Civ. App. 1979).
324. *Cf.* Pfizer, Inc. v. Jones, 272 S.E.2d 43 (Va. 1980).
325. Marcus, *Safe Equipment: A Matter of Selection and Detection,* 8 Hosp. Med. Staff 14 (May 1979).
326. Morris, *supra* note 250.
327. Marcus, *supra* note 325, at 17.
328. *E.g.,* Rose v. Hakim, *supra* note 249.

329. Ardoin v. Hartford Accident & Indemnity Co., 350 So.2d 205 (La. App. 1977), rev'd on other grounds, 360 So.2d 1331 (La. 1978).
330. See W. Prosser, supra note 2, at 662–63.
331. Jorgensen v. Meade Johnson Laboratories, Inc., 483 F.2d 237 (10th Cir. 1973).
332. Roth v. Bell, 24 Wash. App. 92, 600 P.2d 602 (1979).
333. Air Shields, Inc. v. Spears, supra note 323.
334. Woodill v. Parke-Davis & Co., supra note 269.
335. Jones v. Sportelli, supra note 291.
336. G.D. Searle & Co. v. Superior Ct., City of Sacramento, 49 Cal. App.3d 22, 122 Cal. Rptr. 218 (1975).
337. Mink v. University of Chicago, supra note 302.
338. Vaccaro v. Squibb Corp., 52 N.Y.2d 809, 436 N.Y.S.2d 871, 418 N.E.2d 386 (1980).
339. Lindsay v. Ortho Pharm. Corp., supra note 270.
340. E.g., Diamond v. E.R. Squibb & Sons, Inc., 397 So.2d 671 (Fla. 1981).
341. Needham v. White Laboratories, Inc., supra note 270 (C.A. Ill. 1981); G.D. Searle & Co. v. Superior Ct., City of Sacramento, supra note 336; Witherell v. Weimer, 79 Ill. App. 3d 582, 396 N.E.2d 268 (1979); Martinex v. Rosenzweig, 70 Ill. App. 3d 155, 387 N.E.2d 1263 (1979).
342. Mink v. University of Chicago, supra note 302; Morrissy v. Eli Lilly & Co., 76 Ill. App. 3d 753, 394 N.E.2d 1369 (1979); Ferrigno v. Eli Lilly & Co., supra note 256; see also Payton v. Abbott Laboratories, 512 F. Supp. 1031 (D. Mass. 1981)
343. See, W. Prosser, supra note 2, at 663–65.
344. Lyons v. Premo Pharm. Labs, Inc., supra note 277.
345. Bichler v. Willing, 58 A.D.2d 331, 397 N.Y.S.2d 57 (1977).
346. Lemire v. Garrard Drugs, 95 Mich. App. 520, 291 N.W.2d 103 (1980).
347. Mink v. University of Chicago, supra note 302.
348. E.g., Mahr v. G.D. Searle & Co., supra note 255; McEwen v. Ortho Pharm. Corp., supra note 255; Lukaszewicz v. Ortho Pharm. Corp., supra note 312.
349. Gray v. United States, 445 F. Supp. 337 (S.D. Tex. 1978).
350. Abel v. Eli Lilly & Co., 94 Mich. App. 59, 289 N.W.2d 20 (1980).
351. Bichler v. Eli Lilly & Co., supra note 275.
352. Sindell v. Abbott Laboratories, 26 Cal. 3d 588, 163 Cal. Rptr. 132, 607 P.2d 924 (1980); cert. denied, 449 U.S. 912 (1981).
353. Sindell v. Abbott Laboratories, supra note 352; Abel v. Eli Lilly & Co., supra note 350; Namm v. Charles E. Frosst & Co., 178 N.J. Super. 19 (1981); Ferrigno v. Eli Lilly & Co., supra note 256; Lyons v. Premo Pharm. Labs, Inc., supra note 277; see generally Sheiner, DES and a Proposed Theory of Enterprise Liability, 46 Fordham L. Rev. 963 (1978).
354. Id.
355. See, e.g., Payton v. Abbott Laboratories, supra note 342; Sindell v. Abbott Laboratories, supra note 352; Abel v. Eli Lilly & Co., supra note 350; Namm v. Charles E. Frosst & Co., supra note 353; Ferrigno v. Eli Lilly & Co., supra note 256; Bichler v. Eli Lilly & Co., supra note 275.

Chapter III

Defenses

§ 3.10 INTRODUCTION

When a lawsuit is brought charging a physician with malpractice, the law affords the physician certain defenses to the action. Generally, the plaintiff has the burden of proving the allegations made against the physician-defendant; the jury is told that the defendant must prevail unless the patient-plaintiff proves by a preponderance of the evidence each element of his claim.

If the plaintiff succeeds in proving a case, the physician-defendant must then go forward with proof of a defense to the action. The most commonly invoked defense consists of a denial of the elements of the patient-plaintiff's claim. Thus the physician-defendant may prove that he or she possessed the requisite skill and exercised the necessary care (see §§ 1.30, Duty and 1.40, Breach of Duty), deny that his or her conduct caused the patient's injury (see § 1.50, Causation), deny that the patient was actually injured (see § 1.60, Damages), or deny all or any combination of such allegations.

The physician has certain additional defenses to malpractice, which fall into two categories: substantive and procedural. Substantive, or affirmative, defenses relate to the facts or merits of the lawsuit. They include contributory or comparative negligence and assumption of risk. Procedural defenses refer to some aspect or requirement of the legal process that has not been properly complied with by the plaintiff and that, consequently, bars the plaintiff from recovering against the physician. Procedural defenses include statutes of limitation, res judicata, and release from liability agreements. Each of these defenses appears in Table 3.1.

§ 3.20 CONTRIBUTORY NEGLIGENCE

Contributory negligence has been defined as:

> conduct on the part of the plaintiff, contributing as a legal cause to the harm he has suffered, which falls below the standard to which he is required to conform for his own protection . . . although the defendant has violated his duty, has been

§ 3.20   Contributory Negligence   141

negligent, and would otherwise be liable, the plaintiff is denied recovery because his own conduct disentitles him to maintain the action. In the eyes of the law both parties are at fault; and the defense is one of the plaintiff's disability, rather than the defendant's innocence.[1]

Contributory negligence is an affirmative defense, which means that the burden of proof is on the physician-defendant.[2]

CASE ILLUSTRATION

The physician diagnosed the young married patient as pregnant, and she periodically visited him for checkups. Everything developed normally except for the patient's weight gain, about which the physician expressed his concern, warning the patient of the possibility of developing toxemia or eclampsia. A month after this warning, the patient overslept and missed her Friday appointment with the physician. The patient's husband, on returning from work that evening, noticed that his wife was swollen all over, was unable to speak clearly, and was having difficulty walking. The husband contacted the physician, who agreed to see the patient on Monday. The patient's mother arrived Monday to take the patient to the physician's office. At that time, however, the patient went into continuous convulsions and was taken to the hospital, where the physician, who had been notified, met her and diagnosed her condition as acute eclampsia. The baby was delivered dead the next morning. The patient died three days later. The

TABLE 3.1   Physician Defenses

Incomplete Tort Defenses	Substantive Defenses	Procedural Defenses
1. Duty?	1. Contributory negligence*	1. Statute of limitations
2. Breach of duty?	2. Comparative negligence**	2. Release forms
3. Damage?	3. Assumption of risk†	
4. Proximate cause?	4. Standard of care options††	
	a. Best judgment rule	
	b. Respectable minority	
	c. Different schools	

*Both parties considered to be at fault; physician must prove the patient's contribution. Recovery by patient is all or none, none if patient is found contributorily negligent.
**Responsibility for damage is apportioned between patient and physician according to percent of wrongdoing.
†Once patient is informed of the risks and authorizes the treatment, the patient is held to have assumed the risk.
††If the physician complies with the (an) acceptable standard of care, the physician can claim to have used his or her *best judgment*. If there is more than one standard of care, compliance with a *respectable minority* standard is sufficient. Where physicians from *different schools* (for example M.D., D.O., chiropractic) follow the standards of their respective schools and the standards between the schools are different, they will be judged according to their school's standard and not that of another.

patient's husband sued the physician for negligence. The physician alleged that the patient was contributorily negligent in failing (1) to follow instructions regarding weight control, (2) to advise the physician of changes in her condition, and (3) to return to the physician and keep her appointment so as to allow the physician to examine her. The trial court held for the physician; the husband appealed, and the appellate court ordered a new trial. The appellate court, while recognizing the existence of contributory negligence as a defense, held that the instructions given the jury by the trial court judge erroneously suggested that it was necessary for the patient's husband to prove the patient had been free of contributory negligence. The proper rule is that the physician-defendant has the burden of proving the patient-plaintiff's contributory negligence, and this burden does not shift among the parties during the trial (*Kaspar v. Schack*, 1976).[3]

A successful defense of contributory negligence operates to bar *any* recovery by the plaintiff, and therefore the defense has gradually come to be disfavored by the courts.[4]

The defense of contributory negligence has been recognized in cases in which the patient has failed to follow the physician's or nurse's instruction,[5] refused suggested treatment, or given the physician false, incomplete, or misleading information concerning symptoms.[6] The question of whether a patient's actions are contributorily negligent is a question for the jury.

CASE ILLUSTRATION

A patient visited the physician on August 6, 1962. She was given a routine Pap smear. Two weeks later, a report was sent to the physician which stated that the specimen had been "suspicious for malignancy." The physician attempted to reach the patient by telephone several times but was unsuccessful until January 1963, when the patient paid her bill. In February, she was given another Pap smear, which was again "suspicious for malignancy." A biopsy was performed soon after, and was diagnosed as "early, invasive" carcinoma. The patient was given cobalt and radium therapy, which destroyed her ovaries, rendered her sterile, and precipitated symptoms of menopause. The plaintiff brought a lawsuit which alleged that the physician failed to notify her of the results of the first Pap smear and therefore her condition worsened and more drastic treatment was required. Evidence revealed that the plaintiff had moved one month after the initial examination and had had no telephone installed until nine months later. The patient had represented to the physician that she and her husband both worked at the local university, she as a secretary and he as an accountant; actually, she was employed in a different capacity at the university, and her husband was an unemployed accountant. The physician had tried to reach her several times at her home address and through the university. The patient testified that she gave the physician's office her change of address, and she argued that she could have been reached by mail. The jury brought a verdict for the physician-defendant. In a memo denying the patient-plaintiff's motion for a new trial, the trial court stated that "the evidence disclosed, and the jury could have found, that plaintiff, in furnishing defendant information as to her occupation and her husband's occupation and her failure promptly to notify the defendant of a change of address was inconsistent with the behavior to be expected of an ordinarily prudent person and, therefore, negligence." The higher court held that whether the patient was contributorily negligent by giving the physician incomplete and misleading information about her employment status, by maintaining no telephone where she lived, and by failing to inquire about the results of the Pap smear so that the physician was unable to contact her and notify her that the test results showed a possibility of cancer was a question appropriate for the jury to have decided. The court therefore affirmed the verdict (*Ray v. Wagner*, 1970).[7]

Both courts and commentators have emphasized, however, that the availability of a contributory negligence defense in a malpractice case is limited because of the disparity of medical knowledge between the patient and the physician and because of the patient's right to rely on the physician's knowledge and skill in the course of medical treatment. Thus, it has been held that it is not contributory negligence to follow the physician's instructions or to fail to consult another physician when the patient has no reason to believe his or her pain is caused by the physician's negligence. Nor is it contributory negligence for the patient to refuse to submit to a second procedure which is intended to correct the result of the physician's negligent initial treatment.[8] If a physician fails to prove that the patient was contributorily negligent, the patient's claim will not be barred.

CASE ILLUSTRATION

The patient underwent a total abdominal hysterectomy. The wound failed to heal properly, and several months after the removal of the sutures the patient began to experience pain in the area of the incision. She went to a new physician, who determined that one of the stitches inside her abdomen had become infected. The incision was reopened and cleaned and packed with iodoform gauze pads. It was repacked each of the next three days, and three days later the patient made a final visit. The physician told her that he had unpacked the incision and that she should go home and take it easy. Although the medical records from the hospital indicated she was to return to the gynecology clinic two weeks after her discharge, the patient asserted that no one ever told her she was to return for further treatment after her final visit. Approximately six weeks after her discharge from the hospital she suffered pain and went back to the hospital where she was first seen. X rays revealed the presence of a foreign body, and surgery was performed. An iodoform gauze pad was found in the patient's abdominal cavity and was removed from the site of her previous incision. The patient brought suit.

At trial, one of the surgeons testified that this iodoform gauze pad had caused the infection which had precipitated the plaintiff's complaints of pain. The defendant asserted that the patient was contributorily negligent in failing to return to the gynecology clinic during the time her wound was being treated with the gauze packing. The court found that, in view of the patient's unrebutted testimony that no one told her she was supposed to return to the clinic, she was not contributorily negligent in failing to return. The court stated that there was no indication that, had she kept this alleged appointment, the gauze pad would have been discovered and removed. The court held in favor of the patient (*Wells v. Woman's Hospital Foundation*, 1973).[9]

From a strategic standpoint, a defense of contributory negligence probably should not be raised in every case where a plaintiff has done something which aggravates his or her injury. The wisdom of invoking contributory negligence may involve more delicate considerations in malpractice cases than in the general run of tort cases. A jury naturally may resent an attempt to offset a particularly egregious error by a professional with a relatively minor dereliction of a sick layperson. Possibly, too, the phrase "contributory" may in some malpractice cases psychologically imply more than it does generally in tort cases—an admission that the defendant was negligent in the first place. It may be wise, depending on the facts, for the defendant to rely not on contributory negligence but on the defense that the plaintiff's negligence was the *sole* cause of the injury.[10]

Occasions could arise when the patient would be contributorily negligent not in refusing the suggested treatment, but rather in submitting to it (for example, where a patient allows a drunken doctor to give an injection and is injured as a result).[11]

Negligence of the patient prior to the physician's alleged negligence will not bar a claim by the patient. The physician's negligence occurs in treating the patient in the condition in which she presents herself for treatment.[12]

The defense of contributory negligence may not be available if the plaintiff's state of mind or health precludes the capacity to be negligent. Thus, the defense may be rejected where the patient is mentally ill,[13] semiconscious,[14] heavily sedated,[15] or very old.[16]

§ 3.30 COMPARATIVE NEGLIGENCE

The doctrine of comparative negligence relieves the plaintiff from the hardship often imposed by the doctrine of contributory negligence. In contrast to the contributory negligence rule that negligence by the plaintiff will totally bar his or her action, under a comparative negligence scheme damages are divided between the two parties in proportion to their fault for the injury.[17] For example, in a case where the patient suffers $10,000 damages, the jury may find that the physician was responsible for 70 percent of the damages and the patient for 30 percent. In a jurisdiction adhering to the contributory negligence doctrine, the finding that the patient's own negligence was a partial cause of the injury would bar the action,[18] but in a comparative negligence jurisdiction, the physician would be held liable for 70 percent ($7,000) of the damages, and the patient would be required to absorb the remaining 30 percent ($3,000) of the damages.

As the example shows, the doctrines of contributory negligence and comparative negligence are incompatible. All jurisdictions use one or the other of the rules; none uses both. Largely because the contributory negligence rule totally denies recovery to plaintiffs only nominally at fault, an increasing number of jurisdictions are adopting the comparative negligence rule.

The obstacle to adopting comparative negligence is the rigid precedent of case law recognizing contributory negligence.[19] As of 1978, legislatures in 26 jurisdictions had circumvented their courts' adherence to precedent by passing comparative negligence statutes.[20] In still other jurisdictions, the courts are reversing themselves and adopting the comparative negligence doctrine.[21] Application of the rule in those jurisdictions that have adopted it is not uniform. An important question upon which the courts disagree is whether or not a plaintiff who is equally or more at fault than the defendant can recover damages. In other words, if the plaintiff is 50 percent or more at fault for the injury, can he or she recover? Some jurisdictions permit recovery in this situation; others do not. A compromise approach adopted by still other states permits recovery if the plaintiff's fault is 50 percent or less but not if it is more.[22]

Comparative negligence may have particular application in malpractice cases when the patient negligently fails to follow her physician's advice on self-care. In such cases, however, the courts will take into consideration the disparity in medical knowledge between patient and physician. Thus, if the physician negligently fails to give the patient adequate advice on the implications of her condition, the patient's liability for injuries caused by improper self-care will be correspondingly lessened.

CASE ILLUSTRATION

A pathology report following a tubal ligation showed that the patient's left fallopian tube had been removed, but that the tissue removed from the patient's right side was a cross-section of an artery. A hysterosalpingogram was done, and the physician and surgeon concluded that the patient's right tube had been effectively blocked by the suturing done by the surgeon. A conference was then held among the physician, the surgeon, and the patient. The three participants later disagreed about what transpired at the conference. The physician stated that he offered a free vasectomy for the patient's husband and encouraged the operation as an alternative to a second tubal ligation. The surgeon, on the other hand, stated that he saw no need for a vasectomy and so advised the patient. The patient said that she was told that the operation was successful, but that her husband was advised to have a vasectomy in case she was uneasy. The husband did not undergo a vasectomy, and the patient became pregnant.

The patient and her husband brought suit against the physician and the surgeon. The jury returned a verdict dividing fault equally between the plaintiffs and the defendants. The appellate court reversed, stating: "the relevant issue in this case . . . is whether and to what extent plaintiffs may be charged with acting unreasonably in the face of certain statements and advice of defendant doctors. . . . Plaintiff-wife may have acted unreasonably in failing at least to persuade her husband to have a vasectomy, or, in the absence of vasectomy, in failing to continue a regimen of birth control. The record, however, provides only the barest minimum support for these inferences of negligence. . . . The evidence of plaintiff-husband's contributory negligence is plainly insufficient. The only evidence as to his conduct is that he concluded his wife could not become pregnant and he elected not to have a vasectomy." In addition, the court stated that "neither doctor apparently discussed with plaintiff-wife the risks of pregnancy notwithstanding the operation or directly informed her that she could become pregnant again. Under these circumstances, plaintiffs cannot be held equally negligent with the surgeon, because the subject matter of their negligence is the interpretation of medical matters about which the doctors owe a greater duty to them than the plaintiffs owe to themselves. The superior knowledge and skill of the physicians in this case should have been reflected in straightforward, complete, and accurate information and advice to their patients. That patient should not be denied recovery because she did not sift from their equivocation this kind of information and advice." The court therefore ordered a new trial against both defendants on the issues of their negligence, of the contributory negligence of the plaintiffs or plaintiff-wife, and of the damages (*Martineau v. Nelson*, 1976).[23]

Comparative negligence reduces damages to the degree that the plaintiff's negligence increases the extent of his or her injury.[24] Where the fault of the patient was subsequent to the fault of the physician and only served to aggravate the injury, only the amount of damages recoverable by the patient is affected.[25]

§ 3.40 ASSUMPTION OF RISK

The doctrine of assumption of risk recognizes generally that, if a patient has full knowledge of an open and visible condition, appreciates the dangers incident to that condition, and voluntarily acts with reference to that condition, the patient assumes or absorbs the risks of the attendant dangers. It is a matter of the patient's full knowledge and intelligent acquiescence.[26]

There are two basic elements that must be proved in order to successfully raise a defense of assumption of risk:

1. The party assuming the risk must have knowledge of the danger.
2. There must be a voluntary exposure to the known danger.[27]

In the malpractice setting, it is possible to identify two aspects to the application of the doctrine: medical and nonmedical. Nonmedical risks are those that a patient, through common sense or experience, can appreciate without medical information. If a patient appreciates such a nonmedical risk and acts despite the existence of the risk, the patient cannot recover for injury resulting from the actualization of the potential risk. One commentator has asserted that the defense is more likely to be raised in cases involving other than purely medical questions. Under a true application of the doctrine, it would be difficult to assert assumption of medical risk successfully because a patient's medical knowledge usually is not adequate enough for her to realize that she is being treated negligently.[28]

CASE ILLUSTRATION

An elderly patient fell and injured herself in the physician's dressing room; she sued the physician. The patient alleged that the physician was negligent in failing to have a nurse assist her in disrobing. The physician argued that the patient was offered assistance by his nurse, but the patient refused to allow the nurse to assist her and thereby assumed any risk involved. The court rejected the plaintiff's claim that the physician failed to meet the standard of care, because no expert testimony was offered. The court affirmed the jury verdict for the defendant, accepting the defense of assumption of risk (*Levett v. Etkind*, 1969).[29]

Medical risks are tied into the doctrine of informed consent (see § 1.33, Consent and Informed Consent). Specifically, if the physician has fulfilled the duty of informing the patient of risks and expected results of a treatment, then the patient's consent is informed and the patient has assumed the risks of the treatment. If the patient knows and comprehends the danger and voluntarily exposes herself to it, she is deemed to have assumed the risk and is precluded from recovering for a resulting injury.[30] However, the patient never assumes the risk of negligent or improper treatment.[31]

The courts recognize that it is not the patient's duty to set her judgment against that of the physician, an expert in medicine. Consequently, medical risks are not viewed as within the patient's ken to assume. The physician-patient relationship is founded upon trust and confidence, and the patient has a right to rely on the professional skill of the physician.

CASE ILLUSTRATION

Over a period of time, the patient underwent two D&Cs and a major operation, separation of adhesions and supravaginal hysterectomy. She received narcotics after her hysterectomy and during the following months. Six months after her last operation, she was diagnosed as a morphine addict. The patient sued the physician, who raised, as one defense, the patient's assumption of risk of addiction. There was evidence that the patient complained of pain when she was not in pain in order to obtain morphine. The patient and her husband, however, both fearful of the effects of the morphine, had asked the physician about the consequences of too much morphine, and the physician had told them not to worry, that the patient should have it whenever she wanted it. The court affirmed a judgment for the patient and stated that, because the physician had not informed the patient of the risks of addiction and the patient had therefore not given her informed consent to the use of the drug, the physician could not argue as a defense that she had assumed the risk of addiction (*Los Alamos Medical Center v. Coe*, 1954).[32]

Thus in medical malpractice actions, assumption of risk is generally not feasible as a defense. The defense usually arises only in exceptional circumstances, such as where a patient is specifically warned of the risk and refuses to follow, or ignores, the physician's instructions. The superior knowledge and expertise of the physician in medical matters and the limited ability of the patient to comprehend the risk and dangers of certain treatments undermine the effective use of this defense by a physician.

§ 3.50 STATUTE OF LIMITATIONS

A person who has been intentionally or negligently injured by another must bring suit within a specified period after the injury occurred or the law will not permit the suit to be brought at all. The period within which the suit must be brought is specified by a "statute of limitations" and varies according to the nature of the right asserted by the plaintiff. Whereas contract actions, for example, typically may be brought within six years of the date of breach (see § 2.20, Contract Theory), malpractice suits must generally be brought within two to three years. There is a great variation in the statutes of limitations enforced in the various states, and nowhere is this more true than with respect to statutes governing medical malpractice actions (see Table 3.2). It is therefore necessary to set forth the basic rules that apply to such actions (although not all states follow all of the rules) and to remind physicians that they would be well advised to check the particular laws of the state in which they practice.

The most restrictive rule, still followed in a number of jurisdictions, might be described as the date of injury rule. Under such statutes, the patient's right to bring suit accrues on the date of the alleged negligent act or omission, at which time the limitations period also begins to run.[33] Because an injury caused by malpractice may not become apparent until many years after the date of treatment, however, it is quite possible under the date of injury rule for the patient to lose the right to sue before she is even aware of having been injured.[34]

TABLE 3.2 Statutes of Limitation for Malpractice, Contract, and Wrongful Death, by Jurisdiction*

Jurisdiction	Malpractice	Contract[†]	Wrongful Death
Alabama	2 years after date of injury or 6 months after discovery of injury, but within 4 years of date of injury	Same	2 years after death
Alaska	2 years, but no longer than 2 years after disability ceases	6 years	2 years after death
Arizona	3 years after date of injury or discovery	3 years	2 years after death
Arkansas	2 years after date of injury or 1 year from the date of discovery, but within 1 year after disability is removed	3 years	3 years after death
California	3 years after date of injury or 1 year after discovery, but within 4 years of date of injury	2 years	Same as malpractice
Colorado	2 years after discovery, but within 3 years of date of injury	Same	2 years after act resulting in death or within 1 year after death
Connecticut	2 years after date of injury or 2 years after discovery of injury, but within 3 years of date of injury	3 years	2 years after act resulting in death or 2 years after discovery, but within 3 years of act
Delaware	2 years after date of injury or, upon discovery, 3 years after date of injury	2 years	Same as malpractice

Continued

*This table attempts to compare statutory limitations periods pertinent to malpractice actions and offers only a distillation of statutory meaning. Specific statutory language should be consulted for applicability to a particular case.

†Where the malpractice statute specifies a limitations period applicable to contracts, the word "same" appears in the contracts column. Where a different statute applies to contracts, the period is given, even if it is the same.

Table 3.2 Continued

Jurisdiction	Malpractice	Contract†	Wrongful Death
District of Columbia	3 years	3 years	1 year after death
Florida	2 years after date of injury or 2 years after discovery, 4 years of date of injury for fraudulent concealment, but within 2 years of date of injury	3 years	Same as malpractice
Georgia	2 years after date of injury or 1 year after discovery	4 years	2 years after death
Hawaii	2 years after discovery of injury, but within 6 years of date of injury	6 years	Same as malpractice
Idaho	2 years after date of injury or 2 years after discovery of injury, but within 30 years of date of injury	4 years	2 years
Illinois	2 years after discovery, but within 4 years of date of injury	2 years	Same as malpractice
Indiana	2 years after date of injury	Same	2 years after death
Iowa	2 years after discovery, but within 6 years of date of injury	5 years	Same as malpractice
Kansas	2 years after date of injury or upon discovery, but within 4 years of date of injury and an overall limit of 10 years.	3 years	2 years after death
Kentucky	1 year after date of injury, but within 5 years of date of injury	1 year	Same as malpractice
Louisiana	1 year after date of injury or 1 year after discovery, but within 3 years of date of injury	Same	Same as malpractice
Maine	2 years after date of injury	6 years	2 years after death
Maryland	5 years after date of injury or 3 years after discovery, whichever is shorter	3 years	3 years after death
Massachusetts	3 years after date of injury	Same	3 years after death
Michigan	2 years after discontinuing treatment or 6 months after discovery	6 years 3 years for implied contract	2 to 5 years, depending on the facts
Minnesota	2 years after date of injury	Same	3 years after act resulting in death
Mississippi	2 years after date of injury or discovery	3 years	6 years after death
Missouri	2 years after date of injury or 2 years after discovery, but within 10 years of date of injury	5 years	3 years after death
Montana	3 years after date of injury or discovery, but within 5 years of the date of injury	5 years	3 years after death
Nebraska	2 years after date of injury or 1 year after discovery, but within 10 years of date of injury	Same	2 years after death

Table 3.2 Continued

Jurisdiction	Malpractice	Contract†	Wrongful Death
Nevada	4 years after date of injury or 2 years after discovery	4 years	Same as malpractice
New Hampshire	2 years after date of injury or discovery	2 years	2 years after death
New Jersey	2 years after date of injury or discovery	6 years	2 years after death
New Mexico	3 years after date of injury	3 years	3 years after death
New York	2½ years after date of injury; 1 year after discovery of foreign object	6 years	2 years after death
North Carolina	3 years after date of injury or 1 year after discovery, but within 4 years of date of injury; within 10 years of date of injury if foreign object is discovered	3 years	2 years after death
North Dakota	2 years after date of injury or discovery, plus 1 year for fraudulent concealment, but within 6 years of date of injury	6 years	2 years after death
Ohio	1 year after date of injury or discovery, but within 4 years of date of injury or termination of physician-patient relationship	6 years	2 years after death
Oklahoma	2 years after discovery, but within 3 years of date of injury (damages limited after 3 years)	Same	Same as malpractice
Oregon	2 years after discovery, but within 5 years of date of injury	6 years	3 years after death
Pennsylvania	2 years after date of injury, but within 4 years of date of injury	4 years	2 years after death
Rhode Island	2 years after date of injury or 1 year after discovery	10 years	2 years after death
South Carolina	3 years after date of injury or discovery, but within 6 years of date of injury	6 years	6 years after death
South Dakota	2 years after date of injury	Same	3 years after death
Tennessee	1 year after date of injury or 1 year after discovery, but within 3 years of date of injury	Same	1 year after act resulting in death
Texas	2 years after date of injury or discovery	2 years	Same as malpractice
Utah	2 years after discovery, but within 4 years of date of injury	Same	2 years after death
Vermont	3 years after date of injury or discovery, but within 7 years of date of injury	6 years	2 years after death
Virginia	2 years after date of injury; 2 years after date of discovery if injury is fraudulently concealed	2 years	2 years after death
Washington	3 years after date of injury or 1 year after discovery, but within 8 years of date of injury	3 years	2 years

Continued

Table 3.2 Continued

Jurisdiction	Malpractice	Contract†	Wrongful Death
West Virginia	2 years after date of injury; 2 years after date of discovery if injury is fraudulently concealed	5 years	2 years after death
Wisconsin	3 years after date of injury or 1 year after discovery, but within 5 years of date of injury	Same	3 years after death
Wyoming	2 years after date of injury or 2 years after discovery	8 years	2 years after death

To avoid this difficulty, an increasing number of states adhere to what is known as the discovery rule. The discovery rule postpones the start of the limitations period until the patient knows, or in the exercise of reasonable diligence should know, of her injury.[35]

CASE ILLUSTRATION

Two years after undergoing a bilateral tubal ligation, the patient became pregnant. Eleven months after discovering her pregnancy, but more than three years after the operation, the patient brought suit against the operating physician. The applicable statute of limitations required malpractice actions to "be commenced within one year after the cause of action accrued." The court rejected the physician's argument that the statute required the patient to bring her action within one year after the operation. Instead, applying the discovery rule, the court stated that the patient's cause of action did not accrue until she "discovered she was pregnant or, in the exercise of reasonable care and diligence, she should have so discovered." Since the patient had in fact brought suit within one year after discovering her pregnancy, the court held that her suit could go to trial (*Teeters v. Currey,* 1974).[36]

As this case illustrates, the discovery rule significantly extends a patient's ability to recover for malpractice. Nonetheless, adoption of the rule does not eliminate the statute of limitations as an effective defense. The patient who fails to bring suit within a reasonable time after discovering her injury will still find her action barred.

CASE ILLUSTRATION

In early 1972, the physician examined the 19-year-old patient and concluded that she was suffering from multiple sclerosis. He advised her to undergo a sterilization operation. The patient consented, and on May 23,

§ 3.50   *Statute of Limitations*   153

1972, a tubal ligation was performed by an obstetrician-gynecologist. Two years later, the patient was told by another physician that she had never had multiple sclerosis. Another medical opinion suggested that, even if the patient did have the disease, sterilization was probably unnecessary. On November 21, 1974, 2½ years after the operation, the patient brought suit against the original physician and the obstetrician-gynecologist. The applicable statute of limitations required malpractice actions to be brought within two years of the date that the patient's injury first became physically ascertainable. The patient argued that her injury first became ascertainable, and that the statute began to run, when she was informed in 1974 that the sterilization was unnecessary. The court disagreed. Stating that the injury complained of (sterility) was "immediately manifest" upon completion of the operation, the court held that the statute began to run when the sterilization was performed in 1972. So reasoning, the court concluded that the patient had failed to bring her action within the two-year statutory period, and it ordered her case to be dismissed (*Pearson v. Boines,* 1976).[37]

Not all courts agree with the conclusion reached in this case. At least one other case has held that the cause of action for an unnecessary sterilization does not begin to run until the misdiagnosis is discovered.[38]

Under the discovery rule, lack of knowledge of the extent of one's injury generally does not delay the running of the period. Instead, the period begins to run as soon as the patient is, or should be, aware of any injury at all and its possible connection to malpractice.[39] In determining the point at which a patient should have discovered a cause of action for malpractice, the patient's experience, background, and medical skills may be taken into account. Thus a court may impute knowledge of injury to a health care professional who is a patient if, under the circumstances, the professional's special training should have revealed the injury to him or her. This is so even if the available facts would not indicate that anything was amiss to the typical patient.[40]

Determining whether or not a patient has exercised reasonable diligence in discovering an injury is a matter to be decided based on the facts of the particular case. It has been held, however, that a patient has exercised reasonable diligence if she relies upon repeated assurances of recovery made by the treating physician, when no apparent reasons to disbelieve the physician exist.[41]

Having stated the rule generally, it should be noted that some diversity of opinion exists regarding just what must be discovered for the limitations period to begin. A majority of jurisdictions following the rule hold that it is the patient's discovery of injury which is relevant.[42] A minority, however, count the limitations period from the date on which the patient either discovers, or through reasonable diligence should have discovered, the specific acts or omissions of the physician alleged to constitute malpractice.[43]

Certain other doctrines, independent of the date of injury and discovery rules, may toll, or postpone, the running of the statute. A number of states hold that the statute does not begin to run, regardless of the date of malpractice or the status of the patient's knowledge, until the physician-patient relationship ends.[44]

CASE ILLUSTRATION

The patient suffered a vesicovaginal fistula in connection with a panhysterectomy. More than one year after the operation, but less than a year after termination of the physician-patient relationship, the patient brought suit against the physician. The applicable statute established a one-year limitations period for malpractice actions. In refusing to hold the patient's action barred, the court noted that the patient had continued to have the greatest confidence in the physician and had continued treatment with him, including curative attempts for her injury, until a period less than one year before suit was brought. The court also set forth the rationale behind the physician-patient rule, stating that "while the physician-patient relationship continues, the plaintiff is not ordinarily put on notice of the negligent conduct of the physician upon whose skill, judgment, and advice he continues to rely. Thus, in the absence of actual discovery of the negligence, the statute does not commence to run during such period, and this is true even though the condition itself is known to the patient, so long as its negligent cause and its deleterious effect is not discovered" (*Rawlings v. Harris,* 1968).[45]

The patient-physician relationship is a strictly personal one. Thus the statute begins to run as soon as the physician has performed his or her last services for a particular patient. This rule applies when the patient relies upon the physician's referral to another physician or continues to use, without the physician's knowledge, a drug the physician prescribed.[46]

Some states, in refinement of this rule, follow the continuous treatment doctrine. In these states, the mere continuity of a professional relationship between a particular physician and patient is not sufficient to toll the statute. Instead, the statute is suspended only as long as the patient continues to be treated by the physician for the same condition or for a condition related to the one that occasioned the alleged act of malpractice.[47] However, most courts following the continuous treatment doctrine hold that the statute begins to run as soon as the patient discovers, or should have discovered, her injury and its connection to the negligent act.[48] Other courts may not make this exception.[49]

A physician's fraudulent concealment of the results of malpractice will also toll the statute. Thus, if a physician repeatedly and knowingly gives false assurances of recovery or absence of injury, this conduct will suspend the statute, even though without such assurances the patient would be charged with actual or imputed knowledge of injury.[50] Most courts hold that actual knowledge on the part of the physician of a wrong done the patient is essential to a finding of fraudulent concealment in a malpractice action.[51] The courts disagree, however, as to whether an affirmative act on the part of the physician is necessary for such a finding. Some jurisdictions will not find concealment unless knowingly false statements have been made to the patient,[52] while others hold as sufficient proof the fact that the physician failed to disclose material information in his or her possession.[53]

CASE ILLUSTRATION

Two and one-half years after undergoing a tubal ligation, the patient became pregnant. After the birth of her child, the patient brought suit, contending that the operation had been performed negligently and that the physician had knowledge of the negligence but had failed to tell her of it. Evidence at trial showed that, on the day after the operation, a surgical pathological report had been placed in the patient's file showing that the tubal ligation was not complete. The applicable statute of limitations required malpractice actions to be brought within three years of the allegedly negligent act. The court rejected the physician's argument that the statute barred the patient's action, holding that the alleged "fraudulent concealment" had tolled the running of the statute. The court noted that, while ordinarily fraudulent concealment will not be found in the absence of an affirmative act, the physician-patient relationship imposes a duty of disclosure upon the physician which can be breached by mere silence. The court, therefore, allowed the patient's suit to go forward under the general rule that "where the cause [of action] is harm to the injured party, but is of such character as to conceal itself from the injured party, the statutory limitation will not begin to run until the right of action is discovered, or, by the exercise of ordinary diligence, could have been discovered" (*Hardin v. Farris,* 1974).[54]

Courts applying the fraudulent concealment exception are not in agreement whether the statute begins to run on the date the patient actually discovers the fraud[55] or on the date she should have discovered it.[56]

Still other circumstances may toll an otherwise applicable statute of limitations. The statute cannot run against an individual who, at the time his or her cause of action accrued, had a "legal disability" such as mental incapacity[57] or infancy (any age below the age of majority)[58] and was thus unable to bring an action on his or her own behalf. The statute does not begin to run against such a disabled individual until the legal disability is removed by either the recovery of mental capacity[59] or the attainment of the age of majority.[60] Most state statutes require that actions be brought within a specified period after the removal of the legal disability. During the period of legal disability, an action may be brought on behalf of the disabled individual by either a parent or a guardian; such actions may also be used to recompense the parent or guardian for expenses paid in consequence of the disabled individual's injury.[61] However, a parent or guardian's failure to seek recovery for the individual's personal losses within the statutory period does not remove the disabled individual's right to recover his or her own damages.[62]

CASE ILLUSTRATION

The physician performed a cesarean section upon the patient on February 22, 1972. Thereafter, the patient became pregnant again. On October 22, 1974, approximately ten weeks before the expected delivery of her child, the patient suffered an occult rupture of the uterus. During the emergency cesarean section necessitated by the rupture, the patient's baby suffered a period of hypoxia or anoxia, or both, with resultant serious injuries and brain damage. On November 29, 1976, the patient and her husband brought suit against the physician who performed the original cesarean section, contending that his negligent performance of the operation had caused their son's injury. The court held that the parents' action for their own damages was barred by this failure to bring suit within two years of the allegedly negligent act, as required by the statute. The court, however, permitted the action for the infant's personal damages to proceed, holding that the child's minority had tolled the statute with respect to the claim (*Bergstreser v. Mitchell*, 1977).[63]

To toll the statute, the legal disability must exist at the time the cause of action accrues. A disability acquired subsequent to the accrual of the cause of action (as, for example, mental incapacity suffered after an act of malpractice has been discovered) will not toll the statute.[64] An exception may be made, however, if the injury for which recovery is sought caused the disability.[65]

In the event that a foreign object is mistakenly left in a patient's body by the physician, a foreign object rule will be applied in some states. Under this rule, the statute is suspended until the patient either discovers or should have discovered the presence of the object.[66] Although virtually the same as the discovery rule, the foreign object rule may be applied in jurisdictions that do not follow a discovery rule in other types of malpractice cases.[67] Most commonly, the rule is applied in situations where the object involved (for example, a sponge or forceps) was clearly not intended to have been left inside the patient's body.[68] A few jurisdictions however, have applied the rule in cases where the object involved was intentionally inserted in the patient's body but later broke or deteriorated.[69] As with the discovery rule, under the foreign object rule the statute begins to run as soon as the necessary discovery has been made. The fact that the patient may not be immediately aware of the full extent of her injury will not excuse a delay in bringing the action.

CASE ILLUSTRATION

The patient's third child was successfully delivered by the physician in October 1968. Some weeks later, the patient became aware of a large gauze surgical packing which had been left inside her body at the time of delivery. She removed this packing and brought it to the attention of the physician, who assured her that nothing was wrong. The patient's pain and bleeding continued, however, and two D&Cs, together with a variety of prescription drugs, were used to treat her, all to no avail. Finally, when the bleeding continued after delivery of the patient's fourth child, in June 1972, she underwent a complete hysterectomy. The patient brought suit on October 29, 1973. Although the applicable statute of limitations required malpractice actions to be brought within two years of the accrual of the cause of action, the patient contended that her cause of action did not accrue until she had suffered the "ultimate" damage resulting from the physician's alleged negligence—that is, the hysterectomy. The court, however, disagreed, stating that to "delay the commencement of the running of the statute of limitations until plaintiff's ultimate degree of damage becomes known would allow suits to be brought long after the event, contrary to the intent and purpose of such 'statutes'." Instead, said the court, under the foreign object rule the patient's cause of action accrued when she discovered the packing in late 1968. Because the patient had not brought her suit within two years of that discovery, the court held her action to be barred and entered judgment for the physician (*Patrick v. Morin*, 1975).[70]

In a majority of jurisdictions, any action brought by the survivors of a patient who dies in consequence of malpractice will be subject to the statutory period applicable in wrongful death actions, not to the period otherwise used in malpractice cases.[71] A wrongful death action allows the survivors of a person wrongfully killed or fatally injured to recover, on their own behalf, the net economic benefit they would have received from the decedent had he or she lived. Some jurisdictions also permit recovery of damages for loss of society and companionship in wrongful death actions, particularly where the decedent is a child and application of the traditional measure of damages would lead to no recovery at all.[72] The statutory period for wrongful death actions begins to run on the date of death, not on the date of injury leading to death.[73] In some states, however, the death of the patient does not by itself affect the statutory period.

In such states the survivor's action will be subject to the period generally used in malpractice cases.[74]

§ 3.60 RES JUDICATA AND COLLATERAL ESTOPPEL

To promote legal efficiency and economy, and for basic reasons of fairness, established doctrines exist which preclude a party from relitigating a cause of action or an issue which that party has previously litigated to final conclusion. Known as res judicata and collateral estoppel, these doctrines may be pleaded as a special defense in malpractice cases. As will be seen, these two rules of law are distinct and should not be confused.

The doctrine of res judicata states that a valid, final judgment rendered on the merits of the case constitutes an absolute bar to subsequent relitigation between the same parties, or those in privity* with them, of the same claim or demand.[75] As might be expected, problems can arise in individual cases when a plea of res judicata is interposed. Was the original decision based "on the merits" of the case? Did privity exist between the party sought to be precluded and one of the parties to the original suit? Is the present litigation based upon the same claim or demand as the original? For purposes of malpractice, the most important question raised by a plea of res judicata is the latter, and only that question will be given detailed consideration here.

Suppose, for example, a physician negligently uses a drug that causes injury to a patient's sight and hearing. The patient recovers damages for the injury to her sight in a malpractice action, but she does not plead injury to her hearing. Next, in a separate action, the patient seeks to recover for her hearing loss. Can she do so? No. Res judicata precludes relitigation not only of claims actually decided in an earlier action but also of claims that *should* have been determined in the earlier action.[76] Because the patient's claim for hearing loss arose out of the same negligent act as did her earlier claim for loss of sight, the two actions involved the same claim and should have been pleaded together in a single suit. Having failed to so plead, the patient is precluded from subsequently raising the hearing claim. Suppose in the second action the patient does not plead that the physician negligently injured her hearing, but that the physician breached a warranty that the drug would not injure her health. Does the availability to the patient of a second theory upon which recovery could be based get her past the bar of res judicata? No. The fact that the physician's act can be variously characterized does not defeat the identity of the claims.[77]

The doctrine of collateral estoppel, in contrast, applies to factual issues,

---

*Privity refers to a special relationship between parties that is recognized by law to exist when, by virtue of the transactions between the parties, they have mutual or successive rights or interests in the subject matter of the transaction.

not to claims. Collateral estoppel states that, where a question of fact essential to a judgment was actually litigated and determined by valid and final judgment, the issue cannot again be litigated between the same parties in any future lawsuit.[78] Thus collateral estoppel cannot be invoked to preclude litigation of matters that have not already been litigated.[79]

The effect of collateral estoppel might best be seen through a continuation of the example above. Suppose the physician, having been found negligent in the patient's action for loss of sight, brings an action against the patient to recover overdue payments. The patient pleads in defense that she owes no debt because the treatment was negligent. Need the patient once again prove the physician's negligence, or will the physician be permitted to offer proof that his or her actions were reasonable under the circumstances? No. Because the earlier finding of negligence was actually litigated and was necessary to the judgment (the physician could not have been held liable had he or she not been found negligent), the physician will be collaterally estopped from relitigating the issue of his or her negligence, and the patient need not prove the physician's negligence again.

A question of some importance in the law today is whether collateral estoppel may be invoked by someone who is neither a party to the original action nor in privity with someone who was. For example, if patient A successfully recovers from physician B on grounds that B was negligent in administering a certain drug, can patient C, who had the same condition as A and received the same drug from B, recover from B *solely* on the basis of the earlier judgment? Patient C may indeed be able to do so. The U.S. Supreme Court has recently indicated that such "offensive use of collateral estoppel," where the plaintiff seeks to foreclose the defendant from litigating an issue the defendant has previously litigated unsuccessfully in an action with another party, is generally permissible. In deciding whether special circumstances that would bar the use of offensive collateral estoppel exist, wide discretion is left in the hands of the trial judge.[80]

Defensive use of collateral estoppel occurs when a defendant seeks to prevent a plaintiff from asserting a claim that the plaintiff has previously litigated and lost against another defendant. Thus, if physician B is specifically found to have been not negligent in giving a certain drug to patient A, A will be collaterally estopped in attempting to prove physician C's negligence, if C gave A the same drug under the same conditions. Such defensive use of collateral estoppel is widely accepted.[81]

A basic point to remember in all questions of collateral estoppel is that a party not involved in the earlier action, whether in person or through privity, can *never* be collaterally estopped. As seen above, however, such a person may be able to *assert* collateral estoppel against a person who was involved in the earlier action.

§ 3.70 RELEASE FROM LIABILITY FORMS

Persons generally may not contract against the effects of their own negligence, and agreements that attempt to do so are invalid. This is particularly true where public policy requires the duties involved to be performed nonnegligently and when the party releasing his rights holds the weaker bargaining position. It has thus been established, by courts that have passed on the question, that a physician may not, in advance, relieve himself of liability for malpractice.[82] In other words, a contract between patient and physician signed prior to treatment in which the patient releases her right to recover damages in the event of malpractice is invalid and will not be enforced[83] (see Appendix A for an example of an invalid release form).

CASE ILLUSTRATION

Prior to undergoing an abortion, the patient signed a form purporting to release the physician from any legal liability associated with the operation. At a checkup following the operation, the physician assured the patient that "everything was fine." In fact, the patient was still pregnant, a fact she did not discover until it was too late to have another abortion. She gave birth a few months later. The patient sued the physician. At trial, the physician argued that the release form signed by the patient constituted a bar to her suit. The court, however, rejected this defense, holding that an exculpatory contract signed by a patient as a condition of receiving medical treatment is invalid as contrary to public policy and may not be pleaded as a bar to the patient's suit for negligence (*Olsen v. Molzen*, 1977).[84]

Release of liability forms may be given effect, however, if they are signed before the performance of an experimental and inherently dangerous surgical procedure or course of treatment. In such cases, parties may validly contract to exempt medical practitioners from liability for injuries that may arise as consequences of the nonnegligent, proper performance of the procedure. Thus an experimental procedure which, because of its inherent dangers, may ordinarily be in and of itself a departure from customary and accepted practice and thus possibly actionable as malpractice, even if performed in a nonnegligent manner, may be rendered unactionable by a release of liability form. Such an agreement will not, however, exempt the physicians involved from liability for any adverse consequences resulting from the negligent performance of a procedure.[85]

After malpractice has occurred, a patient may validly release her rights to recover in a lawsuit in return for a specified consideration. For any release to be valid, however, the person giving it must not be suffering any legal disability.[86] The release must not be obtained by fraud,[87] misrepresentation,[88] or duress.[89] A physician's knowingly false statements of absence of injury or probable recovery will invalidate a release if the patient entered into the agreement on the basis of those assurances.[90] Mutual mistake will also constitute sufficient grounds to set aside a release.[91] If, for example, both physician and patient believed at the time they executed the agreement that the patient's injuries were minor, but passage of time reveals the injuries to be serious, the release signed by the patient may not bar her action for malpractice.

NOTES

1. W. Prosser, Handbook of the Law of Torts § 65 (4th ed. 1971).
2. *Id.*
3. Kaspar v. Schack, 195 Neb. 215, 237 N.W.2d 414 (1976).
4. W. Prosser, *supra* note 1.
5. Steele v. Woods, 327 S.W.2d 187 (Mo. 1956).
6. Martineau v. Nelson, 311 Minn. 92, 247 N.W.2d 409 (1976).
7. Ray v. Wagner, 176 N.W.2d 101 (Minn. 1970).
8. Martineau v. Nelson, *supra* note 6.
9. Wells v. Women's Hosp. Found., 286 So.2d 439 (La. App. 1973); *writ denied*, 288 So.2d 646 (La. App. 1973).
10. Louisell & Williams, Medical Malpractice, § 9.03, 249–50 (1977).
11. Comment, Contributory Negligence as a Defense to Medical Malpractice in California, 8 U.S.F.L. Rev. 386 (1973) *citing* Champs v. Stone, 74 Ohio App. 344, 58 N.E.2d 803 (1944).
12. Sales v. Bacigaludi, 74 Cal. App.2d 82, 117 P.2d 399 (1941).
13. Bennett v. State, 49 Misc.2d 306, 299 N.Y.S.2d 288 (1969).
14. Bess Ambulance, Inc. v. Boll, 208 So.2d 308 (Fla. App. 1968).
15. Steele v. Woods, *supra* note 5.
16. Clark v. Piedmont Hosp., Inc., 117 Ga. App. 875, 162 S.E.2d 468 (1968).
17. W. Prosser, *supra* note 1, at 417.
18. *Id.* at 436.
19. Mackey v. Greenview Hosp., Inc., 587 S.W.2d 249 (Ky. 1979).
20. Ark. Stat. Ann., §§ 27-1763 – 27-1765 (1979); Colo. Rev. Stat. Ann. § 13-21-111 (Bradford Supp. 1980); Conn. Gen. Stat. Ann. §§ 52-572h (West Supp. 1981); Ga. Code Ann. §§ 94-703, 105-603 (Harrison 1968 & Supp. 1980); Hawaii Rev. Stat. § 663-31 (1976); Idaho Code Ann. §§ 6-801 to 6-806 (1979); Kan. Stat. Ann. §§ 60-258a, 60-258b (1976); Mass. Gen. Laws Ann., ch. 231 § 85 (Supp. 1980); Minn. Stat. Ann. § 604.01 (West Supp. 1981); Miss. Code Ann. § 11-7-15 (1972); Mont. Rev. Code §§ 58-607.1, 58-607.2 (1970 & Supp. 1977); Neb. Rev. Stat. § 25-1151 (1965); Nev. Rev. Stat. § 41.141 (1979); N.H. Rev. Stat. Ann. § 507:7-a (Supp. 1979); N.J. Stat. Ann. §§ 2A:15-5.1 to 2A:15-5.3 (West Supp. 1981–82); N.Y.Civ. Prac. Law §§ 1411 to 1413 (McKinney 1976); N.D. Cent. Code § 9-10-07 (1975); Okla. Stat. Ann., tit. 23 §§ 11, 12 (West Supp. 1980-81); Or. Rev. Stat., §§ 18.470 to 18.510 (1979); R.I. Gen. Laws Ann. §§ 9-20-4, 9-20-4.1 (Supp. 1980); S.D. Comp. Laws § 20-9-2 (1979); Tex. Stat. Ann. art. 2212a, §§ 1,2 (Vernon Supp. 1980–81); Utah Code Ann. §§ 78-27-37 to 78-27-43 (1977); Vt. Stat. Ann., Tit. 12 § 1036 (Supp. 1980); Wash. Rev. Code Ann. § 4.22.010 (Supp. 1981); Wyo. Stat. Ann. § 1-1-109 (1980).
21. *See, e.g.,* Kaatz v. State, 540 P.2d 1037 (Alaska 1975); Nga Li v. Yellow Cab Co., 13 Cal.3d 804, 532 P.2d 1226, 119 Cal. Rptr. 858 (1975); Placek v. City of Sterling Heights, 405 Mich. 638, 275 N.W.2d 511 (1979).

22. Miller v. Trinity Med. Center, 260 N.W.2d 4 (N.D. 1977).
23. Martineau v. Nelson, *supra* note 6.
24. Heller v. Medine, 377 N.Y.S.2d 100, 50 A.D.2d 831 (1975).
25. Bird v. Pritchard, 33 Ohio App.2d 31, 291 N.E.2d 769 (1973).
26. Mainfort v. Giannestras, 49 Ohio Op. 440, 111 N.E.2d 692 (1951).
27. Morrison v. MacNamara, 407 A.2d 555 (D.C. Cir. 1979).
28. D. Harney, Medical Malpractice 243 (1973).
29. Levett v. Etkind, 158 Conn. 567, 265 A.2d 70 (1969).
30. Munson v. Bishop Clarkson Mem. Hosp., 186 Neb. 778, 186 N.W.2d 492 (1971).
31. Mainfort v. Giannestras, *supra* note 26.
32. Los Alamos Med. Center v. Coe, 58 N.M. 686, 275 P.2d 175 (1954).
33. Bolen v. Bolen, 409 F. Supp. 1374 (W.D. Va. 1976); Cook v. Soltman, 96 Idaho 187, 525 P.2d 969 (1974); Laughlin v. Forgrave, 432 S.W.2d 308 (Mo. 1968); Olson v. St. Croix Valley Mem. Hosp., 55 Wis.2d 628, 201 N.W.2d 63 (1972).
34. Laughlin v. Forgrave, *supra* note 33; Peterson v. Roloff, 57 Wis.2d 1, 205 N.W.2d 699 (1973).
35. Teeters v. Currey, 518 S.W.2d 512 (Tenn. 1974); Vilord v. Jenkins, 226 So.2d 245 (Fla. App. 1969); Berry v. Branner, 245 Or. 307, 421 P.2d 996 (1966).
36. Teeters v. Currey, *supra* note 35.
37. Pearson v. Boines, 367 A.2d 653 (Del. Supp. 1976); *aff'd,* 386 A.2d 651 (Del. 1978).
38. Iverson v. Lancaster, 158 N.W.2d 507 (N.D. 1968).
39. Hulver v. United States, 562 F.2d 1132 (8th Cir. 1977); Patrick v. Morin, 345 A.2d 389 (N.H. 1975).
40. Jones v. Sugar, 18 Md. App. 99, 305 A.2d 219 (1973).
41. Toman v. Creighton Mem. St. Joseph's Hosp., 191 Neb. 751, 217 N.W.2d 484 (1974).
42. Hall v. Musgrave, 517 F.2d 1163 (6th Cir. 1975); Anguiano v. St. James Hosp., 51 Ill. App.3d 229, 9 Ill. Dec. 419, 366 N.E.2d 930 (1979); Tomlinson v. Siehl, 459 S.W.2d 166 (Ky. App. 1970); Teeters v. Currey, *supra* note 35.
43. Iverson v. Lancaster, *supra* note 38; Witherell v. Weimer, 77 Ill. App. 3d 582, 33 Ill. Dec. 43, 396 N.E.2d 268 (1979).
44. Lundberg v. Bay View Hosp., 175 Ohio St. 133, 23 Ohio Op. 2d 416, 191 N.E.2d 821 (1963).
45. Rawlings v. Harris, 265 Cal. App. 2d 452, 71 Cal. Rptr. 288 (1968).
46. Millbaugh v. Gilmore, 30 Ohio St. 2d 319, 59 Ohio Op. 2d 383, 285 N.E.2d 19 (1972); Fleishman v. Richardson-Merrell, Inc., 94 N.J. Super. 90, 226 A.2d 843 (1967).
47. Fonda v. Paulsen, 46 A.D.2d 540, 363 N.Y.S.2d 841 (1975).
48. Lopez v. Swyer, 15 N.J. Super. 237, 279 A.2d 116 (1971); *modified,* 62 N.J. 267, 300 A.2d 563 (1973).
49. Hundley v. St. Francis Hosp., 161 Cal. App. 2d 800, 327 P.2d 131 (1958).
50. Swope v. Printz, 468 S.W.2d 34 (Mo. 1968).
51. Kauchick v. Williams, 435 S.W.2d 342 (Mo. 1968).
52. Layton v. Allen, 246 A.2d 794 (Del. 1968).
53. Hardin v. Farris, 87 N.M. 143, 530 P.2d 407 (1974).
54. *Id.*
55. Seitz v. Jones, 370 P.2d 300 (Okla. 1961).
56. Hardin v. Farris, *supra* note 53.
57. Jaime v. Neurological Hosp. Ass'n, 488 S.W.2d 641 (Mo. 1973).
58. Bergstreser v. Mitchell, 448 F. Supp. 10 (E.D. Mo. 1977).
59. Seymour v. Lofgreen, 209 Kan. 72, 495 P.2d 969 (1972).

Notes: Chapter III

60. Ferguson v. Cunningham, 556 S.W.2d 164 (Ky. App. 1977); Canterbury v. Spence, 464 F.2d 772 (D.C. Cir. 1972).
61. Bergstreser v. Mitchell, *supra* note 58.
62. *Id.*
63. *Id.*
64. Roman v. A. H. Robins Co., 518 F.2d 970 (5th Cir. 1975).
65. Chartener v. Kice, 270 F. Supp. 432 (E.D. N.Y. 1967).
66. Flanagan v. Mount Eden Gen. Hosp., 24 N.Y.2d 427, 301 N.Y.S.2d 23, 248 N.E.2d 871 (1969); Berry v. Branner, *supra* note 35; Billings v. Sisters of Mercy, 86 Idaho 485, 389 P.2d 259 (1964).
67. Shrewsbury v. Smith, 511 F.2d 1058 (6th Cir. 1975).
68. Billings v. Sisters of Mercy, *supra* note 66; Spath v. Morrow, 174 Neb. 38, 115 N.W.2d 581 (1962).
69. Murphy v. St. Charles Hosp., 35 A.D.2d 64, 312 N.Y.S.2d 978 (1974).
70. Patrick v. Morin, *supra* note 39.
71. Lambert v. Mitchel, 364 So.2d 248 (La. App. 1978); Jones v. Black, 539 S.W.2d 123 (Tenn. 1976).
72. Selders v. Armentrout, 100 Neb. 275, 207 N.W.2d 686 (1973).
73. Larcher v. Wanless, 18 Cal.3d 646, 135 Cal. Rptr. 75, 557 P.2d 507 (1976).
74. Weiss v. Bigman, 84 Mich. App. 487, 270 N.W.2d 5 (1978).
75. Saylor v. Lindsay, 391 F.2d 965 (2nd Cir. 1968).
76. Tutt v. Doby, 459 F.2d 1195 (D.C. Cir. 1972).
77. Forman V. Wolfson, 327 Mass. 341, 98 N.E.2d 615 (1951).
78. Sanders v. State, 242 So.2d 412 (Miss. 1970).
79. Adfigian v. Harron, 297 F. Supp. 1317 (E.D. Pa. 1969).
80. Parklane Hosiery Co. v. Shore, 439 U.S. 322 (1979).
81. *Id.*
82. Belshaw v. Feinstein, 258 Cal. App. 2d 711, 65 Cal. Rptr. 778 (1968).
83. Olsen v. Molzen, 558 S.W.2d 429 (Tenn. 1977); Meiman v. Rehabilitation Center, Inc., 444 S.W.2d 78 (Ky. 1969).
84. Olsen v. Molzen, *supra* note 83.
85. Colton v. New York Hosp., 414 N.Y.S.2d 866 (N.Y. Sup. 1979).
86. Fleming v. Ponquiani, 24 N.Y.2d 105, 299 N.Y.S.2d 134, 247 N.E.2d 114 (1969).
87. Brady v. Johnson, 512 S.W.2d 359 (Tex. Cir. App. 1974).
88. Hendricks v. Simper, 24 Ariz. App. 415, 539 P.2d 529 (1975).
89. Hylton v. Phillips, 270 Or. 760, 529 P.2d 906 (1974).
90. Central of Georgia Ry. Co. v. Ramsey, 275 Ala. 7, 151 So.2d 725 (1962).
91. *Id.*

Chapter IV

The Lawsuit in Court

§ 4.10 INTRODUCTION

When patients feel they have suffered an injury due to the malpractice of a physician, they may retain legal counsel to investigate the treatment received or file a lawsuit alleging malpractice against the physician, or both. The purpose of such lawsuits is to recover money damages (see § 1.60, Damages) from the physician for the injury caused by the alleged medical malpractice.

Although the courtroom, the suit, and the attendant proceedings are primarily the responsibility of the physician's attorney,* physicians are well advised to familiarize themselves with the mechanics of malpractice suits and the ways of the courtroom. The following delineates a general background, which should prove helpful to any physician confronted with a malpractice suit. References to the Federal Rules will indicate the procedure followed in a majority of courts.†

§ 4.20 PLEADINGS

Pleadings—the patient's complaint and the physician's answer—constitute the first official stage of a lawsuit. They are documents prepared by the attorneys for both parties, and their filing instigates the suit. Essentially, pleadings provide the mechanism that defines the legal and factual issues of the lawsuit. In pleadings, allegations of fact and assertions of law may be presented and sharpened into focus. By the effective use of pleadings, parties may eliminate irrelevant and uncontested claims at the outset of the suit. By the end of the pleading

---

*Usually the attorney representing the physician is chosen and paid for by the physician's malpractice insurance carrier. Increasingly, however, physicians are personally retaining counsel to work with the counsel provided by the insurance company to ensure that their personal interests are protected in the event that the interests of the physician and the insurance company diverge.

†The Federal Rules of Civil Procedure, first adopted in 1938, govern procedure in all federal courts. About half the states have adopted these rules virtually unchanged, and all the others have revised their procedure under the Rules' influence. *See* C. Wright, Law of Federal Courts 294 (3d ed. 1976).

stage, a reasonably accurate blueprint of the issues to be raised and argued at trial will have been established. This serves both the interests of the parties and of the court because it facilitates the efficient resolution of those issues that are truly contested or in doubt.

§ 4.21 The Patient's Complaint

The first step for the patient-plaintiff's attorney in bringing a legal action against a physician-defendant is drafting and filing a complaint. The basic purpose of the complaint is to set forth information. Under the Federal Rules, the essential concern is whether the complaint reveals enough information to allow the physician to respond and to understand the reason for the suit. The usual standard is that the patient-plaintiff must state a claim showing that he or she is entitled to some relief.[1] The Federal Rules system is called notice pleading because its primary concern is that the contents of the complaint give sufficient notice of the suit to the defendant; notice pleading generally avoids elaborate rules. (See Appendix B for a sample complaint.)

Some states require fact pleading, in which the patient must state the essential facts of the case with enough specificity to inform the physician of what the patient proposes to prove in court. This requirement is designed to give the physician (and the attorney) the information necessary to prepare a defense early in the suit. Under notice pleading, the physician would have later access to this information in the discovery phase (see § 4.30, Discovery), which occurs after the pleadings are filed.

§ 4.22 The Physician's Answer

After the plaintiff's complaint has been filed, the physician has a specified time within which to file an answer. Under the Federal Rules,[2] the physician must respond within 20 days. Some states, such as California,[3] allow a longer period (30 days), while others, such as Washington,[4] have a significantly shorter requirement (ten days). (See Appendix B for a sample answer.)

In the answer, the defendant takes issue with the plaintiff and the plaintiff's assertions of fact and law. The defendant may admit certain factual allegations set forth in the plaintiff's complaint (yes, the physician-defendant did treat the patient-plaintiff) and deny others (no, the actions of the physician-defendant were not negligent). As a general rule, a defendant's failure to deny a fact set forth in the complaint constitutes an admission of that fact. The physician's attorney is responsible for responding appropriately to the plaintiff's complaint.

Denials of the facts set forth by the complaint constitute negative defenses. The defendant should also raise affirmative defenses in the answer. Affirmative defenses are claims that other factual circumstances exist which, if proven, would exonerate the defendant, even if the facts alleged by the complaint are true. For instance, a physician may assert as an affirmative defense that the plaintiff-patient assumed the risk of injury when he or she consented to the proposed treatment with full knowledge of the attendant risk of injury (see § 3.40, Assumption of Risk).

§ 4.30 DISCOVERY

Following, or sometimes during, the pleadings stage, the parties may begin discovery. The discovery process entails essentially what its name implies: a discovery of the facts and evidence relevant to the upcoming trial. The American legal system provides a number of mechanisms by which to achieve this goal, including depositions, written interrogatories, subpoenas for production of documents and things, and physical examination.

The avowed purpose of discovery is straightforward: to simplify and clarify the issues and to provide accurate information in advance of the trial. Courts tend to construe discovery requests liberally in order to enable the parties to identify the true facts and circumstances of the case. Liberal discovery serves several purposes. It enables the parties to gather all of the relevant facts and evidence so that each can present the best possible case at trial. Also, the discovery process serves to minimize the chance that one party's ignorance of key facts or an opponent's surprise presentation of unknown evidence will defeat the truth-finding goal of the trial court. Full and open disclosure of facts also encourages settlements, where appropriate. If discovery indicates that one party is likely to prevail at trial, a settlement may save both the court and the parties the additional time, effort, and expense of trial.[5]

Another use of discovery, although illegitimate, may be the harassment of an opponent. Each party is given wide latitude in determining the extent of discovery necessary; abuse of that discretion can subject an opponent to great expenditures of time and money. For example, one party may flood an opponent with hundreds of far-reaching written interrogatories (see § 4.33, Written Interrogatories) in the hope of discovering something important (a "fishing expedition"), while at the same time subjecting the opponent to great effort and cost.

§ 4.31 Depositions

A primary discovery mechanism is the deposition. A deposition is the record of the sworn testimony of a party or a witness taken before an authorized individual, usually an officer of the court;[6] it may be taken after the commencement of an action in any court. All parties and their attorneys have the right to be present and to examine and cross-examine the witness.

Depositions serve several purposes. They develop evidence for use at trial: when a witness will be unable to appear at the trial, the deposition serves as a means of preserving the witness's testimony.[7] Such testimony is entitled to the same consideration by the finder of fact as testimony given in open court.[8] Also,

§ 4.31   Depositions   167

deposition testimony can serve as evidence to impeach the testimony of the witness who actually appears at the trial and contradicts his or her deposition testimony.[9] Depositions primarily enable a party to discover and preserve evidentiary information.[10]

There are three fundamental limitations on the scope of examination under the Federal Rules:[11]

1. The information must be nonprivileged (see § 4.46, The Physician-Patient Privilege).
2. The information must be admissible under the rules of evidence or reasonably calculated to lead to discovery of admissible evidence.
3. The information must be relevant to the subject matter involved in the pending action.

If a deponent refuses to answer based on one of the above three limitations, the court may order the deponent to answer.[12] Deponents should not refuse to answer for insubstantial reasons, for if the refusal is without justification the refusing party may be required to pay the expenses incurred by the examining party in obtaining the order to compel an answer.[13]

Under the Federal Rules, a litigant may discover certain facts known and opinions held by experts the other party intends to call as witnesses or, under certain circumstances, experts the party has retained in anticipation of or to help prepare for the suit.[14] One party can require the other party to identify in written interrogatories (see § 4.33, Written Interrogatories) each expert witness, to state the substance of the facts and opinions on which the expert is expected to testify, and to summarize the grounds for each opinion. The court may also allow further discovery of expert witnesses by other means, such as oral deposition.[15] For an expert retained in anticipation of or in preparation for the suit, but not as a potential witness, the opposing party may discover the expert's facts and opinions only upon showing that it would be impracticable to obtain facts and opinions on the same subject by other means.[16]

In a suit, such as a malpractice action, where the mental or physical condition of the patient is at issue, the physician may request a court order to require the patient to submit to a physical or mental examination.[17] If the court orders the examination, the patient can obtain by discovery the detailed written report of the examining physician, including findings, test results, diagnosis, and conclusions.[18] The party requesting discovery in these situations must pay the expert a reasonable fee for time spent responding to the discovery request "unless manifest injustice would result."[19] In some cases the discovering party must also pay a portion of the fees and expenses the other party incurred in obtaining facts and opinions from the expert.[20]

Federal discovery rules concerning experts attempt to facilitate the presentation and clarification of issues at trial while guarding against the danger that one party will unfairly use the other party's experts to prepare his or her own case.

Some states allow pretrial discovery of experts only at the trial court's discretion.[21] The judge may require the deposing party to pay the expert a reasonable fee for the time involved.[22] In at least one state, Michigan, the state appellate court has ruled that a physician has a property right in his or her professional opinion and need not divulge it even under subpoena.[23]

§ 4.32 Subpoena

A subpoena is an order issued under the seal of the court which commands an individual to attend and give testimony at the time and the place specified.[24] Physicians may resent having to appear in response to a subpoena; some feel a written statement should suffice. However, the American legal system, with its adversarial focus, places a great premium on the face-to-face confrontation of witnesses and the right of cross-examination. This is reflected in the fact that failure to obey a subpoena may subject the subpoenaed individual to a contempt of court citation or other consequences.*

If the physician is subpoenaed on behalf of the party opposing his or her patient, the physician should inform the patient and the patient's attorney. If the state in which the suit is filed honors the physician-patient privilege, the patient's attorney may want to quash the subpoena.

§ 4.33 Written Interrogatories

Written interrogatories are similar to depositions in purpose and scope. Parties may use written interrogatories, like depositions, to take the testimony of any person, including another party, in order to discover information or to use the written information as evidence in the action.[25] Written interrogatories are basically what the name implies. The discovering party drafts a list of written questions; this is sent to the opposing party or witness, who then returns the written answers to the discovering party.

§ 4.34 Production of Documents and Things

Discovery procedures also give a party the right to inspect relevant documents and tangible objects that may be held by or in the possession of an opposing party or witness.[26] If the opposing party refuses to deliver the materials upon

---

*Individuals found to be in contempt of court may be ordered to appear again, to be fined, or to be jailed until they comply with the court's order. Other consequences, where the noncomplying person is a party to the action, include the staying of all further proceedings until the party complies; striking all or part of that party's pleadings; considering the matter which the order dealt with to be established in favor of the party obtaining the order; and requiring the disobedient party to pay all reasonable expenses, including attorney's fees, caused by the failure. *See* Fed. R. Civ. P. 37(b).

§ 4.40 Evidence and Witnesses

request, the discovering party may seek a court order compelling inspection.[27] Generally, the same rules apply to court orders compelling inspection as to orders (subpoenas) compelling depositions. For example, if a state has a statute establishing the physician-patient privilege, a patient may assert the privilege to withhold certain information from the defendant-physician. Under the privilege, the patient could prevent the physician-defendant from inspecting medical records and from directly questioning (by deposition) the patient's other physicians about the injury at issue in the case (see §§ 1.31, The Physician-Patient Relationship and 4.46, Physician-Patient Privilege).

Under the generally recognized work product exception, a party may not ordinarily obtain documents, or work products, prepared in anticipation of litigation or for trial by or for the party. This exception includes work products of the party's attorney, consultant, insurer, or agent. However, if the discovering party can show a substantial need for the materials and that he or she cannot obtain the equivalent of the materials without undue hardship, the court, under the Federal Rules, may order discovery of the requested work products. The Federal Rules also require the court, when ordering discovery, to protect against disclosure of the mental impressions, opinions, or legal theories of an attorney concerning the case.[28]

§ 4.35 Physical Examinations

Under the Federal Rules, a physician-defendant may request the court to require the plaintiff to submit to a physical examination by a physician in order to ascertain the nature, extent, and permanency of any alleged injuries. The decision, however, lies within the discretion of the trial court.[29] To obtain the order, the physician must show that the patient's physical condition is in contention and that the physician has "good cause" to request an examination. Should the trial court order an examination, the plaintiff may have the right to have his or her own physician and attorney present at the examination. If the patient refuses to comply with the court order, he or she may suffer the same consequences as failing to comply with orders to appear for depositions (subpoenas) or to produce documents.

§ 4.36 Protective Orders

Under the Federal Rules, a party may request the court to issue a protective order forbidding or modifying the opposing party's right to discovery of certain matters.[30] The requesting party must show a substantial reason for this, such as protection from annoyance, embarrassment, oppression, or undue expense.

§ 4.40 EVIDENCE AND WITNESSES

In bringing an action for medical malpractice, the patient-plaintiff has the burden of proving by a preponderance of the evidence that the physician violated the requisite standard of care* (see § 1.20, Elements of Negligence). In some jurisdictions, where the doctrine of res ipsa loquitur is recognized (see § 1.52, Res Ipsa Loquitur), the burden may shift to the physician-defendant. In either situation, the physician's testimony, medical records, and other materials prepared in the course of treating the patient may be pertinent to the trial of the case and therefore essential to meeting the burden of proof. Specific legal rules governing the admissibility, presentation, and availability of these items of evidence may affect the outcome of the lawsuit.

§ 4.41 Expert Testimony

As a general rule of evidence, the testimony of the nonexpert witness at a trial is limited to facts and circumstances within his or her own observation, knowledge, or recollection. This basic rule limits the witness's testimony to those facts directly perceived by the witness, as distinguished from opinions, inferences, impressions, or conclusions. The trier of fact, whether judge or jury, must draw conclusions based upon the factual testimony of the witness.

Sometimes, however, the judge or the jury may not be able to derive valid conclusions from factual testimony if that testimony is of a technical nature and involves a subject beyond the comprehension of the layman not schooled in the subject. This is the case with complex medical issues. In these situations, the layman is not equipped by common knowledge and experience to reach accurate judgments and needs the assistance of expert testimony. If the court determines that specialized knowledge will assist the trier of fact in understanding the evidence or in determining the issues of the case, a witness qualified as an expert may testify by giving factual information or an opinion on the subject.[31]

As a general rule, expert testimony is essential to support a cause of action for malpractice.[32] Often, expert testimony is a prerequisite to the patient's right to recover for the alleged malpractice of either a physician or a hospital.[33] Expert testimony is necessary to establish both the appropriate standard of care and the physician-defendant's violation of that standard[34] (see § 1.32, Standard of Care). This requirement for expert testimony is predicated upon the belief that, in cases involving professional service, the layman is not equipped by common knowledge and experience to judge the skill and competence of that service nor to determine whether it conforms with the appropriate standard of medical practice.

The determination of whether a witness qualifies as an expert is left to the discretion of the trial court judge.[35] In most jurisdictions a witness may be classified as an expert on the basis of knowledge, skill, experience, training, or education.[36] There is, however, no presumption that a witness is competent to

---

*This is the general standard for all tort cases in which a plaintiff alleges that the defendant breached a standard of care and that the breach caused the plaintiff harm. Most malpractice cases come under tort law.

qualify as an expert; therefore, the party offering the witness must show that the witness has the necessary qualifications.

As a general rule, any licensed physician is considered to be a medical expert. References to membership in medical societies, appointments, published books or articles, or honors and recognitions, however, may have bearing on the *weight* the trier of fact will give the expert testimony.

Expert Witness Fees: It is ethical and legal for physicians to accept compensation for their services as expert witnesses. The exception to this general rule is the contingent-fee arrangement, in which the physician-witness's fee depends on the outcome of the litigation. This arrangement is unethical because it undermines the physician's impartiality and distorts the truth-finding process of the trial. Contingent fees are also likely to detract from a witness's professional credibility and to cast great doubt on the reliability and veracity of his or her testimony. Expert witnesses may legitimately be cross-examined as to their interest in the case and may be asked if the fee payment depends on the outcome of the case.[37] Expert witnesses should be frank in their responses and not hide the facts surrounding their compensation.

Preparation for Trial: Preparation for the trial is imperative. Examination of the injured party, preparation of a medical report, and a review of the relevant technical literature may all be necessary to assure informed and effective testimony at trial. This preparation also diminishes the potential for embarrassment when the predictable cross-examination comes.

The expert witness should meet before the trial with the attorney for the party who has asked him or her to testify. Such meetings are completely legitimate and are vital to an effective presentation of the expert's testimony. Attorneys should not tell their expert witnesses what their opinions should be, and expert witnesses should not change their testimony to satisfy the attorney. It is proper, however, for attorneys to ask that answers be responsive to the questions asked and that witnesses not volunteer answers where no question has been asked.

The Expert Witness and the Witness Stand: Generally, under the rules of evidence and courtroom procedure there are two types of witness interrogation: direct examination and cross-examination. There are defined limits to the proper nature and scope of questions for each type of interrogation.

Direct examination takes place when one side calls an individual to the witness stand. Questions asked under direct examination may be specific or general, calling for a freer narrative, but should not be leading. A leading question is one that strongly suggests a specific answer to the witness. Attorneys are not ordinarily allowed to use leading questions on direct examination, except under the discretionary approval of the trial judge.[38]

After direct examination by the attorney who called the witness to the stand, opposing counsel cross-examines the same witness. The rules governing cross-examination are less restrictive than those for direct examination and generally allow leading questions.[39] However, the examining attorney must usually restrict questions to the subject matter of the direct examination and to matters relating to the credibility of the witness.[40]

The trial judge plays an important role in supervising the proceedings. The Federal Rules explicitly require the judge to exercise reasonable control over the interrogation of the witnesses to make the interrogation an effective tool in a search for truth and to protect witnesses from harassment or undue embarrassment.[41]

During the trial, expert witnesses are called to the stand by the attorney for the party who has engaged their services. Through direct examination, the attorney questions the expert in order to present the expert's knowledge and opinion to the trier of fact. This is a relatively straightforward process, and if the attorney and expert are properly prepared the expert will be familiar with the questions and will give answers consistent with those given in the past (that is, at deposition or in preparation for trial).

Experts may relate their findings and opinions or respond to hypothetical questions relevant to the medical issues in the case (see § 4.43, Hypothetical Questions and Opinion Testimony).

After direct examination, the counsel for the opposing party will cross-examine the expert witness. This is likely to be the most trying time for the expert witness.

The purpose of cross-examination is to test the expert, the expert's testimony, or the basis of the expert's testimony. In theory this testing process is the adversary system's mechanism for finding the truth. Too often, however, truth gets lost in the testing, and legitimate experts with legitimate opinions feel confounded and attacked. A cross-examining attorney may employ a number of unpleasant techniques in his or her attempt to establish that the witness's knowledge is inadequate or unsound or that the witness is partisan. In this respect the attorney is motivated by his or her ethical duty to employ all available legal means in representing the client's interest in court.[42]

Experts should be prepared for bullying, rude, and rough cross-examinations. They may have to contend with shouting and finger-pointing. Some attorneys choose less harsh tactics, such as questions intended to disturb the witness. Questions about the compensation to be received for testifying are traditional. Cross-examining counsel may pose a series of questions necessitating the recall of picayune medical facts that the expert has had no need to recall since medical school. The attorney may ask the expert a long series of questions requiring an affirmative answer, thus giving the impression of agreement.

In response to such techniques, expert witnesses should remain as calm as possible and answer the questions as honestly as possible. This may be difficult, because courtroom procedure often obfuscates the truth. The best way to counter these difficulties is to anticipate them through pretrial preparation and open

§ 4.41   *Expert Testimony*   173

communication between the expert witness and counsel for the party who engaged the expert's services.

The law department of the American Medical Association has formulated the following guidelines for the physician preparing for an appearance in court:[43]

1. *Do* take the role of the medical witness seriously. The courtroom is a place in which practical men are engaged in the serious work of endeavoring to administer justice. The role of the medical witness is a key one in this endeavor.

2. *Don't* agree to or accept compensation for your services contingent upon the outcome of litigation. This practice is unethical, and disclosure of it would be apt to destroy the value of your testimony.

3. *Do* insist on preparation for your testimony in consultation with the attorney for the party who called you as a witness. He should advise you on what to expect on cross-examination. You have a right to consult with the party and his attorney about the case, so don't be embarrassed if asked about such consultations.

4. *Don't* act as an advocate or partisan in the trial of the case. If the attorney for the party who calls you as a witness needs the advice or guidance of a doctor during the trial, let him employ someone else. Disclosure of partnership of a witness strongly tends to discredit his testimony.

5. *Do* be as thorough as is reasonably necessary under the circumstances in examining a party in preparation for trial. Exhaustion of all possible tests and procedures may not be required, but be prepared to justify any omission.

6. *Don't* exaggerate. Any attempt to puff up your qualifications or to elaborate the extent of the examination you have made is apt to expose you to embarrassment.

7. *Do* inform the attorney for the party who calls you as a witness of all unfavorable information developed by your examination of the party as well as the favorable information.

8. *Don't* try to bluff. If you don't know the answer to a question, don't guess. If you guess wrong, you may be falling into a trap.

9. *Do* be frank about financial arrangements with the party who called you as a witness, with respect to your compensation for both treatment given and services in connection with the litigation.

10. *Don't* regard it as an admission of ignorance to indicate that your opinion is not absolutely conclusive or that you don't have the answer to a particular question. Honesty may frequently require testimony of this nature.

11. *Do* answer all questions honestly and frankly. Any display of embarrassment or reluctance to answer will tend to discredit your testimony.
12. *Don't* use technical terminology which will not be understood by the jury, the attorney, or the judge. If technical terms are unavoidable, explain them as best you can in the language of the layman.
13. *Do* be willing to disagree with so-called authorities if you are convinced they are wrong. If you have sound reasons for disagreement, the contrary opinion of authorities will not necessarily discredit you.
14. *Don't* be smug. A jury is quite likely to react adversely to an attitude of this nature. A modest attitude on the part of the witness is apt to elicit a more favorable response. Leave it to the attorney to bring out your special qualifications.
15. *Do* be courteous, no matter what the provocation. If a cross-examining attorney is discourteous to you, this is apt to win sympathy for you from the jury, provided you don't descend to the same level.
16. *Don't* lose your temper. If a cross-examining attorney can provoke you to a display of anger or sarcasm, he has already substantially succeeded in discrediting your testimony.
17. *Do* pause briefly before answering a question asked on cross-examination, to give the other attorney an opportunity to object to the question if he so desires. Taking a moment for deliberation before answering a question does not indicate uncertainty or embarrassment.
18. *Don't* allow yourself to be forced into a flat yes or no answer if a qualified answer is required. You have a right to explain or qualify if that is necessary for a truthful answer.

§ 4.42 Court-Appointed Expert

To mediate conflict in expert testimony, the trial judge may, at his or her discretion, appoint an independent medical expert to testify.[44] In some cases this may add much to the truth-seeking process because it provides a neutral party in a potentially confusing and divided situation. Physicians are often more willing to testify as an officer of the court than as a partisan witness in a dispute.

If the court decides that an independent expert is needed, it may appoint an expert on its own or ask the opposing parties to nominate mutually agreeable candidates. Court-appointed experts are subject to deposition and cross-examination by both parties.

§ 4.43 Hypothetical Question and Opinion Testimony

As a general rule, witnesses qualified as experts may testify in the form of opinion. The hypothetical question is one of the standard means of eliciting opinion testimony. Basically, a hypothetical question is one that asks for an opinion on the basis of assumed facts.

At one time, physicians who had not treated the patient-plaintiff could not give testimony regarding that patient's treatment, diagnosis, or prognosis because they did not have first-hand knowledge. To skirt this problem, the law created a legal fiction—the hypothetical question. This fiction allows the attorney seeking the opinion to state a series of hypothetical facts that the expert is to assume are true. The expert may then state opinions based on those hypothetical facts. In practice, of course, the facts stated in the hypothetical question mirror the facts of the case under consideration.

A few states have significantly liberalized the restrictions on expert testimony;[45] in these states, much of the original rationale for the use of hypothetical questions is gone. However, attorneys still commonly employ hypothetical questions under both the liberalized and the more traditional rules, so physicians should have some understanding of this interrogation technique.

Once the court has qualified a witness as "expert," the examining attorney may ask hypothetical questions. In many states, the expert may stay in the courtroom during the taking of other testimony; then, when the expert testifies, the examining attorney can simplify the hypothetical question by asking the expert to assume the truth of the previous testimony,[46] or some specified part of it, and to base an opinion on that assumption. Where not grounded on other testimony in the case, hypothetical questions should contain the facts to be assumed by the expert witness and should be complete enough to allow the expert to form an opinion. The hypothetical question does not need to include *all* of the facts in the case, but the facts assumed must be supported by evidence in the case.[47] The hypothetical question must include all of the facts upon which the answer is based.[48] Some states require that the question include all material facts,[49] but the more widely prevailing view rejects that requirement.[50] Where the facts are in dispute, the attorneys posing the hypothetical question may base it on testimony supporting their client's theory of the case, although contradictory testimony may be called to the expert's attention on cross-examination by varying the hypothesis.[51] Although the facts assumed in the hypothetical question do not have to be in evidence at the time the question is posed, the examining counsel must give assurances that they will be.[52] However, on cross-examination, the examining attorney may usually use hypothetical questions to test the expert's skill and knowledge, even though the questions are not based on evidence in the case.[53]

Hypothetical questions are difficult for attorneys to frame, for courts to rule upon, and for juries to understand.[54] "[M]isused by the clumsy and abused by the clever, [they have] in practice led to intolerable obstruction(s) of truth."[55] As one critic put it, a hypothetical question is "perhaps the most abominable form of evidence that was ever allowed to choke the mind of a juror or throttle his intelligence."[56] The primary difficulty is with hypothetical questions not based on facts in evidence. Because these questions need not include all the facts in a case, those facts that are assumed as part of the hypothesis must somehow be drawn from the evidence; in complex trials, attorneys may, if not extremely careful, forget which facts are in evidence and which facts are not. In all of this, the trial court needs, and has, considerable discretion in passing on the propriety of hypothetical questions.[57]

§ 4.44 Textbooks

If the authors of medical textbooks or scholarly articles are not available for cross-examination in a trial, many state courts will not admit statements or extracts as independent evidence bearing on a medical issue in the case.[58] The Federal Rules are more liberal than this, so under some circumstances attorneys in federal court may read textbook materials into evidence.[59]

Most courts do permit attorneys to use learned materials in cross-examination when the witness has already relied on a particular treatise and the cross-examining attorney is attempting to show that the material does not, in fact, support the witness's position.[60] A number of courts also permit cross-examination from learned works other than the one the witness relied on to support his or her opinion. In these cases, once a witness cites a particular treatise as support for a medical opinion, the opposing attorney may use other established works to undermine the credibility of the witness's testimony.[61] A third group allows the cross-examiner to interrogate the witness from treatises the witness has recognized as authoritative in the field, regardless of whether the witness has based his or her opinion on the work in question.[62] A number of courts also allow attorneys on cross-examination to test the witness's competency or qualifications by using textbooks, whether or not he or she has relied on or recognized the authority of the text.[63] As with many questions of evidence and trial procedure, the judge generally has broad discretion in controlling the extent to which attorneys may use medical texts as tools for cross-examination.[64]

Although most states allow the introduction of professional literature only under the limited circumstances described above, there are strong arguments for relaxing the rules and allowing plaintiff and defendant to introduce treatises and texts as substantive evidence on issues of medical practice in the case.[65] Actually, the testimony of experts is often based on information from the professional literature. Allowing the literature into evidence directly could improve the quality of information available to judges and juries. In addition, the judicial emphasis on trustworthiness of evidence would be amply satisfied by the author's desire to write a text respected within the profession.

§ 4.45 Adverse Witness Provisions

In malpractice actions, problems arise when counsel for the physician-defendant chooses not to call the physician-defendant to the stand. Under the normal rules of evidence, if the plaintiff's counsel wanted to question the defendant on the witness stand, he or she would have to call the physician as an ordinary witness; counsel would therefore be limited by the rules of direct examination. This would put the plaintiff's counsel in a position far less advantageous than if he or she could question the physician-defendant in accord with the more liberal rules of cross-examination.

To combat the problem posed by the strict application of the rules of evidence, many states have adverse witness provisions in state statutes or practice rules. Adverse witness rules enable either party in a lawsuit to call the opposing party (or an employee or agent of the opposing party) to the witness stand and to engage in cross-examination.[66] If the plaintiff is permitted to use the testimony of the physician-defendant as the basis for establishing the fact of malpractice, as some courts allow,[67] the adverse witness rule is a very helpful tool for the plaintiff.

§ 4.46 Physician-Patient Privilege

The physician-patient relationship may be described as fiduciary in nature (see § 1.31, The Physician-Patient Relationship). Consequently, the American Medical Association advises physicians to safeguard patient confidences within the constraints of the law.[68] The law recognizes a legally enforceable duty on the part of the physician to maintain the confidentiality of information obtained during the course of the physician-patient relationship.[69] In legal parlance, physician-patient communication is viewed as privileged information: the privilege not to disclose such information is recognized by the law to assure that a patient may speak freely with the physician in procuring treatment. Even though recognized by the law, the physician-patient privilege is given limited application, particularly when the privileged information constitutes evidence in the litigation of a case.

The physician-patient privilege is a creature of state legislation.[70] In states without such a statute, physician-patient communications are not protected; where such statutes do exist, they have been held to extend to information contained in the patient's hospital record.[71] In many of the states that have privilege statutes, a physician ordinarily cannot give in evidence in a court of law information acquired in the discharge of professional duties. Because the privilege is said to belong to the patient, only the patient may waive, or give up, the privilege.[72] Patients may waive the privilege by failing to object to the taking of testimony on information protected under it. Thus, by inaction or inadvertance, patients may lose the statute's protection.

Some states have laws that require automatic waiver when the patient brings an action for personal injuries (such as those resulting from a car accident) or where the patient's physical or mental condition is at issue.[73] Several state courts have held that, under these laws, the patient waives the privilege for discovery proceedings as well[74] (see § 4.30, Discovery). As a result, before the trial a physician-defendant may obtain information regarding medical examinations by other physicians concerning the injury or condition at issue in the case. Other states have statutes providing that the patient necessarily gives up the privilege when he offers himself or any physician as a witness on his behalf in a suit involving personal injuries.[75] Some state courts have decided that, under these statutes, merely beginning a lawsuit involving a patient's physical condition does not mean automatic loss of the privilege.[76] In Michigan, for example, a patient suing for injuries may prevent the deposition of a physician on the basis of the physician-patient privilege, but the patient may not then use that physician as a witness. On the other hand, the patient may give up the privilege, allow the deposition, and use the physician as a witness.[77]

In the absence of a statute specifically governing the conditions of waiver, some state courts have held that the commencement of a personal injury suit, including malpractice, operates to end the privilege for the injuries at issue, both at trial and in discovery.[78] In other states, the courts have found that, in the absence of a specific statute defining conditions of waiver, beginning a suit involving the patient's physical condition does not necessarily operate automatically to cut off the patient's right to insist on the physician-patient privilege.[79] These courts have refused to permit the defendant to discover the patient's medical evidence prior to trial.

In states that have a statute creating the physician-patient privilege, a physician's breach of the privilege may result in legal liability. For example, if a physician wrongfully discloses information regarding a patient's medical condition (such as venereal disease), the patient may sue the physician for damages on a defamation theory (see § 2.60, Liability Arising from Medical Records). Generally, privileged information must not be disclosed without the patient's consent unless public interest or the patient's own interests require it.[80] Thus physicians have not been held liable for disclosing information to insurers[81] or to a third party where the communication discloses a danger to the third party.[82] Physicians should consult an attorney to determine whether their state has a privilege statute and scrupulously protect the confidences of their patients.

§ 4.47 Medical Records

Information in the patient's medical record is subject to laws protecting its confidentiality (see § 4.46, Physician-Patient Privilege), defining the property rights of those with an interest in it (see § 2.60, Liability Arising from Medical Records), and governing its admissibility as evidence in a court of law. Where such information is not privileged, the medical record that contains it is admissible in evidence, subject to the following legal considerations.

In order to assure that the trier of fact, usually the jury, hears both sides of a controversy, the law requires that each party have the opportunity to place a witness under oath, cross-examine the witness, and allow the trier of fact to observe the witness's demeanor on the witness stand. A medical record fails to meet these requirements. Statements on the record are not subject to cross-examination and may be viewed as hearsay,* which cannot be introduced into evidence. However, business records—records made in the regular course of business activity—are admissible as an exception to the hearsay rule in most jurisdictions, and medical records have been recognized as business records by most courts.

The inconvenience or impossibility of introducing certain records into evidence has led to legislation such as the Uniform Business Records Act. In a 1978 decision, a Pennsylvania court considered the admission into evidence of hospital or medical records. The court stated that hospital or medical reports are admissible as business records pursuant to the Uniform Business Records Act if the report meets the following criteria: (1) it is made contemporaneously with the events it purports to relate; (2) at the time it was prepared it was impossible to anticipate reasons for making a false entry into it; and (3) the person responsible for the statements contained in the report is known.[83] Most medical records meet these criteria, therefore it is usually a simple matter to enter medical records into evidence.

Once entered, the records often play a significant role in the evidentiary strategy of the plaintiff's attorney. This is especially true where records have been altered or tampered with. Often, physicians who are sued for malpractice, rather than first contacting an attorney or their insurance company for guidance, attempt to alter or obliterate any evidence in the medical record they consider damaging to their position. In the hands of a skillful plaintiff's attorney, the act of alteration often proves to be even more damaging than the original information. Where alteration is proved, it undermines physician-defendant's credibility and calls into question his or her motive in making the change.

CASE ILLUSTRATION

The patient consulted the physician, a general practitioner, about a lump in her breast. The physician performed no tests, nor did he suggest that she see a specialist. Rather, he told her that the lump was nothing to worry about. Without any significant examinations or tests, he continued to see the patient for an additional two years. The patient then consulted other physicians; a radical mastectomy was performed when a biopsy revealed that cancer had spread from the patient's breast through the lymph glands to the axilla and possibly to other parts of her body.

The patient sued the first physician. When requested during discovery to produce his original clinical records concerning his treatment of the

---

*Hearsay is evidence not proceeding from the witness's personal knowledge but from the repetition of what others were heard to say. It is inadmissible because its veracity is dependent upon the veracity of persons not subject to examination.

plaintiff, the physician-defendant was unable to do so. In answer to interrogatories, he stated that "the original records were recopied in a more legible form . . . said recopied records were taken verbatim from the original records and do constitute the same clinical record." The physician-defendant could not locate the original records and "assumed that they were thrown away." The patient's attorney had evidence that the recopied records were not consistent with the original records. To prevent any evidence of the altered records from being submitted to the jury, the physician admitted negligence. However, the physician denied proximate cause, the real issue in the case, and the patient-plaintiff lost the case on this issue.

The patient appealed the trial court decision. The court of appeals reversed the trial court's decision in favor of the physician and stated:

> The fact that defendant was unable to produce his original clinical record concerning his treatment of plaintiff after he had been charged with malpractice created a strong inference of consciousness of guilt on his part. He apparently claimed to have an innocent explanation: exact copying to make the records look more legible and inadvertent loss of the originals.
>
> . . . a party's . . . suppression of evidence by spoliation . . . is receivable against him as indication of his consciousness that his case is a weak or unfounded one; and from that consciousness may be inferred the fact itself of the cause's lack of truth and merit. The inference thus does not apply itself necessarily to any specific fact in the case but operates, indefinitely though strongly, against the whole mass of alleged facts constituting his cause.
>
> . . . the adversary's conduct may be considered as tending to corroborate the proponent's case generally and as tending to discredit the adversary's case generally.
>
> If defendant destroyed the records under a "consciousness of guilt," why should we assume that such consciousness was irrelevant on the issue of causation? What justifies a belief that his feeling of guilt was provoked only by professional embarrassment over the fact that he had been negligent? Is it not just as reasonable to assume that he had a bad conscience because as a result of that negligence his patient had been caused to suffer harm?

The court of appeals ordered the case to be retried (*Thor v. Boska*, 1974).[84]

Not only may intentional tampering be detrimental to the physician's position in a malpractice suit, but incomplete record keeping may also raise questions. In a 1964 decision, the Alaska Supreme Court stated that "careless habits of record keeping should be viewed as badges of suspicion respecting the accuracy of entries."[85]

In some jurisdictions, alteration or modification of the medical record may constitute a crime.[86] Furthermore, tampering may be held to warrant an award of punitive damages against the physician (see § 1.60, Damages).

It behooves the physician to maintain complete and accurate medical records. Any alterations that must be made due to human error should be entered legibly on the record, and edited, incorrect information should remain legible so as to avoid the appearance that the physician was trying to hide something in making the changes. This may be accomplished by drawing one line only through the statements to be deleted. Otherwise, the medical record, which is generally held to be admissible into evidence in most jurisdictions, could become a damaging piece of evidence that throws suspicion on the physician regardless of the quality of care provided the patient.

§ 4.50 COUNTERSUITS

Physician countersuits against patients or their attorneys are among the most controversial responses to the recent "medical malpractice crisis." In these suits, the physician-defendant in a medical malpractice case sues the patient-plaintiff or the patient-plaintiff's attorney, or both of them, after the physician-defendant has won a jury verdict or the trial court has dismissed the case for the patient-plaintiff's failure to state a cause of action.[87]

Physician-defendant countersuits may be brought on a number of legal theories, including defamation* (the physician claims the patient's wrongful suit injured the physician's reputation or character); malicious prosecution (the patient allegedly filed suit only to torment the physician and without any reasonable basis in fact to support the claim); and abuse of process (the patient or patient's attorney is alleged to have used the courts for a wrongful purpose).

In one of the first successful abuse of process cases, the Supreme Court of Nevada noted that, in order to prevail against the attorney or the patient, the physician must prove an ulterior purpose for bringing the suit and a willful act in the use of process not proper in the regular conduct of the proceeding.[88] Damages recoverable in this type of action include compensation for fears, anxiety, mental and emotional distress, injury to reputation, and inconvenience.[89]

The policy of American jurisprudence tends to protect patients, because the founding fathers valued highly the individual's right to have disputes heard in courts of law. Accordingly, American courts are reluctant to allow countersuits. They fear that recognizing such suits will frighten patient-plaintiffs out of exercising their constitutional right to have disputes heard in court. The counterbalancing policy of protecting physician-defendants from unwarranted suits has traditionally been viewed as of lesser value. However, where the intent or motivation of either the patient or the patient's attorney can be shown to be

---

*Generally, an attorney is absolutely privileged to make defamatory remarks concerning another person in communications preliminary to or during the course of a judicial proceeding or as a part of a judicial proceeding in which he or she participates as counsel, as long as the remarks have some relation to the proceedings. However, in *Bull v. McCuskey*, 615 P.2d 957, 961 (1980), the admission into evidence of the attorney's denigrating comments during the original trial was not reversible error.

malicious (for example, where it can be shown that the patient, because of spite, hate, or ill-will, disregards the rights and interests of the physician), courts may find in favor of the physician. The problem the physician confronts is one of proof. For example, unless the patient has gone on record, in writing or orally before reliable witnesses, the physician is hard put to prove that the patient was motivated by malice. Complicating the problem even further are attorneys' defenses that they owe no duty to the opposing parties and that their first duty is to advocate zealously the interests of their client (the patient). At least one state, Michigan, has adopted this rationale.[90]

Although countersuits are attractive to many physicians, the likelihood of bringing a successful countersuit today is not great. Further, few attorneys will file countersuits on behalf of physicians on a contingent fee basis because no countersuit has yet been won and affirmed at the appellate level. Accordingly, physicians desiring to bring countersuits against patients or their attorneys are usually required to pay substantial retainers, which tends to discourage such actions. It is possible, however, that physician countersuits may be more successful with the emergence of legal standards of care applicable to plaintiffs' malpractice attorneys.

NOTES

1. Fed. R. Civ. P. 8.
2. Fed. R. Civ. P. 12.
3. Cal. Civ. Proc. Code § 412.20 (West 1977).
4. Wash. Rev. Code § 4.28.060 (1974).
5. *See generally* Green, Basic Civil Procedure, ch. 6 (1979); James & Hazard, Civil Procedure § 6.2 (1977).
6. Fed. R. Civ. P. 29(c), (f).
7. *Id.* at 32(a)(3).
8. *Id.* at 32(a).
9. *Id.* at 32(a)(1).
10. *Id.* at 26(a).
11. *Id.* at 26(b)(1).
12. *Id.* at 37(a).
13. *Id.* at 37(a)(4).
14. *Id.* at 26(b)(4).
15. *Id.* at 26(b)(4)(A).
16. *Id.* at 26(b)(4)(B).
17. *Id.* at 35(a).
18. *Id.* at 35(b).
19. *Id.* at 26(a)(4)(C)(i).
20. *Id.* at 26(a)(4)(C)(ii).
21. Dow Chemical Co. v. Superior Court, 2 Cal. App. 3d 1, 82 Cal. Rptr. 288 (1969); Klabunde v. Stanley, 16 Mich. App. 490, 168 N.W.2d 250 (1969), *rev'd on other grounds,* 384 Mich. 276, 181 N.W.2d 918 (1970).
22. *See, e.g.,* J. Honigman & C. Hawkins, Michigan Court Rules Annotated, Rules 302.1, 306.2 (2d ed. 1963); State *ex rel.* Reynolds v. Circuit Court, 15 Wis. 2d 311, 112 N.W.2d 686 (1961), *rehearing denied,* 113 N.W.2d 537 (1962).

23. Klabunde v. Stanley, *supra* note 21.
24. Fed. R. Civ. P. 45.
25. *Id.* at 33.
26. *Id.* at 34.
27. *Id.* at 37(a).
28. *Id.* at 26(b).
29. *Id.* at 35(a).
30. *Id.* at 26(c).
31. *See, e.g.,* Har-Pen Truck Lines, Inc. v. Mills, 378 F.2d 705 (5th Cir. 1967); Pennsylvania Threshermen & Farmers Mut. Ins. Co. v. Messenger, 181 Md. 295, 29 A.2d 653 (1943); Swartley v. Seattle School Dist. No. 1, 70 Wash. 2d 17, 421 P.2d 1009 (1966); Fed. R. Evid. 702.
32. *See, e.g.,* Stephenson v. Kaiser Found. Hosp., 203 Cal. App. 2d 631, 21 Cal. Rptr. 646 (1962); Dimitrijevic v. Chicago Wesley Mem. Hosp., 92 Ill. App. 2d 251, 236 N.E.2d 309 (1968); Morgan v. State, 40 A.D.2d 891, 337 N.Y.S.2d 536 *aff'd*, 34 N.Y.2d 709, 313 N.E.2d 340, 356 N.Y.S.2d 860 (1972), *cert. denied*, 419 U.S. 1013 (1974).
33. *Id.;* Thomas v. Corso, 265 Md. 84, 288 A.2d 379 (1972); Bivens v. Detroit Osteopathic Hosp. 77 Mich. App. 478, 258 N.W.2d 527 (1977).
34. *See, e.g.,* Norden v. Hartman, 134 Cal. App. 2d 333, 285 P.2d 977 (1955); Lince v. Monson, 363 Mich. 135, 108 N.W.2d 845 (1961); Williams v. Chamberlain, 316 S.W.2d 505 (Mo. 1958).
35. *See, e.g.,* Fed. R. Evid. 104(a), 403, 702; Bronaugh v. Harding Hosp., Inc., 12 Ohio App. 2d 110, 231 N.E.2d 487 (1967).
36. *See, e.g.,* Fed. R. Evid. 702; Mich. R. Evid. 702.
37. *See, e.g.,* Fed. R. Evid. 611(b); 3A Wigmore, Evidence § 961 n. 2 (Chadbourn rev. 1970).
38. McCormick's Handbook of the Law of Evidence § 6 (2d ed. 1972); Fed. R. Evid. 611(c).
39. 3A Wigmore, *supra* note 37, at § 773; Fed. R. Evid. 611(c).
40. 6 Wigmore, Evidence §§ 1886–91 (3d ed. 1940); Fed. R. Evid. 611(b).
41. Fed. R. Evid. 611(a).
42. Model Code of Professional Responsibility, Canon 7 (1979).
43. Law Department of the American Medical Association, *Do's and Don't's for the Medical Witness,* Proceedings Medical-Legal Symposium, Miami Beach, Florida 277–79 (November 8–9, 1963).
44. *See, e.g.,* Hunt v. State, 248 Ala. 217, 27 So.2d 186 (1946); Citizens' Bank v. Castro, 105 Cal. App. 284, 287 P. 559 (1930); Fed. R. Evid. 706; Mich. R. Evid. 706.
45. *See, e.g.,* Mich. R. Evid. 703 (based on Fed. R. Evid. 703); Rabata v. Dohner, 45 Wis. 2d 111, 172 N.W.2d 409 (1969); Kan. Civ. Proc. Code Ann. § 60-456 (Vernon 1977); N.J.R. Evid. 57, 58; N.Y. Civ. Prac. Law § 4515 (McKinney 1976).
46. 2 Wigmore, Evidence § 681 (3d ed. 1940).
47. Barnett v. State Workmen's Compensation Comm'r. 153 Va. 796, 172 S.E.2d 698 (1970); Nisbet v. Medaglia, 356 Mass. 580, 254 N.E.2d 782 (1970).
48. *In re* Cottrell's Estate, 235 Mich. 627, 209 N.W. 842 (1928).
49. Stumpf v. State Farm Mutual Auto. Ins. Co., 252 Md. 696, 251 A.2d 362 (1969); Leitch v. Getz, 275 Mich. 645, 267 N.W. 581 (1936); Ames & Webb, Inc. v. Commercial Laundry Co., Inc., 204 Va. 616, 133 S.E.2d 547 (1963).
50. Virginia Beach Bus Line v. Campbell, 73 F.2d 97 (4th Cir. 1934); Pickett v. Kyger,

151 Mont. 87, 439 P.2d 57 (1968); Gordon v. State Farm Life Ins. Co., 415 Pa. 256, 203 A.2d 320 (1964).
51. *In re* McCord, 243 Mich. 309, 220 N.W. 710 (1928).
52. Gibson v. Healy Bros. & Co., 109 Ill. App. 2d 342, 248 N.E.2d 771 (1969); Barretto v. Akau, 51 Hawaii 383, 463 P.2d 917 (1969).
53. Randall v. Goodrich-Gamble Co., 244 Minn. 401, 70 N.W.2d 261 (1955); Seibert v. Ritchie, 173 Wash. 27, 21 P.2d 272 (1933); 2 Wigmore, *supra* note 46, at § 684.
54. Honigman, *The Hypothetical Question Meets Its Answer*, 36 Mich. St. B.J. 12 (Nov., 1957).
55. 2 Wigmore, *supra* note 46, at § 686.
56. Wellman, The Art of Cross-Examination 103 (4th ed. 1963).
57. *In re* Stephen's Estate, 244 Mich. 547, 222 N.W. 128 (1928).
58. *See, e.g.*, Salgo v. Leland Stanford Jr. Univ. Bd. of Trustees, 154 Cal. App. 2d 560, 317 P.2d 170 (1957); Noland v. Dillon, 261 Md. 516, 276 A.2d 36 (1971); O'Connell v. Williams, 17 Misc. 2d 296, 181 N.Y.S.2d 434 (1958).
59. Fed. R. Evid. 803(18).
60. *See, e.g.*, Hope v. Arrowhead & Puritas Waters, Inc., 174 Cal. App. 2d 222, 344 P.2d 428 (1959); Darlington v. Charleston Community Memorial Hosp., 50 Ill. App. 2d 253, 200 N.E.2d 149 (1964); Myers v. St. Francis Hosp., 91 N.J. Super. 377, 220 A.2d 693 (1966).
61. *See, e.g.*, Briggs v. Chicago Great Western Ry. Co., 238 Minn. 472, 57 N.W.2d 572 (1953); Farmers Union Federated Co-Op Shipping Ass'n v. McChesney, 251 F.2d 441 (8th Cir. 1958); Bruins v. Brandon Canning Co., 216 Wis. 387, 257 N.W. 35 (1934).
62. *See, e.g.*, Kaplan v. Mashkin Freight Lines, Inc., 146 Conn. 327, 150 A.2d 602 (1959); St. Petersburg v. Ferguson, 193 So.2d 648 (Fla. App. 1966); Jones v. Bloom, 388 Mich. 98, 200 N.W.2d 196 (1972).
63. *E.g.*, Superior Ice & Coal Co. v. Belger Cartage Service, Inc., 337 S.W.2d 897 (Mo. 1960); Iverson v. Lancaster, 158 N.W.2d 507 (N.D. 1968); Gravis v. Physicians & Surgeons Hosp., 415 S.W.2d 674 (Tex. Civ. App. 1967), *rev'd on other grounds*, 427 S.W.2d 310 (Tex. 1968).
64. *E.g.*, Darlington v. Charleston Community Mem. Hosp., *supra* note 60; Callaway v. Mountain State Mutual Casualty Co., 70 N.M. 337, 373 P.2d 827 (1962); Sutkowski v. Prosperity Co., 7 A.D.2d 660, 170 N.Y.S.2d 166 (1958).
65. *See* 6 Wigmore, *supra* note 40, at §§ 1690–92.
66. *See, e.g.*, Libby v. Conway, 192 Cal. App. 2d 865, 13 Cal. Rptr. 830 (1961); Loggin v. Morgenstern, 60 So.2d 732 (Fla. 1952); Argo v. Goodstein, 438 Pa. 468, 265, A.2d 783 (1970); Fed. R. Evid. 611(b).
67. *See, e.g.*, Daggett v. Atcheson, Topeka & Santa Fe Ry. Co., 48 Cal. 2d 655, 313 P.2d 557 (1957); Ferguson v. Gonyaw, 64 Mich. App. 685, 236 N.W.2d 543 (1975), *appeal denied*, 396 Mich. 817 (1976).
68. American Medical Association, *Principles of Medical Ethics*, § IV in Current Opinions of the Judicial Council of the American Medical Association (1981).
69. Horne v. Patton, 291 Ala. 701, 287 So.2d 824 (1974).
70. *See, e.g.*, Cal. Civ. Proc. Code § 1181 (West 1977); Cal. Penal Code § 1321; Cal. Evid. Code § 990-95 (West Supp. 1967); N.Y. Civ. Prac. Law §§ 352,354 (McKinney 1976); Ohio Rev. Code § 2317.02 (Page 1980).
71. State v. Bedel, 193 N.W.2d 121 (Iowa 1971).
72. *See, e.g.*, Koump v. Smith, 25 N.Y.2d 287, 250 N.E.2d 857, 303 N.Y.S.2d 858 (1969); Sagmiller v. Carlsen, 219 N.W.2d 885 (N.D. 1974).
73. *See, e.g.*, Cal. Evid. Code § 996 (West 1977).

Notes: Chapter IV

74. *See, e.g.,* Hall v. Superior Court, 20 Cal. App. 2d 652, 97 Cal. Rptr. 879 (1937); Lind v. Canada Dry Corp., 283 F. Supp. 861 (D. Minn. 1968) (applying Minn. law).
75. *See, e.g.,* Mich. Comp. Laws Ann. § 600.2157 (1968).
76. *See, e.g.,* Hardy v. Riser, 309 F. Supp. 1234 (N.D. Miss. 1970) (applying Miss. law); D. v. D., 108 N.J. Super. 149, 260 A.2d 255 (1969); Avery v. Nelson, 455 P.2d 75 (Okla. 1969).
77. Roe v. Cherry-Burrell Corp., 28 Mich. App. 42, 184 N.W.2d 350 (1970).
78. *E.g.,* Trans-World Investments v. Drobny, 554 P.2d 1148 (Alaska 1976); State *ex rel.* McNutt v. Keet, 432 S.W.2d 597 (Mo. 1968); Koump v. Smith, *supra* note 72.
79. *E.g.,* Bower v. Murphy, 247 Ark. 238, 444 S.W.2d 883 (1969); State *ex rel.* Lambdin v. Brenton, 21 Ohio St. 2d 21, 254 N.E.2d 681 (1970); Phipps v. Sasser, 74 Wash. 2d 439, 445 P.2d 624 (1968).
80. Horne v. Patton, *supra* note 69.
81. Conyers v. Massa, 512 P.2d 283 (Colo. App. 1973).
82. Tarasoff v. Regents of Univ. of California, 13 Cal.3d 177, 529 P.2d 553, 118 Cal. Rptr. 129 (1974).
83. Sauro v. Shea, 257 Pa. 66, 390 A.2d 259 (1978).
84. Thor v. Boska, 38 Cal. App. 3d 558, 113 Cal. Rptr. 296 (1974).
85. Patrick v. Sedwick, 391 P.2d 453 (Alaska 1964).
86. *See, e.g.,* Cal. Penal Code § 471.5 (West 1970 & Supp. 1983).
87. Cavanaugh, *Countersuit: A Viable Alternative for the Wrongfully Sued Physician?*, 19 Washburn L. J. 450 (1980); Higgs, *Physicians' Countersuits—A Solution to the Malpractice Dilemma?*, 28 Drake L. Rev. 81 (1978–79); Birnbaum, *Physicians Counterattack: Liability of Lawyers for Instituting Unjustified Medical Malpractice Actions,* 45 Fordham L. Rev. 1003 (1977). *See also,* Kerr, *The Countersuit: The Situation in Michigan Today,* Mich. Med. 432 (August, 1978). *See also, infra* note 87.
88. Bull v. McCuskey, 615 P.2d 957 (Nev. 1980).
89. *Id.*
90. Friedman v. Dozorc, 412 Mich. 1, 312 N.W.2d 585 (1981).

Part II

Regulation

Chapter V

Governmental Regulation

§ 5.10 INTRODUCTION

In the general legal sense, regulation involves the application of certain standards of conduct to a field of activity, such as medicine. Malpractice litigation, in that it applies a standard of care (see § 1.32, Standard of Care) to a physician's conduct in a given case, constitutes one form of regulation. Reliance on the occurrence of litigation as a regulatory mechanism, however, is inadequate to achieve a desirable level of quality in the provision of health care services. Litigation fails to identify general standards of minimum competence that a health care practitioner must possess before engaging in practice; instead, litigation focuses on a specific standard applicable to the specific case being litigated. While it may provide a remedy for the individual who institutes a lawsuit, it does nothing to ensure that others will not suffer the same injuries in the future by the same hands. Nor can litigation ensure that physicians be continually exposed to and educated in new methods of treatment for the benefit of their patients.

Regulation is intended to deal with these concerns by defining minimum levels of competence, requiring that these levels be met by practitioners, and enforcing such requirements. Sweeping issues, other than questions of competency, that are peculiar to the practice of medicine may be resolved by regulation, whereas case-by-case resolution is inadequate. Generally, where a problem permeates a field, regulation is viewed as the answer; for example, legislation establishing Professional Review Organizations has been one regulatory solution to the problem of rising health care costs.

Regulation of the health care field originates in a variety of quarters. Government regulation is perhaps the most familiar. In order to protect the public health, safety, and welfare, the government, both state and federal, is empowered to regulate.[1] States achieve this objective through licensure laws as well as through specific public health provisions. Federal regulation generally encompasses broad issues such as the distribution of drugs or controlled substances and the control of the cost of health care. Often the government looks to the profession for guidance in defining standards to be imposed or in identifying areas of professional activity that require scrutiny. Certification standards are derived from professional associations. This is a time-honored mode of regulation in the United States: in the early 1800s, states empowered local medical societies to examine and license prospective physicians; unlicensed physicians were prohibited from collecting fees through court process or were fined for unauthorized practice.[2] Furthermore, the serious medical professional has traditionally shown an interest in legitimating his or her profession by delineating standards of quality professional service. Another source of physician regulation is the hospital. Not only is the hospital itself subject to government regulation, its bylaws generally define and regulate the scope and extent of its medical staff physicians' hospital practice. To maintain their accreditation, most hospitals must provide specified facilities and staff them with professionals who have specified qualifications.

Regulation focuses on the general practice of medicine: very little of it is pertinent to a single speciality. Some specialties are more regulated than others. For example, the anesthesiologist is subject to few governmental regulations dealing solely with the practice of anesthesiology, whereas obstetricians and gynecologists may be subject to governmental strictures regarding such aspects of their practice as abortion, contraception, sterilization, and fetal research. Members of both specialties are subject to specific standards imposed by their respective professional societies.

The following chapter offers a perspective on regulation, both general and specific, governing the practice of obstetrics and gynecology and explores standards of conduct imposed by state and federal governments, as well as by professional associations and hospitals.

§ 5.20 STATE LICENSURE

Licensure is a process by which government grants permission to individuals who have obtained a specified minimum degree of competence to engage in a given profession. This minimum degree of competence is attained upon satisfaction of a variety of express conditions. Traditionally these conditions include such things as academic qualifications, training and experience, passing a licensure examination, and miscellaneous personal qualifications. Thus, licensure provides barriers to entry into the profession and serves to ensure an acceptable level of quality in the services.[3]

The state is empowered to regulate the practice of medicine in order to protect the public health, safety, and welfare.[4] The practice of medicine is viewed as a privilege granted by the state rather than an individual right.[5] The state may not exercise its regulatory power in an arbitrary or capricious manner, and legislation regulating the practice of medicine must bear a reasonable relation to the state's legitimate interest in protecting the public from incompetent practitioners.[6] The rationale underlying recognition of the state's interest is that the state is in a better position than the individual to safeguard his or her interests by evaluating a physician's competence.

To carry out their regulatory functions, states have delegated the responsibility for establishing qualifications, conditions, and requirements of medical licensure to medical licensing boards. Generally, the organization of these governmental bodies, usually called boards of medical examiners, is similar across the United States. Most states combine licensing and disciplinary functions in one board.[7] Some states, however, provide for a separate entity to either conduct or assist the board in conducting disciplinary proceedings.[8] The boards may be independent state bodies or may be included within another state agency.* Some states have departments that regulate and license all professions and include medical licensing boards within them.†[9]

The number and qualification requirements of members of the state medical boards vary slightly. The majority of states have fewer than ten members,[10] while others range between four (Alabama)[11] and 20 members (New York).[12] Physicians comprise a majority of the membership of state licensing boards in every state. In several states, where the board regulates other health care professionals in addition to physicians,[13] board membership includes representatives of other professions. For example, the New Jersey board, which regulates physicians as well as chiropractors, consists of ten physicians, one chiropractor, one podiatrist, one bioanalyst, one laboratory director, one representative from the state executive department, and one member of the public.[14] Many states regulate different types of physicians under one board.[15] For example, the Massachusetts Board of Registration and Discipline in Medicine regulates M.D.s as well as "other professionals" such as osteopathic physicians and chiropractors.[16] A sizable minority of states provides for members of the public to be on the board.[17] For example, the Connecticut Medical Examining Board requires membership of two persons unconnected with medicine.[18]

In most states, the state medical society plays an important role in the selection of board members. This role varies from direct selection of members by the state medical society[19] to submission of a list from which the governor or appointing person is either required[20] or encouraged to select board members.[21] It has been recommended that the system of mandatory selection of members from lists submitted by the medical society be replaced by a system

---

*For example, the licensing board is included in the Department of Consumer Affairs in California, the Department of Health in Maryland, the Department of Education in New York, and the Department of State in Pennsylvania.

†For example, the general licensing board is the Department of Regulatory Agencies in Colorado, the Department of Professional and Occupational Regulation in Florida, the Department of Registration and Education in Illinois, the Division of Registration in Massachusetts, the Department of Licensing and Registration in Michigan, and the Department of Registration and Licensing in Wisconsin.

of selection based on appropriate standards developed by the legislature for appointees.[22] Few states, however, specify minimum qualifications for board membership. Some states require that members must have been in active practice in the state for a specified number of years.[23] Residency may also be a requirement.[24] Various other requirements are less common, such as representation from different congressional districts,[25] graduation from a recognized medical college,[26] and representation from hospital staffs.[27]

Some states require representation from medical school faculties,[28] while other prohibit such representation.[29] The presence of medical school faculty members is likely to add persons of distinction in the profession who are knowledgeable both about recent advances in medicine and practice and about medical education and examinations for competence.[30]

The majority of state boards of medical examiners are funded from legislative appropriations from the state treasury, with all other states relying on licensure and registration fees generated by the board. The source of funding not only has a bearing on the amount of money with which a board can operate, but also on the degree of political control exercised by a state over the board itself.[31]

State statutes delegate a broad range of powers and duties to the licensing boards. These powers and duties generally include examination of applicants, issuance of licenses, definition of standards of practice, enforcement of licensing laws, approval of educational programs and recognition of accrediting agencies.[32]

§ 5.21 Requirements

The basic requirements that a physician must meet to obtain a state license vary from state to state and are specified in the state medical practice laws. Many states allow the state licensing authority to define specific licensure standards in rules. Four types of qualifications are generally used to determine initial competence to be licensed as a physician: academic and educational background, postgraduate training and experience, passing of a licensure examination, and moral and personal fitness.[33]

Education and Postgraduate Training: All states require graduation from an approved medical school as a condition of licensure as a medical doctor (M.D.)[34] and graduation from an approved college of osteopathic medicine as a condition of licensure as a doctor of osteopathic medicine (D.O.)[35] Thirty-six jurisdictions now have a one-year postgraduate "experience" requirement (formerly referred to as an internship) for M.D.s.[36] Thirty-four states have a similar requirement for D.O.s.[37]

Twelve states still require a basic science certificate as a prerequisite to licensure, although the tendency is to eliminate this requirement since basic science is included in all medical curricula.[38]

California's educational requirements are quite comprehensive.[39] Its statute provides that an applicant for a license must submit an official transcript showing that minimum course requirements were met[40] and that he or she has completed at least two years of preprofessional, postsecondary education that includes the subjects of physics, chemistry, and biology. If one of these subjects was not taken, the applicant must take it at an approved institution prior to taking the examination. The applicant must also have completed four years of study at an approved medical school.[41] Finally, the statute specifies areas of study required to be in the medical school curriculum, such as anatomy, anesthesiology, geriatric medicine, and pharmacology. There are approximately 15 such required subjects. California requires a one-year postgraduate training period at an approved hospital.[42] It also provides that when an applicant for admission to the examination is rejected by the Division of Licensing he or she may sue in state court to compel admittance or any other appropriate relief.[43]

Examinations: Generally states impose a written examination requirement for both M.D.s and D.O.s. Some states also have oral examinations[44] or require practical examinations[45] for licensure of M.D.s. Few states require oral examination[46] or practical examination of D.O.s.[47]

In most states the boards of medical examiners do not devise their own exams but use the exams prepared by national organizations. For example, 27 states and the District of Columbia accept successful completion of the National Board of Medical Examiners' examination in lieu of the state examination for M.D.s.[48] Twenty-nine states accept the examination prepared by the National Board of Examiners for Osteopathic Physicians and Surgeons rather than a state examination.[49]

Many states specify the subject matter to be covered in their licensure examinations.[50] Most states require a 75 percent minimum proficiency on the examination for M.D.s to pass.[51] Several states also require 75 percent minimum proficiency for D.O.s.[52]

At least six states limit the number of times an applicant for M.D. licensure may be reexamined,[53] while only three states so limit reexamination of an applicant for D.O. licensure.[54] In some of these states the limitation is only applied to applicants who have not had further education since the previously failed examination.

Personal Qualifications: Most states have miscellaneous licensure requirements addressing personal qualifications such as age, citizenship, and character. Some states require an applicant to be 21[55] or 18[56] years old to be licensed as an M.D. Some states enforce a minimum age of 21 for licensure as a D.O.,[57] while fewer states have an 18-year-old minimum.[58]

About half of the states require the applicant to be a U.S. citizen or to declare an intent to become a U.S. citizen as a condition of licensure as an M.D.[59] Slightly fewer than half the states have a similar requirement for D.O.s.[60] The legality of these requirements is questionable, since similar requirements for lawyers and engineers have been found unconstitutional by the U.S. Supreme Court.[61]

Many states and the District of Columbia require evidence of the applicant's good moral character as a condition of licensure as an M.D. or D.O.[62] A few states have defined what is meant by "good moral character," by general definition applicable to all licensed professions. For example, Michigan law states that "good moral character" means a propensity on the part of the person to serve the public in the licensed area in a fair, honest, and open manner.[63]

Foreign-Trained Physicians: One response to the perceived shortage of physicians in the mid-1960s was to give physicians occupational preference in immigration policy.[64] Between 1963 and 1973, approximately 65 percent of the net increase in the U.S. physician-to-population ratio was attributable to physicians trained in foreign countries.[65] In 1975, foreign medical graduates (FMGs) accounted for 35 percent of new licensees, down from a high of 46 percent in 1972. In 1974 FMGs occupied 29 percent of total filled residencies.[66]

The rapid increase in the number of FMGs in the United States raises questions about the quality of care provided. Particular concerns are raised about the relatively poor performance of FMGs on licensure and credentialing examinations and the comparability of their qualifications to physicians trained in the United States. These concerns led Congress to declare in 1973 that there is no longer an insufficient number of physicians in the United States such that there is a need for affording preference to alien physicians. Subsequently, the date of these restrictions on visas was postponed to 1978.[67]

Some states also took action to assure the quality of care rendered by FMGs. Many states license physicians educated in foreign medical facilities as M.D.s.[68] Only a few states have some special licensure requirements for foreign-trained osteopaths.[69] Several states place conditions on the professional education of foreign-trained M.D.s. For example, California and Maryland require that the professional education of foreign-trained M.D.s be substantially equivalent to that of M.D.s trained in the United States.[70] Florida provides for waiver of formal education requirements if the foreign-trained M.D. applicant is eligible or certified as a specialist.[71] About 30 states may accept certification by the Educational Council for Foreign Medical Graduates in lieu of or in addition to other requirements.[72]

Other state requirements may also be imposed. Michigan, for example, requires that an applicant for licensure in any health profession, including physicians, have a working knowledge of the English language.[73] This requirement responds to the claim that language barriers and cultural differences of foreign-born FMGs are detrimental to providing good medical care.[74]

At least one study has attempted to determine the relationship between medical education and performance (as measured by technical performance and utilization of medical care resources) in offices and hospitals. Differences between medical school training did not have a significant effect except for specialists practicing in their own specialty. This study offered no evidence that graduates of U.S. medical schools provide a higher overall quality of care than FMGs.[75]

In the last 20 years of FMG entry, many states and many facilities, such as those dependent on unaffiliated graduate medical education programs and state mental institutions, have developed a considerable dependency on FMG-delivered medical care. Studies have shown that hospital-based, as well as office-based, FMGs serve certain socioeconomic groups that otherwise might not find medical care readily available.[76]

American-born graduates of foreign medical schools are likely to encounter the same difficulty meeting U.S. licensure and certification requirements that foreign-born FMGs have. American-born graduates of foreign medical schools are also likely to confront stiff competition for graduate positions in the United States.[77]

In 1972, about 500 U.S. citizens went abroad to study medicine. The Association of American Medical Colleges (AAMC) predicts that only about 200 of these will eventually be licensed to practice in the United States.[78] Fewer than ten states have separate licensing provisions for U.S. citizens trained abroad as M.D.s,[79] while no state makes such provision for D.O. applicants.[80] About one-third of the states do not classify Canadians as FMGs for purposes of M.D. licensure.[81]

Reciprocity and Endorsement: As with the procedures for obtaining a license and relicensure, the requirements for reciprocity and endorsement vary from state to state. In many states, licensure by endorsement is a discretionary matter within the purview of the applicable administrative agency.[82] In New Jersey, for instance, a physician who has been examined by the licensing board of another state or who has taken the National Board of Medical Examiners' examination successfully may be granted a license to practice without further examination upon payment of a fee.[83] Some states require that the examination originally taken by the physician be of the same quality as its own and that the applicant's state extend reciprocal privileges.[84] Florida further requires that, unless the license is utilized by the applicant within three years by actively engaging in the practice of medicine in Florida for one year, it is void.[85] Successful completion of the National Board of Medical Examiners' examination is used as a benchmark in licensing out-of-state physicians in a number of states. California, however, requires that the standard of the National Board examination be substantially the same as California's own at the time the certificate was issued.[86] Furthermore, an oral examination is deemed not equivalent to a written examintion for licensure, and the California Division of Licensing will not issue a reciprocity certificate to a physician until he or she takes a comprehensive oral and clinical examination administered by the division.[87]

§ 5.22 Relicensure and Continuing Medical Education

Some states have combined procedures for relicensure with provisions requiring continuing education.[88] Michigan requires anyone seeking to renew a license to have completed coursework of no fewer than 150 hours during the three years immediately preceding his or her application. Such education must be in subjects related to the practice of medicine. Michigan further requires evidence of continuing competence to demonstrate that the licensee continues to meet the educational and practice standards of the profession.[89] Ohio, on the other hand, deals with compulsory continuing education in the context of a suspended or revoked license.[90] There, the state medical board may, at its discretion, require additional training and reexamination as a condition of reinstatement of the physician's license.[91] Similarly, the Florida statute, requiring additional education, applies only to renewal of inactive licenses.[92] Illinois is currently in the process of developing and evaluating a compulsory continuing education program.[93]

Procedures for relicensure vary from state to state, depending on the circumstances. If relicensure is merely renewal, the statutes tend to provide a period of time (California—five years,[94] Florida—one year[95]) within which the license may be renewed as a matter of form. The physician need only apply and pay a late penalty fee. If, however, application for renewal of the license is not made within the specified time, the physician may be required to take 12 hours of course work for each year the license was inactive, to take and pass the examination for initial licensure, or otherwise to establish that he or she is qualified to practice.[96]

A suspended or revoked license is more difficult to renew, although there is great variance from jurisdiction to jurisdiction. Under California law, the physician may not petition for reinstatement for at least one year after the date of the disciplinary action. The petition must be accompanied by a minimum of two verified recommendations from physicians with personal knowledge of the petitioner's activities since the disciplinary action was imposed. Further, the administrative body hearing the case may impose whatever restrictions or terms it deems necessary.[97] At the other end of the spectrum are states such as New Jersey which provide that the physician may, at the discretion of the examining board, be relicensed at any time without an examination.[98] In Ohio, the board may require an examination, whether oral, written, or both, as well as additional training.[99] Texas law provides for a one-year waiting period before application can be made, but reinstatement is otherwise at the discretion of the board of medical examiners.[100] Virginia has only a three-month waiting period.[101]

Some states provide for the reinstatement of the license of a physician who has been found to be mentally incompetent.[102] In Illinois, a judgment by a state court operates as a suspension of the physician's license. The physician may resume practice only upon a finding by the state medical board that the court has found the physician to be recovered and recommends that he or she be permitted to resume practice.[103]

§ 5.23 Disciplinary Proceedings

The due process clause of the Fourteenth Amendment to the U.S. Constitution protects individuals from being deprived of their property by state governments without due process of law. Early legal decisions recognize the right to practice medicine as a valuable property right that may be protected and secured.[104] Consequently, medical licensure boards, as agents of state governments, are required to exercise fundamental fairness in disciplinary proceedings. The U.S. Supreme Court has held that, while the Constitution does not guarantee the unrestricted right to engage in a business, a person may not be excluded from a legitimate occupation without due process.[105]

Procedural Aspects: The type of procedural protection required by due process depends on factors such as the interests of the parties involved, the gravity and potential impact of the decision, the nature of the proceeding, the importance of the particular procedure in assuring the decision's validity, and the possible burden of that proceeding.[106]

If the determinations of medical associations, specialty boards, hospitals, and other nongovernmental bodies take on the character of "state action" (see § 7.90, Medical Staff Privileges), they are subject to due process constraints. Often the disciplinary decisions of these bodies have major and far-reaching impacts on a professional's career.

Most procedural requirements for disciplinary proceedings have evolved from two constitutional mandates: adequate notice that the disciplinary action will take place must be given, and the party to be disciplined must be given the opportunity to be heard.[107] Other aspects of due process have been provided by state statute or imposed by court decision. Many states have adopted legislation similar to the Model State Administrative Procedures Act.[108] Model Act standards include requirements for contents of the notice of hearing, hearing procedures, and criteria for judicial review of administrative decisions. These procedures apply in contested cases involving the grant, denial, renewal, revocation, or suspension of a license.

Notice: Due process requires that proper notice be given in order to afford the physician an opportunity to meet the charges against him or her. Due process is satisfied if the licensee has reasonable notice of the hearing and a reasonable opportunity to be heard and to present his or her claim or defense, subject to due regard being given to the nature of the proceeding and the character of the right that may be affected by it.[109] The statement of charges, or complaint, must be specific enough to enable the accused to prepare a defense, although the exact statutory language under which the charges are brought need not be used.[110] Some courts have held that the notice requirement embraces not only accusations against the licensee, but the disciplinary action contemplated as well.[111] An Illinois court has held that the Constitution requires that the accused be personally notified.[112] Conducting the hearing on unreasonably short notice (for example, two days) violates due process.[113] Unless statutorily required, the notice need not apprise the accused of any right he or she might have to be represented by an attorney.[114]

The required response to the notice of charges varies among the states. Some states require a written answer prior to hearing.[115] Other states make the opportunity to respond optional.[116]

Hearing: At a minimum, due process requires a full, fair, and impartial hearing before an appropriate administrative body.[117] Although this tribunal is required to be impartial, it may handle both the investigative and adjudicative aspects of a disciplinary hearing. The honesty and integrity of the tribunal members is presumed; therefore, the burden of proving bias is on the person alleging its existence.[118] To disqualify the tribunal, any bias that is proved must be shown to be of a personal nature and to lead to a substantially preconceived resolution of the issues. If such bias is shown, a court may review the matter.[119] Bias has been found where the medical or professional society has an undue influence on the disciplinary process or on the board.[120] General bias claims against individual board members or the board as a whole have failed where the result appears fair based on the record.[121]

The person to be disciplined is entitled to be an active participant in the hearing. Participation includes testifying on his or her own behalf and presenting, challenging, and confronting witnesses.[122] The credibility of witnesses is for the board to determine.[123]

Evidence supporting the complaint is heard before the accused presents his or her evidence. If no evidence is offered to support the complaint, it should be dismissed and the accused spared the necessity of presenting evidence.[124] Although evidence presented at hearings must meet minimum standards of reliability, authenticity, and fairness, it need not conform to the strict rules of evidence observed in judicial proceedings. Thus, hearsay evidence is generally admissible where it has some probative value.[125] One court has extended the physician-patient privilege to administrative hearings to prevent the disclosure of confidential information acquired in the course of a patient's treatment where the patient has not waived the privilege[126] (see § 4.46 Physician-Patient Privilege). However, transcripts from prior, related judicial proceedings may be admitted as evidence.[127]

A board's action may be predicated on a physician's guilty plea to criminal charges arising from the same facts.[128] Revoking a physician's license for conduct that resulted in a felony conviction does not violate due process. (Double jeopardy does not apply, since a licensure action is administrative, not criminal, in nature.)[129]

In most jurisdictions, the fact that the physician engaged in wrongful acts must be proved at the hearing by a preponderance of the evidence.[130] Thus, the evidence need only establish the truth of the charges, not prove guilt beyond a reasonable doubt. Establishing guilt beyond a reasonable doubt is generally reserved for hearings in the nature of criminal proceedings that could result in a deprivation of liberty or other interest fundamental to personal welfare. The license to practice medicine is not considered to be such an interest. An intermediate evidentiary standard requiring that improper conduct be shown by clear and convincing evidence is employed in some jurisdictions. In New Jersey, it is used in attorney disciplinary actions, but the less stringent standard, preponderance of the evidence, is applied to physicians. In a 1982 case, a New Jersey allergist challenged this discrepancy of evidentiary standards as violating his constitutional right to equal protection. The New Jersey Supreme Court upheld the practice, drawing a distinction between the two professions primarily on the ground that medical practice, unlike the practice of law, concerns life and death consequences to the public. Consequently, a less stringent burden of proof in a disciplinary hearing against a physician can be viewed as more protective of society's interest in life and health.[131]

After a hearing, the board must publish a statement of its findings. Normally this will include an evaluation of the evidence presented, findings of fact, a statement of offenses committed, if any, and the imposition of a penalty.[132] An order of the board that is not sufficiently specific may be reversed on appeal.[133] As a general matter, the reviewing court will not alter an order of the board that is supported by "substantial evidence"[134] or a preponderance of the evidence.[135] The record of the hearing must contain a factual basis from which the board can make its conclusion regarding the complaint.[136]

Judicial Review: Generally, state statutes allow state courts to review administrative decisions.[137] A state court must examine three criteria before review: jurisdiction, justiciability, and exhaustion of administrative remedies. Jurisdiction is the power of the court to recognize and decide an issue. Federal courts generally do not have jurisdiction in state medical board proceedings.[138]

Justiciability refers to the existence of an actual claim or dispute that requires a solution. Thus, a case may be dismissed as moot where the outcome of the decision would no longer affect the parties because circumstances have changed since the dispute arose.[139]

To exhaust administrative remedies, a party must allow the board to completely review and enter a final order in a case before seeking judicial review. For example, a physician must petition the board for restoration of a suspended license before requesting a court order to require the board to restore it.[140] If the board cannot successfully defend its ruling, the order will be terminated by the reviewing court.[141]

In some cases, a physician may appeal to a court prior to entry of a final order of the board. This is done where no other course is available and judicial review is necessary to ensure the fairness of the board proceedings (for example, when a board denies the accused physician's request for subpoenas to compel disclosure of certain documents prior to the hearing).[142]

Ex Parte Actions: In some states, the board is empowered to temporarily suspend a physician's license without a formal hearing. This power is generally limited to cases where the public health, safety, or welfare requires emergency action.[143] Action taken on this basis is referred to as ex parte action. Some courts have allowed the board to revoke a license without a hearing when the physician was convicted of or pleaded guilty to a felony[144] or was involved in criminal violations of federal or state narcotics laws.[145]

State statutes may provide for automatic suspension of a license based on a formal adjudication of the licensee's mental incompetence.[146]

Grounds: Grounds for instituting a disciplinary action against a physician are usually specified by state statute. These grounds may be specific offenses such as criminal conduct. They may also be general offenses not specifically included in the statute, such as unprofessional conduct.

A statutory offense must be specific enough to inform the licensee of the actions it prohibits. Statutes which are not that specific may be attacked in court as unconstitutionally vague.[147] If such an attack is successful, the statute may not be used as a ground for taking disciplinary action.

Unprofessional conduct is a ground for disciplinary action in all states.[148] Most states specify the types of conduct included within this category. For example, the Michigan statute provides:

> Unprofessional conduct, consisting of any of the following:
>
> a. Misrepresentation to a consumer or patient or in obtaining or attempting to obtain third-party reimbursement in the course of professional practice.
> b. Betrayal of a professional confidence.
> c. Promotion for personal gain of an unnecessary drug, device, treatment, procedure, or service, or directing or requiring an individual to purchase or secure a drug, device, treatment, procedure, or service from another person, place, facility, or business in which the licensee has a financial interest.[149]

Texas gives a general definition of unprofessional conduct and then includes specific examples:

> Unprofessional or dishonorable conduct likely to deceive or defraud the public includes but is not limited to the following acts:
>
> a. Committing any act that is in violation of the laws of the State of Texas if the act is connected with the physician's practice of medicine. A complaint, indictment, or conviction of a law violation is not necessary for the enforcement of this provision. Proof of the commission of the act while in the practice of medicine or under the guise of the practice of medicine is sufficient for action by the board under this section;
> b. Failing to keep complete and accurate records of purchases and disposals of drugs listed in the Texas Controlled Substances Act . . . or of controlled substances scheduled in the Federal Comprehensive Drug Abuse Prevention and Control Act of 1970. . . . A physican shall keep records of his purchases and

disposals of these drugs to include without limitation the date of purchase, the sale or disposal of the drugs by the physician, the name and address of the person receiving the drugs, and the reason for the disposing or dispensing of the drugs to the person. A failure to keep the records for a reasonable time is grounds for revoking, canceling, suspending, or probating the license of any practitioner of medicine;

c. Writing prescriptions for or dispensing to a person known to be a habitual user of narcotic drugs, controlled substances, or dangerous drugs or to a person who the physician should have known was a habitual user of the narcotic drugs, controlled substances, or dangerous drugs. This provision does not apply to those persons being treated by the physician for their narcotic use after the physician notifies the board in writing of the name and address of the person being so treated;

d. Writing false or fictitious prescriptions for dangerous drugs . . . of controlled substances scheduled in the Texas Controlled Substances Act . . . or of controlled substances scheduled in the Federal Comprehensive Drug Abuse Prevention and Control Act of 1970 . . .;

e. Prescribing or administering a drug or treatment that is nontherapeutic in nature or nontherapeutic in the manner the drug or treatment is administered or prescribed;

f. Prescribing, administering, or dispensing in a manner not consistent with public health and welfare dangerous drugs . . . controlled substances scheduled in the Texas Controlled Substances Act . . . or controlled substances scheduled in the Federal Comprehensive Drug Abuse Prevention and Control Act of 1970 . . .;

g. Persistently and flagrantly overcharging or overtreating patients;

h. Failing to supervise adequately the activities of those acting under the supervision of the physician; or

i. Delegating professional medical responsibility or acts to a person if the delegating physician knows or has reason to know that the person is not qualified by training, experience, or licensure to perform the responsibility or acts.[150]

Statutory language that is vague, such as "unprofessional," "unlawful," or "unethical" conduct has been justified when it has been adequately defined by subsequent judicial decisions.[151] For example, a physician was found to have committed acts of unprofessional conduct after he disclosed to medical board investigators that he had sold examination questions and answers to medical licensure candidates.[152] Representations to patients by a physician that he had staff privileges to deliver their babies at a certain hospital when he did not have such privileges have been held to amount to "dishonorable conduct" sufficient to support a two-year suspension of a license.[153] Child molesting[154] and violation of a civil statute prohibiting office abortions[155] have also been found to constitute unprofessional conduct.

CASE ILLUSTRATION

Two osteopathic physicians were charged with knowingly and intentionally making excessive and unwarranted charges to public funds under Medicare claims as medical providers. The physicians contended that their conduct did not constitute grounds for revoking their licenses, because the petition charging them alleged "unethical" conduct, whereas the statute covered "immoral, unprofessional, or dishonorable" conduct. The court found little substantial difference in the terms and held that the charges warranted revocation (*Kansas Board of Healing Arts v. Seasholtz*, 1972).[156]

"Professional incompetence" has recently become a ground for disciplinary action outside the general ground of "unprofessional conduct." Revocation of a physician's license must be supported by evidence of specific acts or a course of conduct showing incompetence.[157] Courts have been less willing to allow the boards' broad discretion in the use of this charge.

CASE ILLUSTRATION

The board alleged that the physician had incorrectly diagnosed and treated seven patients for gonorrhea and charged her with unprofessional conduct in making "misleading, deceptive, or fraudulent representations and with engaging in unethical . . . conduct." The court reversed the board's suspension of the physician's license, finding that the physician was guilty only of faulty diagnoses resulting from the use of a less preferred test. The test conformed to minimum standards of practice, even though it was not the most accurate and currently acceptable method. The court concluded that incorrect diagnoses alone do not constitute medical incompetence unless they result from failure to conform to minimal standards of practice (*Gentry v. Department of Professional and Occupational Regulation*, 1974).[158]

The generic term "immoral conduct" includes cases of sexual impropriety. Courts have split on whether the immoral conduct must be related to the physician's practice.[159] For example, where a physician was charged with moral turpitude for making a homosexual gesture to a police officer in a public rest room, the court agreed with the physician that the issue was whether the claimed conduct would adversely affect future patients. However, the court sustained the board's action (probation) because the board members' expertise placed them in a better position to assess the likelihood of danger to patients.[160]

"Unlawful conduct" includes conviction of a crime, acts for which the physician has been acquitted,[161] and conduct for which criminal prosecution would normally ensue but for some reason has not.[162] Disciplinary action may

§ 5.23 *Disciplinary Proceedings* 203

be imposed for unlawful conduct even though the law has not established guilt.[163] Physicians have unsuccessfully challenged disciplinary actions for unlawful conduct on equal protection grounds, claiming that additional sanctions are imposed on physicians without a valid reason for distinguishing them from other persons who commit the same crimes.[164]

In addition to generic grounds for disciplinary action, most states include other, more specific grounds in their statutes. For example, Michigan lists the following grounds for disciplinary action, including several specific offenses:

I. A. A violation of a general duty, consisting of negligence or failure to exercise due care, including negligent delegation to or supervision of employees or other individuals, whether or not injury results, or any conduct, practice, or condition which impairs, or may impair, the ability to safely and skillfully practice the health profession.
 B. Personal disqualifications, consisting of any of the following:
    i. Incompetence.
    ii. Substance abuse as defined by statute.
    iii. Mental or physical inability reasonably related to and adversely affecting the licensee's or applicant's ability to practice in a safe and competent manner.
    iv. Declaration of mental incompetence by a court of competent jurisdiction.
    v. Conviction of a misdemeanor or felony reasonably related to and adversely affecting the licensee's or applicant's ability to practice in a safe and competent manner. A certified copy of the court record is conclusive evidence as to the conviction.
 C. Prohibited acts, consisting of any of the following:
    i. Fraud or deceit in obtaining a license.
    ii. Permitting the license to be used by an unauthorized person.
    iii. Practice outside the scope of a license.
    iv. Obtaining, possessing, or attempting to obtain or possess a controlled substance without lawful authority; or selling, prescribing, giving away, or administering drugs for other than lawful diagnostic or therapeutic purposes.
 D. Unethical business practices, consisting of any of the following:
    i. False or misleading advertising.
    ii. Dividing fees for referral patients or accepting kickbacks on medical or surgical services, appliances, or medications purchased by or in behalf of patients.
    iii. Fraud or deceit in obtaining or attempting to obtain third party reimbursement.
 E. Unprofessional conduct, consisting of any of the following:
    i. Misrepresentation to a consumer or patient or in obtaining or

attempting to obtain third party reimbursement in the course of professional practice.
  ii. Betrayal of a professional confidence.
  iii. Promotion for personal gain of an unnecessary drug, device, treatment, procedure, or service, or directing or requiring an individual to purchase or secure a drug, device, treatment, procedure, or service from another person, place, facility, or business in which the licensee has a financial interest.
 F. Failure to report a change of name or address within 30 days after it occurs.
 G. A violation, or aiding or abetting in a violation, of the state licensing law.
 H. Failure to comply with a subpoena issued pursuant to law.
 I. Failure to pay an installment of an assessment levied pursuant to law within 60 days after notice by the appropriate board.
II. A. Failure or refusal to submit to an examination which a board is authorized to require after reasonable notice and opportunity constitutes a ground for suspension of a license until the examination is taken.
 B. Additional grounds for disciplinary action may be found in the law dealing with a specific health profession.[165]

Sanctions: Until recently only two options were available to most boards when a licensee was found to have violated a medical practice act—revocation or suspension of the license and reprimand or censure.[166] In many cases the former sanctions were considered too severe, while the latter were too lenient.

Many states now allow their boards to impose sanctions that are differentiated according to the severity of the offense. Generally, the choice of sanction authorized by statute is a matter within a board's discretion, if supported by a preponderance of the evidence.[167]

CASE ILLUSTRATION

A physician without previous disciplinary actions against him was found to have prescribed Desoxyn, a controlled substance, to known drug addicts without first conducting physical examinations. The prescriptions were not issued for monetary gain. The state board charged him with negligence or incompetence on more than one occasion. The hearing panel recommended that the physician's license be revoked but that such revocation be stayed and that he be placed on probation for two years. The board elected to revoke the physician's license in lieu of probation. The physician appealed this decision as too harsh in light of his prior record. The court of appeals sustained the board's action, finding that revocation of the physician's license to practice medicine was not excessive in view of the evidence and that it was within the board's authority to do so (*Widlitz v. Board of Regents,* 1980).[168]

Evidence relied on to impose sanctions on a physician, including the revocation of a license to practice medicine, need not be provided by expert testimony when the hearing body is composed of medical experts. Such a panel is recognized as qualified to exercise medical judgment to determine the propriety of the sanction imposed.

The sanctions usually available to a board are reprimand, probation, requirement for retraining or rehabilitation, limitation on practice, suspension, revocation, and fine. Censure or reprimand is the least intrusive sanction, since it allows the physician to continue to practice without affecting the scope of his or her license, whereas probation and retraining or rehabilitation requirements allow the board to monitor certain of the physician's professional activities. These sanctions also allow the board to use its power for rehabilitative rather than strictly punitive purposes.[169] In a California decision where the board suspended a physician's license for one year unless the physician could pass an oral clinical examination in the management of fluid and electrolyte imbalances, the court held that such a rehabilitative penalty was valid.[170]

In conjunction with probation or retraining, or as a separate action, the board may limit the physician's license. Michigan defines a limited license as a "license to which restrictions or conditions, or both, as to scope of practice, place of practice, supervision of practice, duration of licensed status, or type or condition of patient or client served are imposed by the board."[171] This type of authority allows the board to tailor the sanction to the particular licensee and his or her circumstances.

Some states require the board to impose a mandatory sanction for certain offenses. This type of mandatory sanction removes a significant amount of the board's discretionary power when dealing with more serious offenses. For example, Iowa requires the board to revoke or suspend a license when the licensee is found guilty of any of a series of offenses, including incompetence in the practice of his or her profession.[172]

§ 5.30 PROFESSIONAL REVIEW ORGANIZATIONS

Peer review takes place at many levels in the medical system. Sometimes called utilization review, peer review is conducted in most hospitals in the United States (see § 7.64, Utilization Review Committee and § 7.74, Professional Review Organizations), and a form of peer review is conducted by the states pursuant to their licensure statutes (see § 5.20, State Licensure). For purposes of this section, however, peer review is defined in terms of federally legislated peer review for purposes of determining whether the care rendered to patients whose bills are paid for by the federal government (that is, by Medicare) is of sufficient quality and delivered at a reasonable cost.

The original federal peer review program was created in 1972 by an amendment to the Social Security Act and was titled the Professional Standards Review Organization (PSRO) Act. That program applied to patients whose bills were paid through federal reimbursement programs such as Medicare, Medicaid, and Maternal and Child Health programs.[173]

In 1982, with the passage of the Tax Equity and Fiscal Responsibility Act, the PSRO program was replaced by a similar utilization review program, the Utilization and Quality Control Peer Review Organization (PRO). (Existing PSROs will not be eliminated, however, until the Department of Health and Human Services (DHHS) publishes regulations implementing the new law.)[174]

The PROs appear to be as controversal as PSROs. Recently, for example, the PSRO budget was slashed, in a continuing resolution, from $24 million to $15 million at the insistence of House appropiations DHHS subcommittee chairman William Natcher (D–KY). This funding cut forced the administrator of the program to make a difficult decision. She decided to fund existing PSROs at full budget strength through fiscal 1983. This decision will bankrupt the controversial program by October unless Congress intervenes. The action is likely to prompt a showdown between the Office of Management and Budget (OMB) and Congress over the future of utilization review for Medicare. OMB has flatly refused to ask for PSRO or PRO funding in 1984. These programs, however, are viewed as effective cost savers in the eyes of the Senate Finance Committee.[175] This dispute is but one of many that has surrounded the peer review programs developed by the federal government to combat perceived misuse and abuse by providers whose services are reimbursed by the government.

The PRO act was intended to eliminate many of the structural and procedural requirements governing PSROs, thereby giving the new organizations broader authority in carrying out review activities while giving the DHHS greater responsibility for setting PRO goals and objectives. The legislative goal was to create a tougher program. It is hoped that this new program will be more effective at containing costs and will function cooperatively with the insurance industry rather than focusing equally on cost and quality, as the old program did. PROs are not required, for example, to study profiles of provider care, to undertake quality studies, or to involve as many physicians as possible practicing in the area in the peer review activities. All of these functions and activities were required of the PSROs.[176]

Provisions of the new act include:

1. The new program calls for fewer and larger PRO areas, with most PROs to be statewide. As a result, many of the remaining PSROs will have to merge, subcontract with a PRO, or be dissolved. A qualified PRO must either be composed of a substantial number of licensed doctors representative of the area or have available to it, by contract or other arrangement, sufficient doctors to carry out its review functions. The former type of PRO will have priority over the latter. If, after a

year, there is no qualified PRO in the area, the secretary of the DHHS may contract for review activities with an insurance company or fiscal intermediary. In no instance may a PRO be a provider of health care.

2. The DHHS will enter into two-year contracts rather than grants with PROs. The contracting authorities of DHHS may be carried out without regard to other provisions of federal contract law, and DHHS may use different procedures in different parts of the country. The contract will include "negotiated objectives against which the PRO's performance will be judged and negotiated specifications for use of regional norms" Section 1153(c)(7). This language may put an end to the interminable and conflicting evaluations the PSROs have been undergoing for the past two years.

3. PROs, like their predecessors, will review "some or all of the professional activities in the area, subject to the terms of the contract, of physicians and other health care practitioners and institutional and noninstitutional providers of health care services. . . ." The new Section 1154(a)(1) thus continues review authority over ambulatory and outpatient care, as well as inpatient care. At the same time, the new language makes it clearer that not all PROs will review all activities. The new legislation requires PROs to review only Medicare (Title XVIII) services. State and Medicaid programs may use PROs too, but they are not required to do so. PROs are now expressly, rather than implicitly, required to determine whether care offered on an inpatient basis could be more appropriately performed on an outpatient basis. Specific authority to delegate review functions to hospitals has been eliminated; however, the language of Section 1153(c)(1) would allow a PRO to delegate "review function to a provider by subcontract, if the [PRO] finds that the provider will effectively and efficiently review itself."

4. The obligations of a provider or practitioner to provide appropriate care and the authority of the review organization to recommend sanctions when that obligation is not met remain substantially the same, with only one significant change: in addition to being medically necessary, meeting professionally recognized standards, and being supported by sufficient evidence of necessity and quality, the care must be provided "economically."

5. The situations in which PROs may disclose data have been made more specific. First, the language states that PROs are not federal agencies for the purposes of the Freedom of Information Act, thereby precluding new litigation contending that PRO information is generally available to the public. Second, the PROs are required to disclose data and information in accordance with procedures established by DHHS. In addition, PROs will continue to be obligated to disseminate aggregate data to health planning agencies.

6. "Each PRO shall make available its facilities and resources for contracting with private and public entities paying for health care in its area for review . . ." Section 1154(a)(11). In the same vein, the PRO is to coordinate its activities, including information exchanges, which are consistent with economical and efficient operation or programs among appropriate public and private agencies or organizations.[177]

As might be expected, major controversies are building as the Health Care Financing Administration (HCFA) of the DHHS attempts to draft regulations to implement the new act. One of the options being considered, for example, is to require the use of data collected by the Medicare fiscal intermediaries. Under the old act, PSROs work from a medical discharge abstract. Fiscal intermediaries, on the other hand, get data from the hospital bill. Some HCFA officials believe they can save millions of dollars and improve the quality of data collection by eliminating the separate medical review data collection process and adding diagnostic information to the billing forms. Various interest groups believe this change could pose threats to confidentiality, create administrative problems, and diminish the quality of the data.[178] This and other controversies are bound to follow peer review as it continues to evolve at the federal level.

In contrast to the old act, the act establishing PROs would allow for the negotiation of two-year, performance-based contracts with both profit and not-for-profit peer review organizations. Under the new act, the secretary of DHHS may not contract with a hospital or hospital-affiliated organization. However, hospitals may subcontract with peer review organizations for delegated review purposes. The new act provides that no contracts can be made with fiscal intermediaries or insurance companies for the first 12 months of the program. After that, such contracts can be made only if no other qualified organization exists in the area. Finally, if there is more than one peer review organization available, the secretary of DHHS must give preference to groups composed of physicians.[179]

Review responsibilities are basically the same under both acts. The review organization's determinations are binding on intermediaries and carriers as to matters of appropriateness, necessity, and quality of Medicare-paid services. As to Medicaid, individual states can choose to use PROs. When states so elect, the federal government will share up to 75 percent of the cost. Whether state reviews are binding, however, is not yet clear.

As one authority has noted:

> The essential questions asked by most providers facing this system is how it will interact with diagnosis-related group-based reimbursement in particular and prospective payment in general. The House Ways and Means Committee report provides the answer in its emphasis on admissions review and sanctions for patterns of inappropriate, unnecessary, and poor quality care. The authority of the new organizations to review patterns of care and make sanction recommendations, including expulsion from Medicare and repayment of monies improperly paid, will be highly important.[180]

§ 5.41 *Drugs* 209

Until new regulations are issued by DHHS, a certain amount of chaos is likely to exist. Providers will be faced with increasing ambiguities as PSROs are supplanted by PROs. In the absence of new regulations, the tendency is to rely on old ones. Ambiguities created by this transition place many providers in a bad position. For example, if a provider assumes the regulations will go in one direction and they do not, that provider, based on a single assumption, may be faced with reimbursement or penalty situations that can only be avoided by the prompt promulgation of the new regulations. In the interim, it is likely that Medicare, Medicaid, and Maternal and Child Health patients, providers, and states will be adversely affected by ambiguities not of their own making.

§ 5.40 OTHER REGULATION

In addition to licensing physicians, states impose regulations that affect the practice of medicine. Some of these requirements deal with procedures usually performed by obstetricians or gynecologists (see §§ 5.42, Human and Fetal Research; 5.43, Reporting Requirements; 5.44, Testing Requirements; 5.45, Abortion; and 5.46, Contraception); others are applicable to physicians generally (see § 5.41, Drugs). States may also regulate other types of health personnel (see § 6.22, Nurse-Midwife Legislation), as well as the facilities that relate to the practice of medicine, particularly in the areas of obstetrics and gynecology.

Pertinent federal regulation also exists. Both the Congress and federal agencies authorized to do so may regulate the obstetrician's or gynecologist's practice. Federal legislation governing the dispensation and prescription of controlled substances and Health and Human Services regulations governing fetal research bear on this practice. Furthermore, the U.S. Supreme Court has spoken to issues surrounding abortion, contraception, and sterilization. The controversy surrounding the legal treatment of abortion promises that the Court will be repeatedly faced with new facets of the question in the future.

Thus, from the relatively static and comprehensive regulation imposed by state licensure law to the expanding and amorphous judicial pronouncements governing abortion, the obstetrician and gynecologist, perhaps more than any other medical specialists, must answer to a variety of regulatory demands.

§ 5.41 Drugs

Controlled Substances: Most states[181] have adopted some variation of the Uniform Controlled Substances Act (UCSA), drafted by the National Conference of Commissioners of Uniform State Laws in 1970 and recommended for adoption in all states. The purpose of the UCSA was to assure continued free movement of controlled substances among states while preventing the diversion of these drugs from legitimate sources.[182] By adopting the UCSA, states are assured of having drug laws similar to those of other states and complementary to federal drug laws.

The UCSA requires any person who manufactures, distributes, dispenses, or prescribes a controlled substance to obtain annually a license issued by the state board of pharmacy or its designated or established authority.[183] Thus, most physicians must obtain a license pursuant to the Act.

The UCSA places controlled substances in five schedules. Substances will be placed in Schedule 1 if they have a high potential for abuse and no accepted use in medical treatment (in the United States) or if they lack accepted safety for use in treatment under medical supervision.[184]

Substances are placed in Schedule 2 if they have a high potential for abuse, which may lead to severe psychological or physical dependence, and if they are currently accepted for medical use with severe restrictions.[185] Substances that have less potential for abuse and whose abuse may lead to moderate or low physical dependence or high psychological dependence and that are currently accepted for medical use are placed in Schedule 3.[186] Substances are placed in Schedule 4 if, relative to Schedule 3 substances, they have a low potential for abuse, which may lead to limited physical dependence or psychological dependence, and if they are currently accepted for medical use.[187] Schedule 5 substances have a lower potential for abuse and a currently accepted medical use.[188]

A license issued under the UCSA allows physicians to dispense or prescribe drugs in Schedules 2, 3, 4, and 5. However, the issuance of a license does not authorize a physician to dispense, manufacture, distribute, or prescribe a controlled substance if such activities are not for legitimate and professionally recognized therapeutic, scientific, or industrial purposes or are not in the scope of practice of a practitioner licensee.[189]

A license to manufacture, distribute, prescribe, or dispense a controlled substance may be denied, suspended, or revoked by the administrator of the board of pharmacy upon various grounds, including:

1. Furnishing false or fraudulent information in application for a license to distribute controlled substances
2. Promoting a controlled substance to the general public
3. Not maintaining effective controls against diversion of controlled substances to other than legitimate and professionally recognized therapeutic, scientific, or industrial uses
4. Manufacturing, distributing, or dispensing a controlled substance for other than legitimate or professionally recognized therapeutic, scientific, or industrial purposes or outside the scope of practice of the practitioner-licensee or applicant
5. Violating or attempting to violate, directly or indirectly, assisting in or aiding the violation of, or conspiring to violate any of the rules regulating controlled substances[190]

The administrator of the board of pharmacy may limit revocation or suspension of a dispensing license to the particular controlled substance as to which grounds for revocation or suspension exist.[191]

A person licensed under the UCSA must keep records and maintain inventories as required by federal law and additional rules promulgated by the administrator.[192]

The UCSA regulates the prescription of controlled substances as follows:

1. Except when dispensed directly by a practitioner, other than a pharmacy, to an ultimate user, no controlled substance in Schedule 2 may be dispensed without the written prescription of a practitioner.

2. In emergency situations, as defined by rule of the [appropriate person or agency], Schedule 2 drugs may be dispensed upon oral prescription of a practitioner, reduced promptly to writing and filed by the pharmacy. Prescriptions shall be retained in conformity with the requirements of Section 306. No prescription for a Schedule 2 substance may be refilled.

3. Except when dispensed directly by a practitioner other than a pharmacy, to an ultimate user, a controlled substance included in Schedule 3 or 4, which is a prescription drug as determined under [appropriate state or federal statute], shall not be dispensed without a written or oral prescription of a practitioner. The prescription shall not be filled or refilled more than six months after the date thereof or be refilled more than five times, unless renewed by the practitioner.

4. A controlled substance included in Schedule 5 shall not be distributed or dispensed other than for a medical purpose.[193]

Although the UCSA defines offenses that violate the act, it allows each state to set its own penalties.[194] These vary widely, both in form and in substance. New York has enacted a separate article to deal with controlled substances offenses.[195] Many localities and at least one state have decriminalized the possession or sale, or both, of marijuana.[196]

Despite the goal of uniformity, other areas of state-controlled substance laws vary widely. Five states and the District of Columbia have so far failed to enact any form of the UCSA.[197] Three of these states and the District of Columbia have retained and updated the old Uniform Narcotic Drug Act.[198] The other two states have enacted their own drug acts, which differ materially from the UCSA.[199]

Significant differences exist among states that have adopted the UCSA. A few states require three copies of prescriptions for Schedule 2 drugs, but most states do not.[200] Some states prohibit dispensing samples of all controlled substances. Provisions regulating medical research with controlled substances vary greatly. States are beginning to transfer drugs from one schedule to another and to add drugs to schedules; one state has introduced a Schedule 6, containing all prescription drugs not covered in Schedules 1 through 5.[201]

The Federal Controlled Substances Act (FCSA) was enacted in 1970 to control drug abuse and related matters.[202] The FCSA, like the state acts discussed above, classifies dangerous drugs into five schedules.[203] The federal act also requires registration of drug manufacturers, wholesalers, and retailers and maintenance of records of transactions of drugs in the system.[204] Every physician who administers, prescribes, or dispenses any of the listed drugs must register annually with the Department of Justice, Bureau of Narcotics and Dangerous Drugs.[205]

Generic Equivalents: In an effort to reduce drug costs to the consumer, most states now allow the substitution of a chemically equivalent generic drug for a prescribed name brand drug, although the details of enabling statutes vary from state to state.

In the majority of states, the pharmacist may substitute a generic drug unless the physician instructs otherwise.[206] The physician may do so in a number of ways. If the prescription is delivered orally, the physician may expressly state that no substitution be made.[207] On a written prescription, the prescriber may prohibit substitution by writing "dispense as written,"[208] initialling a preprinted "dispense as written" box[209] on the prescription form, or noting "d.a.w." next to the preprinted space allowing substitution.[210] A stamp may not be used.[211]

A few states provide for mandatory substitution unless the physician indicates otherwise.[212]

Many states permit the substitution of generic drugs only on the instruction of the physician. These states use two-line prescription forms. In the lower right corner of such forms is a line labeled "dispense as written"; opposite this is the label "substitution permitted." The physician must sign next to one or the other label, and the pharmacist must follow these instructions.[213] In New Hampshire, the physician must write "or its generic equivalent drug listed in the New Hampshire formulary" to permit substitution.[214]

Patient approval is required by some states before the pharmacist may dispense a generic substitute.[215] In other states, the selection and substitution of the generic equivalent is within the discretion of the pharmacist and may be done even without the patient's request.[216] The pharmacist must comply with the patient's request for a less expensive generic equivalent.[217] The consumer may also require that the prescription be filled as written or communicated.[218]

When the pharmacist dispenses a drug other than the prescribed brand, the consumer must be notified.[219] This notification may be required to be made orally or as an indication on the label, or both.[220]

Most state laws mandate that all savings realized by generic substitution be passed on to the consumer.[221] Other states specify that a fixed minimum percentage be passed on. For example, Washington requires that at least 60 percent of the savings be passed on to the consumer.[222] Generally, the cost of the substituted drug may not exceed the amount normally charged for that drug or the total charge for the drug product originally prescribed unless the patient consents.[223] In most states, a pharmacist may not substitute a more expensive drug product without the consumer's consent.[224]

Some states require that pharmacists post signs in a location readily visible to customers stating that a less expensive drug may be substituted, or is required to be substituted, for the prescribed drug.[225]

Most states compile a drug formulary that contains either names of drug products that may be substituted for the prescribed brand[226] or names of those which the pharmacist may not substitute.[227] The responsible state agency determines whether or not a particular generic drug is equivalent in quality and effectiveness to the name brand and, if not, whether it would pose a threat to the health and safety of the citizens of the state. If a drug product appears on a prohibited list or fails to appear on an approved list, the pharmacist may not substitute it.[228] The FDA has compiled a list of drug products that have no known bioequivalents.[229] At least one state requires pharmacists to be familiar with this list when dispensing generic drug products.[230] The FDA has also approved the New York formulary as an example of one containing only therapeutically equivalent products with no problems involving bioequivalence or other aspects of quality.[231]

Some states statutorily exempt physicians from liability from injuries arising out of the substitution of generic drugs.[232]

In an effort to standardize drug substitution laws, the Federal Trade Commission (FTC) has recently proposed a model substitution law that contains provisions designed to encourage substitution. The FTC model law (1) allows pharmacists to substitute unless the physician writes "d.a.w." on the prescription, thus adopting the pattern that the majority of states have followed, (2) permits substitution only in accordance with an FDA-developed formulary, (3) requires that the substitute product be lower priced than the prescribed brand name product, although it does not require that all the savings be passed on to the consumer, (4) allows the state to limit a pharmacist's liability for substitution, and (5) requires that the consumer be informed of the substitution.[233]

§ 5.42 Human and Fetal Research

Current debate over the status of the fetus, generated by concern for its protection, has spawned regulation governing research conducted on human fetuses. At the federal level, recommendations submitted by the National Commission for the Protection of Human Subjects of Biomedical and Behavioral Research have been drafted into regulations that apply to all research involving human subjects conducted or supported by DHHS.[234]

Among other things, the regulations specify general requirements for obtaining the informed consent of human subjects (see § 1.33, Consent and Informed Consent). Such consent may be sought only under circumstances that provide prospective subjects or their representatives sufficient opportunity for considering whether to participate and that minimize the possibility of coercion or undue influence. The researcher must explain the purposes of the research in understandable language and must disclose the expected duration of the subject's participation. The researcher must describe anticipated procedures, identifying any that are experimental, together with any expected risks and benefits. The subject must be apprised of any possibly advantageous alternative procedures or causes of treatment that could be employed. The extent to which records will be confidential must also be described. If more than minimal risk is possible, the researcher must explain whether any compensation or any medical treatment is available if injury results. Finally, the researcher must state that participation is voluntary, refusal to participate will impose no penalty or loss of entitlement to any benefit, and the subject may withdraw at any time without repercussion.[235]

Additional protections governing research grants to studies involving the fetus, pregnant women, and in vitro fertilization have been promulgated by DHHS.[236] These regulations advocate limiting the scope of fetal research,[237] and they impose the following restraints on such research:

1. Appropriate studies on animals and nonpregnant individuals must be completed before experimentation on pregnant human subjects may be done.
2. Nontherapeutic research may pose no more than minimal risk to the fetus.
3. Researchers conducting the experiments may not take part in decisions regarding the timing or method of abortion or the viability of the fetus at the termination of the pregnancy.
4. Abortion procedures may pose no more than minimal risk to the fetus or to the pregnant woman.
5. No inducements may be made to terminate the pregnancy.[238]

Research activity directed toward pregnant women must meet the health needs of the mother and pose a minimal risk to the fetus. The father's consent as well as the mother's must be obtained unless the sole purpose of the activity is to meet the mother's health needs or the father is unavailable.[239] Likewise, research conducted on fetuses in utero must meet the fetus's health needs, pose minimal risk to the fetus, and receive the consent of both parents. The research must have as its purpose the development of important biomedical knowledge unobtainable by other means.[240] An ex utero fetus may not be the subject of research without first determining whether it is viable. This determination need not be made if the research poses no added risk and could provide important, otherwise unobtainable biomedical knowledge or if the research activity is conducted to enhance fetal survival. Nonviable ex utero fetuses may not be the subject of research unless (1) their vital functions are not artificially maintained, (2) the procedures employed would not themselves terminate heartbeat or respiration, and (3) the purpose is to develop important, otherwise unobtainable biomedical knowledge. If any such research is conducted, the consent of the mother and the father, if he is available, is required.[241]

Because the federal regulations apply only to federally funded research, several states have enacted legislation curtailing fetal research that is funded from other sources.[242] Federal regulation does not supersede state regulation, therefore a person conducting research with federal money must comply with any applicable state laws, as well as with the federal regulations.[243] There is a wide variance in these statutes, from South Dakota, which liberally allows fetal experimentation, provided the mother consents,[244] to Maine, which flatly prohibits all experimentation on fetuses in utero as well as on all live fetuses ex utero.[245] Some states permit only therapeutic research or diagnostic and remedial procedures used to determine or preserve the life or health of the fetus.[246] About eight states prohibit experimentation on the aborted fetus, without mentioning research on the fetus in utero.[247] Kentucky[248] and Nebraska[249] prohibit all experimentation on the "live or viable" aborted fetus, while other states' statutes make no reference to the viability of the fetus. Some states prohibit all experimentation on fetuses ex utero,[250] while others prohibit such experimenting only on live fetuses, except where it is done to preserve the life or health of a viable fetus.[251]

Federal regulations defer to state or local law with respect to research conducted on the dead fetus.[252] Some states have adopted pertinent legislation. Indiana, Illinois, and Ohio, for example, prohibit experimentation on aborted fetuses.[253] Massachusetts, North Dakota, and South Dakota require that the mother's consent be obtained before experimentation on the dead fetus.[254]

Many of the states that regulate fetal research impose severe penalties for violations. For example, Louisiana provides that violators may be sentenced to five to 20 years at hard labor or fined up to ten thousand dollars, or both.[255] Kentucky requires imprisonment for at least ten but not more than 20 years for anyone who permits a live or viable aborted child to be used for any form of experimentation.[256] Several states provide for imprisonment for up to five years.[257]

§ 5.43 Reporting Requirements

Some states require the reporting of events or conditions usually associated with procedures performed by obstetricians-gynecologists. The sensitive nature of these conditions or procedures may present special problems regarding the confidentiality of records and impose record-keeping requirements on physicians and health facilities.

Birth Registration: All states have some requirement for registration of births.[258] Generally, if a child is born in or en route to an institution such as a hospital, the chief administrator or his or her designated representative must file a birth certificate within five[259] to ten days after the birth,[260] depending on the jurisdiction. The physician, or whoever was in attendance, must provide the medical information and certify the facts of the birth.[261] The time limitation governing the physician's certification varies. For example, Michigan requires the certification to be made within three days of birth,[262] whereas Georgia requires certification within five days of birth.[263]

If a child is born outside an institution, most states require one of the following individuals, listed in order of preference, to certify and file the birth registration: the physician in attendance, any other person in attendance (such as a midwife),[264] one of the parents, or the individual in charge of the premises where the child was born.[265] In some states, if no one is in attendance and neither parent is able to prepare the certificate, the local health officer must prepare it using information secured from any person who has knowledge of the birth.[266] Some states make no distinction as to the place of birth in designating the persons responsible for certification and filing of birth registration.[267]

If a child is born in a moving conveyance, registration generally takes place in the state in which the child is first removed from the conveyance.[268] Most states provide for delayed birth registration and set forth judicial procedures whereby the facts of birth can be established if a delayed certificate is rejected.[269]

States also provide for registration of infants of unknown parentage. Generally, whoever assumes custody must report to the appropriate authority information regarding the circumstances of the discovery; particularized data with respect to the child, such as sex and race; and the ultimate placement of the child. Such a report constitutes the child's birth certificate. If the child is later identified and another birth certificate obtained, the first report is sealed and filed and may be opened only by court order.[270]

If the child's natural parents are not married to each other at the time of birth, requirements as to identification of the father vary. In some states, the name of the putative father may not be entered on the birth certificate without his consent[271] and the consent of the mother,[272] nor may other facts relating to the father be reported.[273] The child will be registered in the surname of the mother.[274] The name of the father may be inserted on the birth certificate if both mother and father sign it prior to the registration[275] or if a final determination of paternity has been made by the court having jurisdiction. In such cases, the father's surname may be used.[276] In Washington, the mother may use any surname she desires, but no father may be specifically named.[277] Michigan requires that the name of the husband at the time of conception or, if none, at the time of birth be registered as the father of the child, although any surname may be designated by the parents.[278]

Most states provide for confidentiality of birth records of illegitimate children. Such records may only be disclosed under court order[279] or applicable regulatory procedures.[280] Some states, such as Indiana, allow a natural parent who has not lost custody of the child to obtain all records relevant to the child's birth.[281]

Fetal Death: Some states have special provisions regarding the reporting of fetal death. This type of reporting allows for analysis of fetal death patterns in order to assess possible environmental or other factors that could be contributing to abnormal fetal death rates. The definition of fetal death varies from state to state. In California, fetal death is defined as death of a fetus that has advanced to or beyond the twentieth week of uterogestation.[282] Michigan defines it as the death of a fetus that has completed 20 weeks of gestation or weighs 400 grams.[283] A number of states have defined it as the death of a product of human conception prior to complete expulsion or retraction from its mother, irrespective of the duration of the pregnancy. Death is indicated by the fact that, after such expulsion or retraction, the fetus does not breathe or show any other evidence of life such as heartbeat, umbilical cord pulsation, or definite movement of voluntary muscles.[284] Thus, in some cases, a fetal death certificate will be required for the product of a spontaneous or voluntary abortion.

Fetal death certification must be filed with the local registrar of the state district where death or delivery occurred within three to five days after the occurrence and prior to the removal of the fetus from the state. If the place of death is unknown, the certificate is to be filed within the state district where the fetus was found.[285] If death occurs in a moving conveyance, the certificate is to be filed where the fetus was first removed from the conveyance.[286]

Generally the certificate is to be prepared by the funeral director, or someone acting in that capacity, who first takes custody of the fetus; in the absence of such a person, the physician or other person in attendance at or after the delivery prepares the certificate.[287] The medical certification of the cause of death is to be completed and signed by the physician in attendance, except where a coroner's inquest is required.[288] A coroner's inquest may be required where circumstances suggest that death was caused by other than natural causes. In such cases, depending on the jurisdiction, the attending physician, the funeral director, or some other specified state officer is required to refer the case to the coroner for investigation.[289] If there is no attending physician, or if he or she fails to do so, the responsibility may rest on the local health officer.[290]

When fetal death occurs without medical attendance of the mother or after delivery, the coroner may be required to investigate the cause of the death and complete the medical certificate within 24 hours after taking charge of the case.[291]

In some states, it is the physician's responsibility to deliver the certificate either to the place where the death occurred or to the attending funeral director at his place of business.[292] In others it is the responsibility of the funeral director to obtain the information from the physician.[293] If the fetus is delivered in an institution, the chief administrator or his representative may be responsible for preparing and filing the fetal death report.[294]

Some states, such as Michigan, maintain fetal death records only for statistical and analytical purposes. Therefore no parental names or common identifiers (such as social security numbers or driver's license numbers) are contained on the forms. Statistical information that may reveal the identity of the biological parents of a fetal decedent is also prohibited.[295]

Venereal Disease: Reporting of cases of venereal disease is required by many states under statutes regulating the control of communicable diseases. Communicable diseases are defined in various ways. Some states define them as any infectious or contagious disease declared to be a communicable disease by law or by a designated state agency.[296] Other states specifically designate the venereal diseases covered by the statute and may include syphilis, gonorrhea, chancroid,[297] lymphogranuloma venerum, or granuloma inguinale.[298]

Any physician or other person who diagnoses or treats venereal disease may be required to report it to the designated state health authority.[299] Other persons who may be required to make such a report include heads of hospitals and other state health institutions, directors of laboratories, nurses, and midwives.[300] In New Jersey, the report must contain the name, address, race, sex, nationality, and approximate age of the patient; the character of the disease; the probable source of the infection; and whether or not the case has been reported previously[301] (see § 5.44, Testing Requirements).

Most states provide that the information contained in the reports is confidential and limit the circumstances under which the information can be divulged. Generally, the information may be disclosed under court order[302] to a person whose official duties entitle him or her to receive information contained in the records,[303] to a physician or health official when it is necessary to protect the public health and safety,[304] or for research purposes subject to strict supervision by health officials to ensure confidentiality.[305] In all cases, necessary public health authorities may have access to the records.[306] Some states provide for the confidentiality of vital statistics information, generally without specifically mentioning venereal disease reports.[307]

§ 5.44 Testing Requirements

Newborns: Phenylketonuria (PKU) is an inherited metabolic disorder caused by the lack of phenylalanine hydroxylase, an enzyme necessary for the digestion of milk and other proteins. Without this enzyme, phenylalanine accumulates in the bloodstream of the newborn and frequently causes mental retardation and neurological abnormalities. Simple blood and urine tests have been developed to test for PKU. The ease of testing, weighed against the severity of the disease, has caused many states to initiate legislation requiring that a PKU test be performed on every newborn infant.[308]

It is the duty of the health professional in charge of a newborn's care or present at the birth of an infant,[309] the staff medical officer,[310] or any other person in charge of an institution caring for newborns[311] to test for PKU. If the test is positive, the health professional usually must report the result to the infant's parents or guardian.[312] In some states, the results must be forwarded directly to the department of health, which must then contact as soon possible any suspected case of PKU for further testing.[313]

In a number of states, there are no specific statutory provisions for the procedures to be followed; the appropriate state agency rather than the legislature is required to develop procedures and regulations for PKU testing.[314] For example, Georgia has provided for PKU testing as part of a comprehensive system designed to prevent mental retardation resulting from inherited metabolic disorders. The state's department of human resources is responsible for screening all newborns and retrieving potentially positive cases for further treatment. The entire process of screening, retrieval, and diagnosis must be completed within the first three weeks of the infant's life.[315] In Arkansas, the board of health may provide by regulation that no birth certificate may be received by the bureau of vital statistics unless proper proof is made that a PKU test has been performed.[316] Most statutes provide that mandatory testing provisions not be applied to any child whose parents object on religious grounds.[317]

Many states require that any person attending upon or assisting at birth treat both eyes of the infant with a prophylactic to prevent ophthalmia neonatorum.[318] Ophthalmia neonatorum is a severe inflammation of the eye which may result from delivery through an infected birth canal.[319] Most states specify a 1 percent solution of silver nitrate to treat the eyes.[320] The various statutes mandate that treatment be performed within such time limits "as soon as practicable after birth,"[321] "within two hours after birth,"[322] or "within one hour after birth or as soon thereafter as the health professional is present."[323] If any redness, swelling, or signs of inflammation appear in the child's eyes or eyelids within two weeks after birth, many states requires the health professional caring for the infant to report it to the local health officer[324] or to a competent physician[325] within six[326] to 24[327] hours of discovery.

All maternity homes, hospitals, and similar institutions where childbirths occur must keep records of all cases of ophthalmia neonatorum occuring or discovered therein.[328]

In some states, the birth certificate must indicate whether precautions against ophthalmia neonatorum were taken.[329] Most states provide that violation of a requirement relating to newborns is a misdemeanor.[330]

Venereal Disease: Because of the possibility of complications during pregnancy or adverse affects on the fetus, all states require a physician attending a pregnant woman to test for venereal disease.[331] The test may be made at the time of the initial examination, unless medically inadvisable,[332] within ten days thereof,[333] or at any time during the period of prenatal treatment.[334] In some states, a physician must keep a record of the dates and results of the tests or the reason why such tests were not administered.[335] The state may also require that this information be included on the birth certificate.[336] In other states, information as to whether or not the proper tests were performed, the date the specimen was taken, and the results of the test are to be entered in the physician's birth report.[337]

Several states require that a person who is attending a pregnant woman, but who is not permitted to take blood samples, ensure that a specimen is taken by a licensed physician and submitted to a laboratory for the necessary tests.[338]

If at the time of delivery no prior test can be proven, the person in attendance may be required to take a blood sample and send it to a laboratory for testing.[339] Such specimen may be taken as soon after delivery as the physician thinks advisable.[340]

Many states require that, before obtaining a marriage license, a couple must submit to a blood test to determine the presence of venereal disease. If the test is positive, treatment is required before the license is granted.[341] Some states allow this requirement to be waived on the basis of an individual's personal religious beliefs.[342]

Prostitutes, or persons taken into custody and charged with any crime involving a sex offense or lewd conduct, may be required to submit to an examination for venereal disease.[343] Health regulations requiring submission to physical examinations have been upheld as a valid exercise of the state's police power.[344]

Many states have special provisions regarding the testing for and treatment of venereal disease in minors. As a general rule, a minor may give a valid and binding consent to medical or surgical care or services for the treatment of venereal disease.[345] This consent cannot later be disaffirmed by reason of his or her minority.[346] The consent of the minor's spouse, parents, or guardian is not necessary.[347] However, in some states a physician may, at his or her discretion, inform the parent or guardian without the consent or over the express objection, of the minor[348] without being subjected to liability for breach of the physician-patient privilege.[349]

§ 5.45 Abortion

The U.S. Supreme Court decided on January 22, 1973, that the constitutional right to privacy protected by the due process clause of the Fourteenth Amendment entails that (1) no law can restrict the right of a woman to have an abortion performed by a physician during the first trimester of her pregnancy; (2) during the second trimester the abortion procedure may be regulated by law only to the extent that the regulation reasonably relates to the preservation and protection of maternal health; (3) at the point at which the fetus becomes viable (not before the beginning of the third trimester), a law may prohibit abortion, subject to an exception permitting an abortion whenever necessary to protect the woman's life or health (including any aspect of her physical or mental health); and (4) no law may require that all abortions be performed in accredited hospitals (where accreditation has no particular concern with abortion as a medical or surgical procedure), that abortions be approved by hospital committee or a second medical opinion, or that abortions be performed on women residing in the state concerned.[350] The effect of this decision was to invalidate some of the laws regulating abortion in every state.

Informed Consent: A number of states have passed statutes requiring that a woman give informed, written consent to the abortion to be performed on her[351] (see § 1.33, Consent and Informed Consent). The Supreme Court held,

§ 5.45   Abortion   221

in *Planned Parenthood of Central Missouri v. Danforth*,[352] that a state may constitutionally require prior written consent for an abortion. The Court stated that:

> It is true that *Doe* and *Roe* clearly establish that the state may not restrict the decision of the patient and her physician regarding abortion during the first stage of pregnancy. Despite the fact that apparently no other Missouri statute [with one noted exception] requires a patient's prior written consent to a surgical procedure, the imposition by [the statute] of such a requirement for termination of pregnancy even during the first stage, in our view is not in itself an unconstitutional requirement. The decision to abort, indeed, is an important and often stressful one, and it is desirable and imperative that it be made with full knowledge of its nature and consequences. The woman is the one primarily concerned, and her awareness of the decision and its significance may be assured, constitutionally, by the State to the extent of requiring her prior written consent.[353]

While the Supreme Court has recognized the authority of the state to require informed consent by statute, such a statute must not impinge on a woman's constitutional rights in its enforcement. Thus, a district court upheld a Montana statute that made it a crime for a physician to perform an abortion on a woman without her informed consent. Informed consent under the statute meant that she be told of the nature of abortion surgery and of alternatives to abortion before she consented.[354] Tennessee has adopted the requirement that a woman be told that her fetus may be viable when she seeks an abortion more than 24 weeks after conception.[355] However, a Missouri statute requiring a physician to inform a woman seeking an abortion of the probable anatomical and physiological characteristics of the unborn child at the time the abortion is to be performed was held to constitute an impermissible intrusion into the privacy of the physician-patient relationship.[356] A city ordinance requiring that persons undergoing abortions be told certain things by the physician, including the "facts" that abortion is major surgery and that human life begins at the time of conception, was held unconstitutional.[357] A district court has invalidated a Nebraska law requiring a woman seeking an abortion to indicate that she had been informed not only of the reasonably possible consequences of abortion, but also of the reasonably possible conquences of pregnancy and childbirth, because the law violated the substantive due process guarantee of the Fourteenth Amendment.[358]

Some states have attempted to impose waiting periods prior to the performance of an abortion, generally of one to two days.[359] A federal court invalidated the Nebraska requirement of a 48-hour waiting period between the time the physician obtained an informed consent and the time the abortion was performed because it imposed an undue burden on the woman's freedom to obtain an abortion.[360] Similarly, the portion of a Maine statute requiring a 48-hour waiting period between physician counseling and an abortion was struck down, although the requirement that the physician counsel the woman was upheld.[361]

Notification or Consent of Spouse or Parent: It is unconstitutional for a state to require the consent of the husband of the woman seeking an abortion during the first trimester.[362] In 1975, the Supreme Court found unconstitutional a section of a Missouri statute that required the written consent of the woman's spouse unless a licensed physician certified that the abortion was necessary to preserve the mother's life. The Court found the statute to be unconstitutional because it did not conform with the standards enunciated earlier in *Roe v. Wade*.[363] The Court also found that the state could not delegate to a spouse the veto power that the state itself is absolutely and totally prohibited from exercising during the first trimester of pregnancy.[364]

> It seems manifest that, ideally, the decision to terminate a pregnancy should be one concurred in by both the wife and her husband . . . but it is difficult to believe that the goal of fostering mutuality and trust in a marriage, and of strengthening the marital relationship and the marital institution, will be achieved by giving the husband a veto power exercisable for any reason whatsoever or for no reason at all.[365]

The court noted that it is obvious that, when the wife and the husband disagree on the question of whether the wife should have an abortion, the view of only one of them can prevail: "Inasmuch as it is the woman who physically bears the child and who is more directly and immediately affected by the pregnancy, as between the two, the balance weighs in her favor."[366]

Relying on *Danforth,* the Supreme Court in another case affirmed in memorandum the circuit court's decision that spousal consent requirements for abortion are unconstitutional. The circuit court identified two interests of the state: one incidental to its general authority to regulate the marriage relationship and one in protecting the right of a husband whose wife desires an abortion. The court stated that it knew of no case that sanctioned state determination of intrafamilial decision-making processes with regard to childbearing decisions.[367] Further, a 1972 case of the Supreme Court specifically held that the married person's right of privacy included the right to be free from unwarranted governmental intrusion into matters as fundamentally affecting a person as the decision of whether to bear or beget a child.[368] The Court found the state's interest in protecting the husband's rights to be substantial but not of sufficient weight that the state may constitutionally require a woman to obtain her husband's consent to obtain an abortion.[369]

Spousal notification requirements have also been invalidated. For example, a Florida statute which required that a married woman intending to seek an abortion give her husband notice of the proposed termination of pregnancy and an opportunity to consult with the wife concerning the procedure, and which required the woman to provide her attending physician with either a written statement that such notice and opportunity had been given or the written consent of her husband, has been declared unconstitutional. The U.S. District Court for the Southern District of Florida questioned whether the notice and consultation requirement furthered the husband's interest in the procreative potential of his marriage. It also found that the statute was too inclusive insofar as it sought to promote marital harmony, because it required notification of the woman's husband in all cases. A woman's husband, said the court, is not necessarily the father of her unborn child.[370]

Regarding parental consent to a minor's obtaining an abortion, the Supreme Court concluded that a state may not impose a blanket provision requiring the consent of a parent or guardian to an abortion for an unmarried minor during the first 12 weeks of pregnancy.[371] However, if a state decides to require a pregnant minor to obtain the consent of one or both of her parents to an abortion, it must also provide an alternative procedure whereby authorization can be obtained, such as judicial consent. The alternative procedure must provide for anonymity of the minor and sufficient speed to provide an effective opportunity for an abortion to be obtained. A state may not impose a consent provision that amounts to the absolute and possibly arbitrary veto power of a parent or guardian.[372]

The U.S. Supreme Court has upheld a Utah statute requiring a physician to "notify, if possible, the parents or guardian of the woman upon whom the abortion is to be performed, if she is a minor."[373] The court found that the statute serves the important considerations of preserving family integrity and protecting adolescents and does not violate any constitutional guarantees as applied to immature and dependent minors.[374]

Abortion Reporting: Some states require physicians to report all performed abortions to the designated state agency within a specified time after the abortion.[375] (For example, Michigan allows seven days,[376] Ohio allows 15.[377]) The reports are to be made on forms provided by the designated state agency, and they are confidential: no state permits the identity of the woman obtaining or seeking an abortion to be revealed. To the extent that these reporting requirements are not utilized or enforced so as to impose an undue burden on the physician or to violate the privacy of the woman, the courts have upheld them.[378] A provision requiring the reporting of "prescribed" abortions has been invalidated.[379] The following Michigan statute is a comprehensive example of the information generally required in abortion reports:

1. The age of the woman at the time of the abortion
2. The marital status of the woman at the time of the abortion
3. The city or township, county, and state in which the woman resided at the time of the abortion
4. The location and type of facility in which the abortion was performed
5. The source of referral to the physician performing the abortion
6. The number of previous pregnancies carried to term
7. The number of previous pregnancies ending in miscarriage or spontaneous abortion
8. The number of previous pregnancies terminated by abortion

9. The period of gestation, in weeks, of the present pregnancy and the first day of the last menstrual period
10. The method used to perform the abortion
11. The weight of the embryo or fetus, if determinable
12. Whether the fetus showed evidence of life when separated, expelled, or removed from the woman
13. The date of performance of the abortion
14. The immediate complications of the abortion procedure
15. The physician's signature and his state license number[380]

Regulation of Facilities in Which Abortions Are Performed: Although the Supreme Court held that a woman's fundamental right to privacy encompassed the right to terminate her pregnancy during the first trimester,[381] it recognized the state's legitimate interest in requiring that the abortion be performed under circumstances ensuring maximum safety for the patient.[382] This interest extends to the performing physician, his or her staff, the facilities involved, the availability of aftercare, and adequate provision for any complication or emergency that might arise.[383] The Supreme Court allows reasonable state regulations not designed to impinge on the abortion decision to be applied to first trimester abortions.[384]

Most states provide for regulation of abortion facilities by statute and by administrative regulation.[385] It is generally accepted that states may require facilities performing first trimester abortions to obtain licenses to operate and may impose appropriate regulations to that end.[386] For example, in 1979 the U.S. Court of Appeals for the First Circuit scrutinized a Massachusetts clinical licensing and regulation scheme as it applied to an abortion clinic. The regulations included requirements that a physician and registered nurse be in attendance at all times during clinic hours and that clinics comply with record-keeping requirements. The court upheld the Massachusetts provisions, finding that they had no "legally significant impact or consequence on the abortion decision or on the physician-patient relationship" but neutrally protected the public health and safety. The Court, however, explicitly censured clinic licensure laws aimed at restricting a woman's right to a first trimester abortion.[387]

Statutes requiring that all abortions be performed in hospitals have been held to be unconstitutional.[388] In one case it was stated that, prior to the end of the first trimester, the physician may exercise his judgment regarding the abortion decision free of interference by the state. Therefore, the U.S. District Court held invalid an Indiana statute that exempted first trimester abortions from criminal penalties only if they were performed in a hospital or in a licensed health care facility that offered the same basic safeguards as a hospital and immediate hospital backup.[389] The Supreme Court ruled that requiring second trimester abortions to be performed solely in hospitals is ". . . a heavy and unnecessary burden on women's access to a relatively inexpensive, otherwise accessible and safe abortion procedure."[390]

A state may regulate first trimester abortion facilities to the same degree that it regulates other clinics which perform surgical procedures requiring approximately the same degree of skill and care.[391] It may not, however, impose more severe standards on abortion facilities in an attempt to eliminate them.[392] A Florida statute requiring all facilities in which pregnancy terminations were performed to be licensed was allowed to stand, but accompanying regulations which provided that each patient admitted to the facility for an abortion must have a confirmed gestation diagnosis of no more than thirteen weeks were struck down. Under these regulations, the statute applied only to physicians and clinics involved in first trimester abortions.[393]

Where the state regulates abortions more than other, similar surgical procedures, the difference in regulation must be shown to be necessitated by the peculiar characteristics of the abortion procedure.[394] New York has extensive statutory rules and administrative regulations that have been upheld as part of a comprehensive plan for the regulation of hospitals and other public and private health facilities.[395] In addition to obtaining written approval from the public health council, a health facility that is found to be a "diagnostic or treatment center" must comply with minimum operating and construction standards.[396] These standards govern items ranging from laboratory requirements and nursing personnel supervision to the availability of public toilet facilities and the width of public corridors. In addition, certain standards are applicable only to facilities in which terminations of pregnancy are performed. These facilities must have:

1. Procedure rooms with minimum dimensions of 12 feet by 15 feet
2. Scrub facilities adjacent to the procedure rooms
3. Separate male and female toilets and locker and dressing rooms
4. A recovery room consisting of two recovery beds for each procedure room and a lounge with sitting space for four patients for each procedure room
5. Stretcher parking area or alcove
6. Patient dressing and toilet facilities
7. Storage space for oxygen and inhalation equipment, in accordance with National Fire Protection Association Code 56B, Standard for Nonflammable Medical Gas Systems[397]

Despite this unique treatment, a federal court upheld the New York regulations on the grounds that they were shown to be necessitated by the nature of the abortion operation.[398]

Some states regulate freestanding surgical outpatient facilities and define them to include abortion clinics. Regulations that apply to all such facilities, without regard to the type of surgery performed, avoid the problem created by statutory and regulatory provisions that single out abortion clinics for more stringent regulation. For example, Michigan defines a "freestanding surgical outpatient facility" as:

> A facility, other than the office of a physician, dentist, podiatrist, or other private practice office, offering a surgical procedure and related care that in the opinion of the attending physician can be safely performed without requiring overnight inpatient hospital care. It does not include a surgical outpatient facility owned by and operated as part of a hospital.[399]

Such facilities in Michigan must adopt certain statutorily specified policies governing the rights of patients. Thus, a Michigan abortion clinic licensed as a freestanding surgical outpatient health facility may not deny appropriate care on the basis of race, religion, color, national origin, sex, age, handicap, marital status, sexual preference, or source of payment. Patients are entitled to inspect or receive copies of their medical records for a small fee and to otherwise have such records afforded confidential treatment. A facility must provide understandable information to a patient about her proposed course of treatment and honor a patient's refusal to undergo treatment. General information regarding any experimental procedure to be performed, billing, identities of those responsible for a patient's care, and facility rules and regulations must also be made available to patients.[400] Michigan abortion clinics are also subject to regulations that require the facility to provide counseling services should the patient request them, to keep certain specified records of all performed abortions, to adopt as policy the rule that only uncomplicated pregnancies of less than 14 weeks duration may be aborted, and to undergo routine inspection.[401]

These and companion regulations have been challenged in federal court by Michigan abortion clinics. In a 1981 decision, the Federal District Court for the Eastern District of Michigan found those regulations mentioned above to be valid. Their validity stemmed from the fact that none of them, either collectively or individually, unduly burdens a woman's right to seek an abortion. Furthermore, they were found to be rationally related to the state's legitimate interest in assuring adequate standards of health care in facilities where outpatient surgery is performed. The court recognized further that, while such regulation is permissible, it may not be delegated to a nongovernmental agency. On this basis the court overruled a separate regulation that required abortion clinics to enter into agreements with nearby hospitals to transfer emergencies because the regulation vested hospitals, whose self-interest would affect their decisions, with the power to effectively veto the existence of such clinics.[402] Other jurisdictions have also invalidated similar transfer agreement requirements.[403]

The U.S. Supreme Court has explained that, in scrutinizing abortion clinic regulations, a court's focus should be on the actual effect of the enactment, not upon the motivation or collection of different motivations which may be difficult for a court to ascertain.[404]

Just as a state may not regulate first trimester abortion clinics out of existence, a city may not impose licensure ordinances not imposed on other, similar facilities.[405] Regulations aimed generally at abortion clinics and which fail to exclude first trimester abortions have been held invalid.[406] Further, city hospitals may not be staffed in such a way as to deny abortions to indigent women who may choose to terminate a pregnancy. For example, under Missouri state law, medical personnel opposed to abortion could not be required to treat or admit for treatment a woman desiring an abortion. By staffing the obstetrics and gynecology clinics in city hospitals only with personnel opposed to abortions, city officials could effectively evade the Supreme Court's mandate, at least with regard to poor women, who would be more likely to use city facilities than private ones.[407]

A federal court held invalid a state department of health rule requiring that a physician performing a first trimester abortion have unsupervised privileges at an accessible hospital. Although there was extensive evidence that the regulations were passed to ensure the continuity of care in the case of emergency, there was no such requirement for other "procedures of similar or greater medical complexity and risk." The court stated that there was no good reason given for the distinction and that there were other ways to ensure that only competent physicians performed the procedure.[408]

Funding Restrictions: Since September 1976, Congress has prohibited (either by an amendment to the annual appropriations bill for DHHS or by a joint resolution) the use of any federal funds to reimburse the cost of abortions under the Medicaid program except under certain specified circumstances. This funding restriction is commonly known as the "Hyde Amendment," after its original congressional sponsor, Representative Hyde. The version of the Hyde Amendment applicable to fiscal year 1980 provides:

> [None] of the funds provided by this joint resolution shall be used to perform abortions except where the life of the mother would be endangered if the fetus would be carried to term; or except for such medical procedures necessary for the victims of rape or incest when such rape or incest has been reported promptly to a law enforcement agency or public health service.[409]

Although lower courts had reached opposite conclusions on the issue,[410] in June 1980 the U.S. Supreme Court declared the Hyde Amendment constitutional. The Court held that, while the government cannot *restrict* a woman's right to choose abortion, it is not obligated to provide her with the funds necessary to obtain an abortion, and it need not remove obstacles to obtaining an abortion, such as indigency, which are not of its own creation. The Court reasoned that the Hyde Amendment leaves the indigent woman with at least the same range of choice in deciding to obtain a medically necessary abortion as she would have if Congress subsidized no health care costs at all. The Court further found the restrictions imposed by the Hyde Amendment to be rationally related to the legitimate government objective of protecting potential life.[411] Many states have also passed statutes limiting Medicaid abortion funding.

In 1977, the Supreme Court ruled that participation in the Medicaid program under Title XIX of the Social Security Act does not obligate a state to pay for nontherapeutic abortions.[412] This ruling was expanded in a 1980 case which held that a state may constitutionally withhold funding not only for nontherapeutic, but also for medically necessary abortions. A state may withhold this funding even though it continues to fund other medically necessary health services. Participation in the Medicaid program does not obligate a state to pay for those medically necessary abortions for which federal funding is denied under the Hyde Amendment.[413]

Although the Supreme Court allows a state to constitutionally withhold all funding for abortions, it does not preclude a state wishing to fund abortions from doing so. A state may also fund through its own Medicaid plan such abortions as are excluded by the Hyde Amendment.

§ 5.46 Contraception

States have the right to regulate private activity to protect public health, safety, and welfare. In the public health field, it is this police power under which government can require vaccinations or impose a quarantine, for example. It is also under this power that states may regulate abortion and sterilization procedures and require parental consent for a minor's care. Poised against the state's right to regulate is the individual's right to privacy, which encompasses both an individual's interest in avoiding disclosure of personal matters and his or her interest in being able to make certain kinds of important decisions independently of state intrusion.[414] The right to control one's fertility falls within the latter area.

Prior to 1965, restrictive legislation existed at both the state and federal levels of government. State laws were modeled on the federal Comstock Law, which prohibited the interstate transport of any "obscene, lewd, or lascivious book, pamphlet, picture, paper, print, or other publication of an indecent character, or any article or thing designed or intended for the prevention of conception or procuring of abortion. . . ."[415] The American birth control movement developed in reaction to these laws. As its interest merged with the movement for women's rights and in alliance with the medical profession, a collision of these two competing interests—the state's right to regulate for the public welfare and the individual's right to privacy—was bound to occur.

In 1965, the U.S. Supreme Court in *Griswold v. Connecticut*[416] held unconstitutional, as violating the individual's right to privacy, a state law prohibiting the use of contraceptives, even by married couples in their own homes. Seven years later, the Court expanded the privacy concept to include single persons as well (in *Eisenstadt v. Baird*).[417] Justice Brennan, speaking for the Court, clearly set forth the principle: "If the right of privacy means anything, it is the right of the *individual*, married or single, to be free from unwarranted governmental intrusion into matters so fundamentally affecting a person as the decision whether to bear or beget a child.[418]

Congressional legislation such as the Family Planning Services and Population Research Act[419] is indicative of the shift toward government approval and support of family planning and the broad dissemination of information regarding contraceptives and contraceptives themselves. The Supreme Court decisions taken with a public policy supportive of family planning and birth control leave little doubt that few, if any, barriers exist to distribution of contraceptives to adults in the United States. Distribution of contraceptives to adults is currently permitted in all states—in pharmacies, through organized family planning programs, and through physicians.[420] The remaining question is whether the same principles are to be applied to minors.

In a significant case concerning a minor's access to contraceptives, the Supreme Court recognized the minor's consensual right to receive contraceptives. *Carey v. Population Services International*[421] concerned a New York law[422] which made it a crime (1) for any person to sell or distribute contraceptives of any kind to a minor under the age of 16; (2) for anyone other than a licensed pharmacist to distribute contraceptives to persons over 16; and (3) for anyone, including pharmacists, to advertise or display contraceptives. The statute was challenged by several population counseling services on the grounds that it violated their rights under the due process clause of the Fourteenth Amendment. In affirming the district court ruling declaring the statute unconstitutional, the Supreme Court concluded, "the decision whether or not to beget or bear a child is at the very heart of this cluster of constitutionally protected choices. . . . For in a field that by definition concerns the most intimate of human activities and relationships, decisions whether to accomplish or to prevent conception are among the most private and sensitive."[423] The Supreme Court also rejected the state's argument that the statute served to emphasize to young people the seriousness with which the state viewed sexual promiscuity at an early age.

Although the decision in *Carey* protected the minor's right of privacy in contraceptive decisions, the language suggested that the freedom of minors to make their own decisions concerning contraceptives might be more limited than that of adults. Specifically, the right of parents to raise their children as they see fit without outside interference must be balanced against the minor's right of privacy. Some states require that minors obtain the consent of their parents before obtaining family planning services.[424]

At least one such statute was struck down by the U.S. District Court for Utah in *Jones v. T. H.* The court held that the provisions of the Utah State Plan for Provision of Social and Medical Services illegally discriminates against minors by requiring prior parental consent for birth control counseling, services, and supplies. By doing so, the state in effect added a condition of parental consent to the requirements of the Social Security Act and at the same time deprived minors of their constitutional right to privacy. The U.S. Supreme Court affirmed the decision of the trial court by summary action on May 25, 1976.[425]

In some states, the decision of whether or not to inform the parents of the treatment requested rests in the sole discretion of the physician, and he or she may notify parents without the minor's consent.[426]

Although the Supreme Court has not yet ruled on the legality of either the consent or notice requirements, lower federal courts have struck down the requirements of several states.[427] In *Doe v. Pickett,* a federal district court considered the policy of the West Virginia Department of Health denying birth control and family planning services to unmarried persons under 18 without parental consent. The court held that the department, being a grantee under Title X of the Public Health Services Act and Titles IV, XIX, and XX of the Social Security Act, could not impose a requirement of parental consent or notice as a condition to family planning services.[428] This brings into question existing interpretations of law, such as the Kansas attorney general's opinion that no state clinic could distribute contraceptives to a single person under 18.[429]

Another recent case concerned a family planning center that dispensed oral contraceptives to minors without the notice or consent of their parents. The sixth circuit court in *Doe v. Irwin* reversed a district court which had held that parents must be allowed a reasonable opportunity to consult with their minor children before the children may obtain contraceptives.[430] However, the state had not passed any law requiring parental notification, so there was no parental right to balance against the minor's right of privacy.

Undoubtedly, a case dealing with parental consent and notification requirements will soon reach the Supreme Court, and the extent of minors' privacy rights to obtain contraceptives and the constitutionality of parental restrictions on these rights will be further defined.

§ 5.47 Sterilization

Government-Funded Elective Sterilizations: The federal government has promulgated extensive regulations governing the use of federal funds for elective sterilizations.[431] The regulations apply to all health service programs and projects administered by the U.S. Public Health Service and supported in whole or in part by federal funds. The regulations are intended, in part, to prevent poor and minority women from being pressured into sterilization operations that they do not want. Heavy emphasis is accordingly placed on the requirement of "informed consent."

Informed consent is not valid under the regulations unless the person seeking sterilization is a mentally competent individual at least 21 years of age.[432] Informed consent also requires the person obtaining the patient's consent to answer the patient's questions and to provide her with basic information and advice. Specifically, the patient must be told that refusal to undergo sterilization will not affect her right to obtain future care or treatment under any federally funded program. She must be told that sterilization is considered irreversible, and available alternative methods of birth control and family planning must be described. The specific sterilization procedure to be performed, and the benefits, risks, and discomforts associated with sterilization, must also be thoroughly explained. An interpreter is to be provided if necessary. Consent may not be obtained if the patient is under the influence of alcohol or other drugs, is in childbirth or labor, or is obtaining or seeking to obtain an abortion.[433] Finally, a consent form approved by DHHS must be used, and all necessary signatures must be obtained.[434]

The regulations prohibit the performance of a hysterectomy for the sole purpose of rendering the patient infertile.[435] They also establish a mandatory waiting period. Except in cases of premature delivery or emergency abdominal surgery, the sterlilization operation must be performed not less than 30 but not more than 180 days after informed consent is obtained.[436] The waiting period is intended to give the patient additional time in which to consider her decision to be sterilized.

Most states do not have extensive regulations pertaining to state-funded sterilization operations. Sterilizations funded by the state of California, however, are governed by a set of regulations patterned after the federal model.[437] The California regulations differ from the federal in establishing a shorter waiting period (14 days in most cases; as little as 72 hours if the patient so requests) and in lowering the age of consent to 18. California also requires that the patient's informed consent be obtained if she is to receive therapy which will result in sterility.

In Minnesota, it is a misdemeanor for any person compensated under a state family planning program to coerce a patient into undergoing an abortion or a sterilization operation by threatening her with the loss of or disqualification for benefits under any state or federal program.[438] Minnesota also requires employees of state-funded programs to notify the parents if they recommend abortion or sterilization to an unemancipated minor.[439]

State Regulation of Elective Sterilization: Most states have no laws specifically regulating privately funded, elective sterilizations. Others, however, have considered it necessary to pass such laws for the protection of the patient or physician, or both.

Statutes in some states require a physician to obtain the patient's informed consent before performing a sterilization operation.[440] Informed consent has been defined as consent that is based upon an understanding of the nature and consequences of sterilization, given by a person competent to make such a decision, and wholly voluntary and free from coercion, expressed or implied.[441] To emphasize to the patient the seriousness of her decision, and to protect the physician from charges of battery, the patient may be required to give her consent in writing.[442] Of course, even in states without specific statutes, the physician may have a common-law duty to obtain the patient's informed consent before performing a sterilization operation (see § 1.33, Consent and Informed Consent).

Some statutes require the patient's spouse to agree to the sterilization operation.[443] The validity of these statutes is in considerable doubt following the Supreme Court decision in *Planned Parenthood of Missouri v. Danforth*.[444] The Court held that a state may not constitutionally require a woman to obtain her spouse's consent before she procures an abortion. At least one court has held that the Supreme Court rationale compels invalidation of sterilization statutes requiring spousal consent.[445] However, there is also authority that a statute requiring a patient to give his or her spouse prior notice, but not requiring spousal consent, is constitutional.[446]

Other states specifically prohibit institutions and medical personnel from considering any special, nonmedical qualifications for sterilization cases that are not considered for other types of operations.[447] Nonmedical qualifications that may not be considered include the patient's age, marital status, and number of natural children.[448] Such statutes are not, however, intended to affect the physician's right to counsel the patient as to whether sterilization is appropriate.

The age at which effective consent can be given to a sterilization operation may be set by statute. Typically, effective consent may be given at 18 years of age,[449] but an unmarried person is not permitted to consent to sterilization until reaching the age of 21.[450] On the other hand, an emancipated minor can give effective consent to surgical procedures, including sterilization, before reaching the age of majority. An emancipated minor is a person under the age of majority who is no longer under the care or custody of parents or other guardian.[451] The usual ways in which a minor is emancipated are by marrige, by judicial decree, by consent of the parents, or by the failure of the parents to meet their legal responsibiliities. Minors will also generally be deemed emancipated if they live apart from their parents, are self-supporting, and exercise general control over their own lives. Statutes in some states embody the emancipated minor's right to give effective consent to medical or surgical treatment.[452] In addition, the age of consent may be less than 18, even for an emancipated minor, if no parent or guardian of the minor is immediately available[453] (see § 1.33, Consent and Informed Consent).

Some states have enacted statutes intended to ensure the safety of sterilization operations. Thus it may be required that sterilization operations be performed only by physicians[454] or only in a hospital or other licensed facility.[455] In addition, a physician may be required to collaborate or consult with at least one other physician before performing a sterilization operation.[456]

State law may specifically provide that a physician cannot be held civilly or criminally liable for performing a nonnegligent sterilization operation in accordance with state statutes.[457] Such laws do not, however, shield the physician from liability for any negligence in the performance of the operation.[458] A physician who *refuses* to participate in sterilization procedures on moral or ethical grounds may also be protected from liability by statute. Commonly called "conscience clauses," statutes protecting physicians from liability for refusal to participate in abortions and, sometimes, for refusal to participate in sterilizations have been enacted by some states (see § 7.65, Abortion and Sterilization). The following New Jersey statute is typical: "The refusal to perform, assist in the performance of, or provide abortion services or sterilization procedures shall not constitute grounds for civil or criminal liability, disciplinary action or discriminatory treatment."[459]

Violation of statutes regulating elective sterilization may constitute grounds for disciplinary proceedings or for sanctions imposed by the state.[460] Statutes regulating elective sterilization are intended to apply only to operations performed for the express purpose of rendering the patient infertile. Operations indicated by sound therapeutic reasons which have the incidental effect of causing sterility do not fall within the scope of such statutes.[461]

Nonelective Sterilization: As one commentator has noted, there has been a long, if not wholly honorable, tradition of eugenic sterilization in the United States.[462] Many states provide for the nonelective sterilization of the retarded, the insane, the feebleminded, or the criminal recidivist[463] upon the application of a parent, guardian,[464] or other designated authority, such as the director of a mental health institution.[465] The courts have generally sustained legislation providing for sterilization of certain types of criminally insane and feebleminded persons.[466] In one case, a sterilization statute designed to prevent procreation of children by mentally ill or retarded individuals who would be unable to take care of their children or who would procreate children with physical, mental, or nervous diseases was upheld where the statute had adequate procedural safeguards to protect the incompetent.[467] Some courts, however, have found that sterilization statutes are unconstitutional because (1) sterilization is cruel and unusual punishment,[468] (2) such statutes amount to unconstitutional class legislation,[469] (3) the statutes deny due process by failing to provide for notice of hearing to the person whose sterilization is proposed,[470] or (4) they violate the equal protection clause of the Fourteenth Amendment.[471] In all cases, a valid order for the sterilization of a mental incompetent must comply with the procedural requirements of the statute. The examining physician may be required to appear before a court for questioning, and a temporary guardian for the incompetent may be appointed within the time specified by the statute.[472]

Although the decisions are not uniform, most courts will not authorize such sterilizations without statutory authority, regardless of the facts before them.[473] Given the complicated legal and sociological issues involved, other mechanisms, such as impartial review committees, are also being developed to ensure that the rights of incompetent persons are fully protected.[474]

The North Carolina sterilization statute gives some idea of the procedural safeguards to which an incompetent person is entitled.

1. The petition for sterilization must contain psychological test results.

2. The incompetent and his guardian must receive notice of the required court hearing.
3. The incompetent has a right to appeal the decision and a right to counsel (provided by the state, if necessary).
4. The evidence must be "clear, strong and convincing" before a court order can be entered.[475]

A federal court in Alabama required similar standards to ensure the protection of three mentally retarded inmates at a state institution, as well as other individuals who would be involved in future sterilization attempts. The court required (1) a determination that the proposed sterilization is in the best interests of the resident (who must be at least 21 years old), (2) written consent of the inmate, (3) an evaluation by the director of the institution as to the inmate's understanding of the nature and consequences of sterilization, and (4) extensive final review of the case by a review committee.[476]

As of 1975, only nine states had statutes dealing with the sterilization of noninstitutionalized, mentally deficient persons.[477] In a recent decision, parents caring for severely retarded and deaf children in their homes were permitted to seek authorization for the sterilization of these children when the same opportunity was afforded parents or guardians of institutionalized children by statute. The judge noted that, if the state may rationally decide to allow sterilization of some individuals to avoid unwanted pregnancy, it makes little sense to contend that the same right should be denied to others in the same situation.[478]

The liability of a physician who performs a eugenic sterilization is usually governed by statute. Most eugenic sterilization statutes contain exculpatory provisions that render the physicians and administrative officials who participate in the proceeding immune to civil or criminal liability, providing they act in accordance with law. Some statutes, however, provide that the exemption from liability does not extend to negligence in the performance of the operation. Several states also impose criminal sanctions for failure to perform the sterilization in accordance with the provisions of the statute.

NOTES

1. Dent v. West Virginia, 129 U.S. 114 (1888).
2. L. Friedman, A History of American Law 163 (1973).
3. Dept. Health, Education & Welfare, Report on Licensure and Related Personnel Credentialing, 54-55 (DHEW Pub. No. HMS 72-11) (1971).
4. Dent v. West Virginia., *supra* note 1.
5. *Id.*
6. *In re* Ariffiths, 413 U.S. 717 (1973); Adams v. Tanner, 244 U.S. 590 (1916).
7. American Medical Association, 5 State Health Legis. Rep. 2 (Sept. 1977) (hereinafter cited as AMA).
8. *See, e.g.,* Cal. Bus. & Prof. Code § 2323 (West 1974 & Supp. 1981); Ill. Ann. Stat. ch. 111, § 4435 (Smith-Hurd 1978 & Supp. 1980–81); Md. Health Code Ann. art. 43, § 120 (Supp. 1980); N.Y. Educ. Law § 230 (McKinney Supp. 1981).

9. U.S. Dept. of Health, Education & Welfare, Report on Medical Disciplinary Procedures 57 (1978) (hereinafter cited as DHEW).
10. *Id.*
11. Ala. Code § 34-24-1 (1977) (Alabama State Licensing Bd. for the Healing Arts).
12. N.Y. Educ. Law § 230 (McKinney Supp. 1981) (New York State Bd. for Medicine).
13. *See, e.g.,* Ill. Ann. Stat. ch. 111, § 4435 (Smith-Hurd 1978 & Supp. 1980–81); Ind. Code Ann. § 25-22.5-2-6 (Burns 1976); Va. Code § 54-282 (1978).
14. N.J. Stat. Ann. § 45:9-1 (West 1978 & Supp. 1981–82).
15. *See, e.g.,* Cal. Bus. & Prof. Code §§ 2000–22 (West 1974 & Supp. 1983); Ga. Code Ann. §§ 84-901–935.2 (1979 & Supp. 1982); Ill. Ann. Stat. ch. 111, §§ 4401–4478 (Smith-Hurd 1978 & Supp. 1983); Ky. Rev. Stat. Ann. § 311.565 (Baldwin 1981); Tenn. Code Ann. § 63–6–204 (1982).
16. Mass. Gen. Laws Ann. ch. 13, §§ 8 *et seq.* (West 1980).
17. *See, e.g.,* Ariz. Rev. Stat. Ann. § 32.1402 (1976); Cal. Bus. & Prof. Code § 2001 (West 1974 & Supp. 1981); Fla. Stat. Ann. § 458.307 (West Supp. 1980); Iowa Code Ann. § 147.14 (West Supp. 1981–82); Wash. Rev. Code Ann. § 18.72.040 (1978).
18. Conn. Gen. Stat. Ann. § 20-8(a) (West Supp. 1981).
19. *See, e.g.,* Md. Health Code Ann. art. 43, § 120 (Supp. 1980); N.C. Gen. Stat. § 90-3 (1975 & Supp. 1979).
20. *See, e.g.,* Del. Code Ann. tit. 24, § 1710 (Supp. 1980); Ga. Code Ann. § 84-903 (1979 & Supp. 1980); Neb. Rev. Stat. § 71-117 (1971); Okla. Stat. Ann. tit. 59, § 482 (West 1971).
21. *See, e.g.,* Ariz. Rev. Stat. Ann. § 32-1402 (1976); Colo. Rev. Stat. § 12-36-103 (Supp. 1980); N.Y. Educ. Law § 230 (McKinney Supp. 1981); Va. Code § 54-284 (1978).
22. DHEW, *supra* note 9, at 60.
23. *See, e.g.,* Ariz. Rev. Stat. Ann. § 32-1402 (1976); Fla. Stat. Ann. § 458-307 (West Supp. 1980); Ga. Code Ann. § 84-902 (1979 & Supp. 1980); Miss. Code Ann. § 73-43-3 (Supp. 1980).
24. *See, e.g.,* Fla. Stat. Ann. § 458.307 (West Supp. 1980); Ga. Code Ann. § 84-902 (1979 & Supp. 1980); Ill. Ann. Stat. ch. 111, § 4435 (Smith-Hurd 1978 & Supp. 1980–81); Wis. Stat. Ann. § 15-405(7) (West Supp. 1980–81).
25. *See, e.g.,* Del. Code Ann. tit. 24, § 1710 (1975 & Supp. 1980); Ga. Code Ann. § 84-902 (1979 & Supp. 1980); Wash. Rev. Code Ann. § 18-72-040 (1978).
26. *See, e.g.,* Ind. Code Ann. § 25-22.5-2-1 (Burns 1976).
27. *See, e.g.,* Conn. Gen. Stat. Ann. § 20-8(a) (West Supp. 1981).
28. *See, e.g.,* Cal. Bus. & Prof. Code § 2007 (West 1974 & Supp. 1981); Neb. Rev. Stat. § 71-115 (1971).
29. *See, e.g.,* Flat. Stat. Ann. § 458.307 (West Supp. 1980); Iowa Code Ann. § 147.14 (West Supp. 1981–82).
30. DHEW, *supra* note 9, at 60.
31. AMA, *supra* note 7, at 18.
32. Dept. Health, Education & Welfare, Public Health Service, Health Resources Admin., State Regulation of Health Manpower 2 (DHEW Pub. No. HRA 77-49) (1976).
33. Dept. Health, Education & Welfare, Public Health Service, Health Resources Admin., State Regulation of Health Manpower 3 (DHEW Pub. No. (HRA) 77-49) (1977) (hereinafter cited as DHEW State Regulation).
34. *Id.* at 157.
35. *Id.* at 171.
36. *Id.* at 157; *see, e.g.,* Ala. Code 34-24-70 (1977); Ariz. Rev. Stat. Ann. § 32-1423

(1976); Conn. Gen. Stat. Ann. § 20-10 (West Supp. 1981); Mich. Comp. Laws Ann. § 333.17031 (1980); Ill. Ann. Stat. ch. 111, § 4411 (Smith-Hurd 1978 & Supp. 1980–81).
37. DHEW State Regulation, *supra* note 33, at 171; Fla. Stat. Ann. § 459.006 (West Supp. 1980); Ill. Ann. Stat. ch. 111, § 4411 (Smith-Hurd 1978 & Supp. 1980–81); N.J. Stat. Ann. § 45.9-14.1 (West 1978 & Supp. 1981–82).
38. *See, e.g.*, Ala. Code § 34-24-24 (1977); Colo. Rev. Stat. § 12-36-107 (Supp. 1980); Tenn. Code Ann. § 63-611 (1976).
39. Cal. Bus. & Prof. Code §§ 2080–89 (West Supp. 1981).
40. *Id.* at § 2082.
41. *Id.* at § 2089.
42. *Id.* at § 2096.
43. *Id.* at § 2087.
44. *See, e.g.*, Alaska Stat. § 08.64.220 (1977); Cal. Bus. & Prof. Code § 2281 (West Supp. 1981); Tenn. Code Ann. § 63-611 (1976); Wyo. Stat. § 33-26-112 (1969).
45. *See, e.g.*, Ariz. Rev. Stat. Ann. § 32-1428 (1976); Cal. Bus. & Prof. Code § 2281 (West Supp. 1981); N.J. Stat. Ann. § 45:9-15 (West 1978 & Supp. 1981–82).
46. *See, e.g.*, Alaska Stat. § 08.64.220 (1977); Cal. Bus. & Prof. Code § 2281 (West Supp. 1981); Iowa Code Ann. § 147.34 (West Supp. 1981–82); W. Va. Code § 30-14-5 (1980); Wyo. Stat. § 33-26-112 (1969).
47. *See, e.g.*, Cal. Bus. & Prof. Code § 2281 (West Supp. 1981); Iowa Code Ann. § 147.34 (West 1981–82); Mont. Rev. Codes Ann. § 37-5-302 (Supp. 1977); N.J. Stat. Ann. § 45.9-14.1 (West 1978 & Supp. 1981–82); Va. Code § 54-300.1 (1977 & Supp. 1980).
48. *See, e.g.*, Cal. Bus. & Prof. Code §§ 2194, 2288 (West Supp. 1981); Fla. Stat. Ann. §§ 458.09, .051 (West Supp. 1980); Mass. Gen. Laws Ann. ch. 112, §§ 2, 2A (1980); Ohio Rev. Code Ann. § 4731.13 (Page 1977); Rules of Ohio State Med. Bd. MB-3-14; Tenn. Code Ann. §§ 63-611, 615 (1976).
49. *See, e.g.*, Ariz. Rev. Stat. § 32-1822 (1976); Cal. Bus. & Prof Code § 2194 (West Supp. 1981); Fla. Stat. Ann. § 459.007 (West Supp. 1980); Minn. Stat. Ann. § 147.02 (West Supp. 1981); N.J. Stat. Ann. § 45.9-13 (West 1978 & Supp. 1981–82).
50. *See, e.g.*, Ariz. Rev. Stat. Ann. § 32-1428(c) (1976); Cal. Bus. & Prof. Code § 2288 (West Supp. 1981); Conn. Gen. Stat. Ann. § 20-18(a) (West Supp. 1981) (specified subjects for D.O.s but not for M.D.s); Mass. Gen. Laws Ann. ch. 112, § 3 (West 1980); Tenn. Code Ann. § 63-611 (1976).
51. *See, e.g.*, Ariz. Rev. Stat. Ann. § 32-1428 (1976); Fla. Stat. Ann. § 459.007 (West Supp. 1980); Ky. Rev. Stat. Ann. § 311.570 (Baldwin Supp. 1980); Minn. Stat. Ann. § 147.02 (West Supp. 1981); Or. Rev. Stat. § 677.110 (1979); S.D. Comp. Laws Ann. § 36-4-17 (1977).
52. *See, e.g.*, Colo. Rev. Stat. Ann. § 12-36-113 (Supp. 1980); Ky. Rev. Stat. Ann. § 311.570 (Supp. 1980).
53. *See, e.g.*, Ala. Code § 34-24-72 (1977); Idaho Code § 54-1810 (1979); Ind. Code Ann. § 25-22.5-4-2 (Burns 1980); N.H. Rev. Stat. Ann. § 329:13 (1966 & Supp. 1979); Vt. Stat. Ann. tit. 26, § 1394 (Supp. 1980).
54. Ala. Code § 34-24-72 (1977); Ind. Code Ann. § 25-22.5-4-2 (Burns 1980); Mont. Rev. Codes Ann. § 37-5-301 (Supp. 1977).
55. *See, e.g.*, Colo. Rev. Stat. Ann. § 12-36-107 (Supp. 1980); N.J. Stat. Ann. § 45:9-6 (West 1978 & Supp. 1981–82).
56. *See, e.g.*, Conn. Gen. Stat. Ann. § 20-10 (West Supp. 1981); Ky. Rev. Stat. Ann. § 311.570 (Baldwin 1977); Ohio Rev. Code Ann. § 4731.08 (Page 1977).
57. *See, e.g.*, N.J. Stat. Ann. § 45:9-6 (West 1978 & Supp. 1981–82).

58. *See, e.g.,* Conn. Gen. Stat. Ann. § 20-10 (West Supp. 1981); Ky. Rev. Stat. Ann. § 311.570 (Baldwin 1977); Ohio Rev. Code Ann. § 4731.08 (Page 1977).
59. *See, e.g.,* Ariz. Rev. Stat. Ann. § 32-1423 (1976); Ill. Ann. Stat. ch. 111, § 4410 (Smith-Hurd 1978 & Supp. 1980–81); Mo. Ann. Stat. § 334.031 (Vernon 1966); N.Y. Educ. Law § 6524 (McKinney 1972 & Supp. 1980–81).
60. *See, e.g.,* Alaska Stat. § 08.64.205 (1977); Ill. Ann. Stat. ch. 111, § 4410 (Smith-Hurd 1978 & Supp. 1980–81); Mo. Ann. Stat. § 334.031 (Vernon 1966); N.J. Stat. Ann. § 45.9-14.1 (West 1978 & Supp. 1981-82).
61. *See In re* Ariffiths, *supra* note 6 (admission to the practice of law); Examining Bd. v. De Otero, 426 U.S. 572 (1976) (admission to the private practice of engineering).
62. *See, e.g.,* Cal. Bus. & Prof. Code § 2168 (West Supp. 1981); Fla. Stat. Ann. § 458.313 (West Supp. 1980); Ill. Ann. Stat. ch. 111, § 4410 (Smith-Hurd 1978 & Supp. 1980–81); Md. Health Code Ann. § 123 (Supp. 1980); N.Y. Educ. Law § 6524 (McKinney 1972 & Supp. 1980–81); Va. Code § 54-305 (1980).
63. Mich. Comp. Laws Ann. § 338.41(1) (Supp. 1981–82).
64. Dept. Health, Education & Welfare, A Report to the President and Congress on the Status of Health Professions Personnel in the United States (DHEW Pub. No. (HRA) 79-93, IV-7) (1978) (hereinafter cited as DHEW Health Professions).
65. *Id.* at IV-8.
66. *Id.* at IV-49.
67. *Id.* at IV-8.
68. DHEW State Regulation, *supra* note 33, at 165–66.
69. *Id.*
70. Cal. Bus. & Prof. Code § 2101 (West Supp. 1981).
71. Fla. Stat. Ann. § 458.05(3) (West Supp. 1980).
72. *See, e.g.,* Ariz. Rev. Stat. Ann. § 32-1424 (1976); Fla. Stat. Ann. § 458.05 (West Supp. 1980); Ohio Rev. Code Ann. § 4731.09 (Page 1977); Wis. Stat. Ann. § 448.03 (West Supp. 1980–81).
73. Mich. Comp. Laws Ann. § 333.16174 (1980).
74. S. Rhee, *U.S. Medical Graduates vs. Foreign Medical Graduates,* 15 Med. Care 568 (1977).
75. *Id.*
76. DHEW Health Professions, *supra* note 64, at IV-9.
77. Association of American Medical Colleges, Medical School Admission Requirements 1979–80 (29th ed. 1978).
78. D. Simmons, The Medical School Game, 61–64 (1975).
79. Ariz. Rev. Stat. Ann. § 32-1421 (1976); Ill. Ann. Stat. ch. 111, § 4411(1)(d) (Smith-Hurd 1978 & Supp. 1980–81); Md. Health Code art. 43, § 123(A) (Supp. 1980).
80. DHEW State Regulation, *supra* note 33, at 171.
81. *Id.; see, e.g.,* Ariz. Rev. Stat. Ann. § 32-1423 (1976); Del. Code Ann. tit. 24, § 1733(C) (Supp. 1980); Fla. Stat. Ann. § 458.05(3) (West Supp. 1980).
82. Fla. Stat. Ann. § 425.00 (West Supp. 1980); N.J. Stat. Ann. § 45:9-13 (West 1978 & Supp. 1981–82); Ohio Rev. Code Ann. § 4731.29 (Page 1977); Tex. Health & Safety Code Ann. § 4498a (Vernon 1976); Va. Code § 54-311.2 (1978).
83. N.J. Stat. Ann. § 45:9-13 (West 1978 & Supp. 1981–82).
84. Cal. Bus. & Prof. Code § 2140 (West Supp. 1981); Ill. Ann. Stat. ch. 111, § 425 (Smith-Hurd 1978 & Supp. 1980–81); 63 Pa. Cons. Stat. Ann. §§ 421.1-18 (Purdon Supp. 1981–82); Tex. Health & Safety Code Ann. § 4498a (Vernon 1976).
85. Fla. Stat. Ann § 458.313 (West Supp. 1980); *see also* N.J. Stat. Ann. § 45:9-13 (West 1978 & Supp. 1981–82); 63 Pa. Cons. Stat. Ann. § 421.1-18 (Purdon Supp. 1981–82).

86. Cal. Bus. & Prof. Code § 2135, 2136 (West Supp. 1981).
87. *Id.* at § 136.
88. Fla. Stat. Ann. § 458.419 (West Supp. 1980); Mich Comp. Laws Ann. § 333.17033 (1980); Ohio Rev. Code Ann. § 4731.222 (Page 1977).
89. Mich. Comp. Laws Ann. § 333.17033 (1980).
90. Ohio Rev. Code Ann. § 4731.222 (Page 1977).
91. *Id.*
92. Fla. Stat. Ann. § 458.319 (West Supp. 1980).
93. Ill. Ann. Stat. ch. 111, § 4412 (Smith-Hurd 1978 & Supp. 1980–81).
94. Cal. Bus. & Prof. Code § 2428 (West Supp. 1981).
95. Fla. Stat. Ann. § 458.319 (West Supp. 1980).
96. Cal. Bus. & Prof. Code § 2428 (West Supp. 1981); Ohio Rev. Code Ann. § 4731.222 (Page 1977); Tex. Health & Safety Code Ann. § 4498a (Vernon 1976).
97. Cal. Bus. & Prof. Code § 2428 (West Supp. 1981).
98. N.J. Stat. Ann. § 45:9-16 (West 1978 & Supp. 1981–82); Ill. Ann. Stat. ch. 111, § 4412 (Smith-Hurd 1978 & Supp. 1980–81); Mich. Comp. Laws Ann. § 333.17088 (1980).
99. Ohio Rev. Code Ann. § 4731.222 (Page 1977).
100. Tex. Health & Safety Code Ann. § 4506 (Vernon 1976).
101. Va. Code § 54-321 (1978).
102. Ill. Ann. Stat. ch. 111, § 412 (Smith-Hurd 1978 & Supp. 1980–81); Ohio Rev. Code Ann. § 4731.221 (Page 1978); 63 Pa. Cons. Stat. Ann. § 410 (Purdon Supp. 1981–82).
103. Ill. Ann. Stat. ch. 111, § 412 (Smith-Hurd 1978 & Supp. 1980–81).
104. *See, e.g.,* Hewitt v. State Med. Examiners, 148 Cal. 590, 84 P. 39 (1906); Hughes v. State Bd. of Med. Examiners, 162 Ga. 246, 134 S.E. 42 (1926); Lawrence v. Biry, 239 Mass. 424, 132 N.E. 174 (1921).
105. *In re* Ruffalo, 390 U.S. 544 (1968).
106. *See e.g.,* Morrissey v. Bruner, 408 U.S. 471 (1972); Goldberg v. Kelly, 397 U.S. 254 (1970).
107. Missouri *ex rel.* Hurwitz v. North, 271 U.S. 40 (1925).
108. *See e.g.,* Mich. Comp. Laws Ann. §§ 24.201-.315 (Cum. Supp. 1967–81).
109. Missouri *ex rel.* Hurwitz v. North, *supra* note 107.
110. Kansas State Bd. of Healing Arts v. Foote, 200 Kan. 447, 436 P.2d 828 (1968).
111. Board of Med. Examiners v. Schutzbank, 94 Ariz. 281, 383 P.2d 192 (1963).
112. Bruni v. Department of Registration & Educ., 8 Ill. App. 3d 321, 290 N.E.2d 295 (1972).
113. Colorado State Bd. of Med. Examiners v. Palmer, 57 Colo. 40, 400 P.2d 914 (1965).
114. Bills v. Weaver, 25 Ariz. App. 473, 544 P.2d 690 (1976); Miller v. Board of Regents, 30 A.D.2d 994, 294 N.Y.S.2d 29 (1968).
115. *See, e.g.,* Ga. Code Ann. § 88-1912 (1979).
116. *See, e.g.,* Alaska Stat. § 08.64.330 (1977).
117. *In re* Ruffalo, *supra* note 105.
118. Withrow v. Larkin, 368 F. Supp. 796 (E.D. Wis. 1973), *rev'd*, 421 U.S. 35 (1975).
119. *See, e.g., id.*; Gibson v. Berryhill, 411 U.S. 564 (1973).
120. *See, e.g.,* LeBow v. Optometry Examining Bd., 52 Wis. 2d 569, 191 N.W.2d 47 (1971); Blanchard v. Michigan Bd. of Examiners in Optometry, 40 Mich. App. 320, 198 N.W.2d 804 (1972).
121. *See, e.g.,* Petrucci v. Board of Med. Examiners, 45 Cal. App. 3d 83, 117 Cal. Rptr. 735 (1975); Clark v. Michigan Bd. of Registration, 367 Mich. 343, 116 N.W.2d 797 (1962).

Notes: Chapter V

122. *See e.g.,* Sos v. Board of Regents, 19 N.Y.2d 990, 228 N.E.2d 814, 281 N.Y.S.2d 831 (1976); D'Alois v. Allen, 31 A.D.2d 983, 297 N.Y.S.2d 826 (1969).
123. De Hart v. State Dept. of Licensing & Regulation, 97 Mich. App. 307, 293 N.W.2d 806 (1980); Glashow v. Allen, 27 A.D.2d 625, 275 N.Y.S.2d 994 (1966).
124. Smith, *Due Process in the Disciplinary Hearing,* 208 J.A.M.A. 2229, 2230 (1969).
125. Eichberg v. Maryland Bd. of Pharmacy, 50 Md. App. 189, 436 A.2d 525 (1981); Kansas State Bd. of Healing Arts v. Burwell, 5 Kan. App. 2d 357, 616 P.2d 1084 (1980); Stammer v. Board of Regents, 287 N.Y. 359, 39 N.E.2d 913 (1942).
126. Davis v. Board of Med. Examiners, 108 Cal. App. 2d 346, 239 P.2d 78 (1951).
127. Elder v. Board of Med. Examiners, 241 Cal. App. 2d 246, 50 Cal. Rptr. 304 (1966); *cert. denied,* 385 U.S. 1001 (1967).
128. Mascitelli v. Bd. of Regents, 32 A.D.2d 701, 299 N.Y.S.2d 1002 (1969).
129. Younge v. State Bd. of Registration for the Healing Arts, 451 S.W.2d 346 (Mo. 1969); *cert. denied,* 397 U.S. 922 (1970).
130. *In re* Polk, 90 N.J. 550, 449 A.2d 7 (1982); Ferguson v. Hamrick, 388 So.2d 981 (Ala. 1980); Sherman v. Commission on Licensure, 407 A.2d 595 (D.C. App. 1979); *In re* Wilkins, 294 N.C. 528, 242 S.E.2d 829 (1978).
131. *In re* Polk, *supra* note 130.
132. Vodicka, *Medical Discipline Part VIII: Procedural Matters,* 235 J.A.M.A. 1051, 1052 (1976).
133. Gentry v. State Bd. of Med. Examiners, 282 So.2d 386 (Fla. App. 1973).
134. Martinez v. Texas State Bd. of Med. Examiners, 476 S.W.2d 400 (Tex. Civ. App. 1972).
135. Sherman v. Commission on Licensure, 407 A.2d 595 (D.C. App. 1979).
136. Hake v. Arkansas State Med. Bd., 237 Ark. 506, 374 S.W.2d 173 (1964).
137. American Medical Association, Disciplinary Digest: Court Decisions in Regard to Disciplinary Actions by State Boards of Medical Examiners, 44 (1967).
138. Prosch v. Baxley, 345 F. Supp. 1063 (M.D. Ala. 1972); Geiger v. Jenkins, 316 F. Supp. 370 (N.D. Ga. 1970).
139. *See e.g.,* Margoles v. Iowa State Bd. of Med. Examiners, 260 Iowa 846, 151 N.W.2d 457 (1967).
140. Bryant v. State Bd. of Med. Examiners, 292 So.2d 36 (Fla. App. 1974).
141. *See, e.g.,* Texas State Bd. of Med. Examiners v. Haney, 472 S.W.2d 550 (Tex. Civ. App. 1971).
142. Shively v. Stewart, 65 Cal. 2d 475, 421 P.2d 65, 55 Cal. Rptr. 217 (1966).
143. *See, e.g.,* Mich. Comp. Laws Ann. § 333.16233 (1980).
144. *See, e.g.,* Mascitelli v. Board of Regents, *supra* note 128.
145. *See, e.g.,* N.J. Stat. Ann. § 45:9-16 (West 1978 & Supp. 1981–82).
146. *See, e.g.,* Ill. Ann. Stat. ch. 111, § 4433 (Smith-Hurd 1978 & Supp. 1980–81); Ohio Rev. Code Ann. § 4731.22.1 (Page 1977); 63 Pa. Cons. Stat. Ann. § 421.14 (Purdon Supp. 1981–82).
147. *See, e.g.,* Czarra v. Board of Med. Supervisors, 25 App. D.C. 443 (1905); *In re* Van Hyning, 257 Mich. 146, 241 N.W. 207 (1932).
148. Vodicka, *Medical Discipline Part VI: The Offenses,* 235 J.A.M.A. 302 (1976).
149. Mich. Comp. Laws Ann. § 333.16221(e) (1980).
150. Tex. Health & Safety Code Ann. § 4495b(4) (Vernon Supp. 1982–83).
151. *See, e.g.,* Kansas State Bd. of Healing Arts v. Acker, 228 Kan. 145, 612 P.2d 610 (1980); Kudish v. Bd. of Regents, 356 Mass. 98, 248 N.E.2d 264 (1969); Sanchick v. State Bd. of Optometry, 342 Mich. 555, 70 N.W.2d 757 (1955).
152. Pepe v. Board of Regents, 31 A.D.2d 582, 295 N.Y.S.2d 209 (N.Y. 1968).
153. Kansas State Bd. of Healing Arts v. Acker, *supra* note 151.

240

Notes: Chapter V

154. Cadilla v. Board of Med. Examiners, 26 Cal. App. 3d 961, 103 Cal. Rptr. 455 (1972).
155. Martinez v. Texas State Bd. of Med. Examiners, *supra* note 134.
156. Kansas State Bd. of Healing Arts v. Seasholtz, 210 Kan. 694, 504 P.2d 576 (1972).
157. Hawkins v. Board of Med. Examiners, 542 P.2d 152 (Or. App. 1975).
158. Gentry v. Department of Prof. & Occupational Regulations, 283 So.2d 95 (Fla. App. 1974).
159. *See, e.g.,* Prosch v. Baxby, *supra* note 138; Margoles v. Wisconsin Bd. of Med. Examiners, 47 Wis. 2d 499, 177 N.W.2d 353 (1970).
160. McLaughlin v. Board of Med. Examiners, 35 Cal. App. 3d 1010, 111 Cal. Rptr. 353 (1973).
161. Younge v. State Bd. of Registration for the Healing Arts, *supra* note 129.
162. Geiger v. Jenkins, *supra* note 138; Strance v. New Mexico Bd. of Med. Examiners, 83 N.M. 15, 487 P.2d 1085 (1971).
163. *See, e.g.,* Strance v. New Mexico Bd. of Med. Examiners, *supra* note 162; *Id.*
164. Weisbuck v. Board of Med. Examiners, 41 Cal. App. 3d 924, 116 Cal. Rptr. 479 (1974).
165. Mich. Comp. Laws Ann. §§ 333.16221, 16224 (1980).
166. F. Grad and N. Marti, Study of Medical Disciplinary Procedures, Legislative Drafting Research Fund 42 (1978).
167. *See, e.g.,* Windham v. Board of Med. Quality Assurance, 104 Cal. App. 3d 461, 163 Cal. Rptr. 566 (1980); Ferguson v. Hamrick, 388 So.2d 981 (Ala. 1980).
168. Widlitz v. Board of Regents, 77 A.D.2d 690, 429 N.Y.S.2d 794 (1980).
169. American Medical Association, Legislative Department, *A Report on Medical Discipline Legislation,* 5 State Health Legis. Rep. 16 (Sept. 1977) (hereinafter cited as AMA Legis. Rep.).
170. Gore v. Board of Med. Quality Assurance, 110 Cal. App. 3d 184, 167 Cal. Rptr. 881 (1980).
171. Mich. Comp. Laws Ann. § 333.16106 (1980).
172. AMA Legis. Rep., *supra* note 169.
173. 42 U.S.C. § 1320c (1974 & Cum. Supp. 1975–80).
174. Tax Equity and Fiscal Responsibility Act of 1982, Pub. L. No. 97-248, 96 Stat. 324 (1982).
175. *PSRO's Face Fiscal Termination,* 40:1 Med. Care Rev. 6–7 1983).
176. *Medicare Peer Review Organizations To Be Established,* 39:4 Med. Care Rev. 243–45 (1982).
177. *Id. See also, Conferees Agree on Health Cuts,* Wash. Rpt. Med. & Health Perspectives (Aug 16, 1982); Price, *Analysis of the New Federal Legislation on Review of Health Care Utilization: PSRO's To Be Replaced by PRO's,* Health Cost Containment Rptr. 5:1–2, (Sept. 1982)
178. *Debate Builds over Peer Review Regulations,* Wash. Rpt. Med. & Health Perspectives, (Oct. 18, 1982).
179. *Headlines,* Hospitals, 21–28 (Nov. 1982).
180. Gosfield, *Utilization and Quality Control Peer Review Organizations: More than PSRO's Revisited,* Health Law Vigil, (Supp. April 1, 1983).
181. Ala. Code Ann. §§ 20-2-1–20-2-93 (1975); Ariz. Rev. Stat. §§ 36-2501–36-2553; Cal. Health & Safety Code, §§ 11000–11651; Conn. Gen. Stat. Ann. §§ 19-43–19-504j (West); Del. Code tit. 16, §§ 4701–4778; Fla. Stat. §§ 893.01–893.15; Ga. Code Ann. §§ 79A-801–79A-834, 79A-9917; Hawaii Rev. Stat. §§ 329-1–329-58; Idaho Code §§ 37-2701–37-2751; Ill. Ann. Stat. ch. 56½, §§ 1100–1603 (Smith-Hurd); Ind. Code §§ 35-48-1-1–35-48-4-14; Iowa Code Ann. §§ 204.101–

204.602 (West); Kans. Stat. Ann. §§ 65-4101–65-4140; Ky. Rev. Stat. §§ 218A.010–218A.990; La. Rev. Stat. Ann. §§ 40.961–40.995 (West); Md. Ann. Code art. 27, §§ 276–302; Mass. Gen. Laws Ann. ch. 94C, §§ 1–48; Mich. Comp. Laws Ann. 333.7101–333.7545; Minn. Stat. Ann. §§ 152.01–152.20 (West); Miss. Code Ann. §§ 41-29-101–41-29-175 (1972); Mo. Rev. Stat. §§ 195.010–195.320; Mont. Rev. Codes Ann. §§ 54-301–54-327 (1947); Neb. Rev. Stat. §§ 28-4,115–28-4,142; Nev. Rev. Stat. §§ 453.011–453.361; N.J. Stat. Ann. §§ 24:21-1–24:21-45 (West); N.M. Stat. Ann. §§ 54-11-1–54-11-39; N.Y. Public Health Law §§ 3300–3396; N.C. Gen. Stat. §§ 90-86–90-113.8; N.D. Cent. Code §§ 19-03.1-01–19-03.1-43; Ohio Rev. Code Ann. §§ 3719.01–3719.99; Okla. Stat. Ann. tit. 63, §§ 2-101–2-610; Or. Rev. Stat. §§ 475.005–475.285, 475.992–475.995; Pa. Stat. Ann. tit. 35, §§ 780-101–780-144 (Purdon); R.I. Gen. Laws §§ 21-28-1.01–21-28-6.02; S.C. Code §§ 44-53-110–44-53-580; S.D. Comp. Laws Ann. §§ 39-17-44–39-17-155; Tenn. Code Ann. §§ 52-1408–52-1450; Tex. Rev. Civ. Stat. Ann. art. 4476-15 (Vernon); Utah Code Ann. §§ 58-37-1–58-37-19; Va. Code Ann. §§ 54-524.1 *et seq.*; Rev. Wash. Code §§ 69.50.101–69.50.608; W. Va. Code §§ 60A-1-101–60A-6-605; Wis. Stat. Ann. §§ 161.001–161.62 (West); Wyo. Stat. Ann. §§ 35-7-1001–35-7-1055.

182. Uniform Laws Annotated, Master Ed., vol. 9, Uniform Controlled Substances Act, Introduction.
183. *Id.* at § 302(2).
184. *Id.* at § 203.
185. *Id.* at § 205.
186. *Id.* at § 207.
187. *Id.* at § 209.
188. *Id.* at § 207.
189. *Id.* at § 302(b).
190. *Id.* at § 303(a).
191. *Id.* at § 304(b).
192. *Id.* at § 306.
193. *Id.* at § 308.
194. *Id.* at Introduction.
195. N.Y. Penal Law, §§ 220.00–220.60.
196. *See, e.g.,* Alaska.
197. Alaska, Colorado, District of Columbia, Maine, New Hampshire, Vermont.
198. Alaska Stat. §§ 17.10.010–17.10.240; Colo. Rev. Stat. §§ 12-22-301–12-22-323 (1973); D.C. Code Encycl. §§ 33-401–33-425 (West); Me. Rev. Stat. Ann. §§ 2361–2380.
199. N.H. Rev. Stat. Ann. §§ 318-13:1–318-13:30; Vt. Stat. Ann. tit. 18, §§ 4201–4225.
200. David, *Interplay of Federal and State Regulatory Programs on the Distribution of Pharmaceuticals—The Legislative Aspects,* 29 Food Drug Comm. L.S. 449, 453 (1974).
201. *Id.* at 454.
202. 21 U.S.C §§ 801 *et seq.*
203. *Id.* at §§ 812–820.
204. *Id.* at §§ 822–824, 827.
205. *Id.* at § 822.
206. *See, e.g.,* Cal. Bus. & Prof. Code § 4047.6 (Deering); Colo. Rev. Stat. § 12-22-118.5; Fla. Stat. § 465.025; Ky. Rev. Stat. § 217.814; Ore. Rev. Stat. § 689.515; Utah Code Ann. § 58-17-31; Mich. Comp. Laws Ann. § 333.17755.

207. *See, e.g.,* Colo. Rev. Stat. § 12-22-118.5; Wash. Rev. Code § 69.41.120; W. Va. Code § 30-5-121; Mich. Comp. Laws Ann. § 333.17755; Pa. Stat. Ann. tit. 35, § 960.3.
208. *See, e.g.,* Alaska Stat. § 08-80-295; Colo. Rev. Stat. § 12-22-118.5; Mich. Comp. Laws Ann. § 333.17755.
209. *See, e.g.,* Alaska Stat. § 08-80-295.
210. Mich. Comp. Laws Ann. § 333.17755.
211. Colo. Rev. Stat. § 12-22-118.5.
212. *See, e.g.,* Fla. Stat. § 465.025; Ky. Rev. Stat. § 217.814; Mass. Gen. Laws Ann. ch. 111, § 12D (West); N.J. Rev. Stat. § 24:6E-6: Pa. Stat. Ann. tit. 35, § 960.3 (Purdon); R.I. Gen. Laws § 5-19-38; W. Va. Code § 30-5-12b.
213. *See,e.g.,* Alaska Stat. § 08.80.295; Ga. Code § 79A-1008; Ill. Rev. Code ch. 111, § 4033; Mass. Gen. Laws Ann. ch. 112, § 12D (West); Wash. Rev. Code § 69.41.120.
214. N.H. Rev. Stat. Ann. § 146:6-b.
215. *See, e.g.,* Alaska Stat. § 08.80.295; Ill. Rev. Code tit. 111, § 4033.
216. *See, e.g.,* Colo. Rev. Stat. § 12-22-118.5; Ark. Stat. Ann. § 72-1048.
217. *See, e.g.,* Ill. Rev. Code tit. 111 § 4033; Mich. Comp. Laws Ann. § 333.17755.
218. *See, e.g.,* Pa. Stat. Ann. tit. 35, § 960.3.
219. *See, e.g.,* Colo. Rev. Stat. § 12-22-118.5; Mich. Comp. Laws Ann. § 333.17755.
220. *See, e.g.,* Ark. Stat. Ann. § 72.1050.
221. *See, e.g.,* Alaska Stat. § 08-80-295; Colo. Rev. Stat. § 12-22-118.5; Fla. Stat. § 465.025; N.J. Rev. Stat. § 24:6E-6; Mich. Comp. Laws Ann. § 333.17755; W. Va. Code § 30-5-12b.
222. Wash. Rev. Code § 69.41.130.
223. *See, e.g.,* Colo. Rev. Stat. § 12-22-118.5; Ark. Stat. Ann. § 72-1048.
224. *See, e.g.,* Colo. Rev. Stat. § 12-22-118.5; Ark. Stat. Ann. § 72-1048.
225. *See, e.g.,* Alaska Stat. § 08.80.295; Ky. Rev. Stat. § 217.894; Wash. Rev. Code § 69.41.160; W. Va. Code § 30-5-12b.
226. *See, e.g.,* Mass. Gen. Laws Ann. ch. 13, § 17; Wis. Stat. Ann. § 140.90 (West).
227. *See, e.g.,* Ark. Stat. Ann. § 72-1049; W. Va. Code § 30-5-12b.
228. *See, e.g.,* Mass. Gen. Laws Ann. ch. 13, § 17; Ky. Rev. Stat. § 217.814.
229. 40 Fed. Reg. 26164-69 (1975).
230. Colo. Rev. Stat. § 12-22-118.5.
231. HEW news press release No. P78-4 (Jan. 23, 1978).
232. *See, e.g.,* Wash. Rev. Code § 69.41.150.
233. Grabowski & Vernon, *Substitution Laws and Innovation in the Pharmaceutical Industry,* 43 J. L. Contemp. Probs. 43 (1979).
234. 45 C.F.R. § 46.101 (1981).
235. 45 C.F.R. § 46.116 (1981).
236. 45 C.F.R. § 46.201 (1981).
237. Toulmin, *Exploring The Moderate Consensus,* 5 Hastings Center Rep. 31 (June 1975).
238. 45 C.F.R. § 46.206 (1981).
239. 45 C.F.R. § 46.207 (1981).
240. 45 C.F.R. § 46.208 (1981).
241. 45 C.F.R. § 46.209 (1981).
242. Cal. Health & Safety Code Ann. § 25956 (Deering, 1980); Ill. Ann. Stat. ch. 38, § 81-18 (Supp. 1980); Ind. Ann. Stat. § 10-112 (Supp. 1980); Ky. Rev. Stat. Ann. § 436.026 (Cum. Supp. 1980); La. Rev. Stat. Ann. § 14:87.2 (West 1980); Me. Rev. Stat. Ann. tit. 22, § 1574 (Supp. 1981); Mass. Ann. Laws ch. 112, § 125 (1980); Mich. Comp. Laws Ann. §§ 333.2685–2692 (1980); Minn. Stat. Ann. §

Notes: Chapter V

145.422 (Supp. 1980); Mont. Rev. Code Ann. § 94-5-617 (1979); Neb. Rev. Stat. § 28-4, 161 Reissue, 1978); N.D. Cent. Code § 14-02.2-01 (1979); Ohio Rev. Code Ann. § 2919.14 (1980); Pa. Stat. Ann. tit. 35, § 6605 (Supp. 1980); S.D. Comp. Laws Ann. § 34-23a-17 (Rev. 1977); Utah Code Ann. § 76-7-310 (1979).
243. 45 C.F.R. §§ 46.101(g), 46.201(b) (1981).
244. S.D. Comp. Laws Ann. § 34-23A-17 (Rev. 1977).
245. Me. Rev. Stat. Ann. tit. 22, § 1574 (Supp. 1981).
246. *See, e.g.*, La. Rev. Stat. Ann. § 14:872 (West 1980); Mass. Ann. Laws ch. 112, § 125 (1980); N.D. Cent. Code § 14-02.2-01 (1979).
247. *See e.g.*, Cal. Health & Safety Code Ann. § 25956 (Deering 1980); Ill. Ann. Stat. ch. 38, § 81-18 (Supp. 1980); Ind. Ann. Stat. § 10-112 (Supp. 1980); Ky. Rev. Stat. Ann. § 436.026 (Cum. Supp. 1980); Mont. Rev. Code Ann. § 94-5-617 (1979); Neb. Rev. Stat. § 28-4, 161 (Reissue 1978); Ohio Rev. Code Ann. § 2919.14 (1980); Pa. Stat. Ann. tit. 35, § 6605 (Supp. 1980).
248. Ky. Rev. Stat. Ann. § 436.026 (Cum. Supp. 1980).
249. Neb. Rev. Stat. § 28-4, 161 (Reissue, 1978).
250. Ill. Ann. Stat. ch. 38, § 81-18 (Supp. 1980); Ind. Ann. Stat. § 10-112 (Supp. 1980); Me. Rev. Stat. Ann. tit. 22, § 1574 (Supp. 1981); Ohio Rev. Code Ann. § 2919.14 (A) (1980).
251. Cal. Health & Safety Code Ann. § 25956 (a) (Deering 1980); La. Rev. Stat. Ann. § 14:87.2 (West 1980); Mass. Ann. Laws ch. 112, § 125 (1980); Mont. Rev. Code Ann. § 94-5-617 (3) (1979); N.D. Cent. Code § 14-02.2-01 (1979); Pa. Stat. Ann. tit. 35, § 6605 (b) (Supp. 1980).
252. 45 C.F.R. § 46.210 (1981).
253. Ill. Ann. Stat. ch. 38, § 81-18 (Supp. 1980); Ind. Ann. Stat. § 10-112 (Supp. 1980); Ohio. Rev. Code Ann. § 2919.14 (A) (1980).
254. Mass. Ann. Laws ch. 112, § 125 (1980); N.D. Cent. Code § 14-02: 2-01 (1979); S.D. Comp. Laws Ann. § 34-23a-17 (Rev. 1979).
255. La. Rev. Stat. Ann. § 14:87.2 (West 1980).
256. Ky. Rev. Stat. Ann. § 436.026 (Cum. Supp. 1980).
257. *See, e.g.*, Me. Rev. Stat. Ann. tit. 22, § 1574 (Supp. 1981); Mich. Comp. Laws Ann. § 333.2691, (1980) N.D. Cent. Code § 14-02.2-01 (1979).
258. *See, e.g.*, Ark. Stat. Ann. § 82-513; Cal. Health & Safety Code § 10101 (Deering); Colo. Rev. Stat. § 25-2-11; Ga. Code Ann. § 88-1709; Kan. Stat. Ann. § 65-2409 *et seq.*; Mich. Comp. Laws Ann. § 333.2822(a).
259. *See, e.g.*, Mich. Comp. Laws Ann. § 333.2822(a).
260. *See, e.g.*, Ark. Stat. Ann. § 82-513.
261. *See, e.g.*, Ark. Stat. Ann. § 82-513; Cal. Health & Safety Code § 10101 (Deering); Colo. Rev. Stat. § 25-2-11; Ga. Code Ann. § 88-1709; Kan. Stat. Ann. § 65-2409 *et seq.*; Mich. Comp. Laws Ann. § 333.2822(a).
262. Mich. Comp. Laws Ann. § 333.2822(a).
263. Ga. Code Ann. § 88-1709.
264. *See, e.g.*, Ga. Code Ann. § 88-1709.
265. *See, e.g.*, Ark. Stat. Ann. § 82-513; Cal. Health & Safety Code § 10101 (Deering); Colo. Rev. Stat. § 25-2-11; Ga. Code Ann. § 88-1709; Kan. Stat. Ann. § 65-2409 *et seq.*; Mich. Comp. Laws Ann. § 333.2822(a).
266. *See, e.g.*, Ind. Code Ann. § 16-1-16-4 (Burns).
267. *See, e.g.*, Ohio Rev. Code Ann. § 3705.14 (Page); Wash. Rev. Code § 70.58.080.
268. *See, e.g.*, Ark. Stat. Ann. § 82-513; Colo. Rev. Stat. § 25-2-11; Ga. Code Ann. § 88-1709; Mich. Comp. Laws Ann. § 333.2823(1).
269. *See, e.g.*, Ark. Stat. Ann. § 82-515; Colo. Rev. Stat. § 25-2-114; Ga. Code Ann. § 88-1711; Ind. Code Ann. § 16-1-16-5 (Burns); Wash. Rev. Code § 70.58.145.

Notes: Chapter V

270. *See, e.g.*, Ark. Code Ann. § 82-514; Ga. Code Ann. § 88-1710; Mass. Ann. Laws ch. 46, § 1A; Ohio Rev. Code Ann. § 3705.16 (Page).
271. *See, e.g.*, Ga. Code Ann. § 88-1709.
272. *See, e.g.*, Mich. Comp. Laws Ann. § 333.2824.
273. *See, e.g.*, Mass. Ann. Laws ch. 46, § 3.
274. *See, e.g.*, Ohio Rev. Code Ann. § 3705.14 (Page); Ga. Code Ann. § 88-1709.
275. *See, e.g.*, Ohio Rev. Code Ann. § 3705.14 (Page).
276. *See, e.g.*, Ga. Code Ann. § 88-1709.
277. Wash. Rev. Code § 70.58.080.
278. Mich. Comp. Laws Ann. § 333.2824.
279. *See, e.g.*, Ark. Code Ann. § 82-528; Ga. Code Ann. § 88-1723; Ind. Code Ann. § 16-1-19-3 (Burns); 35 Pa. Cons. Stat. § 521.15.
280. *See, e.g.*, Ark. Code Ann. § 82-528.
281. Ind. Code Ann. § 16-1-16-6 (Burns).
282. Cal. Health & Safety Code § 10175 (Deering).
283. Mich. Comp. Laws Ann. § 333.2803.
284. *See, e.g.*, Ark. Stat. Ann. § 82-503; Colo. Rev. Stat. § 25-2-102; Ga. Code Ann. § 88-1702; Wash. Rev. Code § 70.58.160.
285. *See, e.g.*, Ark. Stat. Ann. § 82-581; Cal. Health & Safety Code § 10178 (Deering); Colo. Rev. Stat. § 25-2-110; Ga. Stat. Ann. § 8-1716; Wash. Rev. Code § 70.58.160.
286. *See, e.g.*, Ark. Stat Ann. § 82-581; Cal. Health & Safety Code § 10178 (Deering); Colo. Rev. Stat. § 25-2-110; Ga. Stat. Ann. § 8-1716.
287. *See, e.g.*, Ark. Stat. Ann. § 82-581; Ga. Stat Ann. § 8-1716; Ohio Rev. Code Ann. § 3705.27 (Page); Wash. Rev. Code § 70.58.170.
288. *See, e.g.*, Ark. Stat. Ann. § 82-581; Cal. Health & Safety Code § 10180 (Deering); Colo. Rev. Stat. § 25-2-110; Ga. Code Ann. § 88-1716; Ind. Code Ann. § 16-1-17-3 (Burns); Ohio Rev. Code Ann. § 3705.27 (Page); Wash. Rev. Code § 70.58.170.
289. *See, e.g.*, Ind. Code Ann. § 16-1-17-5 (Burns): Ohio Rev. Code Ann. § 3705.27 (Page).
290. *See, e.g.*, Ind. Code Ann. § 16-1-17-4 (Burns).
291. Ark. Stat. Ann. § 82-581; Colo. Rev. Stat. § 25-2-110; Ga. Code Ann. § 88-1716.
292. *See, e.g.*, Cal. Health & Safety Code, § 10180 (Deering).
293. *See, e.g.*, Ark. Stat. Ann. § 82-583.
294. *See, e.g.*, Mich. Comp. Laws Ann. § 333.2834.
295. Mich. Comp. Laws Ann. § 333.2834(3).
296. *See, e.g.*, N.J. Rev. Stat. § 26:4-1.
297. *See, e.g.*, Wash. Rev. Code § 70-24-010.
298. *See, e.g.*, Ga. Code § 88-1601; Mich. Comp. Laws Ann. § 333.5219.
299. *See, e.g.*, Ark. Stat. Ann. § 82-632; Colo. Rev. Stat. § 25-4-402; Ga. Code § 88-1602; Mass. Gen. Laws Ann. ch. 111, § 111 (West); N.J. Rev. Stat. § 26:4-38; 35 Pa. Cons. Stat. § 521.4.
300. *See, e.g.*, N.J. Rev. Stat. § 26:4-38; 35 Pa. Cons. Stat. § 521.4.
301. N.J. Rev. Stat. § 26:4-38.
302. *See, e.g.*, Ark. Stat. Ann. § 82-635; Mass. Gen. Laws Ann. ch. 111, § 119 (West); N.J. Rev. Stat. § 26:4-41; 35 Pa. Cons. Stat. § 521.4.
303. *See, e.g.*, Mass Gen. Laws. Ann. ch. 111, § 119 (West).
304. *See, e.g.*, N.J. Rev. Stat. § 26:4-41.
305. *See, e.g.*, 35 Pa. Cons. Stat. § 521.15.
306. *See, e.g.*, Ark. Stat. Ann. § 82-635; Mass. Gen. Laws Ann. ch. 111, § 119 (West); N.J. Rev. Stat. § 26:4-41; 35 Pa. Cons. Stat. § 521.4.
307. *See, e.g.*, Ind. Code Ann. § 16-1-19-3 (Burns).

Notes: Chapter V

308. Mich. Dept. of Public Health, Maternal & Child Health Division, *Phenylketonuria—General Information*, Children's Bureau Pub. No. 419 (1964).
309. See, e.g., Ind. Code Ann. § 16-1-11-5 (Burns); Mich. Comp. Laws Ann. § 333.5431.
310. See, e.g., Colo. Rev. Stat. § 25-4-303.
311. *Id.*
312. See, e.g., Mich. Comp. Laws Ann. § 333.5431.
313. See, e.g., Colo. Rev. Stat. § 25-4-303.
314. See, e.g., Ark. Stat. Ann. § 82-625; Cal. Health & Safety Code § 309 (Deering); Mass. Ann. Laws ch. 111, § 110A; Ohio Rev. Stat. Ann. § 3701.50.1 (Page).
315. Ga. Code Ann. § 88-1201.2 (Supp. 1982).
316. Ark. Stat. Ann. § 82-625.
317. See, e.g., Ark. Stat. Ann. § 82-627; Mass. Ann. Laws ch. 111, § 110A.
318. See, e.g., Cal. Health & Safety Code § 551 (Deering); Colo. Rev. Stat. § 25-4-303; Ga. Code Ann. § 88-1605; Ind. Code Ann. § 16-1-11-5 (Burns); Ohio Rev. Code Ann. § 3701.55 (Page).
319. R. Benson, Current Obstetric and Gynecologic Diagnosis and Treatment 302 (2d ed. 1978).
320. See, e.g., Mich. Admin. Code § R325.34 (AACS 1979); Fla. Stat. Ann. § 383.04.
321. See, e.g., Colo. Rev. Stat. § 25-4-303.
322. See, e.g., Cal. Bus. & Prof. Code § 551 (Deering 1982 Supp.); Mass. Ann. Laws ch. 111, § 109A.
323. See, e.g., Colo. Rev. Stat. § 25-4-303; Mich. Comp. Laws Ann. § 333.5254.
324. See, e.g., Mich. Comp. Laws Ann. § 333.5524 (1980) Cal. Bus. & Prof. Code § 551 (Deering 1982 Supp.); Mass. Ann. Laws ch. 111, § 110.
325. See, e.g., Colo. Rev. Stat. § 25-4-303.
326. See, e.g., Colo. Rev. Stat. § 25-4-303; Ohio Rev. Code Ann. § 3701.52; Fla. Stat. Ann. § 383.06; Ill. Ann. Stat. ch. 91, § 106 *et seq.* (Smith-Hurd).
327. See, e.g., Cal. Health & Safety Code § 551 (Deering): Mass. Ann. Laws ch. 111, § 110.
328. Ill. Ann. Stat. ch. 111½ § 4703 (Smith-Hurd).
329. See, e.g., Ind. Code Ann. § 16-1-11-6 (Burns).
330. See, e.g., Ohio Rev. Code Ann. § 3701.99 (Page).
331. See, e.g., Ind. Code Ann. § 16-1-11-12 (Burns); Mass. Gen. Laws Ann. ch. 111, § 121A; Ohio Rev. Code Ann. § 3701.46 (Page).
332. See, e.g., Mich. Comp. Laws Ann. § 333.5251.
333. See, e.g., Cal. Health & Safety Code § 3220 (Deering); Ohio Rev. Code Ann. § 3701.50 (Page).
334. See, e.g., Ark. Stat. Ann. § 82-607.
335. See, e.g., Mich. Comp. Laws Ann. § 333.5251; Ind. Code Ann. § 16-1-11-15 (Burns).
336. See, e.g., Ind. Code Ann. § 16-1-11-15 (Burns); Ohio Rev. Code Ann. § 3701.46 (Page).
337. See, e.g., Ark. Stat. Ann. § 82-609.
338. See, e.g., Ark. Stat. Ann. § 82-607; Cal. Health & Safety Code § 3220 (Deering); Colo. Rev. Stat. § 25-4-203; Ga. Code Ann. § 88-1606; Ind. Code Ann. § 16-1-11-14 (Burns); Ohio Rev. Code Ann. § 3701.49 (Page).
339. See, e.g., Ind. Code Ann. § 16-1-11-14 (Burns).
340. See, e.g., Ohio Rev. Code Ann. § 3701.50 (Page).
341. See, e.g., Ga. Code Ann. § 53-215; Ill. Rev. Stat. ch. 40, § 204; Ind. Code Ann. § 31-1-1-7 (Burns); Mich. Comp. Laws Ann. § 333.5241; N.J. Rev. Stat. § 37:1-9; 35 Pa. Cons. Stat. § 521.12.

342. *See, e.g.*, Mich. Comp. Laws Ann. § 333.5242.
343. *See, e.g.*, N.J. Rev. Stat. § 26:4-32; 35 Pa. Cons. Stat. § 521.8.
344. Reynolds v. McNichols, 488 F.2d 1378 (10th Cir. 1973).
345. *See, e.g.*, Mich. Comp. Laws Ann. § 333.5257; Ark. Stat. Ann. § 82-610; 35 Pa. Cons. Stat. § 521.14a.
346. *See, e.g.*, Ark. Stat. Ann. § 82-610.
347. *See, e.g.*, Ark. Stat. Ann. § 82-630; Colo. Rev. Stat. § 25-4-402.
348. *See, e.g.*, Ark. Stat. Ann. § 82-631.
349. *See, e.g.*, Colo Rev. Stat. § 25-4-402.
350. Roe v. Wade, 410 U.S. 113, 164 (1973).
351. *See, e.g.*, Fla. Stat. Ann. § 390.001(4) (West); 40 La. Rev. Stat. Ann. § 1299, 35.6 (West): Va. Code § 18.2-76; N.D. Cent. Code § 14-02.1-02(4); Va. Code § 18.2-76.
352. Planned Parenthood of Central Mo. v. Danforth, 428 U.S. 52 (1976).
353. *Id.* at 66–67.
354. Doe v. Deschamps, 461 F. Supp. 682 (D. Mont. 1976).
355. Tenn. Code Ann. § 39-302.
356. Planned Parenthood Assoc. of Kansas City, Mo., Inc. v. Ashcroft, 483 F. Supp. 679 (W.D. Mo. 1980).
357. Akron Center for Reproductive Health v. City of Akron, ___ U.S. ___ (1983). [Hereafter Akron Center].
358. Womens Services, P.C. v. Thone, 483 F. Supp. 1022 (D. Neb. 1979).
359. *See, e.g.*, N.D. Cent. Code § 14-02.1-02(4); *id.*
360. Womens Services, P.C. v. Thone, *supra* note 358.
361. Women's Community Health Center, Inc. v. Cohen, 477 F. Supp. 542 (D. Me. 1979).
362. Planned Parenthood of Central Mo. v. Danforth, *supra* note 352; Poe v. Gerstein, 517 F.2d 787 (5th Cir. 1975); *aff'd. mem.*, 428 U.S. 901 (1976).
363. Roe v. Wade, *supra* note 350, at 164.
364. Planned Parenthood of Central Mo. v. Danforth, *supra* note 352.
365. *Id.* at 71.
366. *Id.*
367. Poe v. Gerstein, *supra* note 362.
368. Eisenstadt v. Baird, 405 U.S. 438 (1972).
369. Poe v. Gerstein, *supra* note 362.
370. Scheinberg v. Smith, 482 F. Supp. 529 (S.D. Fla. 1979).
371. Planned Parenthood of Central Mo. v. Danforth, *supra* note 352, at 74.
372. Bellotti v. Baird, 443 U.S. 622 (1979).
373. Utah Code Ann. § 76-7-304 (1974).
374. H.L. v. Matheson, 450 U.S. 398 (1981).
375. *See, e.g.*, Mich. Comp. Laws Ann. § 333.2825(2); Mo. Ann. Stat. § 188.052; Mont. Rev. Codes Ann. § 94-5-619; Neb. Rev. Stat. § 28-343 (Supp. 1979); Ohio Admin. Code § 3701-47-03.
376. Mich. Comp. Laws Ann. § 333.2835(2).
377. Ohio Admin. Code § 3701-47-03.
378. Planned Parenthood Ass'n. of Kansas City, Mo., Inc. v. Ashcroft, ___ U.S. ___ (1983).
379. Women's Services, P.C. v. Thone, *supra* note 358.
380. Mich. Comp. Laws Ann. § 333.2835(3) (1978).
381. Roe v. Wade, *supra* note 350.
382. *Id.* at 150.
383. *Id.*

Notes: Chapter V

384. Planned Parenthood of Central Mo. v. Danforth, *supra* note 352.
385. *See, e.g.,* Fla. Stat. Ann. § 390.011 *et seq.*; Mass. Gen. Laws Ann. ch. 111, § 50-57c (West); Mich. Comp. Laws Ann. § 333.20801 *et seq.*; Minn. Stat. § 145.411 *et seq.*; N.Y. Public Health Law § 2800 *et seq.* (McKinney).
386. *See, e.g.,* Baird v. Department of Public Health, 599 F.2d 1098 (1st Cir. 1979); Hodgson v. Lawson, 542 F.2d 1350 (8th Cir. 1976); Westchester Women's Health Org. v. Whalen, 475 F. Supp. 734 (S.D. N.Y. 1979).
387. Baird v. Department of Public Health, *supra* note 386 at 1100, 1101, 1103.
388. Arnold v. Sendak, 416 F. Supp., 22 *aff'd mem.*, 429 U.S. 968 (1976); Word v. Poelker, 495 F.2d 1349 (8th Cir. 1974); Emma G. v. Edwards, 434 F. Supp. 1048 (E.D. La. 1977); Wright v. State, 351 So.2d 708 (Fla. 1977).
389. Arnold v. Sendak, *supra* note 388.
390. Akron Center, *supra* note 357.
391. Hodgson v. Lawson, *supra* note 386; Roe v. Wade, *supra* note 350; Women's Med. Center of Providence, Inc. v. Cannon, 463 F. Supp. 531 (D. R.I. 1978).
392. Friendship Med. Center, Ltd. v. Chicago Bd. of Health, 505 F.2d 1141 (7th Cir. 1974), *cert. denied* 420 U.S. 997 (1975); Baird v. Department of Public Health, *supra* note 386; Hodgson v. Lawson, *supra* note 386.
393. Florida Women's Med. Center, Inc. v. Smith, 478 F. Supp. 233 (S.D. Fla. 1979); Fla. Stat. Ann. § 390.011 *et seq.*
394. Hodgson v. Lawson, *supra* note 386; Word v. Poelker, *supra* note 388; Westchester Women's Health Org. v. Whalen, *supra* note 386; Women's Med. Center of Providence, Inc. v. Cannon, *supra* note 391.
395. Westchester Women's Health Org. V. Whalen, *supra* note 386; N.Y. Public Health Law § 2800 *et seq.* (McKinney Supp. 1978-79).
396. 10 N.Y. C.R.R. §§ 711.7, 750.0-751.16.
397. 10 N.Y. C.R.R. § 711.7(f)(11).
398. Westchester Women's Health Org. v. Whalen, *supra* note 386.
399. Mich. Comp. Laws Ann. § 333.20104(5) (1980).
400. *Id.* at § 333.20201 (1982).
401. Mich. Admin. Code R. 325.3801 *et seq.*
402. Birth Control Centers, Inc. v. Reizen, 508 F. Supp. 1366 (E.D. Mich. 1981).
403. Hallmark Clinic v. North Carolina Dept. of Human Resources, 380 F. Supp. 1153 (E.D. N.C. 1974); *But, see* Westchester Women's Health Organization v. Whalen, *supra* note 386.
404. Palmer v. Thompson, 403 U.S. 217, 224-25 (1971).
405. Mahoning Women's Center v. Hunter 610 F.2d 456 (6th Cir. 1979); *vacated* 447 U.S. 918 (1979).
406. Word v. Poelker, *supra* note 388.
407. *Id.*
408. Women's Med. Center of Providence, Inc. v. Cannon, *supra* note 391.
409. Dept. of Labor and Dept. of Health, Education & Welfare Appropriations Act of 1980, P. L. No. 96-123, § 109, 93 Stat. 923 *amending* 42 U.S. Code §§ 1396 *et. seq.* (1980).
410. Woe v. Califano, 460 F. Supp. 234 (S.D. Ohio 1978); McRae v. Harris, 491 F. Supp. 630 (E.D. N.Y. 1980).
411. McRae v. Harris, 448 U.S. 297 (1980).
412. *Id.*
413. *Id.*
414. Whalen v. Roe, 429 U.S. 589 (1970).
415. An Act For the Suppression of Trade in, and Circulation of, Obscene Literature and Articles of Immoral Use, ch. 258, 17 Stat. 598 (1873).

Notes: Chapter V

416. Griswold v. Connecticut, 381 U.S. 479 (1980).
417. Eisenstadt v. Baird, 405 U.S. 438 (1972).
418. *Id.* at 453.
419. Family Planning Services and Population Research Act, Pub. L. No. 91-572, 84 Stat. 1504 (1970).
420. Isaacs, *The Law of Fertility Regulation in the United States: A 1980 Review*, 19 J. Family L. 65 (Nov. 1980).
421. Carey v. Population Services Int'l, 431 U.S. 678 (1977).
422. N.Y. Educ. Law § 6811(8) (McKinney 1972).
423. Carey v. Population Services Int'l, *supra* note 421, at 685.
424. *See, e.g.*, Colo. Rev. Stat. § 40-2-50(4) (Supp. 1967).
425. T____ H____ v. Jones, 425 F. Supp 873 (D. Utah 1975).
426. *See, e.g.*, Md. Ann. Code, art. 43, § 135; Or. Rev. Stat. § 381; Tex. Fam. Code Ann. tit. 2, § 35.03.
427. Doe v. Irwin, 615 F.2d 1162 (6th Cir. 1980); Doe v. Pickett, 480 F. Supp. 1218 (S.D. W.Va. 1979); Scheinberg v. Smith, 482 F. Supp. 529 (S.D. Fla. 1979).
428. Doe v. Pickett, *supra* note 427.
429. Kansas Op. Att'y. Gen. § 75-450 (1977).
430. Doe v. Irwin, *supra* note 427.
431. 42 C.F.R. § 50.201 (1979).
432. 42 C.F.R. § 50.203 (1979).
433. 42 C.F.R. § 50.204 (1979).
434. 42 C.F.R. § 50.205 (1979).
435. 42 C.F.R. § 50.207 (1979).
436. 42 C.F.R. § 50.203(a) (1979).
437. Cal. Admin. Code tit. 22, §§ 51305.1–51305.6 (1980).
438. Minn. Stat. Ann. § 145.925(8) (1979).
439. *Id.* at § 145.925(4).
440. *See, e.g.*, Ga. Code Ann. § 84-932 (1979); Va. Code § 54-325.3 (1978); W.Va. Code § 16-11-1 (1979).
441. *See, e.g.*, 1979 Conn. Pub.,Acts 543(1)(a) (Jan. Sess. 1979).
442. *See, e.g., id.* at 543; Ga. Code Ann. § 84-932 (1979); Mass. Laws Ann. ch. 112, § 12w (1975); W.Va. Code § 16-11-1 (1979).
443. *See, e.g.*, Ga. Code Ann. § 84-932 (1979); Va. Code §54-325.3 (1978).
444. Planned Parenthood of Central Mo. v. Danforth, *supra* note 352.
445. Coe v. Bolton, No. C76-7854 (N.D. Ga., Sept. 30, 1976, unreported opinion).
446. *See, e.g.*, Jane Doe v. Temple, 409 F. Supp. 899 (E.D. Va. 1976).
447. *See, e.g.*, Cal. Health & Safety Code § 1258 (1979); N.H. Rev. Stat. Ann. § 460:21-a (1979).
448. *Id.*
449. *See, e.g.*, 1979 Conn. Pub. Acts 543 (Jan. Session 1979); Ga. Code Ann. § 84-932 (1979).
450. *See, e.g.*, Va. Code § 54-325.3 (1978).
451. Black's Law Dictionary 468 (5th ed. 1979).
452. *See, e.g.*, Ala. Code tit. 22, § 8-5; Minn. Stat. Ann. § 144.341 (1979).
453. *See, e.g.*, Kan. Stat. Ann. § 38-123b (1973).
454. *See, e.g.*, Ga. Code Ann. § 84-932 (1979).
455. *See, e.g.*, W.Va. Code § 16-11-1 (1979).
456. *See, e.g.*, Ga. Code Ann. § 84-932 (1979).
457. *See, e.g., id.* at § 84-935.1; W.Va. Code § 16-11-2 (1979).
458. *Id.*
459. N.J. Stat. Ann. § 2A:65A-3 (1980).

460. *See, e.g.,* Mass. Laws Ann. ch. 112, § 12W (1975).
461. *See, e.g.,* Ga. Code Ann. § 84-935.1 (1979); Va. Code § 54-325.6 (1978); Winfrey v. Citizens and Southern Nat'l Bank, 149 Ga. App. 484, 254 S.E.2d 725 (1979).
462. Isaacs, *supra* note 420.
463. Ark. Stat. Ann. §§ 59-101–59-502 (Supp. 1979); Cal. Welf. & Inst. Code § 7254 (West 1980); Conn. Gen. Stat. Ann. §§ 17–19 (1980); Del. Code Ann. tit. 16, §§ 5701–5705 (Supp. 1980); Ga. Code Ann. §§ 84-921–84-936 (Supp. 1980); Iowa Code Ann. §§ 145.1–145.22 (Supp. 1980); Me. Rev. Stat. Ann. tit. 34, §§ 2461–2468 (Supp. 1980); Mich. Comp. Laws §§ 720.301–720.310 (West 1980); Minn. Stat. Ann. §§ 256.07–256.08 (Supp. 1980); Mass. Code Ann. 41-45-1–41-45-19 (Supp. 1980); Mont. Rev. Code Ann. §§ 69-6401–69-6406 (1980); N.H. Rev. Stat. Ann. (Supp. 1979); Okla. Stat. tit. 43A, § 341-6 (Supp. 1980); Ore. Rev. Stat. §§ 436.025–436.110 (1980); S.C. Code Ann. §§ 320671–320680 (Supp. 1980); Utah Code Ann. 64-10-1–64-10-14 (Supp. 1979); Vt. Stat. Ann. tit. 18, §§ 8701–8704 (Supp. 1980); Va. Code Ann. §§ 37.1-156–37.1-171 (Supp. 1980); W.Va. Code Ann. §§ 16-10-1–16-10-7 (Supp. 1980); Wis. Stat. Ann. tit. 7, § 46.12 (Supp. 1980).
464. *See, e.g.,* Ark. Stat. Ann. § 59.501 (Supp. 1979); Del. Code Ann. tit. 16, § 5701 (Supp. 1980); Ore. Rev. Stat. § 436.025 (1980); Wis. Stat. Ann. (Supp. 1980).
465. *See, e.g.,* Cal. Welf. & Institution Code § 7254 (West Supp. 1980); Conn. Gen. Stat. Ann. § 17-19 (1980); Va. Code Ann. § 37.1-156 (Supp. 1980).
466. Buck v. Bell, 274 U.S. 200, (1925); *In re* Sterilization of Moore, 289 N.C. 95, 221 S.E.2d 307 (1976).
467. *In re* Sterilization of Moore, *supra* note 466.
468. Mickle v. Henrichs, 262 F. 687 (D.C. Nev. 1918).
469. Haynes v. Lapeer Circuit Judge, 201 Mich. 138, 166 N.W. 938 (1918).
470. Wyatt v. Aderholt, 368 F. Supp. 1382 (M.D. Ala. 1973); Algee v. Hillman Inv. Co., 12 Wash.2d 600, 123 P.2d 332 (1942).
471. Skinner v. Oklahoma, 316 U.S. 535 (1942).
472. Smith v. Wayne Probate Judge, 231 Mich. 409, 204 N.W. 140 (1925).
473. *See, e.g.,* Matter of Guardianship of Eberhardy, 97 Wis.2d 654, 294 N.W.2d 540 (1980); Ruby v. Massey, 452 F. Supp. 361 (D. Conn. 1978); Tulley v. Tulley, 83 Cal. App. 3d 698, 146 Cal. Rptr. 266 (1978), *cert. denied,* 440 U.S. 967 (1979), *contra In re* Sallmaier, 85 Misc.2d 295, 378 N.Y.S.2d 989 (Sup. Ct. 1976); Matter of Grady, 170 N.J. Super. 98, 405 A.2d 851 (1979).
474. Isaacs, *supra* note 420, at 83; *see also* Wyatt v. Aderholt, *supra* note 470.
475. North Carolina Ass'n for Retarded Children v. North Carolina, 420 F. Supp. 451 (M.D. N.C. 1976).
476. Wyatt v. Aderholt, *supra* note 470.
477. Ark. Stat. Ann. § 59-502 (Supp. 1979); Del. Code Ann. tit. 16, § 5702 (Supp. 1980); Ga. Code Ann. § 840933 (Supp. 1980); Iowa Code Ann. § 145.2 (Supp. 1980); Me. Rev. Stat. Ann. tit. 34, § 2461 (Supp. 1980); Mont. Rev. Code Ann. § 69-6403 (1981); N.C. Gen. Stat. § 35–37 (Supp. 1979); Ore. Rev. Stat. § 436.025 (1980); Vt. Stat. Ann. tit. 18, § 8702 (Supp. 1980).
478. Ruby v. Massey, *supra* note 473, at 368.

Chapter VI

Professional Regulation

§ 6.10 SPECIALTY CERTIFICATION

Specialty board certification is not required for a physician to practice medicine, or even to practice a particular specialty. Certification has developed as a voluntary procedure out of the efforts of the medical profession to improve the quality of graduate medical education. Specialty examinations are viewed as a means of differentiating the qualified from the unqualified physician for the purpose of peer recognition.[1]

Although it is a voluntary procedure, specialty board certification is important to a physician, especially where staff privileges are at issue. A DHHS regulation disavows any intention of having certification control staff privileges, but critics assert that the phrasing of the regulation indicates that this factor exerts substantial influence.[2] In 1975, 46 percent of the physicians who were not in training and who were included in the national registry of physicians maintained by the American Medical Association (AMA) were diplomates of a specialty board.[3]

Unlike state licensure of the general practice of medicine, medical specialization is supervised by independent specialty boards, which are private, nonprofit organizations not exercising any governmental authority. The number of members of a board ranges from ten to nearly forty. All boards are composed entirely of physicians. Specialty boards have been described as a mechanism of physicial self-regulation.[4] Physician specialty boards principally view themselves as organizations functioning to assess a physician's competence and knowledge upon his or her initial entry into the specialty.[5] Specialty boards are also beginning to play a role in maintaining physician competence in a specialty through the revocation of certificates and the development of recertification programs.[6]

All 23 primary and joint specialty boards endorse the principle of recertification.[7] As of July 1980, nine boards had received approval for their recertification proposals from the American Board of Medical Specialties, five had completed one cycle, and three proposals were being considered.[8]

Board certification bestows both privileges and liabilities. Public and professional recognition as a specialist leads to increased patient referrals. On

§ 6.11 *Obstetricians and Gynecologists*

the other hand, certification has also subjected physicians to more stringent standards of practice. The current trend in medical malpractice cases is to hold defendant specialists to the standards expected in the specialty nationally[9] (see § 1.32, Standard of Care).

§ 6.11 Obstetricians and Gynecologists

To be eligible for certification in obstetrics and gynecology, a candidate must apply to the American Board of Obstetrics and Gynecology, Inc. (ABOG) (see § 6.12, Professional Organizations). The certification process extends over 3½ years. The candidate must pass both a written and an oral examination and compile a patient list. To take the written examination, a candidate must have a Doctor of Medicine or equivalent degree and an unrestricted license to practice medicine in one of the states or territories of the United States or a province of Canada or have unrestricted privileges to practice medicine in the U.S. armed forces. The candidate must have completed at least four years in accredited clinical programs, with at least three years of progressive responsibility for the care of obstetrical and gynecologic patients, including the time as chief resident. More specifically, the candidate must have completed or be near completion of a graduate education program in obstetrics and gynecology accredited by the residency review committee of the ABOG or the council of the Royal College of Physicians and Surgeons in Canada.[10]

The written examination is a three-hour objective test. Questions are chosen from each of the following areas:

1. Anatomy, embryology, and genetics
2. Physiology
3. Endocrinology, fertility, and infertility
4. Gynecology
5. Obstetrics
6. Medicine, surgery, and psychosomatic problems
7. Pathology
8. Oncology[11]

The candidate must also demonstrate skill in applying basic knowledge to clinical problems. These skills include:

1. Obtaining needed information
2. Interpretation and use of the data obtained
3. Selecting, instituting, and implementing care
4. Management of complications
5. Following and continuing care[12]

To qualify for the oral examination, a candidate must fulfill all requirements for and pass the written examination, in addition to fulfilling requirements for the oral examination. The ABOG has different requirements for candidates who have had personal responsibility for the care of obstetrical and gynecologic patients and for those whose responsibilities have involved only supervision of the care given by others. All candidates must have had medical practice experience acceptable to the ABOG for no less than 12 months prior to the application date. All candidates must also submit a patient list, which the ABOG will use as a basis for questions about patient management.[13]

The oral examination is designed to test the candidate's knowledge and skills in solving clinical problems in obstetrics and gynecology. Approximately half of the examination consists of questions concerning patient management. The examiners freely use the candidate's list of patients for this purpose, but additional basic clinical problems are also included. The remainder of the examination consists of recall of basic knowledge in obstetrics and gynecology and interpretation of growths and microscopic pathology, X-ray films, sonograms, and related material from photographic slides. The knowledge and skills required for the oral examination are the same as those listed for the written examination. The report of the examining team is reviewed by the board of directors, and each candidate is passed or failed by a vote of the board.[14]

It is the candidate's responsibility to seek information concerning current requirements for certification. The ABOG refuses to notify a candidate of changes in requirements which could result in loss of eligibility to take an exam.[15]

A candidate for certification may achieve active candidate status when he or she has fulfilled the requirements to take the examinations. To maintain active candidate status, the candidate must apply and be ruled eligible to take the next regularly scheduled examination, written or oral. A candidate becomes a diplomate of the ABOG when he or she has fulfilled all requirements, has satisfactorily completed the written and the oral examinations, and has been awarded the board's diploma.[16]

The ABOG offers a voluntary recertification evaluation process for all diplomates. It is available to all diplomates who have completed and returned the board's data questionnaire. The evaluation process includes both an audit of practice and a cognitive examination. The audit consists of a pretest and detailed score report from which the candidate may identify areas of strength or weakness. After completing the audit, the candidate may take the cognitive examination. The ABOG determines recertification status based upon a review of the audit as well as performance on the written examination.[17]

Specialty Division Certification: In 1972, the ABOG established three specialty divisions to define qualifications and determine the obstetrician-gynecologist's eligibility for certification of special competence in gynecologic oncology, maternal-fetal medicine, and reproductive endocrinology. The American Board of Medical Specialties authorized the ABOG to certify physicians for special competency in these fields in 1973.[18] To become certified in a specialty division, a candidate must pass both a written and an oral examination. To be eligible to take a written examination, the applicant must have passed the written and oral examinations for basic certification by the ABOG. In addition, the applicant must have satisfactorily completed graduate medical education and training previously approved by the specialty division and supervised by a program director in one or more institutional settings. The candidate must pass the division's written examination before he or she may take the oral examination. In addition, after completing a formal program of graduate medical education in a specialty previously approved by the division, a candidate for certification of special competence in the specialty must have gained and be prepared to document at least two years' experience in practice as a subspecialist in a center providing or having ready access to essential diagnostic and therapeutic facilities.[19]

All three specialty divisions require an applicant for oral examination to submit a list of patients (hospitalized patients in the case of the division of gynecologic oncology and maternal-fetal medicine) in whose care the applicant participated significantly during graduate medical education as a subspecialist.[20] Applicants must also submit copies of a thesis published or in press within the past three years in a peer-reviewed journal. The paper must be on clinical or basic research in the sub-specialty area, and the applicant must be the sole or first author.[21]

An appeal procedure is available for the candidate who feels that he or she has not had a fair oral examination.[22]

Revocation of Diploma or Certificate: When making an application, each candidate signs an agreement concerning disqualification or revocation of his diploma or certificate for cause. Revocation may occur when:

1. The physician was not in fact eligible to receive the diploma or certificate, irrespective of whether or not the facts constituting such ineligibility were known to or could have been ascertained by the ABOG, or its representatives, at or before the time the diploma or certificate was issued

2. The physician violates any rule governing examination for a diploma or certificate, notwithstanding the fact that the violation is not discovered until after the issuance of the diploma or certificate

3. The physician violates the standards of ethical practice accepted by organized medicine in the locality in which he or she practices (forfeiture, revocation, or suspension of the physician's license to practice medicine or the expulsion or suspension of the physician from membership in an organization of his or her professional peers is considered evidence of a violation of the standards of ethical practice of medicine)

4. The physician fails to comply with or violates the bylaws or the rules and regulations of the ABOG

Upon revocation of any diploma or certificate by the Board of Obstetrics and Gynecology, the holder must return his or her diploma or certificate and other evidence of qualification to the secretary, and the physician's name will be removed from the list of certified specialists.[23]

§ 6.12 Professional Organizations

There are a number of organizations of interest to obstetricians and gynecologists in the United States. The following is a brief summary of some important facts about the structure, duties, and functions of various associations and liaison committees.

American College of Obstetricians and Gynecologists: The American College of Obstetricians and Gynecologists (ACOG) is a nonprofit educational and scientific institution. Its stated objectives are to "foster and stimulate improvements in all aspects of the health care of women which properly come within the scope of obstetrics and gynecology." To implement these goals, ACOG sets up practice guidelines, provides comprehensive educational programs, and furnishes educational materials to patients and the public, as well as to practicing physicians.[24] For physicians, ACOG presents postgraduate courses, seminars, and updates in basic and clinical science at its annual clinical meeting. It also offers approximately 35 topic-oriented postgraduate courses across the country. These courses have a preliminary test, course syllabus, and post-course test. Upon completion of the post-course test, continuing medical education (CME) credit is automatically recorded.

A variety of home study media is also available. Two journals—*Precis*, an update of clinically relevant changes in the specialty, and *Obstetrics and Gynecology* (the "green journal"), containing clinical articles—are published. Two audiotape series consisting of seminar discussions and condensed postgraduate course material are published monthly. Slide packages on a particular topic are released quarterly. These audiotape and slide courses carry a post-course test that may be completed and returned for CME credit.

A computer-based system automatically records CME credit for ACOG-sponsored programs and other qualifying activities reported by the physician. Transcripts are mailed to the physician semiannually for use in documenting CME credit, as required by some state licensing boards and medical societies.

The ACOG also publishes *Standards for Obstetric-Gynecologic Services*, a bimonthly *Technical Bulletin*, and policy statements and guidelines on practice issues aimed at improvement of patient care.

The ACOG is organized to benefit the public at large and so performs primarily educational functions. It does not, and under its current tax status cannot, certify individual physicians, as that is an activity presumed to benefit individuals rather than the public at large.[25]

The American Board of Obstetrics and Gynecology: The ABOG has undertaken the responsibility of certifying and recertifying individual physicians on a voluntary basis. As stated in their articles of incorporation, the purposes of the ABOG include:

1. To arrange and conduct examinations or other procedures, or both, to test the qualifications of voluntary candidates for certification and recertification
2. To issue certificates or any other ABOG evidences of competence to eligible physicians whom ABOG considers to have demonstrated special knowledge of and professional competence in obstetrics and gynecology (These certificates or other evidences of competence may, at ABOG's discretion, be valid only for a limited time.)
3. To determine from time to time whether physicians who have been issued certificates or other evidences of competence have continued to maintain their professional qualifications and to issue recertification certificates or other evidences of competence to those physicians who successfully demonstrate continued maintenance of such qualifications[26]
4. To encourage the study, improve the practice, and advance the cause of obstetrics and gynecology, subjects that should be inseparable[27]

To accomplish these objectives, the ABOG arranges and conducts examinations to certify initial candidates or to recertify those who have already received diplomas. Certificates issued or granted by the ABOG do not confer any degree or legal qualifications, privileges, or license to practice obstetrics or gynecology, nor does the lack of such certification interfere with or limit the practice of medicine by any duly licensed physician.[28]

There are currently three subspecialty divisions of the ABOG: gynecologic oncology, maternal-fetal medicine, and reproductive endocrinology. The objectives of the specialty divisions are, in general, to improve the health care of women with special disorders of the reproductive tract or process by:

1. Elevating standards of education and training relating to those areas
2. Enhancing the recruitment of qualified physicians into obstetrics and gynecology and into special areas
3. Improving the organization and distribution of patient services
4. Increasing basic knowledge in the special areas[29]

The Residency Review Committee: The Residency Review Committee is an interorganizational committee responsible for recommending approval of residency programs in obstetrics and gynecology to the Liaison Committee for Graduate Medical Education, which makes the final decision regarding accreditation. The liaison committee also publishes information regarding graduate education programs.[30]

The Council on Resident Education in Obstetrics and Gynecology: The council is an educational organization focusing on improvement of residency programs. It sponsors annual examinations for residents and issues objectives for residency training programs.[31]

A recommended core curriculum and hospital practice privileges in obstetrics and gynecology for family physicians was developed in late 1976. Revisions to this curriculum were made in 1980 by the Council on Resident Education in Obstetrics and Gynecology in conjunction with ACOG, the American Academy of Family Physicians, and the Association of Professors of Gynecology and Obstetrics. These revisions increase the ability of a joint training committee, composed of equal numbers of obstetrics-gynecology and family practice faculty, to assess the individual resident's performance in meeting the objectives of the program. The new curriculum recommends a more complete education in obstetrics and gynecology and intensified experience for physicians practicing in communities without readily available specialist consultation.[32]

The Association of Professors of Gynecology and Obstetrics: The association is composed of faculty in medical school departments of obstetrics and gynecology. It prepares objectives and criteria for undergraduate medical programs and concentrates on departmental, faculty, and undergraduate education development.[33]

The American Medical Association: The AMA is a federation of state and specialty medical societies. It devotes its energy to political and educational activities. It supports the Coordinating Council on Medical Education and pays half the expenses of several liaison committees that work under the Council.[34]

The Coordinating Council of Medical Education: The council is an inter-organizational group with general responsibility for policies and accreditation for all medical education. One of its subsidiary committees, the Liaison Committee for Medical Education, accredits medical schools in the United States and Canada. In 1976, the FTC questioned the role of the liaison committee on the grounds that there was a potential conflict of interest between the accrediting function and the economic interest of the profession. The coordinating council has retained approval of the federal Office of Education, however, and the liaison committee continues to accredit schools.[35]

Table 6.1 contains a summary of the above information, as well as membership and legal status of various obstetrics-gynecology organizations.

§ 6.20 MIDWIVES

When medical licensure came under state control in the nineteenth century, licensure and regulation of midwives was ignored. No regulatory control whatever was exercised on midwives by 20 states as late as 1900. Indifference to regulating the care provided by midwives has been said to reflect the treatment generally afforded the class of society to whom midwives historically provided their services. Midwives served the poor, rural population in the South and the immigrants of the North. In the early 1900s, steps were taken in England, and later in the United States, to train midwives and regulate their practice. This effort, wherever it was instituted, was consistently followed by a dramatic decline in the infant mortality rate.[36]

Measures to promote midwifery were met with opposition; the 1920s saw the outcry of various prominent American physicians criticizing the midwife as part of the ignorance of the past and calling for the legal abolition of the practice. Finally, decreasing immigration after World War I and federal laws providing funds for obstetrical care contributed to the demise of the midwife.[37]

Currently, however, interest in the midwife has been renewed. Seen as a solution to the problem of rising health care costs, midwifery is the subject of educational programs, state regulation, and professional certification. Out of the emerging profession of nurse-practitioner has come the nurse-midwife, a practitioner who superimposes general nursing training upon training in midwifery. While the lay midwife still exists, the nurse-midwife is viewed as the more extensively trained practitioner. Regulation of the two is discussed in the pages that follow.

§ 6.21 American College of Nurse-Midwives

The American College of Nurse-Midwives (ACNM) is the professional organization for nurse-midwives in the United States. It defines nurse-midwifery as:

> The independent management of care of essentially normal newborns and women antepartally, intrapartally, postpartally and/or gynecologically, occuring within a health care system which provides for medical consultation, collaborative management, or referral and is in accord with the *Functions, Standards, and Qualifications for Nurse-Midwifery Practice* as defined by the American College of Nurse-Midwives.[38]

Nurse-midwifery education is currently given after the registered nurse (R.N.) or master's degree has been obtained. The post-R.N. program provides a curriculum of theory and clinical experience in nurse-midwifery, while the degree program offers preparation in nurse-midwifery in conjunction with courses leading to a master's degree. A fully licensed R.N. who graduates from an ACNM-approved program is eligible to take the ACNM national examination for certification. A nurse-midwife certified by ACNM is entitled to use the initials C.N.M. (certified nurse-midwife) after his or her name.[39] Although the actual scope of practice available to a C.N.M. will depend on statutory and regulatory requirements of the jurisdiction in which he or she will practice, the ACNM has issued a broad statement outlining the functions of nurse-midwifery practice as the official policy statement for the professional organization.[40] According to the ACNM, the nurse-midwife:

Table 6.1 Structure and Functions of Obstetrics–Gynecology Organizations

Organization	Responsibilities	Membership*	Legal Status
American College of Obstetricians and Gynecologists (ACOG)	Prepare education programs and practice guidelines, as well as materials for patient and public education	21,000 fellows	Nonprofit scientific and educational corporation 501(c)3
American Board of Obstetrics and Gynecology (ABOG)	Certify and recertify individuals on a voluntary basis	12 members, elected for 6 years only, from among nominees of ACOG, APGO, AGS, AAOG, and AMA	Nonprofit corporation 501(c)6
Residency Review Committee (RRC)	Recommended accreditation of residency programs in obstetrics and gynecology to LCGME	12 members, selected directly for 6 years; 4 each by AMA, ACOG, and ABOG	Interorganizational committee
Council on Resident Education in Obstetrics and Gynecology (CREOG)	Improved residency education programs	12 representatives selected by national obstetrics-gynecology societies serving for 6 years, plus 2 residents	Interorganizational committee
Association of Professors of Gynecology and Obstetrics (APGO)	Improve education programs for medical students	Medical school departments of obstetrics and gynecology and their faculty members	Nonprofit scientific and educational corporation 501(c)3
American Board of Medical Specialties (ABMS)	Develop policies and procedures for specialty certification and recertification	Representatives from all 22 specialty boards (includes ABOG)	Nonprofit corporation 501(c)6

Coordinating Council on Medical Education (CCME)	Develop policies and recommend accreditation for all medical education	Representatives from AMA, AHA, AAMC, CMSS, ABMS, and others	Interorganizational committee
Liaison Committee for Medical Education (LCME)	Accredit U.S. and Canadian medical schools	Representatives from AMA, AAMC, and others (see text)	Interorganizational committee
Liaison Committee for Graduate Medical Education (LCGME)	Accredit residency programs in all specialties in the United States	Representatives from AMA, AHA, AAMC, CMSS, ABMS, and others	Interorganizational committee
Liaison Committee for Continuing Medical Education (LCCME)	Accredit continuing education	Representatives from AMA, AHA, AAMC, CMSS, ABMS, and others	Interorganizational committee

*Other organizations—abbreviations used: AAMC, Association of American Medical Colleges; AAOG, American Association of Obstetricians and Gynecologists; AGS, American Gynecological Society; AHA, American Hospital Association; CMSS, Council of Medical Specialty Societies (ACOG is one of twenty-two member societies).

Source: Pearse, *Spelling out the ABCs of Ob-Gyn Organizations*, 13 Contemp. Ob-Gyn 71, 76 (April 1979).

1. Assumes responsibility for the management and complete care of the essentially healthy woman and newborn related to childbearing processes
2. Develops with the woman an appropriate plan of care attentive to her interrelated needs
3. Participates in individual and group counseling and teaching throughout the childbearing processes
4. Manages, through mutual agreement and collaboration with the physician, that part of care of medically complicated women which is appropriate to the skills and knowledge of nurse-midwives
5. Collaborates with other health professionals in the delivery and evaluation of health care
6. Assesses his or her own professional abilities and functions within identified capabilities
7. Assumes self-determination within the boundaries of professional practice
8. Maintains and promotes professional practice in concert with current trends
9. Utilizes "Standards for Evaluation of Nurse-Midwifery Procedural Functions" in development and evaluation of practice
10. Promotes the preparation of nurse-midwifery students
11. Assists with the education of other health care personnel
12. Supports the philosophy and official policies of the American College of Nurse-Midwives[41]

The ACNM has also issued "Standards for the Practice of Nurse-Midwifery," which have been incorporated in the legislative statutes or agency regulations of 13 states.[42] Under the ACNM standards, nurse-midwifery practice:

1. Strives to provide continuity of care to the woman and her family during the maternity cycle, continuing throughout the childbearing years
2. Fosters the delivery of safe and satisfying care
3. Recognizes that childbearing is a family experience and encourages the active involvement of family members in care
4. Upholds the right to self-determination of consumers within the boundaries of safe care
5. Focuses on health and growth as developmental processes during the reproductive years
6. Stimulates community awareness of and responsiveness to the need for delivery of high quality family-centered care

§ 6.22 *Nurse-Midwife Legislation* 261

7. Takes place interdependently within a health care delivery system
8. Takes place within a formal written alliance with an obstetrician or with another physician or group of physicians who have a formal consultative arrangement with an obstetrician-gynecologist
9. Exists within a framework of medically approved protocols
10. Takes place within the realm of professional competence
11. Requires opportunities for continuing professional growth and development
12. Includes an ongoing process of evaluation[43]

§ 6.22 Nurse-Midwife Legislation

Individual states define and control the actual practice of nurse-midwives through legislation and regulations issued by a state agency. The laws and regulations of many states and jurisdictions either specifically recognize nurse-midwives[44] or allow the functions of nurse-midwives to be performed under extended nurse practice acts.[45] No state or jurisdiction has laws which clearly prohibit nurse-midwifery, although a few states have disallowed full practice by nurse-midwives by interpreting their laws restrictively.[46]

Licensure and qualifications for the practice of nurse-midwifery vary among states. Thirty states and jurisdictions specifically recognize nurse-midwives by statute or official regulation. Thirty-two states recognize certified nurse-midwives (see Tables 6.2 and 6.3).

California regulates the preparation and practice of nurse-midwives to a greater extent than most other states,[47] but, like most other states, it recognizes that the scope of nurse-midwife functions is greater than that of lay midwives. Training requirements are therefore more extensive for nurse-midwives.

Basically, the nurse-midwife assumes direct responsibility for the development and implementation of a comprehensive, supportive plan of care for and with the patient.[48] Nurse-midwifery may include (1) provision of necessary supervision, care, and advice to women during the antepartal, intrapartal, and postpartal periods, (2) counseling for family planning,[49] (3) conducting deliveries on the midwife's own responsibility,[50] (4) determining when physician consultation and assistance are needed and obtaining such assistance.[51]

Training programs are generally designed to prepare the nurse-midwife for managing a normal labor and delivery. Some states specifically enumerate circumstances that require a physician's attendance.[52] Factors such as maternal age (under 16 or over 35, for instance), documented problems in maternal medical history, or findings based on a physical examination indicating increased risk factors (such as significant obesity or poor nutritional status) may require referral to a physician.[53] Management of a normal delivery may include the administration of intravenous fluids, analgesics and postpartum oxytocins, amniotomy during labor, episiotomies, repair of episiotomies and lacerations, and resuscitation

TABLE 6.2 Patterns of Legislation and Actual Practice of Certified Nurse-Midwives (C.N.M.s) in the United States

States and jurisdictions with specific recognition of nurse-midwifery in legislative statutes or official regulations

C.N.M.s practicing fully

Alabama	Hawaii	New Mexico	South Carolina
Alaska	Indiana	New York	Utah
Arizona	Kentucky	North Carolina	Virgin Islands
California	Maryland	Ohio	Virginia
Colorado	Massachusetts	Oregon	Washington
Connecticut	Mississippi	Pennsylvania	West Virginia
Florida	New Hampshire	Puerto Rico	
Guam	New Jersey	Rhode Island	

C.N.M.s not practicing fully

Delaware	Idaho	Michigan	Montana*	South Dakota*

States with permissive laws, but no specific recognition of nurse-midwifery.

C.N.M.s practicing fully

Arkansas	Illinois	Minnesota	Texas
District of Columbia	Louisiana	Missouri	Vermont
Georgia	Maine	Tennessee	Wyoming

C.N.M.s not practicing fully

Iowa	North Dakota*	Oklahoma
Nebraska	Nevada	

States with restrictive interpretation of laws

C.N.M.s practicing fully

Wisconsin

C.N.M.s not practicing fully

Kansas

Source: 25 *J. Nurse-Midwifery* 19 (July-Aug. 1980).
*Exception: nurse-midwives practice in federal government hospitals.

TABLE 6.3 Specific Recognition of Certified Nurse-Midwives in Laws of States and Jurisdictions*

Statutory recognition with or without regulatory recognition

Alabama	Maryland	Montana	Utah
California	Massachusetts	New York	Virginia
Colorado	Michigan	Ohio	West Virginia
Kentucky			

Regulatory recognition only

Alaska	Hawaii	New Jersey	Rhode Island
Arizona	Idaho	New Mexico	South Carolina
Connecticut	Indiana	North Carolina	South Dakota
Delaware	Mississippi	Oregon	Washington
Florida	New Hampshire	Pennsylvania	

Source: 25 *J. Nurse-Midwifery* 19 (July-Aug. 1980).
*Prepared by the Legislation Committee of the American College of Nurse-Midwives, January 1980.

§ 6.23   *Lay Midwives*   263

of the newborn.[54] A nurse-midwife may also be responsible for routine gynecological care, including fitting vaginal diaphragms, inserting IUDs, and selecting contraceptive agents from approved formularies.[55] Some states require that these procedures be done in a physician's office or in a licensed health care facility that employs a full-time physician on the premises during all business hours. Upon approval of the appropriate state agency, a nurse-midwife may dispense family planning medication in a physician's office or in a licensed health care facility having a part-time physician on the premises.[56] Nurse-midwives may not manage labor and delivery in abnormal circumstances, such as premature labor at less than the thirty-seventh week of gestation, failure to make normal progress in labor (New Jersey utilizes the Friedman curve to determine normal progress), or multiple births.[57]

State regulations may require supervision by and association with a licensed physician with current training in obstetrics and gynecology[58] and with hospital privileges.[59] A written agreement may be required specifying such things as (1) criteria for patient ineligibility for care solely by the nurse-midwife, (2) standing orders for medications that the nurse-midwife may dispense (a nurse-midwife may not independently dispense a drug which is categorized as a controlled substance), (3) arrangements for consultation and periodic review of patient files, (4) arrangements for alternative consultants when the supervising physician is unavailable, and (5) hospital referrals and alternative physician supervision accessible to the nurse-midwife's geographic area of practice.[60]

A nurse-midwife generally must be a licensed registered nurse and a graduate of an approved program in nurse-midwifery.[61] Most states provide for alternative methods of certification.[62] A number have adopted the standards promulgated by the ACNM, while others recognize graduates from an ACNM-approved educational program.[63]

In California, applications for certification and examination are considered by a nurse-midwifery committee composed of at least one nurse-midwife and one physician, who have demonstrated familiarity with consumer needs, collegial practice, accompanying liability, and related educational standards in the delivery of maternal-child health care. The committee must also include at least one member of the public and may include any other member that the board of registered nursing deems appropriate.[64] In other states, such committees serve in an advisory capacity.[65]

Nurse-midwives must renew their certificates periodically.[66] The time varies with each state, but usually renewal is required annually or biennially. State regulations also provide for disciplinary action against a nurse-midwife for unprofessional conduct, including, but not limited to, incompetence or gross negligence in carrying out the usual functions of a nurse-midwife.[67]

§ 6.23 Lay Midwives

As one author has noted, the difference between lay midwives and nurse-midwives is one of degree—the nursing degree.[68] As in the case of nurse-midwives, the educational requirements and scope of the lay midwives' practice are legislated by each state.[69]

The practice of lay midwifery can be defined as the furthering of, or the undertaking by any person to assist in, normal childbirth, not including the use of any instrument or the assisting of childbirth by any artificial forcible or mechanical means nor the administering, prescribing, or advising with respect to any drug.[70] Thus, in California a lay midwife may not dispense contraceptives, insert an IUD, or perform an amniotomy during labor, although a nurse-midwife may.[71]

Many states that allow lay midwives to practice regulate their practice closely. Georgia, for example, has extensive regulations specifically detailing the responsibilities of lay midwives and the boundaries of their practice. Applicants must complete a prescribed course of instruction and furnish at least two statements attesting to their good moral character. They must attend continuing education programs after certification. Before a lay midwife may attend a patient, the patient must have obtained a written statement from a physician certifying to the safety of lay midwife delivery in her case. Regulations include conditions that mandate referral to a physician; specifications for conduct of labor, delivery, and the postpartum period; and the equipment the lay midwife is required to have.[72] States also provide for disciplinary action for unprofessional conduct and for certification renewal.[73]

Some states require clinical experience as well as academic training for lay midwives. In Florida, for example, a lay midwife must have attended not less than fifteen cases of labor and cared for at least fifteen mothers and newborn infants during lying-in periods of at least ten days, each under the supervision of a licensed, registered physician.[74] Connecticut has similar requirements. As with nurse-midwives, lay midwives practice under the supervision and direction of an obstetrician, who is responsible for developing written policies and procedures governing the practice.[75]

NOTES

1. Dept. Health, Education & Welfare, Report on Medical Disciplinary Procedures 81–96 (1978) (hereinafter cited as HEW Report).
2. 20 C.F.R. § 405.1023 (1977).
3. American Board of Medical Specialties (ABMS), Annual Report 22 (1975–76).
4. HEW Report, *supra* note 1.
5. *Id.* at 83–84.
6. *Id.* at 82–83.
7. American Board of Medical Specialties (ABMS), Annual Report and Reference Handbook 20 (1980).
8. *Id.* at 22.
9. *See, e.g.,* Naccarato v. Grob, 384 Mich. 248, 180 N.W.2d 788 (1970).
10. American Board of Obstetrics and Gynecology, Inc. (ABOG), Bulletin for 1980 15–16.
11. *Id.* at 15.

12. *Id.*
13. *Id.* at 21–22.
14. *Id.* at 21.
15. *Id.* at 9–10.
16. *Id.* at 7–8.
17. *Id.* at 12–13.
18. American Board of Obstetrics and Gynecology, Inc., Divisions of Gynecologic Oncology, Maternal-Fetal Medicine, and Reproductive Endocrinology, Bulletin 6 (August 1979).
19. *Id.* at 33, 35.
20. *Id.* at 12, 22, 31.
21. *Id.* at 14, 22, 31.
22. *Id.* at 37.
23. *Id.* at 37–38; ABOG, *supra* note 10, at 35.
24. Bylaws of the American College of Obstetricians and Gynecologists (ACOG), art. II, §. 1, *as amended* April, 1979.
25. Pearse, *Spelling Out the ABCs of Ob-Gyn Organizations,* 13 Contemporary Ob-Gyn 71 (1979).
26. ABOG, *supra* note 10, at 6–7.
27. Directory of Medical Specialists 1041 (18th ed. 1977–78).
28. ABOG, *supra* note 10, at 7.
29. ABMS, *supra* note 7, at 6.
30. Residency Review Committee for Obstetrics-Gynecology, Guide for Residency Programs in Obstetrics-Gynecology 1 (1976).
31. Pearse, *supra* note 25, at 73.
32. *ACOG-AAFP Approve Revised Curriculum,* 24 ACOG Newsletter 1–2 (July, 1980).
33. Pearse, *supra* note 25, at 73.
34. *Id.*
35. *Id.*
36. H. Speert, Obstetrics and Gynecology in America: A History 12 (1980).
37. *Id.* at 14, 15.
38. American College of Nurse-Midwives, What Is a Nurse-Midwife? (June, 1979).
39. *Id.*
40. Forman & Cooper, *Legislation and Nurse-Midwifery Practice in the U.S.A.,* 20 J. Nurse-Midwifery 54 (Summer, 1976).
41. *Id.*
42. Arizona, Connecticut, Florida, Kentucky, Montana, New Hampshire, New Jersey, New Mexico, New York, South Dakota, Utah, Virginia, West Virginia; *id.* at 18.
43. *Id.* at 54.
44. *See, e.g.,* Cal. Bus. & Prof. Code §§ 2746 *et seq.* (Deering 1980); La. Dept. Health and Human Resources, Bd. of Nursing R.N. 3.042; Mass. Ann. Laws ch. 112, § 80 C & D (Michie, Supp. 1980); 12 N.J. Reg. §§ 13:35–13:91 *et seq.* (1980).
45. *See, e.g.,* Ga. Rules Bd. of Nursing ch. 410-12-01 *et seq.*; 244 Code Mass. Reg. § 4.21.
46. Kansas, Michigan, Wisconsin; *see,* Langwell, Wilson, Deanne, Black and Chui, *Geographic Distribution of Certified Nurse-Midwives,* 25 J. Nurse-Midwifery (Nov.-Dec. 1980).
47. Cal. Bus. & Prof. Code §§ 2746 *et seq.* (Deering 1980); 16 Cal. Admin. Code §§ 1461 *et seq.* (1979).
48. 16 Cal. Admin. Code § 1463 (1979); 12 N.J. Reg. § 13:35-9.5 (1980).
49. 16 Cal. Admin. Code § 1463 (1979); La. Dept. Health and Human Resources, Bd.

of Nursing R.N. 3.042; 244 Code Mass. Reg. § 4.25; 12 N.J. Reg. § 13:35-9.1 (1980).
50. 16 Cal. Admin. Code § 1463 (1979).
51. *Id.*; 12 N.J. Reg. § 13:35-9.5 (1980).
52. *See, e.g.*, 12 N.J. Reg. §§ 13:35-9.3(c), 13:35-9.5 (1980).
53. 12 N.J. Reg. § 13:35-9.3(c) (1980).
54. 16 Cal. Admin. Code § 1462 (1979); 12 N.J. Reg. § 13:35-9.5 (1980).
55. 16 Cal. Admin. Code § 1462 (1979).
56. *See, e.g.*, 12 N.J. Reg. § 13:35-9.6 (1980).
57. *Id.* at §§ 13:35-9.3, 9.4.
58. 16 Cal. Admin. Code § 1464 (1979); 244 Code Mass. Reg. § 4.22; 12 N.J. Reg. § 13:35-9.3 (1980).
59. 12 N.J. Reg. § 13:35-9.3 (1980).
60. 16 Cal. Admin. Code § 1464 (1979); *id.*
61. *Id.*
62. *See, e.g.*, 16 Cal. Admin. Code § 1460 (1979).
63. *See, e.g., id.*; 12 N.J. Reg. § 13:35-9.2 (1980).
64. *See, e.g.*, 16 Cal. Admin. Code § 1461 (1979).
65. *See, e.g.*, Mass. Admin. Laws ch. 112, § 80D (Michie Supp. 1980); Mich. Comp. Laws Ann. §§ 333.16163, 333.17225 (1979).
66. *See, e.g.*, 16 Cal. Admin. Code § 1461 (1979).
67. *See, e.g.*, Cal. Bus. & Prof. Code § 2746.6 (Deering, 1980).
68. Ventie, *The Lay Midwife,* 22 J. Nurse-Midwifery (Winter, 1978).
69. *See, e.g.*, Cal. Bus. & Prof. Code §§ 2505 *et seq.* (Deering, 1980); Conn. Ann. Stat. §§ 20-75 *et seq.* (1980); Fla. Stat. Ann. §§ 485.011 *et seq.* (Supp. 1980); Ga. Public Health Code §§ 270-5-7-.01 *et seq.* (1979).
70. Cal. Bus. & Prof. Code § 2505 (Deering, 1980); Conn. Ann. Stat. § 20-75 (1980).
71. 16 Cal. Admin. Code § 1463 (1979).
72. Ga. Public Health Code §§ 270-5-7-.01, 270-5-7-.03, 270-5-7-.06, 270-5-7-.08 (1979).
73. *See, e.g.*, Cal. Bus. & Prof. Code § 2506 (Deering, 1980); Conn. Gen. Stat. § 20-86 (1980); Fla. Stat. Ann. § 485.071 (Supp. 1980); Ga. Public Health Code § 270-5-7-.12 (1979).
74. Fla. Stat. Ann. § 485.031 (Supp. 1980).
75. *See, e.g.*, Conn. Public Health Code § 19-13-C22 (1980).

Chapter VII

Hospital Regulation

§ 7.10 INTRODUCTION

This chapter focuses on the physician's perspective in his or her relationship with the hospital and addresses only those legal problems arising from the physician-hospital interface: numerous other legal issues and problems pertinent to hospital activity are not addressed here. The hospital administrative structure is briefly examined, along with the legal requirements imposed on the hospital and its physicians in providing various services and procedures. Emphasis is given to the legal aspects of granting, denying, or revoking hospital privileges and the procedural safeguards to which a physician is entitled in such a situation. It is in this area that most of the conflict between physicians and hospitals is generated.

As hospitals apply objective standards to the evaluation of physician performance, as the number of physicians in the population approaches saturation, as cost containment becomes a higher priority consideration, and as physicians continue to assert their rights through the legal system the likelihood of conflict increases. Accordingly, if predictions are accurate, the interface of physician and hospital will probably generate more legal conflict than any other in the field of medical jurisprudence, with the exception of the physician-patient interface. Because the quality of patient care will be affected by these conflicts, it is important that hospital leaders, physicians, and other involved parties anticipate these problems, engage in preventive measures where appropriate, and seek nonconfrontational resolutions.

§ 7.20 ORIGIN AND DEVELOPMENT

The first hospitals were small, overcrowded, underequipped places for the sick to die. Treatment was rarely given in an effort to cure. The earliest American hospitals appeared in the fifteenth century, during the reign of Montezuma, the last Aztec ruler of Mexico.[1] Hospitals began to appear in the United States and Canada in the seventeenth and eighteenth centuries.[2]

As society changed, so did the concept of hospitals. The growth of organized government brought a corresponding increase in government regulation and government responsibility for the public's health, safety, and welfare. Social factors such as health insurance, corporate law, taxation, the development of medical specialites, new concepts of liability, new professions, and new levels of medical technology influenced the structure and development of hospitals. These factors shifted the focus of hospitals from the acceptance of death to the preservation of life—that is, to the treatment and discharge of admitted patients.

§ 7.30 TYPES OF HOSPITALS

Hospitals can be classified in a number of ways: by type of control, type of services, length of stay of patients, or size and institutional purpose, to suggest a few.[3] The broadest and probably the most useful classification distinction to be made from the standpoint of hospital law is the distinction between public and private hospitals.

Public hospitals are established by a governmental unit. They are always organized as nonprofit institutions, but they may limit services to a specified type of patient—for example, the mentally ill or retarded, the tuberculosis patient, or the elderly. Some are associated with universities as teaching hospitals. Public hospitals are exempt from property, income, and sales taxes.[4]

While it may be stated generally that a nonemergency patient has no legal right to be admitted to a hospital,[5] the public hospital must admit any eligible patient. Eligibility may be determined by the purpose for which the hospital was established, which is generally specified in the statute creating it, or by the purpose defined by the governing board and administration of the hospital. Stated purposes may limit the type of patient the hospital treats by disease, as illustrated above, or other reasonable criteria.[6] However, statutes which require residency in the geographic area in which the hospital is located as a prerequisite to admission have been found unconstitutional by the U.S. Supreme Court.[7] In addition to federal and state civil rights laws prohibiting discrimination, many state licensing laws provide that a public hospital must comply in all phases of its operation with state and federal laws prohibiting discrimination.[8] Other states have inserted prohibitions against discriminatory practices in regulations pertaining to tax-exempt status.[9] Racial discrimination would jeopardize the hospital's funding under both the Medicare and Hill-Burton programs.[10]

In general, all licensed physicians have privileges to treat patients in public hospitals, subject to the rules and regulations of the hospital. According to the law in most states, a publicly owned hospital must have clearly stated, reasonable rules regarding staff appointments and fair procedures pertaining to enforcement of those rules. A physician who applies for membership on the medical staff of a public hospital must be judged in the light of his training, experience, clerical and professional competence, ethical attitudes, and ability to function effectively with patients and colleagues. The general rule is that public hospitals are under a duty not to act arbitrarily, capriciously, or unreasonably in granting, withholding, or restricting medical staff privileges. Each application must be decided upon in view of the merits and the facts of the particular situation.[11]

The Joint Commission on the Accreditation of Hospitals (JCAH) adds further support to the general rule by requiring that professional and ethical criteria, rather than criteria lacking professional justification (such as sex, race, creed, or national origin), be used as the basis for granting medical staff membership.[12]

The Fourteenth Amendment to the U.S. Constitution provides that no ". . . state [shall] deprive any person of life, liberty, or property, without due process of law; nor deny to any person . . . the equal protection of the laws." In order for these due process and equal protection constraints to apply, there must be a finding of state action.* Where state action can be established, a hospital must extend both substantive and procedural due process, as well as equal protection, to a physician in admitting him or her to the hospital staff, discharging him or her from the hospital staff, or reducing his or her staff privileges[13] (see § 7.90, Medical Staff Privileges).

Although the operation of a public or governmental hospital may be found to involve state action for purposes of the Fourteenth Amendment, it is not necessarily a governmental function for purposes of immunity from tort liability. For example, the Supreme Court of Michigan ruled that the defense of governmental immunity from liability in tort may no longer be used by governmental hospitals. The court concluded that the day-to-day operation of the hospital did not constitute a "governmental function" within the meaning of the statute granting immunity to governmental agencies in the exercise or discharge of such a function.[14]

Governmental immunity from liability in tort is still recognized to some extent in twenty states.[15] Allowance of governmental immunity may be limited to nonpaying patients.[16] Other states limit liability to the extent of the defendant's insurance.[17] Several states enforce full liability of governmental units,[18] while no state continues to uphold full immunity for all governmental subdivisions.[19]

Private hospitals may be classified as either profit or nonprofit. The profit classification applies to those hospitals, also referred to as proprietary, owned generally by an individual or corporation and organized for the purpose of making a profit. The proprietary hospital is subject to the same rules, laws, and regulations as any other business operated for profit. The nonprofit private hospital, also referred to as voluntary, is generally owned by a benevolent or nonprofit association or corporation such as a church or other religious organization;

---

* "State action" is a legal concept used to analyze facts and circumstances under which an institution derives support from or relies upon the government to such an extent as to justify classification of the actions of the institution as state action. Government ownership is one indication of state action, but a nongovernment-owned institution may be held to be engaging in state action depending on the extent of its nexus with the government or even the "public" nature of its activities.

it is organized not to make a profit, but to achieve certain goals related to the public interest. The most common example is the charitable hospital, which provides care to all who seek it, regardless of ability to pay.[20]

The state regulates private hospitals under its police power—that is, the broad power of the state to provide for the general health and welfare of the people. This power includes the power to license hospitals, to certify their eligibility for participation in state and federal programs, and to administer a certificate-of-need program (see § 7.70, Regulation of Hospital). The federal government regulates private hospitals indirectly, through funding.

Like public hospitals, private nonprofit hospitals (generally charitable in nature) are exempt from property, income, and sales taxes. They are supported by private funds, including gifts, benefits, and fees for service, rather than by taxes. Unlike public hospitals, private hospitals are not required to admit all nonemergency patients who apply and are eligible for admission; however, once the patient is admitted, the hospital is required to exercise the appropriate standard of care.[21]

Since private hospitals are not generally considered agents of the state, they are not subject to the stringent requirements of the equal protection and due process clauses of the Fourteenth Amendment. They are therefore free to regulate patient admissions and medical staff admissions or discharges through their bylaws. However, numerous cases have been brought in an attempt to apply the due process and equal protection clauses of the Fourteenth Amendment to private hospitals by showing government involvement through licensing, Hill-Burton assistance, and other governmental links.[22] Most federal circuit courts hold these levels of involvement with the state to be insufficient to invoke the requirements of the Fourteenth Amendment,[23] although the Fourth Circuit Court of Appeals has held that the defendant hospital's receipt of substantial amounts of federal funds entitled physicians seeking staff privileges to the equal protection of the law.[24] The requirement that there be state action in order to impose due process protections may gradually give way to the conclusion that due process is also grounded in public policy and common law and applies therefore to private hospitals, regardless of the applicability of the Fourteenth Amendment.[25]

The federal regulations that apply to hospitals participating in the Medicare program,[26] the standards of the JCAH,[27] and a number of state court decisions have imposed requirements on private hospitals similar to those imposed on public hospitals by the Constitution. Therefore, the freedom that private hospitals once had in determining membership on the medical staff has been constrained by notice and hearing requirements similar to those imposed on public hospitals (see § 7.90, Medical Staff Privileges).

Although private hospitals are not exempt from tort liability on the basis of governmental immunity, some states still uphold the doctrine of charitable immunity in limited circumstances. Some states limit the charitable institution's liability to damages for injuries resulting from the negligence of an employee hired through the negligence of an agent of the hospital.[28] Other states limit a charitable hospital's liability to paying patients[29] or to the extent of the institution's insurance.[30] Most jurisdictions, however, have abolished the doctrine of charitable immunity altogether.[31]

§ 7.40 LEGAL BASES FOR HOSPITAL OPERATION

Hospital operations are regulated externally by means of state incorporation statutes, federal and state licensing and certification laws, and the JCAH requirements. Internally, hospitals are regulated to a large extent by their own bylaws. Generally, the organization of a hospital is determined by its corporate or noncorporate, profit or nonprofit status.

§ 7.41 Corporations

Although a hospital may be formed as an association or even a partnership, most hospitals are organized as corporations. In states that have no separate statute regulating incorporation of nonprofit organizations, hospitals may incorporate under the general business corporation act of the particular state. About half of the states, however, have adopted a general nonprofit corporation act.[32] The majority of these states enacted the Model Nonprofit Corporation Act with minor variations.[33]

A for-profit corporation pays income to its shareholders, who are entitled to dividends and to a share in the assets of the corporation. A nonprofit corporation is organized primarily to render a service and does not distribute its income to the members, directors, trustees, or officers. This distinction, however, is not always clear.[34] Nonprofit status does not preclude a corporation from paying salaries or wages to the corporate members, trustees, or officers who are employees of the corporation. The nonprofit corporation uses its profits and reinvests its income for institutional purposes. (Since the nonprofit corporation does not have shareholders, its owners are referred to as members.)

Because the corporation is a legal entity separate and distinct from those who created it or are employed by it, it can sue or be sued as an entity and can hold property in its corporate name.[35] The major advantage of corporate status is the limited liability* of the shareholders, owners, or members of the corporation for the actions of the corporation.

The articles of incorporation define the corporation's basic structure. Generally, they specify such things as how the board is elected, the number of board members, who votes and how, the frequency, time, and place of meetings, the manner of distribution of dividends, and other basics of the operation of the corporation. A copy of the articles of incorporation is filed with the state at the

---

*Limited liability means that the owners or shareholders of the corporation are not held personally liable for the contracts or torts of the corporation.

same time as the application for corporate status.[36] The articles may be amended by a majority of the members or shareholders of the corporation.

Corporations possess express and implied powers. Express powers are granted by statutes, articles of incorporation, and bylaws. Implied powers are those which are reasonably necessary to or convenient for carrying out the express powers.[37]

If the corporation performs outside its powers, it is said to perform ultra vires. For example, a gift made by a nonprofit corporation to another institution for a purpose not included in its own charter would be an ultra vires gift. Ultra vires acts of the board are voidable—that is, challengeable. If unchallenged or otherwise ratified by the shareholders or members, there are no personal consequences to the board members. Successfully challenged ultra vires acts may, however, lead to personal liability of board members. No personal liability arises from good faith mistakes in judgment.[38]

Illegal actions of the governing board are void—that is, they cannot bind the corporation or the institution. For example, employment by a hospital of an unlicensed professional person is an absolutely void act. An employment contract signed subsequent to this illegal hiring cannot bind the corporation.[39]

§ 7.42 Bylaws

A hospital, public or private, may have two sets of bylaws. The first set is adopted by the governing board and includes such things as the role and purpose of the hospital, the specifics of the governing board itself (members, elections, officers, maximum service, duties, frequency of meetings, quorum requirements), the relationship between the governing board and the chief executive officer, and the relationship between the governing board and the medical staff.

A second set of bylaws may be developed and adopted by the medical staff. Medical staff bylaws are generally adopted by the corporate board and, in effect, become part of the corporate bylaws; thus they are binding on the corporation. It should be noted that JCAH requires the development and adoption of both sets of bylaws.[40] The bylaws establish a framework for the operation of the medical staff and its accountability to the governing board.[41] They should reflect the current staff practices of the hospital. The governing board has approval and adoption power over the medical staff bylaws. These bylaws include the qualifications and procedures for appointment and reappointment to the medical staff, various procedures for delineation of privileges, credentials review, organizational structure in departments, frequency and attendance at meetings, mechanisms for effective communication with the governing board regarding quality of care, continuing education requirements, and an ethical pledge.[42]

The medical staff also adopts, subject to governing board approval, rules and regulations specifically related to the role of the medical staff in the care of inpatients, outpatients, emergency patients, and home care patients. These regulations may be specific to a department or generalized to the whole medical staff.

The significance of bylaws from the standpoint of hospital liability is that they are evidence of the standard of care required by the hospital of its medical staff and employees. They reveal what the hospital knew or should have known regarding the practice of its staff and employees.[43] The presence of bylaws with clearly defined and well-monitored procedures is critical to a hospital's avoidance of liability (see § 7.51, Governing Board).

CASE ILLUSTRATION

The patient, an 80-year-old woman, was admitted to the hospital's "special care unit" after suffering a heart attack. Nine days later, she was transferred out of that unit to a double room in a regular patient ward. Her bed there had two pairs of side rails, one pair for the upper half of the bed and the other pair for the lower half. The night she was transferred, a hospital nurse gave the patient 15 milligrams of flurazepam hydrochloride (Dalmane). At midnight, the patient awoke and wanted to go to the bathroom. She was confused and thought she was at home. The upper side rails of her bed were raised, but the lower side rails were down. Without calling for help, the patient got out of bed and headed for the hallway. In the hall she fell and sustained a fracture of her right hip. The hip could not be operated on as soon as it should have been because of the patient's poor general condition. (The patient's physicians suspected that she might have suffered a second heart attack.) Because of the delay, the hip never healed properly, and the patient was never able to walk again unaided or without pain.

The manufacturer of Dalmane provides certain warnings with the drug, one of which states: "Dizziness, drowsiness, lightheadedness, staggering, atoxia, and falling have occurred, particularly in elderly or debilitated persons." The hospital has a regulation which reads: "Bedside Rails. With confused or disoriented patients, beds should be in low position at all times with side rails up, except when nursing care is being given. If patient objects to the side rails being raised, a note to that effect should be included in the nursing notes or the doctor may indicate on the order sheet that he does not want the side rails raised."

The patient sued the hospital and submitted its regulation as evidence of negligence. The hospital argued that expert testimony was required to show that it had acted improperly. The court imposed liability on the hospital, holding that "the hospital regulation is, in a sense, an expert opinion concerning the necessity for raising bed rails in the circumstances to which the regulation applies" (*Polonsky v. Union Hospital,* 1981).[44]

§ 7.50 ORGANIZATION AND ADMINISTRATION

The organization and administration of the hospital define the relationships between various groups. A clear understanding of their respective functions will facilitate communications and contribute to the efficient functioning of the hospital generally.

§ 7.51 Governing Board

The governing board is the major decision-making body of the hospital. In the case of a private hospital, the governing board is the board of directors; for a public hospital, it is the board of trustees. Election or appointment to the governing board is conducted according to the requirements of the articles of incorporation or state statute, or both.

Most state incorporation statutes regulate the duties and responsibilities of hospital governing boards and their members quite specifically.[45] Generally, the governing board develops policy and articulates plans for short- and long-term institutional goals and ultimately controls the performance of both professional and nonprofessional staff.[46]

The following JCAH principle and standards reflect the requirements imposed by most state laws on hospital governing boards:

> *Principle:* There shall be an organized governing body, or designated persons so functioning, that has overall responsibility for the conduct of the hospital in a manner consonant with the hospital's objective of making available high-quality patient care.
>
> *Standard I:* There shall be full disclosure of hospital ownership and control.
>
> *Standard II:* The governing body shall adopt bylaws in accordance with legal requirements and its responsibility to the community.
>
> *Standard III:* Governing body members shall be selected, unless otherwise provided by law, in accordance with the hospital's bylaws and, if applicable, articles of incorporation or charter.
>
> *Standard IV:* The governing body shall provide for the selection of its officers, adopt a schedule of meetings, and define attendance requirements and the method of documenting governing body proceedings.
>
> *Standard V:* The governing body shall provide mechanisms for fulfilling the functions necessary to the discharge of its responsibilities.
>
> *Standard VI:* The governing body shall provide for institutional planning to meet the health needs of the community.
>
> *Standard VII:* The governing body shall appoint a chief executive officer whose qualifications, responsibilities, authority, and accountability shall be defined in writing.
>
> *Standard VIII:* The medical staff bylaws, rules, and regulations shall be subject to governing body approval. This approval shall not be unreasonably withheld.

Standard IX: The governing body shall hold the medical staff responsible for making recommendations concerning initial medical staff appointments, reappointments, termination of appointments, the delineation of clinical privileges, and the curtailment of clinical privileges.

Standard X: The governing body shall require that the medical staff establish mechanisms designed to assure the achievement and maintenance of high standards of medical practice and patient care.[47]

The governing board may appoint an executive committee, which is responsible for the day-to-day operation of the hospital. A number of standing committees may be appointed to advise and make recommendations to the board.

The authority of hospital governing boards is either express or implied. Express authority is granted by the articles of incorporation, which set forth the purpose of the hospital and the powers that the corporation, through the governing board, is authorized to use to fulfill the purpose. Other powers are implicitly authorized in order to carry out any and all acts necessary to exercise the authority expressly granted to the corporation and board.[48]

Ultimate responsibility for the quality of patient care in the hospital rests with the governing board.[49] Part of this responsibility involves the appointment and retention of medical staff and the delineation of privileges for individual physicians. Although the medical staff may advise regarding these matters, the board cannot delegate its responsibility.[50] Failure to exercise reasonable care may result in liability of the hospital.[51]

Members of the governing board are fiduciaries* to the hospital corporation and the shareholders or members. This fiduciary position entails two extra duties—loyalty and responsibility. Loyalty implies that the interests of the institution must be placed above self-interest. Board members are therefore precluded from such things as secret profits, bribes, and competing with the hospital. Responsibility requires the exercise of reasonable care, skill, and diligence in every activity of the board. "Reasonable care" is that which an ordinary, prudent trustee would exercise under similar circumstances.[52]

Breach of fiduciary duties may lead to the individual liability of board members for their own torts, even though carried out in the name of the corporation.

§ 7.52 Hospital Administrator

The hospital administrator is the chief executive officer of the hospital. The governing board appoints this person and confers authority on him or her consistent with the board's goals and objectives. The law does not articulate specific qualifications for the hospital administrator, although the JCAH requires the

---

*A fiduciary relationship involves both formal and informal relations where one person or institution is placed in a position of trust or confidence by another.

administrator to be qualified by education and expertise appropriate to the fulfillment of his or her responsibility.[53]

Basically, the hospital administrator is responsible for planning, developing, and maintaining programs that implement the policies and achieve the goals of the governing board. Specifically, the hospital administrator organizes the administrative functions, establishes accountability, facilitates effective communication between medical staff and departments, organizes the hospital's internal structure, manages the hospital finances, and provides for the appropriate use of the physical resources of the hospital.[54]

The relationship between the administrator and the medical staff is not always smooth and cooperative. Antagonism stems from the seemingly different focus of the two groups. Although both groups are ultimately striving for high quality patient care, the administrator is required to comply with various government and other regulations. These regulations require the imposition of cost-containment measures, red tape, and accountability controls that consume valuable physician time and restrict the freedom and spending of the medical staff.[55] Despite the problems, the hospital administrator is central to the operation of the hospital.

§ 7.53 Medical and Other Staff

The precise legal nature of the medical staff has been questioned in some states. A New Jersey court has held it to be an unincorporated association and therefore capable of being sued as an entity for failing to curtail privileges of an incompetent staff member.[56] The more traditional view is that the medical staff is not a legal entity, but a component of the hospital corporation, which is ultimately responsible to the governing board.[57]

Selection of the medical staff is one of the fiduciary responsibilities of the board. Hospitals may be liable for patient injury resulting from the failure to adequately monitor the qualifications and performance of the medical staff[58] (see § 7.51, Governing Board).

Functions and duties of the medical staff are specified in its bylaws (see § 7.42, Bylaws). The medical staff may be organized into categories such as active, associate, courtesy, consulting, and honorary staff. These categories and the various responsibilities and privileges associated with them should also be specified in the medical staff bylaws.[59]

Generally, the medical staff is composed of active staff and an executive committee, which performs the day-to-day functions of the medical staff and serves as a liaison between the medical staff and the hospital administrator.[60]

Large hospitals may provide for the departmentalization of medical staff. The departments are specified by the bylaws, as is the method of appointing department heads.[61]

The nursing staff is organized into a nursing department and is directed by a nurse-administrator.[62] Unlike the medical staff, the nursing staff are hospital employees. This is a primary source of hospital liability—that is, both the nurse and the hospital are responsible for the negligence of the nurse.[63] The nursing department should have written standards delineating the authority, accountability, and lines of communication between administrative, medical, and nursing staff.[64] These written standards, along with appropriate governmental regulations, define the standard of care to which a nurse in a particular hospital will be held.

Concern over the scope of practice of nurses has stimulated changes in licensing legislation. The effect of those changes has been to recognize a broader range of activity for professional nurses and to eliminate artificial definition and unnecessary restriction of nursing practice.[65]

§ 7.60 SERVICES AND PROCEDURES

JCAH requires that a hospital have at least the following services: dietetic, emergency, medical record, nuclear medicine, pathology and medical laboratory, pharmaceutical, radiological, rehabilitation, respiratory care, social work, and special care[66]. Each of these services must be organized, directed, and integrated with other related services and departments of the hospital. Most of them should have written policies and procedures concerning their scope and conduct.[67]

§ 7.61 Admissions

The governing board establishes admission policies. Beyond the general, non-emergency situation, admission to the hospital is handled on a case-by-case basis. Hospitals generally utilize admission forms containing such things as responsibility for payment, consent for routine medical procedures and diagnostic tests, information regarding the safekeeping of valuables, and consent to release of information to legitimate third parties such as insurers and governmental agencies.[68]

§ 7.62 Emergencies

Governmental hospitals have no right to refuse admission, while private hospitals have no duty to admit patients. These rules do not apply in emergency admissions. Some states require certain hospitals to provide emergency care. These hospitals must provide at least a specified amount of physician coverage, as well as adequate facilities for emergency care. Harm to a patient stemming from failure to provide adequate emergency facilities could result in liability of the hospital.[69] These statutes imply that a hospital which holds itself out as treating emergencies has a duty to treat (or to refer if unable to treat) emergency cases.[70]

The JCAH requires that any individual who comes to the hospital for emergency medical evaluation or initial treatment shall be properly assessed by qualified individuals and that appropriate services shall be rendered within the defined capability of the hospital. The hospital must have some procedure whereby the ill or injured person can be assessed and either treated or referred to an appropriate facility.[71] The degree of evaluation and treatment given to any patient in the emergency care area is the responsibility of a physician.[72] A hospital must have written policies and procedures regarding the following aspects of emergency patient care:

1. The provision of care to an unemancipated minor not accompanied by parent or guardian, or to an unaccompanied unconscious patient
2. The transfer and discharge of patients
3. The emergency medical record, including consent for treatment
4. Specification of the scope of treatment allowed, including the general and specific procedures that may not be performed by medical staff members in the emergency department service, and the use of anesthesia
5. Who, other than physicians, may perform special procedures, under what circumstances, and under what degree of supervision
6. The use of standing order
7. Circumstances that require the patient to return to the emergency department for treatment
8. The handling of alleged or suspected rape and child abuse victims
9. Management of pediatric emergencies
10. Initial management of patients with acute problems such as burns, hand injuries, head injuries, fractures, poisoning, and gunshot and stab wounds[73]

When a hospital exerts control over an emergency patient—that is, when it begins to render aid—it is generally under a duty to use reasonable care under all circumstances.[74]

In determining the private hospital's liability for an emergency patient, older legal cases distinguished between whether or not an admission had been made. If the emergency treatment did not constitute an admission, recovery of damages was denied because the hospital had no duty to accept any patient.[75]

Many states currently follow the rule stated by the Delaware Supreme Court: liability of the hospital may be predicated on the refusal of service to a patient in the case of an "unmistakable emergency."[76] Since courts generally view the extent of the emergency with the benefit of hindsight, the hospital is obligated to adequately screen each emergency patient to determine whether the patient's condition, if left untreated, presents a serious threat to his life, health, or well-being.[77]

A hospital is not required to admit a patient when it is not adequately equipped to provide necessary continuing treatment. The hospital in this case has a positive duty to transfer or refer the patient to a facility where appropriate care can be rendered.[78] Transfers motivated in whole or part by a patient's race, creed, or ability to pay are risky for the hospital.[79]

The emergency admission situation is different from the in-hospital emergency situation. In Michigan, for example, physicians, nurses, or other hospital personnel* who respond in good faith to life-threatening emergencies within the hospital even though their actual duties as defined by hospital rules do not require a response, are exempted by state statute from civil liability for damages resulting from an act or omission unless the act or omission amounts to gross negligence or willful and wanton misconduct.[80] Because of the high standard of care it is required to provide patients, a hospital may be held liable for ordinary negligence in the treatment of a patient by employees if a hospital-patient relationship exists at the time of the negligent act. A Michigan hospital may not claim derivative immunity from the acts of its employees.[81]

(WARNING: *This immunity from liability does not apply to a physician where a physician-patient relationship existed between the patient and the physician prior to the emergency.*[82])

§ 7.63 Discharge

Discharge from a hospital is generally determined by hospital policy and on a case-by-case basis by the treating physician. Two major problems may arise concerning patient discharge. First, the restraint of patients who wish to leave and, second, the release of patients who may endanger themselves or third parties after leaving.[83] The refusal to discharge a patient who insists on leaving but who needs further care constitutes the tort of false imprisonment and subjects the hospital or the physician, or both, to liability.[84] In this situation, the hospital should require the patient (or guardian) to sign a form acknowledging that he or she is acting against the advice of the physician or hospital and releasing them from liability for resulting harm.[85] If the patient refuses to sign, he or she may not be forced to do so, nor may release be withheld pending signature. The form should be filled out and witnessed by hospital personnel with the notation "signature refused."[86] It should be noted that the detention of a patient for inability to pay a bill also constitutes false imprisonment.[87]

In the second situation, the hospital or the physician, or both, may be liable for damages resulting from the improper discharge of patients. This situation usually involves mental patients or patients with contagious diseases. In either case, the hospital is justified in using as much restraint as reasonably necessary.[88] Hospitals have also been held liable when, knowing of the escape of a dangerous patient, they fail to warn forseeable victims.[89] In such cases, the physician-patient privilege ends where public peril begins.[90]

§ 7.64 Utilization Review Committee

A hospital may be required to have a utilization review committee to monitor

---

*The statute applies to a physician, dentist, podiatrist, intern, resident, registered nurse, licensed practical nurse, registered physical therapist, clinical laboratory technologist, inhalation therapist, certified registered nurse-anesthetist, X-ray technician, or paramedic.

the hospitalization of individual patients. If this committee recommends against continued hospitalization and the patient is not discharged, most third-party payers (insurers) will not assume responsibility for the remaining costs.[91] Obviously, this is of critical importance to the patient, the physician, and the hospital (see § 7.74, Professional Review Organizations). Utilization review is especially important to hospitals seeking accreditation from the JCAH (see Appendix C for 1982 JCAH Utilization Review requirements).

§ 7.65 Abortion and Sterilization

Once a state has undertaken to provide general short-term hospital care, it may not prohibit certain surgical procedures that constitute such short-term care where to do so would impinge on fundamental rights: a public hospital, therefore, may not refuse to perform a lawful abortion or sterilization.[92] Since private hospitals are not constrained by the requirements of the Fourteenth Amendment's due process and equal protection clauses, they may refuse to perform abortions or sterilizations regardless of whether or not they receive federal funds.[93]

Some states have enacted "conscience clauses," which allow an institution, physician, or other health practitioner to refuse to perform or participate in the performance of an abortion. For example, Michigan provides:

> A hospital, clinic, institution, teaching institution, or other health facility is not required to admit a patient for the purpose of performing an abortion. A hospital, clinic, institution, teaching institution, or other health facility or a physician, member, or associate of the staff, or other person connected therewith, may refuse to perform, participate in, or allow to be performed on its premises an abortion. The refusal shall be with immunity from any civil or criminal liability or penalty.
>
> A physician or other individual who is a member of or associated with a hospital, clinic, institution, teaching institution, or other health facility, or a nurse, medical student, student nurse, or other employee of a hospital, clinic, institution, teaching institution, or other health facility in which an abortion is performed, who states an objection to abortion on professional, ethical, moral, or religious grounds, is not required to participate in the medical procedures which will result in abortion. The refusal by the individual to participate does not create a liability for damages on account of the refusal or for any disciplinary or discriminatory action by the patient, hosptial, clinic, institution, teaching institution, or other health facility against the individual.
>
> 1. A physician who informs a patient that he or she refuses to give advice concerning, or participate in, an abortion is not liable to the hospital, clinic, institution, teaching institution, health facility, or patient for the refusal.
> 2. A civil action for negligence or malpractice or a disciplinary or discriminatory action may not be maintained against a person refusing to give advice as to, or participating in, an abortion based on the refusal.
>
> A hospital, clinic, institution, teaching institution, or other health facility which refuses to allow abortions to be performed on its premises shall not deny staff

§ 7.65   *Abortion and Sterilization*   281

privileges or employment to an individual for the sole reason that the individual previously participated in, or expressed a willingness to participate in, a termination of pregnancy. A hospital, clinic, institution, teaching institution, or other health facility shall not discriminate against its staff members or other employees for the sole reason that the staff members or employees have participated in, or have expressed a willingness to participate in, a termination of pregnancy.[94]

Georgia's conscience clause was specifically approved by the U.S. Supreme Court.[95] However, a Minnesota statute which provided that no person, hospital, or institution could be coerced, held liable for, or discriminated against in any manner because of a refusal to participate in an abortion was held to be unconstitutional as applied to public facilities.[96] Some state courts have approved their conscience statutes as a means of supporting the First Amendment right to practice one's religion.

CASE ILLUSTRATION

Plaintiff, a certified nurse-anesthetist, was asked to assist in a D&C accompanied by an abortion. Plaintiff's observation of the dissection and part-by-part removal of the fetus caused her to be horrified and upset. She informed the hospital administration the day before her scheduled participation in another tubal ligation that she would not participate. Plaintiff was fired and, upon request, was given a written statement of the reason for her discharge as "untimely refusal to perform customary and needed services." The court concluded that the plaintiff's rights under the conscience statute were not outweighed by the employer's necessity, especially since the procedure was elective and there was no showing that the hospital was unduly prejudiced or that the patient was in danger. The court further held that the plaintiff was not required to specify her reasons for not participating in the procedure (*Swanson v. St. John's Lutheran Hospital,* 1979).[97]

There are essentially two federal conscience clauses. The first[98] provides that the receipt of funds under enumerated federal programs does not authorize any court or public official to require any individual or institutional recipient to perform or assist in the performance of an abortion or sterilization. An institution receiving funds under these programs may not discriminate in employment based on nonparticipation in abortion. The second conscience clause[99] provides that no institution receiving a research grant from DHHS may discriminate in employment based on the performance or nonperformance of a medical procedure because of religious or moral beliefs concerning the activity. No individual may be compelled, in any health service or research program so funded, to participate in any part of the program contrary to his or her religious or moral beliefs.[100]

A physician who refuses to perform an abortion or sterilization based on moral or religious grounds is required to refer the patient to another competent practitioner to perform the procedures.[101]

§ 7.70 REGULATION OF THE HOSPITAL

Hospitals are externally regulated in a number of ways. Generally, noncompliance with requirements of state and federal programs will involve a penalty for the hospital in terms of finances, availability of or eligibility for various funds, or some sanction against the hospital's license. Voluntary compliance with the requirements of the JCAH can provide financial incentives, yet no penalties are given for noncompliance.

§ 7.71 Joint Commission on the Accreditation of Hospitals

The standards adopted by the JCAH relate to the quality of services provided by hospitals. They are optimal yet achievable, and they are the basis of the voluntarism movement across the United States.[102] The standards provide incentives for compliance (such as automatic compliance with Medicare conditions of participation) rather than penalites for noncompliance.[103] These JCAH standards also foster compliance because they are admissible for the jury to consider as evidence in determining the standard of care to which a hospital should be held.[104]

To participate in the accreditation process, a hospital must request and complete an Application for Survey. The hospital will be notified of the survey approximately four weeks in advance.[105] The extent of the hospital's compliance will be assessed through at least one of the following means:

1. Statements from authorized and responsible hospital personnel
2. Certification or other documentation of compliance provided by the hospital
3. Answers to questions concerning the implementation of a standard, or examples of its implementation, that will enable a judgment of compliance to be made
4. On-site observations by Hospital Accreditation Program surveyors[106]

The JCAH will also provide an opportunity during the on-site survey for the presentation of information about the hospital by hospital personnel and staff and public representatives and consumers.[107]

Since the JCAH standards are optimal, 100 percent compliance is not necessary, and a hospital that substantially complies will be accredited.[108]

The development of JCAH standards is an ongoing process. Technological innovations, advancements in knowledge, changes in governmental regulations, or consumer demand for accountability may prompt revision or development of standards. Input for each standard is solicited from specialty organizations and experts in the appropriate area. Feedback is also obtained from concerned governmental agencies, individual health care practitioners, and health care groups.[109]

Accreditation by the JCAH is attractive to many hospitals because it offers benefits in the private and public sectors. Some private insurance companies require accreditation for reimbursement; even if it is not required, accreditation generally smooths the path for private insurance reimbursement.[110] The federal government gives accredited hospitals "deemed status," or automatic eligibility for Medicare-Medicaid reimbursement.[111] Accreditation is one of the criteria for funding decisions such as those made under the terms of the Hill-Burton Act or loans made by private banks, as well as rate-setting for hospital liability insurance premiums. Such internship, residency, or medical specialty programs require JCAH accreditation, and an accredited hospital may have an advantage in recruiting professional staff.[112]

The JCAH interacts with the federal government in several ways. The government validates JCAH's survey findings, even though the government generally uses less stringent standards. Since 1976, PSRO and JCAH have formed a joint task force to avoid duplication of effort and to eliminate potential conflicts in review activities.[113] JCAH and PSRO are not equivalent, however, and JCAH maintains strict confidentiality of its survey results.[114] It is not part of the federal or state government and as yet has no contract of funding from the government.

§ 7.72 Licensure

The passage of the Hill-Burton Act of 1946 led most states to adopt a hospital licensing statute because state licensure was a prerequisite to obtaining federal construction funds and to participating in federal and state Medicare-Medicaid programs. Most standards set forth in these licensing statutes pertain to the adequacy of the construction design and physical plant of hospitals rather than to the quality of care delivered.[115] Some states, however, do cover all aspects of the hospital, including physical plant, services procedures, administration, and medical staff.[116] Some regulations—for example, those which relate to patients' rights—may be worded as recommendations rather than requirements, making enforcement difficult.[117]

§ 7.73 Certificate of Need

By 1973, about half of the states had passed certificate-of-need legislation. This legislation requires a facility to obtain certification that there is a public need for change in or expansion of its services before beginning such change or expansion.[118] As part of the 1972 amendments to the Social Security Act, Section 1122 provided for review of capital expenditures of institutions participating in the Medicare reimbursement program. The National Health Planning and Resources Development Act (Public Law 93-641) established a system for national to local health planning. Part of it includes responsibility and criteria for administering the certificate-of-need program.[119] Basically, the certificate-of-need program attempts to contain health care costs by restricting capital expenditures by health facilities in the form of building, expansion, and acquisition of expensive equipment. The underlying assumption is that unnecessary facilities or services will increase inappropriate utilization and overhead, which ultimately increases the cost of health care.

§ 7.74 Professional Review Organizations

Medical services provided in hospitals have been reviewed and regulated on both a voluntary and involuntary basis for a number of years. Many hospitals engaged in such review activities before private accreditation and federally mandated programs came into existence. The uniform development of this area, however, was prompted principally by two groups, JCAH (see § 7.64, Utilization Review Committee) and the federal government (see § 5.30, Professional Review Organizations).

The goal of professional review and utilization review is to balance cost control and quality of care. As the needs and resources of society fluctuate, however, the emphasis placed on savings may outweigh that placed on quality of care. Review models evolve in response to this fluctuating emphasis. In the face of growing economic restraints, it is likely that the balance will continue to shift toward cost savings at the expense of optimal care. Physicians correctly note, especially as they are forced to respond to federal cost control initiatives, that they are being pushed into a dual standard of care: they may feel pressured to give less than optimal care, yet in a medical malpractice proceeding they will still be held to the optimal standard of care of their specialty (see § 1.32, Standard of Care).

As a result of the values effected by utilization review and its linkage with reimbursement, PROs and other forms of utilization review will probably become increasingly controversial hot spots for patient, physician, hospital, and government interaction.

§ 7.80 OBSTETRIC AND GYNECOLOGIC SERVICES

In addition to the general licensure and accreditation requirements mentioned above, hospitals may be required to comply with specific regulations related to a particular service or procedure. The JCAH allows a hospital to have any of the following four clinical services in order to be eligible for an accreditation survey: medicine, obstetrics-gynecology, pediatrics, or surgery.[120] Therefore, not all JCAH-accredited hospitals will have facilities for obstetrics-gynecology.

§ 7.81 JCAH Standards

Since the JCAH does not require all hospitals to have obstetrics-gynecology services, the standards and requirements related to such services are interspersed throughout the accreditation manual. Indeed, there are no unified JCAH standards for in-hospital obstetrical-gynecological services.

Anesthesia must be available when the hospital provides surgical or obstetrical services. The director of anesthesia services is responsible for monitoring the quality of anesthesia care rendered anywhere in the hospital, including the obstetrical area.[121] Physician-anesthetists must be able to perform accepted procedures commonly used to render the patient insensible to pain during the performance of obstetrical maneuvers.[122] A qualified nurse- or dentist-anesthetist may perform under the overall direction of the surgeon or obstetrician responsible for the patient's care.[123] The anesthesia service must have written regulations for the control of electrical and anesthetic explosion hazards. Pursuant to these regulations, anesthesia personnel must familiarize themselves with the rate, volume, and mechanism of air exchange and humidity control within the surgical and obstetrical suites.[124]

The JCAH requires hospitals to have available an autonomous emergency power source to provide essential service when the normal electrical supply is interrupted. Emergency power must automatically be provided to the operating rooms, delivery rooms, special care units, newborn nursery, and postoperative recovery rooms, among other areas, within ten seconds of failure of the normal power source.[125]

Hospitals must have specific written infection control policies and procedures for all services throughout the hospital. These policies are dictated by the physical layout, personnel, equipment, and type of patient admitted or treated in the area. These policies should be developed in cooperation with the various departments, services, and areas, including the newborn nursery, the obstetrical department or service (see Appendix D for a sample protocol for a department of obstetrics and gynecology), and the surgical suite.[126] In addition, the housekeeping staff must follow specific procedures regarding the cleaning of specialized areas such as the surgical suite, obstetrical suite, and newborn nursery.[127]

An adequate medical record must be maintained for each person evaluated or treated in the hospital or in a hospital-administered home care program.[128] All medical records must contain the following information:

1. Identification data, including the patient's name, next of kin, date of birth, and address
2. The patient's medical history (obstetrical records should include all prenatal information)
3. A report giving a comprehensive, current physical assessment
4. Diagnostic and therapeutic orders
5. Evidence of appropriate informed consent
6. Clinical observations, including progress notes, consultation reports, nursing notes, and entries by specified professional personnel (when

oxygen is prescribed for a newborn, its frequency of use and the concentration used should be recorded, in accordance with the written policies of the newborn nursery)

7. Reports and results of procedures and tests
8. Conclusions at the end of hospitalization, including provisional diagnosis or reason for admission, principal and additional diagnoses, the clinical resume or final progress note, and the necropsy report, if any (in the case of patients with minor problems requiring hospitalization for less than 48 hours and in the case of normal newborn infants and uncomplicated obstetrical deliveries, a final progress note may substitute for the resume)[129]

Nurses' duties must be commensurate with their qualifications, and departments must be structured to meet the needs of patients.[130] Only qualified registered nurses may be assigned as head nurses, supervisors, or circulating nurses in the surgical and obstetrical suites.

Hospitals may establish special care units as determined by the patient needs of the community and only if they can be supported by the resources available to the hospital.[131] An example of this type of special care unit is the neonatal intensive care unit. This unit must be used only for the care of high-risk newborn infants. A plan for the use of the unit should be developed, it should allow for the grouping of infants with similar needs and for the isolation of infants when necessary. The director of the unit must have at least one year of recognized special training and experience, as well as demonstrated competence in neonatology. Nursing care must be supervised by a registered nurse with training, experience, and documented current competence in the care of high-risk infants. The nursing staff must be able to instruct the parents in the care of the infant at home, including the safe use and accurate interpretation of all monitoring equipment. Other policies and procedures shall be developed for conducting patient care activities in the unit. Visiting policies should reflect a sustained commitment to reducing the separation of parent and infant.[132]

§ 7.82 State Regulation

In addition to the JCAH standards and general state hospital licensing requirements, some states specify requirements regarding the obstetrics-gynecology service or department. These requirements are generally included within the hospital licensing regulations.

Some of the regulations deal at length with the physical requirements for obstetrical and gynecological services.[133] For example, New Jersey requires that the labor-delivery and nursery units be set up in such a way that appropriate restrictions may be placed on entry to the units. A separate delivery room should be available for infected patients. No room used as a nursery can communicate directly with any other room used as a nursery. A separate refrigerator must be provided for storage of infant feedings requiring refrigeration. All exterior windows and doors used for ventilation on the units must be effectively screened. Extra equipment may not be stored in the nurseries or nursery accessory rooms.[134] Texas regulates physical plant standards in such detail as to require that the ceilings of labor rooms be acoustically treated.[135]

Staffing requirements are often regulated. Illinois requires that the chief of the obstetric service be a physician qualified in obstetrics. Nursing supervision is to be provided on a 24-hour basis by a registered nurse with education and experience in maternity or neonatal nursing, or both.[136] Most states require that all deliveries in the hospital be attended by a physician or midwife (a certified nurse-midwife may be specified).[137] New Jersey requires that physicians performing obstetrics be classified on the basis of either their ability to perform all types of obstetric procedures and deliveries or their ability to perform only uncomplicated deliveries.[138]

In addition to the basic physical plant and staffing requirements, most states' regulations include provisions for medical records, equipment, and control of infection.[139] Some states also specify procedures to be performed or standards for certain procedures. Blood type and RH determination are commonly required to be made prior to or immediately upon admission.[140] Certain test results may be required to be available within a specified time. For example, Illinois requires that hematocrit blood typing and crossmatching, glucose, bilirubin, Coombs' test, pH, and blood gases test results be available within less than one hour.[141] Other such requirements, as well as staffing and physical plant requirements, may depend on the level of perinatal care available at the facility.[142]

Georgia has developed a system of perinatal care which organizes and coordinates services within a geographic area to assure provision of the appropriate level of care to each patient within the area. For this purpose, Georgia has defined the following three levels of perinatal care:

1. A primary care hospital, which meets the state's minimum standards for hospital maternity and newborn services. All hospitals in Georgia that perform deliveries must meet these standards.

2. Secondary care perinatal units outside a standard metropolitan statistical area, which are responsible for (1) accepting obstetrical and newborn transfers, regardless of the patient's race, creed, or ability to pay, for a defined geographic region, (2) meeting defined standards, (3) having the services of a board-certified (or eligible) obstetrician and pediatrician available 24 hours per day, (4) being able to coordinate transportation of referrals from primary hospitals, (5) having a defined, coordinated relationship with a tertiary level service that includes accepting infants back to a secondary care facility when tertiary care is no longer needed.

3. Tertiary care units, which are the least numerous. They must (1) accept

referrals originated by physicians in primary or secondary units, regardless of the patient's race, creed, or ability to pay, within a defined geographic region, (2) accept responsibility for maternal and neonatal transport systems within their region, (3) make continuing education available to primary and secondary care facilities and (4) meet defined standards.[143]

Increased awareness of natural childbirth methods and the desirability of health education for new mothers has prompted regulations dealing with the presence of fathers in the delivery room,[144] required postpartum instruction in infant care,[145] and infant rooming-in arrangements.[146]

§ 7.90 MEDICAL STAFF PRIVILEGES

Given the realities of contemporary medical practice in this country, affiliation with a hospital is absolutely indispensable to surgeons and other specialists. A physician or surgeon who is denied access to hospital facilities is for all practical purposes effectively denied the opportunity to practice his or her profession fully. Because of the adverse professional and financial effects of not being appointed to or of being removed from the hospital staff, many physicians without staff privileges have gone to court to obtain or retain their appointments. As noted earlier, it is the governing board of the hospital which is ultimately responsible for the quality of patient care; the board therefore controls admission to, or discharge from, the medical staff. This conflict between the responsibility of the hospital and the needs of the physician has spawned considerable litigation in the area of medical staff privileges.

§ 7.91 Substantive Due Process

The U.S. Constitution provides that a state may not deprive any person of life, liberty, or property without due process of law nor deny to any person the equal protection of its laws.[147] These clauses, referred to as the due process and equal protection clauses, seemingly apply only to governmental entities or to entities that have such close connections to the government as to be considered its agents. The significance of the clauses from the standpoint of a hospital medical staff is that they impose certain constraints on hospitals in denying, reducing, or revoking staff privileges. Some state courts have begun to impose similar constraints on private hospitals, based on public policy and common law.[148] In addition, the JCAH[149] and its conditions of participation for hospitals[150] require that physicians be afforded substantive due process and equal protection.

Substantive due process requires that hospital privileges be determined on reasonable, nonarbitrary, and noncapricious standards. This has been interpreted to mean that the standards for determining privileges must be related to such things as clinical standards of patient care, the objectives and purposes of the institution, or the professional, ethical behavior of the physician and be capable of an objective application.[151] Hospitals may not restrict privileges based on vague and arbitrary standards such as "the best interests of the patient and hospital."[152]

Various requirements of admission to the medical staff have been tested in court. Briefly, the following requirements have been upheld:

1. References documenting training, experience, and current clinical competence, as long as they are not required from currently active medical staff members[153]
2. Reasonable geographic limitations regarding the proximity of the hospital to the physician's office, although these limitations cannot require that the office be in the same county as the hospital[154]
3. Documented clinical competence[155]
4. Mandatory medical malpractice insurance[156]
5. Mandatory specialty board certification[157]
6. Documented ability to work with others[158]

Furthermore, hospitals may restrict or delineate privileges if the restriction can be professionally justified.[159] For example, a Michigan appeals court has allowed a hospital to suspend privileges based on the physician's personal behavior—that is, rudeness and unacceptable language directed at patients, staff, and visitors.[160]

In most states, public hospitals may deny privileges to licensed osteopathic physicians and to members of other schools of healing arts.[161] Some states, however, have adopted specific legislation prohibiting discrimination against doctors of osteopathic medicine.[162] Where licensing statutes or other legislation equate physicians of allopathic and osteopathic medicine, osteopathic physicians must be afforded equal substantive rights and opportunities, based on their individual training and qualifications.[163]

Courts have upheld the requirement of AMA-approved residency in a specialty as a prerequisite to admission to the medical staff in that specialty.[164] The JCAH standards specify that delineation of clinical privileges should be based on the staff member's credentials. While one method of delineating clinical privileges is through specialty board certification or current eligibility, as defined by the appropriate board, privilege delineation should be reasonably comprehensive and not identified simply as a specialty designation such as "family practice" or "obstetrics and gynecology."[165] A California family practitioner successfully challenged the action of a hospital board that revoked his obstetrical staff privileges in a 1980 lawsuit. The court that reinstated these privileges did not indicate whether a family practitioner's privileges could be so limited, only that the revocation procedures followed by the hospital violated the family practitioner's rights.[166]

Physician specialists have been excluded from medical staffs on the basis that current staff coverage in their specialty is adequate or that additional coverage would needlessly increase the amount of surgery performed.[167] In these cases, the hospital must be able to support its decision with substantial, credible evidence and may not base such exclusions on fostering the well-being of present staff members.[168]

A lawsuit brought in New Jersey challenged a blanket moratorium on new medical staff appointments (except for limited subspecialties or where an applicant had no hospital affiliation) that was adopted to curb excessive utilization rates. The court held the moratorium to be an abuse of the governing board's discretion when a five-year experience demonstrated its ineffectiveness. The court found that the moratorium only enhanced the economic interests of the current medical staff at the expense of practictioners whose patients would be excluded.[169]

Courts have upheld closed departments or services which restrict from practice in their specialty or service all physicians except those who have an exclusive contract with the hospital for the rendering of that service.[170] In exclusive contract arrangements, the hospital contracts with one or more physicians to provide specialized professional service, closing that service to all other physicians regardless of their qualifications and competence. The hospital must be able to show valid reasons for its decision to enter into an exclusive contract.[171]

§ 7.92 Procedural Due Process

In addition to the reasonableness requirements of due process, certain procedural safeguards are imposed on hospitals in granting, reducing, or revoking staff privileges. Though procedures may vary slightly between initial appointments to the staff and renewals or other actions against the privileges of current staff members, procedural due process generally means that the physician must be granted fundamental fair play under the particular circumstances.[172] At least one state court has specified minimal due process requirements as follows:

1. Written notice of the charges against him or her (or reasons for denial of initial appointment)
2. Opportunity for a hearing
3. A relatively impartial, duly authorized body to conduct the hearing
4. Opportunity to produce positive evidence and witnesses and to refute adverse evidence and testimony
5. Findings based on substantial factual evidence
6. Written notice of the decision, with reasons for it
7. Opportunity to appeal[173]

The JCAH standards require the medical staff to adopt bylaws that include the establishment of a fair hearing and appellate review mechanisms in connection with medical staff recommendations for denial of initial appointments and reappointments, curtailment, suspension, or revocation of staff privileges. These mechanisms should specify the period of time during which a hearing may be requested, the right to introduce witnesses or evidence, the role of legal counsel, and fixed periods of time within which action must be completed, including final action by the governing board.[174]

Some hospitals may grant protection to staff physicians in their bylaws, such as the physician's right to be represented by counsel.[175] Although hospitals may summarily suspend a physician's privileges in order to protect the patient, they must provide the physician with an opportunity for a hearing within a reasonable time after suspension.[176] Whether public or private, a hospital must follow the procedural due process requirements specified in its bylaws.[177]

§ 7.100 EXCLUSIVE CONTRACTS

Hospital contracts for the exclusive services of a single specialist or group of specialists have been repeatedly challenged by physicians seeking hospital privileges in the specialty covered by the contract.[178] The courts will look to the hospital's rationale for the exclusive contract in deciding physicians' suits based on civil rights or antitrust claims. The hospital's reasons for the contract must be related to legitimate hospital concerns.

> CASE ILLUSTRATION
>
> Defendant, a public hospital, was dissatisfied with the anesthesiology services provided to it. It had for some time attempted, unsuccessfully, to assure "on-call" services of anesthesiologists and nurse-anesthetists; as a result, surgery was sometimes performed without an anesthesiologist in attendance. The JCAH had indicated a number of deficiencies in the hospital's anesthesiology services in its annual review. The hospital finally contracted with a professional corporation of three anesthesiologists and a number of nurse-anesthetists to provide 24-hour-per-day, 7-day-per-week services. Plaintiff's application to use hospital facilities to practice his specialty, anesthesiology, was denied because of the existence of the exclusive contract. The court dismissed plaintiff's suit charging violations of the Sherman Antitrust Act, federal civil rights statutes, and the U.S. Constitution.
>
> The court's specific conclusions of law contained the following listing of legal arguments in general support of a hospital's right to enter into an exclusive contract:
>
> 1. A physician has no federal constitutional right to staff privileges at a public hospital merely because of his or her license to practice medicine.
> 2. A hospital has the right to treat physicians of the same calling differently, provided there is a rational basis for the different treatment.

3. A contract between a hospital and some of its staff members to operate a certain specialized facility to the exclusion of other equally qualified physicians is not necessarily unreasonable or arbitrary, depending on the ends to be met thereby.
4. The hospital administered the plaintiff's application with fairness and denied it based on rationale compatible with the hospital's responsibility.
5. The exclusive contract was justified in view of the ends to be accomplished by the hospital and contractors in providing proper care to surgical patients.
6. None of the plaintiff's rights under the Fourteenth Amendment to the U.S. Constitution or the Civil Rights Act (42 U.S.C. § 1983) was abridged as a result of the existence of the exclusive contract (*Capili v. Shott*, 1980).[179]

The above listing is an example of the consideration given an exclusive contract that is being challenged. Other courts have rejected a plaintiff's argument that denial of hospital privileges due to the existence of an exclusive contract entitles plaintiff to a hearing.[180]

Courts will generally uphold the hospital's discretion to adopt a reasonable administrative policy. For example, where a hospital faced with conflicting views chooses to operate a particular unit on a closed-staff basis, the court stated that, where the rule-making or policymaking decision was arrived at in substantively rational and fair proceedings, the court would not substitute its judgment for that of the governing board, even if it disagreed with the board's decision.[181]

NOTES

1. E. Hayt, L. Hayt, & A. Groeschel, Law of Hospital, Physician and Patient 83 (1972).
2. *Id.* at 84.
3. A. Donabedian, Aspects of Medical Care Administration 241 (1973).
4. D. Warren, Problems in Hospital Law 303 (1978); A. Southwick, The Law of Hospital and Health Care Administration 79 (1978).
5. Hill v. Ohio County, 468 S.W.2d 306 (Ky. 1971); *cert. denied*, 404 U.S. 1041 (1972).
6. A. Southwick, *supra* note 4, at 162–63.
7. Memorial Hosp. v. Maricopa County, 415 U.S. 250 (1974).
8. Mich. Comp. Laws Ann. § 333.20152 (1980).
9. *See e.g.*, Okla. Stat. Ann. tit. 68, § 2405(j) (West 1966 & 1980 Supp.); A. Southwick, *supra* note 4, at 431.
10. D. Warren, *supra* note 4, at 86.
11. A. Southwick, *supra* note 4, at 431.
12. Joint Commission on Accreditation of Hospitals, Accreditation Manual for Hospitals 93 (1981) (hereinafter cited as JCAH).
13. Southwick, *Due Process Part 1: The Physician's Right to Due Process and Equal Protection*, 7 Hosp. Med. Staff 30, 31 (May, 1978).

14. Parker v. Highland Park, 404 Mich. 183, 273 N.W.2d 413 (1978); Mich. Comp. Laws Ann. § 691.1407 (Supp. 1981).
15. *See* D. Louisell & H. Williams, 2 Medical Malpractice 528-540.7 (1980).
16. *See, e.g.*, Calomeris v. D.C., 125 F. Supp. 266 (D.D.C. 1954); Strickland v. Bradford County Hosp. Corp., 196 So.2d 765 (Fla. App. 1967).
17. *See, e.g.*, Mo. Ann. Stat. § 71.185 (Vernon 1959); McMahon v. Baroness Erlanger Hosp., 306 S.W.2d 41 (Tenn. App. 1951); Vt. Stat. Ann. tit. 29, §§ 1401 *et seq.* (1965); Collins v. Memorial Hosp. of Sheridan County, 521 P.2d 1330 (Wyo. 1974).
18. *See, e.g.*, Tuengel v. Sitka 118 F. Supp. 399 (D. Alaska 1954); Stone v. Arizona Highway Commission, 93 Ariz. 384, 381 P.2d 107 (1963); Conn. Gen. Stat. Ann. § 7-465 (West 1961, *as amended*, 1963, 1965); Rev. L. Hawaii § 245a-2 (Supp. 1965); Parker v. City of Highland Park, *supra* note 14; Becker v. City of New York, 2 N.Y.2d 266, 140 N.E.2d 262 (1957).
19. *See* Louisell and Williams, *supra* note 15, at 528-540.7.
20. E. Hayt, L. Hayt & A. Groeschel, *supra* note 1, at 91, 93, 95.
21. D. Warren, *supra* note 4, at 303.
22. *Id.* at 53.
23. *See, e.g.*, Waters v. St. Francis Hosp., 618 F.2d 1106, 1107 (5th Cir. 1980); Hodge v. Paoli Mem. Hosp., 576 F.2d 563, 564 (3d Cir. 1978); Barret v. United Hosps., 376 F. Supp. 791 (S.D. N.Y. 1974), *aff'd mem.*, 506 F.2d 1395 (2d Cir. 1974).
24. Sams v. Ohio Valley Gen. Hosp. Ass'n, 413 F.2d 826 (4th Cir. 1969); Simkins v. Moses H. Cone Mem. Hosp., 323 F.2d 959 (4th Cir. 1963), *cert. denied*, 376 U.S. 938 (1964).
25. Southwick, *supra* note 13, at 31.
26. 42 C.F.R. §§ 405.1021 *et seq.* (1979).
27. JCAH, *supra* note 12, at 94-95.
28. Arkansas Midland R.R. Co. v. Pearson, 98 Ark. 399, 135 S.W. 917 (1911); Morton v. Savannah Hosp., 148 Ga. 438, 96 S.E. 887 (1918); Jones v. Baylor Hosp., 284 S.W.2d 929 (Tex. Civ. App. 1955); Norfolk Protestant Hosp. v. Plunkett, 162 Va. 151, 173 S.E. 363 (1934).
29. Sisters of the Sorrowful Mother v. Zeidler, 183 Okla. 454, 82 P.2d 996 (1938); Villarreal v. Santa Rosa Med. Center, 443 S.W.2d 622 (Tex. Civ. App. 1969); Sessions v. Thomas D. Dee Mem. Hosp., 94 Utah 460, 78 P.2d 645 (1938).
30. O'Connor v. Boulder Colorado, Sanitarium Ass'n, 105 Colo. 259, 96 P.2d 835 (1939).
31. Tucker v. Mobile Infirmary Ass'n, 191 Ala. 572, 68 So. 4 (1915); Tuengel v. Sitka, *supra* note 18; Ray v. Tucson Med. Center, 72 Ariz. 22, 230 P.2d 220 (1951); Malloy v. Fong, 37 Cal.2d 356, 232 P.2d 241 (1951); Heimbuch v. President & Directors of Georgetown College, 251 F. Supp. 614 (D. D.C. 1966); Wilson v. Lee Mem. Hosp., 65 So.2d 40 (Fla. 1964); Bill v. Presbytery of Boise, 91 Idaho 60, 297 P.2d 1041 (1956); Darling v. Charleston Community Mem. Hosp., 33 Ill. 2d 326, 211 N.E.2d 253 (1965), *cert. denied*, 383 U.S. 946 (1966); Harris v. Young Women's Christian Ass'n, 237 N.E.2d 242 (Ind. 1968); Haynes v. Presbyterian Hosp., 241 Iowa 1269, 45 N.W.2d 151 (1950); Noel v. Menninger Found., 175 Kan. 751, 267 P.2d 934 (1954); Jackson v. Doe, 296 So.2d 323 (La. 1974); Colby v. Carney Hosp., 254 N.E.2d 407 (Mass. 1969); Parker v. Port Huron Hosp., 361 Mich. 1, 105 N.W.2d 1 (1960); Mulliner v. Evangelischer Diakonniessenverein of Minn. Dist. of German Evangelical Synod of North America, 144 Minn. 392, 175 N.W. 699 (1920); Mississippi Baptist Hosp. v. Holmes, 214 Miss. 906, 55 So.2d 142 (1951); Abernathy v. Sisters of St. Mary's, 446 S.W.2d 599 (Mo. 1969); Howard v. Sisters of Charity of Leavenworth, 193 F. Supp. 191 (D. Mont. 1961); Myers v. Drozda, 180 Neb. 183, 141 N.W.2d 852 (1966); Welch v. Frizbee Mem.

Hosp., 90 N.H. 337, 9 A.2d 761 (1939); Collopy v. Newark Eye and Ear Infirmary, 27 N.J. 29, 141 A.2d 276 (1958); Bing v. Thunig, 2 N.Y.2d 656, 143 N.E.2d 3 (1957); Rickbeil v. Grafton Deaconess Hosp., 74 N.D. 525, 23 N.W.2d 247 (1964); Avellone v. St. John's Hosp., 165 Ohio St. 467, 135 N.E.2d 410 (1956); Hungerford v. Portland Sanitarium & Benevolent Ass'n, 235 Or. 412, 384 P.2d 1009 (1963); Flagiello v. Pennslyvania Hosp., 417 Pa. 486, 208 A.2d 193 (1965); Foster v. Roman Catholic Diocese of Vt., 116 Vt. 124, 70 A.2d 230 (1950); Friend v. Cove Methodist Church, Inc., 65 Wash. 2d 174, 396 P.2d 546 (1964); Atkins v. St. Francis Hosp., 143 S.E.2d 154 (1965); Kojis v. Doctors Hosp., 12 Wis. 2d 367, 107 N.W.2d 131, *modified,* 12 Wis. 2d 367, 107 N.W.2d 292 (1961); Lutheran Hosps. v. Homes Society v. Yepsen, 469 P.2d 409 (Wyo. 1970).
32. A. Southwick, *supra* note 4, at 32.
33. *Id.* at 37.
34. R. Anthony & R. Huzlinger, Management Control in Nonprofit Organizations 2–36 (1975).
35. A. Southwick, *supra* note 4, at 33.
36. *Id.* at 32.
37. *Id.*
38. *Id.* at 35.
39. Manuel Tovar v. Paxton Community Mem. Hosp., 29 Ill. App. 3d 218, 330 N.E.2d 247 (1975).
40. JCAH, *supra* note 12, at 51, 103.
41. *Id.* at 103.
42. *Id.* at 103–4.
43. Darling v. Charleston Community Mem. Hosp., *supra* note 31.
44. Polonsky v. Union Hosp., 418 N.E.2d 620, 622 (Mass. App. Ct. 1966).
45. D. Warren, *supra* note 4, at 27.
46. A. Southwick, *supra* note 4, at 40.
47. JCAH, *supra* note 12, at 51–56.
48. D. Warren, *supra* note 4, at 28.
49. JCAH, *supra* note 12, at 151.
50. Shields, *Guidelines for Reviewing Applications for Privileges,* 9 Hosp. Med. Staff 11 (Sept., 1980).
51. *See, e.g.,* Purcell v. Zimbliman, 18 Ariz. App. 75, 500 P.2d 335 (1972); Joiner v. Mitchell County Hosp. Auth., 125 Ga. App. 1, 2, 186 S.E.2d 307, 308 (1971), *aff'd,* 229 Ga. 140, 189 S.E.2d 412 (1972); Corleto v. Shore Mem. Hosp., 138 N.J. Super. 302, 309, 250 A.2d 534, 537 (1975).
52. A. Southwick, *supra* note 4, at 51.
53. JCAH, *supra* note 12, at 79.
54. *Id.* at 81–82.
55. Blanton, *Physician's Role in Hospital Continues To Grow,* 9 Hosp. Med. Staff 13, 14 (April, 1980).
56. Corleto v. Shore Mem. Hosp., *supra* note 51.
57. Horty & Mulholland, *The Legal Status of the Hospital Medical Staff,* 1979 Spec. L. Dig.: Health Care 19 (April 1979).
38. Warren, *supra* note 4, at 47.
59. JCAH, *supra* note 12, at 99.
60. *Id.* at 101.
61. *Id.* at 102.
62. *Id.* at 115.
63. D. Warren, *supra* note 4, at 71.
64. JCAH, *supra* note 12, at 116.

65. D. Warren, *supra* note 4, at 79.
66. JCAH, *supra* note 12, at xviii.
67. *Id.* at 9, 28, 126, 142, 157, 174, 179, 184.
68. A. Southwick, *supra* note 4, at 164–66.
69. D. Warren, *supra* note 4, at 91.
70. A. Southwick, *supra* note 4, at 186; *see, e.g.,* Mich. Comp. Laws Ann. § 691.1502 (Supp. 1980–81).
71. JCAH, *supra* note 12, at 23.
72. *Id.* at 26.
73. *Id.* at 29–30.
74. *See, e.g.,* Thomas v. Corso, 265 Md. 84, 288 A.2d 379 (1972); Barcia v. Society of N.Y. Hosp., 241 N.Y.S.2d 373, 39 Misc. 2d 526 (Sup. Ct. 1963).
75. Kucera, *Narrow Definition of "Emergency" Can Spell "Litigation,"* 7 Hosp. Med. Staff 21, 23 (Sept. 1978).
76. Wilmington Gen. Hosp. v. Manlove, 54 Del. 15, 174 A.2d 135 (Sup. Ct. 1961).
77. Kucera, *supra* note 75, at 25; *see* Powers, *Hospital Emergency Service and the Open Door,* 66 Mich. L. Rev. 1455 (1968).
78. *See, e.g.,* Carrasco v. Bankoff, 220 Cal. App. 2d 230, 33 Cal. Rptr. 673 (1963).
79. Kucera, *supra* note 75, at 26.
80. Mich. Comp. Laws Ann. § 691.1502 (Supp. 1980–81).
81. Hamburger v. Henry Ford Hosp., 91 Mich. App. 580, 284 N.W.2d 155 (1979).
82. Mich. Comp. Laws Ann. § 691.1502 (Supp. 1980–81).
83. D. Warren, *supra* note 4, at 93.
84. A. Southwick, *supra* note 4, at 179.
85. D. Warren, *supra* note 4, at 95.
86. American Medical Association, (AMA), Office of the General Counsel, Medicolegal Forms with Legal Analysis 6 (1973).
87. D. Warren, *supra* note 4, at 93.
88. *Id.* at 95.
89. Tarasoff v. Regents of the Univ. of California, 118 Cal. Rptr. 129, 529 P.2d 553 (1974); Rum River Lumber Co. v. Minnesota, 282 N.W.2d 882 (Minn. 1979); Comiskey v. State of N.Y., 71 A.D.2d 699, 418 N.Y.S.2d 233 (1979).
90. *Id.*
91. A. Southwick, *supra* note 4, at 181.
92. Greco v. Orange Mem. Hosp. Corp., 513 F.2d 873 (5th Cir. 1975), *rehearing denied,* 515 F.2d 1183, *cert. denied,* 423 U.S.1000 (1975); Nyberg v. City of Virginia, 495 F.2d 1342 (8th Cir. 1973); Hathaway v. Worcester City Hosp., 475 F.2d 701 (1st Cir. 1973), *appeal for stay of mandate denied,* 411 U.S.929 (1973); Doe v. Bridgeton Hosp. Assoc., Inc., 168 N.J. Super. 593, 403 A.2d 965 (App. Div. 1979).
93. Doe v. Bellin Mem. Hosp., 479 F.2d 756 (7th Cir. 1973); Greco v. Orange Mem. Hosp. Corp., *supra* note 92.
94. Mich. Comp. Laws Ann. §§ 333.20181–333.20184 (1980).
95. Doe v. Bolton, 410 U.S. 179 (1973).
96. Hodgson v. Lawson, 542 F.2d 1350 (5th Cir. 1976).
97. Swanson v. St. John's Hosp., 597 P.2d 702 (Mont. 1979).
98. 42 U.S.C. § 300a-7 (1976).
99. 42 U.S.C. § 300a-7(2) (1976).
100. M. Stern, *Abortion Conscience Clauses,* 11 Colum. J. L. Soc. Probs. 571, 591–94 (1975).
101. A. Southwick, *supra* note 4, at 270.
102. JCAH, *supra* note 12, at xi.

103. *Id.* at x.
104. A. Southwick, *supra* note 4, at 370, 412.
105. JCAH, *supra* note 12, at xix.
106. *Id.* at xvii.
107. *Id.* at xx.
108. *Id.* at xxi.
109. *Id.* at xi.
110. Interview with Jan Shulman, Public Relations Dep't, JCAH (Feb. 13, 1980).
111. JCAH, *supra* note 12, at x.
112. Shulman, *supra* note 110.
113. *Id.*
114. JCAH, *supra* note 12, at xxiii.
115. Worthington & Silver, *Regulation of Quality of Care in Hospitals: The Need for Change*, 35 Law & Contemp. Probs. 305, 309 (1970).
116. *See, e.g.*, Mich. Comp. Laws Ann. §§ 333.21501 *et seq.* (1980).
117. G. Annas, The Rights of Hospital Patients 22 (1975).
118. Havighurst, *Regulation of Health Facilities and Services by Certificate of Need*, 59 Va. L. Rev. 1143, 1144 (1973).
119. *See* D. Warren, *supra* note 4, at 263–76.
120. JCAH, *supra* note 12, at xviii.
121. *Id.* at 5.
122. *Id.* at 6.
123. *Id.* at 7.
124. *Id.* at 8–9.
125. *Id.* at 43–44.
126. *Id.* at 75.
127. *Id.* at 77.
128. *Id.* at 83.
129. *Id.* at 84–87.
130. *Id.* at 117.
131. *Id.* at 186.
132. *Id.* at 188–89.
133. *See, e.g.*, Ill. Dept. Pub. Health, Hospital Licensing Act and Requirements §§ 15-2 *et seq.* (Jan. 1981); N.J. Dept. Health, Manual of Standards for Hospital Facilities § 802 (Oct. 1979); Tex. Dept. Health, Hospital Licensing Standards (April, 1969).
134. N.J. Dept. Health, *supra* note 133, at § 802.
135. Tex. Dept. Health, *supra* note 133, at § II Standards for New Construction 24.
136. Ill. Dept. of Pub. Health, *supra* note 133, at §§ 15-2, 15-3.6.
137. *See, e.g.*, Ga. Admin. Code ch. 290-5-6 (May 1977); Conn. Pub. Health Code ch. 4, § 19-13-D14.
138. N.J. Dept. Health, *supra* note 133, at § 801.
139. *See, e.g.*, Conn. Pub. Health Code, *supra* note 137, at § 19-13-D14; Ga. Admin. Code ch. 290-5-6-.17(7); Ill. Dept. Pub. Health, *supra* note 133, at §§ 15-2.5, 15-3.8; N.J. Dept. Health, *supra* note 133, at §§ 802, 803.
140. *See, e.g.*, Conn. Pub. Health Code, *supra* note 137, at § 19-13-D14(f); N.J. Dept. Health, *supra* note 133, at § 803(A)(6).
141. Ill, Dept. of Pub. Health, *supra* note 133, at 76a.
142. *See, e.g.*, Ga. Council on Maternal & Infant Health, Perinatal Standards for Level II and Level III Hospital Units (Feb. 1981); Ill. Dept. of Health, *supra* note 133, at 76a.
143. Ga. Council on Maternal and Infant Health, *id.*

144. *See, e.g.*, Ill. Dept. Health, *supra* note 133, at § 15-3.11.
145. *See, e.g.*, 13 Mo. Code State Regulation ch. 20, Hospitals.
146. *See, e.g.*, Ill. Dept. Health, *supra* note 133, at § 15-5.1; Ga. Admin. Code ch. 290-5-6-.17(8).
147. U.S. Const. amend. XIV.
148. Southwick, *supra* note 13.
149. JCAH, *supra* note 12, at 104.
150. 42 C.F.R. §§ 1021 *et seq.* (1979).
151. Southwick, *supra* note 13, at 32; Gouda v. Detroit-Macomb Hosp. Ass'n. 52 Mich. App. 516, 217 N.W.2d 905 (1974).
152. *See, e.g.*, Milford v. People's Community Hosp. Ass'n. 380 Mich. 49, 155 N.W.2d 835 (1968).
153. Southwick, *supra* note 13, at 32–33.
154. *Id.* at 33.
155. *Id.*
156. *See, e.g.*, Renforth v. Fayette Mem. Hosp., 267 Ind. 326, 383 N.E.2d 368 (1978); Holmes v. Hoemako Hosp., 117 Ariz. 403, 573 P.2d 477 (1978).
157. *See, e.g.*, Berman v. Florida Med. Center, Inc., 600 F.2d 466 (5th Cir. 1979).
158. *See, e.g.*, Huffaker v. Bailey, 540 P.2d 1398 (Or. 1975).
159. Southwick, *supra* note 13, at 33.
160. Anderson v. Caro Community Hosp., 10 Mich. App. 348, 159 N.W.2d 347 (1968); Sosa v. Bd. of Managers of Val Verde Hosp., 437 F.2d 173 (5th Cir. 1971).
161. Hayman v. City of Galveston, 273 U.S. 414 (1927); Hoffman v. Garden City Hosp.-Ostepathic, 115 Mich. App. 773, 321 N.W.2d 810 (1982).
162. *See, e.g.*, Mich. Comp. Laws Ann. § 333.20152(1)(b) (1980).
163. *See, e.g.*, Stribling v. Jolley, 241 Mo. App. 1123, 253 S.W.2d 519 (1952).
164. JCAH, *supra* note 12, at 95.
165. Berman v. Fla. Med. Center, Inc., *supra* note 157.
166. Applebaum v. Bd. of Directors of Barton Mem. Hosp. 104 Cal. App. 3d 648, 163 Cal. Rptr. 831 (1980).
167. *See, e.g.*, Guerrero v. Burlington County Mem. Hosp., 70 N.J. 344, 360 A.2d 334 (1976); Davis v. Morristown Mem. Hosp., 106 N.J. Super. 33, 254 A.2d 125 (1969).
168. Southwick, *The Physician's Right to Due Process in Public and Private Hospitals: Is There a Difference?*, 9 Medicolegal News 4, 6 (Feb., 1981).
169. Walsky v. Pascack Valley Hosp., 145 N.J. Super. 393, 367 A.2d 1204 (1976).
170. Dattilo v. Tucson Gen. Hosp., 23 Ariz. App. 396, 533 P.2d 700 (1975) (nuclear medicine); Blank v. Palo Alto-Stanford Hosp. Center, 234 Cal. App. 2d 377, 44 Cal. Rptr. 572 (1965) (diagnostic radiology); Lewin v. St. Joseph Hosp., 82 Cal. App. 3d 368, 146 Cal. Rptr. 892 (1978) (renal hemodialysis); Rush v. City of St. Petersburg, 205 So.2d 11 (Fla. App. 1968) (pathology); Adler v. Montefiore Hosp. Ass'n., 254 Pa. 60, 311 A.2d 634 (1973) (cardiac catheterization).
171. Southwick, *supra* note 4, at 6.
172. Southwick, *Due Process Part 2: The Elusive Concept of Procedural Due Process*, 7 Hosp. Med. Staff 19, 20 (June, 1978).
173. Silver v. Castle Mem. Hosp., 53 Hawaii 475, 484 (1972).
174. JCAH, *supra* note 12, at 104.
175. *See, e.g.*, Bylaws of the Medical Staff of the University of Michigan, § ix-4 (Jan., 1979).
176. Southwick, *supra* note 4, at 24.
177. Margolin v. Morton F. Plant Hosp. Ass'n, 348 So.2d 57 (Fla. App. 1977).

178. Hyde v. Jefferson Parish Hosp. Dist., 513 F. Supp. 532 (E. D. La. 1981) *rev'd on other grounds*, 686 F.2d 286 (5th Cir. 1982).
179. Capili v. Shott, 620 F.2d 438 (4th Cir. 1980)
180. Centeno v. Roseville Community Hosp., 167 Cal. Rptr. 183 (Cal. App. 1979).
181. Lewin v. St. Joseph Hosp., *supra* note 170.

MEDICAL-LEGAL ASPECTS OF OBSTETRICAL AND GYNECOLOGICAL CARE

Introduction to Parts III–V

Parts III through V of *Obstetrics/Gynecology and the Law* are unique in today's medical-legal literature. Each drug, device, and treatment regimen for which obstetricians and gynecologists have been found liable for malpractice is identified and discussed.

As discussed in Part I, the patient-plaintiff must prove that the defendant-obstetrician or gynecologist deviated from the accepted obstetrical or gynecological standards of care before malpractice can be found (see § 1.32, Standard of Care). Because standards of care are so elusive and because most physicians do not know what standard of care applies until they are accused of breaching it, Parts III through V attempt to present a variety of standards from a variety of sources. Therefore, this book in general, and Parts III through V in particular, may be useful as a risk management tool.

The sources of obstetrical and gynecological standards of care used in this text include (1) the published guidelines of the American College of Obstetricians and Gynecologists, (2) interpretations and customary practice, as written by the medical authors, and (3) appellate court reports of trial-jury decisions which found that a particular obstetrical or gynecological standard of care applied after having heard expert testimony based on a specific set of facts.

The obstetrical and gynecological standards of care are not offered to direct care. Rather, they are offered to help practicing obstetricians and gynecologists avoid known medical-legal pitfalls and to stimulate a standard-of-care debate. It is the authors' view that an open discussion of standards of care will promote quality care by keeping physicians up to date and at the same time providing protection against the penalties of ignorance. Because standards of care are constantly evolving in response to technological advances and increases in knowledge, such discussion is essential.

Because they present standards of care, Parts III through V will be controversial. Controversy will come from those who believe that standards of care are antithetical to the art of practicing medicine. It will also come from those who may propose a different standard for a given drug, device, or treatment regimen. Comments from the latter are welcomed by the authors and may be reflected in updates of this text. Those who believe that standards of care are antithetical to the art of practicing medicine, however, should be prepared for the intrusion of reality.

Part III

Contraception and Conception

Chapter VIII

Contraception

§ 8.10 ORAL CONTRACEPTIVES

Liability may be imposed on a physician prescribing oral contraceptives for the failure to take a complete patient history, the failure to thoroughly examine the patient, the failure to adequately warn the patient of the risks involved, the failure to monitor the patient for the symptoms of adverse reactions, or the failure to recommend a waiting period between the use of oral contraceptives and becoming pregnant.

Basic Standard of Care: The American College of Obstetricians and Gynecologists has set forth the following indications and contraindications for oral contraceptives.[1]

Oral contraceptives are indicated for

1. Contraception
2. Menorrhagia
3. Dysmenorrhea

Oral contraceptives are possibly indicated for

1. Benign functional cysts of the ovary
2. Selected areas of endometriosis

Oral contraceptives are contraindicated for

1. Thrombophlebitis, thromboembolic disorders, cerebral vascular disease, coronary occlusions, or a past history of these conditions
2. Markedly impaired liver functions
3. Known or suspected estrogen-dependent neoplasia
4. Known or suspected carcinoma of the breast
5. Undiagnosed abnormal genital bleeding
6. Known or suspected pregnancy

Interpretation and Customary Practice: Oral contraceptives are hormonal compounds that prevent pregnancy by inhibiting ovulation. They are relatively convenient and highly efficacious, factors that have led to their widespread use in those societies where they have been introduced. In the United States, oral contraceptives have been marketed since 1960 and currently are being taken by an estimated 10 million women; worldwide, some 54 million women use them.[2] Were it not for the concern in the medical profession over the safety and long-term effects of oral contraceptives, they would most likely be used by even greater numbers of women.

Legal attitudes have responded to the increase in the general use of contraceptives. Courts have declared unconstitutional most state restrictions on the individual's freedom of choice in the areas of contraception and family planning, basing their decisions on the individual's right to privacy.[3] Certain social changes, such as the influx of women into the work force and the increase in premarital sexual intercourse, have accompanied the increased use of various methods of birth control.[4]

Most oral contraceptives contain two hormonal agents, estrogen and a progestin. Together, they induce a pseudopregnant condition in the user. This can lead to various side effects, the most common of which are nausea, vomiting, bleeding between menstrual periods, weight gain, and breast tenderness.[5] These side effects may be annoying, but they pose no real health hazard to the user.

Unfortunately, the use of oral contraceptives has been positively associated with a number of adverse reactions, including thrombophlebitis and thrombosis, pulmonary embolism, myocardial infarction and coronary thrombosis, cerebral thrombosis, cerebral hemorrhage, hypertension, gallbladder disease, and benign adenomas and other hepatic lesions, with or without intra-abdominal bleeding. In addition, the use of oral contraceptives has been tentatively associated with such other adverse reactions as mesenteric thrombosis, Budd-Chiari syndrome, and various neuro-ocular lesions—retinal thrombosis and optic neuritis, for example. Women for whom oral contraceptives are prescribed should be encouraged to refrain from smoking. The serious side effects of oral contraceptives, particularly fatal cardiovascular disorders, occur several times more often in smokers than in nonsmokers. Oral contraceptive use may also harm fetuses, and the hormonal agents contained in oral contraceptives appear in the milk of mothers taking them.[6]

In rare instances, oral contraceptives fail to prevent pregnancy, and lawsuits have been brought against both physicians and manufacturers to recover damages for wrongful conception or wrongful birth[7] (see § 2.40, Birth-Related Causes of Action). Most lawsuits involving oral contraceptives, however, arise when the user suffers an adverse reaction to the drug. Typically, the user will bring a products liability action against the manufacturer, on the theory that its oral contraceptive was defective and caused her injury[8] (see § 2.70, Products Liability). Almost as often, she will name her physician as a defendant in the same suit, on a medical malpractice count alleging negligent prescription, diagnosis, or treatment. As these allegations suggest, the physician's legal responsibilities toward the patient who is seeking or using oral contraceptives are extensive.

When a patient first requests that a physician prescribe an oral contraceptive, the physician must perform a thorough physical examination and take a complete medical and family history.[9] In the examination, the physician should make special reference to blood pressure and the condition of the breasts, abdomen, and pelvic organs, and he or she should include a Pap smear and relevant laboratory tests.[10] Overall, the physician should check for any of the following contraindicated conditions: hypertension, thrombophlebitis, thromboembolic disorders, cerebral vascular disease, myocardial infarction or coronary artery disease or a past history of these conditions; known or suspected carcinoma of the breast; known or suspected estrogen-dependent neoplasia; undiagnosed abnormal vaginal bleeding; known or suspected pregnancy; markedly impaired liver function; and past or present benign or malignant liver tumors.[11] Severe hypertension and insulin-dependent diabetes may also contraindicate the use of oral contraceptives. Very few cases are brought, and even fewer are decided, on the grounds that a physician knew or should have known that the patient's physical condition or medical history made it improper to prescribe an oral contraceptive.[12] Nevertheless, the physician who fails to examine a patient thoroughly and to take her complete history breaches an obvious and fundamental duty to that patient.

Once a physician has determined that a patient may receive oral contraceptives, the physician must discuss with the patient the possible side effects and dangers of the drug.[13] Physicians are provided with a variety of warnings from the manufacturers of oral contraceptives—by the manufacturers' detail men (field representatives), by informative insertions in the *Physicians' Desk Reference*, by product cards distributed to physicians and available at medical conventions and hospital exhibits, and by "Dear Doctor" letters. Physicians must convey to their patients, in language that will be comprehensible to them, any relevant information they have obtained by these means.[14] As the courts put it, physicians serve as "informed intermediaries" between the manufacturer and the user;[15] their special expertise is necessary for the safe use of prescription drugs.[16] Each patient's psychological as well as physiological needs are unique and usually known only to the physician. Thus the primary duty to warn the patient of the risks involved in using oral contraceptives is the physician's, not the manufacturer's.[17] Although the FDA now requires the manufacturer to warn the oral contraceptive user directly, by means of a Patient Package Insert dispensed with the product,[18] this in no way affects the physician's own duty to warn. More than one party can be held legally responsible for a patient's failure to receive adequate warnings prior to using oral contraceptives.[19] In short, the physician's duty in this area is a specialized manifestation of the general duty to obtain the patient's informed consent (see § 1.33, Consent and Informed Consent).

If the patient wishes to receive an oral contraceptive, the choice of a particular drug and dosage are matters left to the physician's independent medical judgment.[20] Similarly, if the patient has been suitably warned, the physician may prescribe an oral contraceptive for purposes other than preventing pregnancy. As in all matters involving discretion, however, the physician can be found to have acted negligently with respect either to the choice of drug or to the purpose for which it is intended.[21]

CASE ILLUSTRATION

A physician prescribed Ovulen-21 for his patient, a 19-year-old woman who was seeking a method of birth control. The patient was experiencing primary amenorrhea: she had never had a normal menstrual period. The physician prescribed the drug both to induce menstruation and to prevent pregnancy. Although the physician informed the patient about alternative methods of birth control, he did not inform her of any possible side effects from taking the oral contraceptive. Further he did not tell her (1) that, because primary amenorrhea generally indicates infertility, the chances of her becoming pregnant were slight; (2) that the birth control pill he prescribed was not a treatment for the underlying cause of her primary amenorrhea; or (3) that the longer the underlying cause of the primary amenorrhea remained undiagnosed and untreated, the less chance she had of ever becoming pregnant. The patient took the contraceptive for approximately 17 months. During that time, she experienced nausea, dizziness, and headaches, which were diagnosed as flu or upper respiratory infection. Eventually, she had a massive bilateral stroke, which left her partially paralyzed. She brought a medical malpractice suit against her physician. Expert testimony at the trial established that (1) the oral contraceptive does not constitute a treatment of any of the disease entities underlying primary amenorrhea, (2) the standard of care in the medical profession requires a prompt diagnosis of the underlying disease, (3) the oral contraceptive can be used as a diagnostic tool to establish whether the uterus can, in fact, bleed, and (4) when used in this manner, the oral contraceptive should not be prescribed for more than six months. A jury awarded the plaintiff $1.1 million in damages. The verdict was upheld by the Washington Court of Appeals. In addition to several other bases for its holding, the court found that the physician-defendant had presented no testimony that prescribing birth control pills was considered a proper method of treatment. Thus he was not entitled to a jury instruction recognizing his discretion to choose among different methods of treatment viewed as proper by physicians of ordinary skill and learning (*Klink v. G.D. Searle & Co.*, 1980).[22]

Before determining whether or when to prescribe an oral contraceptive, the physician should consult the most recent medical literature on the subject, as a supplement to whatever data the manufacturer supplies.[23] Furthermore, if the physician decides to go ahead with the prescription, he or she should prescribe at the outset a preparation with the lowest effective estrogen-progestin content. In the *Klink* case, for example, it may have been unnecessary to prescribe such a strong contraceptive as Ovulen-21, since there was little danger of pregnancy in the plaintiff's situation.

The physician's responsibilities continue after the patient has begun to take an oral contraceptive. Periodically during the administration of the drug, the physician should repeat the initial physical examination. He or she should be on the alert for the presence of certain conditions which, although they do not necessarily contraindicate the use of oral contraceptives, call for continued close observation and possibly for discontinuing the prescription to see whether the symptom is drug-related. These conditions include mental depression; fluid retention, which can aggravate convulsive disorders, migraine syndrome, asthma, and cardiac, hepatic, and renal dysfunction; cholestatic jaundice; hypertension; and diabetes.[24] The physician may choose to alter the dosage or the relative proportions of estrogen and progestin.

The physician's most important duty is to monitor the symptoms of adverse reactions to the oral contraceptive and to take the patient off the drug if such reactions seem to be occurring.

CASE ILLUSTRATION

When the patient, who for two years had been taking two different types of birth control pills, moved to Denver, she consulted a physician to see if she should continue taking oral contraceptives. The physician saw no reason why she should stop and changed her prescription to Ovulen. When the patient subsequently returned, complaining of increasing migraine headaches, the physician advised her to continue using the contraceptive. On neither occasion did the physician tell the plaintiff of any adverse effects she might experience, nor did he give her any booklets or literature. Some time later the patient suffered a stroke. The patient sued her physician for negligent failure to warn her of the risk of blood clots and for negligent failure to terminate her prescription upon learning she was experiencing severe and frequent headaches. The trial court dismissed the suit against the physician, but the Colorado Court of Appeals reversed, holding that the physician's duty to disclose the possible hazards of the contraceptive was imposed by law and did not require expert testimony to establish. The issue, therefore, should have been submitted to the jury. The court also held that, although some physicians would continue to prescribe an oral contraceptive despite a patient's severe headaches, these physicians did not constitute a respectable minority; thus a jury could infer that the defendant's choice to continue the prescription was negligent.* Finally, the court held that, despite the absence of testimony from the plaintiff that she would not have taken the oral contraceptive had she been advised of the risk of clotting, the jury should decide what a reasonable person would have done if warned (*Hamilton v. Hardy*, 1976).[25]

As the *Hamilton* case indicates, the physician's duty to diagnose a patient's adverse reactions and to take appropriate corrective action is one of a series of interrelated duties that physicians owe to users of oral contraceptives. It should be noted that patients have certain duties themselves. For example, a patient must report to her physician any premonitory symptoms of a stroke; otherwise, the physician may not be expected to treat the patient differently or to discontinue her prescription for oral contraceptives.[26] Furthermore, the experience, background, and medical skills of a patient may be taken into consideration in determining at what point she should have discovered the existence of a cause of action for medical malpractice. A nurse engaged in teaching, who suffered a stroke while using oral contraceptives but who did not bring a lawsuit within her state's two-year statute of limitations period because she did not realize that the drug might have caused her injury, has properly been held to be barred from bringing suit[27] (see § 3.50, Statute of Limitations).

When a patient who has been using an oral contraceptive discontinues her prescription with the intention of becoming pregnant, her physician should advise her to use an alternative form of contraception for a period of time before attempting to conceive. A two- or three-month period is commonly suggested. There is some evidence that triploidy and possibly other types of polyploidy and chromosomal anomalies are increased among abortuses (fetuses weighing less than 500 grams at the time they are expelled from the uterus and thus having no chance of survival) from women who become pregnant soon after stopping oral contraceptives. Embryos with these anomalies are virtually always aborted spontaneously. Whether there is an overall increase in spontaneous abortion of pregnancies begun soon after stopping the use of oral contraceptives is unknown. Similarly, the safety of continuing to use this product during pregnancy has not been demonstrated.[28] Nevertheless, the courts have been willing to recognize a cause of action where a mother, who has taken oral contraceptives (Oracon) right up to the time of becoming pregnant, subsequently delivers a live child with Down's syndrome.[29] The prudent physician, therefore, should recommend a waiting period to the patient before she attempts to conceive.

---

*A physician need not follow a course of treatment preferred by a majority of physicians. The courts recognize that physicians have different opinions about what should be done in a given situation. If expert testimony at the trial establishes that a "respectable minority" of physicians would approve of the physician-defendant's choice of action, no negligence on the defendant's part can be inferred. There is, however, no fixed number or percentage of physicians which constitutes a respectable minority; it is decided on a case-by-case basis (see § 1.32, Standard of Care).

Pregnancy, of course, should be ruled out before initiating or continuing the contraceptive regimen. Pregnancy should always be considered if withdrawal bleeding does not occur. For any patient who has missed a period, further use of oral contraceptives should be withheld until pregnancy has been ruled out. If pregnancy is confirmed, the patient should be apprised of the potential risks to the fetus; the advisability of continuing the pregnancy in light of these risks should be discussed.[30]

§ 8.20 INTRAUTERINE DEVICES

Liability may be imposed on a physician regarding the use of IUDs for the failure to inform and continue to inform the patient of the risks associated with use, the failure to take a complete patient history and perform a thorough examination, negligent insertion or removal of the device, negligence in determining that the device is properly in place, the failure to advise and warn a patient about risks associated with pregnancy occurring while the IUD is in place, or the failure to adequately monitor the patient for possible adverse reactions associated with the use of the device.

Basic Standard of Care: The American College of Obstetricians and Gynecologists has identified the following concerns surrounding the use of intrauterine devices.[31]

The patient should indicate her preference for this method and should be informed of the effectiveness rates, as well as the potential side effects associated with it. Possible major contraindications of the insertion of an IUD include:

1. Pelvic infections
2. Known or suspected cervical or uterine malignancy, including unresolved, abnormal Pap smears
3. Pregnancy—relative contraindications include:
    a. Uterine abnormalities
    b. Hypermenorrhea
    c. Dysmenorrhea

Special consideration is required for women who are within the eighth postpartum week or who have valvular heart disease, susceptibility to infections, or coagulopathy or use anticoagulant drugs.

The technique of insertion varies with the type of device, but general guidelines have been established to assure an appropriate evaluation of uterine size and shape and a check for contraindications to insertion.

If a string of the IUD cannot be seen and the patient is not aware of the IUD's having been expelled, three potential situations must be considered and explored:

1. *Pregnancy*—this possibility must be evaluated in the usual ways (history, pelvic examination, and appropriate laboratory tests).

2. *Unnoticed Expulsion*—if there are no signs of pregnancy, the presence or absence of the IUD and its position must be determined using one or more of the following methods: probe the uterus for retracted string or the presence of the IUD, or both; ultrasonography; PA; and lateral X rays of the pelvis with the position of the uterine cavity indicated by one of the following methods:
   a. Metal uterine sound
   b. Radiopaque dye via catheter
   c. Insertion of another IUD of a different type
   d. Hysterogram
3. *Perforation*—perforation is a known risk with IUD insertion. The perforation rate varies with the experience of the individual performing the insertion, ranging from 0.5 per 1,000 insertions to 10 per 1,000 insertions. Most reports indicate that the range of perforation is around 0.5 to 3 per 1,000 insertions. In some instances when perforation occurs at the time of insertion, it is immediately recognized. However, it may be partially initiated at the time of insertion, remain partial, proceed to a full perforation, or become embedded in the uterine wall. Perforation of the cervix or lower segment of the uterus with the vertical arm of certain devices can occur spontaneously in a small percentage of cases. If the IUD is found to be outside the uterine cavity and free in the abdominal cavity, it should be removed by laparoscopy, culdoscopy or laparotomy. If it is a copper-bearing device, its removal should be effected promptly because of the likelihood that dense adhesions will form around it.

A complete evaluation is important in assessing any potential pregnancy with the IUD in place. Particular consideration should be given to the possibility of an ectopic pregnancy, as this occurs with relatively greater frequency in the presence of an IUD. Removal of an IUD when pregnancy is detected results in a reduction of spontaneous abortion from an unexpected rate of approximately 50 percent to 25 percent. Removal also minimizes the risk of septic abortion, known to be a hazard when the IUD remains in place.

It is important to determine whether the pregnancy occurs as a result of spontaneous, unnoticed expulsion or whether the IUD is still present, as well as the type of device. If the gestation is 10 to 12 weeks or more, it is possible the string of the IUD may have been drawn up inside the enlarging uterus. Ultrasonography for IUD identification is preferred, particularly when the patient may elect to carry the pregnancy. X-ray diagnosis may be necessary, but generally, X rays should be avoided during pregnancy. If the IUD is present, an informed decision should be made by the patient, with awareness of the risks of all options. It is important that she be made aware of the increased hazard of septic abortion, including death (particularly if the device has a multifilament tail), if the pregnancy continues with the device in place. If the patient elects to continue the pregnancy, she must be closely observed. She should be advised to report all abnormal symptoms, such as flu-like syndrome, fever, abdominal cramping and pain, or bleeding, as symptoms may be insidious. Death has been known to occur within 72 hours of the onset of symptoms. If symptoms occur, aggressive treatment must be instituted. Steps must be taken immediately to evacuate the contents of the uterus. Concomitant antibiotic therapy, effective against anaerobes, must also be initiated. In rare instances, hysterectomy may be necessary.

Interpretation and Customary Practice: The IUD is an ancient form of contraception.[32] Until recently, however, it was not sufficiently safe to be used universally. The metal IUDs introduced in the late 1800s and used through the early decades of this century caused severe and often fatal pelvic infections in many users; antibiotics were not yet available as a remedy. Only with the development, around 1960, of stainless steel and polyethylene IUDs did the device attain a reliable degree of safety. Both materials decreased the risk of infection. In addition, the polyethylene devices were flexible and could be inserted without dilating the cervix.[33] By the mid-1970s, more than 15 million IUDs had been distributed throughout the world, the majority to developing nations.[34]

The exact mechanism by which the IUD prevents conception has not been conclusively demonstrated, but it seems to produce changes in the endometrial lining of the uterus which make it unsuitable for implantation of the fertilized ovum.

Although far safer than the original models, today's IUDs can cause a variety of problems. The reported adverse reactions include: endometritis, spontaneous abortion, septic abortion, septicemia, perforation of the uterus and cervix, embedment in the uterine wall, fragmentation of the IUD, pelvic infection, vaginitis, leukorrhea, cervical erosion, pregnancy, ectopic pregnancy, difficult removal, complete or partial expulsion of the IUD, intermenstrual spotting, prolongation of menstrual flow, anemia, pain and cramping, backaches, dyspareunia, and neurovascular episodes, including bradycardia (slowing of the heart beat) and syncope (temporary unconsciousness). Perforation into the abdomen has been followed by abdominal adhesions, intestinal penetration, intestinal obstruction, and cystic masses in the pelvis. Urticarial allergic skin reaction (hives) has been reported in connection with IUDs containing copper.[35]

Women injured by IUDs often sue both their physician and the manufacturer of the device. Whereas manufacturer liability in oral contraceptive cases is usually based upon failure to warn of dangerous side effects, IUD manufacturers are more frequently charged with producing a defectively designed product[36] (see § 2.70, Products Liability). As for physicians, their legal responsibilities are generally similar to those they are deemed to have when oral contraceptives are involved with some differences due to the mechanical nature of the IUD.

Like oral contraceptives, IUDs are available only by prescription. When a patient first consults a physician, nurse, or other trained health professional about obtaining an IUD, she should be provided with the patient brochure required by the FDA.[37] She should be given the opportunity to read the brochure and to discuss fully any questions she may have concerning the IUD, as well as other methods of contraception.[38] The physician must inform her of the risks and dangers involved in using an IUD, although he or she will be held only to that knowledge about the safety of IUDs common in the general medical community at the time the IUD is prescribed.[39] Again, at this stage of the physician's relationship with the patient, the initial duty is to obtain the patient's informed consent (see § 1.33, Consent and Informed Consent).

Also at this preliminary stage, the physician must take a complete medical history and perform a thorough physical examination—including a pelvic examination, Pap smear, and, if indicated, a gonorrhea culture and appropriate tests for other forms of venereal disease—in order to determine whether it is safe for the patient to use an IUD.[40] The physician should not insert an IUD when the following contraindicated conditions exist: pregnancy or suspicion of pregnancy; abnormalities of the uterus resulting in distortion of the uterine cavity; acute salpingitis or a history of repeated pelvic infections; postpartum endometritis, recent infected abortion; known or suspected uterine or cervical malignancy, including unresolved, abnormal Pap smear; genital bleeding of unknown etiology; untreated acute vaginitis or cervicitis until infection is controlled; diagnosed Wilson's disease; or known allergy to copper (for IUDs that contain copper).[41]

Furthermore, physicians should use IUDs with caution in those patients who have an anemia or a history of menorrhagia or hypermenorrhea. Patients experiencing menorrhagia or metrorrhagia, or both, following insertion of an IUD may be at risk for the development of hypochromic microcytic anemia. Physicians should also use IUDs with caution in patients receiving anticoagulants or having a coagulopathy. Patients with valvular or congenital heart disease and those with heart valve prostheses are prone to develop bacterial endocarditis; an IUD may serve as a source of septic emboli in such patients.[42]

To reduce the possibility of inserting an IUD in the presence of an existing undetermined pregnancy, the physician should insert the IUD during or shortly following a menstrual period. The physician usually should not insert an IUD after delivery or abortion until involution of the uterus is completed. The risk of perforation or of subsequent expulsion is increased if the uterus has not yet returned to its normal state.[43] For all patients, of course, the physician must perform the preliminary fitting procedures outlined in the manufacturer's instructions with great care;[44] negligent failure to insert an IUD safely is a common allegation in the malpractice suits in this area.[45] Physicians also should be warned that syncope, bradycardia, or other neurovascular episodes may occur during insertion or removal of IUDs, especially in patients with a predisposition to these conditions.[46]

The patient should be told at the time of insertion that some bleeding and

§ 8.20 *Intrauterine Devices* 315

cramping may occur during the next few weeks, but that, if her symptoms continue or if they are severe, she should report them to her physician. She should be instructed on how to check after each menstrual period to make certain that the thread attached to the IUD still protrudes from the cervix, and she should be cautioned that there is no contraceptive protection if the IUD is expelled. She should be cautioned, too, not to pull on the thread and displace the IUD. If partial expulsion occurs, removal is indicated, and a new IUD may be inserted. Women wearing an IUD that contains copper may develop a copper-induced urticarial allergic skin reaction. If symptoms of such an allergic response occur, the patient should be instructed to tell the consulting physician that a copper-bearing device is being worn.[47]

The physician's responsibilities to the IUD user continue after insertion of the device.[48] Since an IUD may be expelled or displaced, the physician should examine the patient shortly after her first postinsertion menses but definitely within three months after insertion.[49] At that time, and at all subsequent check-ups, it is the physician's duty to ascertain that the IUD is still in place.

CASE ILLUSTRATION

On January 6, the physician inserted an IUD into the patient's uterus. On February 15, the patient asked the physician to inspect the device, and he complied, apparently finding that it was still in place. On May 25, the patient asked for another inspection; the physician had X rays taken. The next day, when the patient called him, the physician told her that "the X ray was just fine . . . [the IUD] was in place." At some point, however, the IUD perforated the patient's uterus and passed into her abdomen. She became pregnant and had to undergo both an abdominal operation to remove the IUD and a cesarean section to deliver the child. The patient sued her physician for malpractice. Among other things, she alleged that at the February appointment the physician-defendant incorrectly and negligently diagnosed the position of the IUD and failed to take X rays to locate it; that at the May appointment he negligently failed to read or view the X rays, to read the X-ray report made by the radiologist, to advise her of the facts disclosed by the X rays, and to treat her for the injury and condition disclosed by them; and that she was harmed by reason of such failure and negligence. The physician-defendant argued that the patient-plaintiff's expert testimony failed to establish a standard against which to judge her allegations, and the district court agreed, dismissing her suit. The Supreme Court of Wyoming reversed. It held that the patient-plaintiff's experts *had* established a standard of care. For example, one expert had testified that, if an IUD is found floating in the abdominal cavity, it is "probably" the doctor's obligation, in the exercise of reasonable care, to inform the patient "if she were available." In the circumstances of the plaintiff's case, the court concluded, a genuine issue existed as to whether the defendant's acts were consistent with this standard of care, and a new trial was ordered to be held (*Godard v. Ridgway*, 1968).[50]

Another, more recent case has emphasized the physician's duty to locate the lost IUD by studying the X ray.

CASE ILLUSTRATION

After delivering the patient's third child in 1973, the physician inserted an IUD. However, seven months later the physician confirmed that the patient was once again pregnant. The physician agreed to remove the IUD and to perform an abortion and a tubal ligation. During surgery, the physician was unable to locate the IUD. He ordered X rays, which were taken by the hospital radiologist, immediately after surgery. When the patient asked him about the IUD, he told her it was gone and not to worry. During the next two years the patient experienced pain in the abdomen and lower back, periods of dizziness, spots before her eyes, headaches, and increasing difficulty with urination. She eventually entered a hospital, where X rays revealed that the IUD was in her peritoneal cavity. Hospital physicians discovered that the 1973 X rays also showed that the IUD was in the peritoneal cavity. The physician surgically removed the IUD, and the patient's symptoms disappeared. At trial, the physician contended that he had no duty to read the X-ray report in 1973, but that it was the duty of the hospital radiologist to inform him of any abnormalities. The court held that the standard of care required that a physician who is unable to locate an IUD must order X rays to see if it is in the peritoneal cavity. Further, the physician has a duty to personally examine the X rays or reports and relay the information to the patient. Since the physician had not done so, and since there was adequate evidence that the patient's injuries would have been avoided had the IUD been removed in 1973, the court held that the patient's claim could go to trial (*Killebrew v. Johnson*, 1980).[51]

Failure to inform the patient of the continuing presence of an IUD after an abortion may constitute negligence. However, the physician cannot be held liable for the patient's subsequent hysterectomy and bilateral salpingo-oophorectomy unless the retained IUD was a proximate cause of the injury.

CASE ILLUSTRATION

The patient obtained an abortion while an IUD was present. The physician was informed that the device was present but did not remove it. Four months later, the patient was hospitalized for abdominal pain. While the patient was being treated for a uterine infection, X rays revealed that the IUD was still present. The IUD was surgically removed, and, because infection was still evident, a D&C was performed. Since the infection did not respond to treatment, the patient underwent a total hysterectomy and bilateral salpingo-oophorectomy. The patient brought suit against the physician for failure to remove the IUD prior to the abortion and for failing to inform her that it was still in place. The patient-plaintiff's expert witness testified that the physician-defendant breached the applicable standard of care by failing to inform the patient-plaintiff that the IUD was still in place. However, the physician-defendant was held not liable on a directed verdict because the patient-plaintiff's expert witness could not testify to "a reasonable medical certainty" that the physician-defendant's action was the proximate cause of the hysterectomy. The expert had stated that "The infection caused the hysterectomy. The IUD made the infection worse." The court noted that the expert could not state that hysterectomy would have been unnecessary if the IUD had been removed (*Sponaugle v. Pre-Term, Inc.*, 1980).[52]

If at any time the physician determines that the IUD is no longer in place, he or she must take immediate steps to locate and remove the device if it is still in the patient's body. If the physician fails to locate or remove the IUD, his or her negligence is said to continue up to the time of such failure. This is the time, not the time of insertion, that the courts use in determining whether the physician's last alleged act of negligence occurred within the time permitted by the appropriate statute of limitations[53] (see § 3.50, Statute of Limitations).

The physician is under a continuing duty to inform the patient of risks known to be associated with IUDs.[54] Women with IUDs in place should be seen at least once a year for a complete physical examination, including all appropriate medical and laboratory tests;[55] they should be informed of newly discovered risks at such a visit, even though they are having no problems at the time. This means that the physician is responsible for knowing the current status of medical research on IUDs and for conveying pertinent information to the patient.

CASE ILLUSTRATION

The physician inserted a Dalkon Shield into the patient in 1972. At that time, it was one of the most popular and reputedly safe IUDs on the market. Serious questions about its safety were first raised and acknowledged in the general medical community two years later. It was withdrawn from the market soon afterwards. In 1975, the patient was injured by the Dalkon Shield she was using. In her suit against the physician, the patient-plaintiff alleged: (1) that he prescribed and inserted a Dalkon Shield for temporary contraceptive purposes without proper investigation to determine its safety and (2) that he failed to warn her that the Dalkon Shield was a health hazard when he subsequently acquired actual knowledge of the danger. Concerning the first allegation, the physician-defendant answered that the Dalkon Shield was a generally acceptable IUD to use in 1972 and that thereafter he had provided the plaintiff with a copy of the manufacturer's package insert, which described the Dalkon Shield and potential problems and complications. The plaintiff did not respond to the defendant's answer, so the trial court dismissed this allegation for lack of a triable issue; the California Court of Appeals affirmed. Concerning the second allegation, the defendant answered, without further factual averments, that at all pertinent times his conduct was within the standard of practice of the community. The trial court dismissed this part of the plaintiff's case, too, but the court of appeals reversed, holding that the defendant's answer was not sufficient to negate an allegation that his duty to warn had been breached. Noting that the manufacturer has no sure way to reach the patient, the court asked, "Who then is to tell the patient of the hazards newly discovered and not known at the time of the original patient-physician contact when the drug or medical appliance was prescribed?" The court concluded that in her second allegation the plaintiff *had* stated a triable issue, one based upon "the imposed continuing status of physician-patient where the danger"—that is, the IUD first prescribed and later thought to be suspect— "arose from that relationship" (*Tresemer v. Barke*, 1978).[56]

In another case, a plaintiff was found to have stated a triable issue where she alleged that her physician assured her he knew of no pregnancy or infection problems associated with the Dalkon Shield, at a time when medical journals had already been publishing studies confirming the association and when earlier in the month the plaintiff herself had read an article on the subject in the *New York Times*.[57]

The long-term effects of an IUD upon offspring are unknown. Thus, when pregnancy occurs with an IUD in place, physicians have special responsibilities. Reports have indicated an increased incidence of septic abortion associated in some instances with septicemia, septic shock, and death in patients becoming pregnant with an IUD in place. Most of these reports have been about women in the second trimester of pregnancy. In some cases, the initial symptoms were insidious and not easily recognized. If pregnancy should occur with an IUD in place, the IUD should be removed, if the string is visible, or, if removal proves to be or would be difficult, termination of the pregnancy should be considered and offered to the patient as an option, bearing in mind that risks associated with an elective abortion increase as the pregnancy advances.[58]

If the patient chooses to continue the pregnancy, she must be warned of the increased risk of spontaneous abortion and of the increased risk of sepsis, including death, if the pregnancy continues with the IUD in place. The patient must be closely observed, and she must be advised to report all abnormal abdominal cramping and pain, bleeding, or vaginal discharge immediately, because generalized symptoms of septicemia may be insidious.[59]

A pregnancy that occurs with an IUD in place is more likely to be ectopic than is a pregnancy occurring without an IUD in place. Accordingly, patients who become pregnant while using the IUD should be carefully evaluated for the possibility of an ectopic pregnancy. Special attention should be directed to patients who have delayed menses; who have slight metrorrhagia or pelvic pain, or both; or who wish to terminate a pregnancy because of IUD failure; these women may have an ectopic pregnancy.[60]

In general, once the IUD is in place, the physician has a continuing duty to monitor the patient for possible adverse reactions of all sorts. If pelvic infection is suspected, appropriate aerobic and anaerobic bacteriological studies should be done, and antibiotic therapy should be initiated. If the infection does not show a marked clinical improvement within 24 to 48 hours, the IUD should be removed and the continuing treatment reassessed, based upon the results of culture and sensitivity tests. The possibility of perforation must be kept in mind at the time of subsequent examinations, as well as during insertion. If perforation has occurred, the IUD should be removed.[61] Whenever a patient complains of abnormal side effects, diagnosis and treatment should be scheduled promptly.[62]

A physician who performs a tubal ligation renders an IUD (or any other form of birth control) useless, and he or she should remove the device to avoid complications.[63] Finally, the physician who inserts an IUD for purposes other than birth control has a special duty to supervise the patient's condition during use, to determine if the treatment is successful and to diagnose whether an IUD could cause whatever symptoms the patient might report.[64]

§ 8.30 STERILIZATION

Liability may be imposed on a physician in connection with a tubal ligation when: (1) the informed consent of the patient is not obtained, (2) the operation is unnecessary (having been performed as treatment for a mistakenly diagnosed illness), (3) the operation is negligently performed and the patient suffers additional injury, or (4) the patient is mentally incompetent and proper legal authority is not obtained.

Basic Standard of Care: The American College of Obstetricians and Gynecologists has set forth the following standards governing the welfare of a patient considering sterilization.[65]

Women desiring elective surgical sterilization should be fully counseled about the implications of this surgery. Informed consent requires that the patient understand the following:

1. That the procedure is intended to be permanent
2. That there can be no guarantee of the effectiveness of the procedure
3. That the restoration of fertility by a subsequent operation is uncertain

Consultation is not necessary if sterilization is requested by the patient and her physician agrees to perform this surgery. If the decision for sterilization is complicated by medical or psychiatric problems, the opinion of a knowledgeable consultant may be desirable. Sterilization should not be a precondition for appropriate medical care.

Interpretation and Customary Practice: Sterilization of the female patient is most often accomplished by tubal ligation, that is, ligating or severing the fallopian tubes. Tubal ligation may be done in conjunction with any indicated abdominal operation or as a primary procedure. One method employed is laparoscopic tubal cautery, which requires only brief hospitalization and a minimal period of disability.[66] Methods most often employed include Madlener, Pomeroy, Irving, Uchida, and Aldridge techniques. When performed in conjunction with a cesarean section the Madlener technique has a failure rate as high as two percent, whereas the Uchida and Irving methods have failure rates of less than 0.1 percent. While the physician generally makes his or her final choice as to which technique to employ after inspecting the condition of the uterus and tubes, he or she may be able to avoid legal liability by informing the patient in advance of the various technique options and their expected failure rates.[67] Liability may be imposed if the physician tells the patient that the sterilization operation was successful when the physician knows that it was not.[68] Cases with facts such as these have also been brought under legal theories other than the informed consent doctrine. Wrongful conception and wrongful birth theories are applicable where a sterilization procedure is ineffective and the patient subsequently becomes pregnant (see § 2.40, Birth-Related Causes of Action).

While sterilization may be accomplished by hysterectomy, this method is generally considered too radical a procedure for such purposes and is more typically indicated for treatment of specific gynecological disturbances. Therefore this discussion will be confined to a consideration of tubal ligation (see § 13.20, Hysterectomy).

Sterilization is considered to be a simple procedure. Consequently, only a few lawsuits[69] have been instituted to recover for physical injuries incurred during tubal ligation, for example bowel perforation.[70] In such cases, standard negligence principles would apply (see § 1.20, Elements of Negligence).

Sterilization is often indicated when pregnancy is hazardous and contraceptive methods are likely to be harmful or unsuccessful. In addition, if a therapeutic abortion is necessary, sterilization may be indicated: most intractable disorders in the mother (such as extreme, inoperable congenital heart disease) that are serious enough to require an abortion will threaten future pregnancies as well. Additional indications for sterilization include:

1. Neuropsychiatric—any neuropsychiatric condition that will prevent proper care of children or make pregnancy dangerous, such as feeble-mindedness, advanced schizophrenia, severe epilepsy
2. Medical—familial blood, dyscrasia, marked cardiovascular or renal disease, severe diabetes mellitus, chronic leukemia, and other medical conditions that make pregnancy hazardous
3. Obstetric—extreme anti-Rh sensitization in the woman whose husband is Rh-positive, uncorrectable uterine abnormality, habitual abortion
4. Surgical—carcinoma of the breast[71]

Any of the conventional sterilization procedures may be performed immediately after labor, concomitantly with an induced abortion, or during any phase of the menstrual cycle. While there are medically recognized motivational, logistic, and practical advantages to performing sterilization at the same time as delivery or abortion,[72] legal liability may be imposed where consent for the concurrent sterilization is not expressly obtained. Consent of a patient; express or implied, is required before any surgical operation, and the surgeon who operates without such consent may be held liable in damages. The exception is in the case of an emergency requiring immediate surgery for preservation of life or health under circumstances in which it is impractical to obtain the consent of the patient or someone authorized to assume such responsibility. In the absence of an emergency, no husband or wife may grant permission to a physician for the sterilization of his or her spouse.[73] No case has held that one spouse's consent is necessary for the other to undergo a sterilization procedure.

CASE ILLUSTRATION

The patient had entered the hospital in premature labor for the birth of her third child. She had consented to the delivery procedure and, possibly, a cesarean section. There was a known blood incompatibility between the patient and her husband, and she was fully aware of the problems presented, having been so informed by the physician during her first two pregnancies. The physician had suggested a hysterectomy to the patient, which she had rejected as "too final." The patient and the physician had also discussed tubal ligation on numerous occasions. However, the patient maintained she had never expressly or implicitly consented to the ligation but in every instance had told the physician she would think about it and let him know. Upon admission to the hospital, the patient was asked by the admitting nurse to sign a "consent to operation, anesthetics, and other medical services" form provided by the hospital. The form contained, among others, the following provisions: "I am aware that sterility may result from this operation. I know that a sterile person is incapable of becoming a parent." This provision, at the patient's insistence, was stricken from the form. The form accompanied the patient's chart into the operating room, as altered, and was present there during the surgical procedure. The physician was assisted in the delivery by an obstetrician-gynecologist, who asked the physician whether the patient's tubes were to be tied. Because the patient was under anesthesia and no hospital tubal ligation consent form was found on her chart, the physician obtained a form and the signature of the patient's husband. A tubal ligation was performed, and the patient brought suit. Although there was a conflict of testimony on the pivotal issue of consent, the court concluded that the physician had entertained some doubt as to whether the patient had consented. Although there was no evidence that the physician was aware of the deletion made on the form that the patient signed on admission, the form was available to the physician in the operating room. The court reasoned that, had the physician consulted the chart and noted these deletions, this would have raised questions as to whether the patient had desired a ligation and should have alerted him to the possibility that, even if the patient had previously given such consent, she had changed her mind. In addition, if the physician were certain that the patient had given express verbal consent, as he contended, there would have been no need to request the husband's consent. The husband's consent was not held to be a defense sufficient to excuse the physician from liability for performing a tubal ligation without the express or implied consent of the patient, notwithstanding the fact that the operation was skillfully performed (*Beck v. Lovell,* 1978).[74]

A patient may argue that her consent to an operation was not binding because she was inadequately informed about the operation, its consequences, and alternatives to it; or because she was misinformed about the need for the operation. Cases involving the first argument turn upon the doctrine of "informed consent" (see § 1.33, Consent and Informed Consent).

A patient's consent is "informed" only if it is given after the patient has received a fair and reasonable explanation of the contemplated treatment or procedure.[75] It is incumbent upon the physician to reveal to the patient the nature of her ailment and the proposed treatment, the probability of success of the contemplated therapy and alternatives to it, and the risk of unfortunate consequences associated with such treatment.[76] Thus, a physician who recommends or performs a sterilization operation upon a willing patient may face malpractice liability if he or she fails to consider the duty of disclosure.

CASE ILLUSTRATION

Because severe complications had necessitated delivery by cesarean section in both of the patient's first two pregnancies, her obstetrician-gynecologist recommended that she consider sterilization. The patient consented, and when the obstetrician-gynecologist delivered the patient's third child by cesarean section, he performed a bilateral tubal ligation upon her, using the Madlener technique. Although the obstetrician-gynecologist assured the patient and the patient's husband that she could not become pregnant again, the operation was unsuccessful, and the patient became pregnant approximately two years later. The patient brought suit, contending that her consent to the operation was ineffectual because it had been given on the basis of inadequate information. Specifically, the patient contended that the obstetrician-gynecologist was negligent in failing to inform her that the operation might not succeed and that alternative methods of sterilization were available. Evidence at trial indicated that the obstetrician-gynecologist had not told the patient that tubal ligation could be performed in a number of different manners or that the technique which he planned to use, while the simplest, had a relatively high risk of failure (2 percent). He did not tell her that the risk of failure would be less if the operation were performed at some time other than immediately following cesarean birth, and he did not discuss the possibility of vasectomy with either her or her husband. Stating that "unless a person has been adequately apprised of the material risks and therapeutic alternatives incident to a proposed treatment, any consent given, be it oral or written, is necessarily ineffectual," the court held that the patient's claim could go to the jury. Given the patient's interest in avoiding both damage to her health and the financial burden of another child, said the court, a jury could reasonably find that she would not have consented to the operation actually performed had she been told of the risk of failure or of alternative methods of sterilization. The fact that before the operation the patient had signed, without reading, a hospital consent form providing that she understood sterilization operations were "not effective in all cases" was held not to bar her action. The patient's signature on the form, said the court, was simply another fact for the jury to consider in determining whether she had been given adequate information to make an informed decision (*Sard v. Hardy,* 1977).[77]

Not all courts agree with the conclusion reached in this case. In another case, a patient became pregnant following the unsuccessful but not negligent performance of a tubal ligation. She sought recovery from her physician on the ground that he had not informed her that the operation might fail. The court affirmed the judgment for the physician, holding that at most the physician was guilty of an honest error in judgment, for which he could not be held liable. The court also stated that it was inconceivable that the patient would not have talked with her physician about the possibility of failure before consenting to the operation.[78]

In another case, the Pomeroy method was used, the pathologist positively identified that the tubal canal had been cut, but the patient subsequently became pregnant. The court absolved the physician of liability, reasoning that the operation had been successful, as the physician represented, in that the fallopian tubes had been cut and ligated. Furthermore, the patient had been apprised of the operations's failure rate.[79]

While the informed consent requirement for a sterilization procedure must be met, any evidence of the patient's consent, even if only implied, will prevent the physician from being held liable.

CASE ILLUSTRATION

In the course of performing a cesarean section, the physician tied off the patient's fallopian tubes. The patient brought suit, contending that the tubal ligation had been performed without her consent. Evidence at trial showed that the cesarean section and the tubal ligation were discussed with the patient as a "package deal" and that there was a tacit understanding that the ligation would be performed unless the patient expressed a contrary intention. In affirming a judgment for the physician and hospital, the court noted that consent could further be implied from the facts that the patient made no protest when told that the ligation had been performed and that she had continued under the physician's care without complaining (*Haywood v. Allen,* 1966).[80]

A physician may face liability if a patient consents to sterilization on the basis of the physician's incorrect diagnosis of her condition. In such cases the patient may not discover the inaccuracy of the physician's diagnosis until long after the operation is performed. The relevant statute of limitations (see § 3.50, Statute of Limitations) may therefore have an important effect upon the outcome of the case.

CASE ILLUSTRATION

The patient first saw the physician in July 1957 for treatment of hypertension. The physician advised the patient that, because of her hypertension, she should not become pregnant. The patient consented to a recommended sterilization and underwent a successful hysterectomy in February 1959. She continued to see the physician following the hysterectomy, and on June 27, 1962, he discovered that her hypertension was the result of a coarctation of the aorta. Corrective surgery eliminated the hypertension. On June 23, 1964, the patient brought suit, contending that the physician had been negligent in failing to discover the cause of her hypertension at an earlier date and that as a result of his negligence she had been unnecessarily sterilized. The state statute of limitations required malpractice actions to be brought within two years "after the cause of action has accrued." The trial court dismissed the case. Upon appeal, the court rejected the physician's argument that the patient's cause of action accrued when she was sterilized in 1959 and was therefore barred by the statute.

Instead, said the court, the cause of action in malpractice cases does not arise until the patient discovers, or in the exercise of reasonable diligence should discover, the physician's alleged negligence. Stating that the present patient could not reasonably have discovered the physician's alleged misdiagnosis until she was informed by him of the coarctation of her aorta, the court held that the patient's suit was timely filed. The court therefore remanded the case to the trial court for further consideration of the physician's alleged negligence in his diagnosis of the patient's condition and his recommendation of sterilization (*Iverson v. Lancaster,* 1968).[81]

The approach taken in this case is not universally followed. In another case, the patient consented to an unnecessary sterilization when her physician incorrectly advised her that she was suffering from multiple sclerosis. Rejecting the patient's argument that the statute began to run when she discovered the inaccuracy of the diagnosis, the court held that, since the injury complained of (sterility) was "immediately manifest" upon completion of the operation, the statute began to run at that time.[82]

The consent issue in sterilization often gives rise to other legal issues, particularly where the sterilization may be viewed as performed under the auspices of or in conjunction with governmental authority. Such a case puts the physician in the legal posture of an "agent of the state," and his or her liability is often determined by this legal role. In such cases, both the state and its agents may be liable.

CASE ILLUSTRATION

A deaf-mute unmarried mother of two children instituted a civil rights action for an alleged conspiracy to sterilize her against her will. The suit was instituted against the physician who performed the operation and several social service workers employed by various governmental agencies. The threshold question confronting the court of appeals was whether the private community hospital in which the sterilization was performed could be considered a "state actor" for purposes of imposing liability for depriving the plaintiff of her civil rights. The court then determined that the hospital and the town were sufficiently intertwined to make the hospital an arm for the state. The court also determined that the physician's action constituted state action, since he was not simply a private physician making use of the hospital but was its chief of staff, with major supervisory and organizational duties designated by the hospital's bylaws. The court then turned to the question of qualified immunity, a theory under which some government officials whose jobs require the exercise of discretion are shielded from liability for official actions taken "in good faith" so that they may perform their duties without fear of liability. Such immunity would protect the physician, said the court, if he negligently interpreted the plaintiff's communication as indicating consent. Under the facts of this case, however, the court suggested that the physician reasonably could have known that his conduct amounted to an unconstitutional deprivation of the plaintiff's rights and that, by deliberately disregarding her and her fiance's protests, he could be found to have a malicious motive, thus destroying his "good faith" immunity (*Downs v. Sawtelle*, 1978).[83]

If the court finds that the physician was not acting as an agent of the state, there can be no civil rights liability.

CASE ILLUSTRATION

An obstetrician refused to treat Medicaid patients (or any other patients unable to pay for their bills privately) for their third pregnancy unless they voluntarily submitted to sterilization following delivery. The court held that the obstetrician was not acting "under color of state law" in a way that violated the federal civil rights law, since the defendant was only expressing his personal economic philosophy, the patients were aware of his attitude, and he did not force his views on any patient (*Walker v. Pierce*, 1977).[84]

NOTES

1. American College of Obstetricians and Gynecologists, Technical Bulletin No. 41 (July 1976).
2. Population Information Program Reports, The Johns Hopkins University, Series A, No. 5, Oral Contraceptives A–133 (Jan. 1979).
3. *See, e.g.,* Roe v. Wade, 410 U.S. 113 (1973) (abortion); Griswold v. Connecticut, 381 U.S. 479 (1965) (contraceptives); Hathaway v. Worcester City Hosp., 475 F.2d 701 (1st Cir. 1973) (sterilization).
4. A. Guttmacher, Pregnancy, Birth and Family Planning, 304–43 (1973).
5. Physician's Desk Reference 1595 (34th ed. 1980).
6. *Id.* at 1594–95.
7. *E.g.,* Whittington v. Eli Lilly & Co., 333 F. Supp. 98 (S.D. W.Va. 1971).
8. *See, e.g.,* McKenna v. Ortho Pharmaceutical Corp., 622 F.2d 657 (3d Cir. 1980).
9. *See* Carmichael v. Reitz, 17 Cal. App. 3d 958, 95 Cal. Rptr. 381 (1971).
10. Physician's Desk Reference, *supra* note 5.
11. *Id.* at 1591–92.
12. *See, e.g.,* Hayes v. Weyrens, 15 Ill. App. 3d 365, 304 N.E.2d 502 (1973).
13. Carmichael v. Reitz, *supra* note 9.
14. Lindsay v. Ortho Pharmaceutical Corp., 637 F.2d 87 (2d Cir. 1980).
15. *Id.*
16. Dunkin v. Syntex Laboratories, Inc., 443 F. Supp. 121 (W.D. Tenn. 1977).
17. *Id.*
18. 21 C.F.R. § 310.501 (1980). *See,* Lukaszewicz v. Ortho Pharmaceutical Corp., 510 F. Supp. 961 (E.D. Wis. 1981).

Notes: Chapter VIII

19. Ortho Pharmaceutical Corp. v. Chapman, 388 N.E.2d 541 (Ind. App. 1979).
20. Leibowitz v. Ortho Pharmaceutical Corp., 224 Pa. Super. 418, 307 A.2d 449 (1973).
21. Carmichael v. Reitz, *supra* note 9.
22. Klink v. G.D. Searle & Co., 26 Wash. App. 951, 614 P.2d 701 (1980).
23. Leibowitz v. Ortho Pharmaceutical Corp., *supra* note 20; *see also* Ortho Pharmaceutical Corp. v. Chapman, *supra* note 19.
24. Physician's Desk Reference, *supra* note 5.
25. Hamilton v. Hardy, 549 P.2d 1099 (Colo. App. 1976). *See also* Witherell v. Weimer, 77 Ill. App. 3d 582, 33 Ill. Dec. 43, 396 N.E.2d 268 (1979); Klink v. G.D. Searle & Co., *supra* note 22.
26. Vaughn v. G.D. Searle & Co., 536 P.2d 1247 (Or. 1975).
27. Hayes v. Weyrens, *supra* note 12.
28. Physician's Desk Reference, *supra* note 5, at 1594.
29. Jorgensen v. Meade Johnson Laboratories, Inc., 483 F.2d 237 (10th Cir. 1973).
30. Physician's Desk Reference, *supra* note 5, at 1594.
31. American College of Obstetricians and Gynecologists, Technical Bulletin No. 40 (June 1976).
32. McCombs and Szaller, *The Intrauterine Device: A Criticism of Governmental Complaisance and An Analysis of Manufacturer and Physician Liability,* 24 Clev. St. L. Rev. 247 (1975).
33. Population Information Program Reports, The Johns Hopkins University, Series B, No. 3, Intrauterine Devices B-51-52 (May 1979).
34. *Id.* at B-90-91.
35. 21 C.F.R. § 310.502 (1981).
36. *See in re* A.H. Robins Co., Inc., "Dalkon Shield" IUD Products Liability Litigation, 406 F. Supp. 540 (Judicial Panel on Federal Multiple District Litigation 1975).
37. *See* 21 C.F.R. § 310.502 (1981) (patient information). *See also* Terhune v. A.H. Robins Co., 90 Wash.2d 9, 355 P.2d 975 (1978) (upholding physician's discretion not to give manufacturer's brochure to plaintiff).
38. Physician's Desk Reference, *supra* note 5, at 1579; *see also in re* A.H. Robins Co., Inc., *supra* note 36.
39. Tresemer v. Barke, 86 Cal. App. 3d 656, 150 Cal. Rptr. 384 (1978). *See also* Godard v. Ridgway, 445 P.2d 757 (Wyo. 1968).
40. Physician's Desk Reference, *supra* note 5, at 1579.
41. 21 C.F.R. § 310.502 (1981).
42. *Id.*
43. *Id.*
44. *In re* A.H. Robins Co., Inc., *supra* note 36.
45. *E.g.,* Newberry v. Tarvin, 594 S.W.2d 204 (Tex. App. 1980); Terhune v. A.H. Robins Co., *supra* note 37; Godard v. Ridgway, *supra* note 39.
46. 21 C.F.R. § 310.502 (1981).
47. *Id.*
48. Tresemer v. Barke, *supra* note 39; Martinez v. Rosenzweig, 70 Ill. App. 3d 155, 26 Ill. Dec. 335, 387 N.E.2d 1263 (1979); Newberry v. Tarvin, *supra* note 45.
49. 21 C.F.R. § 310.502 (1981).
50. Godard v. Ridgway, *supra* note 39.
51. Killebrew v. Johnson, 404 N.E.2d 1194 (Ind. App. 1980).
52. Sponaugle v. Pre-Term, Inc., 411 A.2d 366 (D.C. 1980).
53. *See* Martinez v. Rosenzweig, *supra* note 48.
54. Gugino v. Harvard Community Health Plan, 403 N.E.2d 1166 (Mass. 1980).

Notes: Chapter VIII

55. 21 C.F.R. § 310.502 (1981).
56. Tresemer v. Barke, *supra* note 39.
57. Gugino v. Harvard Community Health Plan, *supra* note 54.
58. 21 C.F.R. § 310.502 (1981).
59. *Id.; see also* Terhune v. A.H. Robins Co., *supra* note 35.
60. 21 C.F.R. § 310.502 (1981).
61. *Id.*
62. Gugino v. Harvard Community Health Plan, *supra* note 54.
63. Green v. Lilliewood, 272 S.C. 186, 249 S.E.2d 910 (1978).
64. Newberry v. Tarvin, *supra* note 45.
65. American College of Obstetricians and Gynecologists, Standards for Obstetric/Gynecologic Services 49 (5th ed. 1982).
66. R. Willson & E. Carrington, Obstetrics and Gynecology 179 (6th ed. 1979).
67. *See* Sard v. Hardy, 281 Md. 432, 379 A.2d 1014 (1977); Brocato v. Leggio, 393 So.2d 183 (La. App. 1980).
68. Pritchard v. Neal, 139 Ga. App. 512, 229 S.E.2d 18 (1976).
69. *See, e.g.*, Johnson v. Northwestern Mem. Hosp., 74 Ill. App. 3d 695 (1979); Raitt v. Johns Hopkins Hosp., 274 Md. 489, 336 A.2d 90 (1975).
70. Raitt v. Johns Hopkins Hosp., *supra* note 69.
71. R. Benson, Handbook of Obstetrics and Gynecology 430 (1977).
72. R. Benson, Current Obstetric and Gynecologic Diagnosis and Treatment 474 (1978).
73. Beck v. Lovell, 361 So.2d 245 (La. App. 1978).
74. *Id.*
75. *See, e.g.*, Cobbs v. Grant, 8 Cal. 3d 229, 104 Cal. Rptr. 505, 502 P.2d 1 (1972); Natanson v. Kline, 187 Kan. 186, 354 P.2d 670 (1960).
76. Natanson v. Kline, *supra* note 75.
77. Sard v. Hardy, *supra* note 67.
78. Bennett v. Graves, 557 S.W.2d 893 (Ky. App. 1977).
79. Brocato v. Leggio, *supra* note 67.
80. Haywood v. Allen, 406 S.W.2d 721 (1966).
81. Iverson v. Lancaster, 158 N.W.2d 507 (N.D. 1968).
82. Pearson v. Boines, 367 A.2d 653 (Del. Sup. 1976); *aff'd*, 386 A.2d 651 (Del. 1978).
83. Downs v. Sawtelle, 574 F.2d 1 (1st Cir. 1978).
84. Walker v. Pierce, 560 F.2d 609 (4th Cir. 1977).

Chapter IX

Genetic Counseling

§ 9.10 PRE-CONCEPTION COUNSELING

Liability may be imposed on a physician for failing to refer a patient to a qualified genetic counselor and on a genetic counselor for failing to correctly diagnose a genetic condition that is later manifested in the patient's offspring or for failing to inform a patient of the consequence of being a carrier of a genetic defect.

Basic Standard of Care: The Council on Scientific Affairs of the AMA has identified the following indications for referring a patient to a genetic counselor:[1]

1. Genetic or congenital anomaly in a family member
2. Family history of an inherited disorder
3. Abnormal somatic or behavioral development in a child
4. Mental retardation of unknown etiology in a child
5. Pregnancy in a woman over the age of 35
6. Specific ethnic background suggestive of a high rate of genetic abnormality
7. Drug use or long-term exposure to possible teratogens or mutagens
8. Three or more spontaneous abortions, early infant deaths, or both
9. Infertility

Interpretation and Customary Practice: Genetic counseling involves the communication by one or more specially trained and skilled individuals to a counselee and his or her family about the diagnosis, genetic mechanism, prognosis and alternate courses of action available to manage a genetically determined disorder.[2] Such counseling differs from the conventional physician-patient situation in that the disorders involved result from abnormalities of the genes, the focus of decisions to be made is on future children, and the family or couple rather than an individual is the "patient."

Most persons seeking genetic counseling, however, are parents of a child with a birth defect who are concerned that future offspring might be affected by the same defect.[3] The obstetrician-gynecologist should assess his or her own qualifications for offering such counseling. In a 1976 case, the New York Court of Appeals refused to impose upon all obstetricians the duty of becoming genetic counselors. The court expressed the fear that a contrary holding would (1) compel all obstetricians to take lengthy genealogical histories of both parents, whether they requested it or not and whether medical circumstances indicated cause for alarm or not and (2) burden obstetricians with inevitable legal liability should the infant be born with a genetic deformity.[4] Nonetheless, the obstetrician still has a general legal duty to refer the patient to a specialist[5] in the field of genetic counseling.

In pre-conception genetic counseling, the counselor estimates the probability of recurrence of the genetic defect, informs the prospective parents, and assists them in deciding what action is appropriate.[6] If the woman is already pregnant, the genetic counselor may advise amniocentesis (see § 9.30, Amniocentesis), depending on the severity of the genetic defect and the risk of its recurrence. Amniocentesis is also used to monitor the pregnancy of a couple known to be at risk for a particular genetic defect.[7]

Genetic counseling not only predicts the risk of disease for a specific couple, it may also apply to relatives and future offspring of the couple seeking advice. The genetic counselor arrives at a prognosis through information derived from an extensive family history, diagnosis, and knowledge of genetic principles.[8] Taking the family history involves constructing a pedigree and listing the patient's near relatives by sex, age, and state of health, with particular reference to the occurrence of relevant diseases in the family.[9]

Accurate diagnosis of the potential disease is essential: various genetic diseases often share symptoms but occur because of differing factors, factors that specifically affect risk and probability. For example, some forms of muscular dystrophy have similar manifestations, but the modes of inheritance are entirely different. An individual afflicted with the facioscapulohumeral form can transmit the disorder to 50 percent of his or her children, whereas the limb-girdle variety is transmitted only if the affected person's mate carries the same defective gene.[10]

The degree of risk attached to a particular genetic disease depends upon the mode of inheritance. The random risk of any pregnancy resulting in a defective child is 1 in 30.[11] Generally, the more definite and clear-cut the genetics, the greater the accuracy of a prognosis.

Genctic counselors recognize three categories of risk.[12]

1. Random risk is when the chance of recurrence is little more than the risk for any pregnancy in the population at large; these situations generally result from environmental conditions and are not likely to recur in future pregnancies. Examples include defects resulting from maternal rubella, toxoplasmosis, or ingestion of a teratogenic drug such as thalidomide.

2. High risk is when there is a chance of recurrence of at least 1 in 10 and more often 1 in 4. The majority of such instances is due to mutant genes; a minority is due to chromosomal aberrations in which a parent has a similar anomaly. Examples of the latter include D/G translocation Down's syndrome, polydactyly, or achondroplasia.
3. Moderate risk is when the chance of recurrence is less than 1 in 10 but greater than the random risk of 1 in 30. This is the largest group and is composed of fairly common conditions. Risk estimates in this group are empirical; that is, they are based not on genetic theory, but on experience and observation of frequency of occurrence. Diseases in this category are caused by environment as well as inherited predisposition. Examples include congenital dislocation of the hip, clubfoot, cleft lip, cleft palate, and central nervous system malformations such as anencephaly, spina bifida, and hydrocephalus.

After evaluating the risk of recurrence of a genetic disease, the genetic counselor communicates the diagnosis and associated risk in a nondirective manner to the patient. The failure to exercise due care in such counseling (for example, providing the patient with erroneous information) may result in legal liability.

CASE ILLUSTRATION

In June 1969, the patient gave birth to a baby who lived for only five hours. The cause of death was determined to be polycystic kidney disease, a fatal hereditary disease. There exists a substantial probability that any future baby of the same parents will be born with it. The patient asked her physician if there was any risk of a subsequent child being born with the same affliction. The physician responded that the chances of having another baby with polycystic kidney disease were "practically nil," inasmuch as the disease was not hereditary. The patient and her husband relied on this advice and gave birth to another baby in July 1970. This baby, too, was born with polycystic kidney disease and lived for about 2½ years before dying. The patient sued the physician on behalf of the child for wrongful life, alleging that the infant suffered the damage of having been born in a defective condition that rendered it susceptible to the pain, suffering, and eventual death associated with polycystic kidney disease. The patient also sued the physician for the damages he had inflicted on her in the form of the mental suffering and the medical costs incurred in treating the infant. The court rejected the wrongful life cause of action but recognized the patient's right to seek recovery for the sums expended for the care and treatment of her child until the child's death, in that the court recognized that such damages were both ascertainable and the result of a breach of the duty owed by the physician to the patient (*Park v. Chessin*, 1978).[13]

At this writing, few cases involving pre-conception genetic counseling have been reported. This may be due to the fact that genetic counseling is a relatively new field and that pre-conception counseling is available on a relatively limited basis. As the field grows and, perhaps, as the public places greater reliance on physicians for genetic counseling, the incidence of cases such as the one illustrated above may increase. The legal perception of such a case is offered by the following excerpt from the intermediate appellate opinion in the case set out above:

> No new duty is imposed on any physician in these circumstances; rather, validating the parents' cause of action in the . . . case merely extends to a physician a pre-existing duty widely recognized in numerous fields of classic tort law, that one may not speak without prudence or due care when one has a duty to speak, knows that the other party intends to rely on what is imparted, and does, in fact, so rely to his detriment. The injuries that flow therefrom include the economic injuries represented by provable medical and support expenses incurred during the lifetime of the child.[14]

A later Michigan Court of Appeals decision reinforces this statement. In the case of *Dorlin v. Providence Hospital,* the patient was diagnosed as a carrier of sickle-cell anemia but was not informed of the consequences of such a diagnosis. When the patient gave birth to a daughter suffering from sickle-cell anemia, she brought suit. The court denied recovery because the suit was not brought within the period required by the statute of limitations (see § 3.50, Statute of Limitations) but stated that such a case, if brought in a timely manner, is governed by familiar legal principles of negligence.[15]

Medical science has made significant progress in controlling diseases caused by nutritional deficiency and infection. This has provided a new perspective for diseases in which genetic factors predominate. With the eradication of other threats to neonatal health, physicians have begun to devote greater attention to genetic defects. At present, more than half of the infant mortality rate is attributed to congenital malformations.[16] Furthermore, new technologies for the identification, treatment, and control of hereditary defects are being developed. The young field of genetic counseling is experiencing an accelerated growth and a developing recognition by the public of its potential. In the United States, ten genetic counseling centers existed in 1951, 25 in 1961, and 400 in 1974.[17] The public will increase its expectations of the genetic counselor in the future. When less than expert counseling is provided, patients become victims, and those victims may seek restitution through legal channels.

§ 9.20 GENETIC SCREENING

> *With respect to genetic screening, physcian liability may be imposed for negligence such as incorrect diagnosis, the failure to obtain informed consent to the screening procedure, the failure to disclose test results to the*

person screened and the unauthorized disclosure of results to persons other than the person screened.

Basic Standard of Care: The American College of Obstetricians and Gynecologists recognizes that genetic screening attempts to prevent genetic disease, a goal thought to be attainable in cases where:

1. The disease occurs predominately in a defined population
2. Carriers can be identified simply and accurately
3. The disease can be detected in utero early in pregnancy

In addition to these criteria, the mode of inheritance should be known if meaningful genetic counseling is to be undertaken.[18]

Interpretation and Customary Practice: Genetic screening identifies particular population groups at risk for certain genetic anomalies or diseases and tests for them.

The more prevalent genetic anomalies include Tay-Sach's disease, which most commonly afflicts Ashkenazic Jews, sickle-cell anemia, which occurs most commonly in the black population, and phenylketonuria (PKU), which is not population-specific but which can be identified in newborns. Testing programs designed to identify children with PKU early enough to treat the disease and save them from the mental disorders that accompany it have been enacted by a majority of states.[19] Screening programs for sickle-cell anemia have also been established. Unlike PKU, however, sickle-cell anemia is a hereditary disorder that cannot be treated; it can be eliminated only if carriers do not marry or if they marry and remain childless. Thus, screening programs for sickle-cell anemia are designed to identify and warn carriers of the risk of bearing children with an incurable genetic disease.

In May 1972, Congress enacted the National Sickle-Cell Anemia Control Act, which provided for the establishment and operation of screening and counseling programs and the development and dissemination of relevant information to health care providers and the public at large.[20] A number of states have also passed laws relating to sickle-cell anemia.[21] In contrast to the federal law, some of these states make participation in such screening programs mandatory for certain classifications of people.[22] The laws have been written in a manner that avoids specific racial classifications, while ensuring that those groups most likely to be affected are tested. Illinois, for example, allows school authorities, when they deem it necessary, to require sickle-cell screening as part of those health examinations required of all students.[23] California empowers its department of health to require a test for "any identifiable segment of the population" which the department determines is disproportionately susceptible to sickle-cell anemia.[24] Similarly, Massachusetts requires a test for all school children whom the commissioner of public health determines are "susceptible to the disease known as sickle-cell anemia."[25] Other states have instituted programs based on voluntary participation and cooperation of individual citizens.[26] A number of states have enacted laws providing for sickle-cell testing prior to marriage.[27] In some states participation is voluntary,[28] in others it is mandatory. New York, for example, requires a test for a marriage license applicant who is not of the "Caucasian, Indian or Oriental race." However, the application cannot be denied "solely" on the basis of a positive test result (no explanation is given for the use of the word "solely," nor are any additional criteria for denial provided) nor is lack of a test grounds for invalidating a marriage.[29] Georgia has set up a program for mandatory testing of infants.[30]

It has been pointed out that there is no real public health justification for mass screening for sickle-cell anemia, since neither the disease itself nor the genetic trait is contagious, and the disease is not treatable.[31] Thus the laws would not enable individuals afflicted with the disease to seek treatment for it, nor would they serve to protect the public at large. Because misunderstanding may surround the sickle-cell trait, it is argued that such programs publicly identify victims, thereby subjecting them to serious prejudice and stigmatization. For example, airline employees identified as possessing the trait were at one time grounded because of uninformed fears that, if the plane depressurized, they would go into a sickling crisis; insurance companies were charging sickle-cell carriers higher premiums; and the armed forces considered deferment of carriers, closing off valuable job opportunities.[32] Further, since the rationale for mass screening programs is to identify carriers and dissuade them from either marrying each other or having children, the black population has been skeptical of programs that may be perceived as the first step toward reproductive control of the race.

No court has yet dealt with the issue of the liability of physicians for malpractice with respect to screening programs themselves, although cases have been brought regarding a physician's failure to diagnose PKU in small children. Where a physician negligently fails to diagnose the condition, thereby delaying necessary treatment to the patient's detriment, damages may be assessed against the physician.[33]

A number of commentators have also addressed the issue of legal liability with respect to genetic screening.[34] Professor Jon R. Waltz has set forth four areas in which problems are most likely to arise: (1) professional negligence, including incorrect diagnosis; (2) failure to obtain informed consent to the screening procedure; (3) failure to disclose the results of screening; and (4) unauthorized disclosure of screening results to persons other than the person screened.[35]

The first of these problems is not likely to occur very often or to be very serious, given the uncomplicated procedures used in genetic testing. As Waltz notes, "there is a limit to how much can go wrong during a simple blood test to determine whether a person has the recessive trait for such diseases as sickle-cell anemia or Tay-Sachs."[36] Further, physicians can accurately diagnose the likelihood of a defective child based on the results of blood tests. However, should a physician make a faulty diagnosis prior to pregnancy and a defective child is born, some law exists to indicate he or she may be liable for damages. In related cases, one court has held a physician liable for incorrectly interpreting the results of amniocentesis, where the physician represented the test to be foolproof, and a defective child was born.[37] In other cases, physicians have been held liable for failing to inform a patient, at risk for conceiving a genetically defective child, of the availability of amniocentesis.[38] The reasoning in some of these cases may be applicable in cases of negligence in genetic screening (see § 9.30, Amniocentesis).

The confidentiality problem (that is, unauthorized disclosure of results) may occur in two areas. One involves disclosure of results with respect to a particular person, the other involves disclosure of results for research and statistical purposes that incidentally reveal particular information about particular persons. As discussed above with respect to testing for sickle-cell anemia, such revelations may result in serious problems for persons involved. As with most of the issues in this area, answers to the knotty confidentiality problems inherent in genetic screening and counseling are neither clear nor easily ascertainable. And just as much of the tort law may be carried over from other areas of medical malpractice, so much of the law respecting the right of privacy, confidentiality, and even defamation will form the basis for future decisions in this particular area.

§ 9.30 AMNIOCENTESIS

Liability may be imposed on a physician for the negligent performance of amniocentesis, the failure to make appropriate disclaimers concerning the safety and effectiveness of the procedure, or the failure to inform a patient at risk of producing genetically impaired offspring of the availability of amniocentesis.

Basic Standard of Care: The American College of Obstetricians and Gynecologists has identified the following conditions and prerequisites for undertaking amniocentesis for the prenatal diagnosis of genetic disorders:

1. An appropriate indication exists
2. Duration of pregnancy is appropriate
3. The information obtained will be useful to the patient and her family for decision making
4. The technique for the particular disorder has been established
5. There has been appropriate counseling of the patient and her family with regard to the risk of the disorder, the risks of the procedure, and the nature of the information to be obtained[39]

If amniocentesis is performed in an ambulatory setting, ultrasound equipment for placental localization and an appropriate method of fetal heart rate monitoring should be available. When amniocentesis is performed in the third trimester, cesarean delivery capabilities should be readily available.[40]

Interpretation and Customary Practice: In 1960 Riis and Fuchs, two scientists studying inherited diseases, developed a technique for retrieving cells desquamated by the fetus into the surrounding amniotic fluid. Because it was assumed at the time that the desquamated cells contained a chromosomal complement identical to that of other fetal cells, the desquamated cells were thought to promise specific genetic information for accurate diagnosis of genetic defects. Upon implementation of the technique, the assumptions were proved correct, and the promise was fulfilled. Riis and Fuchs called their technique "amniocentesis."[41] Since its development, amniocentesis has received such accolades by medical commentators as "the most useful tool for prenatal diagnosis now available"[42] and has become, in recent years, a fairly common procedure.[43] While amniocentesis is most commonly employed around the sixteenth week of gestation,[44] it has been performed within the range of 13 and 21 weeks' gestation.[45]

In amniocentesis, about one-third of an ounce of amniotic fluid is removed from the amniotic cavity by perforating the abdominal and uterine walls with a long needle. The amniotic fluid is centrifuged in order to isolate its component cells, which are compounded with calf serum and grown for two to four weeks in a culture medium.[46] At this point the cells may be examined by karyotyping and biochemical analysis. Karyotyping involves locating and photographing chromosomes through a microscope and systematically grouping them on the basis of physical characteristics.[47] Karyotyping can detect the doubling or absence of a particular chromosome, the absence of a fragment of a chromosome, or the mutual exchange of fragments between two broken chromosomes, all of which can result in severe congenital defects.[48] Biochemical analysis of the cells comprising the amniotic fluid can identify the fetus's genetic constitution and certain genetic defects manifested by abnormal enzyme activity.[49] Hereditary diseases that may be diagnosed prenatally include at least seven lipidoses (Gaucher's, Tay-Sach's, Fabry's, and so on), at least six mucopolysaccharidoses (Hurler's, Hunter's, and so on), at least 11 aminoacidurias (cystinosis, homocystinuria, maple syrup urine diseases, and so on), at least eight diseases of carbohydrate metabolism (glucose-6-phosphate dehydrogenase deficiency, glycogen storage disease, and so on), and other diseases (such as adrenogenital syndrome, Lesch-Nyhan syndrome, and Down's syndrome).[50]

Genetic amniocentesis may be indicated under the following circumstances:

1. When one parent is a carrier of chromosome translocation
2. When a couple has already produced a trisomic child
3. When the pregnant woman is over the age of 35
4. When the fetus is at risk of being born with X-linked disorders

5. When there is a parental or family history of certain metabolic diseases
6. When it is necessary to determine alpha-fetoprotein levels in preganancies with potential for neural tube anomalies[51]

Certain legal principles come into play with respect to amniocentesis. Injury resulting from negligent performance of the technique will give rise to a cause of action.[52] While a search of the legal literature reveals no reported cases involving physical injuries sustained as a result of the procedure, the medical liaterature describes many. Maternal risks associated with amniocentesis include uterine infection, perforation of the intestine, and Rh sensitization of the Rh-negative mother by blood from an Rh-positive fetus if the placental vessels are perforated as the needle is inserted.[53] In addition, the procedure may create unavoidable anxiety because it takes four to five weeks to obtain the test results.[54] Risks to the fetus appear to be greater than those for the mother.[55] They include fetal death from infection of the amniotic fluid,[56] infection of the amniotic membrane,[57] perforation of the fetal blood vessels in the umbilical cord,[58] and perforation of the fetal blood vessels in the placenta.[59] If the needle punctures the fetus, it can produce injuries ranging from insignificant skin lesions,[60] to damage to the cerebrospinal system,[61] to ocular trauma resulting in blindness.[62]

Although specific risks have been identified, amniocentesis is generally thought to be a low-risk procedure.[63] One study has determined the risk to the mother or fetus to be as low as one to two percent.[64] Another study has found the risk of cutaneous injury to the fetus to be nine percent but has qualified this figure by stating that nearly half of the patients contacted failed to return with their children for examination. It was felt that those who failed to return probably had infants without injuries.[65] Other studies have reported a spontaneous abortion rate of about 1.5 percent before 28 weeks' gestation.[66] Although this rate was equivalent to the rate to be expected at that time of gestation,[67] a small proportion of the losses were directly attributed to amniocentesis.[68] All of these risk figures are considered to be quite low, and it is certain that the babies of couples whose histories indicate a risk of a serious genetic defect are at greater risk from the defect than from anmiocentesis.

Risks of injury from anmiocentesis are further reduced when it is performed with real-time ultrasound guidance so that the advancing needle can be seen and the fetus avoided. Furthermore, it has been recommended that amniocentesis be postponed until at least the sixteenth week of pregnancy, at which time there is 50 percent more amniotic fluid than there is at 14 weeks and cell culture failure is reduced because of the greater quantity of desquamated fetal cells present in the amniotic fluid. A greater quantity of fluid and fetal cells reduces the probability that additional taps will be needed; multiple attempts at amniocentesis have been associated with a greater risk of fetal injury.[69]

Although such risks are currently recognized, the risk of injury should diminish as amniocentesis is further refined and developed. Eventually, some of these injuries may result only if the procedure is performed negligently. Then the physician performing amniocentesis might be held liable for ensuing physical injury. In any event, it is already necessary for the physician to obtain the informed consent of the patient who is about to undergo amniocentesis (see § 1.33 Consent and Informed Consent). The consent process should expose any misconceptions the prospective parents may have, not only about the actual procedure, but also regarding what information amniocentesis can provide.[70] Specifically, a negative chromosomal analysis should not be viewed as a guarantee that the fetus will be born normal. The physician should explain that, although highly reliable, amniocentesis does occasionally yield erroneous diagnoses.[71] One consent form that has been designed for amniocentesis provides a brief description of the procedure, then states that there are no guarantees that:

1. The procedure will not injure the mother or fetus
2. The attempt to obtain amniotic fluid will always be successful
3. The attempt to obtain usable cultures will always be successful
4. Even if a genetically balanced karyotype is found, the child will be born normal[72]

If the physician fails to make disclaimers of this kind and amniocentesis yields an erroneous diagnosis, the physician may be held liable.

CASE ILLUSTRATION

The pregnant patient and her husband consulted the physician for the treatment, care, and supervision of the patient's pregnancy. Tests ordered by the physician established that both the patient and her husband were carriers of Tay-Sach's disease. The patient informed the physician that she and her husband would not go through the preganancy unless they were totally assured that the fetus was not afflicted with Tay-Sach's disease. The physician recommended amniocentesis and *"explicitly guaranteed"* that the test results would determine whether or not the fetus would have Tay-Sach's disease. Amniocentesis was performed, and the patient was informed that the results "eliminated *any possibility*" that the fetus would have the disease. The physician recommended that the patient proceed with the pregnancy, stating that any possibility that the fetus would be afflicted with Tay-Sach's had been ruled out by amniocentesis. The patient subsequently gave birth to a male child afflicted with Tay-Sach's disease.

The patient and her husband brought suit against the physician and the hospital in which the amniocentesis was performed, both for wrongful life on behalf of the child and on their own behalf. The court rejected the cause of action for wrongful life brought on behalf of the child but recognized the parents' claim for damages for medical expenses and emotional suffering. The court stated that a causal relationship existed between the performance and interpretation of the amniocentesis and the subsequent birth of the child with Tay-Sach's. The inaccurate interpretation, coupled with the representation that the interpretation was guaranteed to be determinative, prevented the parents from exercising their right to obtain an abortion. The court held that such a legal claim may be brought against a physician under these facts (*Gildiner v. Thomas Jefferson University Hospital,* 1978).[73]

For purposes of maintaining amniocentesis as a low-risk procedure, the future may see restrictions of performance to the hospital setting, defining it as a privilege belonging only to obstetricians or such other practitioners with the required skill and with access to adequate equipment such as sonography. State statutes and regulations may be passed regulating the functions of laboratories to further assure quality control and the production of accurate test results. Medical commentators emphasize the importance of having the procedure performed by an experienced obstetrician and having the analysis carried out by a qualified laboratory experienced in culturing amniotic fluid cells and performing the particular diagnostic tests.[74]

American courts have also awarded recovery to prospective parents who are not informed of the availability of amniocentesis by their physicians. Failure to inform deprives the patient of diagnostic information that might prompt her to obtain an abortion, if warranted under the circumstances, and avoid the medical expense and emotional suffering occasioned by the birth of a defective child. In the late 1960s, courts refused to impose liability for the failure to inform of the availability of amniocentesis: medical knowledge of amniocentesis at that time was not widespread, therefore the physician's failure to inform was a permissible exercise of medical judgment rather than a departure from accepted medical practice.[75] This resolution of the issue basically involved a determination of standard of care—that is, the standard existing then did not require disclosure concerning the availability or the use of amniocentesis (see § 1.32 Standard of Care).

Currently, the physician's decision to inform his or her patient of the availability of the procedure might be considered a medical decision or a determination of the standard of care, depending upon the patient. Commentators have noted that a patient who is at low risk of producing an offspring with a specific genetic defect might not be a proper candidate for amniocentesis, because she would be subjected to the unnecessary pain and expense accompanying the procedure, and she would place herself and her fetus at risk of sustaining physical injury.[76] However, because the law traditionally requires the physician to provide treatment consistent with the skill, care, knowledge, and attention ordinarily possessed and exercised by practitioners under like circumstances,[77] the current state of medical knowledge probably mandates that the pregnant patient known to be at any risk of producing genetically defective offspring should at least be informed of the availability of amniocentesis. This may be so even if the patient abuses the information. A medical case has been reported in which a pregnant patient, already the mother of two girls and one boy, underwent amniocentesis because she was medically determined to be at risk of producing a child with Down's syndrome. Amniocentesis revealed that she was carrying a genetically normal female fetus, which she decided to abort because she did not want another female child.[78] Such use of information is difficult to anticipate, and, whereas it may offend the physician's ethical and moral attitudes, the fact that information has been communicated preserves the legal rights of the parties involved.

If the physician fails to inform the patient of the availability of amniocentesis and a genetically defective infant is born, the patient may bring a suit for wrongful birth on her and her husband's behalf, as well as a suit for wrongful life on behalf of the infant[79] (see § 2.40, Birth-Related Causes of Action). The wrongful life suit argues that the physician should compensate the infant for the damage of having been born defective because of the physician's failure to inform the infant's parents of the availability of amniocentesis, thereby precluding them from aborting the fetus based on test results. With the exception of two California decisions and a decision from Washington state, the suit for wrongful life has not been generally recognized, and such claims have been dismissed.[80] On the other hand, the wrongful birth cause of action, which seeks compensation for the parents' damages in failing to have been informed of the availability of amniocentesis, has been recognized.[81]

The courts' reception of such a claim has been guarded, and different jurisdictions may recognize different items of damages. In New York, the courts originally expressed the view that to award damages for the emotional injury suffered by the parent in giving birth to a defective infant would extend the "perimeter of liability" beyond acceptable boundaries.[82] Intermediate appeals courts in New York have allowed such damages in subsequent cases,[83] but it remains unclear as to whether the New York court of last resort, the Court of Appeals, has settled the issue. The fact that other jurisdictions allow emotional damages[84] compounds the confusion. Furthermore, the jurisdictions are divided as to whether the cost of raising and caring for a genetically defective child are compensable.[85] As the dust of inconsistency settles in this area, a duty, already recognized by some courts,[86] will most likely emerge requiring the physician to provide the patient with proper medical care during her pregnancy by informing her of the availability of amniocentesis.

CASE ILLUSTRATION

The patient was 38 years old at the time of her pregnancy. During the course of the pregnancy, the patient's physician never informed her of the availability of amniocentesis. The patient gave birth to a female child afflicated with Down's syndrome and sued the physician on behalf of herself and her child. The court recognized a cause of action by the patient against the physician for emotional damages resulting from the birth of a defective child but rejected the child's cause of action for wrongful life. The court stated that, in failing to inform the patient of the availability of amniocentesis, the physician directly deprived her and her husband of the option to accept or reject a parental relationship with the child and thus caused them to experience mental and emotional anguish upon their realization that they had given birth to a child afflicted with Down's syndrome. However, the court rejected the patient's claim for medical and other expenses that would be incurred in order to properly raise, educate, and supervise the child, because, although the court recognized that these costs were "caused" by the physician's negligence in failing to inform, awarding such damages would allow the patient to obtain all the benefits inherent in the birth of the child—that is, the love and joy she would experience as a parent—while saddling the physician with the enormous expenses attendant upon rearing the child (*Berman v. Allan*, 1979).[87]

Berman v. Allan was decided in a jurisdiction, New Jersey, that recognized one element of damages and rejected another. The *Becker v. Schwartz* case, decided in New York, reached the opposite conclusion with respect to damages.

CASE ILLUSTRATION

The patient was 37 years old when she became pregnant. Despite this fact, the physician who treated her failed to inform her of the availability of amniocentesis. The patient gave birth to a female child afflicted with Down's syndrome and brought suit against the physician on her own behalf and on behalf of the child. The court rejected the child's cause of action but allowed recovery by the patient for the cost of the care and treatment of the infant. The court stated, in traditional tort language, that, but for the physician's breach of duty to advise the patient of the availability of amniocentesis, the patient would not have been required to assume these financial obligations. The court held that the patient had stated a cause of action predicated upon a breach of a duty flowing from the physician to the patient as a prospective parent, resulting in damages to the patient for which compensation could be readily fixed. The court further stated that the recovery of damages for psychic or emotional harm must necessarily be circumscribed. The court expressed the view that, although the birth of a child afflicted with an abnormality would cause the parents to suffer certain emotional anguish, they might also experience a love that even an abnormality could not entirely dampen. Furthermore, the court held that the calculation of such damages was too speculative to permit recovery (*Becker v. Schwartz*, 1978).[88]

NOTES

1. American Medical Association, Council on Scientific Affairs, *Genetic Counseling and Prevention of Birth Defects,* 248 J.A.M.A. 221 (July 9, 1982); *see also* McCormack, *Medical Genetics in Family Practice,* 20 Am. Fam. Physician 142–51 (1979).
2. Fraser, *Genetic Counseling,* 26 Am J. Human Genetics 636 (1974).
3. Simpson, The Prenatal Diagnosis of Genetic Disorders, 25:4 Clin. Obstet. Gynecol. 635 (1982); J. Nora and F. Fraser, Medical Genetics: Principles and Practice 351 (1974); L. Whaley, Understanding Inherited Disorders 180 (1974).
4. Howard v. Lecher, 53 A.D.2d 420, 386 N.Y.S.2d 460 (1976), *aff'd,* 42 N.Y.2d 109, 397 N.Y.S.2d 363, 366 N.E.2d 64 (1977); *see also* Park v. Chessin, 60 A.D.2d 80, 400 N.Y.S.2d 110 (1977).
5. *See* Richardson v. Holmes, 525 S.W.2d 293 (Tex. 1975); Wilson v. Gilbert, 25 Cal. App. 3d 607, 102 Cal. Rptr. 31 (1972); Largess v. Tatem, 291 A.2d 398 (Vt. 1972); Morgan v. Engles, 13 Mich. App. 656, 164 N.W.2d 702 (1968).
6. J. Nora & F. Fraser, *supra* note 3; R. Eggen, Chromosome Diagnostics in Clinical Medicine 150 (1965).
7. J. Nora & F. Fraser, *supra* note 3, at 261.
8. L. Whaley, *supra* note 2, at 182; American College of Obstetricians and Gynecologists, Standards for Obstetric/Gynecologic Services, 50, 51 (5th ed. 1982).
9. J. Nora & F. Fraser, *supra* note 3, at 352.
10. L. Whaley, *supra* note 2, at 182.
11. J. Roberts, An Introduction to Medical Genetics, ch. 12 (5th ed. 1970).
12. *Id.*
13. Park v. Chessin, 46 N.Y.2d 401, 413 N.Y.S.2d 895, 386 N.E.2d 807 (1978).
14. Park v. Chessin, *supra* note 4.
15. Dorlin v. Providence Hosp., 118 Mich. App. 831, 325 N.W.2d 600 (1982).
16. L. Whaley, *supra* note 2, at 178.
17. Herrmann and Opitz, *Genetic Counseling,* 67 Postgrad. Med. 233 (1980).
18. American College of Obstetricians and Gynecologists, Technical Bulletin No. 34 (Jan. 1970).
19. Mich. Dept. of Public Health, Maternal & Child Health Division, Phenylketonuria—General Information, Children's Bureau Pub. No. 419 (1964).
20. National Sickle-Cell Anemia Control Act, 86 Stat. 136 (codified in scattered sections of 42, 33 U.S.C. Supp. II, 1972).
21. *See, e.g.,* Cal. Health & Safety Code § 325-27 (West Supp. 1980); Ill. Ann. Stat. ch. 122 § 27-8.1 (Smith-Hurd Supp. 1979); Va. Code Ann. §§ 32.1-68, 32.1-69 (Supp. 1980); N.Y. Educ. Law § 904 (McKinney Supp. 1980); Mass. Gen. Laws Ann. ch. 76 § 15A (Supp. 1980); Miss. Code Ann. §§41-24-1—41-24-5 (Supp. 1980).
22. *See, e.g.,* Cal. Health & Safety Code § 325 (West Supp. 1981); Ill. Rev. Stat. ch. 40, § 204 (Smith-Hurd 1980); Mass. Gen. Laws Ann. ch. 76, § 15A (West Supp. 1980); N.Y. Dom. Rels. Law § 13-aa (McKinney Supp. 1980).
23. Ill. Ann. Stat. ch. 122 § 27-8.1 (Smith-Hurd Supp. 1979).
24. Cal. Health & Safety Code § 326 (West Supp. 1980).
25. Mass. Gen. Laws Ann. ch. 76 § 15A (Supp. 1980); *see also* Miss. Code Ann. § 41-24-3 (Supp. 1980).
26. *See, e.g.,* Va. Code Ann. § 32.1-68, 32.1-69 (Supp. 1980).
27. *See, e.g.,* Cal. Health & Safety Code § 325 (West Supp. 1980); Ga. Code Ann. § 53-216 (Supp. 1980); Ill. Rev. Stat. ch. 40 § 204 (Smith-Hurd 1980); Mass Gen. Laws Ann. ch. 76, § 15A (West Supp. 1980); N.Y. Dom. Rels. Law § 13-aa (McKinney Supp. 1980).

28. *See, e.g.,* Cal. Health & Safety Code § 325 (West Supp. 1980); Ga. Code Ann. § 53-216 (Supp. 1980); Ill. Rev. Stat. ch. 40, § 204 (Smith-Hurd Supp. 1980).
29. N.Y. Dom. Rels. Law § 13aa (McKinney Supp. 1980).
30. Ga. Code Ann. § 88-1201.1 (Supp. 1980).
31. Waltz & Thigpen, *Genetic Screening and Counseling: The Legal and Ethical Issues,* 68 Nw. U.L. Rev. 696 (1973); P. Reilly, Genetics, Law and Social Policy 70 (1977).
32. Reilly, *supra* note 31, at 74; Comment, The Constitutionality of Mandatory Genetic Sceening Statutes, 31 Case W. Res. L. Rev. 897 (1980-81).
33. Naccarato v. Grob, 384 Mich. 248, 180 N.W.2d 788 (1970); Lewis v. Owen, 305 F.2d 537 (10th Cir. 1968).
34. Waltz & Thigpen, *supra* note 31; M. Shaw, *The Potential Plaintiff: PreConception and Prenatal Torts,* in 2 Genetics and the Law 48 (1980); J. Waltz, The Liability of Physicians and Associated Personnel For Malpractice in Genetic Screening, in 1 Genetics and the Law 39 (1975).
35. Waltz & Thigpen, *supra* note 31, at 140.
36. *Id.*
37. Gildiner v. Thomas Jefferson Univ. Hosp., 451 F. Supp. 692 (E.D. Pa. 1978).
38. Berman v. Allan, 80 N.J. 421, 404 A.2d 8 (1979); Becker v. Schwartz, 46 N.Y.2d 401, 413 N.Y.S.2d 895, 386 N.E.2d 807 (1978). See also Jackson, Guidelines for Amniocentesis and Genetic Counseling, 85:6 Penn. Med. 35(1982).
39. American College of Obstetricians and Gynecologists, *supra* note 8, at 19.
40. *Id.* at 24.
41. Turner, Hayashi, & Pogoloff, *Legal and Social Issues in Medical Genetics,* 134 Am. J. Obstet. Gynecol. 83, 84 (1979).
42. Epley, Hanson, & Cruikshank, *Fetal Injury with Midtrimester Diagnostic Amniocentesis,* 53 Obstet. Gynecol, 77 (1979).
43. Merin & Beyth, *Uniocular Congenital Blindness as a Complication of Midtrimester Amniocentesis,* 89 Am. J. Ophthal. 299 (1980).
44. Nadler, *Prenatal Detection of Genetics Defects,* 74 J. Pediat. 132, 135 (1969).
45. Epley, Hanson, & Cruikshank, *supra* note 42.
46. Nadler, *supra* note 44.
47. Howell & Moore, *Prenatal Diagnosis in the Prevention of Genetic Disease,* 70 Tex. Med. 79-80 (1974).
48. Brody, *Prenatal Diagnosing Is Reducing Risk of Birth Defects,* N.Y. Times, June 3, 1971, 53, col. 5.
49. *Diagnostic Amniocentesis,* 14 Med. Letter on Drugs and Therapeutics 53 (1972).
50. R. Benson, Current Obstetric and Gynecologic Diagnosis and Treatment 520 (1978).
51. *Id.*
52. Gildiner v. Thomas Jefferson Univ. Hosp., *supra* note 37.
53. J. Willson & F. Carrington, Obstetrics and Gynecology 33 (6th ed. 1979).
54. Fletcher, *Parents in Genetic Counseling: The Moral Shape of Decision-Making in Ethical Issues in Human Genetics: Genetic Counseling and the Use of Scientific Knowledge,* 318 Fogarty Int'l. Center Proceedings No. 13 (1973).
55. Hyman, Oepp, Pakravan, Stinson & Allen, *Pneumothorax Complicating Amniocentesis,* 41 Obstet. Gynecol. 43 (1973).
56. Bang & Northeved, *A New Ultrasonic Method for Transabdominal Amniocentesis,* 114 Am. J. Obstet. Gynecol. 599 (1972).
57. Gerbie, Nadler, & Gerbie, *Amniocentesis in Genetic Counseling,* 109 Am. J. Obstet. Gynecol. 765, 766 (1971).
58. Riis & Fuchs, *Antenatal Determination of Foetal Sex in Prevention of Hereditary Diseases,* 2 Lancet 2 (July 23, 1960).
59. Fuchs, *Amniocentesis: Techniques and Complications, Early Diagnosis of Human*

Genetic Defects: Scientific and Ethical Considerations, 13 Fogarty Int'l. Center Proceedings No. 6 (1971).
60. Epley, Hanson, & Cruikshank, *supra* note 42.
61. Bang & Northeved, *supra* note 56, at 599.
62. Merin & Beyth, *supra* note 43.
63. Fost, Prenatal Diagnosis of Down's Syndrome, 242 J.A.M.A. 2326(1979); Milunsky, *Risk of Amniocentesis for Prenatal Diagnosis,* 293 New Eng. J. Med. 932 (1975).
64. Gerbie, Nadler, & Gerbie, *supra* note 57, at 767.
65. Epley, Hanson, & Cruikshank, *supra* note 42, at 80.
66. Golbus, Loughman, Epstein, Halsbasch, Stephens & Hall, *Prenatal Genetic Diagnosis in 3000 Amniocenteses,* 300 New Eng. J. Med. 157 at 162 (1979); Simpson et al., *Prenatal Diagnosis of Genetic Disease in Canada: Report of a Collaborative Study,* 115 Canadian Med. Assoc. J. 739 (1976); Giljaard, *European Experience with Prenatal Diagnosis of Congenital Disease: A Survey of 6121 Cases,* 16 Cytogenet. Cell Genet. 453 (1976).
67. French & Bierman, *Probabilities of Fetal Mortality,* 77 Public Health Rep. 835 (1962).
68. Golbus, Loughman, Epstein, Halsbasch, Stephens & Hall, *supra* note 66.
69. Epley, Hanson, & Cruikshank, *supra* note 42, at 80.
70. Lieberman, *Psychosocial Aspects of Selective Abortion,* 7(5) Birth Defects 20 (1971).
71. Golbus, Loughman, Epstein, Halsbasch, Stephens & Hall, *supra* note 66.
72. MacIntyre, *Chromosomal Problems of Intrauterine Diagnosis,* 7(5) Birth Defects 14 (1971).
73. Gildiner v. Thomas Jefferson Univ. Hosp., *supra* note 37.
74. Nadler, *supra* note 44.
75. Johnson v. Yeshiva Univ., 42 N.Y.2d 818, 396 N.Y.S.2d 647, 364 N.E.2d 1340 (1977).
76. Turner, Hayashi, & Pogoloff, *supra* note 41.
77. *See, e.g.,* Zoterell v. Repp, 187 Mich. 319, 153 N.W. 692 (1915).
78. Stenchever, *Abuse of Prenatal Diagnosis,* 22 J.A.M.A. 408 (1972).
79. Curlender v. Bio-Science Laboratories, 106 Cal. App. 3d 811, 165 Cal. Rptr. 477 (1980). *But see* Turpin v. Sortini, 182 Cal. Rptr. 337 (1982) limiting damages in wrongful life cases. *See also* Harbeson v. Parke-Davis Inc., No. 48331-1 (Wash. January 6, 1983) recognizing wrongful life.
80. *See, e.g.,* Becker v. Schwartz, 46 N.Y.2d 401, 413 N.Y.S.2d 895, 386 N.E.2d 807 (1978).
81. *See, e.g.,* Gildiner v. Thomas Jefferson Univ. Hosp., *supra* note 37; Phillips v. United States, 508 F. Supp. 544 (D.S.C. 1981); Berman v. Allan, *supra* note 38; Park v. Chessin, *supra* note 4, *modified sub nom.,* Becker v. Schwartz, *supra* note 38; Jacobs v. Theimer, 519 S.W.2d 846 (Tex. 1975); Dumer v. St. Michael's Hosp., 69 Wis.2d 766, 233 N.W.2d 372 (1975).
82. Howard v. Lecher, 42 N.Y.2d 109, 397 N.Y.S.2d 363, 366 N.E.2d 64 (1977).
83. Karlsons v. Guerinot, 57 A.D.2d 73, 394 N.Y.S.2d 933 (1977).
84. Berman v. Allan, *supra* note 38.
85. *Compare* Berman v. Allan, *supra* note 38, and Becker v. Schwartz, *supra* note 38.
86. Karlsons v. Guerinot, *supra* note 83.
87. Berman v. Allan, *supra* note 38.
88. Becker v. Schwartz, *supra* note 38.

Part IV

Pregnancy and Birth

Chapter X

Pregnancy

§ 10.10 DIAGNOSIS

A physician is most likely to be subject to legal liability in connection with the diagnosis of pregnancy where (1) the physician fails to detect an existing pregnancy, or (2) the physician incorrectly diagnoses as pregnancy a different, pathological condition.

Basic Standard of Care: The American College of Obstetricians and Gynecologists has not published specific guidelines for the diagnosis of pregnancy.

Interpretation and Customary Practice: Because pregnancy causes a variety of physical changes, some pronounced, others subtle, diagnosis depends upon the analysis of a number of signs, symptoms, and laboratory tests. Signs are indicators that may be ascertained objectively and that are, therefore, discoverable by the obstetrician. Symptoms are subjective indicators, which may be apparent only to the patient. The following signs and symptoms are presumptive evidence of pregnancy, but even two or more are not diagnostic.

Symptoms of Pregnancy:[1] The earliest symptom of pregnancy is usually amenorrhea, or cessation of menses. Whenever a normally menstruating woman misses a period, she should be presumed to be pregnant until proven otherwise. Amenorrhea may not be a reliable indicator of pregnancy in a woman who has irregular periods. Other conditions, such as abnormal ovarian function, thyroid disorders, hypopituitarism, the patient's fear of possible pregnancy, a change in environment, or menopause, may cause amenorrhea. Furthermore, about 25 percent of pregnant women experience slight, painless bleeding in the first trimester.

Nausea and vomiting, distaste for food, queasiness, and other digestive disturbances are reported by almost half of pregnant women during the first three months. Because it is most often noted upon arising, this reaction is called morning sickness; in some patients, however, it may occur only in the evening. These symptoms usually disappear late in the first trimester.

Fullness or engorgement of the breasts and a corresponding sensitivity or tingling in the nipples are frequent complaints during early pregnancy but are of doubtful value in its diagnosis.

Estrogens and progesterone increase the turgescence of the bladder and urethra. Bladder irritability, urinary frequency, and nocturia are common symptoms during the first trimester. These symptoms decrease during the second trimester, as the uterus rises out of the pelvis, but during the third trimester the pressure of the presenting part reduces the capacity of the bladder and symptoms of frequency and pressure often recur. Constipation often develops early in pregnancy as a symptom resulting from changing eating habits or hormone-mediated hypoactive peristalsis. However, if a woman keeps her fluid intake up, true constipation should not occur.

Some woman complain of distention of the lower abdomen early in their pregnancies. This may be due to uterine enlargement and as such constitutes a symptom of pregnancy. However, enlargement of the abdomen could also be caused by factors not related to pregnancy (such as obesity or a pelvic tumor); therefore, great reliance should not be placed on this symptom. During pregnancy there is usually a steady gain in weight from about the tenth to the thirty-sixth week, when weight gain tends to level off. The physician should note whether weight has been average and stable in recent months. It is desirable for a normal woman to gain about 25 pounds during pregnancy.

Fatigue and lassitude are symptoms noted by many pregnant women soon after the first missed period.

Quickening, or the perception of fetal movement by the mother, is usually noted between the sixteenth and eighteenth weeks.

Signs of Pregnancy:[2] Pelvic signs are manifested by changes in the uterus, cervix, and vagina. One of the earliest signs, which may occur two to three weeks after the first missed period, is a softening of the lower uterine segment and cervix. The softening results in compression of the area between the cervix and fundus to such a degree that these areas appear to be two distinct entities rather than opposite poles of the same organ. This is known as Hegar's sign. Enlargement or softening of the fundus, which occurs between eight and twelve weeks, also signifies pregnancy. The enlargement is progressive and therefore easily discernible by repeated examination. Vascular congestion is thought to cause both a softening of the cervix (Goodell's sign) and a bluish discoloration of the vagina or cervix (Chadwick's sign). These signs appear later than Hegar's sign. Ballottement of the fetus may be accomplished by pushing the fingers against the lower uterine pole, thereby causing the fetus, which is floating in a large amount of amniotic fluid, to bump against the distal uterine wall and rebound. This is considered a definite sign of pregnancy, and it may be obtained as early as the fourth or fifth month.

Enlargement and vascular engorgement of the breasts begins at about the sixth or eighth week after conception. The areola may darken and Montgomery's follicles may become more prominent. About the end of the first trimester, colostrum may be secreted.

An abdominal sign of pregnancy is a soft blowing sound, referred to as a uterine souffle, which may be heard with a stethoscope over the large vessels on one or both sides of the uterus after the sixteenth week. The fetal heartbeat is perhaps the most reliable sign of pregnancy. The fetal heart may be heard after the eighteenth week, beating at a much faster rate than the maternal pulse; it has been described as resembling the sound of a watch ticking under a pillow.

Facial melasma (chloasma) and darkening of the skin over the forehead, the bridge of the nose, and the malar prominences ("mask of pregnancy") occur to a variable degree in most pregnant women after the sixteenth week. Pigmentation of the nipples and areolas appears at about the same time. The linea nigra (pigmented linea alba) may be noted after the third month.

Tests for Pregnancy:[3] Laboratory tests are seldom necessary and should not be relied upon as the sole basis for a diagnosis of pregnancy. However, in situations in which the history and physical findings are inconclusive or in which a complication such as threatened abortion or ectopic pregnancy is suspected but not confirmed, tests for human chorionic gonadotropin (HCG) may be an invaluable aid in diagnosis.

Biologic tests for pregnancy, which depend upon stimulation of ovulation in animals by HCG from the urine or serum of pregnant women, have been replaced by the less expensive and faster immunologic tests. Immunologic pregnancy tests are based on the reaction of urinary HCG with chorionic antitropin antiserum obtained from rabbits. Most pregnancy tests use the hemagglutination inhibition principle as an indicator: either latex particles (slide tests) or sheep erythrocytes (test tube assay) are employed.

The hemagglutination inhibition test, which is a two-hour test, is more sensitive and accurate than the two-minute slide test. The hemagglutination inhibition tests are sufficiently sensitive to detect 0.5 to 1.0 international units of HCG per milliliter of urine, while the slide test can detect no fewer than 2.0 international units.

A radioimmunoassay for the polypeptide beta subunit receptor of HCG is the most sensitive (earliest) pregnancy test, however it is expensive and is impractical as a routine test. It may be positive as early as the second day after implantation of the ovum, or the twenty-third day of the menstrual cycle in which a pregnancy occurs. Other, less accurate radioimmunoassays of HCG also measure luteinizing hormone, which contains a fragment similar in structure to HCG.

An oblique X-ray view of the abdomen directed through the greater sacrosciatic notch may reveal fetal bones as early as the twelfth week. An anteroposterior film may not disclose a definite skeleton until the sixteenth week because of the interference of bowel shadows and the variable density of the sacrum. However, X-ray diagnosis should rarely be used because of the possibility of fetal or gonadal damage, which could result in genetic abnormalities.

Ultrasonography may be used to diagnose pregnancy after only four to six weeks' gestation—even before much enlargement of the uterus has taken place. Sound waves are passed through tissues, meet with varying densities, and are reflected back as an echo, which is measured and converted into a two-dimensional picture.

A wide variety of testing methods is available. Although some of them are more reliable than others, there is always the possibility of a false positive or false negative result. The standard hormone tests for pregnancy are about 98 percent accurate when carried out by hemagglutination inhibition procedures and when performed properly more than two weeks after the missed period.[4]

Where a physician can prove that means and methods accepted by the profession were used in arriving at a diagnosis, even though the diagnosis was mistaken, the courts will generally not impose liability when the patient sues for misdiagnosis.[5] The accepted means and methods of the profession will invariably require the physician to conduct a physical examination, and such tests as are indicated by the circumstances of the case. A physician need not utilize precisely the same tests or the same examination procedures as do other physicians. The courts have recognized that it is only reasonable to expect that physicians differing in background and experience will hold differing opinions on the efficacy and advisability of available medical techniques. Thus the courts have held that a mere difference of professional opinion as to methods of diagnosis or treatment is not enough to establish negligence. The patient must show that the procedure used by the physician constituted a breach of the duty of care the physician owed to her.[6] As long as the physician used a method of diagnosis or treatment considered valid within the profession, the patient who experienced a bad result may have a difficult time proving breach of duty.

CASE ILLUSTRATION

The patient had her last menstrual period on February 14. She consulted the physician on March 27, complaining of pelvic pain and difficulties. On the basis of the patient's history and an examination involving bimanual palpation of the uterus, the physician diagnosed a "retroverted, moderately enlarged fibroid-type of uterus and probable cervical stenosis." He prescribed tablets for a Gestest pregnancy test. Four days later, the physician gave the patient another pelvic examination and palpation. In obtaining an endometrial biopsy, the physician noted the existence of a tight, stenotic cervix. A pathologist who examined the biopsy tissue returned a diagnosis of "late secretory endometrium," a diagnosis which indicated the absence of pregnancy. The Gestest tablets, however, had not induced menstruation in the patient. This result indicated pregnancy. When the patient continued

§ 10.10   *Diagnosis*   351

to experience heavy pain in her pelvis and back, the physician recommended a hysterectomy, to which the patient consented. In the course of the operation it was discovered that the patient's uterus had the appearance of a pregnant uterus. The incision was closed, and the patient was returned to her room. A urine test confirmed the pregnancy. It was later discovered that the patient was not naturally pregnant, in that she suffered from a blighted ovum; as a result, she later aborted spontaneously. The patient brought suit. Although she did not allege that the spontaneous abortion was in any manner due to an act or omission of the physician, she contended that, because of negligence by the physician she had undergone an unnecessary exploratory laparotomy and had suffered emotional damages. At trial, both parties agreed the physician had a duty to rule out pregnancy before performing a hysterectomy; they disagreed as to whether that duty had been fulfilled. The patient's expert witness testified that an endometrial biopsy test was not acceptable under the applicable standard of care, while the physician presented evidence to the contrary. The jury found for the physician, and the court affirmed. The court stated that, while physicians apparently disagreed on the relative merits of various pregnancy tests, there was nonetheless sufficient evidence that the tests conducted by the physician-defendant were consistent with recognized standards of medical practice (*Hoglin v. Brown*, 1971).[7]

Of course, a physician should not blindly rely on the results of any laboratory test, no matter how commonly used, if reason exists to doubt the test's accuracy in a particular case. Thus if a physician orders a laboratory test and the results are inconsistent with the physician's observation or clinical knowledge of the patient, it may be negligence not to order subsequent tests to rule out the possibility of laboratory error.[8]

Suspected pregnancy should be differentiated from a number of conditions that simulate the signs and symptoms of pregnancy.[9] Cystic ovarian neoplasms, situated either in the posterior cul-de-sac or in the anterior pelvis, may resemble a pregnant uterus. However, ovarian neoplasms do not often cause amenorrhea, are separable from the uterine fundus, and do not increase in size as rapidly as the pregnant uterus.

Uterine fibromyomas, particularly a large single tumor located in the fundus of the uterus, may be quite difficult to differentiate from pregnancy. Uterine tumors do not cause amenorrhea, however, and because of the slow rate at which these tumors grow, repeated examinations at intervals of two to three weeks will reveal little or no change in the uterus. Pregnancy and fibromyomas often occur simultaneously. It is in situations of this sort that it may be necessary to use every possible diagnostic aid. In women who have missed one or more periods or whose periods had been normal but who are now experiencing irregular bleeding, pregnancy must be considered even though a fibromyoma, an ovarian cyst, or another obvious lesion is present. Pregnancy tests and sonography may be particularly helpful in diagnosing early pregnancy in such women. X-ray examination is of no value at this stage and is contraindicated if early pregnancy is suspected.

Pseudocyesis (pseudopregnancy) may be accompanied by amenorrhea and by enlarged, firm breasts that may secrete colostrum. The abdomen increases in size, but the navel retains its normal depression (in contrast to pregnancy, during which the umbilicus flattens or may even evert). Weight gain, greater than that during an actual, normal pregnancy, causes the abdomen to enlarge. This may be caused by subconscious muscular distention which may disappear under anesthesia or hypnosis. Patients with pseudocyesis experience all the subjective symptoms of normal pregnancy, often to an exaggerated degree. For example, quickening may be reported earlier than it would occur in a normal pregnancy. Pseudocyesis is most common in older women, but it may occur at any age. It usually results from an intense emotional need for an infant. Pseudocyesis can be suspected if changes in the pelvic organs characteristic of pregnancy are not detectable; the diagnosis can be confirmed by a negative pregnancy test, sonography, or by the failure of the uterus to enlarge progressively.

In certain situations, a final diagnosis cannot be made on the basis of a single examination or a single battery of tests.[10] In such cases it may be necessary to observe or examine the patient over an extended period. Failure to conduct or arrange for whatever further examinations or tests are needed to confirm a diagnosis may result in liability, even if the physician exercised due care in making his initial diagnosis.

CASE ILLUSTRATION

The patient became ill in late April. The physician decided her troubles were caused by a fibroid tumor of the uterus. The patient entered the hospital for surgery on April 28. X rays revealed no fetal skeleton or other sign of pregnancy. The physician, however, was concerned that the tumor could be hiding an early pregnancy. Although clinical examination of the patient was partially hampered by the size of the tumor, a laboratory test for pregnancy returned a positive result. The physician concluded that the patient was pregnant, and she was released from the hospital on May 2. Fetal heart tones could not be heard during a second examination on June 19, but a laboratory test for pregnancy again returned a positive result. The patient insisted she could not be pregnant because she was having regular menstrual periods. The physician told her to wait several months until the diagnosis of pregnancy could be verified, but a specific return appointment was not made. The patient returned for another examination on October 29. When X rays taken at that time did not reveal a fetal skeleton, the physician informed the patient that the earlier diagnosis of pregnancy was incorrect. The patient eventually underwent an operation to remove the tumor at a different hospital and then brought suit. At trial, expert testimony indicated that an early pregnancy could not be detected by clinical examination or X ray, that the laboratory test was properly administered and its positive results properly relied upon, that many women continue to bleed regularly throughout their pregnancies, that there were no other means of confirming the pregnancy, that the patient's life would have been endangered by surgery had she been pregnant, and that, therefore, the physician's decision to wait several months before operating accorded with proper standards of medical practice. On the basis of this testimony, the court concluded that the patient had failed to demonstrate that the diagnosis of pregnancy was negligent. However, an expert witness also testified that a woman in the patient-plaintiff's condition should be re-examined and her condition re-evaluated within no more than four months after the initial examination. The witness testified that continuing observation was particularly important in a case such as the patient's because of the likelihood of spontaneous abortion. Since more than four months had elapsed between the second pregnancy test in June and the October examination, and more than six months between the April and October examinations, the court held that the physician's failure to keep a closer check on the patient after her June visit may have constituted negligence. It therefore ordered the case to go to trial on that issue alone (*Stephenson v. Kaiser Foundation Hospitals*, 1962).[11]

Where a physician properly conducts appropriate tests and provides proper follow-up evaluation, an incorrect diagnosis will not automatically subject him or her to liability. Because pregnancies are not all the same and many other gynecological conditions simulate the symptoms of pregnancy, an incorrect diagnosis is not, in itself, negligence.

CASE ILLUSTRATION

The patient complained to the physician of nausea, cramps, and a bloody vaginal discharge experienced more than one month after her last menstrual period. The physician conducted a general pelvic examination for pregnancy and concluded that the patient was "probably pregnant." He gave her an injection for cramping and a prescription for the drug Norlutate to prevent involuntary abortion. At an examination four months later, the physician became concerned because a palpable fundus could not be found. Subsequent X rays revealed no fetal skeleton. A gynecologist then examined the patient and diagnosed her condition as an endometrioma of the umbilicus. The patient brought suit, contending that the first physician's diagnosis of probable pregnancy was so obviously negligent as to be "determinable by laymen." The court disagreed, and when the patient failed to produce expert testimony to support her case, it entered judgment for the physician. In fact, said the court, "the defendant's diagnosis of 'probable pregnancy' was based not only upon the test results, but also upon the consideration of the symptoms related to him . . . and an actual pelvic examination for pregnancy. Certainly, a layman is in no position to determine that the defendant's diagnosis of probable pregnancy under these circumstances constituted a violation of defendant's duties to exercise that skill and knowledge normally possessed by the average members of his profession" (*Kleinman v. Armour,* 1970).[12]

Where an incorrect diagnosis is arrived at without conducting appropriate tests, the omission may constitute negligence if the incorrect diagnosis causes the patient to suffer some harm or injury.

CASE ILLUSTRATION

Without administering any tests or X rays, the physician diagnosed a uterine tumor and advised the patient to undergo surgery. He did not conduct any tests for pregnancy, although the patient exhibited symptoms compatible with pregnancy and had raised the possibility with him during their discussions. In the course of an operation for the suspected tumor, it was discovered that the patient was in fact six to eight weeks pregnant. Twenty-two days after the operation, the patient suffered a miscarriage. Upon the patient's appeal from a judgment for the physician, the court noted that "miscarriages may result from myriad causes. There is nothing . . . to establish probably, rather than merely possibly, that the operation was the cause in this particular instance. Accordingly, we conclude that there was insufficient evidence of causation." The court found, however, that the patient was entitled to a new trial on the basis of evidence that the unnecessary operation itself, as opposed to the miscarriage, was the result of a negligent diagnosis (*Jarboe v. Harting,* 1965).[13]

This case raises another issue: whether it is necessary to test routinely for pregnancy in all patients of childbearing age who present with some symptoms of pregnancy. One commentator has suggested that routine pregnancy testing may eventually emerge as a standard of care.[14] Studies disclose that some hospitals screen for pregnancy routinely (four percent of 236 hospitals studied in one report[15]); in one study of such hospitals it was found that as many as 41 percent of the women who were pregnant were unaware of the fact.[16] In light of these facts and the amount and variety of litigation arising from the failure to diagnose pregnancy, commentators assert that the duty to test routinely for

§ 10.10   Diagnosis   355

pregnancy could be viewed by courts as the standard followed by a respectable minority of practitioners[17] (see § 1.32, Standard of Care). If courts adopt this approach, it will have implications for physicians as well as hospitals.[18] This is not to suggest that physicians should engage in testing and procedures clearly not indicated by the patient's condition. Courts will not impose a standard recognized by a respectable minority on a physician-defendant whose conduct conforms with another acceptable standard recognized as sound practice by the profession. Nevertheless, where pregnancy might be a reasonable differential diagnosis, its presence or absence should be ascertained before beginning a treatment (for some other condition) that would injure the fetus or the mother.

CASE ILLUSTRATION

The married, 36-year-old patient saw her physician and complained of spotty vaginal bleeding; she reported that her last menstrual period had occurred 47 days before the examination. The patient had also experienced abdominal pain and nausea for the past month. Without testing for pregnancy, the physician performed a D&C. Five days later, the patient underwent a gallbladder operation. When she returned to the surgeon two weeks after the operation because a small blood clot had formed on her stomach, she told him that her stomach and breasts were enlarging. She asked if she could possibly be pregnant, and the physician told her that pregnancy was physically impossible after what she had been through. Seven months later, the patient gave birth and then brought suit. The trial court decided in favor of the physician-defendants and the patient appealed. The court of appeals concluded, "[T]here was competent evidence from which the jury could find that the medical profession . . . does not perform the operations here involved on a woman of childbearing age without first determining whether she is pregnant; that this admittedly was not done in this case, and although the patient did not miscarry and the fetus was not injured by the surgery, the health of plaintiff-wife was impaired and she suffered mental anguish concerning possible injury to the unborn child." The appellate court ordered the case retried (*Gridley v. Johnson*, 1972).[19]

It may be necessary to test for pregnancy before carrying out other diagnostic procedures when the patient is of childbearing age and the other diagnostic procedures could harm the mother or fetus. This is particularly applicable to the use of X rays for diagnostic purposes.

CASE ILLUSTRATION

The patient complained to the physician, who was a board-certified internist, of nausea, weakness, and other symptoms. The physician ordered the patient hospitalized. In the hospital, the patient was given numerous diagnostic X rays but was not tested for pregnancy. When the patient's symptoms continued unabated after her release from the hospital, she consulted another physician. This physician discovered that the patient was ten weeks pregnant. He advised her that there was a serious risk that her fetus had been damaged by the X rays. The patient decided to terminate her pregnancy, and she procured an abortion. At trial, the jury found that the first physician was negligent in not conducting pregnancy tests before administering the X rays. The jury returned a verdict for the physician, however, on the ground that his negligence was not the cause of the patient's abortion or mental and physical suffering. On appeal, the court reversed in part, stating that, since the patient had decided to procure an abortion in natural consequence of the physician's negligence, it followed that the negligence was indeed a substantial cause of the abortion. Adhering to the general rule that damages for emotional suffering are not recoverable in the absence of physical contact or injury, the court found that the irradiation constituted sufficient physical contact to permit recovery of emotional damages. Accordingly, the court ordered a new trial on the issue of damages alone, telling the jury to determine what damages would compensate the patient for her mental and physical pain and suffering (*Deutsch v. Shein*, 1980).[20]

Not all courts have reached this conclusion.[21] In such cases, it is necessary for the parties to establish, through expert testimony, whether X rays have a deleterious effect on the fetus and warrant termination of the pregnancy. The outcome of such cases will often depend on which party's expert the jury believes, as well as such relevant facts as the amount of radiation the patient is exposed to or the gestational age of the fetus.

CASE ILLUSTRATION

The 36-year-old patient, a mother of four, sought the services of a neurosurgeon because of persistent pain in her lower back. After performing an examination consisting of a series of exercises and a nerve reflex test, the neurosurgeon suspected that the patient might have a spinal cord tumor and ordered that X rays be taken of the patient's lower back and pelvic region. No pregnancy test was given. The patient underwent three X rays. Three days later, she consulted an obstetrician because she wasn't feeling well, she was fearful that the medication the neurosurgeon had prescribed was making her ill, and she suspected a vaginal infection. The obstetrician's examination revealed the patient was 5½ weeks pregnant. Upon discovering that the patient had been subjected to X rays three days earlier, the obstetrician recommended a therapeutic abortion because of possible radiation damage to the fetus. The abortion was performed, and the patient sued the neurologist, alleging that he had negligently failed to examine her and obtain an adequate medical history and that he had negligently prescribed an inappropriate medical procedure by ordering the X rays. At trial, the patient produced no direct medical evidence on the medical standard of care, arguing that the risk of injury to a fetus from the use of X rays is so obvious that it is common knowledge that a physician exercising ordinary care will inquire as to whether a woman of childbearing age is pregnant before ordering them. The obstetrician who recommended the abortion testified at trial that he could not give a specific percentage of fetuses that might be damaged by X-radiation. He further testified that there was a marked difference of opinion between the American College of Obstetricians and Gynecologists and the American College of Radiologists as to the propriety of subjecting a pregnant woman to X-radiation and that this difference had recently been resolved in favor of doing X rays. The neurologist testified that the risk of fetal deformity from X rays is 0.1 percent. The court held that the evidence did not support the patient's contention of the obviousness of the risk and absolved the physician from liability (*Cox v. Dela Cruz,* 1979).[22]

Lawsuits have also been brought for a physician's failure to test for pregnancy and for incorrectly informing the patient that she is not pregnant, thereby precluding her from obtaining an abortion. Such cases generally fall under the rubric of "wrongful birth" (see § 2.40, Birth-Related Causes of Action) and involve the birth of a normal, healthy child. The action is basically malpractice, the long-recognized remedy for damages sustained as the result of a physician's failure to exercise reasonable care in diagnosis.

CASE ILLUSTRATION

The 14-year-old patient, complaining of dizzy spells, fainting, and missed menstrual periods, went to the obstetrician, accompanied by her mother. The obstetrician concluded that these symptoms were a manifestation of obesity and low blood pressure. The patient saw the obstetrician on six occasions; at no time was she tested for pregnancy. The patient was in fact pregnant and gave birth to a normal boy. She sued the obstetrician for damages for the care of the child, alleging that, if she had known she was pregnant, she would have obtained an abortion. At trial, an expert testified that the failure to conduct tests ruling out the possibility of pregnancy in a case such as the patient's constitutes substandard care. In addition to this evidence, the court noted that, where a "physician's conduct is such that a layperson could ascertain that the medical practitioner's acts were negligent, [expert] testimony is not needed." Other evidence at trial included the admission by the obstetrician-defendant that he suspected from the initial visit that the patient was pregnant. The patient's mother testified that she assumed a pregnancy test had been conducted, since the probable cause of her daughter's condition was obvious; however, when the obstetrician said nothing about the possibility of pregnancy, she did not concern herself with it. The court held the obstetrician liable for the requested damages (*Clapham v. Yanga,* 1981).[23]

In a 1974 decision delivered by a New York appellate court, a similar resolution was reached where an obstetrician who had prescribed contraceptives for a patient failed to test for pregnancy, despite the presence of obvious signs and symptoms. The patient's pregnancy was discovered too late to allow a "safe" abortion, but the court noted that the right to have an abortion may not be converted to an obligation to have one.[24] Thus, under the reasoning of this case, a physician who negligently fails to test for pregnancy may be held liable, regardless of when the pregnancy is discovered.

It is not surprising, then, that in recent years physicians engaged in the diagnosis of pregnancy have been faced with a new source of potential liability: liability for failure to diagnose pregnancy soon enough to permit abortion. In these cases, the patient seeks recovery for wrongful birth; that is, she seeks damages for the birth of a child that would have been aborted had the physician exercised reasonable care in making his diagnosis (see § 2.42, Wrongful Birth). Damages typically requested include medical expenses incurred during the pregnancy and delivery and the expected costs of raising and educating the child.

The courts are not in agreement, however, as to whether an allegation of this nature constitutes a valid cause of action. The Wisconsin Supreme Court, with an eye to protecting the physician from potentially disastrous liability, refused to recognize the claim in 1974.

CASE ILLUSTRATION

After examining the patient, the physician diagnosed her condition as a "condition other than pregnancy." He prescribed medication for her and told her she was not pregnant. Two months later, the patient consulted a second physician, who advised her that she was 17 weeks pregnant. The patient subsequently gave birth to a normal child. The patient and her husband brought suit, contending that she would have undergone an abortion had her condition been correctly diagnosed by the first physician and that, by the time her pregnancy was diagnosed, it was too late to abort. The plaintiffs requested damages from the physician and his clinic sufficient to cover the anticipated cost of rearing the child. The court concluded that the patient and her husband should not be permitted to enjoy the love, pride, and other advantages of parenthood without having to bear its costs. The damages requested, said the court, "would be wholly out of proportion to the culpability involved . . . [and] the allowance of recovery would place too unreasonable a burden upon physicians, under the facts and circumstances here alleged." Thus, finding that the complaint was "well beyond" the outer limits of physician liability for failure to diagnose pregnancy, the court ordered the case to be dismissed (*Rieck v. Medical Protective Co.*, 1974).[25]

This case may not be representative of what the future may hold for physicians whose untimely failure to diagnose pregnancy prevents the patient from obtaining an abortion. As long as abortion is recognized as a legal right in the United States, the courts may generally be expected to safeguard that right.

§ 10.11 Extrauterine Pregnancy

Liability may be imposed on the physician for the failure to use accepted diagnostic tests and procedures and to exercise reasonable medical judgment regarding a patient exhibiting symptoms of extrauterine, particularly ectopic, pregnancy.

Basic Standard of Care: The American College of Obstetricians and Gynecologists has not published guidelines for the diagnosis and treatment of extrauterine pregnancy.

Interpretation and Customary Practice: An extrauterine pregnancy is one in which a fertilized ovum is implanted somewhere other than the uterus. While pregnancies can occur in the peritoneal cavity, the incidence of this is extremely rare. At least 90 percent of extrauterine pregnancies occur in a uterine tube and are referred to as ectopic, or tubal, pregnancies. The incidence of ectopic pregnancy is about 1 in 200 pregnancies. Ectopic pregnancy may occur at any time from menarche to menopause, but 40 percent occur in women between the ages of 20 and 29. Ectopic pregnancies occur more frequently in infertile women, women in lower socioeconomic groups, and women who have experienced a previous ectopic pregnancy. Women who have received treatment for salpingitis or who have had a tuboplasty are more prone to ectopic pregnancy.[26]

No specific symptoms or signs are indicative of ectopic pregnancy, but a combination of findings may be suggestive. Ectopic pregnancy should be suspected whenever a woman experiences abnormal bleeding accompanied by abdominal pain, even when she says she has not missed a menstrual period. Ectopic pregnancies may result in ruptured uterine tubes, with acute intra-abdominal hemorrhage, or tubal abortion, with episodes of intra-abdominal bleeding occurring over a period of several days or even weeks. Ectopic pregnancies that do not result in ruptured tubes are not often diagnosed.

Two or more of the following symptoms and signs are usually present:

1. Secondary amenorrhea, although many women do not experience a delay in menstruation

2. Abnormal uterine bleeding, resulting from inadequate secretion of estrogen and progesterone
3. Pelvic or lower abdominal pain, associated with intraperitoneal bleeding or stretching of the tube as the pregnancy advances
4. Subdiaphragmatic pain or sharp shoulder pain, along with extensive intra-abdominal bleeding
5. Palpation of a cul-de-sac or adnexal mass, although a definite mass often may not be felt because the examination is so painful that the patient cannot relax
6. Lower hemoglobin and hematocrit counts because of blood loss, with normal or only slightly elevated white blood cell counts

Standard pregnancy tests are not reliable in diagnosing ectopic pregnancy, because they are positive in no more than 35 to 40 percent of cases. Radioreceptor assays and radioimmunoassays can detect minute amounts of chorionic gonadotropin and are almost always positive with ectopic pregnancies, even those that have been expelled from the tube.

Several procedures should be used to confirm a diagnosis of ectopic pregnancy.[27]

1. Pelvic examination under anesthesia is more accurate in detecting masses than is examination without anesthesia because the patient is not in pain.
2. Culdocentesis may reveal free blood in the cul-de-sac. Failure to detect free blood does not rule out ectopic pregnancy, however. Abdominal paracentesis may be helpful if there is a considerable amount of intraperitoneal bleeding. The presence of blood confirms the need for a definitive operation, although it cannot identify the source of the bleeding.
3. Laparoscopy or culdoscopy permits direct inspection of the tubes.
4. Posterior colpotomy permits accurate diagnosis and may even permit the removal of an early tubal pregnancy.
5. Sonography may reveal a gestational sac in the tube or no evidence of pregnancy in the uterus, or both.
6. A D&C should be performed if profuse and prolonged vaginal bleeding has occurred. This affords an opportunity for careful pelvic examination under anesthesia and may rule out an ectopic pregnancy if placental tissue is obtained from the endometrial cavity. If the curettings grossly resemble those from a normal endometrium, further investigation is indicated.
7. Diagnostic laparoscopy or exploratory laparotomy provides the most specific diagnostic procedure to establish the presence or absence of

ectopic (but not cervical) pregnancy. Laparotomy is indicated when the presumptive diagnosis of ectopic pregnancy has been made based on the presence of blood in the peritoneal cavity or when it is obvious that the patient has suffered massive intraperitoneal bleeding.

Although it is usually possible to diagnose a ruptured tubal pregnancy with reasonable accuracy, an unruptured tubal pregnancy presents such a varied clinical picture that the following conditions must be differentiated:[28]

1. Threatened or incomplete abortion—A longer period of amenorrhea usually precedes the onset of symptoms followed by spotting and brisk vaginal bleeding. The pain is usually less severe with threatened abortion, it occurs in the midline, and it resembles cramps. Tenderness is present, but an adnexal mass usually is not. When differentiation is difficult, the physician may have to resort to D&C and laparoscopy or colpotomy to establish a diagnosis.
2. Salpingitis—The symptoms accompanying salpingitis usually appear at the time of the menses rather than after a period of amenorrhea. The pain, tenderness, and palpable tubal enlargement are usually bilateral. A temperature of 100 to 101 degrees is common with salpingitis but not with ectopic pregnancy, and leukocytosis is much greater with salpingitis. Pregnancy tests will be negative.
3. Appendicitis—A patient with appendicitis will usually have a history of epigastric pain moving to the right lower quadrant, accompanied by such digestive disturbances as nausea and vomiting. Neither amenorrhea nor bleeding will be present. No adnexal mass will be present unless an appendiceal abscess has developed. Pregnancy tests will be negative.
4. Corpus luteum cysts—These develop when the corpus luteum fails to regress at the expected time. The mass is usually larger and more globular than the mass in an ectopic pregnancy. It is also less painful and less tender. However, amenorrhea, mild lower quadrant pain, and an adnexal mass may all accompany corpus luteum cysts.
5. Ruptured graafian follicle with excessive bleeding—Amenorrhea does not usually accompany a ruptured graafian follicle, which occurs most often at midcycle, the time of ovulation. Pregnancy tests will be negative.

Treatment for ectopic pregnancy with a ruptured tube consists of immediate surgical removal of the affected uterine tube and replacement of the blood lost. Unilateral salpingectomy is the usual operation, although some physicians recommend excising the ovary along with the affected tube. An early pregnancy (before rupture of the tube) in the isthmus may be treated by salpingostomy, in which the conceptus is evacuated through a linear incision made in the tube.

The need for promptness in the diagnosis and treatment of ectopic pregnancy cannot be overemphasized. Approximately 11 percent of maternal deaths that occur each year in the United States are due to ectopic pregnancy.[29] Usually the deaths occur because the pregnancy was not diagnosed or because prompt surgical intervention was not instituted. An untreated rupture of a uterine tube may lead to extensive loss of blood and death.

Ectopic pregnancy will recur in about ten percent of the women who have experienced it. Approximately half of the patients who have undergone surgery for ectopic pregnancy are rendered infertile. Of these, about 30 percent become sterile. About half of the patients who have had one ectopic pregnancy are able to achieve normal pregnancies.[30]

A physician who fails to use accepted diagnostic tests and procedures when a patient exhibits symptoms suggestive of ectopic pregnancy may face legal liability.[31] No matter how many tests or examinations a physician conducts, if the possibility of ectopic pregnancy is not considered when the patient's symptoms so indicate or if reasonable skill and care are not used in the confirming or excluding of such a diagnosis, liability may result.

CASE ILLUSTRATION

The patient experienced vaginal bleeding that differed from her ordinary periods in that its duration was longer: nine days. Shortly thereafter, she began to experience nausea, dizziness, and sharp abdominal pains. When these symptoms persisted, the patient was taken to the hospital, where a general practitioner diagnosed her condition as endometritis. The general practitioner than consulted an obstetrician-gynecologist. Although a D&C performed by the physicians gave no indication as to the patient's condition, the physicians decided the symptoms were caused by hyperplasia of the endometrium. Another examination two weeks later revealed a lump or mass on one side of the patient's abdomen which the physicians diagnosed as an ovarian abscess. The physicians did not give the patient a pregnancy test at this time. The patient next consulted a third physician, who performed a laparotomy after giving her pregnancy tests. The operation revealed a rupture of the patient's left fallopian tube caused by an ectopic pregnancy. The rupture had caused severe internal bleeding and clotting. The physician removed the patient's tubes, ovaries, and uterus. The patient brought suit against the general practitioner and the obstetrician-gynecologist, contending that their misdiagnosis was the result of negligence. The court held the case could go to trial, stating: "[T]here is ample evidence . . . from which it can be inferred that defendants did not consider the possibility of a tubal pregnancy where reasonable skill and care would have required such a consideration." The court noted that if the patient's condition had been diagnosed earlier it might have been possible to save one or both of her tubes and ovaries (*Pugh v. Swiontek*, 1969).[32]

Of course, the mere existence of a bad result will not establish negligence. However, where there is admittedly a misdiagnosis, the law inquires whether the misdiagnosis was reached after the exercise of reasonable medical judgment or whether it was arrived at without the exercise of appropriate care. Liability will only be imposed in the latter case.

CASE ILLUSTRATION

The physician was called because the patient was suffering from abdominal cramps and had fainted. The physician did not conduct a pelvic examination but diagnosed the patient's condition as salpingitis. He administered an injection of penicillin and Demerol. During the evening, the patient's symptoms became increasingly severe. She suffered fainting spells, cramps, chills, and fever. She could not walk without assistance. Contacted shortly before dawn, the physician prescribed Empirin and codeine to ease the patient's pain and Nembutal to induce sleep. When the patient had difficulty catching her breath in the morning, her husband took her to the hospital. She died almost immediately upon arrival. The autopsy revealed that the peritoneal cavity contained five pints of blood and that the patient had bled to death because of an ectopic pregnancy that resulted in a ruptured right uterine tube. The physician testified at trial that he did not conduct a pelvic examination because the patient was obese and an examination would not have revealed the presence of an ectopic pregnancy. He also testified that the patient's blood pressure was normal when he examined her and that the treatment he provided would have been of no value whatsoever to a woman with an ectopic pregnancy. A jury verdict for the physician was reversed and a new trial ordered. The trial judge had instructed the jury that there could be no liability for the choice of one of two or more equally recognized methods of diagnosis or treatment. The court of appeals held that this instruction was reversible error since there was no evidence that the treatment actually given to the patient was a proper or recognized one for ectopic pregnancy. The court found that the jury should only have considered whether there had been a negligent failure to diagnose the patient's condition (*Smith v. Shankman*, 1962).[33]

§ 10.20 MANAGEMENT

Liability for improper management of pregnancy will be imposed on a physician if his or her treatment of a particular condit͏̇ pregnancy does not conform with the relevant standard of c 10.26 for discussion of specific conditions).

Basic Standard of Care: The American College of Obste cologists has published the following guidelines governing pr ment. The evaluation of pregnancy should include a full history, physical examination, and laboratory studies. The history should include factors that help identify the patient at high risk, such as age, vaginal bleeding, edema, urinary infection, rubella, exposure to radiation, use of medication, and use of alcohol, tobacco, and other addicting substances. A review of past obstetric experiences, with specific reference to any complications, should also be conducted. A previous administration of RH immune globulin should be specifically noted. The patient's family history, social history, and nutritional status should be evaluated. The physical examination on the initial visit should be comprehensive and include an evaluation of height, weight, blood pressure, head, neck, breasts, heart, lungs, abdomen, pelvis, rectum, and extremities. During the pelvic examination, attention should be given to the size of the uterus and the configuration and capacity of the bony pelvis. Routine laboratory tests should include:

1. Hemoglobin or hematocrit
2. Urinalysis
3. Blood group and Rh type
4. Irregular antibody screen
5. Rubella antibody titer
6. Cervical cytology
7. Syphilis screen

Additional laboratory evaluation may be necessary depending on historical factors or unusual findings derived from history or physical examination. Those patients determined to be at high risk upon initial evaluation may require further evaluation, consultation, or referral. The frequency of follow-up visits should be determined by the woman's individual needs and risk assessment. In general, the woman with an uncomplicated pregnancy should be seen every four weeks for the first 28 weeks of pregnancy, every two to three weeks until 36 weeks' gestation, and weekly thereafter. Weight, blood pressure, urinalysis, fundal height, abdominal findings, and character and location of fetal heart tones should be determined at each visit. The hemoglobin or hematocrit, or both, should be determined between 28 and 36 weeks' gestation. Patient education and nutritional advice are important aspects of prenatal care. In high-risk situations, consultation or transfer to special centers may be necessary.[34]

Interpretation and Customary Practice: Special problems or factors that will affect the management of pregnancies which present these concerns are considered in the pages that immediately follow.

§ 10.21 Rubella

Liability may be imposed on a physician for the failure to diagnose rubella and advise a pregnant patient of its possible effects on the fetus.

Basic Standard of Care: The American College of Obstetricians and Gynecologists has recommended the following practices for diagnosing rubella.[35]

1. If exposure to rubella or infection is suspected at any time during pregnancy in a patient known to be immune [on the basis of prior serological testing, such as the Hemagglutination-inhibiting (HI) antibody test], there is no apparent risk to the fetus.

2. If exposure to rubella or infection is suspected at any time during pregnancy in a known serologic negative patient, a second serum specimen, preferably for HI testing, should be obtained preferably three to four weeks after exposure or ten to 14 days after the onset of the rash to determine if seroconversion to rubella has occurred. If so, appropriate counseling about the possible risk of fetal abnormalities is in order.

3. If a patient of unknown immune status presents within one week after exposure to a rash illness, an HI titer should be obtained. The absence of HI antibody (that is, an HI titer of 1:8 or less) in the first serum specimen followed by a seroconversion in three to four weeks indicates a rubella infection, and appropriate counseling is necessary.

4. If a patient of unknown immune status presents one to five weeks after exposure to a rash illness or up to three weeks after the onset of a rash, an HI titer should be obtained. If the HI titer is considered negative, the procedure as outlined should be followed. If the HI titer is 1:8 to 1:32, a second serum specimen should be obtained in two weeks and HI titers on both repeated. A fourfold or greater rise in HI titer in two weeks, along with rash illness is reliable evidence of an acute rubella infection.

   If at the time of the two-week sample there is no significant change in titer, a complement fixation (CF) test on both sera should be obtained. The absence of CF antibodies in both specimens indicates that there is no evidence of acute rubella infection, while a fourfold or greater rise in CF titers indicates that there is. If the CF titer is unchanged—that is, if there is a stable, positive titer, rubella-specific IgM should be obtained on serum specimens. In this setting, absence of rubella-specific IgM antibody in the specimens indicates there is no evidence of acute rubella. If rubella-specific IgM is present, this is evidence of acute rubella infection, and appropriate counseling regarding the risk to the fetus and management of the pregnancy is necessary.

5. If a patient of unknown immune status presents five weeks after exposure to a rash illness or three weeks after a rash onset and the HI titer is 1:8, the patient is susceptible to rubella and has no evidence of an acute infection. If the HI titer is 1:8 to 1:32, there is evidence of a previous rubella infection, but the date of infection cannot be deter-

mined and the risk to the fetus is unknown. In such instances, it is necessary to consider the historical and epidemiologic information regarding the likelihood of infection during the pregnancy.

Interpretation and Customary Practice: The physician is responsible not only for a diagnosis of pregnancy, but also for the diagnosis of any condition of the mother that might bear upon her ability to deliver a full-term normal child. Much of the current litigation in this area concerns a physician's liability for failure to diagnose rubella, or German measles. Failure to identify rubella in a pregnant woman is particularly distressing because of the risk of birth defects caused by the disease.

Generally a mild, brief illness for the mother, rubella has a teratogenic impact on the fetus. The risk of congenital anomalies is greatest when the fetus is exposed to the rubella virus during the first trimester of pregnancy. Although the risk of birth defects decreases after the twelfth week of pregnancy, it is still a distinct possibility during the second trimester. The general risk for the fetus is greater during rubella epidemics than during sporadic infections. Fetal defects caused by rubella include congenital heart disease, cataracts, deafness, and mental retardation. It may take one to two years before the seriousness of the infant's defects can be established with any certainty.[36] An exact clinical diagnosis of rubella is difficult, particularly in retrospect, because the course of rubella resembles that of several other viral infections. A precise diagnosis can be made only on the basis of antibody studies. HI antibodies, which are absent in susceptible persons, can be detected within 48 hours after the appearance of the rash; the number of these antibodies peaks within two weeks. Thus rubella can be differentiated from other, nonteratogenic viral infections with HI antibody titers. Rubella is characterized by an increased concentration of HI antibodies after the acute infection. Therefore, the titer must be determined within two or three days after the rash appears and again about two weeks later. A significant increase in titer on the second test indicates that the infection was actually rubella. A high titer on a single test performed one or two weeks after a presumed rubella infection is of no diagnostic value because one cannot determine whether the elevated titer was in response to an infection that occurred years or days before the test.[37]

A test for complement-fixation antibodies may be useful. These antibodies appear a few days after the onset of the rash, reaching peak concentrations four to eight weeks later. Concurrently increased concentrations of HI and complement-fixation antibodies indicate a recent infection. An elevated HI titer without detectable complement-fixation antibodies suggests a remote infection, which will not affect the embryo.

The physician should perform a rubella antibody study at the initial prenatal visit. If antibodies are revealed, the patient is immune. If no antibodies are present, she is susceptible, and the appearance of antibodies subsequent to an acute illness will be diagnostic of rubella. Fewer than ten percent of women of childbearing age are susceptible to rubella.[38]

Preventing maternal rubella infection and the subsequent teratogenic effects on the fetus is the major objective of rubella immunization programs. In the United States, the primary target population has been preschool and school age children of both sexes, with secondary emphasis on selective vaccination of women of childbearing age. Although this strategy has resulted in a marked decrease in the total number of reported cases in children under 15, few changes have been noted in the incidence of rubella in those 15 years and older. The persistence of susceptibility rate to rubella of ten to 20 percent among adolescents and young adults is consistent with the continuing outbreaks in these populations. A substantial, immediate decrease in congenital rubella cannot be expected unless susceptible adults of childbearing age, as well as children, are vaccinated. Rubella antibody tests should be performed prior to conception and if the patient is found susceptible she should be immunized before she becomes pregnant.

The only vaccine available in the United States is the RA 27/3 strain,* a live, attenuated rubella virus vaccine produced in human diploid cell cultures. This vaccine simulates natural infection more closely than previously used rubella vaccines. Concentrations of RA 27/3-induced antibodies in the blood, which are present in at least 95 percent of persons vaccinated, have been shown to persist for at least six years without substantial decline. The rubella vaccine virus can be recovered from the respiratory secretions of recipients up to 28 days after subcutaneous or intranasal administration; however, studies have documented the lack of communicability of the vaccine virus. Even though the vaccine virus may be excreted in the mother's milk and seroconversion in the feeding infant may occur, there appears to be no contraindication for vaccinating the susceptible mother if she plans to breastfeed her infant.

Some recipients may develop mild and brief rubella-like signs and symptoms such as fever, rash, and lymphadenopathy seven to 21 days after vaccination. Pain in the joints may occur in up to 40 percent of persons vaccinated, but frank arthritis is rare.[39]

Rubella vaccine virus is known to cross the placenta and may infect the fetus during the early stages of its development. Although the observed risk of congenital malformations following rubella vaccination—regardless of the vaccine strain—is zero, the theoretical risk may be as high as four percent. While this risk is no greater than the risk of malformations occurring by chance, definitive conclusions regarding the long-term risk to the fetus still cannot be drawn. Nonetheless, because the vaccine can infect the fetus, the patient should be immunized only when pregnancy can be excluded and avoided for three

---

*When the RA 27/3 vaccine is administered prior to or during a pregnancy, the physician should report this to the Centers for Disease Control (404) 329-3096 so more cases can be followed.

months after vaccination. Thus, a negative pregnancy test may be required, or the vaccine may be administered during a menstrual period or immediately after childbirth. Women who have been vaccinated should use an effective contraceptive method for three months after the inoculation. Vaccination may not provide complete protection to the fetus; during rubella epidemics as many as 80 percent of vaccinated persons develop subclinical infection.[40]

If the patient contracts rubella within the first 20 weeks after the onset of her last menstrual period, therapeutic abortion should be considered unless the patient and her husband want to accept the risk of birth defects. Patients who become infected after the twentieth week of pregnancy should also consider therapeutic abortion, despite the decreased risk of defects.

Gamma globulin is not an effective treatment. Even if given before exposure, it may only prevent the rash, not the viremia, of rubella. The virus will remain as a serious threat to the fetus.

Because a patient who gives birth to a defective child may claim that she would have undergone an abortion had she been informed of her rubella, courts in recent years have been confronted with the difficult question of whether a patient may recover the cost of rearing the defective child. This issue, though similar to the damages problem raised by an allegation of negligent failure to diagnose pregnancy within a reasonable time (see § 10.10, Diagnosis), has been viewed by the courts in a somewhat different light. In general, the courts appear more willing to permit the parents some measure of damages if their child is born deformed than if it is born normal. Again, however, legal resolution of this issue is not uniform. Some courts have permitted the parents to recover the full cost of childrearing in wrongful birth cases[41] (see § 2.42, Wrongful Birth), while others have refused to allow any damages at all.[42] A compromise approach permits recovery of the extra expenses necessitated by the child's deformity, but not of the general expenses that would have been incurred even if a normal child had been born.[43]

CASE ILLUSTRATION

The patient entered the hospital emergency room for treatment of an upper body rash. She told the physician that she thought she had rubella. The physician diagnosed her condition as an allergic reaction, and he had her discharged. At this time the patient was about one month pregnant. She did not tell the physician she was pregnant because she did not know it herself. Eight months later, the patient's child was born suffering from "rubella syndrome." The child's injuries included permanent physical and mental retardation, cataracts, and heart malfunctions. The patient brought suit for herself and her child, contending that the physician was negligent in failing to test for and diagnose rubella, in failing to inquire as to pregnancy, and in failing to advise her of the possible effects of rubella upon an unborn child and of the availability of abortion. The court held that the child's damages were not compensable because they could not be rationally calculated. The law cannot be expected, said the court, to estimate the difference in value between life in a deformed body and the "void of nonexistence" that follows abortion. The physician's failure to advise the patient of the availability of abortion was not negligence, because at the time of the examination most abortions were illegal. However, the court also found that the physician may have been negligent in failing to diagnose rubella, in failing to inquire as to pregnancy, and in failing to inform the patient of the possible effects of rubella. In ordering the case to be retried, the court stated that, if the patient proved these allegations of negligence and if she also proved that she would have aborted had she been properly diagnosed and informed, then she would be entitled to recover the additional medical, hospital, and support expenses she had incurred and would incur in raising a deformed, as opposed to normal, child (*Dumer v. St. Michael's Hospital,* 1975).[44]

Most courts have acted consistently with the holding in this case in refusing to allow the child itself a cause of action for wrongful life[45] (see § 2.43, Wrongful Life). As one court stated, the law as yet does not recognize a "fundamental right of a child to be born as a whole, functional being."[46] Infants born with deformities caused by rubella or other conditions of the mother may, therefore, be precluded from personally recovering damages for having been brought into the world.

§ 10.22 Preeclampsia and Eclampsia

Liability may be imposed on a physician for negligence in the treatment of preeclampsia if (1) he or she fails to conform to the applicable standard of obstetrical practice in performing tests to diagnose the presence of the condition and (2) the treatment administered does not conform to standard practice and such treatment causes harm to the patient.

Basic Standard of Care: The American College of Obstetricians and Gynecologists has not specifically promulgated guidelines for care of eclamptic patients. These patients, however, should be considered high-risk patients.

Interpretation and Customary Practice: Preeclampsia is a complication occuring during pregnancy. The condition is characterized by hypertension (a rise in blood pressure), edema (increase in body water), and proteinuria (excretion of protein in the urine). Eclampsia is a more severe form of preeclampsia and is evidenced by convulsions or coma.[47]

The symptoms of preeclampsia develop after the twentieth week of pregnancy. The first sign is usually excessive weight gain—more than two pounds (one kilogram) per week. The gain is often sudden because it is due to fluid retention. Edema first appears in the lower legs; as the condition progresses, puffiness develops around the eyes and the fingers swell.[48]

Another sign of preeclampsia is hypertension. Overall blood pressure is not necessarily a reliable indicator of the severity of the condition, however a diastolic pressure of 90 millimeters of mercury indicates a critical level.[49] In addition, any increase of more than 15 millimeters of mercury in diastolic blood pressure or 30 millimeters of mercury in systolic blood pressure should be diagnosed as hypertension.[50]

Finally, proteinuria is usually persent in women with preeclampsia. The amount of protein in the urine increases as the condition becomes more severe. Significant proteinuria exists if examination reveals more than 300 milligrams per liter in a sample collected over a 24-hour period.[51]

Women suffering from severe preeclampsia may also experience headaches, blurred vision, hyperreflexia, and decreased renal function.[52]

Eclampsia is a continuation of the symptoms of preeclampsia, with the addition of coma or convulsions or both. Eclampsia may occur before labor, during labor, or within 24-hours after delivery.[53]

Failure to recognize and respond to changes in these symptoms may constitute negligence. In one case, the physician was sued for failing to diagnose preeclampsia when the patient, already suffering from excessive weight gain, reported that she was swollen, stumbling, and could not speak clearly.

CASE ILLUSTRATION

The patient regularly visited the physician during the course of her pregnancy. At one of these periodic examinations, the physician admonished the patient about her excessive weight gain and warned of the possibility of eclampsia. After missing one of her regularly scheduled appointments, the patient's condition deteriorated. That evening she appeared swollen, could not speak clearly, and stumbled. The patient's husband contacted the physician, who told the patient to come to her office Monday morning. Over the weekend, the patient's condition remained the same. On Monday, the patient went into convulsions. The patient went to the hospital where the physician diagnosed acute eclampsia and noted that the patient had gained 15 to 20 pounds since her last visit. The baby was delivered dead; the patient died a few days later. The patient's husband brought suit, alleging that the physician was negligent in failing to recognize and treat the symptoms when first reported. The physician-defendant claimed that the patient was contributorily negligent in failing to follow instructions, in failing to keep her appointment, and in failing to report changes in her condition. The court reversed a judgment for the physician-defendant and ordered

§ 10.22   *Preeclampsia and Eclampsia*   371

that a new trial be held on the grounds that the trial court had given conflicting jury instructions regarding which party must prove contributory negligence. The court noted that contributory negligence is an affirmative defense and thus the burden of proof rests with the defendant (*Kaspar v. Schack*, 1976).[54]

The cause of preeclampsia is not well understood. The condition occurs most often in patients with the following conditions:

1. Chronic cardiovascular renal disease
2. Multiple pregnancy
3. Primigravidity
4. Hydatidiform mole
5. Dietary deficiency
6. Diabetes mellitus[55]

When diagnosing preeclampsia, the physician must differentiate among several other conditions:

1. Chronic hypertensive vascular disease—Hypertension is transient in a patient with preeclampsia; if hypertension is present before pregnancy or if it continues for more than three months after delivery, the patient has chronic hypertensive vascular disease.[56]
2. Primary renal disease—Laboratory tests of urine specimens are necessary to distinguish between chronic renal disease and infection; pus or bacteria in the urine indicate a urinary infection.[57]
3. Convulsive disorders—Convulsions can be caused by several conditions, including epilepsy, infections, thromboembolism, and drug intoxication; these convulsive disorders can be readily distinguished from eclampsia because they are accompanied by other symptoms and usually do not coincide with edema and proteinuria.[58]

Good prenatal care is the most appropriate means of minimizing the incidence and effect of the condition. The physician should examine the patient at frequent intervals for weight, hypertension, proteinuria, and edema.[59] A physician may face a malpractice suit for failure to adequately test for these symptoms.

CASE ILLUSTRATION

The patient, in her eighth month of pregnancy, fell and injured her neck. Complaining of neck pain, the patient visited her regular physician. Various witnesses presented totally conflicting accounts of the patient's symptoms and appearance while at the physician's office. The physician administered an injection of Talwin to relieve the pain and spasm resulting from the patient's neck injury and conducted a general examination. The physician took the patient's blood pressure, which he found to be within normal limits; checked the fetus's heartbeat, which he found to be satisfactory; and analyzed the patient's urine by smearing a multipurpose urinalysis "dipstick" in the patient's vagina, which he found to be quite moist, a condition that is not unusual at that stage of pregnancy. The physician did not obtain a fresh urine sample, nor did he weigh the patient. The patient returned home and died later that evening. The patient's husband brought suit, alleging that the physician-defendant was negligent in failing to test for, diagnose, and treat preeclampsia. Specifically, the measures taken by the physician to analyze the patient's urine were claimed to be inadequate to determine the presence and amount of protein. Failure to adequately test resulted in failure to diagnose and treat preeclampsia. At trial, the husband-plaintiff submitted the coroner's report as evidence that the cause of the patient's death was eclampsia. Under the heading "Anatomical Diagnosis" the report stated: Acute cerebral edema—patchy atelectasis of lungs, congestion of liver, spleen, and kidneys. Intrauterine pregnancy (3rd Tri). Eclampsia (pending histological exam of tissue)." The autopsy report was also submitted. Under the heading "Anatomical Diagnosis" it stated:

"1. ACUTE CEREBRAL EDEMA
2. Patchy atelectasis of lungs
3. Congestion of liver, spleen, and kidneys
4. Intrauterine pregnancy (3rd Tri)
5. ECLAMPSIA (pending histological exam of tissue)"

In a section of the autopsy report entitled "Final Note," the following observation was made: "The histological findings in the tissue are consistent with eclampsia. The findings, however, are not diagnostic and are nonspecific."

The court noted that the coroner's report was based on information obtained by a clerical worker from conversations with the patient's family, who did not conduct the autopsy or participate in the medical aspects of the case in any way. Furthermore, the court observed that the eclampsia diagnosis was qualified by the same parenthetical statement in the reports, which raised questions as to its conclusiveness. Thus, the court held that the cause of death had not been conclusively proved by competent evidence to be eclampsia. Consequently, the court would not impose liability on the physician, because, without adequate proof that eclampsia caused the patient's death, the physician's failure to diagnose and treat the condition would not result in a legally compensable injury (*Couto v. Oms*, 1975).[60]

§ 10.22   *Preeclampsia and Eclampsia*   373

There are four major objectives in treating preeclampsia:

1. To prevent eclampsia
2. To reduce vasospasm
3. To avoid vascular accidents
4. To ensure delivery of a normal, live baby [61]

Patients with preeclampsia should be restricted to bed rest and their diets should be carefully monitored to allow for high protein and restricted salt intake. Sedatives may be used in mild cases. In more severe cases, magnesium sulfate may be used as an anticonvulsant. The decisive cure for preeclampsia and eclampsia is termination of pregnancy. If patients with preeclampsia do not respond to treatment within 24 to 48 hours, the baby must be delivered, regardless of the length of the pregnancy. Delivery may be brought about by induced labor or cesarean section.[62]

A physician may be subject to a suit for negligent treatment of preeclampsia and eclampsia. In one case, the physician was sued for negligent treatment when the eclamptic patient died after the physician had terminated the pregnancy and administered magnesium sulfate to control convulsions.

CASE ILLUSTRATION

The patient, pregnant with her second child, complained of headache, nausea, vomiting, and blurred vision. Upon examination, the physician determined that the patient had edema, elevated blood pressure, and thick brownish urine with a plus-three albumin level. The physician diagnosed preeclampsia, and the patient was admitted to the hospital. After being informed that the patient had not begun to convulse, the physician prescribed ten milliliters of magnesium sulfate. Before the magnesium sulfate was administered, the patient suffered her first convulsion. The physician then ordered two additional doses of magnesium sulfate. The patient lost consciousness. A second physician performed a cesarean section, delivering a stillborn baby girl. The patient's condition continued to deteriorate. Approximately one week later, an encephalogram indicated that the patient's brain had ceased to function. After life support systems were removed the patient died. The patient's husband sued the physician. The husband-plaintiff alleged that the physician-defendant was negligent in failing to diagnose in timely fashion the patient's condition, claiming that the patient had experienced symptoms of preeclampsia before the crisis that resulted in her death. Secondly, the plaintiff alleged that the physician-defendant was negligent in treating the patient's condition. The court dismissed the plaintiff's action on the ground that plaintiff failed to offer sufficient expert evidence on the issues of negligence and causation. On appeal, the court affirmed the dismissal, noting that "the plaintiff here must introduce expert testimony as to both the standard of care and the defendant doctor's departure from the standard." Further, "plaintiff's claims required expert testimony to show that [physician's] action or inaction was a direct cause of the decedent's death." The court noted that, without such expert testimony, the jury would have to speculate whether earlier diagnoses or different treatment would have effected a cure (*Smith v. Knowles*, 1979).[63]

§ 10.23 Fetal Condition

Liability may be imposed on the physician for the failure to recognize changes in the pregnant patient that indicate the need to assess the status of the fetus.

Basic Standard of Care: The American College of Obstetricians and Gynecologists has published guidelines governing the various methods available for determining and monitoring the condition of the fetus. Various forms of biochemical or biophysical monitoring may be required to determine the integrity of the fetal-placental unit in high-risk patients; these may be conducted in an ambulatory setting. When amniocentesis is performed in the third trimester, cesarean delivery capabilities should be readily available.[64] Facilities needed to monitor the status of the mother or the fetus will vary with the seriousness of the particular disease process, its known risk, and the care that the hospital is prepared to provide. Services may include ultrasonography, electronic monitoring of the fetal heartbeat, amniocentesis, and a special laboratory test to monitor maternal and fetal well-being. Ultrasonography should be available to all physicians providing care for obstetric patients either directly or on a referral basis. Medical supervision of this diagnostic service should be under the direction of a physician who has an interest in obstetrical diagnosis and complications. Technical personnel should be trained adequately in the obstetric application of ultrasound. Equipment for monitoring the fetal heartbeat should be available for such antenatal evaluation as nonstress and stress testing of the fetal-placental unit. Physicians using electronic fetal monitoring for antenatal surveillance must understand the indications, limitations, and interpretation of these tests. Amniocentesis should be available to establish fetal maturity or to measure the optical density of amniotic fluid. Amniocentesis should be performed only by a physician trained in the procedure. It is best done after the location of the placenta and the position of the fetus have been established by ultrasonography.[65]

Interpretation and Customary Practice: There are a number of reasonably accurate biochemical or biophysical tests for assessing fetal maturity and determining the condition of the fetus before labor, while the membranes are still intact. These tests may be conducted in an ambulatory setting and are of greatest value when intrauterine growth retardation is suspected (for example, in women with chronic hypertensive cardiovascular disease and cyanotic heart disease) or when the possibility of postmaturity exists. These tests may also be valuable in managing the pregnancies of diabetic patients or patients with other metabolic disorders that may affect fetal development.[66]

Among the tests for suspected growth retardation and for determining fetal condition are the following:[67]

1. Sonography—Biweekly sonographic measurement of the biparietal diameter of the fetal skull is indicated if growth retardation is suspected and if the patient suffers from chronic hypertensive cardiovascular disease. Failure of the head to grow, particulary when other signs of growth retardation exist, generally indicates the need to terminate the pregnancy in order to prevent intrauterine death. Transthoracic diameter and truncal measurements at the umbilicus provide correlative data.

2. Estriol excretion—Estriol production increases as the fetus grows and decreases when growth ceases. Concentrations of estriol in the mother's urine should be measured from about the thirtieth week of pregnancy in all women with diabetes or whenever growth retardation is suspected. Serial determinations are essential for accurate evaluation of fetal condition.

3. Fetal-maternal electronic monitoring—The oxytocin challenge test is designed to test the reaction of the fetus to uterine contractions. An oxytocin infusion is started, and the flow rate, as measured by an infusion pump, is increased until uterine contractions are occuring at three- to four-minute intervals. External recording devices monitor fetal heart rate and uterine contractions. No change in fetal heart rate should occur if placental function is normal. A nonstress, or fetal activity, test will also help in assessing fetal condition. The heart rate of the healthy fetus accelerates slightly whenever it moves. If no change in heart rate can be found when the fetus moves, it may be in jeopardy. A nonreactive fetal activity test should be followed by an oxytocin challenge test. Nonstress and oxytocin challenge tests are most appropriate in women suspected of having placental dysfunction or insufficiency, for example in women with chronic hypertensive cardiovascular disease or diabetes, and when growth retardation or postmaturity is suspected. The tests should be repeated weekly.

Tests most often used to determine fetal maturity and age include:

1. Amniotic fluid examination—This may be useful in determining fetal age because the number of orange-staining "fetal fat" cells in amniotic fluid increases as the fetus matures. When amniocentesis is performed in the third trimester, cesarean delivery capabilities should be readily available.

2. Creatinine—The infant is presumed to be mature when the concentration of creatinine in the amniotic fluid is higher than 2 milligrams per 100 milliliters.
3. Lecithin-sphingomyelin ratio—A high concentration of lecithin indicates fetal lung maturity. Consequently, if the ratio of lecithin to sphingomyelin is at least 2 to 1, the lung if probably mature, regardless of fetal size, and there is little likelihood that serious respiratory distress will develop. In diabetic patients, a lecithin-sphingomyelin ratio of 2.5, rather than 2.0, may be a better indicator of fetal maturity. This ratio is a more sensitive indicator of fetal viability than either creatinine concentration or the number of orange-staining cells in the amiotic fluid.
4. X-ray examination—The appearance of ossification centers can be used to estimate fetal age. At the thirty-sixth week of pregnancy, the distal femoral epiphysis is present in 80 percent or more of infants, and the proximal tibial epiphysis is present in 70 to 75 percent of infants at term. The presence of these ossification centers confirms the duration of pregnancy, but their absence does not preclude fetal maturity. Other indications of fetal maturity include well-developed cortical bone in the skull and long bones and a well-developed fat line, particularly when combined with good bony ossification and the presence of epiphysis. X-ray examination should be used only when other tests are inconclusive or unavailable.

The most accurate assessment of fetal maturity and condition can generally be made by using all available and appropriate tests rather than by relying on a single one.

The diagnosis of fetal death may be based on a number of indicators. Early in pregnancy, the most significant indicator of fetal death is cessation of uterine growth. When a pregnancy test that was positive becomes negative on two subsequent occasions and uterine growth has ceased, fetal death is likely though not certain. In later pregnancy, the first abnormal symptom noted by the mother is usually cessation of fetal movement. The uterus may fail to enlarge. Fetal heart tones or cardiac activity may no longer be detected, even with a Doppler device or ultrasound. The signs and symptoms of pregnancy may subside. An X ray of the fetus may show evidence of fetal death: overlapping skull bones, gas in the circulatory system, and abnormal posture. If X-ray findings are equivocal, further observation or examination should be performed. If amniocentesis reveals concentrated, dark brown fluid, this may be diagnostic of fetal death.[68]

Failure to recognize changing conditions in the pregnant woman as indications that steps should be taken to assess whether the status of the fetus has changed may result in lawsuit. The hurdle that a patient-plaintiff must overcome with such a suit is establishing causation; she must show that the physician's conduct caused the injury.

§ 10.23 *Fetal Condition* 377

CASE ILLUSTRATION

Approximately three months into the patient's pregnancy, she experienced abdominal pain, low-grade fever, and vaginal spotting. These symptoms persisted for a month before the patient began to miscarry and was hospitalized. During this period the patient had visited her obstetrician several times and complained of pain or a dull ache at a specific site in her abdomen. In the hospital, it was determined that the fetus was dead and heavily infected. An unsuccessful attempt was made to induce the completion of the miscarriage. It then became necessary to operate. The uterus could not be opened in the abdomen without spreading the infection, so a complete hysterectomy was performed. The patient sued the obstetrician, alleging that his negligent failure to diagnose the fetus's condition resulted in the loss of the patient's ability to have children and the pain and damages suffered during her final hospitalization. At trial, the obstetrician testified that, during her visits, the patient reported no pain other than abdominal cramping. He explained that there was a medical difference between cramping and constant pain and said that if he had been told of the latter he would have made further evaluation and, perhaps, required more tests. The court noted this discrepancy in each party's version of the facts. It based its decision, however, on the issue of causation: "Whatever could be decided as to negligence, there is no evidence tending to prove that [the patient's] ultimate adversity would probably have been avoided if a further evaluation or test had been pursued." Because the law requires the patient-plaintiff to prove the physician-defendant's negligence and its causal connection with the injuries suffered, which the patient had failed to do, the court exonerated the physician from liability (*Glenn v. Prestegord*, 1970).[69]

Because a diagnosis of fetal death usually causes the patient to react emotionally, the physician is well advised to be certain of the diagnosis. Even the mere suggestion may give rise to emotional distress. Whether such distress constitutes a legally compensable injury usually depends upon the nature of the physician's statements and whether physical repercussion accompanies emotional distress.

CASE ILLUSTRATION

A patient sued her physician for the emotional distress she suffered when he told her that he could not detect a fetal heartbeat. The physician made this statement after he had examined the patient during her fourth to fifth month of pregnancy. The physician asked the patient to return in a week for a further examination. The patient interpreted the information as a diagnosis that her baby was dead, and she consulted another obstetrician. The second obstetrician was also unable to detect a fetal heart tone but assured the patient that her pregnancy was normal, stating that in some pregnancies the tone is inaudible until after the fifth month. The patient brought suit against the first physician after she had given birth to a normal child. The court refused to impose liability on the physician for negligent misdiagnosis of fetal condition, finding that the evidence showed the physician had informed the patient only of his inability to detect heart tones; the patient, herself, had concluded that the fetus was dead (*Morgan v. Aetna Casualty & Surety Company,* 1960).[70]

Besides evaluating fetal maturity and development, the physician may find it necessary, depending on the history of the patient, to investigate the effect genetic factors may have on a particular fetus. Negligent treatment in this context may give rise to liability (see § 2.40, Birth-Related Causes of Action, and Chapter IX, Genetic Counseling).

Few cases have been brought involving misdiagnosis of fetal condition. Often fetal status must be evaluated with respect to management of parturition; when litigation results, fetal diagnosis is seen as part of the larger issue of parturition mismanagement (see Chapter XI, Parturition). Generally, the death of a fetus due to misdiagnosis can be pleaded as a cause of action. If the child is born alive but dies in consequence of a negligent misdiagnosis made during the fetal stage, the parents will have an action for wrongful death. A wrongful death action permits the survivors to recover the economic benefit which they might reasonably have expected to receive from the decedent in the form of support, services, or contributions during the remainder of his or her lifetime if death had not occured.[71] If the fetus dies before birth, most jurisdictions permit the action only if the fetus was viable at the time of death.[72] Some jurisdictions, however, deny the parents a wrongful death action even if viability was attained,[73] while others allow the action even if viability was not attained[74] (see § 2.50, Legal Status of the Fetus).

§ 10.24 Spontaneous Abortion

Liability may be imposed on the physician for the negligent treatment of a patient who threatens to miscarry, for the erroneous diagnosis of complete abortion, for the negligent misdiagnosis of pregnancy followed by spontaneous abortion, or for the negligent treatment after a miscarriage, including failure to use a particular technique or medical practice.

Basic Standard of Care: The American College of Obstetricians and Gynecologists has not published guidelines for the diagnosis and treatment of spontaneous abortion.

Interpretation and Customary Practice: Abortions that occur because of some maternal or ovular defect are termed spontaneous. Possible etiological factors include the following: defective germ plasm, defective nidation (implantation of the conceptus), maternal disease, abnormalities of reproductive organs, physical trauma, endocrine problems, psychogenic factors, and blood group incompatibilities. The reason for a particular spontaneous abortion cannot always be established because it is impossible to analyze all causative factors.[75]

The precipitating cause of spontaneous abortion is the death of the embryo or its failure to develop normally. The loss of the stimulus of the growing embryo results in a series of fairly characteristic stages that can usually be recognized clinically. These are classified as threatened, inevitable, incomplete, and complete.[76] Abortion may also be categorized as missed or habitual.

In threatened abortion, the previable fetus is in jeopardy, but the pregnancy continues. During early pregnancy, the patient will experience slight bleeding and possibly some cramping. There is no change in the cervix at this stage.[77] A physician may face legal liability for the negligent treatment of a patient who threatens to miscarry. For example, if a patient exhibits symptoms of a threatened abortion, the physician's failure to keep the patient hospitalized or to personally attend her may give rise to a negligence suit.

CASE ILLUSTRATION

The physician agreed to take responsibility for the patient's medical care during her pregnancy and childbirth. He had the patient hospitalized when she threatened to miscarry. After the patient had been in the hospital for ten days, the physician gave her instructions on self-care and conduct and permitted her to return home. That night the patient experienced additional pain and cramping. Advised of her condition, the physician did not go to the patient's house but gave instructions for her care over the telephone. Before the night was over, the patient had miscarried. She brought suit, contending that the physician was negligent in ordering her release from the hospital and in failing to attend her at home when informed of her symptoms. Although the patient presented expert testimony, the court found that none of it tended to support her allegations of negligence. The patient's failure to produce supporting expert testimony was, in the court's view, fatal to her case: "The question of just when and under what circumstances a physician treating a woman threatened with a miscarriage should keep her in the hospital or be at her side is not, in our opinion, one that can be answered on the basis of common knowledge." Thus concluding that the patient had failed to show that the physician's conduct was "negligent or inconsistent with the standard of care that would have been exercised by other physicians in similar circumstances," the court entered judgment for the physician (*Stokes v. Haynes,* 1968).[78]

Abortion is inevitable when two or more of the following are noted: (1) moderate effacement of the cervix, (2) cervical dilatation of more than two centimeters, (3) rupture of the membranes, (4) bleeding for longer than seven days, (5) persistence of cramps despite narcotics, and (6) signs of termination of pregnancy.[79]

In incomplete abortion, portions of the conceptus have already passed, but some placental tissue remains in the uterus. Bleeding and cramping continue until the remaining tissue is expelled or removed.[80] If the retained fragments are not expelled, they should be removed.[81]

In complete abortion, all the conceptus is expelled. Complete abortions are more common during the first six weeks.[82] A physician may be threatened with a malpractice suit for an erroneous diagnosis of complete abortion. However, the physician will not be liable if the only evidence of negligence is that a second physician later diagnosed and treated the patient for an incomplete abortion.

CASE ILLUSTRATION

The patient was admitted to the emergency room complaining of pain, cramps, and vaginal bleeding. The diagnosis was "threatened abortion"; bed rest was prescribed. Later that day, the patient went to a second hospital and was diagnosed as having had an incomplete abortion. The patient was transferred to a third hospital with the recommendation that she receive a D&C. The physician at the third hospital (the defendant in the suit) examined the patient, diagnosed a complete abortion, and discharged the patient. Two days later, the patient returned to the second hospital with vaginal bleeding. The diagnosis was again "incomplete abortion"; a D&C was performed four days later. The patient brought suit against the physician who diagnosed a complete abortion, alleging that the diagnosis was erroneous and that a D&C should have been performed at that time. The court held in favor of the physician-defendant because the patient-plaintiff failed to produce expert testimony that the physician's diagnosis and failure to order an immediate operation were incorrect actions (*Acosta v. City of New York*, 1971).[83]

In missed abortion, the fetus has been dead for at least one month but the conceptus has not been expelled. The symptoms of pregnancy disappear. The patient often experiences a brown vaginal discharge but there is usually no bleeding or cramping. The cervix will probably be closed and firmer than in normal pregnancy. The uterus becomes smaller and firmer; the adnexa are normal.[84]

The term "habitual abortion" is applied to the expulsion of a dead or nonviable fetus in three or more consecutive pregnancies. Habitual abortion can sometimes be prevented if a medical condition (such as hypothyroidism) is detected and can be treated before a pregnancy is initiated. Some cases of repeated second trimester abortion are caused by incompetent cervical os. Most of these cases can be prevented by surgical procedures that close the dilating cervix.[85]

A physician may be threatened with a lawsuit if, after a misdiagnosis of pregnancy, the patient suffers a spontaneous abortion. In one case, a patient who had been informed by her physician that she was not pregnant was later admitted to the hospital with a diagnosis of inevitable abortion. Although the court held against the patient, the physician was forced to introduce evidence showing that her initial diagnosis was not negligent and that her actions did not cause the impending abortion.

CASE ILLUSTRATION

The patient, who wanted to know if she was pregnant, went to the physician's office for a physical examination. After informing the patient that she was not pregnant, the physician diagnosed the patient's condition as menstrual irregularity. The physician prescribed the drug Synthroid as treatment for the patient's condition. Approximately two months later, the patient began to experience severe abdominal cramps. The patient was admitted to the hospital, and her condition was diagnosed by the attending physician as inevitable abortion. The next morning, the attending physician performed a D&C to ensure complete abortion. This physician noted later that the patient was six to seven weeks pregnant at the time of the abortion. The patient brought suit against the first physician, alleging that the physician-defendant negligently failed to diagnose the patient-plaintiff's pregnant condition and, as a result, prescribed the drug Synthroid, which caused the abortion. Secondly, the patient-plaintiff alleged that the physician-defendant was negligent in failing to instruct the patient to come in for further examinations, thus resulting in a failure to diagnose and prevent the abortion. The court affirmed a judgment for the physician-defendant, noting that there was ample evidence to support a finding that the patient was not pregnant at the time of her initial physical examination and that the drug would not have caused an abortion (*Schlesselman v. Gouge*, 1967).[86]

A physician who has misdiagnosed a patient's pregnancy will not be liable for injuries suffered in a spontaneous abortion if his negligent diagnosis was not the cause of the abortion. For example, if the physician performs surgery for a misdiagnosed uterine tumor on a pregnant patient, he will not be liable for a spontaneous abortion occurring three weeks later unless there is evidence that the operation probably caused the miscarriage.

CASE ILLUSTRATION

The physician made a physical examination of the patient and concluded that she suffered from a fibroid tumor of the uterus. The physician then performed an exploratory laparotomy and discovered that the patient did not have a tumor but was six to eight weeks pregnant. The patient recovered, returned home, and 22 days later suffered a miscarriage. The patient and her husband sued the physician for damages incurred because of the operation and for the wrongful death of the aborted child. The court concluded that there was insufficient evidence that the operation caused the miscarriage and thus held in favor of the physician-defendant on the wrongful death claim. The court stated that the patient-plaintiff had introduced "no medical testimony that the operation probably did cause the miscarriage, nor was there any evidence of any signs or symptoms of impending abortion between the time of the operation and the occurring of the miscarriage" (*Jarboe v. Harting*, 1965).[87]

The majority of spontaneous abortions are due to maldevelopment of the embryo and cannot be prevented. Once an abortion is classified as "inevitable," there is no way to reverse the process. If the uterus does not empty itself spontaneously, its contents should usually be removed surgically.

If the patient has suffered an incomplete abortion, the physician should take a complete history and perform physical and pelvic examinations. The examinations should include blood count, intracervical culture, and determination of antibiotic sensitivity in case of infection. The physician must procure blood for possible transfusion, and the uterus should be emptied as soon as possible.[88]

A physician may be confronted with legal liability for negligent treatment *after* a miscarriage. For example, a physician will be liable for negligently failing to remove placental material following a spontaneous abortion.

CASE ILLUSTRATION

The patient was admitted to the hospital by her regular physician after she complained of vaginal bleeding. At this time, the physician discovered that the patient was two to three months pregnant. Two days later, in her hospital bed, the patient suffered a spontaneous abortion and expelled a fetus. The physician examined her and began procedures to deliver the placenta. Because of the patient's condition, the physician decided he could not use physical methods. A few days later, the physician performed a D&C and determined that he removed 90 to 95 percent of the placental material. The patient continued to suffer pain and bleeding. A few months later, a second physician attempted another D&C. However, when the curet entered the patient, she began to hemorrhage and went into shock. Because of the danger to the patient's life, the second physician performed an abdominal hysterectomy and removed the uterus. The uterus contained necrotic and calcified placental material attached to its wall. This placental material was the apparent cause of the complaints that necessitated the removal of the uterus. The patient filed a malpractice suit against the first physician, alleging that his negligence in failing to remove the placental material resulted in her hysterectomy. Although the physician-defendant introduced expert testimony that his D&C procedure was in accordance with the standards employed in the locality, the court found that the physician-defendant negligently failed to remove the retained placenta. The court's decision was based on a finding that, if the physician was not negligent, the amount of placental material later found in the patient-plaintiff's uterus would not have existed (*Carpenter v. Gauthier*, 1972).[89]

A more recent case also indicates that a physician may be liable for negligence in failing to adequately remove all placental material after a miscarriage.

CASE ILLUSTRATION

The patient miscarried in the fifth month of her pregnancy, as she had done in five previous pregnancies. The physician removed placental material both manually and through suction curettage. During the five weeks following the miscarriage, the patient suffered hemorrhaging and fever. When the hemorrhaging became massive, the physician recommended a hysterectomy. The operation was performed by the physician's partner. The patient brought suit, contending that the physician negligently allowed placental material to remain in her uterus and that had he not done so the hysterectomy would not have been necessary. An expert witness for the patient stated that too much placental material had been left behind and that the physician had not met the applicable standard of care. The physician presented expert opinion that the patient's hemorrhaging was caused by placenta accreta and that the placenta could not have been removed through any "accepted medical procedures." Because the conflicting affidavits created a question as to whether the physician has been negligent, the court held that the patient's claim could go to trial (*Nelson v. Marrus*, 1977).[90]

Few cases have been concerned with which particular medical techniques or practices should or should not be followed by the reasonable physician in diagnosing and treating spontaneous abortions. One case, however, indicated that the standard of care *may* require the use of ring forceps to remove placental material following a missed abortion. Because the physician-defendant had not used ring forceps, but had instead performed a D&C, the court held that there was sufficient evidence of negligence for the case to go to trial.

CASE ILLUSTRATION

The physician determined that the patient had had a missed abortion. The physician performed a D&C and removed the lower parts of a macerated fetus. The placenta was not found. Two days later, the upper portion of the fetus was removed. Three weeks later, the patient developed additional bleeding. The patient contacted a second physician, who removed huge amounts of degenerated placental tissue. Because of continued bleeding, the second physician performed an abdominal hysterectomy and found a degenerative placental polyp in the uterus. The patient brought suit, alleging that the first physician mistreated her condition of missed abortion, thus causing the need for a hysterectomy. The physician-defendant's motion for summary judgment was denied because an expert witness's deposition stated that good medical practice would require the use of ring forceps rather than scraping to remove the fetal and placental material. Thus, the court found that the physician-defendant's use of the D&C might be considered negligence and could have been the proximate cause of the patient-plaintiff's hysterectomy (*Johnson v. Hunt*, 1975).[91]

§ 10.25 Administration of Drugs

Liability may be imposed on the physician who administers and prescribes drugs during pregnancy, if the physician fails to regard the manufacturer's warning, fails to examine the patient, fails to diagnose pregnancy before prescribing a drug, or fails to become familiar with a drug before prescribing it.

Basic Standard of Care: The American College of Obstetricians and Gynecologists has not published specific guidelines for the use of drugs during pregnancy. It has recognized, however, that certain therapeutic modalities may pose risks to the fetus and that it would be prudent to keep drug administration in pregnancy to a minimum.

Interpretation and Customary Practice: Although it is generally recognized that drugs administered during pregnancy can have teratogenic effects upon the fetus, many physicians still give too little thought to the possibilities of disturbing embryonic development when they prescribe medication for their pregnant patients. As a general rule, no medication, no matter how innocuous it is presumed to be, should be prescribed during pregnancy unless there is a specific indication for its use and unless the patient may be harmed if it is not used.[92] Women in our society take an average of 4.5 drugs during a pregnancy.[93]

§ *10.25* *Administration of Drugs* 385

While this complicates the determination of the medical cause of an individual deformity, the effects upon fetal development of some of the substances that are used during pregnancy are believed to be known. Physicians, therefore, should be familiar with these substances and their effects—both from a medical standpoint and with a view to understanding the legal ramifications of any injuries caused by the drugs they prescribe.

Physicians commonly obtain information about the potential teratogenic effects of a drug from the manufacturer, who is legally reponsible for warning the medical community of such effects (see § 2.70, Products Liability). The physician who deliberately disregards a manufacturer's warning in favor of his or her own supposed knowledge of the drug is guilty of malpractice.[94] So, too, is the physician who knows a drug is contraindicated for pregnancy but who fails to examine the patient or to diagnose her condition before prescribing the drug.[95] The physician who is simply unaware of information contained in available literature from the manufacturer, however, and who prescribes the drug for a patient known to be pregnant presents a less clear-cut case. As a general rule, however, the physician is responsible for knowing the information in the package insert (also contained in the Physician's Desk Reference) and may be held liable for failing to act consistently with that information.

CASE ILLUSTRATION

The patient, suffering from phlebitis, was hospitalized in October 1972. Her physician, who had earlier confirmed the patient's suspicions that she was pregnant, prescribed dicumarol, an anticoagulant. The plaintiff received dicumarol while in the hospital and later as an outpatient. Her child was born in April 1973 with severe and irreparable birth defects, including brain damage and partial paralysis.

The patient-plaintiff sued two hospitals and four physicians for medical malpractice and three pharmaceutical companies on theories of products liability, alleging that the birth defects resulted from bleeding in the fetal brain caused by her ingestion of dicumarol. The physicians claimed that they had not been adequately warned by the drug manufacturers of the dangers of dicumarol to pregnant women. The drug manufacturers claimed their package inserts provided adequate warning and that the physicians caused the harm to the plaintiff's child by disregarding the inserts and failing to consult available reference material on dicumarol before prescribing it.

At trial, the following facts were established: by 1963 it became generally accepted in the medical community that dicumarol crossed the placental barrier and therefore posed a serious risk to the fetus when given to a pregnant woman. Consequently, in 1964, defendant Eli Lilly and Company amended its package insert for dicumarol to include a "warning" that "when pregnant women are treated with this drug, fetal bleeding diathesis *may* occur and cause fetal death *in utero.*" In 1970, the National Academy of Sciences-National Research Council issued an efficacy report on dicumarol which strongly recommended that the risk of fetal hemorrhage be stressed and that heparin be considered the drug of choice whenever anticoagulation therapy is required for a pregnant patient. In response, Lilly again amended its package insert, this time stating "the drug is contraindicated for pregnant patients and for breastfeeding mothers" and recommending heparin for such patients. The statement of contraindication appeared in Lilly's package inserts at the time the plaintiff's cause of action arose. As an additional measure, Lilly for a time published information on dicumarol in the *Physician's Desk Reference*. From 1964 through 1966, Lilly's advertisement for dicumarol in the *Physician's Desk Reference* stated, among other things, that the drug "is probably contraindicated during pregnancy." In 1967, the contraindication was deleted and replaced by a "warning" concerning the possibility of fetal bleeding diathesis and fetal death in utero. The next year, however, Lilly inexplicably withdrew its *Reference* statement entirely. Hence, by the autumn of 1972, Lilly included a contraindication for pregnant women in its dicumarol package inserts but published no corresponding statement of any sort in the *Physician's Desk Reference* or any other reference work.

At an examination before the trial, the plaintiff's physician testified that when he prescribed the dicumarol he was unaware that it could cross the placental barrier and pose a threat to the fetus. He had never before prescribed the drug for a pregnant patient and had not read anything about the drug for the preceding five years. He did not consult the package insert or any other source of information on dicumarol before ordering it for the plaintiff.

Based upon the physician's testimony and upon the contents of its own package inserts, Lilly moved to dismiss the complaint. The lower court denied the motion, and the New York State Appellate Division affirmed. "[T]he physician upon whom the patient most directly relies may himself lack a complete knowledge of the potential hazards of each of the myriad of drugs at his disposal. Standards of competent medical care require the physician to obtain such knowledge before administering the drug, but he likewise must rely on others to provide the information in the first instance. This responsibility properly falls most heavily on the manufacturer, who stands in the best position to recognize and cure defects, and the law generally acknowledges the physician's right to rely on the drug manufacturer's representations concerning its own products." Noting that pharmacists often discard package inserts before physicians can read them, the court went on to hold that the manufacturer had not adequately warned the medical profession of the dangers of dicumarol. The physician's failure to search the literature for warnings was not an intervening cause of harm, because it was foreseeable to the manufacturer (*Baker v. St. Agnes Hospital*, 1979).[96]

Though the precautions a physician can take to protect the pregnant patient from drugs with potentially harmful effects upon the fetus are limited by the information available within the medical community, the physician should nevertheless make every effort to obtain such information before prescribing a drug for the pregnant patient.

In some cases, the drug industry itself may not be aware of the risks a particular product poses to pregnant women. If the industry does not then alert the medical community to these risks, physicians cannot possibly know of them and cannot be legally responsible for the harm that results when the product is prescribed. Such a case is now before the courts in many separate lawsuits involving DES (see § 2.70, Products Liability). More than 100 clear cell adenocarcinomas of the vagina and numerous instances of adenosis, cervical lesions, and transverse vaginal septa have been diagnosed in women between the ages of 14 and 25 whose mothers were treated with DES during the pregnancies that resulted in their births.[97] The lawsuits allege that the manufacturers of DES should be liable for (1) failing to test the drug adequately when preliminary reports indicated possible dangers when prescribed for pregnant women to prevent miscarriage, (2) suppressing such results in order to market the product for that purpose, and (3) failing to warn of the danger inherent in such use.[98] To date, most of the litigation is tied up in problems concerning the identity of the manufacturer of the particular DES the plaintiff's mother ingested and concerning a suitable theory of liability where the identity of the manufacturer is not known.[99] Almost uniformly, the defendants in these cases are the manufacturers themselves, not the physicians who prescribed the drug. Where pregnant patients were given DES without their knowledge, however, as part of a university study to determine the value of DES in preventing miscarriages, those who administered the drug have been found guilty of battery for not having obtained the patients' informed consent (see § 1.33, Consent and Informed Consent). In the absence of physical injury, patients' claims for mental anxiety over the dangers to their daughters' health have not been upheld.[100]

Many obstetrical patients regularly receive a birth control pill as a daily contraceptive. This medication is contraindicated during pregnancy. Consequently, the patient under such a regimen should be informed of its hazards and counseled as to the proper procedure for its discontinuance if she desires to become pregnant. Lawsuits have been brought where oral contraceptives have been alleged to have a teratogenic effect upon the patient's offspring (see § 8.10, Oral Contraceptives).

§ 10.26 Substance Abuse

Liability may be imposed on the physician for the negligent failure to diagnose and treat alcohol or drug abuse in a pregnant patient or the failure to refer the patient for appropriate treatment.

Basic Standard of Care: Alcohol and drug abuse in pregnant women pose problems for both the obstetrician and the neonatologist. Although a wide variety of drugs may be used, including sedative-hypnotics, tranquilizers, and illicit drugs, the American College of Obstetricians and Gynecologists has focused its greatest attention upon the abuse of heroin, with its risk of potentially severe withdrawal phenomena in the newborn.

The first concern is the identification of the patient as an addict and the identification of what drugs are being used, including an estimate of the doses employed. In the sufficiently motivated patient, detoxification may be attempted, preferably in a residential program or controlled environment because of the high rate of recidivism during pregnancy. Where detoxification is not feasible, a methadone maintenance program may be of benefit.

The second problem is to identify medical problems associated with addiction. Viral hepatitis is common in intravenous drug abusers, and addicts account for 50 percent of all cases of tetanus. Bacterial endocarditis, thrombophlebitis, and pulmonary infections are also commonly associated with drug abuse. Serologic evidence of syphilis occurs in 15 to 20 percent of addicted patients, and 30 percent will have hemoglobins less than 10 grams during pregnancy.

Antepartum hospital care for counseling, psychiatric evaluation, treatment of medical problems, and detoxification is recommended, as are weekly visits to a special prenatal clinic for addicts, if available. Urine testing for drugs should be done on all patients suspected of using drugs.

Obstetrical complications may be associated with narcotic abuse. Premature labor occurs in one-third of such pregnancies. Low birth weight occurs in half of the babies of addicted mothers and may contribute to the higher incidence of breech presentations. Toxemia occurs with a higher than expected frequency and the incidence increases with lack of prenatal care. Labor is likely to be short: Presumably the fear of a long labor without heroin leads addicts to wait until the last possible moment to leave home, and they take a last dose just before leaving. This behavior may result in a precipitous delivery or even a home delivery.

In addition to low birth weights, infants may be addicted with symptoms of narcotism or narcotic withdrawal. Neonatal morbidity is markedly increased, and mortality is approximately three to five percent. Deaths are related to prematurity, respiratory distress syndrome, and withdrawal.

Although not specifically addressed by ACOG, the pregnancies of alcoholics and other substance abusers can be managed using similar principles.[101]

§ 10.26

Interpretation and Customary Practice: Alcohol and drug abuse by pregnant women is receiving increased attention within the medical profession. The Department of the Treasury and DHHS have recently met with representatives of several medical societies to discuss setting up a program of clinical research and public and professional education aimed at alerting both patients and health professionals about the dangers alcohol represents to adults and their offspring.[102] Gynecologists-obstetricians should be able to recognize the basic symptoms of both alcohol and drug abuse and should be aware of the deleterious effects such abuse may have on pregnant women and their unborn children.

Alcoholism: "Alcoholism" denotes addiction to alcohol. As defined by the National Council on Alcoholism, it is a chronic, progressive, relapsing disease characterized by the development of chronic tolerance to alcohol, a withdrawal syndrome on cessation of its ingestion, or various disorders including anorexia, diarrhea, weight loss, and personality changes. A direct connection exists between alcoholism and organ and tissue damage, such a peripheral neuropathy, fatty deterioration of the liver, and mental deterioration. Abstinence is essential for recovery from the disease.[103]

Physicians should be alert for the signs and symptoms of alcoholism in their female patients. Clues to the diagnosis include the following:

1. Unexplained bruises, particularly on the shins, from stumbling around
2. Unexplained fractures
3. Signs of withdrawal, ranging from tremors to a lacerated tongue (the result of an unremembered convulsion)
4. Marital problems
5. Problems with children
6. Frequent loss of job
7. Hypertension
8. Tachycardia
9. Arrhythmias
10. Anemia

The comments of a spouse or a child may arouse suspicions. The patient's regular requests for excuses for absences from work when no illness has been attended to by the physician may also point to a diagnosis of alcoholism.[104] A test for alcohol in the blood may be useful to corroborate suspected alcoholism.

The AMA has published the following guidelines on the diagnosis, treatment, and referral of alcoholic patients.[105]

1. Recognize as early as possible alcohol-caused dysfunction in the biological, psychological, and social areas.

2. Be aware of those medical complications as well as symptoms and syndromes by which alcoholism is commonly presented.
3. Ensure that any complete health examination includes an in-depth history of alcohol and other drug use.
4. Evaluate patient requirements and community resources so that an adequate level of care can be prescribed, with patient needs matched to appropriate resources.
5. If there are medical needs, including severe withdrawal, refer patient to a resource that provides adequate medical care.

While an occasional cocktail *may* cause no ill effect, clinical research has demonstrated that excessive drinking by an expectant mother has devastating and irreversible effects on the fetus. Alcohol is harmful to the fetus's rapidly developing tissues and severely taxes the mother's excretory system. In addition, alcohol may engender a false sense of security and cause the mother to become careless.

Between one-third and one-half of all children born of alcoholic women suffer from fetal alcohol syndrome. There is an unusually high perinatal mortality, and the intellectual capacity of many of those who survive is stunted for life. These children may also exhibit an identifiable pattern of craniofacial, limb, and cardiovascular defects associated with prenatal and postnatal growth retardation. Many of these problems do not become evident until the child is two to three years old. There is no known treatment for these children.[106]

A few cases of the syndrome of acute withdrawal from alcohol (delirium tremens) have been described in the newborn infants of alcoholic mothers. The affected newborn is depressed at birth but soon becomes extremely hyperactive, with sweating, tremors, and episodes of generalized twitching of the face and extremities. The mother is also likely to suffer delirium tremens after delivery.[107]

Treatment of an alcholic mother consists of slow withdrawal of alcohol and its replacement with paraldehyde, phenothiazines, or chlordiazepoxide. Delivery may be accomplished without additional anesthesia if the parturient is acutely alcoholic.

Drug Abuse: Marijuana, or cannabis, a drug of uncertain physiological effects, is the illicit drug most commonly used by American women. It is surprising, then, that aside from occasional case reports no systematic human studies on the teratogenic effects of marijuana have been carried out.[108] Most animal studies performed have shown no teratogenic effects; and studies with microorganisms, rodents, and man have failed to detect any increase in rates of mutation.[109] The National Institute on Drug Abuse concedes that marijuana has not been shown to have serious deleterious effects on either the fetus or the mother during pregnancy or on the newborn after birth.[110]

Despite the lack of adverse findings, the institute cautions against using marijuana when pregnant. Tetrahydrocannabinol (THC), the active principle of cannabis, and its metabolites cross the placental barrier, although there is evidence that the transfer is limited somewhat by placental interference.[111] THC is known to depress the testosterone level of men. It has been hypothesized that lowering the testosterone level of the male fetus around the eighth to tenth week of gestation might interfere with the differentiation of the urogenital system.[112] There is as yet no evidence that this actually occurs, but the drug abuse institute believes the use of marijuana by pregnant women to be especially unwise since the implications of its use in humans have not been adequately explored.[113]

Even though used by comparatively few women, "hard" drugs such as opium derivatives, amphetamines, and barbiturates remain a major problem and pose a serious threat to both women and their unborn children. The problem is exacerbated by the fact that drug users often do not seek prenatal care, and, if they do, they are unlikely to volunteer information regarding their drug use. Needle scars may be the first clue to a patient's addiction to opiates.[114]

Women who take hard drugs expose themselves and their offspring to a variety of risks: accidental overdose is common; the suicide rate of drug addicts is greatly in excess of that of the general population; and LSD (lysergic acid diethylamide) has been shown to significantly increase the risk of spontaneous abortion.[115] Faulty injection techniques may lead to local infection, septicemia, or infectious hepatitis. Operating on persons who inject drugs exposes the operator to the risk of contracting infectious hepatitis as well.[116]

Heroin addicts expose their offspring to a variety of serious risks. One study found the risks of the following complications of pregnancy to be increased two to six times among pregnant women who used heroin: low birth weight (less than 2,500 grams, or 5.5 pounds) caused by prematurity, growth retardation, or both; pregnancy-induced hypertension; bleeding in late pregnancy; malpresentations; and puerperal morbidity. Accelerated fetal lung maturation, manifested by a high lecithin-sphingomyelin ratio in the amniotic fluid and by a low incidence of idiopathic respiratory distress in the newborn, is also characteristic of pregnancies complicated by maternal heroin addition.[117]

Sometimes it is possible to capitalize on the advent of pregnancy to persuade the addict to undergo drug withdrawal in the hospital. If this is not done, more than one-half of newborn infants of heroin addicts will develop withdrawal symptoms. Without treatment, an appreciable number of these infants will die. The newborn infant must be closely watched during the first week of life for irritability, convulsions, nasal congestion, vomiting, diarrhea, tachypnea, and fever. Treatment has included paregoric, phenobarbital, and chlorpromazine. Therapy is slowly withdrawn but is reinstituted if symptoms recur. Treatment may be required for many days to weeks.[118]

Methadone treatment programs have commonly included pregnant women. The newborn infant of the methadone-treated mother is very likely to demonstrate similar withdrawal symptoms.

Multiple addictions may exist, and these can complicate the clinical picture. Approximately 25 percent of heroin addicts and many amphetamine and alcohol addicts also use barbiturates or meprobamate. Other combinations of drugs have been encountered with less frequency. The possibility of multiple addiction must be considered when unusual withdrawal symptoms are noted. When treating these patients, the physician may withdraw the addictive drugs simultaneously or consecutively but care must be taken to treat each withdrawal appropriately; ordinarily, opiate addiction is treated first, followed by barbiturate addiction.[119]

Seizures may follow the sudden withdrawal of drugs that depress the central nervous system, for example anticonvulsants, barbiturates, alcohol, and meprobamate. Such withdrawal seizures are most frequent in patients who sharply reduce the amount of anticonvulsant medication without medical supervision.[120]

Liability: The potential liability of an obstetrician-gynecologist for the negligent diagnosis or treatment of a patient addicted to alcohol or drugs is rarely discussed in reported case law. However, the obstetrician-gynecologist who undertakes the care of such a patient will be held to the standard of care applied to other phases of his or her practice; the physician must exercise that degree of care which would be exercised by a reasonable practitioner operating under the same or similar circumstances (see § 1.32, Standard of Care). Failure to exercise such care may give rise to liability.

Normally, a physician will not be liable for failing to diagnose and treat a condition that the patient does not disclose or attempts to conceal. The doctrines of contributory negligence or comparative negligence are available to physicians as affirmative defenses to malpractice charges (see Chapter III, Defenses). However, if an addiction is obvious, the patient's failure to disclose or attempt to conceal it may not relieve the physician of a duty to treat the addiction. Whether the physician may be liable to the fetus is an unanswered question (see § 2.50, Legal Status of the Fetus).

Further, in other situations, the law has recognized a physician's duty of referral. If a patient addicted to alcohol or drugs entrusts her general physical well-being to an obstetrician-gynecologist and the obstetrician-gynecologist realizes that he or she does not have the skills or resources to treat the patient's condition, it may constitute negligent practice not to refer the patient to some other practitioner or facility capable of providing her with adequate treatment.

§ 10.30 ABORTION

Liability may be imposed on a physician for the negligent performance of an abortion, including the failure to successfully terminate the pregnancy, thereby causing injury to the woman, or for abandoning a woman or failing to perform an abortion despite knowledge that continued pregnancy would be dangerous to the woman's life.

§ *10.30*   *Abortion*

Basic Standard of Care: The American College of Obstetricians and Gynecologists has stated that in the event of an unwanted pregnancy, the patient should be counseled about her options of continuing the pregnancy to term and keeping the infant, offering it for legal adoption, or abortion. If the patient elects abortion, she should be counseled for future reference that abortion is not recommended as a primary method of family planning. When the termination of a pregnancy is recommended by the physician for medical or psychiatric indications, counseling may be appropriate.[121] Ambulatory care facilities providing abortion facilities should meet the same standards of care as those recommended for other surgical procedures performed in the physician's office and outpatient clinic or the freestanding and hospital-based ambulatory care setting. Physicians performing abortions in their offices should provide for prompt emergency treatment or hospitalization in the event of an unanticipated complication. In general, abortions in the physician's office or outpatient clinic should be restricted to 14 weeks from the last day of the menstrual period. This time limit may be extended to 18 weeks from the last menstrual period if the abortion is performed in a hospital-based or freestanding ambulatory surgical facility. Determination of Rh sensitivity should be made, as well as the usual and customary history, physical examination, and laboratory procedures. If fetal parts are not identified with certainty, the tissue specimen should be sent for further pathologic examination and the patient must be alerted to the possibility of an ectopic pregnancy.[122] If definitive embryonic or fetal parts can be identified, the physician should record a description of the gross products. Under these circumstances, tissue need not be submitted to a pathologist for examination. However, unless definitive embryonic or fetal parts can be identified, the products of elective abortions must be submitted to a pathologist for gross and miscroscopic examination.[123]

Interpretation and Customary Practice: Induced abortion is the intentional termination of pregnancy in a manner designed to assure that the fetus or embryo will not survive. In 1973, the U.S. Supreme Court ruled that laws restricting the availability of abortions were invalid because they placed an unconstitutional burden on the individual's right to privacy. The Court held that states cannot interfere with a woman's decision to have an abortion during the first trimester of pregnancy. During the second trimester, states may regulate the abortion procedure in ways that are reasonably related to maternal health. In the third trimester, the state has an interest in the viable fetus and may regulate and even proscribe abortions, except those necessary to preserve the life and health of the mother.[124]

Induced abortions may be performed either because of the woman's personal decision to terminate her pregnancy (elective abortion) or because of certain medical indications (therapeutic abortion). Physicians should recommend therapeutic abortion when the pregnancy adds a significant risk of death for the mother or if there is great risk of death or serious malformation of the fetus. The most common maternal medical conditions indicating therapeutic abortion are hypertensive cardiovascular disease, congenital or rheumatic heart disease, chronic kidney disease, severe diabetes mellitus, and psychiatric disorders. The most common fetal indications include a variety of congenital anomalies or metabolic disorders, maternal rubella, and Rh isoimmunization.[125]

During the first trimester, the abortion may be performed by suction curettage. The uterus is evacuated by dilatation of the cervix with instruments or a hydrophilic Laminaria tent and removal of the conceptus with a suction cannula. In addition, many physicians will use light instrumental curettage. Suction is preferable to surgical curettage because it empties the uterus more rapidly, reduces the incidence of uterine perforation, and minimizes blood loss. The physician must ascertain the size and position of the uterus and the volume of its contents in order to avoid injury to the mother. Abortions performed in early pregnancy by suction curettage have a very low failure rate; the rate of infection or excessive bleeding is under two percent, and the rate of uterine perforation is under one percent. The mortality rate for legal abortions during the first 12 weeks is less than two per 100,000 patients. If suction curettage equipment is not available, surgical curettage can be used for first trimester abortions. Surgical curettage is performed as a standard D&C. When surgical curettage is used, blood loss, duration of surgery, and the likelihood of cervical or uterine damage are increased.[126]

A physician may be liable for an unsuccessful abortion if the patient can show that the physician departed from customary procedure in performing the abortion. For example, a physician will not be liable for failing to use a sharp curet after having used a suction device if prevailing practice does not require that both procedures be performed.

CASE ILLUSTRATION

The physician performed an abortion that failed to terminate the patient's pregnancy. The patient gave birth to a normal, healthy baby and then brought a malpractice action against the physician, alleging that he was negligent in failing to use a sharp curet after suction curettage (which would have been a departure from his normal practice). All the expert witnesses testified that use of either the suction method or the sharp curet was in accordance with customary practice and that both procedures were not required. The court found that the physician-defendant was not negligent. Further, the court noted that there was no evidence establishing that use of the curet would have increased the likelihood of success (*Koehler v. Schwartz*, 1979).[127]

During the second trimester, the method of abortion is determined by the duration of the pregnancy and the size of the uterus. From the twelfth through the sixteenth weeks of pregnancy, an experienced operator can perform the abortion by dilating the cervix and evacuating the contents of the uterus. Later in the second trimester, abortion can be accomplished by injecting prostaglandins, saline solutions, or urea solutions into the amniotic cavity. The principal complications associated with prostaglandin inductions are uterine or cervical tears and retained placenta. The most significant complications associated with intra-amniotic saline injections are infusion into the maternal bloodstream (producing salt intoxication) and the development of disseminated intravascular coagulation. Abortion during the second trimester may also be accomplished by abdominal hysterectomy. Because of increased morbidity, abdominal hysterectomy should only be used if other methods are inappropriate.[128]

Care of the patient after an abortion depends on the method of abortion, the amount of blood lost, and the presence (or not) of infection. Patients who receive uncomplicated elective abortions with little blood loss can be discharged a few hours after the uterus is evacuated. Patients who experience more complications should remain in the hospital. After discharge, the patient should be instructed to report any fever or unusual bleeding and to avoid sexual intercourse or the use of tampons or douches for one week. The physician should examine the patient after the abortion to rule out endo- and parametritis, salpingitis, failure of involution, or continued uterine growth.[129]

A physician will not be legally liable for an injury caused by the abortion procedure if the injury is one that could occur even when reasonable care is exercised. For example, in a case where a patient's uterus was perforated during an abortion, the physician was not held negligent because expert testimony established that perforation could occur despite the exercise of reasonable care.

CASE ILLUSTRATION

The physician performed an abortion on a woman who was six to eight weeks pregnant. There were no complications during the course of the abortion, and the woman drove herself home 90 minutes later. She received printed instructions upon leaving the clinic. By the time she arrived at home, she was not feeling well and was bleeding fairly heavily. The patient phoned the physician, who prescribed Methergine to reduce bleeding. The patient promptly filled the prescription and took the medication; the bleeding was reduced. Seven days after the abortion, the patient went on vacation. During her flight she began to bleed profusely and was taken to a hospital upon arrival at her destination. She had lost a lot of blood and was given a transfusion. The physicians at the hospital performed exploratory surgery and found a large hematoma in her peritoneum. A hysterectomy was performed. The patient brought suit against the physician who performed the abortion. At trial, the physician who performed the hysterectomy testified that there was a perforation in the uterus which caused the bleeding. Most of the physicians who testified felt that this was the underlying cause of the patient's problem. The expert witnesses agreed that "perforation of the uterus does occur in the process of abortion . . . despite the exercise of reasonable care on the part of the physician" because the insertion of instruments is a blind procedure and the anatomical makeup of some women could make the uterus more susceptible to tearing. Thus, the court concluded, the physician-defendant avoided a malpractice conviction.

The court also rejected the patient-plaintiff's claim that she had not given valid consent to the abortion because she was not informed of the risk of perforation. The court refused to apply the informed consent doctrine because the patient-plaintiff failed to show that she would have foregone the abortion if she had known of the risk. Finally, the patient-plaintiff claimed that the instruction sheets given her when she left the abortion clinic were misleading. The court held that the documents were part of the postoperative care and that the physician-defendant would be liable if they were misleading and caused subsequent injury. The court stated that, although the documents were poorly written, there was no evidence that the poor quality of the documents had caused the injury. The court also noted that the patient-plaintiff would have had the same problems if she had not taken a vacation (*Reynier v. Delta Women's Clinic, Inc.* 1978).[130]

A physician who abandons a woman and refuses to perform an abortion knowing that the pregnancy endangers her life may be held liable for her injuries if there is sufficient proof of a causal connection between the abandonment and the injury.[131]

The physician may be under a duty to determine whether the abortion procedure has been successfully completed. Thus, if a physician who has reason to suspect that an abortion has failed neglects to conduct tests or examinations necessary to confirm termination (or nontermination) of pregnancy, he or she may face liability.

CASE ILLUSTRATION

On June 10, 1969, the patient visited a physician, a specialist in obstetrics and gynecology, who confirmed her pregnancy. Because the patient suffered emotional problems, the physician recommended a therapeutic abortion. The abortion was performed on July 8. Approximately two days after the abortion, the physician received the pathology report, which indicated that gross examination of the material removed from the patient's uterus revealed "placental tissue." Microscopic examination showed no placental tissue, however, and the pathologist concluded that the specimen was

§ 10.30   Abortion

"decidua" (the inner lining of the uterus). This diagnosis indicates an unsuccessful abortion. After the abortion, the patient moved out of town. On or about August 8, the patient went to another physician for a checkup and for birth control pills. This physician told her that he thought she was pregnant, and a urine test confirmed the diagnosis. The patient then phoned a third physician (her old family doctor) and told him of the abortion and the result of the new pregnancy test. The third physician contacted the physician who had performed the abortion and learned of the pathologist's report. The third physician contacted the patient and stated that she had been completely aborted and explained that the affirmative pregnancy test could be due to the fact that her "body chemistry" had not returned to normal. This third physician prescribed birth control pills, Enovid-E, to regulate the patient's menstrual period. The patient took the pills, beginning August 19, for 20 days. After discontinuing the pills, the patient did not have a menstrual period. She visited the third physician, who confirmed that she was pregnant. The patient visited a fourth physician, who examined her on September 30 and concluded that she was 23 to 24 weeks pregnant. At this point, abortion was no longer advisable, because the legal deadline had passed and because it was medically unsafe. Abortion would have been possible on August 11, when the second physician diagnosed pregnancy. The patient gave birth to a normal baby boy and brought suit against the first physician (the one who performed the abortion) and the third physician (the one who advised the patient that her pregnancy test was due to "body chemistry" and prescribed birth control pills). The court ruled that the patient-plaintiff had produced enough evidence to go to trial against the first physician. In reviewing the evidence against the first physician, the court stated:

> In the opinion of plaintiff's expert, the diagnosis of "decidua" by the pathologist at least suggested the possibility that the abortion had not been successful. [The physician-defendant] did not agree with the diagnosis, believing that the abortion had been successfully completed. He ordered no further study of the tissue, made no effort to communicate with [the patient-plaintiff], and even after learning . . . that [another] doctor had found [the patient-plaintiff] to be pregnant, he persisted in his belief that his treatment of [the patient-plaintiff] had accomplished the desired objective. These facts, among others, raised questions which required resolution by the jury.

The court also ruled that the question of the third physician's negligence should be submitted to the jury and that expert testimony was not needed to resolve the issue. The court held that, if the patient-plaintiff received a verdict in her favor, she could recover ordinary tort damages, presumably including the cost of raising and educating the child (*Stills v. Gratton*, 1976).[132]

The extent of a physician's liability for negligent failure to abort is an unsettled issue. Some courts will allow recovery of the costs and expenses of raising the child.[133] Others allow the patient to recover damages only for medical and other costs associated with the unwanted pregnancy and for any personal injury suffered as a result of the pregnancy.[134]

In a jurisdiction that allows recovery of the costs of raising the child, a physician faces potentially huge liability. For example, one court allowed an action for expenses for the care and treatment of a child who suffered from a crippling disease.

CASE ILLUSTRATION

The father and his two children were afflicted with neurofibromatosis. The couple decided to limit the size of their family because they were afraid future children would also suffer from the disease. The father had a vasectomy. The operation was unsuccessful, and the mother became pregnant. The mother then sought an abortion. The abortion was unsuccessful. The physicians continued to assure the couple that the pregnancy had been terminated, even though the mother felt the pregnancy was continuing. She delivered a female baby who suffered from neurofibromatosis. The court ruled that the parents could bring suit against the physicians to recover all the pecuniary expenses they had borne and would bear in the future for the care and treatment of the child (*Speck v. Finegold*, 1979).[135]

Before the decision in *Roe v. Wade*[136] eased the restrictions against abortions, most states had laws making abortion a criminal offense. The courts were in disagreement as to whether a woman who had procured an illegal abortion could sue the physician for negligence in performing the abortion. Some courts barred the action on the theory that the woman was an accomplice or had voluntarily participated in the illegal act. Other courts allowed such actions, either because the woman's participation did not contribute to her injuries[137] or because there was a lack of adequate consent.[138] In a recent case based on a statute in effect before *Roe v. Wade,* a New York court refused to allow a woman's suit for injuries suffered during an abortion where both the physician and the patient were guilty of violating the criminal abortion statute. The court stated that the patient-plaintiff, "having participated in an illegal act, may not profit therefrom."[139]

§ 10.40 SURROGATE PARENTING

Although no appellate decisions reporting on medical malpractice actions stemming from surrogate parenting exist as of this writing, it is foreseeable that medical malpractice actions may be brought against physicians as a result of surrogate parenting.

§ *10.40* Surrogate Parenting

The American College of Obstetricians and Gynecologists recognizes that there is current interest in the reproductive alternative known as surrogate motherhood. Accordingly, the College has issued a Statement of Policy on the subject and identified ethical issues in surrogate motherhood. These are presented in Appendix E, Ethical Issues of Surrogate Motherhood.

NOTES

1. R. Benson, Handbook of Obstetrics and Gynecology 37, 38 (6th ed. 1977); K. Niswander, Obstetrics 61, 62 (1976); D. Reid, A Textbook of Obstetrics 218–22 (1962); E. Taylor, Beck's Obstetrical Practice 117 (1971); R. Willson & E. Carrington, Obstetrics and Gynecology 248 (6th ed. 1979).
2. R. Benson, *supra* note 1, at 38–42; K. Niswander, *supra* note 1, at 62–65; E. Taylor, *supra* note 1, at 118–21; R. Willson & E. Carrington, *supra* note 1, at 248–50.
3. K. Niswander, *supra* note 1, at 65–68; D. Reid, *supra* note 1, at 222–24; E. Taylor, *supra* note 1, at 121–23; R. Willson & E. Carrington, *supra* note 1, at 26–28.
4. D. Reid, *supra* note 1, at 222; R. Willson & E. Carrington, *supra* note 1, at 29.
5. Crovella v. Cochrane, 102 So.2d 307 (Fla. App. 1958).
6. Hoglin v. Brown, 4 Wash. App. 366, 481 P.2d 458 (1971).
7. *Id.*
8. Price v. Neyland, 320 F.2d 674 (D.C. Cir. 1963).
9. E. Taylor, *supra* note 1, at 126; R. Willson & E. Carrington, *supra* note 1, at 251, 252.
10. E. Taylor, *supra* note 1, at 125.
11. Stephenson v. Kaiser Found. Hosp., 203 Cal. App. 2d 631, 21 Cal. Rptr. 646 (1962).
12. Kleinman v. Armour, 12 Ariz. App. 383, 470 P.2d 703 (1970).
13. Jarboe v. Harting, 397 S.W.2d 775 (Ky. App. 1965).
14. Hirsh, *Routine Pregnancy Testing: Is It a Standard of Care?*, 73 S. Med. J. 1365 (1980).
15. Brish, *Routine Pregnancy Testing Is a Must*, 1 Lab '79 10 (1979).
16. *When a Hospital Is Blind to Pregnancy*, 19 Med. Tribune 27 (1978).
17. Hirsh, *supra* note 14.
18. *See* Gridley v. Johnson, 476 S.W.2d 475 (Mo. 1972).
19. *Id.*
20. Deutsch v. Shein, 597 S.W.2d 141 (Ky. 1980).
21. *See* Salinetro v. Nystrom, 341 So.2d 1059 (Fla. App. 1977).
22. Cox v. Dela Cruz, 406 A.2d 620 (Me. 1979).
23. Clapham v. Yanga, 102 Mich. App. 47, 300 N.W.2d 727 (1981).
24. Ziemba v. Sternberg, 45 A.D.2d 230, 357 N.Y.S.2d 265 (1974).
25. Rieck v. Medical Protective Co., 64 Wis.2d 514, 219 N.W.2d 242 (1974).
26. R. Benson, *supra* note 1, at 654.
27. R. Willson & E. Carrington, *supra* note 1, at 207.
28. K. Niswander, *supra* note 1, at 189, 190; R. Willson & E. Carrington, *supra* note 1, at 208.
29. May, Miller, & Greiss, *Maternal Deaths from Ectopic Pregnancy in the South Atlantic Region, 1960 through 1976*, 132 Am. J. Obstet. Gynecol. 140–47 (1978); Breen, *A 21-Year Survey of 654 Ectopic Pregnancies*, 106 Am. J. Obstet. Gynecol. 1004–19 (1970); Powers, *Ectopic Pregnancy: A Five-Year Experience*, 73 S. Med. J. 1012 (1980).
30. R. Benson, *supra* note 1, at 657.

31. Spooner v. Austin, 153 Conn. 1, 213 A.2d 310 (1965).
32. Pugh v. Swiontek, 115 Ill. App. 2d 26, 253 N.E.2d 3 (1969).
33. Smith v. Shankman, 208 Cal. App. 2d 177, 25 Cal. Rptr. 195 (1962).
34. American College of Obstetricians and Gynecologists, Standards for Obstetric/Gynecologic Services 9–14 (5th ed. 1982).
35. American College of Obstetricians and Gynecologists, Technical Bulletin No. 62 (July 1981).
36. R. Benson, *supra* note 1, at 816–17.
37. R. Willson & E. Carrington, *supra* note 1, at 266.
38. *Id.* at 266–67.
39. American College of Obstetricians and Gynecologists, *supra* note 35.
40. R. Willson & E. Carrington, *supra* note 1, at 266.
41. Becker v. Schwartz, 46 N.Y.2d 401, 413 N.Y.S.2d 895, 386 N.E.2d 807 (1978).
42. Gleitman v. Cosgrove, 49 N.J. 22, 227 A.2d 689 (1967).
43. Jacobs v. Thiemer, 519 S.W.2d 846 (Tex. 1975); Dumer v. St. Michael's Hosp., 69 Wis.2d 766, 233 N.W.2d 372 (1975).
44. Dumer v. St. Michael's Hosp., *supra* note 43.
45. Becker v. Schwartz, *supra* note 41; Gleitman v. Cosgrove, *supra* note 42; *see also*, Strohmaier v. Associates in Obstetrics & Gynecology, 122 Mich. App. 116 (1983).
46. Becker v. Schwartz, *supra* note 41.
47. R. Willson & E. Carrington, *supra* note 1, at 355.
48. R. Benson, *supra* note 1, at 693.
49. MacGillvray & Campbell, *The Relevance of Hypertension and Oedema in Pregnancy*, 2 Clin. Exper. Hypertension 897, 898 (1980).
50. R. Willson & E. Carrington, *supra* note 1, at 338.
51. R. Benson, *supra* note 1, at 693.
52. *Id.*
53. R. Willson & E. Carrington, *supra* note 1, at 339.
54. Kaspar v. Schack, 195 Neb. 215, 237 N.W.2d 414 (1976).
55. R. Willson & E. Carrington, *supra* note 1, at 339–40.
56. R. Benson, *supra* note 1, at 695.
57. *Id.*
58. *Id.* at 696.
59. *Id.* at 698.
60. Couto v. Oms, 331 So.2d 236 (La. App. 1976).
61. R. Benson, *supra* note 1, at 698.
62. R. Willson & E. Carrington, *supra* note 1, at 343.
63. Smith v. Knowles, 281 N.W.2d 653 (Minn. 1979).
64. American College of Obstetricians and Gynecologists, *supra* note 34, at 12.
65. *Id.* at 24.
66. R. Willson & E. Carrington, *supra* note 1, at 432–33.
67. *Id.* at 256–58, 433–34.
68. R. Benson, *supra* note 1, at 531.
69. Glenn v. Prestegord, 456 S.W.2d 901 (Tex. 1970).
70. Morgan v. Aetna Casualty & Surety Co., 185 F. Supp. 20 (E.D. La. 1960).
71. W. Prosser, Handbook of the Law of Torts 906 (4th ed. 1971).
72. *See, e.g.*, Libbee v. Permanente Clinic, 268 Or. 258, 518 P.2d 636 (1974); Renslow v. Mennonite Hosp., 40 Ill. App. 3d 234, 351 N.E.2d 870.
73. Justus v. Atchison, 19 Cal. 3d 564, 139 Cal. Rptr. 97, 565 P.2d 122 (1977).
74. Presley v. Newport Hosp., 356 A.2d 748 (R.I. 1976).
75. R. Willson & E. Carrington, *supra* note 1, at 181.
76. *Id.* at 184.

Notes: Chapter X

77. *Id.*
78. Stokes v. Haynes, 428 S.W.2d 227 (Ky. 1968).
79. R. Benson, *supra* note 1, at 649.
80. R. Willson & E. Carrington, *supra* note 1, at 184-85.
81. E. Taylor, *supra* note 1, at 313.
82. R. Willson & E. Carrington, *supra* note 1, at 185.
83. Acosta v. City of New York, 67 Misc. 756, 324 N.Y.S.2d 137 (1971).
84. E. Taylor, *supra* note 1, at 315.
85. R. Willson & E. Carrington, *supra* note 1, at 189-90.
86. Schlesselman v. Gouge, 163 Colo. 312, 431 P.2d 35 (1967).
87. Jarboe v. Harting, 397 S.W.2d 775 (Ky. 1965).
88. R. Willson & E. Carrington, *supra* note 1, at 186-89.
89. Carpenter v. Gauthier, 266 So.2d 504 (La. App. 1972).
90. Nelson v. Marrus, 343 So.2d 740 (La. App. 1977).
91. Johnson v. Hunt, (Okla 1975), unreported case published at 46 Okla B.A.J. 422 (1975).
92. R. Willson & E. Carrington, *supra* note 1, at 426.
93. Bleakley & Peters, *Bendectin,* Trial 58 (May 1980).
94. *See, e.g.,* Mulder v. Parke-Davis & Co., 288 Minn. 332, 181 N.W.2d 882 (1970).
95. *See* Physician's Desk Reference 1591, 1594 (34th ed. 1980).
96. Baker v. St. Agnes Hosp., 70 A.D.2d 400, 421 N.Y.S.2d 81 (1979).
97. R. Willson & E. Carrington, *supra* note 1.
98. *See* Sheiner, *DES and a Proposed Theory of Enterprise Liability,* 46 Fordham L. Rev. 963 (1978).
99. *See, e.g.,* Payton v. Abbott Laboratories, 512 F. Supp. 1031 (D. Mass. 1981); Sindell v. Abbott Laboratories, 26 Cal. 3d 588, 163 Cal. Rptr. 132, 607 P.2d 924 (1980); Abel v. Eli Lilly & Co., 94 Mich. App. 59, 289 N.W.2d 20 (1980); Namm v. Charles E. Frosst & Co., 178 N.J. Super. 19, 427 A.2d 1121 (1981); Ferrigno v. Eli Lilly & Co., 175 N.J. Super. 551, 420 A.2d 1305 (1980); Bichler v. Eli Lilly & Co., 79 A.D.2d 317, 436 N.Y.S.2d 625 (App. Div. 1981).
100. Mink v. Univ. of Chicago, 460 F. Supp. 713 (N.D. Ill. 1978).
101. American College of Obstetricians and Gynecologists, Technical Bulletin No. 21 (Apr. 1973).
102. American College of Obstetricians and Gynecologists Newsletter, vol. 24, No. 5 (May 1980), at 2.
103. Seixas, *New Trends in Treating Alcohol/Drug Addiction,* Female Patient 70 (Apr. 1980).
104. *Id.*
105. American Medical Association, Council of Scientific Affairs, *Guidelines for All Physicians with Clinical Responsibility: Diagnosis and Referral,* Guidelines for Alcoholism: Diagnosis, Treatment and Referral (Oct. 8-9, 1978).
106. S. De Lee, Safeguarding Motherhood 66-67 (1976).
107. J. Pritchard & P. MacDonald, Williams Obstetrics, 258 (15th ed. 1976).
108. Matsuyama & Jarvik, *Effects of Marihuana on the Genetic and Immune Systems,* Marihuana Research Findings: 1976 Nat'l. Inst. on Drug Abuse, U.S. Dept. of H.E.W., Monograph 14, 181 (1977).
109. Falek, *Genetic Studies of Marijuana: Current Findings and New Directions,* in Marijuana and Health Hazards, p. 6 (1975).
110. Matsuyama & Jarvik, *supra* note 108.
111. Falek, *supra* note 109.
112. Kolodny, *Research Issues in the Study of Marijuana and Male Reproductive Physiology in Humans,* in Marijuana and Health Hazards, 78 (1975).

113. Petersen, *Summary, Marihuana Research Findings: 1976,* Marihuana Research Findings 14 (1976).
114. J. Pritchard & P. MacDonald, *supra* note 107.
115. S. De Lee, *supra* note 106, at 67.
116. J. Brown & G. Dixon, Antenatal Care 424 (11th ed. 1978).
117. J. Pritchard & P. MacDonald, *supra* note 107, at 817–18.
118. *Id.* at 818.
119. J. Rovinsky & A. Guttmacher, Medical, Surgical, and Gynecological Complications of Pregnancy 469 (2d ed. 1965).
120. *Id.* at 419.
121. American College of Obstetricians and Gynecologists, *supra* note 34, at 48.
122. *Id.* at 54.
123. *Id.* at 66.
124. Roe v. Wade, 410 U.S. 113 (1973).
125. R. Willson & E. Carrington, *supra* note 1, at 197.
126. R. Benson, *supra* note 1, at 478.
127. Koehler v. Schwartz 48 N.Y.2d 807, 424 N.Y.S.2d 119, 399 N.E.2d 1140 (1979).
128. R. Willson & E. Carrington, *supra* note 1, at 198.
129. R. Benson, *supra* note 1, at 481.
130. Reynier v. Delta Women's Clinic, 359 So.2d 733 (La. App. 1978).
131. Pritchard v. Neal, 139 Ga. App. 512, 229 S.E.2d 18 (1976).
132. Stills v. Gratton, 55 Cal. App. 3d 698, 127 Cal. Rptr. 652 (1976).
133. *Id.*
134. Wilczynski v. Goodman, 73 Ill. App.3d 51, 29 Ill. Dec. 216, 391 N.E.2d 479 (1970).
135. Speck v. Finegold, 268 Pa. Super. 342, 408 A.2d 496 (1979).
136. Roe v. Wade, *supra* note 124.
137. Gaines v. Wolcott, 119 Ga. App. 313, 167 S.E.2d 366 (1969).
138. Joy v. Brown, 173 Kan. 833, 252 P.2d 889 (1953).
139. Reno v. D'Javid, 42 N.Y.2d 1040, 399 N.Y.S.2d 210, 369 N.E.2d 766 (1977).

Chapter XI

Parturition

§ 11.10 LABOR

Liability may be imposed on the physician for the failure to adequately attend the patient or to properly monitor the progress of the fetus during labor.

Basic Standard of Care: The American College of Obstetricians and Gynecologists has specified that the data obtained at the time of admission to the labor suite should include: the date of the last menses and expected date of delivery; gravidity and parity; weight and height; vital signs; fetal heart tones; frequency, onset, and duration of contractions; status of membranes; presence of bleeding; station, dilation, effacement, and fetal position; time and content of last meal; allergies; the presence of glasses, contact lenses, or dentures; and preferred anesthetics. Laboratory studies should include examination of hemoglobin, hematocrit, and urine for protein and sugar. Any woman in labor should be closely attended by a person able to identify and inform the responsible physician immediately of any untoward sign or symptoms and to determine whether labor is progressing normally and when delivery is imminent.[1]

Interpretation and Customary Practice: Normal labor has three stages. The first stage lasts from the onset of labor pains until complete cervical dilation occurs. While membrane rupture usually occurs at the end of the first stage, it may take place earlier or at delivery. The second stage begins with complete cervical dilation and ends when the baby is delivered. The third stage begins with delivery of the baby and ends with delivery of the placenta. During normal labor, force is exerted by the uterus from the fundus to the cervix. As labor advances, the upper uterine segment progressively shortens, its walls thicken, and individual muscle fibers retract. The ascending inferior border of the upper segment exerts traction on the lower segment and the effaced cervix. These structures are pulled upward around the presenting part as it is simultaneously pushed through the gradually enlarging opening.[2]

Measures should be taken during labor to assuage the apprehension and discomfort of patients, which is experienced even by women who have had more than one child. Ideally, a physician or nurse should remain with each patient throughout her labor; in practice, however, this is usually impossible. Medical personnel should visit the patient periodically and record certain observations. Fetal heart sounds, which indicate the condition of the fetus, should be counted and recorded at least every 30 minutes during the first stage of labor* and more frequently during the second stage. Maternal blood pressure, which may increase markedly during labor, should also be checked and recorded at 30-minute intervals. The attendant should check the length, duration, and intensity of uterine contractions and the interval between them. The patient's perception of a uterine contraction is unreliable because she feels the contraction for a period lasting several seconds after it has begun to several seconds before it ceases. Abdominal palpation should be employed to make these determinations. Vaginal examinations must be made to determine the progress of cervical dilation and descent of the fetus, but they should be minimized in order to reduce the possibility of infection.[3]

The failure to adequately attend the patient during labor has given rise to litigation. Where the mother is injured as a result, liability may be imposed if the care provided her is shown to be substandard.

CASE ILLUSTRATION

The 24-year-old patient entered the hospital in labor for the birth of her second child after notifying her obstetrician. She was taken to the labor room, where she was prepared for delivery. The nurse on duty instructed the patient's husband to watch the clock and time the length of and the interval between pains and, as the pains came closer together, to notify the nurse, who was in an office up the hall from the labor room, reading a magazine. About 7:30 a.m., 12 hours after the patient had been admitted to the hospital, the husband told the nurse that the patient's pains were getting harder and closer together. The nurse continued to read the magazine but finally checked the patient and said it would be some time before delivery since the patient's cervix was only dilated 7 centimeters. The husband told the nurse that his first child had been born immediately after his wife had dilated to 8 centimeters, but the nurse told him not to worry. At 8:30 a.m. the pains were getting harder and closer together. The husband again informed the nurse, who continued to read her magazine and said that she would "be there in a minute." When she did check the patient, she found her cervix to be dilated to 8 centimeters and told the husband, who requested that the nurse call the obstetrician. The patient's mother,

---

*An alternate view is that the fetal heart rate should be checked at least every 15 minutes. J. Pritchard & P. MacDonald, Williams Obstetrics 329 (15th ed. 1976).

§ *11.10*   *Labor*   405

who had given birth to 16 children, was also present at that time and asked the nurse whether she had called the obstetrician. The mother stated, "I know childbirth, and I knew she [the patient] should have been in the delivery room." She observed that the baby was on the patient's right side and there was a big knot. The nurse told the mother she had called the obstetrician. The husband checked his wife again at 9:00 a.m. Again the nurse continued to read a magazine and stated she would "be there in a minute." When she did examine the patient, dilation was still at 8 centimeters. The husband asked the nurse to call the obstetrician, and she replied that she was in charge and would do what was necessary. She also said, "This hospital has never lost a father yet, so you just go back there and sit down." She then returned to her magazine. Ten minutes later, the patient screamed, "I am going to have that baby right now." The husband went for the nurse. The nurse continued reading her magazine for a while, then went to the labor room and left the labor room immediately to call the obstetrician, telling him, "We are having a baby right now." The nurse ran back to the labor room, pushed the patient into the delivery room on a cart, and told the patient to get off the cart and onto the delivery table. The patient did so, unassisted. The nurse rushed into the hall to find a physician, telling the patient, "Pant like a dog and don't have that kid yet." The nurse grabbed a physician who was walking down the hall, but because the physician was not scrubbed, the nurse ultimately delivered the baby. The patient, when she had climbed from the cart to the delivery table and had placed her own feet in the stirrups, looked in the mirror in the delivery room and saw the baby's head and shoulders being delivered from her body. She fainted. Upon regaining consciousness, the physician was suturing her. She asked him to stop as she had had no anesthetic, but he continued. At this time, the patient's obstetrician arrived, administered an anesthetic and completed the sutures. The patient suffered multiple lacerations on her vagina and labia, some of which were not sutured.

    The patient sued the nurse and the hospital, alleging negligence in failing to notify the patient's obstetrician when birth was imminent. The patient's obstetrician testified that the point at which the nurse should notify the physician depended on several factors, including the measurement of dilation, the speed at which dilation was occurring, and the severity of the uterine contractions. The obstetrician stated that a nurse should use her professional judgment and that there was nothing wrong with the conduct of this nurse. The nurse-defendant argued that the patient must provide expert testimony regarding medical negligence. The court noted that nonexpert witnesses can testify to external appearances and manifest conditions observable by anyone. The court looked to the testimony of the patient's husband and mother to support a finding of negligence. The nurse-defendant further argued that there was no evidence that the patient's injuries, vaginal lacerations, would not have occurred if circumstances had been different. However, the court noted the testimony of the obstetrician regarding the patient's first delivery, during which an episiotomy had been performed to avoid just such an injury. The court held for the patient (*Hiatt v. Groce*, 1974).[4]

When the baby sustains an injury, the resulting lawsuit may claim that the progress of the fetus during labor was improperly monitored.[5] The normal fetal heart rate ranges from 120 to 160 beats per minute, diminishing at least ten beats during a contraction of the uterus. A drop of more than 20 beats or a rate of less than 100 beats per minute signifies the possibility of hypoxia. When the uterus is relaxed, a change in rate is difficult to detect until hypoxia is well advanced. Electronic monitoring is available to continuously assess fetal heart tones.[6] Care of the infant who manifests signs of fetal distress must conform with current medical standards in order for the obstetrician to escape liability for injury.

CASE ILLUSTRATION

The patient notified her obstetrician that she was in labor, and he instructed her to go to the hospital. In the hospital labor room, the patient's obstetrician left orders that the patient be given 50 milligrams of Demerol and 25 milligrams of Phenergan if she became uncomfortable. He also left orders that he be advised when the patient's dilation reached 7 to 8 centimeters. The fetal heart tones were checked with a fetoscope six times, at decreasing intervals of time, within the ensuing two hours and were found to be within normal limits on each occasion. On or about the third examination, the patient heard an attendant, after checking heart tones, instruct a nurse to get in touch with the obstetrician because of a problem. At this time, upon vaginal inspection, the attendant found the patient's cervical dilation to be 3 to 4 centimeters and her contractions to be two minutes apart. He anticipated that her labor would take another three or four hours. Because the patient was beginning to feel uncomfortable, the Demerol and Phenergan were administered. The obstetrician was notified and arrived at the hospital. Within an hour of receiving medication, the patient's cervix had dilated to 10 centimeters. The fetal heart tones were found to be normal at this time, and the patient was transferred to the delivery room.

Upon arrival in the delivery room, fetal heart tones were recorded at 80 beats per minute, faint, and irregular. The obstetrician was notified, and he administered a pudendal block and a local anesthetic; he then performed a left mediolateral episiotomy. The baby was born with no

§ *11.11*   *Induction of Labor*   407

heartbeat and no respiration, and he was flaccid. At this time, the obstetrician ordered that the patient be given a general anesthetic. As the baby was being delivered, the obstetrician suctioned his mouth, nasal pharynx, and nose with a bulb syringe. Upon delivery, the obstetrician placed the baby on a flat surface and put a folded towel under the baby's neck to extend his head. The physician then placed a DeLee tracheal catheter in the baby's larynx and down his trachea. The physician positioned the catheter by placing one finger of his left hand in the baby's mouth. He had his right hand on the baby's chest, with two fingers between the upper and lower third of the sternum. The physician held the catheter between his teeth and held the baby's chin up. The anesthesiologist assisting the obstetrician delivered oxygen to the obstetrician's mouth with the oxygen tube, and the obstetrician delivered oxygen through the catheter to the infant's lungs. There was no resuscitator or anesthesia bag in the delivery room. After ten minutes of this procedure, the baby's color changed from blue to pink, and he began taking breaths independently, although he would stop if the obstetrician stopped. Finally a Bennett resuscitator was brought to the delivery room, the baby was connected to it, and another physician repaired the patient's episiotomy. The baby suffered permanent, irreparable brain damage, and the patient sued the hospital and all medical personnel in attendance.

  The patient claimed that, although the hospital record reflected that the situation was otherwise, when the attendant stated something was wrong, the obstetrician should have been notified immediately and emergency measures implemented. Various experts testified that the care actually rendered was in accordance with medical standards. The court held that the jury could choose to believe the record rather than the patient's version of the facts. The patient also contended it was negligent not to have resuscitative equipment available in the delivery room. The court relied on expert testimony that such equipment need not be obtained until actually needed. The patient argued that the physicians were negligent in failing to deliver the baby earlier, failing to intubate under direct vision with an endotracheal tube, and failing to perform closed chest massage and administer sodium bicarbonate. Expert testimony established that the actions of the physicians met the standard of care in effect at the time of the baby's birth; administration of sodium bicarbonate was not done at that time. The court upheld a jury verdict in favor of all medical personnel (*Northern Trust Co. v. Skokie Valley Community Hospital,* 1980).[7]

§ 11.11 Induction of Labor

Liability may be imposed on the physician for negligence in performing an amniotomy or in performing an amniotomy for inadequate reasons, for negligent drug induction of labor (including contraindicated or premature administration), or for the failure to properly monitor a patient and infant in induced labor.

Basic Standard of Care: The American College of Obstetricians and Gynecologists has specifically addressed the topic of induction or augmentation of labor with oxytocin in the following manner.[8]

Oxytocic agents should be used only when required for the benefit of the mother or fetus. The obstetrician should review the course of labor, examine the patient, and establish the need for augmentation of labor. Examination of the patient may be delegated to another physician or a qualified nurse if the obstetrician has examined her within the last four hours. In cases where the attending physician does not have privileges to manage complications resulting from oxytocic agents, a qualified obstetrician must be consulted. Personnel familiar with the effects of oxytocic agents and with the maternal and fetal complications that may result should be in attendance while such agents are being administered. A responsible physician should be present in the labor area during the first 20 minutes of infusion to manage any unexpected effects. Thereafter, the obstetrician should be readily accessible for the management of any complications that may arise. Oxytocin should be administered intravenously only, and a written protocol for the preparation of oxytocin solutions should be established by the obstetrics department. Electronic fetal monitoring should be used to record fetal heartbeat and uterine contractions continuously when oxytocin is administered. If this equipment is not available, fetal heartbeat, rate frequency and character of contractions, rate of oxytocin flow, and maternal pulse should be recorded at regular intervals, preferably no less than every 15 minutes. Maternal blood pressure should be recorded at least every half hour but more frequently if indicated.

Interpretation and Customary Practice: The reasons for inducing labor fall into two categories. First, when a patient has a history of rapid labor or lives far from the hospital, planned induction can avoid unattended delivery outside the hospital and assure closer supervision of the patient by the obstetrician and hospital personnel. This type of induction is called elective induction and has been used for other reasons as well, such as the physician's convenience or convenience in organizing family household matters. The second category is medically indicated induced labor—that is, labor required by certain medical conditions. The most common of these indications include premature rupture of the membranes, hypertension, diabetes mellitus, prediabetes, Rh sensitization, recurrent pyelonephritis, repeated intrauterine fetal death, and prolonged pregnancy.[9]

Induction is contraindicated whenever labor would endanger either the mother or the infant. Contraindications include abnormal fetal position or presentation, fetopelvic disproportion, previous uterine scars, and a history of previous traumatic delivery.[10]

§ 11.11   Induction of Labor   409

The most common methods of inducing labor are by amniotomy, administration of oxytocin, amniotomy accompanied by oxytocin, and administration of prostaglandins.

Amniotomy is the artificial rupture of the fetal membranes. Most women will begin labor shortly thereafter if the fetal head is engaged and the cervix is "ripe."[11] Sometimes oxytocin is administered as a supplementary aid at the time of rupture. It can also be administered if labor has not begun within six hours after amniotomy.[12]

The most significant complications of amniotomy are prolapse of the cord and the development of infection if labor does not progress. The longer the period from the rupture of membranes to delivery, the greater the risk of infection (see § 11.24, Rupture of the Amnion). Premature infants are particularly susceptible to infection. Hence, it is generally desirable for delivery to occur within 24 hours of rupture of the membranes. If induction fails, cesarean section is indicated.[13]

Plaintiffs have sometimes alleged that a physician was negligent because he or she performed an amniotomy for inadequate reasons. The courts have recognized that amniotomy may be justified by considerations of convenience as well as by strict medical considerations.

CASE ILLUSTRATION

The physician, a specialist in obstetrics and gynecology, undertook to deliver the patient's third child. On January 6, the patient and the physician agreed that the physician would induce labor on January 14. On January 14, the physician performed an amniotomy, and 2½ hours later delivered a healthy 6-pound infant. The patient began to bleed from the vagina after delivery. The physician attempted to stop the bleeding with massage and administration of oxytocin. When this was unsuccessful, he performed an emergency hysterectomy. During the hysterectomy, the patient was transfused with incompatible blood. The patient and her former husband sued the physician, alleging several counts of negligence. One claim was that the physician had been negligent in employing elective induction—that is, induction based on "convenience" rather than medical reasons. The plaintiffs presented a general practitioner at trial who testified that labor should be induced only for specific medical or surgical reasons. The physician-defendant testified that the patient's first child had been born six hours after labor had begun and that her second child had been born three hours after labor had begun. This indicated to him that the third pregnancy would have an even shorter period of labor. He considered it desirable to have the patient in the hospital when labor began in order to avoid an at-home delivery. The physician-defendant also testified that he had performed an amniotomy in connection with the patient's second delivery and that this delivery had been without complications. He testified that, at the time he performed the amniotomy, the patient was "ripe" for delivery. He testified that (1) the patient was within two weeks of the estimated arrival date; (2) the baby was sufficiently large; (3) the cervix was dilated; (4) the baby's head was well down in the pelvis; and (5) the fetal membrane was distending the cervix. Several experts testified that the physician-defendant was correct in inducing labor under the circumstances. They testified that inducing labor by amniotomy under the circumstances of the case was a widely practiced procedure throughout the country and was accompanied by no increase in danger to the patient. The court thus upheld the jury's finding that the physician-defendant had not been negligent in inducing labor by amniotomy under the circumstances of the case (*Parker v. St. Paul Fire and Marine Insurance Co.*, 1976).[14]

In another case, a father alleged that an obstetrician had negligently overestimated an infant's weight, thus causing him to perform an amniotomy five weeks prematurely. The court upheld a jury verdict for the obstetrician-defendant because the evidence showed that he was aware of the correct weight and had performed the amniotomy only because the mother was in irreversible premature labor.[15]

The physician will be liable if he or she performs an amniotomy negligently and this negligence harms the fetus or the mother.

CASE ILLUSTRATION

On April 25, the patient visited the physician, who performed an amniotomy with an unsterile glove. The physician then attempted to induce labor by injecting "some substance," presumably oxytocin, into her veins. This attempt was unsuccessful. On this date, the infant was moving and its heartbeat was audible. The physician sent the patient away. On each subsequent visit, the physician told her to return only when she was in labor. The patient began to suffer from a profuse discharge. She consulted another physician, who sent her to the hospital. At the hospital she was treated with antibiotics for an infection. On May 5, she was delivered of a stillborn child by another physician. The patient sued the physician who performed the amniotomy. The patient-plaintiff offered expert testimony that the death of the fetus was caused by intrauterine infection, that the infection was caused by the amniotomy and lack of subsequent care, and that the actions of the physician-defendant breached the applicable standard of medical care. The court upheld the jury's finding that the physician-defendant was liable for the death of a viable fetus (*Rice v. Rizk*, 1970).[16]

§ 11.11   *Induction of Labor*   411

Oxytocin causes uterine contractions and is often used to induce labor. It may be used alone or in combination with amniotomy. It may also be administered following premature rupture of the membranes.

Ideally, oxytocin should be administered intravenously with an infusion pump. It is difficult for a physician to estimate beforehand the dose of oxytocin that will produce proper uterine contractions. The amount delivered to the patient per unit of time must be cautiously and carefully monitored, since too large a dose will cause excessive uterine contractions which can injure the fetus or rupture the uterus.[17] It is necessary to continuously monitor the uterine contractions, patient pulse and blood pressure, and the fetal heart rate. The goal is to produce normal uterine contractions, occurring at intervals of two to three minutes and lasting 60 to 90 seconds.[18]

One advantage of induction by administration of oxytocin is that the membranes remain intact if the uterus is unresponsive. The chief disadvantage is that the administration is difficult to monitor, and an excessive dose can injure mother and fetus. Oxytocin also has an antidiuretic effect and can produce maternal water intoxication.[19]

A physician can usually induce uterine contractions with prostaglandins. They are employed infrequently, however, and further study must precede their general clinical use.[20]

Liability for negligent induction of labor with drugs can occur in several ways. A physician will be liable if he administers oxytocin to a patient when medical standards require an alternative method of delivery. In one case, a physician administered Pitocin to a patient who subsequently died of pulmonary edema due to an amniotic fluid embolism during delivery. The court reversed a summary judgment in favor of the physician-defendant in light of testimony of the plaintiff's expert witness. The plaintiff's expert indicated that the physician-defendant should have obtained an obstetrical consultation, which might have led to a cesarean section because of the patient's overweight and prior history of miscarriages. The expert hypothesized that the administration of Pitocin caused an excessive uterine contraction in the patient, resulting in the amniotic fluid embolism.[21]

A plaintiff may also contend that drugs were administered prematurely. In one case, the plaintiff introduced an expert who testified that Tocosamine, an oxytocic drug, was negligently administered before the baby's head was engaged.[22]

Another frequent complaint by plaintiffs is that the physician or hospital, or both, negligently failed to properly monitor the administration of oxytocin. In some cases, the plaintiff alleges that the failure caused injury to the mother.

CASE ILLUSTRATION

The patient was under the care of three physicians associated in a medical partnership. She was admitted to the hospital for the birth of her fourth child. She was initially cared for in the delivery room by a nurse and a resident. The patient's hospital chart indicated that she began to receive oxytocin intravenously at 2:45 a.m. The hospital chart contained no notation that the administration of the oxytocin was monitored. The chart indicated that the patient's condition was checked at 5:15 a.m. and at 7:05 a.m. An 8:00 a.m. notation indicated that one of the patient's physicians was attending the delivery. The patient delivered but suffered a ruptured uterus which necessitated an emergency hysterectomy. The patient was subsequently released from the hospital but was shortly thereafter readmitted for treatment of severe infectious hepatitis. The patient alleged that medication she received during the second hospitalization caused a partial hearing loss. The patient sued the physicians individually and as partners, as well as the hospital, alleging that the ruptured uterus and her subsequent injuries were the result of a negligent failure to monitor administration of the oxytocin. The jury decided in favor of the patient-plaintiff and the defendants appealed. The appeals court affirmed. The court noted that the patient-plaintiff offered expert testimony that her injuries were caused by failure to monitor the administration of oxytocin and that the failure was a breach of applicable standards of care. The court then ruled that the jury could reasonably conclude from the absence of notations on the hospital chart that the administration of oxytocin was not monitored. Thus, the defendants were held jointly and severally liable (*Stack v. Wapner*, 1976).[23]

Plaintiffs have also advanced the theory that failure to monitor the administration of oxytocin injured the infant.

CASE ILLUSTRATION

The patient entered the hospital to give birth to her thirteenth child. At 4:45 a.m., she was admitted to the labor room. At 5:05 a.m., the physician performed a vaginal examination and an amniotomy. He instructed the nurse on duty to monitor the contractions and the fetal heart tones. By 7:05 a.m., the infant began to pass meconium. The nurse contacted the physician, who returned to the labor room and performed a vaginal examination. He noted nothing unusual except the meconium staining. At 8:05 or 8:15 a.m., the physician performed another vaginal examination. At 8:20 a.m., the nurse began an intravenous drip of oxytocin to accelerate labor. The evidence at trial established that (1) the only way to monitor contractions at the hospital was by having a nurse feel the patient's abdomen to determine their frequency and intensity, and (2) the hospital nurses were charged with the duty of monitoring the effects of oxytocin unless the attending physician was present and personally monitoring the patient. Hospital regulations required the prescribing physician to be in the

§ 11.20   Delivery   413

hospital while oxytocin was being administered but did not require the physician to be with the patient. The patient testified that no one continuously monitored her contractions between 8:20 a.m. and 10:20 a.m., at which time the infant was born. Her hospital chart contained no notation of monitoring. The patient was transferred to the delivery room at 9:00 a.m. She was given a saddle block anesthetic. The physician arrived, but by 9:40 a.m. the patient had not delivered. At 9:46 to 9:50 a.m., the patient experienced a severe abdominal pain and developed a Bandl's ring. The physician removed the patient to the operating room at 10:15 a.m. By the time the physician performed a cesarean section, the patient's uterus had ruptured and the infant had been expelled into the abdomen. This caused the infant's oxygen supply to be cut off and caused her to be born with cerebral palsy. The evidence indicated that oxytocin was administered continuously from 8:20 a.m. to 10:50 a.m. The infant, through her father, sued the physician and the hospital. The jury decided in favor of the physician-defendant. The jury returned a verdict against the hospital, but the trial court overrode the jury and entered judgment for the hospital. The court of appeals affirmed the judgment for the physician-defendant but reversed the judgment in favor of the hospital-defendant. The court of appeals held that the jury could have reasonably concluded that the physician-defendant was not negligent in administering or monitoring the oxytocin. The court also concluded that the jury could have found that hospital personnel had been negligent in failing to monitor the contractions. Thus, the trial court was wrong in overriding the jury's verdict against the hospital-defendant. In support of its conclusion, the court noted that the hospital admitted that the nurses were responsible for monitoring unless the physician was present and monitoring the patient personally. Since the physician did little, if any, monitoring, the duty fell to the hospital. The court also noted that the jury could have found that the failure to monitor caused the uterine rupture and the infant's neurological impairment (*Long v. Johnson,* 1978).[24]

§ 11.20 DELIVERY

Liability may be imposed on the physician attending a delivery for an injury to the mother or the child if the injury results from the physician's failure to provide treatment that conforms to the relevant standard of care (see §§ 11.21-11.27 for discussion of specific complications and procedures relating to delivery).

Basic Standard of Care: The American College of Obstetricians and Gynecologists recommends that when delivery is imminent, the patient should not be left unattended under any circumstances. No attempt should be made to delay birth by physical restraint, anesthesia, or any other means beyond normal control of delivery. During delivery, the patient's blood pressure and pulse should be recorded every ten minutes, and fetal heart tones should be evaluated at least every ten minutes if electronic fetal monitoring is not being used. The patient should not be left unattended in the immediate postdelivery period. Provisions should be made for postpartum care, and care should be continued through the puerperium (see Chapter XII, Postpartum Complications).[25]

ACOG has not formulated specific guidelines or medical standards regarding the diagnosis and treatment of individual complications during delivery. In general terms, the quality of care available should be sufficient to recognize and treat complications of childbirth, and provisions should be available for appropriate consultation or referral.

Interpretation and Customary Practice: A variety of complications may occur during delivery. Medical treatment appropriate for such complications as breech presentation, dystocia, anomalous placental conditions, and rupture of the amnion is discussed in the pages that follow. When these conditions or other factors indicate that unassisted vaginal delivery is not possible, the obstetrician may be faced with performing a cesarean section or a forceps delivery. The legal implications of these techniques, as well as of the more commonly performed episiotomy, are also considered.

§ 11.21 Breech Presentation

Liability may be imposed on the physician for the failure to properly treat and manage injuries to both mother and infant resulting from breech presentation and for negligence in failing to perform a cesarean section where indicated.

Basic Standard of Care: The American College of Obstetricians and Gynecologists has not published specific guidelines for managing a breech presentation.

Interpretation and Customary Practice: A breech presentation is one in which the pelvis of the infant or one or both of the infant's lower extremities descend through the birth canal first. Breech presentations occur in 3.5 percent of all births, if premature births are included. If only term births are included, breech presentations account for about 2.6 percent of all births. Breech presentations are more common in women who have been pregnant more than once than in women undergoing their first pregnancies.[26]

Breeches are thought to be due to small fetal size relative to the size of the uterine cavity, because the smaller fetus does not conform to or fit snugly in the uterine shape. In a vertex, or normal, presentation, the larger mass of fetal buttocks, feet, and legs is contained in the upper uterine segment, which is wider than the lower uterine segment. Breech positions are relatively common before the thirty-second week of pregnancy. Up to this time, because the volume of amniotic fluid is relatively greater than it will be later, the fetus's movement within the uterus is fairly unrestricted. After the thirty-second week, the fetus may adapt to the vertex position. A breech presentation may result from any interference with this adaptation, such as prematurity, fetal death, extension of fetal legs, excessive amniotic fluid, multiple pregnancy, cornual-fundal implantation of the placenta, placenta previa, uterine fibroids, or hydrocephalus.[27]

In the breech presentation, the fetus may take a variety of attitudes, or positions. In a double, or complete breech, the fetus assumes an attitude of complete flexion: the feet present with the buttocks, and the hips and knees are both flexed. With the more common frank, or single, breech, the fetus's hips are flexed on the abdomen and the legs extend upward so that the feet are positioned directly in front of the face. The less common incomplete breech, or footling, attitude involves the presentation of one or both feet through the cervix first, with hips and knees partially extended.[28]

Breech birth poses certain problems for the mother, although maternal mortality should not vary from normal rates if the birth is properly managed. The manipulation and anesthesia sometimes necessitated by breech delivery may increase maternal morbidity. The most common complications are cervical and vaginal lacerations and uterine rupture. Pulling the infant's aftercoming head through the cervix before it is fully dilated may cause deep cervical lacerations, particularly when the cervix becomes constricted around the child's neck. These lacerated and ruptured structures cause bleeding and predispose the patient to infection.[29] When such injuries occur, the physician may be sued if he or she fails to properly treat and manage them.

CASE ILLUSTRATION

The patient gave birth to her first child with a breech delivery. Mother and child progressed satisfactorily and were discharged from the hospital two days later. Approximately ten days later, the patient discovered that urine was leaking from her vagina. The patient returned to her obstetrician, who was unable to determine the cause of the leakage and told her that her problem "was due to a birth-related phenomenon." The obstetrician referred her to a surgeon colleague, who suggested that she consult a urologist and gave her a note to take with her which read, "To GU [urology] Department. Please see this girl for urethral sphincter problems as a result of childbirth." The urologist's examination revealed a 1.5-centimeter hole near the neck of the bladder down into the vagina. The urologist told the patient that it was not uncommon for this condition to develop following the birth of a woman's first child. The urologist inserted a catheter in the patient's bladder to divert the leakage and to give the affected area an opportunity to regenerate to the point that a plastic repair could be undertaken, a period of some three months.

When this point in her treatment was reached, the patient was told by the urologist that she was ready for surgery and that surgery would cost $250. Unable to raise that amount, the patient elected to postpone corrective surgery. Nine months later, the patient visited a surgeon for the needed surgical repair. The repair progressed in stages for a period of 11 months, after which the patient completely recovered. The patient sued her obstetrician in the last month of her repair. The jurisdiction in which the patient brought the suit [Kentucky] had a one-year statute of limitations. The court interpreted the statute to require the patient to bring her suit within one year of the discovery of the harmful effect manifested by the negligence complained of. The court stated that the patient became aware of the harmful effects of the obstetrician's alleged negligence within two weeks after delivery and was advised of the specific problem and the required surgical repair some 21 months before the filing of the initial complaint. The court dismissed the suit and exonerated the obstetrician (*Hall v. Musgrave*, 1975).[30]

The majority opinion in this case never got beyond the legal issue of the timeliness of the suit itself. It is consequently impossible to determine whether the physician would have been held liable in such a situation without expert testimony and a more complete presentation of the facts. The case, however, does support the conclusion that maternal injuries sustained during a breech birth may give rise to litigation.

Hazards to the infant posed by breech delivery include a neonatal death rate that is four to five times that of babies in the vertex presentation. There is an increased incidence of prolapsed cord presentation, which may subject the infant to periods without oxygen and consequent neurological damage. Prolapse of the cord is found among complete and footling breech presentations but less often among frank breech births because the position leaves little extra room for the cord to prolapse. It is thought that failure to deliver the head within five minutes of the appearance of the umbilical cord at the vulva will result in irreparable fetal asphyxia. Thus, most physicians recognize the necessity for quick delivery.[31] In such a situation, the physician is in a difficult position: failure to respond quickly is likely to result in injury to the baby, as is too quick a response.

CASE ILLUSTRATION

The patient went into labor, attended by the physician, and the baby presented in the breech position. When the baby had been delivered as far as its abdomen, the physician noticed that the cord was not pulsating, which meant that the baby was not receiving oxygen from its mother. Since the baby's nose and mouth were not then delivered, there was no passage for air. The physician stated later that at the time he felt he had no choice: he had to interfere in the birth by manipulating the baby and risk damaging its arms or brachial plexus; otherwise, the baby might have suffocated. Having made this decision, the physician manipulated the baby's left arm in an attempt to deliver the baby's head and create an air passage. As he did so, he felt the baby's left humerus snap. The patient brought suit, alleging negligent delivery and postdelivery care of the infant. Prior to trial, the physician submitted an affidavit to support his request that the case be decided in his favor. The affidavit stated, "I performed my services skillfully and efficiently and in keeping with acceptable medical standards of other physicians and surgeons practicing in this general community." The trial court decided in favor of the physician on the basis of this statement, and the patient appealed the decision. The court of appeals noted that it was necessary for the physician to show through expert testimony what skills, means, and methods are necessary and customarily followed in a given case—the affidavit provided only a conclusion of the physician. Furthermore, the court noted that the affidavit failed to answer the claim regarding postdelivery care of the child. The court reversed the holding of the lower court and ordered that a trial be held (*Brooks v. Serrano*, 1968).[32]

Breech presentation may result in unassisted spontaneous delivery, but it most often requires assistance in the form of manipulation and traction on the presenting parts. Traction may result in injury to the infant's brachial plexus, upper appendages (as in the preceding case), head, and neck. In performing traction, pressure should be applied to bones rather than soft tissue. Downward traction is applied to the pelvic girdle, and the baby's body is pulled downward gradually. The baby's anterior arm is born first by manipulating it across the infant's chest; the body is gently lifted upward and the posterior arm is delivered. The head can usually then be delivered by manual manipulation.[33] All manipulations should be as gentle as possible to avoid injury. If undue force is applied and the infant is injured, litigation may ensue. For example, a suit decided in 1972 was brought after a physician performed a partial breech extraction and the infant was born with a ruptured spinal cord at a point between the eighth cervical and first thoracic vertebrae, resulting in paralysis from the chest down. The patient claimed that the injury was caused by the application of excessive force in effecting delivery of the infant's head. The decision did not resolve the issue of liability but ordered the case retried on the basis of inadequate expert testimony.[34]

The following case contains facts relating to practically all of the complications and considerations associated with the breech position and delivery treated above. The case involves an intrauterine growth retarded (IUGR) baby, one who has been carried in the uterus the full gestational period, yet who has a relatively low weight at birth. Characteristically, an IUGR baby has wasted, flaccid buttocks but a head of normal size. Such babies have a fairly high mortality rate;

in those that survive, there is an increased risk of neurological abnormalities. Because of their small size, they are prone to present in the breech position.

CASE ILLUSTRATION

The patient sued her obstetrician for negligently inflicted injuries to her infant. Her theory for recovery was based upon her obstetrician's failure to realize that the baby was in a breech position until one hour prior to his delivery. She also contended that the obstetrician's administration of spartocin, which speeded up her contractions, and a spinal anesthetic created an emergency situation in the delivery room. Furthermore, the patient claimed the obstetrician erred by performing a total breech extraction rather than a partial breech extraction and that the obstetrician improperly applied forceps to the child. The obstetrician maintained that it is common to be unable to ascertain whether a child is in a vertex or breech presentation until after the amniotic sac bursts. In the present case, the obstetrician made a breech diagnosis after the sac burst. The obstetrician further claimed that spinal anesthetic and spartocin, which makes contractions more efficient rather than accelerating them, are used without complication in partial breech extractions, which the obstetrician claimed the patient's delivery was. Also, the obstetrician stated that the use of forceps was required in order to deliver the child immediately. Finally, the obstetrician claimed that the patient's child was an IUGR baby, which further complicated the delivery. At trial, an expert testified that IUGR babies weighing as little as the patient's (less than 2500 grams, or 5.5 pounds) with a gestation period of more than 37 weeks have a 95 percent mortality rate. IUGR babies who weigh over 2500 grams have only a seven percent mortality rate. The jury delivered a verdict for the obstetrician.

The patient appealed on the basis of an article found after the trial. It refuted the statistics the expert provided, stating that IUGR babies weighing less than 2500 grams and being over 37 weeks old have a 2.6 percent death rate. The court refused to allow the new evidence, however, because it could have been obtained before the trial in the exercise of reasonable diligence. The article had been published five years prior to the trial and the patient knew that IUGR babies would be discussed at trial. Consequently, because the jury had been presented with legally sufficient evidence to determine that the obstetrician was not negligent, the court upheld the jury verdict (*Freed v. Priore*, 1977).[35]

Another aspect of the case that should be noted is the allegation of late diagnosis of breech. Diagnosis may be made by abdominal palpation, through which the head and pelvic regions of the fetus may be distinguished. If the cervix is partly dilated, breech positioning may be identified by vaginal inspection.[36]

Diagnosis of breech is necessary in order to determine whether the baby should be delivered vaginally or by cesarean section (see § 11.26, Cesarean Section). Often lawsuits involving injuries sustained by breech babies are based on allegations that the physician negligently failed to perform a cesarean section. Generally, vaginal delivery is indicated if:

1. The gestational age is greater than 36 weeks
2. The estimated fetal weight is greater than 5.5 pounds (2500 grams) but less than 8 pounds (3,175 grams)
3. The presenting part is at or below station −1 when labor begins*
4. The cervix is soft, effaced, and dilated more than 3 centimeters
5. The patient has an ample gynecoid or anthropoid pelvis
6. The patient has a history of a previous breech delivery of a baby weighing more than 7 pounds or a previous vertex delivery of a baby weighing more than 8 pounds (3,630 grams)
7. The obstetrican is experienced in performing vaginal breech deliveries

The necessity of a cesarean delivery of a breech presentation is strongly suggested if:

1. The gestational age is less than 36 weeks
2. The estimated fetal weight is greater than 8 pounds
3. The presenting part is at or above station −2
4. The cervix is firm, incompletely effaced, and dilated less than 3 centimeters
5. The patient does not have a history of prior vaginal delivery or has a history of a difficult prior vaginal delivery
6. The patient has an android or flat pelvis
7. The baby presents in the footling or complete breech position, which predispose to prolapse of the umbilical cord
8. The fetal head is hyperextended (ascertainable by X ray)[37]
9. The obstetrician has had limited experience in vaginal breech delivery

Where the conditions surrounding a particular breech include one of the indications for a cesarean section and a cesarean section is not performed, the physician may face liability if the baby is injured (see § 11.26, Cesarean Section).

---

*The station, or location, of the presenting part of the fetus in the birth canal is designated by numbers from −5 to +5; the higher the number, the farther the fetus has moved into the canal.

CASE ILLUSTRATION

The patient was admitted to the hospital for the birth of her first child. At that time she was experiencing normal labor. Five hours after the patient's admission, a nurse reported to the obstetrician in charge of the labor facilities that the baby was in a breech position. X rays were ordered, and the patient's husband was informed that there was ample room in the patient's pelvis for a vaginal delivery. The obstetrician failed to inform the patient or her husband that the baby's head was severely bent backwards toward the spine. One hour later, the patient's chosen obstetrician came on duty and was told by the first obstetrician of the baby's hyperextended neck. The second obstetrician also failed to reveal this condition to the parents. The second obstetrician delivered the baby vaginally. Several months after the birth, it was discovered that the baby was quadriplegic, with virtually no movement or feeling below the shoulders. The patient sued the two obstetricians, alleging negligence in their failure to deliver the baby by cesarean section based on their findings that his neck was hyperextended and on their failure to inform the parents of the cesarean delivery option or to obtain their consent to a vaginal delivery. At trial, when asked whether the facts surrounding the circumstances of the impending birth should have been communicated to the parents, one of the obstetricians responded unequivocally in the negative. Earlier, during his deposition, the same obstetrician had testified that the parents were entitled to have the facts of the baby's condition and the risks of a vaginal delivery presented to them. The trial court had refused to allow the jury to consider this prior, inconsistent statement as a reflection on the obstetrician's credibility. The state supreme court held that failure to admit this evidence warranted a new trial. Because medical opinions are required in a jury resolution of the issue of informed consent, the inconsistency of this obstetrician's opinion, as expressed both prior to and during trial, affected the weight the jury would attach to it. Consequently, the court reversed the judgment in favor of the obstetricians and ordered a new trial (*Young v. Group Health Cooperative of Puget Sound*, 1975).[38]

§ 11.22 Dystocia

Liability may be imposed on the physician where inadequate or inaccurate pelvimetry (measurement of the pelvis) causes injury to an infant or where there is negligent management of dystocia.

Basic Standard of Care: The American College of Obstetricians and Gynecologists has not formulated specific guidelines for the management of dystocia.

Intepretation and Customary Practice: Dystocia refers to a long or difficult labor. Normal labor is said to have a maximum duration of 24 hours. Any labor

§ *11.22* *Dystocia* *421*

that lasts longer than this is referred to as prolonged; some physicians consider a second or subsequent labor that lasts longer than 18 hours to be prolonged.[39]

Prolonged labor is not the primary concern in dystocia—the cause of the prolonged labor is. Generally, a dystocia may arise from any of three causes, as identified by Benson: the passage, the power, and the passenger. In other words, alterations in the structure of the birth canal or obstructions such as an ovarian tumor (the passage), ineffective uterine contractions (the power), or excessive size, abnormal presentations, or maldevelopment of the baby (the passenger) may precipitate dystocia. The placenta may also be a factor in dystocia if it blocks or interferes with the descent of the presenting part (see § 11.23, Placental Anomalies).[40]

The obstetrician must consider a number of factors in predicting dystocia and deciding how it will be managed. An estimation of pelvic shape and size, pelvimetry, can be conducted clinically or by X ray. Clinical pelvimetry does not provide accurate measurements of the pelvis, but it offers a fairly accurate assessment of the shape and capacity of the pelvic cavity. X-ray pelvimetry provides more precise information than a clinical examination, particularly with respect to the relation between pelvic capacity and fetal size. Even so, X-ray pelvimetry does not often make it possible to accurately predict the outcome of the pregnancy. X-ray pelvimetry is most informative when performed late in the pregnancy or during labor in the following circumstances:

1. During a dysfunctional labor, particularly if the physician is considering the use of oxytocin
2. After a vaginal examination has been performed early in labor if there is any question of pelvic adequacy in patients with abnormal clinical measurements
3. During a trial labor for contracted pelvis before deciding to use oxytocin or to perform a cesarean section
4. When breech or other abnormal fetal positions are suspected
5. In patients who have had injury or disease involving the hips or bony pelvis
6. In patients with histories of protracted labors or large babies
7. When there is an indication of disproportion, such as a floating head in a primigravida during early labor[41]

Nevertheless, many physicians consider pelvimetry to be a poor way to predict whether vaginal delivery is possible; the diagnosis of "failure to progress" is used more often than "cephalo-pelvic disproportion." Most decisions regarding delivery are based on other factors such as presentation, maturity and failure to progress.

With respect to the fetus, the obstetrician should also determine its position, its weight, the extent of head flexion, head size, and the dimensions of the effective plane of the fetal head. The character of uterine contractions and the progress of effacement and cervical dilation should also be assessed. When these factors are considered, the decision on whether to proceed with a vaginal birth or a cesarean section can be made. Where inadequate or inaccurate pelvimetry can be shown to have caused an injury to an infant, the physician may face liability. A causal connection between the physician's conduct and the injury resulting from dystocia must be shown by the plaintiff, however, if the plaintiff is to prevail.

CASE ILLUSTRATION

Suit was brought against the delivering obstetrician on behalf of an infant suffering from cerebral palsy, spastic paraplegia, and mental retardation. It was alleged that the obstetrician allowed a prolonged labor to occur and that this resulted in perinatal asphyxia, causing the cerebral palsy. The infant-plaintiff provided evidence that the obstetrician had clinically examined the mother prenatally and had recorded the transverse measurement of her pelvic outlet as 8 centimeters. Furthermore, the infant weighed 9 pounds at birth. The infant-plaintiff asserted that these two measurements indicated cephalopelvic disproportion, which should have led the obstetrician to diagnose cervical dystocia. (The obstetrician did diagnose cervical dystocia after the birth.) The obstetrician-defendant presented evidence that the mother had had X-ray pelvimetry performed four years after the birth and that this pelvimetry indicated that the anteroposterior measurement was 7.6 centimeters and the transverse measurement was 11.9 centimeters. The obstetrician argued that these measurements were relevant despite the fact that they were taken four years after the incident resulting in the lawsuit because bony pelvic measurements do not change and because X-ray pelvimetry produces more accurate measurements than does clinical pelvimetry. The obstetrician argued that it was difficult to ascertain the size of the infant's head before birth, but a correlation could be made between weight and head size. Though the infant's weight was greater than normal, the mother's pelvic proportions could arguably accommodate its head. The infant-plaintiff further asserted that labor had lasted 72 hours. On the first day the mother had had light pains, which had become irregular; there had been a slow, minimal dilation of the cervix. The obstetrician administered Pitocin to induce contractions; it strengthened them but had no effect on dilation. During the second day the mother was alternately crying and dozing as labor pains continued on an irregular basis. Her cervix was 3 to 4 centimeters dilated. On the third day dilation progressed and the contractions strengthened. After 16 hours of these strengthened labor contractions, she gave vaginal birth, aided by an episiotomy.

§ 11.22 *Dystocia* 423

The obstetrician-defendant contended that all labor prior to the strengthened pains of the third day constituted false labor and that actual labor, beginning early on the third day, lasted only 16 hours, which is within normal limits. The infant-plaintiff maintained and introduced expert testimony to the effect that the contractive forces of the pelvis on the fetal head and placenta of a prolonged, active labor over a 72-hour period would greatly increase the risk of insufficient oxygen supply to the fetus. A decreased supply of oxygen to the fetus could result in asphyxia or perinatal cerebral anoxia, permanently destroying brain cells; the infant-plaintiff claimed that such damage caused the cerebral palsy. One expert testified on behalf of the obstetrician that cerebral palsy could be caused by hereditary factors or in utero infections. There was evidence that the mother may have suffered such an infection. There was further evidence of genetic defects spread over several generations and several branches of the infant's family. A CAT scan was performed on the infant to determine whether a congenital anomaly or a genetic defect existed. The CAT scan proved normal. The infant-plaintiff asserted that this result ruled out a genetic cause of the cerebral palsy. The obstetrician contended that the scan would show only structural defects and would not disclose anything about a genetic origin unless it was manifested as a structural defect. The court noted that, in order to succeed on the malpractice claim, the infant-plaintiff must prove that his cerebral palsy was caused by the manner in which the obstetrician managed the delivery or that it could have been avoided by some other, more appropriate management. The court held that the evidence failed to show causation by a fair preponderance or to support the infant's contention that a cesarean delivery would have avoided the injury. The court held in favor of the obstetrician (*Dick v. Lewis*, 1980).[42]

Most of the lawsuits arising out of injuries caused by dystocia have been generated by characteristics of the passenger. Litigation most often arises from injuries to the infant's shoulder.[43] The size of the infant is an important consideration in predicting shoulder dystocia. The average weight of an infant at term is slightly more than 7 pounds (3,200 grams); the average length is about 19.5 inches (50 centimeters). Approximately ten percent of infants weigh at least 9 pounds (4,000 grams), but no more than one or two percent weigh over 10 pounds (4,500 grams). Because birth weight often increases with each subsequent pregnancy, it is erroneous to assume that a multiparous woman will deliver without difficulty simply because her previous deliveries were uneventful. If the mother suffers from diabetes, fetal size will most likely be excessive. Generally, a weight gain of more than 30 pounds in a pregnant woman indicates the possibility of a large baby.[44]

Injuries to the shoulder as a result of dystocia occur when the head descends and is delivered, but the baby's shoulders are too broad to pass through. This condition requires prompt delivery, otherwise the baby may die because its chest is compressed, preventing respiration and reducing circulation through the cord. Usually, the posterior shoulder descends below the promontory of the mother's sacrum, but the excessive width of the infant's shoulders prevents the anterior shoulder from entering the pelvis. When this occurs, forceful downward traction on the infant's head could injure the infant's brachial plexus or fracture the cervical spine, while doing little to facilitate the delivery. The infant's anterior shoulder should first be pushed into the pelvis by direct pressure through the mother's abdominal wall. If this maneuver fails, the physician's hand should be inserted into the vagina until the first and second fingers can be hooked in the infant's posterior armpit. The posterior shoulder should be simultaneously rotated towards the anterior and pulled downward. If this succeeds, the anterior shoulder should be rotated into the true pelvis below the sacral promontory while the posterior shoulder is delivered anteriorly from underneath the symphysis.[45] Where indications that dystocia may occur because of excessive shoulder width are not heeded and appropriate delivery techniques are not utilized, the physician may face liability for negligent management of the delivery.

CASE ILLUSTRATION

The patient was 29-years-old and weighed over 200 pounds when her baby boy, who weighed 10 pounds and 14 ounces, was born. The patient had previously given uneventful birth to an 8-pound 6-ounce girl and an 8-pound 12-ounce boy. Urine tests for diabetes had always been negative, although the patient's obstetrician was aware of diabetes in the patient's family. The obstetrician had not run a glucose tolerance test, which is more conclusive; a glucose tolerance test conducted several months after the birth established that the patient had diabetes.

Labor before the birth of the patient's third child was neither extended nor eventful until after the head was delivered. Because of the baby's size, his right shoulder, presenting anteriorly, became lodged behind the pubic symphysis. The obstetrician applied downward pressure on the baby's head in an effort to glide the shoulder beneath the symphysis. He then rotated the shoulders in an unsuccessful attempt to find a more accommodating diagonal diameter. During part of this time, two attending nurses applied fundal pressure by pushing on the patient's abdomen. The obstetrician then reached into the birth canal and extracted the left arm and shoulder. This delivery of the left shoulder caused the right shoulder to drop from behind the symphysis, and delivery was completed. The obstetrician clamped and severed the umbilical cord and circumcised the baby. He noticed that the baby's right arm was flaccid. Another physician later arranged for the baby to be examined at the Mayo Clinic. Physicians there diagnosed his condition as severe injury to the brachial plexus of the right arm (Erb-Duchenne, or Klumpke's paralysis), constituting traumatic nerve damage to the cervical area of the spinal column, where nerves from the head and arm enter the spinal cord. Despite various surgical repairs and splints, the baby's arm was permanently deformed and 85 percent disabled. The patient sued the obstetrician. Several experts testified at trial, most concurring that a brachial plexus injury would not result unless excessive traction had been applied to the infant's head or some other negligent act had occurred. Other expert testimony criticized the use of fundal pressure unaccompanied by downward pressure on the symphysis. Another expert emphasized that dystocia should have been anticipated because of the previous births of large infants, the possibility of diabetes in an obese mother, and estimations of the child's size. The obstetrician-defendant testified that traction put on the infant's head caused the brachial plexus injury. He nevertheless felt he had properly carried out accepted techniques in remedying the dystocia and characterized the amount of traction he had applied to the baby's head as moderate. The court held that the evidence relating to the cause of the injury overwhelmingly indicated traction applied to the baby's head in the course of his birth. While the evidence linking the obstetrician's negligence to the causes of the injury was only circumstantial, it was sufficient under the doctrine of res ipsa loquitur to hold the obstetrician-defendant liable (*Reilly v. Straub*, 1979).[46]

Other courts have decided cases with similar facts in favor of the physician. Those courts are impressed by the difficulty of anticipating dystocia and the hindsight aspect of expert testimony. Courts recognize the existence of different but equally proper courses in dealing with dystocia, and, where the physician has taken appropriate measures, the court will not allow hindsight testimony that another course might have been more successful to determine the outcome of the case.

CASE ILLUSTRATION

The obstetrician determined late in the patient's pregnancy that her uterus may have been developing larger than normal. X-ray studies ruled out any congenital abnormality or multiple birth. Clinical pelvimetry revealed that the patient's intertuberous measurement was 8 centimeters, which the obstetrician considered to be adequate for vaginal delivery. Moreover, the physician considered that the patient had already given birth to a baby of average size without any difficulty. The patient entered the medical center at approximately 11:30 p.m. in the early stages of active labor. After two hours of labor the head had become engaged, and within three hours the cervix was fully dilated, completely effaced, and the membrane ruptured. At this point no abnormalities had been noted by the attending physicians, and there was no reason to expect anything other than a normal vaginal delivery. However, at 2:23 a.m., approximately four hours after labor had begun, fetal distress was noted. The fetus was low in the pelvis and in an occiput posterior (face up) position rather than the more common occiput anterior position (face down). After several unsuccessful attempts to manually rotate the head, the physician decided that a midforceps delivery was necessary. The baby's head was delivered by intermittent traction and relaxation. On delivery of the head it was discovered that the umbilical cord was wrapped around the baby's neck and that he was cyanotic, the probable cause of the fetal distress. The umbilical cord was removed, and manual traction was applied in an attempt to complete the delivery. It was then observed that the baby's shoulders were not being delivered: the right shoulder had overridden the pubic bone and was obstructed by it. Because the baby was partly delivered, a cesarean section was impossible. He had to be delivered vaginally, and, because he had difficulty breathing, his shoulder had to be freed within a few minutes. The obstetrician applied gentle traction to the head to extract the baby; each physician attempted to rotate the shoulder by the corkscrew method—that is, by manual rotation of the fetus. Another physician applied fundal pressure on the mother's abdomen, and the obstetrician inserted his hand to accomplish the delivery of the posterior (left) shoulder first, permitting the right shoulder to slip under the pubic bone. The baby sustained a 2 millimeter depressed occipital fracture, injury to the upper and lower brachial plexus resulting in paralysis, and a fractured clavicle. The patient sued the physicians, alleging negligence in their failure both to predict dystocia and to manage it properly. The court reviewed the testimony and concluded:

1. The failure to perform X-ray pelvimetry in light of an intertuberous diameter of 8 centimeters did not constitute negligence. "Shoulder dystocia cannot be forecast by X-ray pelvimetry, or any other diagnostic tests, and therefore such procedure would not have avoided the problem."

2. It was not malpractice to proceed with a vaginal delivery rather than a cesarean delivery, because the former was one of two acceptable techniques and the use of the latter became preferable only in retrospect.

3. It was not malpractice to use forceps to deliver the child in the face-up position, nor was there a deviation in the type of forceps used or in the actual application of the forceps.

4. It cannot be said that excessive force was used to deliver the

shoulder merely because the child was paralyzed. The presence of an injury does not automatically mean there was negligence.

The court concluded that much of the expert testimony was "based largely, if not entirely, on . . . hindsight judgments as to what should have been done." Because the court stated the physician-defendants should be judged on the facts as they existed when the patient was in labor and not in light of subsequent events, it reversed a judgment for the patient and ordered a new trial (*Henry v. Bronx Lebanon Medical Center,* 1976).[47]

§ 11.23 Placental Anomalies

Liability may be imposed on a physician for the failure to inform a patient of the existence of placenta previa and the option to undergo a cesarean section or the negligent treatment of abruptio placentae and placenta accreta.

Basic Standard of Care: The American College of Obstetricians and Gynecologists has not published guidelines for management of placental anomalies.

Intepretation and Customary Practice: In a normal birth sequence labor begins, the baby is delivered, and the placenta follows. Delivery of the placenta marks the end of the last stage of labor. Occasionally, the placenta will introduce complications.

One such complication is placenta previa. Placenta previa refers to the implantation of the placenta in the lower portion of the uterus rather than the upper, active section. The single most reliable sign of placenta previa is painless bleeding in about the thirty-second week of pregnancy. The location of the placenta interferes with vaginal delivery, and cesarean section is usually indicated unless only a small portion of the placenta is involved. Low implantation of the placenta may cause early spontaneous abortion, postpartum hemorrhage, and puerperal infection. Hemorrhage results because the lower portion of the uterus does not contract as effectively as the upper portion and therefore cannot control bleeding as well. Increased susceptibility to infection results because the placenta is so close to the vagina, from which organisms may be transferred. The baby may not survive delivery because of prematurity, intrauterine anoxia due to placental separation or respiratory distress.[48]

As soon as a diagnosis of placenta previa is made, the physician should inform the patient of the condition. The physician should present the patient with enough information to make an informed choice between vaginal delivery or cesarean section so that, if the patient chooses a cesarean section, it may be performed soon enough to minimize the risks to both mother and child.

CASE ILLUSTRATION

The mother made regular visits to her obstetrician prior to the birth of her child. The obstetrician estimated the probable date of birth to be December 8. Approximately five weeks before that time, the mother experienced episodes of painless bleeding and other symptoms indicating placenta previa. On December 7, the physician rotated the fetus from a breech position. Birth did not occur on the expected date. On December 21, the mother was admitted to the hospital because of bleeding and was examined by the obstetrician. She was taken to the delivery room, where the obstetrician confirmed the diagnosis of partial placenta previa. The obstetrician then attempted, unsuccessfully, to induce labor by administering a drug. In the early afternoon poor fetal heart tones were noted and a cesarean section was performed. The child was limp at birth and suffered from anoxia; the anoxia caused spastic quadriplegia and cerebral palsy. The patient sued the physician, alleging, among other things, that he had failed to inform her of the medically appropriate option of a cesarean section and that this failure caused the damage the child suffered. At trial, an expert testified that it was the duty of obstetricians, when placenta previa occurs, to tell their patients of the risks to both mother and child associated with normal birth. The jury found for the physician on two of the negligence issues presented by the patient (failure to diagnose placenta previa and timely perform a cesarean section). However, the jury was not instructed as to the physician's duty to inform the patient of the cesarean section option. This constituted the basis for a new trial, where not only the negligence of the physician in failing to inform the patient of the alternative procedure would be at issue, but also his negligence with respect to diagnosing the condition and performing the operation earlier (*Holt v. Nelson*, 1974).[49]

Abruptio placentae, the second placental anomaly mentioned above, is a complication of later pregnancy. In such cases, the placenta is separated from its implantation site in the upper segment of the uterus before delivery of the baby. Separation may be complete or partial. Bleeding occurs, accompanied by pain that varies in severity. The blood may be darker than with placenta previa because it is retained in the uterus temporarily before it is discharged into the vagina. The uterus feels firm but tender. The fetus's heart tones may become weak, irregular, or absent. Management of this complication requires consideration of cesarean section. Vaginal delivery is appropriate in patients with less severe forms. Patients who receive liberal transfusions and whose resulting coagulation defects are recognized and corrected have the best chance of survival. Fetal death may be caused by anoxia from placental separation, the complications of prematurity, and maternal toxemia.[50] Proper treatment includes controlling the bleeding, replacing the lost blood, and emptying the uterus. Failure to adequately treat this precarious complication may give rise to litigation.

CASE ILLUSTRATION

The patient, who was in her first pregnancy, was admitted to the hospital with abnormally heavy vaginal bleeding, increased uterine tonus, and a

§ 11.23   *Placental Anomalies*   429

fetal heart rate of 106 beats per minute. Partial placental separation was diagnosed. The patient's obstetrician examined her and returned to his home. The patient received no further care from him throughout the night. During the night, the patient was repeatedly observed to be crying, in pain, and uncontrollable by the single attending nurse in the hospital. The nurse examined the patient but did not recognize evidence of labor. At 6:30 a.m. the patient, unattended, spontaneously delivered a 7-pound 5-ounce baby. The diagnosis of partial placenta separation was confirmed by examination of the placenta and lacerations suffered by the patient. Within four or five hours, the baby experienced severe respiratory distress, and thick, bloody mucus was sucked from his lungs. The baby died at the age of 29 hours. The patient sued her obstetrician, among others. The obstetrician moved for a judgment prior to trial, claiming that the baby died of hyaline membrane disease, a condition beyond his control. The patient, however, submitted the expert testimony of a physician who had examined the record and concluded that, based upon the unsterile conditions at birth, the baby had died of pneumonia. The expert further stated that hyaline membrane disease occurs in premature babies, whereas this baby was mature. Furthermore, the diagnosis was unwarranted by the microscopic findings at the autopsy. The expert contended that a cesarean section should have been performed to deal with the placental separation and to provide a sterile environment for the birth. The court noted this testimony and concluded that an issue of fact existed that should be resolved by the submission of further expert testimony to the jury. The court held that the obstetrician was not entitled to a judgment in his favor prior to trial of the case (*Hogan v. Almand,* 1974).[51]

Another anomaly of the placenta that has given rise to litigation is placenta percreta. This is a rare condition involving penetration of the myometrium by placental villi. A more common, related condition is placenta accreta, which is abnormally firm adherence of the placenta to the uterine wall. Placenta increta also involves penetration of the myometrium by the placental villi but not as far as in placenta percreta. These conditions come about when the decidual elements of the placenta are so insufficient that large numbers of placental villi penetrate the uterine musculature, attaching the placenta to the uterine wall (accreta), invading the uterine wall (increta), or going entirely through the uterus to its peritoneal covering (percreta). With placenta percreta, there is little bleeding. The placenta cannot be removed manually because the maternal surface of the placenta cannot be separated from the uterine wall. A hysterectomy is usually required as treatment.[52] The following case resulted from an incident of placenta percreta.

CASE ILLUSTRATION

The patient became ill in the seventh month of her pregnancy, complaining of chills, diarrhea, and abdominal pain. These symptoms were consistent with an illness prevalent in the patient's town at the time. The examining physician found that the patient had normal vital signs under the circumstances, was lucid, and had not experienced vaginal bleeding. He ruled out abruptio placenta after manually examining the uterus and hearing fetal heart tones. He concluded that the patient was mildly dehydrated, was suffering from gastroenteritis that was probably viral, and was possibly anemic. The physician had the patient admitted to the hospital and ordered appropriate treatment and laboratory tests. A laboratory report the following morning revealed a low blood count. The physician ruled out rectal or uterine bleeding and thought that gastrointestinal bleeding was the most likely cause of the blood loss. He sought to obtain a second opinion before ordering invasive surgery. Later that morning, while still in her room, the patient suffered a cardiac arrest and could not be resuscitated. The cause of death was determined to be cardiac arrest caused by intra-abdominal hemorrhage from placenta percreta. An autopsy revealed that the placenta had grown through the wall of the patient's uterus, creating a 3-centimeter tear in the uterine artery. The patient's husband sued the physician, alleging negligence in failing to timely diagnose and properly treat the patient's condition. At trial, the physician testified, without contradiction, that placenta percreta is an extremely rare condition in pregnancy and that only 37 cases similar to the patient's had ever been reported. Other expert witnesses testified that the diagnosis of gastroenteritis was reasonable under the circumstances. The experts testified further that the laboratory tests which the physician had ordered conformed with proper medical practice and custom; the monitoring of vital signs that he ordered was sufficient; the dosage of medication was moderate and appropriate; hemorrhage was not indicated by the patient's symptoms; and her demise was caused by an acute episode of placenta percreta, causing rapid, massive internal hemorrhaging which filled the retroperitoneal space with 4,000 cubic centimeters of blood within minutes. A jury verdict that the physician was not negligent in his diagnosis or treatment of the patient was upheld (*Eckert v. Smith,* 1979).[53]

§ 11.24 Rupture of the Amnion

Liability may be imposed on a physician for the failure to follow approved medical practices in treating a patient with amnionitis, including the failure to take precautions to control infection and avoid termination of the pregnancy.

Basic Standard of Care: The American Collge of Obstetricians and Gynecologists has not published guidelines for management and treatment of amnion rupture.

§ 11.24   *Rupture of the Amnion*

Interpretation and Customary Practice: Rupture of the amnion, or membrane surrounding the fetus, may lead to infection. If labor does not begin within 24 hours after the rupture, there is an increased risk of amnionitis, or infection of the amnion. The organisms usually associated with amnionitis are gram-negative bacteria, including *Escherichia coli, Aerobacter aerogenes,* and *Proteus vulgaris.* Streptococci and staphylococci have also been found. Vasomotor collapse, acute renal tubular necrosis, and death can result from the endotoxins found in gram-negative bacteria. The patient with amnionitis may also develop hypotension, shock, hypotonic or absent bowel sounds, and oliguria (reduced output of urine). The fetus may develop pneumonia from aspiration of infected amniotic fluid, the umbilical cord extending to the fetal liver may become infected, or the fetus may have septicemia. The symptoms of amnionitis include foul discharge, elevated temperature, and raised pulse. If the patient develops amnionitis, the pregnancy should be terminated by either inducing labor or performing a cesarean section.[54]

A physician may be threatened with legal liablity for failure to follow approved medical practices when treating a patient with amnionitis. In one case, for example, the patient experienced symptoms that included broken water, significant weight loss, and vaginal discharge. The baby was stillborn. The physician, who took no action to treat these symptoms, was sued for medical malpractice because the baby's death was "possibly" caused by amnionitis.

CASE ILLUSTRATION

A physician examined the patient late in her pregnancy. At that time, the patient weighed 188.5 pounds. A few days later, the patient's water broke, but she did not go into labor. A second physician examined the patient the next day and found that her weight had dropped to 183.5 pounds. The physician did not take her temperature or prescribe any medication. At that time, the patient could feel the baby move. The following day, the patient experienced sharp abdominal pains and bloody discharge. The next morning, she noticed a thick green and black discharge. She was examined by the first physician, who told her she was having a false labor and should come back in one week. The patient's weight had dropped to 180 pounds. For the next five days, the patient suffered severe pain and continued to experience the green and black discharge. The physician examined her again and sent her to the hospital for an X ray. Later that day, the physician checked for fetal heartbeat and told the patient she would have a breech birth. The hospital notes indicated that later that evening there was no fetal heart tone. The next morning, the baby was delivered stillborn. The delivering physician's notes stated that "at delivery pt. had prolapsed cord tight around right thigh of infant; severe amnionitis with gross pus noted when head delivered, running from the vagina." Evidence also showed that the baby's skin was macerated. The cause of death was listed as prolapsed umbilical cord with amnionitis as a possible contributing factor. The patient continued to suffer pain and remained in the hospital for ten days.

The patient brought suit against the first two physicians, alleging that they were negligent in providing prenatal care. Specifically, the patient-plaintiff introduced expert testimony that the green and black substance which the patient-plaintiff discharged was meconium, a substance contained in the unborn fetus's intestinal tract that cannot escape unless the amnion has ruptured. In response to hypothetical questions, the expert stated that the membrane ruptured when the patient first experienced a gush of water; that the fetus might have died from infection; that the patient-plaintiff's pain might have been caused by amnionitis; and that a fetus will not have skin maceration unless it has been dead for 24 to 48 hours. Although the jury found that the physician-defendants were negligent, the appellate court found that there was insufficient evidence to support a finding of malpractice, because the patient-plaintiff's expert witness did not state what the physician-defendants should or should not have done to conform with approved medical practices. Further, the patient-plaintiff did not establish by expert testimony that the child would not have been stillborn if the physician-defendants had followed the approved practices. The court granted a new trial (*Lindsey v. The Clinic for Women*, 1979).[55]

The physician may cause infection through negligent examination. While manual examination is used during pregnancy, manipulations must be gentle and kept to a minimum in order to avoid infection and termination of the pregnancy.[56] A physician may face legal liability if negligent examination causes infection that results in a stillborn child.

CASE ILLUSTRATION

While examining the pregnant patient, the physician used an unsterilized glove, broke the patient's water, and unsuccessfully attempted to induce labor by injection. On the day of the examination, the patient could feel the fetus moving, and she had been told by the physician that there was a fetal heartbeat. On subsequent visits, the physician told the patient to come back only when she was in labor. Because she was experiencing profuse discharge, the patient visited a second physician, who sent her to the hospital. Upon entering the hospital, she was found to be suffering from infection and was treated with various antibiotics. The patient delivered a stillborn child. The patient brought suit against the first physician, alleging negligence. At trial, the physicians who treated and examined the patient at the hospital testified that the cause of fetal death was intrauterine

§ 11.25　　　　　　　　　　　　　Forceps Delivery　　　　　　　　　　　　　433

infection. They further stated that the physician-defendant's treatment of the patient was poor and that he failed to recognize "a medical problem that was progressing to an undesirable end," which a physician of ordinary competence would not have done. Further testimony was offered that the patient's condition "could not have developed without having rupture of the membrane as a precursor to her condition." The jury found for the patient-plaintiff, but the appellate court granted a new trial on all issues because the jury had failed to award damages for the destruction of the child's earning power, a proper award in a wrongful death action involving an infant where negligence has been shown (*Rice v. Rizk,* 1970).[57]

§ 11.25　Forceps Delivery

Liability may be imposed on a physician for injury to the mother or infant resulting from the unnecessary or negligent use of forceps during delivery.

Basic Standard of Care: The American College of Obstetricians and Gynecologists has not published guidelines for the use of forceps in delivery.

Interpretation and Customary Practice: Obstetric forceps have two uses: they can be used to extract an infant from the birth canal when the physician deems termination of labor necessary for either the mother or the infant, and they can be used to rotate the infant from an abnormal position.

Over 600 types of obstetric forceps have been designed, many for specific delivery problems.[58] Forceps deliveries are commonly grouped into categories based on the stage and position of the presenting part at the time of application of the forceps.[59] The most common classification includes:

1. Low forceps (used when the fetal head is in an occiput anterior position and is visible during each contraction)
2. Midforceps (used when the lowest part of the head has descended below the level of the ischial spines; it usually has not rotated to an anterior position)
3. High forceps (used when the head is engaged)

Forceps delivery is indicated only when it is necessary to terminate labor and use of forceps is safer and easier than other methods of termination. Oxytocin stimulation will sometimes be preferable to a low forceps delivery, and cesarean section may be preferable to some midforceps deliveries and most high forceps deliveries.[60]

Common maternal indications for forceps delivery are inadequate uterine contractions, exhaustion, cardiac or pulmonary problems, hypertension, and hemorrhage. The most important fetal indication for termination of labor is fetal distress.[61] A common accepted use of forceps is the so called "elective" forceps which are used to shorten the second stage of labor in the absence of fetal or maternal complications.

There are several well-recognized conditions for forceps extraction. The cervix must be completely dilated, and the membranes must be ruptured. The head must be engaged and must present in a position that will permit delivery. There can be no significant cephalopelvic disproportion. The mother's bladder should be empty. Finally, the physician must be trained in and familiar with the use of forceps and have the proper type available.[62]

Improper use of forceps can result in many kinds of injuries to both mother and infant. Maternal complications include lacerations and uterine rupture with consequent hemorrhage and infection. Potential injuries to the infant include fracture of the skull, intracranial hemorrhage, seventh nerve palsy, and laceration of the soft tissue.[63] Injuries in forceps deliveries are caused both by lack of technical skill and by errors in judgment. Judgmental error often consists of failure to heed the outlined conditions for forceps delivery or proceeding prematurely or without adequate indication. Injury can also occur when a physician persists in applying forceps when difficulty indicates the need for an alternative approach, such as cesarean section.[64]

Plaintiffs commonly complain that forceps have been used unnecessarily or negligently, or both, during delivery. Most of these cases concern injury to the infant.

CASE ILLUSTRATION

The patient entered the hospital during her third pregnancy in the early stages of labor. Sometime earlier, the first physician had conducted X-ray studies and a clinical pelvimetry and had decided that the patient's pelvis was adequate for delivery. The patient was attended in the delivery room by the second physician, who was her private obstetrician, and a second-year resident. The patient was admitted to the hospital at 11:30 p.m. Within two hours, the fetus's head was engaged. Within three hours, the cervix was completely dilated and the membranes had ruptured. At 2:23 a.m., the physicians noted fetal distress. At this time, the fetus was facing up rather than down. The physicians attempted to manually rotate the head of the fetus but were unsuccessful. The obstetrician then decided that a midforceps delivery of the fetus was necessary. The resident performed the forceps extraction. He testified that more force than usual was required because the infant was facing up but that he had used no more force than was necessary. When the infant's head was delivered, the physicians noted that the umbilical cord was wrapped around the infant's neck and that the infant was cyanotic. The physicians removed the cord and attempted to complete the delivery by exerting manual traction on the infant's head. At this time, the physicians discovered that the infant's shoulders were causing dystocia, which was restricting his breathing. Since the infant was partially delivered, a cesarean section was impossible. The physicians therefore delivered the infant vaginally with a combination of manual traction and rotation and fundal pressure. The infant was delivered with a depressed occipital fracture, injury to the upper and lower brachial plexus, and a fractured clavicle. The infant, through his father, sued the hospital and the medical group to which the first physician and the obstetrician belonged. The jury returned a verdict for the plaintiffs, finding, among other things, that the forceps delivery was negligently performed and that the delivery by the vaginal route rather than by cesarean section was negligent once it was discovered that the fetus was face up and could not be rotated. The lower court entered judgment on the verdict, but the higher court reversed and remanded for a new trial. It ruled that the jury's findings were against the weight of the credible evidence. The court stated that the plaintiffs' expert had essentially testified that, in retrospect, considering what had actually occurred, a cesarean section would have been preferable to vaginal delivery. The court stated that at the time of the emergency the physicians followed an acceptable delivery procedure. The court ruled that the testimony of the plaintiffs' expert that a cesarean section could have been set up in five minutes was not believable, since the witness knew nothing about the conditions of the hospital, particularly as they existed at 2:30 a.m. The court also noted that the plaintiffs' expert admitted that fetal distress justified the use of forceps and that the type of forceps used was proper. Furthermore, the court held that there was no evidence that the actual application of the forceps was negligent (*Henry v. Bronx Lebanon Medical Center,* 1976).[65]

In *Wale v. Barnes,*[66] the testimony of the plaintiffs' expert was significantly stronger and caused the Supreme Court of Florida to reverse a directed verdict for the physician-defendants. The obstetrician used Tucker-McLean forceps in a midforceps delivery of the infant. The infant suffered bruises on the cheeks and a scalp laceration and subsequently underwent surgery for subdural hematomas. The expert testified that Tucker-McLean forceps were inappropriate because the infant had a molded, or elongated, head and that use of the wrong forceps resulted in a traumatic delivery and caused the chronic subdural hematomas.

In another case, forceps were used to deliver an infant when the infant's head became arrested in a transverse position. When the infant was delivered, swelling was present around the right eyelid and cheek. It was later determined that the infant was totally blind in the right eye. The plaintiffs introduced a number of experts who testified that the blindness was caused by negligent application of forceps. The defendant's experts testified that the blindness was caused by an intrauterine infection. The court entered judgment for the plaintiffs in the amount of $100,000. In support of its conclusion, the court noted that there was expert testimony that the physicians should have taken X rays and delivered by cesarean section, in addition to the testimony that there was actual negligence in the application of the forceps.[67]

Occasionally, plaintiffs allege that negligent and unnecessary use of forceps has caused injury to the mother.

CASE ILLUSTRATION

The patient entered the hospital at 3:00 a.m. The obstetrician delivered her infant at about 8:15 p.m., after at least 12 hours of true labor and more than three hours of second-stage labor. The obstetrician conducted forceps rotation of the infant from the transverse position during delivery. The patient sustained a laceration of the uterus, a bladder tear, a torn urethra, a torn vagina, and subsequently developed a urethrovaginal fistula. The patient sued the obstetrician, alleging that he had been negligent in (1) allowing labor to continue for an excessive period of time; (2) failing to perform a cesarean section; (3) failing to submit the patient-plaintiff to X-ray pelvimetry during labor; and (4) incompetently performing the forceps delivery. The jury returned a verdict for the patient-plaintiff, and the lower court entered judgment on it. The higher court reversed and ordered a new trial. The higher court reasoned that a new trial was warranted because the evidence presented by the patient-plaintiff showed only that cesarean section was a proper alternative to forceps delivery, not that it was required. Furthermore, the patient-plaintiff offered no testimony that X-ray pelvimetry was required by standards of reasonable medical care or that the actual performance of the forceps delivery violated applicable standards (*Schreiber v. Cestari*, 1972).[68]

Plaintiffs have also sought to establish that the physician used forceps without the consent of the parents and is therefore liable for battery and breach of the duty to obtain informed consent.[69]

CASE ILLUSTRATION

The first physician diagnosed the patient's pregnancy and cared for her for seven months. An obstetrician recommended by the first physician cared for the patient thereafter and consulted with her and her husband on several occasions. He found nothing abnormal about the patient's pelvic region. During one meeting, the patient told the obstetrician that she feared the use of forceps in delivery. She had once seen forceps marks on a newborn's face, and this had disturbed her. However, she also expressed her willingness to rely on the obstetrician for medical decisions and trusted him to do the best thing for her and her baby. The patient subsequently went into labor and was admitted to the hospital. A resident initially cared for her.

He administered an epidural anesthetic and notified the obstetrician. The delivery proceeded normally until the head became visible at the introitus. At this time, further progress ceased because of obstruction by the coccyx. The obstetrician arrived and determined that the infant's head was "riding on the coccyx." He announced to everybody in the room that he was going to use forceps to lift the head over the coccyx. The patient's husband, who was in the room, said nothing and testified that he was willing to leave the judgment as to the use of forceps to the obstetrician. The patient said the single word, "Forceps?" The patient testified that she was willing to leave medical judgments concerning the delivery to the obstetrician. The baby was delivered, but the patient's coccyx was dislocated. The patient and her husband sued the obstetrician, alleging, among other things, battery and lack of informed consent. The court upheld a verdict for the obstetrician-defendant, finding that there was no evidence to support the plaintiffs' theories. The court conceded that the patient had a fear of forceps or at least disliked them. The court nevertheless held that the parents had consented to their use. The court also relied on expert testimony that the use of low forceps is so common and free of risk that reasonable medical practitioners do not obtain specific consent to their use (*Charley v. Cameron*, 1974).[70]

Another variety of plaintiff complaints is that the physician was negligent in failing to have available or to use forceps.

CASE ILLUSTRATION

The patient went into labor and was admitted to the hospital. Her physician, a general practitioner, performed an amniotomy. He then discovered that the infant was in a breech position. The general practitioner did not have full obstetric privileges at the hospital. Hospital guidelines required that members without full privileges obtain consultation in difficult cases, including "primi breech" (a baby in a breech position in a primigravida). The general practitioner considered consultation but then decided to follow the patient's progress and base further decisions on further findings. He also considered conducting X-ray pelvimetry but instead merely conducted a clinical pelvic examination of the patient. The general practitioner did not seek consultation when the fetal heart rate later registered 168. He testified that he considered the rate to be just slightly above normal and that he decided to have the mother lie on her side and check the heart tones again. The general practitioner also testified that he did not perform a cesarean section because the labor was progressing without difficulty, and the patient's pelvis was of normal size. The delivery progressed normally until the infant's legs and trunk had been delivered. At this time, the general practitioner had difficulty delivering the head. He performed the accepted Mauriceau's maneuver and delivered the head. This procedure took about ten minutes. The infant did not breathe spontaneously after delivery. The infant was resuscitated for 12 to 15 minutes and taken to the nursery. The general practitioner then consulted a specialist. Although the specialist treated the infant, the infant died about four hours later. The infant's parents sued the general practitioner. The jury returned a verdict for the physician-defendant, and the lower court entered judgment on it. The higher court ruled that the jury could reasonably have found that the general practitioner's failure to consult during delivery was not negligent and was not the proximate cause of the infant's death. The court noted that the physician-defendant believed that the delivery was progressing normally and that consulting a specialist is no guarantee of success. The court also ruled that the jury could reasonably have concluded that the physician-defendant's decision not to perform a cesarean section and X-ray pelvimetry was a reasonable medical judgment. The court then ruled, however, that the physician-defendant was liable for failing to have available and to use Piper forceps when the Mauriceau maneuver was not successful. The plaintiffs' experts and the physician-defendant agreed that Piper forceps should have been available for use. There were none in the delivery room. One expert testified that Piper forceps should have been used immediately when the head was delayed; another testified that they should have been used immediately after the Mauriceau maneuver proved difficult. The specialist who treated the infant testified that death was due to lack of oxygen during the ten-minute delay in delivering the head. The physician-defendant offered no significant testimony to rebut this evidence. Hence, the court found him liable and remanded for a new trial to determine the amount of damages only (*Carmon v. Dippold*, 1978).[71]

§ 11.26 Cesarean Section

Liability may be imposed on a physician for negligence in the performance of a cesarean section, failure to inform a patient of the operation of cesarean section, failure to adequately attend the patient, negligence causing injury to the infant, premature performance of the procedure, or failure to successfully perform sterilization after a cesarean section.

Basic Standard of Care: The American College of Obstetricians and Gynecologists has not published guidelines for performing a cesarean section.

Interpretation and Customary Practice: Cesarean section, sometimes referred to as abdominal hysterotomy, is the delivery of a fetus, placenta, and membranes through incisions in the abdominal and uterine walls. This procedure is generally performed when a vaginal delivery promises to be hazardous to either the mother or the baby. The frequency of its performance has increased steadily as improved techniques and procedures have yielded decreasing rates of morbidity and mortality.[72]

Cesarean section may be preferable to vaginal delivery in a number of circumstances. Some patients with diabetes mellitus should have their babies delivered by cesarean section several weeks before term to avert fetal death in utero during the last three weeks. A patient over the age of 35 who is pregnant for the first time need not have a cesarean section because of her age unless there are complications to the pregnancy. If the patient has had previous cesarean sections, vaginal repair for such things as uterine prolapse or cystocele, or a poor obstetrical history, delivery by cesarean section is advisable.[73]

Cephalopelvic disproportion, uterine dysfunction, or obstruction of the birth canal can bring about dystocia, which may necessitate a cesarean section, particularly where the specific complication renders a vaginal delivery physically impossible (see § 11.22, Dystocia). Placental anomalies may also indicate a cesarean section. It is the treatment of choice in cases of placenta previa and may be performed to control profuse bleeding associated with abruptio placenta. If the fetal heart rate is slow and irregular, cesarean section alone will not save the infant; these factors suggest that the fetus is already damaged and may die before it can be delivered[74] (see § 11.23, Placental Anomalies).

The position or status of the fetus may necessitate delivery by cesarean section. Cesarean section is indicated for most babies in a stable transverse or breech presentation, particularly if the baby is large (see § 11.21, Breech Presentation). Fetal distress may also indicate the need for a cesarean section. Fetal distress refers to a weakening or irregular fetal heartbeat, the presentation of a prolapsed cord, or some other development indicating that the fetus is in jeopardy.[75]

Many pregnancies have progressed to term and the babies have been delivered vaginally where some of the above-mentioned complications have been present, with no injury to mother or child. When injury to either or both results from a complicated birth, however, a common allegation in any ensuing lawsuit is that the physician negligently failed to perform a cesarean section or to inform the parents that such an option was available.[76] The following case is typical of such lawsuits.

CASE ILLUSTRATION

The patient entered the hospital with mild labor contractions after a spontaneous rupture of her membranes and the secretion of amniotic fluid several hours earlier. About four hours later, when the patient's obstetrician examined her, the baby's head had not yet descended into the birth canal, but the patient was having contractions every five minutes. The obstetrician administered an oxytocic drug, Tocosamine, to stimulate contractions. Forty-five minutes later, the patient was having mild to moderate contractions every three minutes, but the baby's head had still not descended through the pelvic opening. The obstetrician ordered another injection of Tocosamine. Forty-five minutes later, moderately strong contractions were occurring two to three minutes apart. The fetal heart rate was 160 beats per minute, on the high side of normal. An attending nurse observed and recorded the presence of meconium. Two and a half hours later, the patient's condition had not changed and the obstetrician ordered another injection of Tocosamine. Within five minutes, the patient was taken to the delivery room with a completely dilated cervix. Twenty-five minutes later, the obstetrician administered another oxytocic medication, Syntocinon. The baby presented in the vertex position, but, because of the baby's size, the obstetrician had to use a vacuum extractor to bring it into the birth canal. The obstetrician removed the vacuum extractor, applied forceps, and delivered the baby. The baby was in a depressed state following delivery and was given an Apgar score of 1. He had marked molding of the head and had a number of seizures while in the hospital.

Ten years earlier, the same obstetrician had delivered the patient's third child. Because that child was large, weighing 9 pounds 3 ounces, the delivery was impeded by its shoulders and the child consequently suffered paralysis of one of its arms. The obstetrician had estimated the weight of the present baby to be between 9 and 10 pounds. Eventually it was discovered that this baby suffered from spastic quadriparesis and anoxic cerebral palsy. The patient sued the obstetrician, claiming he was negligent in failing to perform a cesarean delivery. Expert testimony was offered both supporting and refuting this contention. The jury returned a verdict for the patient and awarded $1.5 million in damages. The trial judge set aside the verdict as excessive and determined that the jury's sympathy for the patient and her child probably motivated not only the large award but also the finding of negligence and liability. The court ordered a new trial (*Rutherford v. Zearfoss*, 1980).[77]

If the physician is able to show that the method actually employed is a medically acceptable alternative procedure and is proper under the circumstances (such as a manual forceps rotation of a baby in the transverse position), liability may not be imposed[78] (see § 1.32, Standard of Care).

In some cases, the allegation may not be that the physician failed to perform the cesarean, but that he or she failed to perform it soon enough.[79] This allegation is generally refutable as a matter of professional judgment.

CASE ILLUSTRATION

The patient entered the hospital in labor, passing meconium-stained amniotic fluid from her vagina. The attending physicians were advised of her condition by telephone by the monitoring nurses, but they did not arrive to deliver the baby by cesarean until 17 hours had passed. The infant was born with chronic neurological disability, which manifested itself as weakness in his right arm and leg, a mild reduction in the acuity of his vision in the right eye, a defect on the left side of the brain, and a reduction in intellect. Suit was brought against the physicians on behalf of the infant, alleging that they were negligent in failing to come to the mother's aid sooner and seeking damages for the infant's resulting injuries. During the discovery proceedings prior to trial, the infant's expert witness attributed the infant's injuries to an episode of perinatal distress, indicated by the meconium-stained fluid leaking from the mother as she entered the hospital. However, the infant's expert noted that the record showed the fetus had maintained an adequate heart rate throughout, and he declined to criticize the care provided by the hospital nursing staff or the decision to perform the cesarean section. He was equivocal as to whether the leaking of the meconium-stained fluid from the mother in itself required an immediate cesarean section and stated that such staining did not preclude the possibility of vaginal delivery. He noted that this was the patient's first pregnancy and that performing a cesarean section would require cesarean sections in all the patient's subsequent pregnancies. He also testified that another reason for performing a cesarean section was prolonged labor, a condition not present in this instance. Accordingly, the attendant physicians might reasonably have postponed the decision to perform a cesarean section, since the fetus did not lose movement or heartbeat, in order to see whether the progress of labor would be adequate to allow vaginal delivery. The court noted that the infant's expert characterized the attending physician's failure to act more promptly as a matter he might question but that the remainder of his testimony indicated that he considered the attending physician's conduct to be reasonable and appropriate. Further, a matter of professional judgment was involved in the delay; the court noted that evidence had been offered explaining why a delay may have been appropriate. The court concluded that an allegation of negligence on the basis of a delay in performing the cesarean section was insufficient to present a genuine issue of fact for trial, and the entry of judgment for the physicians by the trial judge was upheld (*Buck v. Alton Memorial Hospital*, 1980).[80]

Two types of cesarean section that may be performed are the classic section and the low cervical section. The classic section is performed through a vertical incision above the dome of the bladder into the upper, contractile portion of the fundus. This method causes the greatest loss of blood, and the scar it leaves is more apt to rupture in subsequent pregnancies; furthermore, peritoneal infection is more likely. The classic section may be performed more quickly, however, and it is therefore appropriate in emergency situations. It may also be preferable if the bladder is adhered to the uterus, if the baby is in the transverse lie, if placenta previa occurs, or if the patient has carcinoma of the cervix. Because of its disadvantages, however, it is less often performed than the low cervical section.

The low cervical section is performed by making a transverse incision in the thin, lower segment of the uterus after the peritoneum has been cut and the bladder has been separated and pushed downward from its attachment to the anterior wall of the uterus. The time involved in separating the bladder makes this procedure lengthier than the classic section. Advantages of the low cervical section include the decreased likelihood of infection and the lower incidence of scar rupture in subsequent pregnancies.[81]

Complications have given rise to lawsuits. Thus, patients who have suffered from a kinked cecum,[82] a bowel obstruction,[83] or peritoneal streptococcus infection[84] after a cesarean section have sued their obstetricians. The failure of the uterine wound to heal properly has also given rise to litigation.

CASE ILLUSTRATION

The patient consulted the physician in connection with her first pregnancy. Although a vaginal delivery was anticipated, it became necessary to deliver the fetus by cesarean section because of the patient's acute pelvic angulation and tense vaginal musculature. A transverse incision was made in the lower segment, but the baby's head was deep in the birth canal and delivery was impossible. An incision was made in the midline, extending upward, and the infant was successfully delivered in the breech position. The mother's postoperative course was uneventful, and her stitches were removed by her physician, who saw the infant a few times more for routine injections. The physician told the patient that he did not know what had caused her difficulty and assured her that a cesarean section did not mean she could not have more children. Approximately nine months later, the patient discovered that she was again pregnant. Her child's pediatrician referred her to another obstetrician. The patient subsequently miscarried. She became pregnant again some three months later, but again miscarried. When the patient became pregnant for the third time since the cesarean section had been performed, the obstetrician attended her closely. In the fifth month of the pregnancy, he observed that her cervix had begun to dilate, and he performed a Shirodkar operation in an attempt to prevent dilation. The procedure did not succeed, however, and another miscarriage occurred. In an examination either at that time or subsequently, the obstetrician discovered a scar in the wall of the uterus resulting from the longitudinal incision made during the cesarean section. Because of the defect in the uterine wall, the patient could not carry a pregnancy to term. The obstetrician attempted to repair the defect surgically. However, the patient was unable to carry

§ 11.26 *Cesarean Section* 443

a subsequent pregnancy to term, and the obstetrician elected to deliver the fetus by cesarean section. The patient sued the physician involved in her first pregnancy, alleging that, because of the delay in performing the surgery, the child became so deeply placed in the pelvis that a single incision was not adequate to permit delivery and that the second incision produced a weakness in the uterine wall which caused the subsequent miscarriages. The physician claimed that too much time had passed and that the statute of limitations prevented the patient from making her claim. The patient claimed that the physician's assurance that she could have more children amounted to a fraudulent concealment of her injury, which would vitiate the limitations defense. The court stated that an allegation of fraudulent concealment must be supported by evidence of knowledge and intent to conceal. Because the physician had not attended the patient's subsequent pregnancies, had stated that he did not know what caused the initial problem, and there was no evidence to indicate that the statement was made in an effort to conceal anything from the patient, the court held for the physician (*Kauchick v. Williams*, 1968).[85]

Infections, such as those of the urinary tract, that often accompany vaginal delivery and that require care during the postpartum period (see Chapter XII, Postpartum Complications) may also occur after a cesarean section. Because the bladder is traumatized during delivery and becomes atonic after delivery, it provides a particularly susceptible medium for the development of infection. Postpartum urinary tract infections may include cystitis or acute pyelonephritis. Acute pyelonephritis, which occurs in two to three percent of pregnant women, results from an ascending infection that causes inflammation of the connective tissue of the kidney. The onset is frequently abrupt, with symptoms of acute cystitis, backache, fever, and chills. Secondary gastrointestinal symptoms and fever may occur as well.[86] Where there are indications that the cesarean procedure has aggravated a previous problem or given rise to one, the physician should attend the patient closely.

CASE ILLUSTRATION

The patient's first child was born by cesarean section. The patient subsequently suffered painful urination and required catheterization. When her second child was due to be born, the patient agreed to try a vaginal childbirth, but a cesarean section was necessary. During the procedure, the patient's uterus and bladder ruptured. A catheter was inserted for approximately one week, and the patient did not have control of her bladder for about four days. Three months later, the patient was hospitalized for treatment of a neurogenic bladder. She developed a fever of 105 degrees, had a deep rattling in her chest, and her body ached. Her husband was advised that the patient suffered from an acute kidney infection with a diagnosis of pyelonephritis. The patient's husband told her of the diagnosis and that the infections had been caused by the catheterizations that were performed on her in the hospital. Nevertheless, she underwent additional catheterizations, as well as X-ray and medical treatment, for her bladder infection throughout the remainder of that year and the next. The following year, she experienced frequent urination and headaches. Further testing revealed that she suffered from focal pyelonephritis, chronic, left upper pole. In early 1973, the frequency and irritation of urination caused her to consult with another physician. He told her that the urine from her bladder was backing up into her left kidney. The patient ultimately filed her claim against the physicians who performed the second cesarean section, stating that she was not aware of her condition until informed by the last physician. In holding that the patient had waited too long to file the claim, the court noted that she was reasonably aware of the facts giving rise to her condition, beginning with her uterus and bladder rupture in 1965, particularly since the patient was a registered nurse. She had been given permanent possession of all of her medical records in 1970; these contained a physician's diagnosis dated February 12, 1969, of chronic pyelonephritis of the left kidney and diffuse clubbing of the right kidney. The patient had had the records for three years prior to filing her claim and could not therefore argue that she had not discoverd the possible malpractice until 1973. The court refused to toll the running of the statute of limitations and dismissed the patient's claim (*Sanders v. United States*, 1977).[87]

Other injuries that a patient may incur stem from the general risks of surgery. One patient sued her obstetrician when, after four years of suffering from progressively increasing pain following a cesarean section, she underwent an operation to remove what was thought to be a tumor. The tumor was in fact a sponge, left behind during the performance of the cesarean section.[88] In another case, a hypodermic needle was left in the mother's body close to the incision.[89]

Occasionally, the infant delivered by cesarean section suffers an injury that precipitates a lawsuit. A cause of action was recognized in a case where the obstetrician cut the fetus's face during the operation, leaving a permanent, disfiguring scar running from a point near the right ear to a point near the right eye.[90] In another case, the court ordered that trial be held where the mother contended that the physician miscalculated the duration of her pregnancy, performed a cesarean section two months too early, and delivered premature twin fetuses, both of whom died within a day of delivery.[91]

Sterilization of the patient may be performed after delivery by cesarean section. A cesarean hysterectomy may be indicated when the uterus is heavily infected, when excessive bleeding cannot be controlled, or where any of the other indications for hysterectomy exist (see § 13.20, Hysterectomy). If sterilization is the main objective, hysterectomy should not be considered an equally acceptable alternative to tubal ligation. Tubal ligation has a lower morbidity and mortality rate than does hysterectomy.[92] The issues litigated in lawsuits arising out of sterilizations performed in conjunction with cesarean sections parallel those involved in sterilization generally (see § 8.30, Sterilization). Thus, cases have been brought where a cesarean sterilization was ineffective[93] and where the patient claims that her consent was not obtained prior to the sterilization.[94]

CASE ILLUSTRATION

The patient had entered the hospital in premature labor for the birth of her third child. She had consented to the delivery procedure and to a possible cesarean section. There was a known blood incompatibility between the patient and her husband, and she was fully aware of the problems presented, having been so informed by the physician during her first two pregnancies. The physician had suggested a hysterectomy to the patient, but she had rejected it as "too final." The patient and the physician also discussed tubal ligation on numerous occasions. The patient maintained that she had never expressly or implicitly consented to the ligation but had in every instance told the physician she would think about it and let him know. Upon admission to the hospital, the patient was asked by the admitting nurse to sign a "consent to operation, anesthetics, and other medical services" form provided by the hospital. The form contained, among others, the following provisions: "I am aware that sterility may result from this operation. I know that a sterile person is incapable of becoming a parent." This provision, at the patient's insistence, was stricken from the form. The form accompanied the patient's chart into the operating room, as altered, and was present there during the surgical procedure. The physician was assisted in the delivery by an obstetrician-gynecologist who asked the physician whether the patient's tubes were to be tied. Because the patient was under anesthesia and no hospital tubal ligation consent form was found on the patient's chart, the physician obtained a form and the signature of the patient's husband. A tubal ligation was performed, and the patient brought suit.

Although there was a conflict of testimony on the pivotal issue of consent, the court concluded that the physician had entertained some doubt as to whether the patient had consented. Although there was no evidence that the physician was aware of the deletion on the form and signed by the patient on admission, the form was available to the physician in the operating room. The court reasoned that, had the physician consulted the chart and noted these deletions, questions as to whether the patient had desired a ligation would have been raised. The chart also would have alerted him to the possibility that, even if the patient had previously given such consent, she had changed her mind. Further, if the physician had been certain that the patient had given express verbal consent, as he contended, there would have been no need to request the husband's consent. The husband's consent was not held to be a defense sufficient to excuse the physician from liablity for performing a tubal ligation without the express or implied consent of the patient, notwithstanding the fact that the operation was skillfully performed (*Beck v. Lovell*, 1978).[95]

Cases have also been brought where a hysterectomy was performed after a cesarean section as an emergency measure to stop copious bleeding. Despite the lack of express consent, liability has not been imposed where such an action was a proper response to a life-threatening situation.[96]

CASE ILLUSTRATION

The patient was expecting her second child. She consulted a physician, who advised that the baby be delivered by cesarean section because of its size and position within the womb. The patient and her husband agreed to the procedure and also requested that the physician perform a tubal ligation during delivery. When the patient was admitted to the hospital, she signed a consent form authorizing the cesarean section and tubal ligation, as well as "such additional operations or procedures as are considered therapeutically necessary on the basis of findings during the course of said operation." The physician and his partner performed the cesarean section, and a healthy, normal child was born. The patient was bleeding both at the incision and within the uterus from the placental implantation site. To minimize blood loss, the physicians sutured the incision. Because of the patient's age (36), the large size of the child, and the presence of numerous fibroid tumors throughout the uterus, the patient's uterus was contracting at a slower than normal rate and she was losing more than a normal amount of blood. The physicians then discovered a grapefruit-sized tumor involving the patient's right ovary, which was adherent to her uterus. They removed the tumor and sent it to the laboratory for analysis. The laboratory reported that the tumor was benign. However, removal of the tumor entailed heavy loss of blood from the point where it had adhered to the uterus. This blood loss, combined with the blood loss from the cesarean incision and the placental site, caused the physicians to believe that the patient's life was in danger. When suturing and administration of oxytocin were ineffective in controlling the bleeding, the physicians performed an abdominal hysterectomy.

The patient sued the physicians, alleging, among other things, that removal of her uterus was done without her consent and constituted an assault and battery. The physician-defendants claimed that the signed surgery authorization form established their defense of consent. The patient testified that she had read and understood the language of the consent form but claimed that the hysterectomy was not therapeutically necessary. The court observed that the standard for determining whether a procedure is therapeutically necessary is whether the physician "exercised that degree of care, skill, and diligence which any other surgeon would be required to employ in reaching a decision under the same or similar circumstances." All expert medical testimony, including that offered on behalf of the patient, concurred that, once the sutures and oxytocin had failed, a hysterectomy was the next indicated step to stop the flow of blood. The court held in favor of the physicians (*Davidson v. Shirley,* 1980).[97]

Adequate facilities should be available for performing a cesarean section. A well-equipped hospital, a reliable supply of blood, an able anesthesiologist, and capable assistants are considered essential.[98] In one case, failure to provide adequate facilities for cesarean sections as part of a clinic for obstetrical care resulted in the assessment of $10,000 in exemplary damages as well as $10,000 in actual damages against the clinic. The court noted that there was sufficient evidence to establish that the patient had not been advised that the small, 14-bed obstetrical clinic lacked cesarean facilities and that the physicians involved were aware that a certain percentage of all deliveries required cesarean section and had acted with conscious indifference to the patient's welfare. The clinic had apparently attempted to cover cesarean births by employing a physician with staff privileges at a nearby hospital to which the patient could be transferred. However, no employee of the clinic accompanied this patient to the hospital nor took medical steps to assist her once she was placed in the ambulance. (At this point she had been in labor for some time, and the attending physician had attempted to deliver the child by performing a version and extraction, a manual attempt to turn the child in such a way as to permit normal delivery, but was unsuccessful.) Upon the patient's arrival at the hospital, the physicians in the emergency room determined that the fetus was dead.[99]

§ 11.27 Episiotomy

Liability may be imposed on a physician for the negligent performance of an episiotomy.

Basic Standard of Care: The American Collge of Obstetricians and Gynecologists has not published guidelines for performing an episiotomy.

Interpretation and Customary Practice: In order to avoid injury to supporting maternal structures during delivery, episiotomies are often performed. An episiotomy is an incision in the perineum and the underlying supporting structures designed to prevent serious posterior wall injury by laceration. An incision is preferable to a laceration because the straight edges of the incision are easier to repair than irregular, lacerated edges; the well-timed incision may avoid injury to the perineal musculature and vaginal lacerations high in the vaginal vault; and the incision avoids the battering of the baby's head against the perineum as it dilates the vaginal opening.

Episiotomy may be performed either with an incision from the midline of the fourchette toward the left or right ischial tuberosity (mediolateral episiotomy) or with an incision running from the posterior fourchette straight toward the anus until the anal sphincter becomes visible (median, or midline, episiotomy). The median episiotomy provides greater room per inch of incision, can be repaired more easily, results in less loss of blood, and is less uncomfortable for the mother as it heals. However, the median episiotomy is more likely than the mediolateral to result in perineal laceration through the anal sphincter (third degree) or even through the rectal mucosa (fourth degree).[100] Rectovaginal fistulas can also occur. If such an injury results from the improper performance of the episiotomy, the obstetrician may face liability.

CASE ILLUSTRATION

The patient engaged the obstetrician to deliver her second child, agreeing to allow his partner to deliver in his absence. At eight months of pregnancy, an examination disclosed that, as the obstetrician recorded it in the patient's medical record, the patient's cervix was "very soft, indicative of rapid delivery after onset of labor." When labor began one month later, the patient's husband notified the obstetrician, who ordered that the patient be taken to the hospital, told the husband that it was his partner's night on duty and that the hospital nurses would evaluate the patient's condition, and then notified his partner. A first-year resident was waiting for the patient when she arrived. A brief examination established that she was at term, and the resident ordered that the patient be brought to the nearest delivery room. A more detailed examination disclosed that the patient's cervix was fully dilated and that the baby's heartbeat was irregular, indicating fetal distress. Concluding that the baby should be delivered without delay, the resident prepared the patient and performed an episiotomy. After delivery of the child, it was noticed that the patient's sphincter had been disrupted. The resident attempted to repair the episiotomy and the associated disruption. The obstetrician's partner arrived at the hospital as the resident was in the process of placing superficial sutures to complete the repair. Several days later the wound opened, infection set in, and the repair was rendered ineffective. Two subsequent operations to correct the patient's condition also failed, and she was left with chronic rectal incontinence.

The patient sued the two obstetricians and the resident, alleging that they were negligent and that the two obstetricians breached their contract

§ 11.27   Episiotomy   449

to perform the patient's delivery. The trial court found in favor of the obstetricians and the resident, and the patient appealed. With respect to the allegation of negligence, the appellate court concluded that the jury could decide from the evidence that the obstetricians failed to respond to the husband's call promptly enough, in light of the condition of the patient's cervix and the conclusion that birth would occur quickly after labor commenced. With respect to the resident, the appellate court upheld the favorable jury verdict because the patient introduced no conclusive evidence that the torn sphincter was due to the incision, as opposed to a laceration precipitated by labor. Furthermore, although the patient alleged that, in the repair of the sphincter the torn ends were not approximated, she failed to prove this fact with sufficient evidence. With respect to the breach of contract allegation, the appellate court held that the patient was entitled to seek and contract for the services of a specific physician. The appellate court ordered that the case be retried with respect to the two obstetricians but upheld the verdict in favor of the resident (*Alexandridis v. Jewett*, 1968).[101]

Episiotomy results in few complications, but, because it is an operation, general complications of surgery may occur. If these complications can be proved to be the result of the obstetrician's negligence, liablity may be imposed.

CASE ILLUSTRATION

The patient consulted the physician when she was pregnant with her third child. Her history indicated that her previous pregnancies had been normal and that no complications had resulted. To facilitate the delivery of the patient's third child, the physician performed a mediolateral episiotomy, following the scar of prior episiotomies running from the vagina toward the back of the right leg. In repairing the incision, the physician used a curved needle into which was crimped a length of gut about 27 inches long. While in the hospital, the patient complained of pain in the area of the sutures and was given drugs for pain. The patient complained of pain persistently (for which the physician prescribed aspirin) until, three months after the delivery, he refused to see her. The patient continued to see a number of physicians for her pain, which she described as "sudden, shooting, jagged, and sharp." She was found to have hemorrhoids by a second physician, but she was told that, in the absence of a fissure, hemorrhoids would not cause such pain. Just before a scheduled hemorrhoidectomy, ten months after delivery, the patient visited a third physician, complaining of a hard object in her thigh. This physician removed a suture needle from the patient's inner right thigh, about two inches from her vagina. The patient's pain ceased, and she sued the first physician. At trial, the physician-defendant testified that a suture needle should not be left within a patient's body in the course of repairing an episiotomy. The physician appealed the jury verdict for the patient, arguing that the patient failed to provide any expert testimony during the trial to establish negligence. The court noted that the physician-defendant was himself a qualified expert and that he provided evidence which was clearly sufficient to support a verdict in favor of the patient (*Console v. Nickov,* 1968).[102]

Where a general surgical complication occurs, there must be a showing that the complication caused some injury to the patient (see § 1.60, Damages). If this requirement is not met, the physician's conduct does not amount to negligence for which liablity will be imposed.

CASE ILLUSTRATION

The patient was admitted to the hospital and gave birth to a premature daughter weighing 4 pounds, 15 ounces. The obstetrics resident performed an episiotomy to facilitate the delivery. The hospital records reflected that, on the third day after the delivery, a speculum examination was conducted because of a foul-smelling vaginal discharge; one gauze sponge was discovered and removed from the patient's vagina. The patient was discharged two days later. The patient sued the obstetrics resident. At trial, the obstetrics resident testified that he believed the sponge had no adverse effect on the patient's health. At most, the sponge caused the vaginal seepage to develop a foul odor: once the sponge was removed, the odor vanished rapidly. The court noted this testimony and observed that the presence of the sponge was similar to the common female use of the tampon. Because the patient failed to prove the obstetrics resident's conduct had caused any compensable damage, the court held in favor of the resident (*Malinowski v. Zalzal,* 1974).[103]

§ 11.30 OBSTETRICAL ANALGESIA AND ANESTHESIA

Liability may be imposed on a physician administering obstetrical analgesics or anesthetics for the failure to observe the manufacturer's recommendations for use, negligent administraion, or the failure to properly monitor the patient.

Basic Standard of Care: The American College of Obstetricians and Gynecologists recommends that general anesthesia for obstetrics be administered only by those individuals with the proper training and skill to do so. This will usually be an anesthesiologist or certified, registered nurse-anesthetist. General anes-

§ 11.30   Obstetrical Analgesia and Anesthesia   451

thesia is rarely required for vaginal deliveries but may be necessary for cesarean sections.[104]

If major regional anesthesia, such as spinal or lumbar epidural block is to be administered by an obstetrician, either he or she must be qualified to recognize and manage potential complications, or a qualified anesthesiologist or nurse-anesthetist must be immediately available. For the most part, obstetricians are not qualified to manage the infrequent but occasionally life-threatening complications of major regional anesthesia.

The obstetrician who is properly trained may perform pudendal and paracervical blocks or administer sedatives or analgesic drugs. Inhalational analgesia should be avoided by obstetricians because of its potential for progressing to anesthetic depths. Where drugs are used, the minimum effective doses should be employed.

In general, in order to ensure the safest and most effective anesthesia for obstetrical patients, the director of anesthesia services, with the approval of the medical staff, must develop and enforce written policies regarding the provision of obstetrical anesthesia, that is, who may do what and under what circumstances.[105]

Interpretation and Customary Practice: The alleviation of pain associated with labor and delivery has been surrounded by controversy. Initial objections were religious: in the Bible, the book of Genesis directs, "In sorrow ye shall bring forth children." In the middle of the nineteenth century, however, chloroform was first used to assuage obstetrical pain. Opposition to this practice gradually dissipated after Queen Victoria accepted chloroform during the delivery of her eighth child.[106] Contemporary resistance to obstetrical anesthesia is based primarily on the fear that the drugs may harm the baby; thus, many women wish to undergo "natural" childbirth. Some women also fear that paralysis will result from spinal anesthesia.

Obstetrical analgesia and anesthesia are not without hazards. Most of the drugs administered systemically for such purposes are cerebral depressants. Because these drugs cross the placental barrier, they affect the fetus's brain as well. If the exchange of respiratory gases across the placenta continues normally, the effect on the fetal brain is of little consequence. At birth, however, the infant must breathe for itself, and any depression of the infant's respiratory center may delay spontaneous respiration.[107]

The terms "anesthesia" and "analgesia" refer to distinct states or conditions. Anesthesia involves the loss of feeling or sensation, and it is induced to allow the performance of surgery or other painful procedures.[108] Analgesia refers to the absence of sensibility to pain, particularly relief from pain without loss of consciousness.[109]

Providing analgesics during labor should not be considered a "routine" procedure. No single method can or should be applied to all women, since some women do not want analgesic medication (which should never be forced on the patient), some women do not need it, and for some women it may be contraindicated. Analgesic preparations should not be administered until labor is well established. Thus, in a primigravida, contractions should occur at regular two- to three-minute intervals, and the cervix should usually be dilated to 4 to 5 centimeters before an analgesic is given. Because labor progresses more rapidly in multiparas, analgesics may be administered to these women somewhat earlier. Systemic analgesics are administered to alleviate discomfort and to reduce it to a tolerable level; this allows the patient to relax and rest between painful contractions. Phenergan and Demerol are two drugs commonly used for this purpose. Demerol, which relieves pain and acts as an antispasmodic, does cross the placenta and can cause depression in the newborn if an excessive dose is given. Too large a dose of Phenergan may result in hypotension (abnormally low blood pressure). Other possible complications associated with excessive doses of systemic analgesics include reduced efficiency of uterine contractions, inability of the patient to cooperate, and depression of the newborn's respiratory center resulting in apnea neonatorum. These complications may be avoided by administering small doses of analgesics and by attempting to plan the last injection to be given no later than two hours before delivery. Furthermore, neutralizing agents such as Narcan and Nalline may be used to counteract the narcotizing effect these analgesics may have on the newborn. Nalline is only effective with respect to morphine-like drugs and may increase the depression produced by barbiturates.[110]

CASE ILLUSTRATION

The patient had been treated by the obstetrician for three years prior to her pregnancy. She had a history of infertility, menstrual irregularity, and a miscarriage. Her current pregnancy proceeded normally except for a large weight gain and a viral infection during the week prior to delivery. On December 16, approximately two months before the expected delivery date, the patient called her obstetrician and complained of constipation. She was told to take two tablespoons of milk of magnesia. She called again later that evening and told the obstetrician she was having contractions and a bloody show. He told her to go to the hospital. Upon admission, the patient stated that she had given herself two enemas at home. The obstetrician arrived at the hospital at about 5:00 a.m. and was advised of the patient's admission at 2:15 a.m. on December 17. He was told that her cervix was dilated to 3 centimeters. He ordered the oral administration of three grains of Seconal, a barbituate used as a sedative to ease apprehension, and ordered an X ray, which disclosed the presence of excessive amniotic fluid. He then ordered the administration of 50 milligrams of Demerol and 25 milligrams of Phenergan, an obstetrical sedative, both of which were administered by intramuscular injection at 5:10 a.m. At birth, the female infant weighed 4 pounds (1,850 grams) and appeared to be six

§ 11.30 *Obstetrical Analgesia and Anesthesia* 453

or seven weeks premature. The child could not breathe on her own at birth and was given an Apgar rating of 1. She was connected to a resuscitator almost immediately and was treated by the anesthesiologist. Ten minutes after her birth, 0.2 milligrams of Nalline were administered to the child. She took her first voluntary breath some 20 minutes after birth and was subsequently transferred to the newborn nursery. She suffered a cyanotic episode at 10:30 that morning and was transferred to a newborn intensive care unit at another hospital, where she remained for 80 days. During that time, she suffered mental retardation, with spastic quadriparesis and cerebral palsy.

The father sued the obstetrician and anesthesiologist on behalf of his child, alleging that they knowingly deviated from the manufacturers' instructions and recommendations on the use of the drugs administered. More specifically, he charged that use of Seconal was absolutely contraindicated in cases of premature labor, that the dosages of the Demerol and Phenergan were excessive, and that the Nalline might have increased rather than decreased the child's respiratory depression. The plaintiff theorized that the drugs had crossed the placental barrier, thereby causing the child's injuries. The court noted that the manufacturers' instructions as to the use of the drugs were ambiguous. With respect to the Seconal, the manufacturer's instructions contained no warning against its oral use in cases of *premature* delivery, but rather against parenteral administration. The instructions for use of Phenergan in the presence of barbiturates were unclear. Further, where the instructions were unambiguous, the court found the physicians had not deviated from them. For example, the manufacturer's instructions called for a one-quarter to one-half reduction in the dosage of Demerol when it was administered with Phenergan. The usual dosage of Demerol was 100 milligrams—the mother received 50 milligrams. The recommended dosage of Nalline was 0.2 milligrams, the amount administered to the child. On these facts, the court could find no basis for a finding that the physicians failed to observe clear and explicit recommendations with respect to the drugs administered to both mother and child (*Lhotka v. Larson*, 1976).[111]

This case was instituted against two parties commonly involved in the administration of obstetrical anesthetics: the obstetrician and the anesthesiologist or anesthetist. Here, responsibility for the mother and newborn was clearly delineated: the obstetrician ordered the analgesics, the anesthesiologist treated the infant. Division of responsibility is often not so clear-cut; indeed, even in this case one may ask whether the obstetrician's actions caused the infant's respiratory depression. Furthermore, the legal doctrine of vicarious liability (see § 2.30, Vicarious Liability) may often be relevant in cases such as these. Generally, the obstetrician will not be held liable for the actions of an anesthesiologist or nurse-anesthetist who exercises independent judgment and who is not subject to the obstetrician's control.

CASE ILLUSTRATION

The patient was admitted to the hospital for the delivery of her child. Prior to the actual delivery, an anesthetic was administered by the certified nurse-anesthetist. The administration of the anesthetic involved the insertion of an airway into the patient's mouth. In addition to the airway, a catheter was inserted into her mouth, through the airway, and into her throat. During the delivery, the patient suffered damage to her teeth and mouth. Her mouth was either struck by a metal device while the anesthetic was being administered, or she bit down on an unprotected metal device while vomiting. The patient sued the obstetrician and the hospital, alleging that the obstetrician was responsible for the acts of the nurse-anesthetist. The patient also alleged that the obstetrician was negligent in failing to advise the nurse-anesthetist that the patient had recently eaten, increasing the possibility of vomiting and thereby misleading the anesthetist in her choice of anesthetic. The jury found the obstetrician to be liable, and the obstetrician appealed. The appellate court held that the anesthetist did not become the legal servant or agent of the obstetrician merely because she received instructions from him as to the work to be performed. The court observed that, during the administration of the anesthetic and the dynamics of the childbirth, nothing in the record warranted a finding that the obstetrician undertook to exercise control over the nurse-anesthetist's activities. The court reversed the jury verdict and ordered a new trial on the issue of the obstetrician's personal negligence, stating that the jury upon retrial "will not be permitted to find . . . [the obstetrician] vicariously liable for the conduct of the anesthetist" (*Sesselman v. Muhlenberg Hospital*, 1973).[112]

Regional analgesics may be used during labor and delivery to block the transmission of nerve impulses, thus controlling pain without narcotizing the mother. She remains awake and comfortable, and the fetus is rarely depressed. Since there is a high mortality rate where major nerve block techniques are carelessly used, an experienced individual is needed to administer the anesthetic and to supervise the patient during the birth. Analgesia by paracervical block is one of the most popular methods used for relief from pain in the first stage of labor because it is easy to master and has minimal technical demands. It is administered when the cervix is dilated four inches or more, and it relieves pain until the presenting part reaches the lower vagina. The chief advantages of the paracervical block are simplicity, ease of administration, effectiveness, and relative safety. There has been some criticism of it, based on the incidence of fetal bradycardia shortly after the administration of the anesthetic. Some reports sug-

gest that the incidence of this condition is 20 to 25 pe⟨
it between eight and 18 percent. However, fetal bradyc⟨
reduced by decreasing the dosage of the drug used an⟨
cially in the vaginal wall. Other disadvantages inclu⟨
bleeding, fetal trauma, and the short duration of the bl⟨

Epidural analgesic techniques are well suited t⟨
Either a single injection or multiple injections throug⟨
may be used. Patient safety is enhanced by the latter, since smaller doses may be used to obtain the desired effect. The needle is inserted into the extradural space between two lumbar vertebrae. As with nerve blocks generally, epidural anesthesia should not be used unless an experienced individual can perform the insertion and remain in attendance throughout the entire labor, since complications may develop.[114] The following case, arising out of the administration of epidural anesthesia, was brought against the anesthesiologist, although its legal principles pertain as well to the obstetrician who performs such a procedure.

CASE ILLUSTRATION

One day after the patient entered the hospital for the delivery of her child, labor was induced, her contractions subsequently became regular, and she went into "good" labor. Her obstetrician requested an epidural, or caudal, anesthetic, and the anesthesiologist was called by the nurse on duty in the labor room to administer it. When the anesthesiologist entered the labor room, he identified himself and told the patient he had been notified that she desired an epidural. He said something to the effect that "I understand you're ready for an anesthetic" or "Would you like to have one now?" The patient responded affirmatively, and he described the procedure to her. She would be put on her side, a local anesthetic would be injected in her back, a needle through which the epidural anesthetic would be injected would then be inserted, and she should expect to become numb from the waist down. He also told her that there was some risk involved with any kind of anesthetic, but that the risk of serious complications was one in a thousand. He asked if she had any questions; she did not. The patient was in much discomfort at that time and was anxious to receive an anesthetic. The anesthesiologist determined that the patient understood the nature of his questions and there was no impairment of her ability to consent to the anesthetic.

Shortly after the anesthetic was administered, the patient started to show signs of difficulty in breathing and her blood pressure dropped. She became cyanotic and went into cardiac arrest, which lasted for less than a minute. In response to the drop in blood pressure, the anesthesiologist administered the drug ephedrine through an intravenous device set up and placed in the operating room prior to administration of the anesthetic. He first used an oxygen mask and then an ambu-bag to assist the patient in breathing until she was able to resume breathing on her own. The fetus was born subsequently without further complications.

The patient sued the anesthesiologist, alleging that he negligently failed to obtain her informed consent to epidural anesthesia and, in conjunction with the hospital's negligent failure to have necessary emergency equipment on hand, negligently failed to adequately deal with the emergency. With respect to the consent issue, the court noted that consent to medical treatment may be oral or written. Under the facts, the patient's consent was adequate to protect the anesthesiologist from liability. The patient claimed she had no memory of the exchange between herself and the anesthesiologist regarding consent. The court noted that the patient had not presented any evidence that she had suffered any brain damage or that the anesthesiologist's treatment caused an impairment of memory. Without an explanation as to why the patient could not remember the consent conversation, the allegation could not overcome the strength of hospital records and testimony that it had taken place. Consequently, the court held for the anesthesiologist on the consent issue. The court was persuaded by expert testimony that the anesthesiologist was not negligent. The testimony concluded that the actions of the anesthesiologist and the hospital were in full accord with proper procedures for treating such emergencies. The patient failed to offer any testimony to refute this analysis. The court held in favor of the anesthesiologist and the hospital on all issues (*Patterson v. Van Wiel*, 1977).[115]

The use of continuous catheterization for regional anesthesia offers great flexibility. The catheter may be inserted early in labor and the dosage of anesthetic regulated to parallel the needs of the patient. Further, the epidural block may be extended to cover the second stage of labor. The timing must be carefully calculated, however, since ten to twelve minutes are required for a good nerve block to develop after the injection is made.[116] Complications can be avoided by scrupulous adherence to necessary precautions. The most serious complications include massive spinal anesthesia, meningitis, epidural abscess, intravenous injection, and needle or catheter breakage. Contraindications include skin infection near the proposed site, the presence of nervous or spinal disease, severe bleeding, or shock.[117]

Pain in the second stage is best controlled by nerve block techniques, including the epidural block, the subarachnoid block, and the pudendal block. The subarachnoid block may be performed with the patient either sitting or reclining laterally, although the latter position is far more comfortable for the patient. Sensory and motor nerve impulses are blocked rapidly after the anesthetic is administered, and changes in sensory level and blood pressure must be carefully monitored. Blood pressure must be recorded every two or three minutes tient's straining). The physician should also be alert for signs of trouble after, as well as during, the delivery.

CASE ILLUSTRATION

The patient was 31 years old and in good health at the time of her pregnancy and at the time of the birth of her child. She was admitted to the hospital on the evening of November 6 and was taken to the delivery room at approximately 6:00 the following morning. Her physician arrived at the hospital about an hour later and attended her until the baby was born. At 9:48 a.m. a resident physician administered a saddle block spinal anesthetic at the attending physician's direction. The injection was in the lower part of the spine, between the fourth and fifth lumbar vertebrae. Shortly thereafter, the patient gave birth to a normal baby boy. At 11:20 a.m. that day the patient complained of intermittent chills, at 11:45 a.m. she complained of shortness of breath, and at 12:30 p.m. the nurse noted that the patient was rigid, the movement of her arms was spastic, and she was nauseated. At 8:00 p.m., shortness of breath and difficulty in breathing was noted. At approximately 7:00 the next morning, the patient had a convulsion and became completely unconscious. Her physician was notified and returned to the hospital immediately. At 8:30 a.m. the patient's breathing stopped completely. Her entire body was limp; her neck, face, and extremities were flaccid. A tracheotomy was done and a tube was inserted and connected with a respirator, thus restoring the patient's respiration. A working diagnosis of myasthenia gravis was made, and on November 27 the patient was transferred to a medical school hospital, where she remained until May 1961. Although there was some improvement in her condition, she remained partially paralyzed from the neck down and could breathe only with artificial assistance—a respirator during the day and a mechanical rocking bed at night.

The patient sued the physician, alleging among other things that the anesthetic caused her injuries. There was conflicting evidence as to whether or not a pillow had been placed under the patient's head to prevent the anesthetic from ascending the spinal canal and attacking the phrenic nerve, which controls the diaphragm and the nerves in the cranial area. Expert witnesses for the physician testified that the patient's paralysis could not have been caused by the anesthetic, for a number of reasons. The patient suffered no impairment of the sensory nerves, but only of the motor nerves: if the damage to the motor nerves had been caused by the anesthetic, the sensory nerves should have been affected as well. They testified that the patient's retention of sensory function was demonstrated by the fact that she had some sensation when her extremities were pricked by a needle shortly after the birth of her child. Further, there had been no drop in the for the first ten minutes after the anesthetic is administered to insure that hypotension does not go unnoticed. Subsequent recordings may be made every five minutes for 30 minutes.[118]

The subarachnoid block has certain advantages over the epidural block. The anesthetic takes effect immediately, and, because it is deposited in the subarachnoid space in small quantities, there is no transfer of the drug to the fetus. Further, the technique is simple to perform. Disadvantages include a more rapid and pronounced incidence of hypotension and more frequent nausea and vomiting.[119]

Maternal hypotension is a problem common to all forms of regional anesthesia. These techniques block the sympathetic nerves, leading to peripheral vasodilation, decreased venous return, and the drop in blood pressure, which, if not caught and treated immediately, can be hazardous to both mother and child. A 10- to 20-milligram intravenous injection of ephedrine is the generally accepted treatment. The risk of hypotension may be minimized by adequate hydration, infusion of 500 to 1,000 milliliters of a balanced salt solution before administration of the anesthetic, and avoidance of the supine hypotensive syndrome.[120]

The pudendal nerve block is perhaps the simplest of the procedures. No anesthesiologist is needed, the procedure is safe and easy to learn, it requires no expensive machinery, and it is suitable for most normal deliveries. However, the physician should be knowledgeable in the patterns of sensory distribution to the perineum in order to avoid inadequate perineal analgesia. A good bilateral pudendal block will generally effect almost complete perineal analgesia for a normal vaginal delivery. To effect complete perineal analgesia, a superficial injection of the triangular area between the middle of the symphysis pubica and midway to the spinous process should be made in conjunction with the pudendal block. Inhalation analgesia may be used in combination with the block to permit the physician to perform more extensive procedures, such as a midforceps rotation.[121]

The pain of delivery and the third stage of labor can also be alleviated by a spinal anesthetic. Prolonged spinal anesthesia is not recommended for obstetric use; rather, a brief time or minimal dosage of anesthetic should be used. Although spinal anesthesia has a number of advantages, including minimal blood loss, lack of fetal hypoxia in the absence of hypotension, the elimination of any need for inhalation anesthetics or analgesics, prompt effectiveness, and few complications, it has been considered a dangerous method because of the high mortality rate when the technique is improperly used. The low spinal, or saddle, block is used most often and is administered with the patient sitting up. One of the primary complications associated with spinal blocks are headaches, which occur in five to ten percent of patients.[122] More serious complications include arachnoiditis, nerve root injury, and respiratory failure (which may result from the anesthetic's ascending the spinal cord because of rapid injection or the pa-

patient's blood pressure during the delivery: had the anesthetic ascended to the cranial nerves, it would have affected the sympathetic nerves, resulting in an immediate drop. Other reasons for ruling out the spinal anesthetic as the cause of the patient's condition included a lack of any significant increase in the protein count and white blood cells in the patient's spinal fluid shortly after the delivery. The patient's expert—a general practitioner with some experience in administering spinal anesthetics—testified that he felt the anesthetic was the cause of the paralysis because the sequence of events between the administration of the anesthetic and the development of the paralysis were too close to be ignored. It was also pointed out that, although the patient's blood pressure did not drop immediately, less than three hours after the delivery her pressure dropped to 104 over 80. He further testified that the symptoms of damage from within the spinal canal sometimes occur after anesthesia has worn off and that it might be as much as four hours before that happens. The physician-defendant admitted that there might be a delayed reaction from the anesthetic. The court also took note of the patient's own testimony that during the delivery "everything collapsed," that she was unable to reach up for the food brought to her after she returned to her private room, and that she could not move her arms thereafter. The court also noted that the physician's expert had admitted that a lack of white cells and elevated protein count in the spinal fluid were not conclusive evidence: such signs appear in the majority of cases but not in all cases. Although the trial resulted in judgment for the physician, the court of appeals reversed that decision on the basis that one of the instructions given to the jury by the trial judge was prejudicial to the patient. The court of appeals ordered a new trial (*Mayor v. Dowsett*, 1965).[123]

Local or regional analgesia, as well as local or general anesthesia, may be used to relieve pain during a cesarean section. The choice depends on many factors, including patient preference, whether or not the mother has a full stomach, the need for rapid delivery due to fetal or maternal distress, and the physician's preference.[124]

A local analgesic is injected along the line of incision or by making a wheal along either side of the incision with the analgesic. Technical expertise, careful selection of patients, and careful preparation are factors in the degree of success achieved if sufficient time is allowed for the local to act.[125]

There is some debate as to whether or not regional techniques are appropriate for cesarean section in patients with mild or moderate uteroplacental compromise. It is argued that, since a larger sympathetic and analgesic block is required to perform a cesarean section, the risk of maternal hypotension increases, possibly leading to fetal compromise. Basically, if the fetus is already at risk, the physician should carefully consider whether to use any technique that might increase that risk.[126]

§ 11.40 FATHERS IN THE DELIVERY ROOM

Liability may result from allowing fathers in the delivery room where an injury to the mother or child resulting from the negligence of attending personnel subjects the father to emotional distress.

Basic Standard of Care: If the patient desires and hospital protocol permits, the father or other support person may be allowed to be with the patient during her labor and, with the consent of the obstetrician, in the delivery room. A dress code that conforms to that of professional personnel in the delivery room should be followed. Adequate information of the normal events and procedures encountered in the labor and delivery room should be provided. Whether the support person may be present at cesarean birth will depend on the judgment of the obstetric staff, the individual obstetrician, the anesthesiologist, and the policies of the hospital. A written policy is recommended.[127]

Interpretation and Customary Practice: Perhaps as a reaction to modern medicine, manifested in obstetrics by procedures and drugs to reduce discomfort and shorten labor, "natural childbirth" has gained popularity with the public. It is asserted by proponents of natural childbirth that the ill-considered use of techniques ranging from elective induction of labor to continuous conduction analgesia-anesthesia and prophylactic forceps delivery may complicate parturition and deprive the mother of a significant, natural experience. Changing social definitions of the roles of men and women, combined with the values espoused by natural childbirth programs, advocate the father's active participation in the birth process. Consequently, today's expectant father may enter the delivery room along with the mother.

Natural childbirth programs attempt to ease labor by alleviating fear and tension. Such programs acknowledge that women who are self-assured, relaxed, and cooperative experience easier labor. These qualities are gained by teaching the patient about the natural physiologic changes to expect throughout her pregnancy and by training her to breathe properly and to employ relaxation techniques during labor. The father participates in this education and should emerge from the training as a knowledgeable assistant who can time contractions, aid in performing breathing exercises, and provide appropriate emotional support. Both the patient and her husband should gain an understanding of the nature and progress of labor and delivery and of the expected appearance and reactions of the newborn.

The two best known natural childbirth methods are Lamaze and Leboyer. Lamaze involves the individual instruction of both husband and wife, the presentation of films of actual deliveries, visits to labor and delivery rooms, and prenatal explanation by the attending physician. The patient receives training in various exercise techniques. Exercises to strengthen the muscles include squatting and contracting the muscles of the abdomen and pelvic floor. Relaxation exercises focus on contracting and relaxing specific muscle groups on command. Breathing exercises teach chest as opposed to abdominal breathing, enabling the patient to use her intercostal muscles while relaxing the diaphragm. Comfort aids, with which the husband assists, include light back massage, pressure on the sacrum, and positioning the mother on the side of the fetal occiput. The Leboyer method calls for birth to take place in a darkened room devoid of harsh lighting and for the immediate immersion of the newborn in tepid water, a simulation of the fetal environment. These measures are taken to reduce the shock of transition from the uterus to the world outside. The mother strokes and cuddles the infant to achieve "bonding," which is further sought by putting the infant to breast while the mother is still on the delivery table. The father is also encouraged to hold and caress the newborn.[128]

Participation by the father in the birth process has been challenged on the grounds that it could lead to increased puerperal and neonatal infection. Implementing proper aseptic conditions, such as requiring that proper gowning and hand-washing procedures be followed by the father, can minimize this risk. Proper education should prevent the father from fainting or becoming an obstacle if an emergency should arise. Nonetheless, these concerns, among others, were expressed by a Montana hospital administrator and executive committee who adopted a rule prohibiting fathers from being present in the delivery room. An obstetrician and his patient's husband, both of whom wished to deliver the patient's baby using the Lamaze method, sued the hospital, but the Montana Supreme Court upheld the rule in a 1974 decision. The court noted that the necessity of such a rule was debatable, but for the court to avoid "tak[ing] on the escutcheon of Caduceus" it must defer to the competent medical opinion that formulated the rule, as long as the decision was not arbitrary or capricious but related to the orderly management of the hospital. In this case, medical opinion had identified the following risks and concerns associated with allowing fathers to be present in delivery rooms.

> [I]ncreased possibility of infection; concern about malpractice suits; inadequate physical facilities which do not allow room for fathers to change their clothes without possible bothering of the doctors; increased costs, which though they may not be great have to be taken into account, such as additional nursing time, providing gowns, masks, booties, etc.; greater tension in the delivery room caused by the presence of the father which might cause some of the nurses to not perform as well; lack of privacy to other women getting ready to deliver; the strict policy concerning visitors in surgical areas favored by the state board of health; and the furtherance of harmony between physicians so that there would always be cover should [the obstetrician] be absent.[129]

The Montana hospital was a private hospital. When private hospitals in other jurisdictions have adopted rules excluding fathers from delivery rooms, courts have treated challenges to such rules much as the Montana court did: if the rule is not arbitrary or capricious, relates to orderly management of the hospital, and is consistent with sound medical judgment, it will not be disturbed.[130] If the hospital adopting such a rule is a public or state-owned institution, its rule may be challenged on constitutional grounds. The argument that such a rule violated their due process and marital privacy rights was brought by a group of couples against an Indiana hospital that prohibited fathers from its delivery rooms. The Seventh Circuit Court of Appeals rejected the argument that marital privacy was violated and upheld the rule.[131]

Where fathers have been admitted to delivery rooms and have witnessed an injury to mother or child, suit has been brought. Actions are generally for wrongful death (which may not be brought for the death of a fetus, depending upon the jurisdiction) or for the father's emotional distress in witnessing the injury. The only reported decisions as of this writing focus on emotional distress.

CASE ILLUSTRATION

The patient's husband was present in the delivery room to assist in the delivery of their child. The patient died during the delivery procedure. Immediately after her death, her husband was able to feel life in the as-yet-unborn child; he asked the attending physician and nurses to deliver the child, but they refused. The child died; the husband was able to ascertain its death by feeling his wife's body. The husband sued the hospital and the attending physician on a number of legal theories. The trial court entered judgment against the husband-plaintiff on all theories, but the court of appeals ordered a new trial on the husband's claim of emotional distress for injury to a third party, his baby. The court noted that factors to be considered in such an action included: "(1) Whether plaintiff was located near the scene of the accident as contrasted with one who was a distance away from it. (2) Whether the shock resulted from a direct emotional impact upon plaintiff from the sensory and contemporaneous observance of the accident, as contrasted with learning of the accident from others after its occurrence. (3) Whether plaintiff and the victim were closely related, as contrasted with an absence of any relationship or the presence of only a distant relationship." The court concluded that the husband-plaintiff met each of the three requirements and ordered the case to be retried (*Austin v. Regents of the University of California,* 1979).[132]

One of the judges deciding this case wrote a vigorous dissent. He referred to a 1977 California Supreme Court case, *Justus v. Atchison,* with similar facts that denied recovery for emotional distress. The majority opinion in the *Austin* decision differentiated the two cases by finding that, in the *Justus* decision, the father, although present in the delivery room where he witnessed the death of his child resulting from a prolapsed umbilical cord, did not know the baby had died until he had been told so by the obstetrician. Thus, he failed to meet all three requirements. The father in *Austin*, however, determined himself that his baby had died. The dissenting justice saw no merit in this distinction. The *Justus* decision focused on the fact that damages for emotional distress for injury to a third party are only awarded to plaintiffs who are involuntary witnesses to the incident. Fathers in delivery rooms are there by choice. The court noted:

> Surely a layman who voluntarily observes a surgical operation must be prepared for the possibility of unpleasant or even harrowing experiences. This is no less true of the procedure of childbirth, which, although unlikely to be traumatic, is always subject to complications.

The court expressly declined to apply the doctrine of assumption of risk (see § 3.40, Assumption of Risk) but acknowledged the ever-present possibility of emotional distress under such circumstances.[133]

It might be reasonable to expect the natural childbirth phenomenon to present greater potential for liability and lawsuit for reasons unanticipated even by the board of the Montana hospital mentioned above. In fact, few cases have been brought. This may be the result of hospital rules forbidding the practice of fathers attending births, however no statistics or studies are available to support this contention. Equally unsupportable, and equally plausible, is the perspective that the lack of litigation attests to the success of the various natural childbirth programs in training the prospective parents and readying them for the unexpected.

NOTES

1. American College of Obstetricians and Gynecologists, Standards for Obstetric/Gynecologic Services 25–31 (5th ed. 1982).
2. R. Willson & E. Carrington, Obstetrics and Gynecology 387 (6th ed. 1979).
3. *Id.* at 390.
4. Hiatt v. Groce, 215 Kan. 14, 523 P. 2d 320 (1974).
5. *See, e.g.* Swanek v. Hutzel, 115 Mich. App. 254, 320 N.W.2d 234 (1982).
6. R. Willson & E. Carrington, *supra* note 2, at 390.
7. Northern Trust Co. v. Skokie Valley Community Hosp., 401 N.E.2d 1246 (Ill. 1980).
8. American College of Obstetricians and Gynecologists, *supra* note 1, at 29.
9. Tricomi, *Induction of Labor—A Contemporary View,* 16 Clinic. Obstet. Gynecol. 226–42, 233, 234 (1973); R. Willson & E. Carrington, *supra* note 2, at 403.
10. Tricomi, *supra* note 9, at 234; R. Willson & E. Carrington, *supra* note 2, at 404.
11. R. Willson & E. Carrington, *supra* note 2, at 403.
12. *Id.*
13. *Id.* at 402–403.
14. Parker v. St. Paul Fire & Marine Ins. Co., 335 So.2d 725 (La. App. 1976), *cert. denied,* 338 So.2d 700 (La. 1976). *See also* Carmon v. Dippold, 63 Ill. App. 3d 419, 379 N.E.2d 1365 (1978).
15. Gamell v. Mount Sinai Hospital, 34 A.D. 2d 981, 312 N.Y.S. 2d 629 (1970).
16. Rice v. Rizk, 453 S.W.2d 732 (Ky. App. 1970).
17. Tricomi, *supra* note 9, at 238–39.

18. R. Willson & E. Carrington, *supra* note 2, at 403.
19. Tricomi, *supra* note 9, at 241.
20. R. Willson & E. Carrington, *supra* note 2, at 403–404.
21. Lab v. Hall, 200 So.2d 556 (Fla. App. 1967). *See also* Roberts v. Tardif, 417 A.2d 444 (Me. 1980); Freed v. Priore, 247 Pa. Super. 413, 372 A.2d 895 (1977).
22. Rutherford v. Zearfoss, 272 S.E.2d 225 (Va. 1980).
23. Stack v. Wapner, 244 Pa. Super. 278, 368 A.2d 292 (1976).
24. Long v. Johnson, 381 N.E.2d 93 (Ind. App. 1978).
25. American College of Obstetricians and Gynecologists, *supra* note 1, at 29,30.
26. K. Niswander, Obstetrics 297 (1976); E. Taylor, Beck's Obstetrical Practice 243 (1971); R. Willson & E. Carrington, *supra* note 2, at 480.
27. *Id.*
28. R. Willson & E. Carrington, *supra* note 2.
29. E. Taylor, *supra* note 26, at 247, 248; R. Willson & E. Carrington, *supra* note 2.
30. Hall v. Musgrave, 517 F.2d 1163 (6th Cir. 1975).
31. R. Benson, Current Obstetric and Gynecologic Diagnosis and Treatment 868 (2d ed. 1978); E. Taylor, *supra* note 26, at 248; R. Willson & E. Carrington, *supra* note 2, at 480.
32. Brooks v. Serrano, 209 So.2d 279 (Fla. App. 1968).
33. R. Willson & E. Carrington, *supra* note 2, at 487–89.
34. Norland v. Washington Gen. Hosp., 461 F.2d 694 (8th Cir. 1972).
35. Freed v. Priore, 247 Pa. Super. 413, 372 A.2d 895 (Pa. Super. 1977).
36. R. Willson & E. Carrington, *supra* note 2, at 482.
37. R. Benson, *supra* note 31, at 871.
38. Young v. Group Health Co-op., 85 Wash. 2d 332, 534 P.2d 1349 (1975).
39. R. Willson & E. Carrington, *supra* note 2, at 443.
40. R. Benson, *supra* note 31, at 824.
41. R. Willson & E. Carrington, *supra* note 2, at 459–68.
42. Dick v. Lewis, 506 F. Supp. 799 (D.N.D. 1980).
43. *See* Register v. Wilmington Medical Center, 377 A.2d 8 (Del. 1977); Samii v. Baystate Medical Center, 395 N.E.2d 455 (Mass. 1979); Mulligan v. Shuter, 71 A.D.2d 669, 419 N.Y.S. 2d 13 (1979).
44. R. Willson & E. Carrington, *supra* note 2, at 448, 449.
45. *Id.*
46. Reilly v. Straub, 282 N.W.2d 688 (Iowa 1979).
47. Henry v. Bronx Lebanon Medical Center, 53 A.D.2d 476, 385 N.Y.S.2d 772 (1976).
48. E. Taylor, *supra* note 26, at 478–83; R. Willson & E. Carrington, *supra* note 2, at 349–56.
49. Holt v. Nelson, 11 Wash. App. 230, 523 P.2d 211 (1974).
50. R. Willson & E. Carrington, *supra* note 2, at 358–62.
51. Hogan v. Almand, 131 Ga. App. 225, 205 S.E.2d 440 (1974).
52. J. Pritchard and P. MacDonald, Williams Obstetrics 749–51 (1971); E. Taylor, *supra* note 26, at 330.
53. Eckert v. Smith, 589 S.W.2d 533 (Tex. Civ. App. 1979).
54. E. Taylor, *supra* note 26, at 328–29.
55. Lindsey v. Clinic for Women, 40 N.C. App. 456, 253 S.E.2d 304 (1979).
56. E. Taylor, *supra* note 26, at 161.
57. Rice v. Rizk, *supra* note 16.
58. D. Danforth, *Operative Delivery,* in Current Obstetric and Gynecologic Diagnosis and Treatment 853 (1978).
59. *Id.* at 852–53.

Notes: Chapter XI

60. R. Willson & E. Carrington, *supra* note 2, at 496-98.
61. D. Danforth, *supra* note 58, at 852; R. Willson & E. Carrington, *supra* note 2, at 496-97.
62. D. Danforth, *supra* note 58, at 852; R. Willson & E. Carrington, *supra* note 2, at 497.
63. R. Willson & E. Carrington, *supra* note 2, at 500.
64. D. Danforth, *supra* note 58, at 864.
65. Henry v. Bronx Lebanon Medical Center, *supra* note 47. *See also* Roberts v. Tardif, 417 A.2d 444 (Me. 1980), Freed v. Priore, *supra* note 21.
66. Wale v. Barnes, 278 So.2d 601 (Fla. 1973).
67. Larabee v. United States, 254 F. Supp. 613 (S.D. Cal. 1966). *See also* Robbins v. Footer, 553 F.2d 123 (D.C. Cir. 1977).
68. Schreiber v. Cestari, 40 A.D.2d 1025, 338 N.Y.S.2d 972 (1972).
69. Roark v. Allen, 633 S.W.2d 804 (Tex. 1982).
70. Charley v. Cameron, 215 Kan. 750, 528 P.2d 1205 (1974).
71. Carmon v. Dippold, *supra* note 14.
72. R. Benson, *supra* note 31, at 881; R. Willson & E. Carrington, *supra* note 2, at 502.
73. R. Benson, *supra* note 31, at 883; E. Taylor, *supra* note 26, at 557-58; R. Willson & E. Carrington, *supra* note 2, at 503, 504.
74. *Id.*
75. *Id.*
76. Haught v. Maceluch, 681 F.2d 291 (5th Cir. 1982); Holt v. Nelson, 11 Wash. App. 230, 523 P.2d 211 (1974).
77. Rutherford v. Zearfoss, *supra* note 22.
78. Schreiber v. Cestari, *supra* note 68.
79. Bunch v. Mercy Hosp., 404 So.2d 520 (La. App. 1981).
80. Buck v. Alton Mem. Hosp, 86 Ill. App. 3d 347, 407 N.E.2d 1067 (1980).
81. R. Benson, *supra* note 31, at 888; R. Willson & E. Carrington, *supra* note 2, at 504, 505.
82. Comte v. O'Neil, 125 Ill. App. 2d 450, 261 N.E.2d 21 (1970).
83. Carpenter v. Campbell, 149 Ind. App. 163, 271 N.E.2d 163 (1971).
84. Murphy v. Conway, 277 N.E.2d 681 (Mass. 1972).
85. Kauchick v. Williams, 435 S.W.2d 342 (Mo. 1968).
86. K. Niswander, *supra* note 26, at 114-15.
87. Sanders v. U.S., 551 F.2d 458 (D.C. Cir. 1977).
88. Gaddis v. Smith, 417 S.W.2d 577 (Tex. 1967).
89. Seitz v. Jones, 370 P.2d 300 (Okla. 1962).
90. Graham v. Sisco, 248 Ark. 6, 449 S.W.2d 949 (1970).
91. Bates v. Ulrich, 38 Ill. App. 3d 203, 347 N.E.2d 286 (1976).
92. R. Benson, *supra* note 31, at 889, 890; R. Willson & E. Carrington, *supra* note 2, at 505.
93. Sard v. Hardy, 281 Md. 432, 379 A.2d 1014 (1977).
94. Haywood v. Allen, 406 S.W.2d 721 (Ky. App. 1966).
95. Beck v. Lovell, 361 So.2d 245 (La. App. 1978).
96. Davidson v. Shirley, 616 F.2d 224 (5th Cir. 1980).
97. *Id.*
98. R. Willson & E. Carrington, *supra* note 2, at 504.
99. Hernandez v. Smith, 552 F.2d 142 (5th Cir. 1977).
100. K. Niswander, *supra* note 26, at 264-65; R. Willson & E. Carrington, *supra* note 2, at 513-15.
101. Alexandridis v. Jewett, 388 F.2d 829 (1st Cir. 1968).

102. Console v. Nickow, 156 Conn. 268, 240 A.2d 895 (1968).
103. Malinkowski v. Zalzal, 113 R.I. 90, 317 A.2d 875 (1974).
104. American College of Obstetricians and Gynecologists, *supra* note 1, at 30.
105. American College of Obstetricians and Gynecologists, Technical Bulletin No. 57 (Jan. 1980).
106. R. Willson & E. Carrington, *supra* note 2, at 405.
107. *Id.*
108. Dorland's Illustrated Medical Dictionary 86 (25th ed. 1974).
109. *Id.* at 78.
110. R. Willson & E. Carrington, *supra* note 2, at 407.
111. Lhotka v. Larson, 307 Minn. 121, 238 N.W.2d 870 (1976).
112. Sesselman v. Muhlenberg Hosp., 124 N.J. Super. 258, 306 A.2d 474 (1973).
113. R. Benson, *supra* note 31, at 604–05.
114. R. Willson & E. Carrington, *supra* note 2, at 408–9.
115. Patterson v. Van Wiel, 91 N.M. 100, 570 P.2d 931 (1977).
116. R. Benson, *supra* note 31, at 608.
117. R. Willson & E. Carrington, *supra* note 2, at 409.
118. R. Benson, *supra* note 31, at 608.
119. *Id.* at 617.
120. R. Dripps, J. Eckenhoff, & L. Vandam, Introduction to Anesthesia, The Principles of Safe Practice 352 (5th ed. 1977).
121. R. Benson, *supra* note 31, at 608.
122. R. Willson & E. Carrington, *supra* note 2, at 410–12.
123. Mayor v. Dowsett, 240 Or. 196, 400 P.2d 234 (1965).
124. R. Dripps, J. Eckenhoff, & L. Vandam, *supra* note 120, at 354.
125. R. Benson, *supra* note 31, at 616.
126. *Id.* at 617.
127. American College of Obstetricians and Gynecologists, *supra* note 1, at 30.
128. R. Benson, *supra* note 31, at 645–46.
129. Hulit v. St. Vincent's Hosp., 520 P.2d 99 (Mont. 1974).
130. Baier v. Woman's Hosp. Foundation, 340 So.2d 360 (La. App. 1976).
131. Fitzgerald v. Porter Mem. Hosp., 523 F.2d 716 (7th Cir. 1975).
132. Austin v. Regents of the Univ. of California, 89 Cal. App. 3d 354, 152 Cal. Rptr. 420 (1979).
133. Justus v. Atchison, 19 Cal.3d 564, 565 P.2d 122, 139 Cal. Rptr. 97 (1977).

Chapter XII

Postpartum Complications

§ 12.10 HEMORRHAGE AND HYPOVOLEMIC SHOCK

Liability may be imposed on a physician for negligence in the discovery and treatment of excessive postpartum bleeding, the failure to follow recognized methods for treating the resultant shock, the administration of incompatible blood, and the failure to properly attend a patient who is hemorrhaging.

Basic Standard of Care: The American College of Obstetricians and Gynecologists recommends that following delivery, the patient should be transported to a recovery area where she should be constantly attended and closely observed for postpartum complications. Vital signs should be recorded at least every 15 minutes during the first hour and more frequently if warranted by her immediate postpartum status. Fluid intake and output should be recorded, and the uterine fundus should be frequently examined to determine if it is well contracted and to check for excessive bleeding. The patient should remain in the recovery area for at least one hour or until she is recovered from anesthesia. Nursing personnel assigned to observe postpartum patients should be qualified to recognize postpartum emergencies and problems as they occur and should have no other obligations. Patients recovering from major conduction or general anesthesia should be discharged at the discretion of the attending physician or anesthesiologist in charge of the recovery area.[1]

Interpretation and Customary Practice: Maternal bleeding following delivery is fairly common; excessive bleeding is a frequent cause of maternal death. In a study conducted in Texas between 1969 and 1973, 111 of 501 maternal deaths in childbirth were related to postpartum hemorrhage.[2]

There are several causes of postpartum hemorrhaging. The most important are uterine atony and soft tissue injury. Bleeding originates in the sinuses of the placental site when the uterus fails to contract properly or in blood vessels of the birth canal that were torn during delivery.[3]

Excessive bleeding may also be caused by retained products of conception, coagulopathy, or uterine inversion.[4]

When the postpartum hemorrhage is mild, the physician can usually treat the patient by stimulating the uterus to contract by massaging the fundus and administering Pitocin or Methergine; in addition, the physician should inspect the cervix, vagina, and labia for lacerations and explore the uterus for retained products of conception. When confronted with severe hemorrhaging, it is necessary for the physician to determine whether the uterus has ruptured. If it has, repair of the defect, ligation of the internal iliac artery, or a hysterectomy may be necessary to control the hemorrhage[5] (see § 13.20 Hysterectomy).

Hypovolemic shock, which refers to shock resulting from loss of circulating blood, often accompanies serious hemorrhage. In such cases, the physician must first arrest the patient's bleeding and then replace lost plasma volume with blood. He or she can administer crystalloids until blood is available, at which time transfusion should begin.[6] Shock also commonly follows inversion of the uterus.[7]

Postpartum hemorrhage and accompanying hypovolemic shock can occur either in the first 24 hours after delivery or be delayed. Uterine atony or a laceration usually results in early hemorrhage; bleeding due to retained portions of placenta may not begin for several days. Bleeding from subinvolution of the placental site commonly begins between the twelfth and twenty-first days.[8]

Lawsuits have been brought in which patients have alleged negligence in the discovery and treatment of excessive postpartum bleeding. If the physician follows proper medical procedures in treating excessive bleeding, liability may not be imposed, even if the treatment was the cause in fact of some damage to the patient.

CASE ILLUSTRATION

The physician delivered the patient's child. While the physician was preparing to leave the delivery room, the patient had a sudden, massive vaginal hemorrhage. Several inches of blood were standing in a pan beneath the delivery table before the physician could get his gloves back on. The physician checked for retained placenta and cervical lacerations but found none. The physician then inserted five yards of gauze bandage into the patient's uterus in an attempt to control the bleeding. This effort was unsuccessful. By this time, the patient was clearly exhibiting symptoms of shock. The physician called for assistance. He and his assistant administered blood through a catheter into a vein in the patient's left ankle and fibrinogen and Amicar into a vein in the right ankle. These agents were administered to aid clotting of the patient's blood. The patient also received oxygen, Decadron, AquaMEPHYTON, Ergotrate, and Pitocin. After one unit of blood was administered into the left ankle, the physician found that a second unit would not begin to drip. The left leg was swollen and cold. The catheter was removed from the left leg, and the right passageway was thereafter used to administer blood and drugs. The patient survived and, except for her left leg, her condition improved. The leg remained swollen despite the administration of drugs intended to reduce swelling, to dilate blood vessels, and to counteract infection. After several days, the patient's left leg was amputated. An examination revealed a clot in the popliteal artery, with necrosis of tissues from the knee downward.

The patient sued the physician, alleging that his negligence in performing the transfusion procedure caused the loss of the leg. The lower court entered judgment on a jury verdict for the physician-defendant. The higher court affirmed. It ruled that there was sufficient evidence from which the jury could conclude that everything possible had been done to save the patient-plaintiff's leg, in light of the conditions existing and the primary goal of saving her life, and that the physician-defendant had not been negligent in his handling of the grave emergency. In particular, the court noted that during the first two or three hours after delivery it was necessary to administer clotting agents to remedy a clotting defect of the patient (known as afibrinogenemia or hypofibrinogenemia) and that preparations to relieve clotting such as that later found in the popliteal artery were definitely contraindicated (*Chapman v. Carlson*, 1970).[9]

In another case, the patient began to bleed from her vagina after delivery and expulsion of the placenta. The physician first massaged the uterus in an effort to induce contraction. He then inspected for tears or lacerations in the uterus and vagina but found none. The physician thereafter administered Pitocin and performed bimanual compression of the uterus in a further effort to control the bleeding. When all these methods proved ineffective, the physician decided to perform a hysterectomy. The court upheld a jury verdict that the physician had not been negligent in treating the hemorrhage. In so doing, the court referred to the testimony of several expert witnesses that the physician-defendant had taken the proper conservative measures and that the decision to proceed by hysterectomy when these measures failed had been correct.[10]

A physician may be held liable when he or she fails to properly discover a postpartum hemorrhage or fails to follow recognized methods for treatment of resultant shock.

CASE ILLUSTRATION

The obstetrician-gynecologist delivered the patient of her fourth child. Twenty minutes later, the anesthesiologist advised the obstetrician-gynecologist that the patient was experiencing a rapid drop in blood pressure and had a rapid pulse. The patient went into shock. The obstetrician-gynecologist first suspected internal bleeding but, after performing a physical examination of the patient, ruled out internal bleeding as the cause of shock. He then suspected that the cause was either pulmonary embolism or amniotic fluid embolism. He consulted an internist, who diagnosed the probable cause of shock as pulmonary embolism. The patient subsequently lapsed into unconsciousness and died. The actual cause of the shock was severe internal bleeding due to a ruptured intrauterine artery. Neither the obstetrician-gynecologist nor the internist discovered the bleeding.

The patient's widower sued the obstetrician-gynecologist, the internist, the anesthesiologist, and the hospital. The jury found in favor of the anesthesiologist and the hospital but against the obstetrician-gynecologist and the internist in the amount of $400,000. The lower court entered judgment on the verdict, and the higher court affirmed. The court held that the jury could have concluded (1) that the patient had exhibited the classic symptoms of severe internal bleeding but that the physician-defendants had negligently failed to diagnose the condition; (2) that the physician-defendants had failed to follow any recognized methods for the treatment of shock; and (3) that the physician-defendants had failed to remain in constant attendance upon the patient while she was in critical condition, in violation of their duty to do so (*Katsetos v. Nolan*, 1976).[11]

Patients have also alleged that hospitals or physicians, or both, have been negligent in their postpartum care by administering incompatible blood for treatment of a hemorrhage. In one case, there was a dispute over whether incompatible blood was in fact administered. Hospital records stated that the patient's type was AB positive; reports from the Georgia Department of Public Health indicated that the type was O positive but contained the language: "Results insufficient for adequate pretransfusion testing." The court held that the jury was justified in finding that the correct type was AB positive and that incompatible blood was not in fact administered for the treatment of postpartum bleeding and shock.[12] In another case, a physician performed a hysterectomy on the patient to control excessive bleeding after delivery. During the operation, an employee of the hospital brought some A positive blood to the operating room. The blood was incompatible with the patient's O positive blood. After the patient had received about 600 cubic centimeters of the incompatible blood, the physician noticed the error, ordered the correct type, and began to administer other fluids to the patient. The court upheld the jury's finding that the physician-defendant was not negligent in failing to check the match of the blood before transfusing. The medical evidence indicated that it would have been improper for him to divert attention from the operation, and the court held that he was entitled to rely on the accuracy of the hospital employees. The court held that the hospital was liable for damages caused by the error.[13]

§ 12.20 INFECTION

Liability may be imposed on a physician for negligence in the diagnosis and treatment of postpartum infection, including the failure to properly close incisions and failure to promptly treat a known infection.

Basic Standard of Care: The American College of Obstetricians and Gynecologists has not published guidelines for the treatment of postpartum infection.

Interpretation and Customary Practice: Infection is another relatively common postpartum occurrence. In a medical study conducted in Michigan, 725 of 6,436 patients (roughly 12 percent) exhibited puerperal infectious morbidity.[14] Infections most commonly develop in the uterus, urinary tract, surgical wounds, breast, episiotomy, and lacerations.[15]

The most common site of postpartum-infection is the uterine cavity, and the most frequent infection is endometritis. Myometritis, parametritis, salpingitis, pelvic abscess, septic pelvic thrombophlebitis, septicemia, and septic shock are late complications of infection.[16] A number of factors have been identified as increasing the risk of puerperal uterine infection. These include delivery by cesarean section, prolonged rupture of the membranes, frequent pelvic examinations during labor, use of forceps in delivery, and manual removal of the placenta.[17] In a study published in 1979, researchers demonstrated that the incidence of endometritis could be lowered by the use of simple preventive measures, including careful washing of their hands by nurses and physicians, frequent changes of scrub clothes, and restricted staff movement from infected to noninfected patients.[18] Treatment of postpartum uterine infection usually consists of antibiotics, bed rest, hydration, decompression of the bowel, and maintenance of electrolyte balance.[19]

Postpartum urinary tract infection occurs in about five percent of patients.[20] In some patient groups studied, the urinary tract has been a more common site of puerperal infection than has the uterine cavity. Most urinary tract infections are due to coliform bacteria and can be treated with appropriate antibiotics.[21]

Breast infection, in the form of mastitis, occurs most frequently in the primiparous nursing patient. Treatment often consists of the discontinuance of nursing, application of local heat or cold, and the administration of antibiotics. Breast infection that is left untreated often progresses to breast abscess. Incision and drainage are necessary for treatment of an abscess.[22]

Sepsis continues to be a major cause of postpartum maternal death. In most instances, death can be prevented by early recognition of the complication and vigorous treatment with antibiotics and appropriate supportive measures. Early treatment of puerperal infection is frequently essential. Where the patient is injured as a result of negligent treatment, it may be the hospital rather than the patient's physician that is held liable, because of the failure of hospital employees to properly recognize and manage patient complications.

CASE ILLUSTRATION

On June 7, the obstetrician performed a cesarean section on the patient and delivered a normal baby girl. On June 10, the patient developed a fever. She received antibiotics and her fever subsided. On June 13, the patient's temperature was below 100 degrees, but at 4:00 p.m. she complained to hospital personnel of soreness in the jaw and difficulty in opening her mouth. A resident at the hospital examined the patient and ordered the administration of codeine, Nembutal, and oil of wintergreen. The resident did not inform the obstetrician of the patient's symptoms at this time. The obstetrician first learned of them on his hospital visit the next day at 10:00 a.m. The obstetrician made a tentative diagnosis of possible severe neuritis, possible throat infection, possible tooth infection, and possible tetanus. He consulted specialists and began to administer tetanus antitoxin. In addition, he remained in close attendance on the patient throughout June 14 and June 15, administered anticonvulsants, assigned a special nurse to the patient, and introduced airways to enable the patient to receive oxygen. At 11:30 a.m. on June 14, 3,000 units of tetanus antitoxin were administered; at 4:30 p.m., 1,500 units; at 1:30 p.m. on June 15, 50,000 units. At 9:15 p.m. on June 15, the patient suffered a convulsion and died. The cause of death was laryngospasm (spasmodic closing of the larynx) resulting in collapse of the lungs.

The patient's husband sued the obstetrician and the hospital. He alleged negligent introduction of tetanus spores into the patient's body during the operation and negligent failure to diagnose the nature of the infection thereafter. The lower court entered judgment on a jury verdict against the defendants. The higher court upheld the judgment against the hospital but held that the complaint against the obstetrician should have been dismissed. The court noted that there was no evidence of negligence in the obstetrician's treatment of the patient. The court also stated that the evidence established that the obstetrician had correctly, continuously, and intensively treated the patient for a tetanus infection once he had learned of the relevant symptoms on June 14. The court stated, however, that the jury could have concluded that the 18-hour delay in treatment caused by the failure of hospital personnel to inform the obstetrician of the symptoms was negligent and the proximate cause of the patient's death. Hence, the judgment against the hospital was proper (*Garafola v. Maimonides Hospital of Brooklyn*, 1964).[23]

The epidemic form of puerperal infection, which is rare, is caused almost exclusively by beta-hemolytic streptococci from an exogenous source. The source may be the hospital environment, the organisms residing in the nasopharynx or infected skin wounds of labor attendants, or even the patient's own cervix. The course of infections caused by beta-hemolytic streptococci includes an abrupt rise in temperature to 102 to 104 degrees Fahrenheit (39 to 40 degrees centigrade) within the first 12 hours after delivery. The patient feels acutely ill and looks it.[24] In a 1970 Nebraska case, a patient died 31 hours after delivery of a severe beta-hemolytic streptococcus infection. The Supreme Court of Nebraska overruled a directed verdict for the hospital-defendant and remanded for a new trial. Five hours after delivery, the patient had a temperature of 102.2 degrees, a pulse of 126, and a respiration rate of 28. The court ruled that the following acts and omissions by hospital personnel raised a jury question of negligence: (1) failure to take a medical history, which would have revealed infection at the time of admittance to the hospital; (2) failure to notify the attending physician of the abnormal vital signs; (3) administration of codeine and application of ice to the patient's abdomen in contravention of the attending physician's orders; and (4) delay in taking a blood count ordered by the physician.[25]

Peritonitis is an infectious disease that may occur during the puerperium, but it is relatively uncommon as a sequel to delivery. It ranges in severity from relatively mild infection of the peritoneal covering of the broad ligaments to generalized, widespread infection. With widespread infection, the patient usually has an elevated body temperature and an extremely tender abdomen, but, due to abdominal muscle relaxation following delivery, muscle spasm may be absent. Other prominent symptoms include paralytic ileus, vomiting, and distention of the abdomen. If antibiotic treatment is not initiated, the patient could die quickly. An abscess may form in the pelvic cul-de-sac, eventually fluctuating and draining through the rectum. With peritonitis, blood cultures are most often positive.[26] Failure to treat peritonitis promptly may not only pose grave medical consequences for the patient, it may have certain legal implications for the physician.

CASE ILLUSTRATION

On August 13 the physician (an obstetrician-gynecologist) delivered the patient of a premature male infant. On August 14 the patient complained of cramping abdominal pain. On August 15 the patient complained of severe pain in the left lower portion of her abdomen, with associated pain in the left shoulder and back. A resident noted that the patient screamed occasionally, but he attributed this to a postpartum psychosis and prescribed Compazine. At 5:00 p.m. on August 15, the resident informed the physician of the patient's condition, but the physician ordered no evaluatory procedures. By 8:00 p.m. the patient's pain had increased and had rendered her incapable of walking. Her husband called the physician. The physician indicated that the symptoms were normal postpartum cramps, magnified by a low pain threshold. During the day of August 15, the patient had received Librium, Compazine, Miltown, a Darvon compound, codeine, and two APC (acetylsalicylic acid, phenacetin, and caffeine) tablets. At

11:30 p.m. on August 15, the patient was discovered in profound shock. She had no measurable pulse or blood pressure, was cold and clammy, and had a distended abdomen. Two interns were summoned, but the patient's chart reported no therapeutic measures between 11:30 p.m. and 1:00 a.m. The physician was notified of the patient's condition by telephone at 1:00 a.m. He ordered an intravenous infusion of glucose and water with Aramine. One intern testified that the attempts to start the infusion were unsuccessful. The physician arrived at 1:15 a.m. He testified that the infusion was started but that the needle subsequently came out of the vein. There was a dispute in the testimony over whether it was started again. No cutdown was attempted. The physician examined the patient, and the following measures were taken: removal by suction of vomitus, administration of oxygen, application of heat, and elevation of the feet. The patient was pronounced dead at 3:30 a.m. The autopsy revealed a diverticulitis of the sigmoid colon, with rupture of the diverticulum resulting in peritonitis.

The administrator of the patient's estate sued the physician. A jury returned a verdict in favor of the plaintiff. In response to the physician-defendant's challenge of the verdict, the court ruled that the jury could have reasonably found that the physician-defendant's inaction between 5:00 p.m. on August 15 and 1:00 a.m. on August 16 and his failure to take proper measures after 1:00 a.m. constituted negligence in light of the information he possessed. In support of this conclusion, the court referred to testimony of the plaintiff's expert that the physician-defendant failed to meet accepted standards of care in failing to take the following measures after the patient lapsed into shock: blood studies, crossmatching of whole blood for transfusion, X-ray studies of the abdomen, vigorous intravenous fluid infusion, use of plasma, venous cutdown to administer fluids if vein puncture was delayed, administration of antibiotics by vein, and a laparotomy. The court also ruled that the jury could find that all the residents and interns who attended the patient were agents of the physician-defendant (*Schuler v. Berger*, 1967).[27]

Infection of abdominal surgical wounds is a relatively common complication in patients undergoing cesarean section. These infections, as well as infections of episiotomies and lacerations, can often be treated by drainage.[28] The rate of wound infections can be lowered by using the preventive measures discussed earlier and by isolating infected patients.

In a Missouri case decided in 1979, the patient-plaintiff alleged that, during delivery of her child, the physician made several incisions in the area of her vagina, birth canal, rectum, colon, peritoneum, and lower intestinal tract and that he failed to close them properly. She visited the physician and his partner on three occasions after the delivery and complained of severe abdominal pain, stool leakage into her vagina, and inability to control her bowel movements, but on each occasion the physicians merely told her that her condition was nothing to worry about and that it could be rectified in the future with a few sutures. When the patient was unable to raise the money for this subsequent procedure, she consulted another physician, who informed her that the failure to close the incisions properly had resulted in a mix of feces and urine with organs and muscle tissue in her pelvis and that her organs had become "atrophied, degenerated, fouled, and decayed"; numerous surgical procedures would be required to correct the condition, and she would be rendered sterile. The court reversed a summary judgment in favor of the first physician and his partner. They had contended that the statute of limitations (see § 3.50, Statute of Limitations) barred the patient-plaintiff's claim. The court held that the patient-plaintiff had raised the question (which should be answered at the trial of the case) whether the assurances given by the physician-defendants to the patient-plaintiff constituted fraudulent concealment of the seriousness of her condition, which would toll the statute of limitations.[29]

§ 12.30 INJURY TO THE CHILD

Liability may be imposed on a physician for the failure to use proper resuscitative techniques and for the negligent infliction of retrolental fibroplasia on the newborn child.

Basic Standard of Care: The American College of Obstetricians and Gynecologists recommends that the individual who delivers the baby be responsible for the immediate postdelivery care of the newborn until another person assumes the duty. Routine care of the healthy newborn may often be delegated to appropriately trained nurses. The newborn should be examined for any abnormalities, and the Apgar scores should be determined, evaluated, and recorded. Care of the eyes and cord and identification of the newborn should be provided according to written hospital procedures and local statutes. Recognition and immediate resuscitation of the distressed infant requires an organized plan of action and immediate availability of qualified personnel and equipment. Planning must include specific identification and immediate in-house availability of qualified personnel on a 24-hour basis.[30]

Interpretation and Customary Practice: The condition of newborn infants is commonly assessed by the Apgar scoring method (see Table 12.1). The infant is given a score of 0, 1, or 2 for each of five criteria, and evaluations are made at one and five minutes after birth. Normal infants score between 7 and 10. The lower the score, the greater the degree of asphyxia and depression.[31] Scores of 1 to 3 indicate severe asphyxia. Low scores also correlate with a higher rate of subsequent neurologic abnormality.[32]

Newborn infants may fail to breathe after birth for a number of reasons, including intrauterine hypoxia, drug narcosis, and birth injuries.[33] To resuscitate the infant, the physician should first suction the infant's nasopharynx. Oxygen

TABLE 12.1 The Apgar Scoring Chart

Sign	Score 0	Score 1	Score 2
Heart rate	Absent	Slow (below 100)	Over 100
Respiratory effort	Absent	Slow, irregular, hypoventilation	Good, crying lustily
Muscle tone	Flaccid	Some flexion of extremities	Active motion, well flexed
Reflex irritability	No response	Cry, some motion	Vigorous cry
Color	Blue, pale	Body pink, hands and feet blue	Completely pink

Source: J. Hughes, Synopsis of Pediatrics 238 (1980).

is delivered to the lungs through an intratracheal tube, and respiration is supported artificially until the infant starts to breathe by itself. Those infants already breathing spontaneously can be provided supplemental oxygen by mask, with external cardiac massage if necessary.[34] Resuscitative efforts must also include prevention of excessive loss of body heat.[35] Stimulant drugs are generally not indicated in the resuscitation.[36]

Plaintiffs have sometimes alleged that the physicians performing a delivery used improper resuscitative techniques. The courts have ruled that the physicians are not liable as long as their actions were reasonable, even if the plaintiff demonstrates that they could have taken alternative measures.

CASE ILLUSTRATION

The patient was in the ninth month of her first pregnancy. She went into labor and was admitted to the hospital at 2:30 a.m. At 2:40 a.m. she was placed in the labor room under the care of a nurse, two obstetrical technicians, and the first physician. The second physician, the patient's obstetrician, was not present but was notified that the patient had arrived at the hospital. The attending personnel examined the patient at regular intervals between 2:40 a.m. and 6:00 a.m. In addition, fetal heart tones were checked with a fetoscope every half hour. The patient testified that the nurse listened to the fetal heart tones between 4:45 a.m. and 5:00 a.m., went to the labor room door, and stated that there was a problem and that the patient's obstetrician should be notified. No other evidence, including the patient's hospital chart, indicated that any problem or emergency was detected at this time. At 5:58 a.m. or 6:00 a.m. the patient was transferred to the delivery room. The nurse then checked the fetal heart tones. The rate was low (80), and the tones were faint and irregular. At about this time, the patient's obstetrician arrived in the delivery room. The nurse advised him of the abnormal heart tones. He checked the tones, ordered oxygen, and took over the delivery. At 6:15 a.m. the anesthesiologist arrived. At 6:18 a.m. the obstetrician delivered the infant, who had no heartbeat or respi-

§ 12.30   *Injury to the Child*   477

ration and was flaccid. The obstetrician requested the anesthesiologist to put the patient under general anesthesia, and the anesthesiologist did so. The obstetrician suctioned the infant's mouth, nasopharynx, and nose with a bulb syringe. He then placed the infant on a flat surface, extended the infant's head, and inserted a DeLee tracheal catheter. He placed his right hand on the infant's chest to check for bilateral inspiration and heartbeat. The obstetrician held the catheter between his teeth and with his left hand held the infant's chin up. The nurse delivered oxygen to the obstetrician's mouth with the oxygen tube, and the obstetrician delivered the oxygen to the infant through the catheter. The resuscitation continued for ten minutes. The infant's color changed from blue to pink. He began to breathe on his own but would stop when the obstetrician stopped breathing for him. The obstetrician asked the anesthesiologist to insert an endotracheal tube. The anesthesiologist intubated the infant under direct vision, using a laryngoscope and an endotracheal tube. The infant was then connected to a Bennett resuscitator, which the nurse had brought to the delivery room. The infant suffered permanent brain damage.

The infant's special guardian and his parents sued the three physicians, among others. The jury returned a verdict for the three physicians, and the lower court entered judgment on it. The higher court affirmed. The plaintiffs alleged that the first physician was negligent in failing to deliver the infant earlier. The court held that the jury could have reasonably concluded that there was in fact no emergency or problem before 6:00 a.m. The court then ruled that, since there was expert testimony that the first physician had in all respects acted properly, it could not overturn the jury's verdict in his favor. The plaintiffs alleged that the obstetrician was negligent in failing to order intubation immediately and in failing to administer sodium bicarbonate. The court refused to overturn the jury's verdict in favor of the obstetrician since there was expert testimony that temporary use of the DeLee catheter was proper, that administration of sodium bicarbonate was not part of the standard of care required of an obstetrician at the time of the delivery (1967), and that the actions of the obstetrician were proper in all respects. There was also testimony that the infant's neurological deficit was not due to the resuscitative efforts. The plaintiffs alleged that the anesthesiologist was negligent in not taking charge of resuscitating the infant. The court upheld the jury's verdict for him, since the expert testimony indicated that the duty of the anesthesiologist was to stay at the mother's side while she was under general anesthesia (*Northern Trust Co. v. Skokie Valley Community Hospital*, 1980).[37]

Newborn infants with respiratory difficulties often require oxygen therapy. A significant complication of excessive oxygen therapy is retrolental fibroplasia. Retrolental fibroplasia is a retinal vascular disorder that occurs primarily in premature infants who receive a high concentration of oxygen and who weigh less than 3.3 pounds (1,500 grams) at birth.[38] The condition is characterized by disorganized retinal vascular overgrowth in the presence of oxygen, followed by anoxia when the oxygen is removed; this can lead to retinal detachment and the formation of a white membrane behind the lens.[39] In less severe cases, myopia and strabismus can result.[40] The incidence of retrolental fibroplasia has increased in recent years because of the increased use of oxygen therapy for the treatment of respiratory distress syndrome, and it has produced a large amount of litigation.[41] Although retrolental fibroplasia usually occurs in infants who have received supplementary oxygen, it sometimes occurs in infants who have not; conversely, not every premature infant who receives oxygen therapy develops the condition. Cases in which negligent infliction of retrolental fibroplasia is alleged frequently feature directly conflicting expert testimony about the propriety of treatment methods and about causation.

CASE ILLUSTRATION

The infant was born approximately three months prematurely and weighed 1 pound 13 ounces at birth. She was afflicted with respiratory distress syndrome. The physician in charge of her treatment administered oxygen therapy in order to preserve her life. By the time the infant was four months old, she had retrolental fibroplasia in both eyes. The infant, through her father, sued the hospital and the treating physician. At the time of trial she was permanently blind. The testimony at trial was conflicting as to whether the method of oxygen therapy used by the pediatrician-defendant was in accord with applicable medical standards. The plaintiff's experts testified that the pediatrician-defendant administered oxygen at excessively high levels for excessive lengths of time; that he should have treated the respiratory distress syndrome with short periods of therapy; that he failed to properly monitor the absorption of oxygen into the blood; that he failed to properly interpret the tests he did perform; and that the infant's blindness resulted from his negligence. The pediatrician-defendant's experts testified that the oxygen therapy was necessary to save the infant's life; that the pediatrician-defendant administered the proper amount of oxygen and properly monitored oxygen levels in the blood; and that the infant's blindness was caused by a congenital defect unrelated to the oxygen therapy. The pediatrician-defendant's experts also disputed the testimony of the plaintiff's experts as to the cause-and-effect relationship between supplemental oxygen and retrolental fibroplasia.

The jury returned a verdict for the pediatrician-defendant, and the lower court entered judgment on it. The higher court reversed, because the lower court instructed the jury that testimony by an expert that he would have treated the infant differently was not sufficient to establish

§ 12.30   *Injury to the Child*   479

negligence. The higher court held that, while this was an accurate statement of the law, it had been misleading in the context of the case: the plaintiff's experts testified in form as to what they would have done, but in substance their testimony attempted to establish the requisite standard of medical care applicable to the case (*Greenberg v. Bishop Clarkson Memorial Hospital,* 1978).[42]

It is difficult for a physician to gauge the amount of oxygen he or she can safely administer to an infant. Infants vary drastically in their ability to assimilate atmospheric oxygen into their blood. Furthermore, the development of retrolental fibroplasia is not directly related to the concentration of oxygen in the incubator; the correct index is the arterial oxygen tension. Experts have not determined precisely what amount is toxic, but they generally recommend that the partial pressure of oxygen in arterial blood be kept below 90 to 100 millimeters of mercury.[43] If the physician has no device for measuring arterial oxygen tension, he or she must protect against overexposure through some other means. Retrolental fibroplasia occurs only infrequently when the concentration of oxygen in the incubator is kept below 40 percent, but maintaining the concentration at or below this level is no guarantee of success.[44] While the physician must attempt to keep the concentration of oxygen low enough to prevent the development of retrolental fibroplasia, it must be high enough to avoid respiratory problems or brain damage. The cases that have been brought frequently deal with this dilemma of the physician.

CASE ILLUSTRATION

The infant was born prematurely, after 28 weeks of gestation, at 3:00 p.m. on February 9. The pediatrician began to treat her at 3:30 p.m. The pediatrician diagnosed the infant as suffering from either hyaline membrane disease or respiratory distress syndrome. The pediatrician ordered oxygen at "5 to 8 liters per minute or higher if necessary to keep *pink.*" The infant received oxygen until 12:00 p.m. on Feburary 16 (7 days). She developed retrolental fibroplasia and became totally blind. The evidence established that in 1968, the year of the infant's birth, the hospital had no gauges for monitoring the amount of oxygen in the blood. The infant, through her father, sued the pediatrician. The plaintiff presented experts who testified that oxygen should have been administered by means of titration. Under this system, the oxygen concentration is lowered until the infant becomes cyanotic. Then the concentration is raised slightly until the infant becomes pink. The process is repeated periodically. The plaintiff also introduced evidence from the American Academy of Pediatrics which noted that the oxygen concentration "should be kept at the lowest possible level that will relieve the symptoms for which it is given. If possible, it should not be over 40 percent." The records of the nurses reflected that, from 8:30 a.m. on Feburary 12 to 5:00 p.m. on February 15, the oxygen concentration was almost always above, and never below, 40 percent. The pediatrician-defendant offered expert testimony that his own method of oxygen therapy was adequate. He "worked down" from concentrations that were adequate instead of "working up" from inadequate concentrations. Some of the pediatrician-defendant's experts testified that the titration method would actually have been harmful under the circumstances. The evidence established that for at least 40 hours the infant received high concentrations of oxygen without any testing, up or down. The jury returned a verdict for the pediatrician-defendant. The lower court entered judgment on it.

The higher court reversed. It ruled that the trial court had failed to explain to the jury that the plaintiff's allegation of negligent supervision by the pediatrician-defendant was different from an allegation of improper therapeutic procedure. The court noted that there was evidence that the pediatrician-defendant had in fact failed to order or to supervise periodic reduction in oxygen if the infant remained pink. The court ruled that the trial court should have given the following kind of instruction to the jury:

> If you find that [the pediatrician-defendant] believed that continuous administration of oxygen to [the infant] in an amount greater than that necessary to maintain her pink color would be harmful to her and that the dosage was continued in amounts higher than that necessary to maintain her pink color and you further find that the doctor failed to ascertain that the nurses were not periodically testing the oxygen level, as he anticipated, to determine the minimum level of oxygen, then you should find such failure by him not to be in accord with the accepted standards of care and diligence required of physicians, and if such failure on his part contributed to cause or to aggravate the injury to [the infant], you should return a verdict against the doctor.

(*Poulin v. Zartman*, 1975).[45]

NOTES

1. American College of Obstetricians and Gynecologists, Standards for Obstetric/Gynecologic Services 31, 32 (5th ed. 1982).
2. Gibbs & Locke, *Maternal Deaths in Texas, 1969 to 1973,* 126 Am. J. Obstet. Gynecol. 687–92 (1976).
3. R. Willson & E. Carrington, Obstetrics and Gynecology 420 (6th ed. 1979).
4. Watson, *Postpartum Hemorrhage and Shock,* 23 Clin. Obstet. Gynecol. 985–1001 (1980).
5. *Id.* at 991.
6. *Id.* at 990.
7. R. Willson & E. Carrington, *supra* note 3, at 423.
8. *Id.* at 422.
9. Chapman v. Carlson, 240 So.2d 263 (Miss. 1970).
10. Parker v. St. Paul Fire & Marine Ins. Co., 335 So.2d 725 (La. App. 1976); *cert.*

denied, 338 So.2d 700 (La. 1976). *Compare* Stack v. Wapner, 244 Pa. Super. 72, 368 A.2d 292 (1976).
11. Katsetos v. Nolan, 170 Conn. 637, 368 A.2d 172 (1976).
12. Steversen v. Hospital Auth., 129 Ga. App. 510, 199 S.E.2d 881 (1973).
13. Parker v. St. Paul Fire & Marine Ins. Co., *supra* note 10.
14. Sweet & Ledger, *Puerperal Infectious Morbidity,* 117 Am. J. Obstet. Gynecol. 1093–1100, 1094 (1973).
15. Eschenbach & Wager, *Puerperal Infections,* 23 Clin. Obstet. Gynecol. 1003–37 (1980).
16. *Id.* at 1004; M. Novy, *The Puerperium,* in Current Obstetric & Gynecologic Diagnosis and Treatment 765 (1978).
17. Eschenbach & Wager, *supra* note 15, at 1004.
18. Iffy, Kaminetzky, Maidman, Lindsey, and Arrata, *Control of Perinatal Infection by Traditional Preventive Measures,* 54 Obstet. Gynecol. 403–11 (1979).
19. Novy, *supra* note 16, at 765.
20. *Id.*
21. Sweet & Ledger, *supra* note 14, at 1096.
22. M. Novy, *supra* note 16, at 765.
23. Garafola v. Maimonides Hosp. of Brooklyn, 22 A.D.2d 85, 253 N.Y.S.2d 856 (1964); *aff'd.,* 19 N.Y.2d 765, 226 N.E.2d 311, 279 N.Y.S.2d 523 (1967).
24. K. Niswander, Obstetrics 435 (1976); R. Willson & E. Carrington, *supra* note 3, at 534.
25. Foley v. Bishop Clarkson Mem. Hosp., 185 Neb. 89, 173 N.W.2d 881 (1970).
26. K. Niswander, *supra* note 24, at 436; R. Willson & E. Carrington, *supra* note 3, at 535.
27. Schuler v. Berger, 275 F. Supp. 120 (E.D. Pa. 1967); *aff'd.,* 395 F.2d 212 (3d Cir. 1968).
28. Sweet & Ledger, *supra* note 14, at 1097.
29. Brewington v. Raksakulthi, 584 S.W.2d 112 (Mo. App. 1979).
30. American College of Obstetricians and Gynecologists, *supra* note 1, at 31.
31. R. Willson & E. Carrington, *supra* note 3, at 440.
32. J. Hughes, Synopsis of Pediatrics 237 (1980).
33. R. Willson & E. Carrington, *supra* note 3, at 440.
34. J. Hughes, *supra* note 32, at 238.
35. *Id.* at 239.
36. R. Willson & E. Carrington, *supra* note 3, at 441.
37. Northern Trust Co. v. Skokie Valley Community Hosp., 81 Ill. App.3d 1110, 401 N.E.2d 1246 (1980).
38. H. Silver, C. Kempe, & H. Bruyn, Handbook of Pediatrics 372–73 (1980).
39. J. Hughes, *supra* note 32, at 831.
40. Ellis, *Eye,* in Current Pediatric Diagnosis and Treatment 230 (1978).
41. *See, e.g.,* Comley v. Emanuel Lutheran Charity Bd., 35 Or. App. 465, 582 P.2d 443 (1978); Ohler v. Tacoma Gen. Hosp., 92 Wash.2d 507, 598 P.2d 1358 (1979); Hill v. Boles, 583 S.W.2d 141 (Mo. 1979); Ikenn v. Northwestern Mem. Hosp., 73 Ill. App. 3d 694, 392 N.E.2d 440 (1979); Penetrante v. United States, 604 F.2d 1248 (9th Cir. 1979); Romo v. Estate of Bennett, 97 Cal. App. 3d 304, 158 Cal. Rptr. 635 (1979); Lampiasi v. St. Vincent's Hosp., 71 A.D.2d 203, 422 N.Y.S.2d 81 (1979), *aff'd,* 51 N.Y.2d 913, 434 N.Y.S.2d 993 (1980); Donadio v. Crouse-Irving Mem. Hosp., 75 A.D.2d 715, 427 N.Y.S.2d 118 (1980).
42. Greenburg v. Bishop Clarkson Mem. Hosp., 201 Neb. 215, 266 N.W.2d 902 (1978).
43. J. Hughes, *supra* note 32, at 254.

44. H. Silver, C. Kempe, H. Bruyn, *supra* note 38, at 373.
45. Poulin v. Zartman, 542 P.2d 251 (Alaska 1975); *aff'd on rehearing,* 548 P.2d 1299 (Alaska 1976).

Part V

Aspects of Gynecology

Chapter XIII

Diagnosis and Treatment

§ 13.10 PHYSICAL EXAMINATION AND EVALUATION

Liability may be imposed on a physician for the failure to perform an adequate examination of a patient who presents symptoms indicative of the need for an examination, the failure to adequately warn a patient of the risks of foregoing a recommended test, the negligent failure to inform the patient of the results of a test or examination, and negligent misdiagnosis.

Basic Standard of Care: For most women, the gynecologist is the principal source of her health care and may be the only physician providing continuity of care. When the gynecologist serves as the primary physician, the American College of Obstetricians and Gynecologists recognizes that a more comprehensive evaluation will be required than when the gynecologist serves as a consultant.

A woman's first visit to the gynecologist should occur by the age of 18 years, at the onset of sexual activity, and before her first pregnancy. A comprehensive evaluation should also be performed when the woman transfers to a new physician. The American College of Obstetricians and Gynecologists suggests that the basic components of a comprehensive gynecological evaluation should include:

1. History
   a. Purpose of the visit
   b. Present illness
   c. Menstrual and reproductive history
   d. Past medical, past surgical, emotional, social, family, and sexual history
   e. Medications
   f. Allergies
   g. Contraception
   h. Systems review

2. Physical Examination
   a. Weight, nutritional state, blood pressure
   b. Head and neck
   c. Heart
   d. Lungs
   e. Breasts
   f. Abdomen
   g. Extremities
   h. Lymph nodes
   i. Pelvis (external and internal genitalia)
   j. Rectum
3. Laboratory
   a. Urine—sugar and protein
   b. Hemoglobin-hematocrit
   c. Cervical cytology
   d. Rubella titer (if the patient is of reproductive age)

Periodic evaluations need not be as complete as the initial comprehensive evaluation but should include:

1. History
   a. Purpose of the visit
   b. Interval history, including systems review
   c. Menstrual history
   d. Emotional history
2. Physical Examination
   a. Weight, nutritional state
   b. Thyroid
   c. Breasts
   d. Abdomen
   e. Pelvis (external and internal genitalia)
   f. Rectum
   g. Other areas as indicated by the interval history
3. Laboratory
   a. Urine—sugar and protein
   b. Cervical cytology

Additional laboratory tests should be performed as indicated, based on the history, physical examination, and risk factors.[1]

Interpretation and Customary Practice: When a patient presents herself for gynecological or obstetrical care, the physician should elicit a medical history that includes a detailed description of the present complaint or illness.[2] The physician would then proceed to a physical examination of the patient. The physician should perform a complete general physical examination unless the patient has been referred by another physician only for gynecological evaluation. The standard gynecological examination consists of recording the patient's weight and blood pressure and performing breast, abdominal, vaginal, and rectal examinations.[3]

In examining the breasts, the physician inspects them for size, contour, and the condition of the skin; he or she also looks for nodularity or dimpling suggestive of an underlying mass. The physician then palpates the breasts and the axillas.[4] X-ray mammography on an annual basis is recommended for women over the age of fifty.

The abdominal examination begins with inspection of contour and color. The physician auscultates for intestinal activity and then palpates the abdomen, feeling for rigidity, masses, and unusual tenderness. The physician should also perform percussion of the abdomen to identify organ enlargement, tumor, or ascites.[5]

The pelvic examination begins with inspection of the external genitalia and urethra. The physician checks perineal support by inserting two fingers into the vagina and instructing the patient to "bear down." The vagina and cervix are both palpated and visually examined with the aid of a speculum. The physician also collects material from the cervix for cytologic examination (see § 14.10, Cancer). The physician can investigate the adnexal structures and the body of the uterus by bimanual examination: two fingers of one hand are inserted into the vagina while the opposite hand presses against the abdominal wall.[6]

The basic gynecological examination should always include a rectal or rectovaginal examination. This procedure is useful for evaluating some posterior pelvic structures and for revealing rectocele and other lower bowel lesions.[7]

Many specific diagnostic procedures can be performed in the physician's office. These include the fern test for ovulation, the Schiller test for abnormalities of the cervix, and sounding of the cervix and body of the uterus. The physician can also make slides of vaginal "smears" and biopsy suspicious lesions. More complicated procedures, such as laparoscopy, are performed in the hospital with the patient under general anesthesia.[8]

Many cases have discussed the physician's duty to properly perform gynecological and obstetrical examinations on patients who present themselves for examination. The courts have ruled that a physician is liable if he or she fails to perform an examination on a patient with symptoms that indicate an examination is necessary.

CASE ILLUSTRATION

The patient was 14 years old and was suffering from dizzy spells, fainting, and missed menstrual periods. The patient's mother took her to a general practitioner, who attributed the symptoms to obesity and low blood pressure. In fact, the patient was pregnant. The patient saw the general practitioner six times between October 14, 1974, and January 28, 1975. However, at no time did the general practitioner perform a pregnancy test or indicate to the patient or the mother that the patient might be pregnant. The patient gave birth to a child and then sued the general practitioner, alleging that he had been negligent in failing to diagnose her pregnancy. The patient-plaintiff called an obstetrician-gynecologist as an expert witness. He testified that it was a breach of the standard of care for a general practitioner in obstetrical care to fail to conduct a pregnancy test on a person with the patient-plaintiff's symptoms. Furthermore, the general practitioner-defendant admitted that he had suspected pregnancy during the patient-plaintiff's initial visit. The lower court entered judgment on a jury verdict for the patient-plaintiff. The higher court affirmed. The higher court ruled that, even in the absence of expert testimony on the requisite standard of care, a jury could find that a physician who fails to perform a pregnancy test on a patient who exhibits the symptoms exhibited by the patient-plaintiff is negligent. The court noted that this was particularly true in light of the general practitioner-defendant's admission that he had suspected pregnancy (*Clapham v. Yanga*, 1980).[9]

A physician will not be liable for failing to perform a gynecological test if he or she has not assumed the general gynecological care of the patient and the patient does not present any symptoms relating to her pelvic organs.

CASE ILLUSTRATION

From April 1972 until April 1975, the general practitioner treated the patient for various acute problems. In March 1974, the patient spent six days in the hospital with complaints of coughing, shortness of breath, bronchitis, and fever. In July and August 1974 and in March 1975, the patient entered the hospital with complaints of diarrhea and associated pain in the abdomen. The patient did not at any time present to the general practitioner any symptoms relating to her reproductive organs. In October 1975, the patient began to experience vaginal bleeding. She consulted a gynecologist, who diagnosed cancer of the cervix. The patient underwent radiation therapy, surgery, and chemotherapy, but she died on July 14, 1976. Her husband sued the general practitioner, alleging that he had been negligent in failing to perform a Pap smear on his wife. At the trial court level, the jury reached a verdict in favor of the physician-defendant. The appeals court upheld this decision, holding that there was sufficient evidence to support the jury's verdict. The physician-defendant had offered several expert witnesses who testified that, under normal medical practice, when a woman presents a complaint unrelated to her reproductive organs, a general practitioner does not perform a pelvic examination or Pap smear and elicits only enough medical history necessary to treat the patient's specific complaint. Hence, the actions of the physician-defendant conformed to the requisite community medical standards (*Lambert v. Michel*, 1978).[10]

In *Truman v. Thomas*,[11] The Supreme Court of California ruled that a physician is liable if he or she does not adequately warn the patient of the risks of failing to undergo a test that the physician has recommended. In this case, a family physician had undertaken the general gynecological care of the patient, who subsequently died of cervical cancer. Her family sued the physician, claiming that he should have performed a Pap smear on the patient. The physician testified that he continually suggested to the patient that she undergo a Pap smear, but she persistently refused. The court ruled that the physician had a duty to warn the patient of the risks involved in refusing to undergo the Pap smear. The court rejected the argument that these risks are a matter of common knowledge and that no warning is needed. The holding in this case, requiring what amounts to "informed *refusal*" when a patient declines a diagnostic test, is somewhat harsh and has not been followed in jurisdictions other than California as of this writing.

A physician can also be held liable for failing to inform the patient of the results of a test or examination that has been performed.

CASE ILLUSTRATION

The first physician, an obstetrician-gynecologist, performed a Pap smear on the patient in the course of a general postnatal examination. The smear tested out as "Class III," indicating either dysplasia or cancer in situ. The physician performed a D&C and cold conization. The physician believed that he had adequately treated the patient with these procedures and instructed her to return every three months for further Pap smears. The patient subsequently had two smears that proved to be Class I, negative. When the first physician retired, the patient visited a second physician, who was also an obstetrician-gynecologist. This second physician took a Pap smear of the patient. He then informed her that the D&C and cold conization performed by the first physician could not have eliminated her cancer and that a hysterectomy was necessary. The second physician performed a total abdominal hysterectomy. The tissue report showed no cancer. The patient sued the second physician and alleged that his failure to inform her of the negative result of the Pap smear constituted a breach of the duty to obtain informed consent and contributed to her decision to undergo an unnecessary hysterectomy. At the trial, the jury returned a verdict for the physician-defendant. The appeals court reversed and granted judgment for the patient-plaintiff. The appeals court held as a matter of law that the failure by the physician-defendant to inform the patient-plaintiff that the result of the last Pap smear was negative breached his duty of disclosure to her (*Steele v. St. Paul Fire and Marine Insurance Co.*, 1979).[12]

A physician may not be held liable for failing to inform the patient of the unfavorable results of a test if the patient makes it so difficult for the physician to locate her that the physician cannot, with the exercise of reasonable efforts, provide her with the results. Thus, in *Ray v. Wagner*,[13] the physician performed a routine Pap smear on a patient who had requested an IUD. The report on the smear was "suspicious for malignancy," and the patient eventually had to be treated for cervical cancer. When the patient sued the physician, the court held that the physician was not liable for failing to inform the patient of the result: the patient had given false employment information, had moved without informing the physician of her new address, and had no telephone at her new home. Despite his failure to promptly inform the patient of the result, the physician had made a reasonable effort to do so.

The courts have also ruled that a physician may be liable when he or she performs an examination that is unreasonably cursory. Thus, when a patient presents a specific complaint, the physician must perform tests adequate for evaluating the complaint; the physician cannot merely perform the type of examination he or she would perform on an asymptomatic patient.

CASE ILLUSTRATION

The patient discovered a lump in her left breast. She consulted an obstetrician-gynecologist. He could not find a mass, but he did note some tenderness. Since he believed that the tenderness might be due to the patient's approaching menstrual period, he instructed her to return for another examination in ten days. The patient testified that when she returned the physician had forgotten about her specific breast complaint and had merely performed a routine physical examination that happened to include an examination of her breasts. The physician testified that he was aware of the patient's specific complaint and that he performed a complete physical examination in addition to a breast examination because the patient's medical history indicated that she was due for a physical examination. The obstetrician-gynecologist determined that the patient's breasts were normal. Eighteen months later, the patient began to experience pain in her left arm. Another physician diagnosed breast cancer, and the patient underwent a modified radical mastectomy and subsequent chemotherapy, radiation therapy, and hysterectomy. The patient sued the obstetrician-gynecologist, alleging that he had been negligent in failing to diagnose her breast cancer. The lower court held that the physician-defendant had not been negligent. The higher court reversed. The higher court ruled that the lower court was incorrect when it found that the standard of care for a routine breast examination is identical to that for a breast examination conducted to diagnose a specific breast problem. The higher court ruled that the physician-defendant had a duty to be aware of and attempt to resolve the patient-plaintiff's complaint. The breast examination must be geared to the specific complaint of the patient, and the physician must attempt to locate the lump the patient has found. Since the lower court had based its judgment on the failure to distinguish a routine examination from an examination for a specific complaint, a new trial was necessary (*Hernandez v. United States*, 1980).[14]

A physician will also be liable if he or she makes a misdiagnosis after examining the patient and the misdiagnosis is a breach of requisite medical standards of care.[15] Negligent misdiagnosis of pregnancy is a common complaint (see § 10.10, Diagnosis). As in all cases of alleged negligent misdiagnosis, it is not sufficient for the patient to show that the physician has in fact made an incorrect diagnosis that injured her: she must also prove that the physician breached the applicable standards of medical care.

CASE ILLUSTRATION

The patient suspected that she was pregnant and on August 14 contacted the physician's office. An associate of the physician prescribed Produosterone as a test for pregnancy. The patient was told to take the drug: if she was not pregnant, her menstrual period would begin within 72 hours. On August 21, the patient noticed a bloody discharge from her vagina. On August 28, the patient consulted the physician. He took a medical history, noted the patient's symptoms, and performed a pelvic examination for pregnancy. The physician concluded that the patient was "probably pregnant." The patient complained of nausea and cramping and continued vaginal discharge. The physician gave her an injection for cramping and prescribed Norlutate to prevent involuntary abortion. The cramping and bleeding stopped temporarily, but began again on September 11. The physician instructed the patient to go to the hospital. At the hospital, a second physician performed a vaginal examination and concluded that the patient was 1½ to 2 months pregnant. He attributed her symptoms to a threatened abortion. The patient continued to take Norlutate, with her original physician's consent and permission. On January 8, the patient again visited her physician. He could not find a palpable fundus and told the patient to return on January 22. On this date, the physician performed a pelvic examination and found no indication of pregnancy. He then ordered X rays, which also proved negative. The patient subsequently consulted a gynecologist, who diagnosed an endometrioma of the umbilicus. The gynecologist excised the endometrioma.

The patient sued her physician, alleging that he had been negligent in incorrectly diagnosing pregnancy and in improperly treating her for threatened abortion rather than for endometriosis. At trial, the patient-plaintiff offered no expert testimony. The court entered judgment on a directed verdict in favor of the physician-defendant. The appeals court affirmed. The patient-plaintiff argued that a layperson could conclude that the results of the Produosterone test were negative and that the physician-defendant had been negligent in diagnosing pregnancy in spite of these results. The appeals court rejected this argument. First, it noted that the defendant's expert testimony indicated that the bloody discharge of August 21 was a possible indication of attempted involuntary abortion and was not inconsistent with a diagnosis of probable pregnancy. Second, the court pointed out that the physician-defendant's diagnosis of probable pregnancy was based not only on the test results but also on an evaluation of the patient-plaintiff's symptoms and a pelvic examination for pregnancy. The court reasoned that a layperson could not determine as a matter of common knowledge that a diagnosis of probable pregnancy after these procedures was negligent. In addition, the concurring diagnosis of the second physician suggested that the physician-defendant's diagnosis was reasonable when it was made. Since the patient-plaintiff failed to introduce expert testimony that the physician-defendant's diagnosis was negligent in light of the examinations he performed or that different or more frequent examinations were necessary, a directed verdict against the patient-plaintiff was held to be proper (*Kleinman v. Armour*, 1970).[16]

Examination of Sexual Assault Victims: Although most victims of sexual assault are treated in hospital emergency rooms, a physician may occasionally be confronted with a patient-victim outside the emergency room. Treatment is likely to involve psychological trauma for the patient and anxiety for the physician. In the case of a reported assault, the physician has a responsibility to society, as well as to the patient.[17] For these reasons, it is critical that the physician understand the legal, forensic, and medical aspects of sexual assaults so that he or she can competently handle the situation personally or refer the patient to someone who can. Most large cities now have crisis intervention centers, which can be called to assist the physician or the victim, or both, in dealing with a sexual assault.

Rape has traditionally been defined by law as forcible vaginal penetration

§ *13.10* *Physical Examination and Evaluation* 493

without consent.[18] Most states* still have traditional rape laws.[19] A few states** also require the victim to exert utmost[20] or earnest[21] resistance, while others† have expressly removed the resistance requirement.[22] Since 1974, there has been a trend toward reform of state rape laws. Some states†† have passed legislation that provides for more than one degree of forcible rape.[23] Others‡ have limited the requirement that the victim's testimony be corroborated by other evidence.[24] Half the states‡‡ have placed limits on the admissibility of evidence of the victim's prior sexual conduct.[25] More and more states§ are defining sexual crimes so that both men and women can be either victim or perpetrator.[26]

Rape is a crime that, by its nature, is seldom witnessed. Therefore, the corroborating evidence gathered during the examination of an alleged victim is crucial for successful prosecution. This is especially true in those states that require proof of sexual penetration or resistance. It is incumbent upon the physician to conduct the examination in a thorough and competent manner. Some states supply forms, kits, or both to aid physicians in collecting evidence.[27] (See Appendix F for an example of one state's medical report forms.)

The physician responsible for treating a sexual assault victim has several potential areas of concern:

1. Taking a medical history as well as a history of the assault;
2. Making a physical examination;
3. Collecting and preserving evidence;
4. Treating injuries and psychological trauma; and
5. Preventing disease and pregnancy.[28]

---

*Alabama, Alaska, Arizona, the District of Columbia, Georgia, Illinois, Indiana, Maine, Maryland, Mississippi, Missouri, Nevada, New Jersey, North Carolina, Oklahoma, Oregon, Pennsylvania, Rhode Island, South Carolina, Tennessee, Texas, Utah, Vermont, Virginia, West Virginia, and Wyoming.

**Arizona, Louisiana, Kentucky, New York, Texas, and West Virginia.

†Iowa, Michigan, Minnesota, Ohio, and Pennsylvania.

††Indiana, Michigan, New Hampshire, New Mexico, and Ohio.

‡Connecticut, Delaware, Iowa, Minnesota, New Mexico, New York, Pennsylvania, Texas, and Washington.

‡‡Alaska, California, Colorado, Florida, Georgia, Indiana, Iowa, Kentucky, Louisiana, Maryland, Michigan, Missouri, Montana, Nebraska, Nevada, New Hampshire, New Mexico, North Dakota, Oklahoma, Pennsylvania, South Dakota, Tennessee, Texas, Washington, and West Virginia.

§Arkansas, Colorado, Connecticut, Florida, Indiana, Iowa, Massachusetts, Michigan, New Mexico, Ohio, South Dakota, Washington, and Wisconsin.

Personal support and empathy should be provided the patient throughout the examination by the physician and, whenever possible, by a trained support person or a family member or friend. The patient should be afforded as much privacy as the situation will permit. Since the patient-victim has already undergone one trauma, the physician should take care not to compound it or cause a second trauma during the examination and treatment.

History: In addition to a general medical history, a narrative history of the assault should be taken and recorded in the patient's own words. The physician should also record observations of the patient such as general demeanor, the state of clothing and makeup, general appearance, bruises, lacerations, and so on. It should be noted that there is a wide range of emotional responses a victim may exhibit, so the physician should be careful to avoid inaccuracies in recording the victim's frame of mind. A victim may be disturbed even though she seems calm and lucid at the time.[29] (See Appendix F for a detailed list of information to be included in the medical history.)

The physician should express no conclusions, opinions, or diagnosis to the patient or in the patient's record. The record should describe only the physician's findings and examination procedure. Phrases such as "suspected rape" or "alleged rape" may be used where necessary, but the physician should not conclude that a crime has occurred. Negative findings are as important as positive ones and may assist in protecting an alleged assailant who is innocent.[30] Since both the physician and the record may be subpoenaed, the information should be detailed and exact.

Physical Examination: A written and witnessed consent form must precede the physical examination. The form should include consent to the examination, the collection of specimens, the taking of photographs, and the release of information and evidence to the proper authorities.[31] A step-by-step explanation of the procedures to be performed may also minimize the trauma of the examination. (See Appendix H for an example of general office procedures.)

The examination involves three areas: general appearance, external genitalia, and speculum exam. The body as a whole should be examined for obvious signs of trauma or violence as well as for hidden injuries such as a fractured skull.[32] Fingernail scrapings should be taken. The external genitalia should be examined for trauma, and the pubic area should be combed for hairs of the rapist.[33] The vagina should also be examined for injury, and a speculum moistened with water (no other lubricant) should be inserted and foreign materials suctioned up for laboratory examination.[34]

Seminal fluid can be detected in vaginal secretions by an increase in the concentration of acid phosphatase. This must be detected within a reasonable time of the alleged assault: 50 percent of tests run 12 hours after intercourse show acid phosphatase concentrations in the normal range. The test is especially important if the assailant has had a vasectomy, since no sperm will be found.[35]

§ 13.10   *Physical Examination and Evaluation*   495

Preserving Evidence: All specimens should be obtained by a physician in the presence of a witness and personally handed to the pathologist or technician who will make the test. This is done in order to preserve the chain of evidence. All samples should be clearly labeled with the patient's name, the date, the time of the test, and the physician's initials in order to avoid mistakes or exchange of specimens.

Ideally, clothing should be removed by the patient in the presence of the physician. Each article should be examined for stains, soiling, and damage; if any is present, notes should be made to that effect. Ultraviolet light is recommended when examining clothes for stains, particularly semen stains. After examination, each article of clothing should be dried and stored in a separate, clearly labeled, clean paper bag.[36] This evidence should be personally turned over to the proper authorities in return for a detailed receipt. The time at which the evidence was delivered and the person to whom it was delivered should be noted in the patient's record.[37]

Tests now being developed will increase the likelihood of identifying the assailant or clearing an innocent party. It is now possible to determine the blood type of many persons from substances and certain bodily fluids such as seminal fluid or vaginal secretions.[38] Bloodstains can be analyzed for many types besides A, B, and O, and many enzymes can be more accurately analyzed to increase the weight of evidence offered as to the assailant's identity.

Similarly, neutron activation of hair samples can produce an analysis of trace metals that is most likely unique to one person. In the future, genetic material from the spermatozoa may pinpoint the assailant.[39]

Although increasingly sophisticated tests are available, they are rarely fully utilized or promptly performed, for a variety of reasons. Many hospitals are reluctant to treat patient-victims because of the likelihood of time-consuming court appearances for their personnel. Although speed is imperative in gathering evidence of the alleged rape, some private hospitals have a policy of turning rape victims away, and many patient-witnesses are faced with long waits in hospital emergency rooms.[40] In addition, only a few states* will pay for the rape victim's medical care and examination.[41] As a result, fingernail scrapings are often not taken, and the victim herself is requested to perform some procedures (such as combing the pubic area for foreign hairs) by physicians who are reluctant to do anything that might later require them to appear in court.[42] Even more serious are reports of physicians filling out report forms incompletely or inaccurately in order to minimize the possibility of being subpoenaed to appear in court. Some physicians view court appearances as nothing but subpoenas, postponements, and the canceling of office appointments.[43]

Failure to collect all of the evidence against an alleged rapist is not only

---

*California, Minnesota, Nevada, and Ohio.

a tremendous disservice to the community in which the physician lives, it can lead to the physician's losing his license to practice medicine.

Treatment of Injuries and Psychological Trauma: The physician should not be so engrossed in the individual as a victim that he or she ignores the individual as a patient. Lacerations or other injuries should be treated promptly, where indicated. If the victim is in shock, a concussion or fracture may go unnoticed without a thorough examination.

The physician should attempt to minimize trauma wherever possible. The presence of support persons from the local crisis center, the patient's family, or her friends should be considered and provided if the patient desires. The physician should be alert to signs of severe psychological damage (see item 43, form B, Appendix E) and should be prepared to refer the patient to an appropriate mental health professional. The patient should be made aware of normal feelings following the experience so that she knows what to expect and where to go to get help if needed. Sedatives or tranquilizers may be indicated in some cases.[44]

Prevention of Disease and Pregnancy: Prophylactic antibiotic therapy may be given to prevent venereal disease when the patient is advised of its necessity and consents to its use.[45] The physician should recommend a follow-up test for syphilis six weeks after the rape. Tetanus toxoid may be indicated for victims with minor wounds.[46] The use of DES to prevent pregnancy is approved by the FDA under such conditions as rape and incest.[47]

Examination and treatment of a child who is the victim of a sexual assault is similar to that of an adult, with some modifications. First, the physician should realize that the child generally does not seek treatment voluntarily and is less familiar with procedures than an adult. In some states, parental consent is needed before the child may be treated. Other states allow physicians to provide immediate medical treatment without obtaining parental consent.[48] If the child is injured and requires immediate medical attention, no parental consent is necessary.

It is necessary for the physician to establish rapport with the child before examining or questioning her. Taking a medical history and description of the incident depends largely on the age and understanding of the child. The physician may need to prompt the child for answers and descriptions, but he or she should be careful not to put words into the child's mouth.[49]

The physical examination proceeds as in the case of an adult, except that a detailed internal examination may not be necessary in the case of a young child where no evidence of assault is present upon examination of the external genitalia. It has been observed that, because of the anatomic proportions of a female child, sexual penetration occurs in only a fraction of assaults; when it does occur, the resultant injury is obvious and serious.[50] Prophylactic treatment for disease or pregnancy depends on the age of the child and the nature of the assault, but it should be performed where indicated.

§ 13.20 Hysterectomy

The physician should note that children often take behavioral cues from adults, and therefore it may be reasonable and necessary to separate emotionally overwrought parents from the child until they can be calmed. For this reason also, psychiatric follow-up care should involve the family as a unit.[51] The physician should also be aware of the special need for privacy of young victims and be careful to explain the steps of the examination in detail.

Sexual abuse of a child is a form of child abuse when the assailant is responsible for the health and welfare of the child, and suspected child abuse should be reported to the authorities. The presence of venereal disease in a child under the age of 12 is reasonable cause to suspect child abuse and should be reported.

At some point, the physician who examines and treats a victim of criminal sexual conduct may be called on to testify regarding the physical examination of the victim. While lack of a physical examination does not prevent the jury from finding the defendant guilty,[52] the evidence from the examination is often crucial to the determination of the case. Therefore, the examination should be meticulous and well documented, although it is not necessary to preserve the actual slides used in tests.[53] On the other hand, the results from a slide that is not properly labeled may not be admissible as evidence.[54]

The physician should review the records of the examination before appearing in court in order to refresh his or her memory and preclude the chance of being embarrassed at the hands of the attorneys.[55] Generally, the physician will be called as a witness for the prosecution. The physician-witness should bear in mind that, although the prosecution and defense are interested in advancing their respective cases and therefore will ask different questions, the physician's aim should be to help find the truth, not to help convict or acquit the defendant[56] (see § 4.41, Expert Testimony). Occasionally an examining physician will not be available to testify in court; in such a case, the examination results may be inadmissible as evidence because of the hearsay rule. The prosecution may attempt to get the examination and test results into court under the business records exception to the hearsay rule. Courts are divided as to the admissibility of such evidence,[57] but it is clear that records which include dates and times, which are signed, and which have the signature witnessed stand a greater chance of being admitted.[58] Therefore, the physician should take care to document thoroughly all examinations of sexual assault victims as a matter of course.

§ 13.20 HYSTERECTOMY

A physician may face liability arising out of the performance of a hysterectomy where (1) preoperative counseling of the patient was negligent, either because the physician's diagnosis was inaccurate and led to an unnecessary hysterectomy or because the physician failed to obtain the patient's informed consent; (2) the operation resulted in injury to an organ or structure outside the operative field; or (3) the physician failed to provide adequate postoperative care.

Basic Standard of Care: The American College of Obstetricians and Gynecologists has not identified specific standards governing hysterectomy.

Interpretation and Customary Practice: Hysterectomy is the removal of the patient's uterus. It may be indicated in the following circumstances:

1. Inherent disease in the uterus
    a. Leiomyoma uteri
    b. Adenomyosis
    c. Endometriosis
    d. Carcinoma or sarcoma of the endometrium
    e. Carcinoma of the cervix
2. Disease of the adnexa
    a. Carcinoma of the ovaries or tubes
    b. Extensive, chronic inflammation of the pelvis
3. Traumatic conditions of the uterus
    a. Obstetrical rupture
    b. Uncontrollable postpartum bleeding
    c. Abruptio placentae
    d. Septic abortion
    e. Necrosis of the myometrium
4. Abnormal uterine bleeding (unresponsive to conservative management)
5. Prolapse of the uterus
6. Sterilization

Leiomyoma uteri is characterized by the formation of benign tumors in the uterus. Hysterectomy may be indicated when the tumors cause excessive pain, bleed, and enlarge rapidly or to such an extent that they press on adjacent organs or structures. Adenomyosis alone, or when associated with endometriosis, may be treated by hysterectomy if pain cannot be controlled with ordinary, nonnarcotic medications. Premalignant conditions of the cervix (severe dysplasia), carcinoma in situ, invasive carcinoma of the cervix and corpus, and sarcoma of the uterus may be treated in this manner as well.[59]

Diseases of the adnexa that would indicate hysterectomy as partial therapy include carcinoma of the ovaries or tubes. Obstetrical complications that traumatize the uterus may require a hysterectomy. Such complications would include rupture of the uterus accompanied by copious hemorrhage, uncontrollable postpartum hemorrhage, and cases of abruptio placentae that are unresponsive to more conservative treatment.

Hysterectomy may also be indicated as the treatment of choice for prolapse of the uterus. This condition may also be treated by amputation of the cervix, suspension of the uterus, or occlusion of the vagina, but all of these methods risk the retention of a potentially malignant uterus. Menstrual irregularities in the patient who is unresponsive to curettage or hormonal therapy may be alleviated by hysterectomy.[60]

Hysterectomy may not be indicated where the physician is unfamiliar with the operative technique, where the diagnosis is uncertain, or where, as a treatment for cancer, the evaluation is incomplete. Patients who desire a larger family or who are subject to extreme manifestations of psychological factors such as fear or depression are not good candidates for hysterectomy,[61] and the operation should be avoided unless there is no alternative.

Hysterectomy may be performed vaginally or abdominally. Each procedure has its own indications and advantages. (See Appendix I for a flowchart illustrating the decision process for choosing between the two methods). Vaginal hysterectomy involves less loss of blood and may be performed more quickly than an abdominal hysterectomy, reducing the need for lengthy administration of anesthesia. Furthermore, a vaginal hysterectomy entails less handling of the bowels, thereby diminishing the possibility of paralytic ileus, omental or intestinal adhesions, and peritonitis. The patient will not be left with an abdominal scar, is more likely to be ambulatory sooner, and will have a shorter recovery period than if abdominal surgery had been performed. The vaginal hysterectomy is indicated for treating a prolapsed uterus with associated cystocele, rectocele, or enterocele. It may also be the appropriate treatment for carcinoma in situ of the cervix or any of the other indications for hysterectomy generally. It may also be appropriate if the patient is obese, elderly, or a poor risk.[62]

Abdominal hysterectomy is preferred over vaginal hysterectomy if there is any suggestion of invasive malignant disease in the patient or if there is any pathology present in the patient's pelvis or abdomen which requires further assessment at the time of the operation. Thus, endometriosis and chronic inflammation of the pelvis should be treated abdominally, particularly if the uterus is fixed. Ovarian cysts are best managed by an abdominal approach. If the cysts are malignant, their decompression by drainage to permit vaginal removal could spread the disease. Generally, abdominal hysterectomy provides a better view of surrounding pelvic and abdominal structures and allows for a more radical procedure, if such is indicated by the condition of the structures, than does the vaginal approach. Vaginal hysterectomy may be contraindicated if the uterus is too large to be removed easily. Prior surgery associated with ileus and peritonitis or intestinal obstruction also contraindicates a vaginal hysterectomy.[63] Generally, the abdominal hysterectomy is favored for the treatment of malignancies in the reproductive organs, large myomatous tumors, ovarian lesions, and conditions in which the uterus is fixed.

As with any other treatment, the physician must take all necessary steps to ascertain that the diagnosis is correct before performing a hysterectomy. If the hysterectomy is unnecessary, the patient's symptoms will most likely not be alleviated, and the physician may face liability for the performance of unnecessary surgery.

CASE ILLUSTRATION

The patient suffered from chronic, severe back pain. She contacted the first physician, who admitted her to a hospital. This physician performed several unspecified tests, all of which were negative. He diagnosed a tumor of the right ovary and retroflexion of the uterus. The first physician then consulted the second physician, a specialist in surgery and gynecology. The second physician made an examination limited to the patient's "female organs" and her heart and blood pressure. A few days later, the second physician performed three surgical procedures on the patient: total hysterectomy, right salpingo-oophorectomy, and appendectomy. The patient continued to experience back pain. She consulted an orthopedic surgeon, who diagnosed her condition as a chronic, low-grade lower back syndrome caused by a discrepancy in the length of her legs, with associated scoliosis. The patient's pain was eliminated with a heel lift and exercises.

The patient sued the first and second physicians, alleging, among other things, that they were negligent in their misdiagnosis of her condition. On appeal, the higher court considered the lower court's judgment for the first physician (the second physician was no longer a party to the action). The higher court held that judgment was improperly entered and that there must be a trial on the issue of negligent diagnosis. The ruling was based on the fact that the patient-plaintiff introduced expert testimony that (1) the diagnostic tests used by the physician-defendant were inappropriate for the patient-plaintiff's complaints; (2) the discrepancy in leg lengths, and the scoliosis were visible on X-ray film taken in the hospital prior to the surgery; and (3) the physician-defendant purported to diagnose retroflexion of the uterus without using the more conservative therapy of insertion of a pessary (*O'Grady v. Wickman*, 1968).[64]

In another case, the patient alleged that the physician negligently failed to diagnose the cause of her hypertension as coarctation of the aorta and that this failure caused her to undergo an unnecessary hysterectomy. The Supreme Court of North Dakota reversed the trial court's dismissal of the patient-plaintiff's case and remanded for a new trial on the issue of negligent misdiagnosis. The court ruled that, if the physician breached the applicable standard of care in failing to diagnose the coarctation of the aorta, the patient could recover damages for an unnecessary hysterectomy.[65]

§ 13.20 Hysterectomy 501

A patient may also complain where a physician proposes or performs a hysterectomy as treatment for a condition that he or she negligently fails to diagnose as pregnancy; in such a case, the physician may be held liable for damages[66] (see § 10.10, Diagnosis).

In recent years, critics of the medical profession have complained of an increase in the number of "unnecessary" hysterectomies. One authority has responded that it is misleading to rely on statistics alone to substantiate the criticism, since an increase in the rate of hysterectomies is just as likely to be the result of better patient education, coupled with the increasing realization that hysterectomies can be used for relieving symptoms and for sterilization as well as for anatomic reasons.[67] However, "unnecessary hysterectomy" may refer not to the accuracy of the diagnosis itself, but to the appropriateness of hysterectomy as treatment for the patient's condition. The decision to perform a hysterectomy is often a matter of the individual physician's discretion and choice, based on his or her own experience and background. So long as hysterectomy does not clearly constitute inappropriate treatment in a given case, the fact that one physician may propose more conservative treatment for the same symptoms will not be interpreted by the courts to mean that the physician who performs a hysterectomy as the treatment of choice is negligent.

CASE ILLUSTRATION

The physician's examination of the patient disclosed a lump on one of her breasts. The patient had undergone a D&C twice before the examination. She had been unable to achieve a successful pregnancy. She also indicated that she had experienced vaginal bleeding in the past. Physical examination revealed that a mass was present in the abdominal area and that it was sensitive to pressure. The physician also discovered several fibroid growths. Surgical procedures were tentatively scheduled for the removal of the breast mass, as well as to determine the status of the patient's pelvic and abdominal regions, but the patient failed to return until eight months later. At that time she expressed concern about renewed growth of the lump in her breast. The patient signed a consent form authorizing (1) the removal of the lump in her breast and (2) a laparotomy, with permission to perform a hysterectomy if the physician deemed it necessary. The patient was operated upon, and the growth in her breast was successfully excised. Upon performing the laparotomy, the physician found several growths in and about the uterus that might obstruct the ureter and result in danger to the urinary system, particularly the kidney; he also found chronic inflammation of the pelvis, with numerous fluid-filled cysts. The physician concluded that a hysterectomy was necessary, and he removed the patient's uterus.

The patient subsequently sued the physician, alleging, among other things, that her conditions did not warrant a hysterectomy. The evidence presented at trial indicated that the largest of the fibroid growths removed was 3 centimeters in diameter and that, at the time of the operation, the patient was not suffering from uterine bleeding or discomfort, had a negative Pap smear, and was otherwise asymptomatic; a physician called by the patient as an expert witness, stated that, under these circumstances, he would keep the growth under observation and not resort to surgical excision. The court noted, with respect to this testimony, "At no time did the medical expert state what was the usual and accepted procedure in the medical profession for a patient who had previously undergone two D&Cs, was afflicted with a large number of matted fibroid masses throughout the walls of the uterus, a chronic pelvic inflammatory disease with numerous fluid-filled cysts, and where there was presented cause for particular concern because of one myoma located on the upper left aspect of the uterus that presented an apparent real danger to blockage of the ureter as it entered the bladder with concomitant danger to the entire urinary system and the kidney." The physician would not extend his treatment of the hypothetical patient to the patient-plaintiff in this case, so the court concluded that, in the absence of specific medical testimony to the contrary, there was no evidence that the physician-defendant performed his medical and surgical services in any other than a professional and an acceptable manner. Thus, the court held the physician not liable (*Slack v. Moorhead*, 1979).[68]

That hysterectomy as the treatment of choice is a matter within the physician's discretion is true, with one qualification: such a choice can only be made after the consent of the patient is obtained. Thus, hysterectomy performed on a woman who desires a larger family may be contraindicated for legal as well as medical reasons. An understanding of the legal requirement that consent be obtained is particularly pertinent to the hysterectomy procedure because it is often performed in emergency situations where there is no time to obtain the specific consent needed (see § 1.33, Consent and Informed Consent). Hysterectomy may be indicated as an emergency measure to treat uterine trauma in difficult childbirths: for example, when a uterus ruptures during labor, hysterectomy may be the most effective measure available to stop the flow of blood quickly. If a life-threatening situation makes the hysterectomy necessary immediately and the patient's consent cannot be obtained, the physician will not be held liable for his or her failure to obtain the patient's consent.[69] Furthermore, the physician will not be held liable where the patient specifically consents to a procedure other than a hysterectomy but also agrees that the physician may perform additional procedures he or she finds necessary in the course of the primary operation, as long as the conditions for the additional procedure are satisfied and there is no legal reason, such as fraud, to invalidate the consent.[70]

§ 13.20 Hysterectomy 503

CASE ILLUSTRATION

The patient was expecting her second child. She consulted a physician, who advised that the baby be delivered by cesarean section because of its size and position within the womb. The patient and her husband agreed to the procedure and also requested that the physician perform a tubal ligation during delivery. When the patient was admitted to the hospital, she signed a consent form authorizing the cesarean section and tubal ligation, as well as "such additional operations or procedures as are considered therapeutically necessary on the basis of findings during the course of said operation." The physician and his partner performed the cesarean section, and a healthy, normal child was born. The patient was bleeding both at the incision and within the uterus from the area of placental attachment. To minimize blood loss, the physicians sutured the incision. Because of the patient's age (36), the large size of the child, and the presence of numerous fibroid tumors throughout the uterus, the patient's uterus was contracting at a slower than normal rate and she was losing more than a normal amount of blood. The physicians then discovered a grapefruit-sized tumor covering the patient's right ovary, which was adhered to her uterus. The physicians removed the tumor and sent it to the laboratory for analysis. The laboratory reported that the tumor was benign. However, removal of the tumor entailed heavy loss of blood from the point where it had adhered to the uterus. This blood loss, combined with the blood loss from the cesarean incision and the removal of the placenta, caused the physicians to believe that the patient's life was in danger. When suturing and administration of oxytocin were ineffective in controlling the bleeding, the physicians performed an abdominal hysterectomy. The patient sued the physicians, alleging, among other things, that removal of her uterus was done without her consent and constituted an assault and battery. The physician-defendants claimed that the signed surgery authorization form established their defense of consent. The patient testified that she had read and understood the langauge of the consent form but claimed that the hysterectomy was not therapeutically necessary. The court observed that the standard for determining whether a procedure is therapeutically necessary is whether the physician "exercised that degree of care, skill, and diligence which any other surgeon would be required to employ in reaching a decision under the same or similar circumstances." All expert medical testimony, including that offered on behalf of the patient, concurred that, once the sutures and oxytocin had failed, a hysterectomy was the next indicated step to stop the flow of blood. The court held in favor of the physicians (*Davidson v. Shirley,* 1980).[71]

A general consent to further procedures deemed advisable has also been held to authorize a hysterectomy, even when a physician cannot claim that immediate action was necessary. If such a consent is obtained and the hysterectomy performed is medically indicated, the physician may escape liability.

CASE ILLUSTRATION

The patient was presented with consent forms while she was in a labor room after having received pain-relieving medication. The forms authorized a tubal ligation, which she had requested her physician to perform on several previous occasions, and a cesarean section. The forms also contained the following language:

> If any unforeseen conditions arise in the course of the operation, calling on his [the physician's] judgment, for procedures in addition to or different from those now contemplated, I further request and authorize him to do whatever he deems advisable.

The patient signed the forms. The cesarean section resulted in a very large incision in the uterus. Because of the size of the incision; an atypical Pap smear in the past; the presence of cervicitis; the patient's diabetic tendency, high blood pressure, and obesity (indicating high risk for cancer of the uterus); and the patient's request for sterilization, the physician decided to perform a hysterectomy. The patient sued the physician, alleging lack of consent. The jury returned a verdict for the physician-defendant and the court upheld the verdict, finding that there was sufficient evidence to sustain a finding of effective consent (*Offut v. Sheehan*, 1976).[72]

These cases do not consider the legal doctrine of informed consent in the context of hysterectomy. Generally, the doctrine requires that the physician inform the patient of all risks and possible results associated with any proposed treatment (see § 1.33, Consent and Informed Consent).

One risk or complication associated with hysterectomy involves injury to the urinary tract. Such an injury is more likely where there is technical difficulty with the hysterectomy itself, where there are dense adhesions from prior surgery, or where a disease that obscures the anatomy is present, such as endometriosis or inflammation of the pelvis. During an abdominal hysterectomy, the bladder may be injured as the abdomen is entered, particularly when the bladder has been pulled up by previous surgery or as the bladder is released from the cervix. Bladder injury may also occur during a vaginal hysterectomy as the bladder is stripped from the cervix.

Urinary tract infection and retention of urine are frequent sequels to hysterectomy, particularly vaginal hysterectomy. The ureter may occasionally be kinked or tied during a vaginal hysterectomy, but such an injury is a more common sequel to abdominal hysterectomy. Fistulas may also develop, presenting as leakage of urine or feces into the vagina.[73]

The development of a post-hysterectomy fistula gave rise to the case illustrated below. The issue considered by the court was whether a fistula is a risk commonly associated with hysterectomy; if so, the physician would have had to have apprised the patient of the risk in order to have obtained her informed consent. Courts rely on expert testimony to determine which risks a physician should disclose,[74] and they generally do not impose liability for the failure to disclose risks that are considered remote.[75] It should be noted that, in this case, evidence presented to the court convinced the court that the possibility of a fistula was remote; this may not be true of every patient.

CASE ILLUSTRATION

The physician performed a hysterectomy on the patient. After the patient was discharged, she became incontinent due to the development of a ureterovaginal fistula. The patient sued the physician, alleging that he had failed to warn her of the risk of a ureterovaginal fistula and that she therefore did not effectively consent to the operation. The physician-defendant admitted that he had not warned the patient-plaintiff of this risk but testified that he did not do so because the complication was rare. The physician-defendant testified that he had performed over 3,000 hysterectomies but had never before encountered a postoperative ureterovaginal fistula. He also testified that medical texts placed the frequency of this complication at 1 to 12 percent of hysterectomy cases, with the larger figure applicable to patients with cancer. The patient-plaintiff did not have cancer. The court noted that courts in other jurisdictions had imposed liability on physicians who failed to disclose risks with an incidence as low as 1 percent but expressed the opinion that the seriousness of the risk involved is paramount to any percentage of occurrence. The court held that "the development of a fistula in an area not associated with the surgery was not the type of risk that the [physician-]defendant was bound to disclose nor was it of such a material nature that the lack of that particular information could be considered as an invalidation of the consent previously given." Accordingly, the court held that the physician was not liable (*Longmire v. Hoey*, 1974).[76]

The development of a fistula after a hysterectomy has generated a number of lawsuits. The outcomes of these suits are not uniform because of the various legal theories at play and the varying constructions put on these theories by courts in different jurisdictions. Where the suit is based on principles of negligence, as opposed to consent, the courts have generally been consistent in requiring that proof of negligence come from expert testimony. The development of a fistula after a hysterectomy is not the kind of injury that the jury may determine as a matter of common knowledge is the result of negligence.[77]

CASE ILLUSTRATION

The patient was suffering from a prolapsed uterus. She consulted a gynecologist, who recommended a vaginal hysterectomy. The patient consented to the procedure. During the operation, the gynecologist accidently entered the patient's bladder while attempting to separate it from the uterus, to which it was joined by multiple adhesions. The gynecologist consulted a urologist and then repaired the incision. Ten days after the patient was released from the hospital, she returned to the gynecologist for a postoperative examination. The gynecologist discovered a vesicovaginal fistula. The gynecologist referred the patient to a urologist, who repaired the fistula. The patient sued the gynecologist, alleging negligence in the performance of the hysterectomy. The patient-plaintiff offered no expert testimony to support the allegation of negligence. The only testimony offered on the issue was that of two physicians, both of whom stated that a vesicovaginal fistula is a recognized hazard of all hysterectomies and may occur without negligence, even when the surgery is performed under ideal conditions, by the most skillful surgeon. The court held in favor of the physician-defendant, stating that negligence could not be inferred from the fact that the complication occurred. Further, the jury could not find as a matter of common knowledge that the puncturing of the bladder was negligent; rather, the patient-plaintiff was required to introduce expert testimony that the actions of the physician-defendant fell below the requisite standard of medical care. As no such evidence was offered, the judgment in favor of the physician was upheld (*Sims v. Helms*, 1977).[78]

The patient who suffers a urinary complication following a hysterectomy frequently contends that the doctrine of res ipsa loquitur is applicable. As a legal theory upon which to structure a hysterectomy case, res ipsa loquitur is certainly pertinent, since it relates to cases in which the legal cause is difficult to ascertain or may be shown only by circumstantial evidence and the plaintiff is deserving of some compensation because of the nature of the injury suffered (see § 1.52, Res Ipsa Loquitur). The disposition of cases in which res ipsa loquitur is raised varies, since some states do not recognize the doctrine as applicable to medical malpractice at all and those that do recognize it apply it inconsistently. The court's decision to apply the doctrine to a given case usually depends on the strength of the patient-plaintiff's expert testimony that the urinary complication would probably not have resulted in the absence of negligence. Thus, if the patient-plaintiff offers no testimony at all that a ureterovaginal fistula is the result of negligence, the doctrine is usually held to be inapplicable.[79] The courts have also held the doctrine to be inapplicable when the plaintiff's experts testify that the urinary complication resulted from one of several causes, some of which constitute negligence and some of which do not.

CASE ILLUSTRATION

The patient suffered excessive bleeding during her menstrual periods. She consulted the gynecologist, who performed a D&C. The patient's problems were still unresolved, and the gynecologist, after a further examination, advised the patient that her trouble was caused either by a fibroid tumor or by a narrowing of the womb. After another pelvic examination two years later, the gynecologist informed the patient that he had located a fibroid tumor and advised her to undergo an abdominal hysterectomy, which he performed. Two weeks after the operation, the patient began to pass urine through her vagina. The gynecologist referred the patient to a urologist, who discovered a vesicovaginal fistula. The urologist subsequently repaired the fistula surgically. The patient sued the gynecologist, alleging that he had negligently performed the hysterectomy. The patient also claimed that the doctrine of res ipsa loquitur was applicable. The patient-plaintiff's evidence included the testimony of the gynecologist-defendant and two other physicians. The three physicians agreed that a fistula could be caused by (1) cutting the bladder; (2) clamping the bladder and vagina together; (3) stitching or suturing the bladder and vagina together; (4) a cancer of the vagina or of the bladder and a complication of radium, cobalt, and X rays; or (5) the presence of an abscess with no visible evidence of any infection. The physicians agreed that the patient-plaintiff's fistula did not result from the first or fourth causes. They further agreed that the second and third causes constituted negligence but that the fifth cause was a complication that could develop without negligence. The physicians agreed that the patient-plaintiff's fistula resulted from one of three causes and that there was no way to determine which one. The gynecologist-defendant testified that he did not stitch or clamp the bladder and vagina together. The lower court refused to instruct the jury on the doctrine of res ipsa loquitur, and the jury returned a verdict for the gynecologist-defendant on the issue of negligence. On appeal, the higher court upheld the jury verdict and ruled that the doctrine of res ipsa loquitur was not applicable. The court held that the doctrine was inapplicable because the evidence indicated possible alternative causes of the fistula, one of which did not stem from any negligence on the part of the gynecologist-defendant (*Tatro v. Lueken*, 1973).[80]

Typically, for res ipsa loquitur to apply to a given case, the plaintiff must show that the injury is an unusual event that must be explained by the defendant if that party is to avoid liability. Where the defendant performs this evidentiary task, the doctrine will not serve to impose liability.

CASE ILLUSTRATION

The patient consulted the physicians for a routine medical examination. A

Pap smear and subsequent biopsy revealed that the patient had cancer of the cervix, stage I, grade 3. The patient received cobalt and radium therapy. Several weeks later, the physicians performed a modified radical hysterectomy on the patient. During the hysterectomy, the physicians inadvertently clamped and severed the patient's right ureter. The physicians immediately called for a urologist, who attempted to sew the ureter together. Several days later, the urologist noted that fluid was leaking from the patient's vagina. The urologist determined that it was necessary to remove the patient's right kidney rather than make a second operative attempt to repair the ureter, because he felt the patient was physically unable to withstand such an operation. After the patient consented, he performed this procedure. The patient sued the two physicians who performed the hysterectomy, alleging that they had negligently severed her ureter. The court noted that the severing of the ureter was an "unusual event" which required the physician-defendants to prove that they had not been negligent. However, the court stated that the expert testimony established that the physician-defendants had not been guilty of negligence. No expert testified that the physician-defendants failed to exercise the requisite degree of skill and care in performing the operation. In addition, several experts testified that it is especially easy to sever a ureter, despite the exercise of due care, during the performance of a modified radical hysterectomy on a patient with cancer. This is so because in a modified radical procedure the physician must remove most tissue around the uterus, in addition to the uterus itself; and it is inadvisable to dissect or strip the ureter from surrounding tissue when the patient is suffering from a malignancy. The court upheld a judgment for the physician-defendants (*Bryant v. St. Paul Fire and Marine Insurance Co.*, 1973).[81]

California has liberally applied the doctrine of res ipsa loquitur to malpractice cases. Even within this jurisdiction, however, the doctrine has not been applied uniformly with respect to cases involving the development of a fistula subsequent to a hysterectomy. In a case decided in 1962, *Siverson v. Weber*, the California court refused to apply the doctrine, noting that:

[F]istulas result from devascularization and necrosis (cutting off of the blood supply and death of tissue) in the place where the fistula is formed; a number of factors can contribute to the devascularization and necrosis, and ordinarily it cannot be determined which of them [was] operative in a specific case. Among these factors are bruising of the bladder during the necessary separation of the uterus from the bladder, sutures or ligatures in the wall of the bladder to control bleeding caused in the separation, infection present in the cervix of the uterus and the vaginal vault adjacent to the bladder, and the tissue reaction of the individual to surgery and suture materials. Tissue reaction may be affected by previously existent weakness of the area, impairment of the blood supply in the area, and prior X-ray treatment administered to any part of the patient's body. (About one year prior to the hysterectomy, plaintiff had X-ray therapy in connection with the treatment of a malignancy of the breast.)

There is nothing to indicate that, if the fistula was caused by any of the factors listed above or any combination of them, the injury sustained by plaintiff was a result of negligence.[82]

Seven years later, the court decided the following case and allowed the use of the doctrine. It distinguished the earlier *Siverson* case from the following case on the basis of more persuasive evidence of negligence.

CASE ILLUSTRATION

The patient consulted a general practitioner for a physical examination. A Pap smear and a subsequent biopsy confirmed cancer of the cervix. The pathologist's report indicated the possibility that the malignancy had been completely removed by the biopsy. Nevertheless, the general practitioner referred the patient to a gynecologist. The gynecologist recommended a hysterectomy, calling for the removal of the entire uterus, including the cervix, the right tube, and the right ovary. The operation was performed abdominally. During the course of the operation, the gynecologist cut first around the side of the vagina to separate it from the uterus. As he cut around the left side, profuse bleeding from a branch of the uterine artery occurred, which obscured the operative field and hid the bleeding vessel from view. The gynecologist grasped what he thought was the bleeding vessel; he clamped and ligated it. The operation was completed. The patient later developed a ureterovaginal fistula, necessitating corrective surgery. The patient brought suit. At trial, the gynecologist testified that he damaged the patient's left ureter while performing the hysterectomy but that he did not actually know how the injury had occurred. During the operation he had encountered marked bleeding, which obscured his operative field. He could not see the bleeding vessel, since it may have retracted somewhat, so, using a clamp, he "blindly grasped" where he thought the vessel was. In his opinion, the damage to the ureter was done when he clamped the bleeder, possibly because the clamp was placed on the ureter. One expert witness called on the gynecologist's behalf testified that, when confronted with a bleeding artery, the surgeon has "many guides" to the location of the bleeding vessel. He listed touch, seeing the pulsation of the artery, or seeing the origin of the bleeding. He contraindicated "blind clamping." Other expert witnesses concurred with this assessment. Noting this testimony, the court concluded that the patient had proved, with the gynecologist's own experts, that hers was an injury that would not have occurred in the absence of negligence, a prerequisite to the use of res ipsa loquitur. The court held that the doctrine was applicable and, because the lower court judge had failed to properly instruct the jury as to its applicability, ordered that a new trial be held (*Klinger v. Henderson*, 1969).[83]

In another California case where a vesicovaginal fistula developed following a hysterectomy, the court upheld the applicability of res ipsa loquitur, stating that the jury may determine whether facts exist that would justify the application of the doctrine.* In light of expert testimony presented at trial that fistulas are "always caused by negligence," the court reversed the judgment of the lower court, which had been in favor of the physician.[84]

Cases have been brought where a urinary complication arises after a hysterectomy and the patient seeks compensation for negligence in treating the complication, not in causing it.

CASE ILLUSTRATION

Two gynecologists performed a hysterectomy on the patient on October 6, 1967. She began experiencing back pain after the operation but was discharged from the hospital on October 16. Between this time and December 28, the patient consulted the two gynecologists four times. On one occasion, the plaintiff reported that she had passed a large quantity of fluid through her vagina. One of the gynecologists began a series of tests to determine if a fistula was present. The tests proved negative. On January 3, 1968, the patient underwent an intravenous pyelogram, which revealed a blocked left ureter. A urologist then began to treat the patient's urinary system. He initially performed a nephrostomy and then attempted to surgically repair the blocked ureter and reinsert it into the bladder. On April 21, he removed the patient's left kidney, which had been overcome by chronic infection. The patient sued the gynecologist who had directed most of her postoperative care, alleging that he had negligently failed to recognize the cause of her back pain. The patient claimed that either a fistula or blockage had developed after the physician tied off or sutured the left ureter during the hysterectomy and that the physician had failed to recognize the patient's complaint of backache as evidence of the blockage until the blockage had existed for so long that the kidney became incurably infected, leading to its eventual loss.

The patient-plaintiff presented a general practitioner and a surgeon at trial. They testified that the gynecologist-defendant should not have discharged the patient while she was experiencing postsurgical backaches without ruling out a urinary complication. The general practitioner further testified that the gynecologist-defendant had been negligent in failing to

---

*Allowing the jury, rather than the judge, to determine whether res ipsa loquitur is applicable is referred to as "conditional res ipsa loquitur" (see § 1.52, Res Ipsa Loquitur).

§ 13.20   Hysterectomy   511

perform an intravenous pyelogram when the complaints of backache arose shortly after surgery. The defense presented testimony from the patient-plaintiff complained was not significant enough to suggest kidney block-testified that the probable cause of the ureter blockage was the development of scar tissue. He stated that the postoperative pain of which the patient-plaintiff complained was not significant enough to suggest kidney blockage. He stated that kidney blockage is usually accompanied by a fever, from which the patient did not suffer. He further stated that the patient-plaintiff did not experience a urinary discharge from the vagina until nine weeks after the operation. The length of this period supported his conclusion that blockage caused by the development of scar tissue was the source of the patient's problem, not a fistula resulting from an inadvertent suturing of the ureter during the hysterectomy. The obstetrician-gynecologist agreed with the conclusion of the urologist. He further testified that a backache is the most frequent post-hysterectomy complaint and that nothing in the patient's complaints indicated that an intravenous pyelogram should have been run on her before her discharge. The gynecologist-defendant testified that the patient-plaintiff's complaint of backache was vague in nature and that her difficulty seemed to be normal low back and muscle pain, routine after a hysterectomy. The court affirmed a judgment for the gynecologist-defendant. In so doing, the court emphasized that the testimony given by the urologist and obstetrician-gynecologist was persuasive, since they regularly encountered the difficulty experienced by the patient-plaintiff. The court also emphasized that the urologist and the gynecologist-defendant had become thoroughly familiar with the patient-plaintiff's case in the course of treating her (*Alleman v. Seventh Ward General Hospital,* 1974).[85]

It is clear from a review of such cases that the imposition of liability depends upon whether the facts of the case show a marked deviation from the standard of practice and upon how that standard is defined by the expert medical testimony presented at trial.

Patients frequently complain that negligence has caused a gastrointestinal injury or complication. In a medical study of 6,435 hysterectomies conducted in 1979, there were 51 cases of intestinal obstruction and 9 of bowel injury.[86] Injury to the bowel can occur during surgery because of its proximity to the uterus. Mechanical obstruction occurs more often after abdominal hysterectomy, although it may follow a vaginal procedure if a portion of the bowel becomes agglutinated to the wall of the vagina. It has been suggested that using large abdominal packs to keep the bowel out of the way during an abdominal hysterectomy can itself cause extensive damage; it is better to use the Trendelenberg position, in which the patient's torso is tilted downward, because it permits the bowel to gravitate out of the operative field.[87] Generally, gastrointestinal complications following hysterectomy include nausea and vomiting, intestinal obstruction, and paralytic ileus. The risk of gastrointestinal complication is greater when the patient has had infection in the reproductive organs or previous surgery; these can result in adhesion of the bowel to the anterior abdominal wall, to the omentum, to the uterus, or to other parts of the bowel, and the adhesions must be separated during the hysterectomy.

Cases dealing with gastrointestinal complications are similar to those dealing with urinary complications. Generally, the patient-plaintiff must introduce expert testimony that the complication is the result of negligence.[88]

CASE ILLUSTRATION

The patient suffered from recurrent inflammation of the pelvis. The physician performed a hysterectomy on her. The patient subsequently developed a rectovaginal fistula, which caused fecal matter to drain from her vagina. The fistula persisted for two years before another physician was able to repair it surgically. The patient sued the physician who performed the hysterectomy, alleging that his negligence during surgery caused the fistula. She contended that the doctrine of res ipsa loquitur was applicable. The lower court disagreed and refused to instruct the jury on the doctrine. The higher court reversed the ruling of the lower court. It stated that the jury could have concluded that the fistula was more probably than not the result of negligence. Since the other prerequisites for the application of the doctrine were satisfied, the jury could infer that the negligence of the physician-defendant caused the fistula. In support of its conclusion, the higher court noted that the plaintiff's expert witness testified that a rectovaginal fistula was not an expected consequence of a hysterectomy and that the physician-defendant inappropriately operated when the patient-plaintiff's pelvic inflammation was acute. The court stated that this testimony indicated more than that the fistula was an unusual occurrence: it indicated that the expert thought that it was more probably than not due to the physician-defendant's negligence (*Spidle v. Steward*, 1980).[89]

Cases have been brought in which hysterectomy patients have complained that a gastrointestinal complication was exacerbated by negligent postoperative care by a physician.

CASE ILLUSTRATION

The family physician assisted the gynecologist in performing a vaginal hysterectomy on the patient on September 4. The patient developed abdominal distention, fever, and a paralytic ileus after the operation. The two physicians treated these complications with a nasogastric tube and several slush enemas. The patient's complications persisted. On September 26, an

§ 13.20   Hysterectomy   513

internist was consulted; he ordered X rays of the patient, examined her, and recommended immediate surgery. A surgeon examined the patient the same day and considered scheduling surgery for September 27 but postponed it because of the patient's poor physical condition. The patient's condition continued to deteriorate, however, and on October 1 the surgeon performed an exploratory laparotomy. The surgeon discovered that the patient's vaginal cuff was infected. The patient's colon was adhered to this infection and was itself infected. He removed about two feet of the colon and attempted to clean out the remaining infection, but the patient died on October 4 from a massive pelvic infection and congestive heart failure.

The patient's husband and children sued the family doctor and the gynecologist. The lower court directed a verdict for the family doctor; the jury returned a verdict for the gynecologist. On appeal, the plaintiffs contended that they were improperly precluded from raising certain issues at trial. Specifically, the plaintiffs claimed that the trial court was wrong in failing to instruct the jury that they could find negligence in the defendants' (1) failure to perform vaginal examinations; (2) failure to cease use of the nasogastric tube and enemas; (3) failure to obtain additional bacteria cultures after September 10; (4) failure to use other drugs; and (5) failure to obtain more timely and adequate examination of the patient. The higher court ruled that the lower court was correct in refusing to instruct the jury on these issues. The court ruled that the plaintiffs offered no expert testimony that the physician-defendants' actions failed to meet the standard of good medical practice. The testimony that was offered showed, at most, that these courses of action might have been taken, not that they should have been taken as a matter of proper medical care. The court held in favor of the physicians (*Seeley v. Eaton,* 1974).[90]

Wound complications often result from hysterectomy. Dehiscence (a splitting open of the surgical wound) is a possible sequel to abdominal hysterectomy, particularly in a patient with predisposing factors of age, obesity, hypoproteinemia, anemia, chronic disease, carcinoma, or poor hemostasis. Postoperative coughing often triggers the incident, but an improperly closed wound may also initiate the process. This complication may cause or be accompanied by infection, with attendant fever and pelvic pain.[91] While the occurence of wound complications does not automatically constitute negligence, particularly in a high-risk patient, dehiscence may indicate substandard care; it should be managed properly.

CASE ILLUSTRATION

A general practitioner and a gynecologist performed a hysterectomy on the patient. The patient was febrile and began vomiting on the first day after the operation. The general practitioner inserted a nasogastric tube toward the end of the second day. On the third day after the operation, he ordered an X ray, from which the patient's condition was interpreted as "paralytic ileus." The patient's vomiting and pain persisted. On the basis of the patient's elevated temperature and the results of her blood tests, the general practitioner decided on the sixth day that she had an "infection such as peritonitis." On the ninth day, a foul brown discharge was noted on the dressings; X rays were ordered for the first time in six days. The interpretation of these X rays is not described in the decision, but the patient was transferred immediately to a second hospital.

The specialist (a surgeon) to whom she was referred opened the incision that day. He noted an extensive dehiscence, with a loop of black gangrenous bowel trapped between layers of the abdominal fascia. Exudate around the bowel indicated that it had been there "for some time" (at least 12 hours, according to testimony during the trial). The surgeon testified that he had not suspected a complete obstruction prior to opening the incision because of the quality of the aspirate from the nasogastric tube and partial results from an enema. The patient's alert, cooperative mental state "belied the severity of her disease." He testified that even though she did not have abdominal rigidity or distention, as he would have expected in an obstruction, or even an ileus, he was certain the patient had had a paralytic ileus for some time after the operation. He noted that a paralytic ileus could sometimes last as long as a week. The patient, who was a nurse, was sure that she had vomited no fecal material. The surgeon testified that the bowel was "not inadvertently sewed into the fascia. There is no way to tell what caused it. It could be the result of an infection. . . ." The surgeon noted that he had removed 80 percent of the patient's bowel, and he testified that she had done well after this operation. A little more than more than one week after the surgeon operated, the patient died. An autopsy showed extensive brain changes, inflammatory changes, bronchial pneumonia, pulmonary abscesses, multiple thromboembolisms in mesenteric and retroperitoneal veins, and evidence of vascular disease.

The patient's husband sued the general practitioner, alleging that the general practitioner had been negligent in his failure to obtain consultation earlier, failure to repeat X rays for a six-day period, and delay in transferring the patient to a hospital in which she could receive specialized care. Expert medical witnesses called by the plaintiff testified that the general practitioner-defendant should have asked for an opinion from a specialist by, at the latest, the seventh day after the operation. One expert thought that the general practitioner should have been suspicious of paralytic ileus by the fifth or sixth day. This expert testified that the ordinary, occasional abdominal surgeon encounters problems of this nature, lasting more than three to four days postoperatively, so rarely that, unless he has special skills, he cannot be conversant with the problem. The jury found

§ 13.20 Hysterectomy 515

that the delay in transfer, the failure to obtain earlier consultation, and the failure to obtain X rays during a six-day period constituted negligence on the part of the general practitioner-defendant and that such negligence was the proximate cause of the patient's death. The lower court entered judgment on the jury verdict and the higher court affirmed, finding sufficient evidence to support the jury verdict (*Richardson v. Holmes*, 1975).[92]

Nerve injury may also occur during either abdominal or vaginal hysterectomy. Often it is the positioning or exposure of the patient that causes the injury, rather than the procedure itself. The femoral nerve may be injured during abdominal hysterectomy by the lateral wings of the self-retaining retractor. Lower back injury may result from the vaginal procedure, since the lower extremities are elevated and abducted, causing pressure on the ligaments of the lower back. Pressure against the bar that supports the leg holder may also injure the peroneal nerve.[93] Cases have been brought by hysterectomy patients who have sustained nerve injuries.

CASE ILLUSTRATION

The patient underwent an operation for hysterectomy and anterior and posterior vaginal repair. In preparation for the operation, the physician placed the patient in the lithotomy position—lying flat on her back with her legs suspended in stirrups. The physician used this position in order to provide necessary exposure to conduct the operation. After the operation, the patient developed common peroneal palsy of the right foot. The patient sued the physician, alleging that negligence regarding the suspension of her right leg in the stirrup caused the injury. All of the medical testimony at trial indicated that use of the lithotomy position was required by the operation and that nothing unusual had occurred during the operation: the legs were properly suspended, the straps on the stirrups did not slip, and nothing struck the legs during the procedure. The patient-plaintiff's expert witness testified only that the cause of the peroneal palsy was a combination of pulling on the lower sciatic nerve and pressure on the outer aspect of the knee. It was undisputed that the standard lithotomy position required a slight bend in the knee, which is the source of some pressure or stretching of the peroneal nerve. Another expert stated that the lithotomy position, which is the proper, required position for the operation, exerts a combination pulling (or stretching) and pressure. The patient-plaintiff argued that she had had no problems with her leg before the surgery, therefore, because peroneal palsy is not an expected outcome of a hysterectomy, her injury must be due to negligence during the procedure. The court rejected this argument, stating that it relied on circumstantial evidence which failed to show that negligence was more likely than not the cause of the injury.

Furthermore, the court took notice of testimony that the injury could be caused by proper positioning or, as suggested by another witness, could have resulted when the patient was in the recovery room, where she might have hit her leg upon awakening. Based on this reasoning, the court found in favor of the physician (*Louis v. Parchman,* 1973).[94]

In another case,[95] the patient suffered permanent paralysis below her waist because of a transverse myelitis (injury to the spinal cord) at the eleventh thoracic vertebra. The patient-plaintiff sought to recover damages under the doctrine of res ipsa loquitur. The higher court ruled that the lower court had properly held the doctrine inapplicable. The court noted that the expert testimony indicated that the cause of the injury was probably a blood clot in the anterior spinal artery, a plaque, or anatomical configuration; none of these would indicate negligence on the part of the physician-defendant.

While these cases are representative of litigation arising from complications of hysterectomy, they do not cover all the possible complications that may occur (see Table 13.1). Furthermore, simply because no recent case has been brought arising out of, for example, hemorrhagic shock resulting from hysterectomy (whether based on negligent performance leading to the injury, negligent postoperative management of the injury, or failure to inform the patient that such a risk exists when obtaining her consent), there is no reason to believe that liability may not be imposed for this complication. Finally, basic procedures common to any operation may be performed negligently during a hysterectomy and result in liability. In one case, the patient-plaintiff complained of "sticking pains" in her abdomen following a hysterectomy. The physician-defendant prescribed painkilling medication. Another physician subsequently found steel suture material in the area of the incision and removed it, eliminating the pain. The court imposed liability on the physician, ruling that a jury could infer negligence as a matter of common knowledge when there are continual complaints of pain by a patient over substantial periods of time and the physician fails to examine the patient in any manner whatsoever.[96]

§ 13.30 DILATION AND CURETTAGE

Liability may be imposed on a physician for the negligent performance of a D&C, as manifested in a resulting perforation of the uterus or the failure to adequately complete the procedure.

Basic Standard of Care: The American College of Obstetricians and Gynecologists has not identified specific standards of care governing the performance of a D&C.

Interpretation and Customary Practice: A D&C consists of dilating the cervix and scraping the uterus with a curet. It is used both as a diagnostic tool

TABLE 13.1   Complications Associated with Hysterectomy*

Postoperative bleeding
Reaction to transfusion
Pulmonary complications
   Atelectasis
   Pneumonitis
   Pulmonary embolus
Urinary complications
   Injury (immediate injury to the bladder or ureter, delayed injury to the bladder (including vesicovaginal fistula), delayed ureteral fistula, or obstruction from kinking or scar)
   Retention of urine
   Infection of the urinary tract
Venous complications (phlebothrombosis-thrombophlebitis)
Gastrointestinal complications
   Injury to bowel
   Intestinal obstruction
   Paralytic ileus
Wound complications
   Infection
   Hematoma
   Dehiscence
Infection
   Peritonitis
   Pelvic abscess
Nerve Injury
Other complications or injuries
   Granulation tissue at vault of vagina
   Dyspareunia
   Prolapse of the uterine tube, vaginal vault, or ovaries
   Disfigurement
   Emotional injury

*No list can be complete enough to cover *all* possible complications.

and as a treatment for certain gynecological and obstetrical conditions.

There are many different indications for D&C. The most common include menstrual disturbance, intermenstrual or postcoital bleeding or discharge, postmenopausal bleeding or discharge, dysmenorrhea, abnormal cytological smears, and infertility evaluation.[97] A D&C may also be used for abortion,[98] and for removing retained products of conception after parturition.[99]

A D&C is often performed on an outpatient basis. Those patients who are hospitalized are usually discharged within 24 hours after the procedure is performed.[100] The most common complications of D&C are perforation of the uterus, laceration of the cervix, infection, and excessive postoperative uterine bleeding. In younger, nulliparous patients, a D&C may be undesirable because of the possibility of later cervical incompetence; in such cases, diagnostic aspiration curettage will often be preferable.[101]

In a few cases, patients have complained that negligent performance of the D&C caused them injury.

CASE ILLUSTRATION

The patient was suffering from heavy, frequent vaginal bleeding. She had experienced abnormal uterine bleeding in the past because of endometritis, and she had undergone at least two D&Cs. She consulted a physician and subsequently underwent another D&C. While the physician was performing the D&C, he noticed a loss of tension on the curet. He immediately consulted another physician, who performed a laparotomy and discovered a perforation of the uterus. The second physician sutured the uterus. The patient suffered further incidents of abnormal bleeding after her discharge from the hospital. She sued the physician who performed the D&C, alleging, among other things, that he had been negligent in perforating her uterus and that the perforation was the cause of her continued abnormal bleeding. The physician-defendant moved for summary judgment. He offered a deposition of the second physician, in which the second physician stated that (1) the physician-defendant had exercised the requisite degree of care and skill in performing the operation; (2) perforation of the uterus during a D&C can occur despite the exercise of the proper degree of skill and care; and (3) the patient-plaintiff's continued bleeding was caused by chronic endometritis, not by the perforation. The lower court granted summary judgment for the physician-defendant and the higher court affirmed. The court held that summary judgment was proper since the patient-plaintiff had failed to support her allegation of negligence with expert testimony, and because the existence of the perforation would not support a finding of negligence as a matter of common knowledge (*Dickerson v. Hulsey*, 1976).[102]

While the physician in this case was exonerated from liability, in other, similar cases a patient who is injured in the same manner may be able to obtain expert testimony that perforation is a result of negligence. Such expert testimony would overcome the obstacle placed before the patient in this case.

Cases have been brought where patients have complained that the physician was negligent in failing to adequately complete the D&C.

CASE ILLUSTRATION

The patient experienced abnormal vaginal bleeding for several weeks. On January 26, the physician admitted her to the hospital. It was then discovered that the patient was two to three months pregnant. On January 28, the patient suffered a spontaneous abortion. The physician noted that the placenta was not expelled. He attempted several unspecified procedures in an effort to expel the placenta, but they were unsuccessful. On February 4, the physician performed a D&C for the removal of the retained placental material. The patient thereafter continued to suffer bleeding and pain. On April 27, she consulted a second physician, who noted the bleeding, discovered an enlarged uterus, and referred the patient to an obstetrician-gynecologist. On May 8, the obstetrician-gynecologist attempted to perform a D&C. When he inserted the curet, the patient suffered a hemorrhage and went into shock. He then performed an emergency abdominal hysterectomy and discovered placental material attached to the wall of the uterus. The material was necrotic and calcified.

The patient sued the physician who performed the original D&C, alleging that he had negligently failed to remove the retained placenta during the initial procedure. The lower court entered judgment for the patient-plaintiff and the higher court affirmed, ruling that there was sufficient evidence to support a finding that the physician-defendant had been negligent. The physician-defendant testified that he had removed 90 to 95 percent of the placenta during the D&C. He testified that the large amount of placental material discovered after the hysterectomy was the result of a pregnancy that had begun after the first D&C. He further testified that this material was not traceable to the first D&C, since the placental material could not have been retained for the period of three months between the first D&C and the hysterectomy. The court ruled, however, that there was sufficient evidence to rebut this testimony. There was expert testimony that, whereas the patient could not possibly have become pregnant for at least one month after her initial discharge from the hospital, the size of the uterus and placental material at the time of the hysterectomy correlated with a 12- to 16-week gestation period. Also, at the time of the hysterectomy, there was no evidence of a fetus or a recent abortion. Furthermore, the placenta was calcified, indicating that it had been dead tissue for a substantial period of time. Thus, the lower court was justified in concluding that the placenta subsequently found was not the result of a subsequent pregnancy. There was also testimony that, although it is unusual for placental material to be retained for three months, it does occasionally happen; further, the patient exhibited the symptoms that normally accompany such an extended retention (*Johns v. Gauthier*, 1972).[103]

NOTES

1. American College of Obstetricians and Gynecologists, Standards for Obstetric/Gynecologic Services 45–48 (5th ed. 1982).
2. Long, *Gynecologic History, Examination, and Diagnostic Procedures,* in Current Obstetric and Gynecologic Diagnosis and Treatment 80–81 (R. Benson, ed., 1978).
3. J. Willson & E. Carrington, Obstetrics and Gynecology 12 (6th ed. 1979).
4. Long, *supra* note 2, at 82.
5. *Id.*
6. *Id.* at 82–86.

7. J. Willson & E. Carrington, *supra* note 3, at 14.
8. Long, *supra* note 2, at 87–98.
9. Clapham v. Yanga, 102 Mich. App. 47, 300 N.W.2d 727 (1980).
10. Lambert v. Michel, 364 So.2d 248 (La. App. 1978); *cert. denied*, 366 So.2d 917 (La. 1978).
11. Truman v. Thomas, 27 Cal. 3d 285, 611 P.2d 902, 165 Cal. Rptr. 308 (1980).
12. Steele v. St. Paul Fire & Marine Ins. Co., 371 So.2d 843 (La. App. 1979); *cert. denied*, 374 So.2d 658 (La. 1979).
13. Ray v. Wagner, 176 N.W.2d 101 (Minn. 1970).
14. Hernandez v. United States, 636 F.2d 704 (D.C. Cir. 1980).
15. *See, e.g.*, O'Grady v. Wickman, 213 So.2d 321 (Fla. App. 1968).
16. Kleinman v. Armour, 12 Ariz. App. 383, 470 P.2d 703 (1970).
17. Schiff, *How To Handle the Rape Victim*, 71 So. Med. J. 509 (May 1978).
18. Ireland, *Reform Rape Legislation: A New Standard of Sexual Responsibility*, 49 U. Colo. L. Rev. 186 (Winter 1978).
19. Ala. Code tit. 14, § 396 (1958); Alaska Stat. § 11.15.120 (1976); Ariz. Rev. Stat. Ann. § 13-612 (1956); D.C. Code Encycl. § 22-2901 (West 1967); Ga. Code Ann. § 26-2001 (1972); Ill. Ann. Stat. ch. 38, § 11-1 (Smith-Hurd Supp. 1977); Ind. Code § 35-42-4-1 (Supp. 1976); Me. Rev. Stat. Ann. tit. 17A, § 251 (Supp. 1976); Md. Crim. Law Code Ann. art. 27, § 461 (1976); Miss. Code Ann. § 97-3-65 (Supp. 1976); Mo. Ann. Stat. § 566.030 (Vernon Supp. 1977); Nev. Rev. Stat. § 200.364 (1973); N.J. Stat. Ann. § 2A:138-1 (West 1969); N.C. Gen. Stat. § 14-21 (Supp. 1975); Okla. Stat. Ann. tit. 21, § 1111 (West 1958); Ore. Rev. Stat. § 163.375 (1975); 18 Pa. Cons. Stat. Ann. § 3121 (1973); R.I. Gen. Laws § 11-37-1 (1969); S.C. Code § 16-71 (1962); Tenn. Code Ann. § 39-3701 (1975); Tex. Penal Code Ann. tit. 5, §§ 21.01(3), 21.02 (Vernon 1974); Utah Code Ann. § 76-5-401 (Supp. 1976); Vt. Stat. Ann. tit. 13, § 3201 (1974); Va. Code § 18.1-44 (1975); W.Va. Code § 61-88-1 (1977); Wyo. Stat. § 6063 (Supp. 1975).
20. Ariz. Rev. Stat. § 13-611 (1956); La. Rev. Stat. Ann. § 14:42 (West Supp. 1977).
21. Ky. Rev. Stat. Ann. § 510.010(2) (Supp. 1976); N.Y. Penal Law § 130.00 (McKinney 1975); Tex. Penal Code Ann. § 21.02 (Vernon 1974); W.Va. Code § 61-8B-1 (1977).
22. 1976 Iowa Leg. Serv. 595; Mich. Stat. Ann. § 28.788(9) (Supp. 1977); Minn. Stat. Ann. § 609.347 (West Cum. Supp. 1977); Ohio Rev. Code Ann. § 2907.02(c) (Page Spec. Supp. 1973); 18 Pa. Cons. Stat. Ann. § 3107 (Purdon Cum. Supp. 1977–78).
23. Ind. Code § 35-42-4-1 (1976); Mich. Stat. Ann. § 28.788 (Supp. 1977); N.H. Rev. Stat. Ann § 632-A (Supp. 1975); N.M. Rev. Stat. Ann. §§ 40A-9-20–40A-9-26 (Supp. 1975); Ohio Rev. Code Ann. §§ 2907.01–2907.11 (Page Supp. 1975).
24. Some states have abolished statutory corroboration requirements: Conn. Gen. Stat. Ann. § 53a-68 (West 1974) (repealed); Del. Code tit. 11, § 772(c) (1974) (repealed); Iowa Code Ann. § 782.4 (West 1974) (repealed). Other states have enacted statutes specifying that no corroboration is required in rape cases: Minn. Stat. Ann. § 609.347 (West Supp. 1977); N.M. Stat. Ann. § 40A-9-25 (Supp. 1975); N.Y. Penal Law §§ 130.15-16 (McKinney 1975) (repealed 1972); 18 Pa. Cons. Stat. Ann. § 3106 (Purdon Supp. 1977); Tex. Code Crim. Prac. Ann. art. 38.07 (Vernon Supp. 1976); Wash. Rev. Code Ann. § 9.79.150. (1977).
25. Alaska Stat. § 12.45.045(a) (Cum. Supp. 1976); Cal. Evid. Code § 1103 (West Supp. 1977); Colo. Rev. Stat. § 18-3-407 (Cum. Supp. 1976); Fla. Stat. Ann. § 794.022 (West 1976); Ga. Code Ann. § 38-202.1 (Supp. 1976); Ind. Code Ann. § 35-1-32.5-1 (Burns Supp. 1977); Iowa Crim. Code ch. 2, § 1301, Rule 20(b) (Supp. 1977); Ky. Rev. Stat. Ann. § 510.145 (Baldwin Cum. Supp. 1976); La Rev.

Stat. Ann. § 15:498 (West Cum. Supp. 1977); Md. Ann. Code art. 27, § 461A (West Cum. Supp. 1977); Mich. Stat. Ann. § 28.788(10) (Supp. 1977); 1977 Mo. Leg. Serv. Vernon, Act 87, H.B. 502; Mont. Rev. Codes Ann. § 94-5-50-3(5) (Crim. Code Supp. 1976); Neb. Rev. Stat. § 28-408.05 (1975); Nev. Rev. Stat. § 48.069 (1977); N.H. Rev. Stat. Ann. § 632-A:6 (Supp. 1975); N.M. Stat. Ann. § 40A-9-26 (Supp. 1975); N.D. Cent. Code Ann. § 12.1-20-14 (1976); Okla. Stat. Ann. tit. 22, § 750 (West Cum. Supp. 1977); 18 Pa. Cons. Stat. Ann. § 3104 (Purdon Supp. 1977); S.D. Comp. Laws Ann. § 23-44-16.1 (Supp. 1977); Tenn. Code Ann. § 49-2455 (Cum. Supp. 1976); Tex. Penal Code Ann. tit. 5, § 21.13 (Vernon Supp. 1978); Wash. Rev. Code Ann. § 9.79.150 (1977); W.Va. Code § 61-8B-12 (1977).
26. Ark. Stat. Ann. § 41-1803 (Supp. 1976); Colo Rev. Stat. § 18-3-402 (Supp. 1976); Conn. Gen. Stat. §§ 53a-65, 53a-70 (1977); Fla. Stat. Ann. § 794.011 (West 1976); Ind. Code § 35-42-4-1 (Supp. 1976); 1976 Iowa Legis. Serv. 594; Mass. Ann. Laws ch. 265, § 22 (Supp. 1975); Mich. Stat. Ann. § 28.788 (Supp. 1977); N.M. Stat. Ann. § 40A-9-21 (Supp. 1975); Ohio Rev. Code Ann. § 2907.02 (Page 1973); S.D. Comp. Laws Ann. § 22-22-1 (Supp. 1977); Wash. Rev. Code Ann. § 9.79.170 (Supp. 1977); Wis. Stat. Ann. 940.225 (West Supp. 1977–78).
27. *See* Baltimore County Task Force on Rape Control, Report to the County Council, 34 (1975).
28. Schiff, *supra* note 17, at 509.
29. Welch, *Rape and the Trauma of Inadequate Care,* Prism 21 (Sept. 1975).
30. American College of Obstetricians and Gynecologists, Technical Bulletin No. 14 (July 1970).
31. *Id.*
32. Schiff, *supra* note 17, at 510.
33. Stone & Stone, *Scientific Evidence in Rape Cases,* 41 Tex. B. J. 521 (June 1978).
34. American College of Obstetricians and Gynecologists, *supra* note 30.
35. Stone & Stone, *supra* note 33.
36. Paul, *The Medical Examination of the Live Rape Victim and the Accused,* Legal Med. Ann. 145 (1977).
37. American College of Obstetricians and Gynecologists, *supra* note 30.
38. Stone & Stone, *supra* note 33, at 518.
39. *Id.* at 522.
40. Gold & Wyatt, *Rape System: Old Roles and New Times,* 27 Catholic U.L. Rev. 706 (Summer 1978).
41. Cal. Govt. Code, § 13961.5 (West Supp. 1975); Minn. Stat. Ann. § 241.51 (West Supp. 1977); Nev. Rev. Stat. §§ 217.280–217.350, 440.244 (1975); Ohio Rev. Code Ann. § 2907.28 (Page Supp. 1975).
42. Gold & Wyatt, *supra* note 40, at 708.
43. Baltimore Evening Sun, Oct. 14, 1976, § C at 4, col. 6.
44. Welch, *supra* note 29.
45. American College of Obstetricians and Gynecologists, *supra* note 30.
46. Welch, *supra* note 29.
47. Schiff, *supra* note 17, at 511.
48. Gold & Wyatt, *supra* note 40.
49. Schiff, *Attending the Child "Rape Victim,"* 72 So. Med. J. 906–07 (Aug. 1979).
50. *Id.* at 908–09.
51. *Id.* at 910.
52. State v. Whelan, 189 N.W.2d 179 (Minn. 1971).
53. Burke v. State, 238 N.E.2d 1 (Ind. 1968).
54. State v. Heffernan, 367 P.2d 848 (Wash. 1962).

55. Halbert & Jones, *Medical Management of the Sexually Assaulted Woman*, 20 J. Reprod. Med. 274 (1978).
56. Bornstein, *Investigation of Rape: Medicolegal Problems*, Med. Trial Technique Q. 238 (1963).
57. State v. Paulette, 158 Conn. 22, 255 A.2d 855 (1969), ruling evidence admissible under business record exception; State v. Fisher, 178 N.W.2d 380 (Iowa 1970), ruling evidence inadmissible.
58. State v. Paulette, *supra* note 57.
59. Joel-Cohen, *The Place of the Abdominal Hysterectomy*, 5 Clin. Obstet. Gynecol. 526 (1978); Amirikia & Evans, *Ten-Year Review of Hysterectomies: Trends, Indications, and Risks*, 134 Am. J. Obstet. Gynecol. 431–37 (1979).
60. Hassid, *Indications and Contraindications for Vaginal Hysterectomy*, 15 Clin. Obstet. Gynecol. 698 (1972).
61. Poma, *Hysterectomy: Indications and Contraindications*, 158 Ill. Med. J. 18 (1980).
62. Hassid, *supra* note 60, at 697–98; E. Novak, Gynecology 50 (1971); Mitchel, *Vaginal Hysterectomy: Anterior and Posterior Colporrhaphy; Repair of Enterocele; and Prolapse of Vaginal Vault*, in Gynecologic Surgery 44–46 (J. Ridley, ed., 1974).
63. Hassid, *supra* note 60, at 701; Joel-Cohen, *supra* note 59, at 529.
64. O'Grady v. Wickman, *supra* note 15.
65. Iverson v. Lancaster, 158 N.W.2d 507 (N.D. 1968).
66. Burks v. Baumgartner, 72 N.M. 123, 381 P.2d 57 (1963).
67. Poma, *supra* note 61, at 15.
68. Slack v. Moorhead, 152 Ga. App. 68, 262 S.E.2d 186 (1979).
69. Rogers v. Lumbermens Mutual Casualty Co., 119 So.2d 649 (La. App. 1960).
70. Winfrey v. Citizens & Southern Nat'l Bank, 149 Ga. App. 488, 254 S.E.2d 725 (1979).
71. Davidson v. Shirley, 616 F.2d 224 (5th Cir. 1980).
72. Offut v. Sheehan, 168 Ind. App. 491, 344 N.E.2d 92 (1976).
73. Levinson, *Hysterectomy Complications*, 15 Clin. Obstet. Gynecol. 812–17 (1972); E. Novak, *supra* note 62, at 52–54.
74. Thomas v. Berries, 348 So.2d 905 (Fla. App. 1977).
75. Stauffer v. Karabin, 30 Colo. App. 357, 492 P.2d 862 (1971).
76. Longmire v. Hoey, 512 S.W.2d 307 (Tenn. App. 1974).
77. Hart v. Steele, 416 S.W.2d 927 (Mo. 1967); Thomas v. Berries, 348 So.2d 905 (Fla. App. 1977); Tant v. Women's Clinic, 382 So.2d 1120 (Ala. 1980).
78. Sims v. Helms, 345 So.2d 721 (Fla. 1977), *accord.,* Halligan v. Cotton, 193 Neb. 331, 227 N.W.2d 10 (1975).
79. Riedisser v. Nelson, 111 Ariz. 542, 534 P.2d 1052 (1975).
80. Tatro v. Leuken, 212 Kan. 606, 512 P.2d 529 (1973).
81. Bryant v. St. Paul Fire & Marine Ins. Co., 272 So.2d 448 (La. App. 1973), *accord,* Faulkner v. Pezeshki, 44 Ohio App. 2d 186, 337 N.E.2d 158 (1975).
82. Siverson v. Weber, 57 Cal.2d 834, 22 Cal. Rptr. 337, 372 P.2d 97 (1962).
83. Klinger v. Henderson, 276 Cal. App.2d 774, 81 Cal. Rptr. 305 (1969); *see also* Faulkner v. Pezeshki, *supra* note 81.
84. Rawlings v. Harris, 265 Cal. App.2d 452, 71 Cal. Rptr. 288 (1968), *accord.,* Tomei v. Henning, 67 Cal.2d 319, 431 P.2d 633, 62 Cal. Rptr. 9 (1967).
85. Alleman v. Seventh Ward Gen. Hosp., 295 So.2d 503 (La. App. 1974).
86. Amirikia & Evans, *supra* note 59, at 433.
87. Joel-Cohen, *supra* note 59, at 529.
88. Hoeffel v. Campbell, 16 Ariz. App. 577, 494 P.2d 777 (1972); Cline v. Lund, 31 Cal. App.3d 755, 107 Cal. Rptr. 629 (1973).

89. Spidle v. Steward, 79 Ill.2d 1, 402 N.E.2d 216 (1980).
90. Seeley v. Eaton, 506 S.W.2d 719 (Tex. Civ. App. 1974).
91. Levinson, *supra* note 73, at 820, 821.
92. Richardson v. Holmes, 525 S.W.2d 293 (Tex. Civ. App. 1975).
93. Levinson, *supra* note 73, at 822, 823.
94. Louis v. Parchman, 493 S.W.2d 10 (Tex. Civ. App. 1973).
95. Hunter v. Robison, 488 S.W.2d 555 (Tex. Civ. App. 1972); *see also* Faris v. Doctors Hosp., Inc., 18 Ariz. App. 264, 501 P.2d 440 (1972).
96. Revels v. Pohle, 101 Ariz. 208, 418 P.2d 364 (1966), *accord.,* Turney v. Anspaugh, 581 P.2d 1301 (Okla. 1978).
97. MacKenzie & Bibby, *Critical Assessment of Dilatation and Curettage in 1029 Women,* 2 (8089) Lancet 567 (1978); Poma, *Indications for Dilatation and Curettage: New Trends,* 63 Int. Surg. 63 (1978).
98. J. Pritchard & P. MacDonald, Williams Obstetrics 603 (16th ed. 1980).
99. MacKenzie & Bibby, *supra* note 97, at 566–67.
100. Poma, *supra* note 97, at 64.
101. MacKenzie & Bibby, *supra* note 97, at 566–68.
102. Dickerson v. Hulsey, 138 Ga. App. 108, 225 S.E.2d 464 (1976). *See also* Eckley v. St. Therese Hosp., 62 Ill. App.3d 299, 379 N.E.2d 306 (1978).
103. Johns v. Gauthier, 266 So.2d 504 (La App. 1972); *cert. denied,* 263 La. 376, 268 So.2d 260 (1972).

Chapter XIV

Diseases

§ 14.10 CANCER

Liability may be imposed on a physician for negligent diagnosis of cancer, including failure to make a timely diagnosis and misdiagnosis, failure to obtain the patient's informed consent, and negligent treatment of the condition.

Basic Standard of Care: The American College of Obstetricians and Gynecologists has stated that the frequency of cancer screening examinations depends on the risk status of the patient. Cancer screening should include examination of the thyroid, breasts, abdomen, pelvis, and rectum. Cervical cytology should be instituted at the onset of sexual activity or age 18. Uterine cytology and screening for colorectal cancer should be performed for women over the age of 40. A baseline mammogram is recommended for women between the ages of 35 and 50. Abnormal findings obtained during such screening tests require further evaluations.[1]

Interpretation and Customary Practice: Allegations of negligence in the context of breast, ovarian and cervical cancer can be grouped into three general categories. First, the patient may allege negligent diagnosis. This claim has two forms: in the first, the patient alleges that the physician failed to diagnose her malignancy in a timely fashion; in the second, the patient alleges that a benign condition has been negligently misdiagnosed as malignant. Second, the patient-plaintiff's theory of recovery may be lack of informed consent; alleged failure to inform can occur either in the diagnosis or in the treatment stage of the physician-patient relationship. Third, the patient may allege improper treatment of her condition.

Breast Cancer: Failure to timely diagnose and incorrect diagnosis are the most common complaints in suits dealing with malignancy and suspected malignancy of the breast. In general, the courts have upheld a finding of negligence when the physician has unreasonably failed to detect a breast abnormality upon examination and when the physician has failed to go further than a simple clinical evaluation of a suspicious breast abnormality. Conversely, the courts have recognized that not every incorrect diagnosis is the result of negligence.

Many kinds of cancer originate in breast tissues, but most of them are uncommon. During the early stages, the malignant growth is confined to the tissue in which it originated (carcinoma in situ). However, by the time they are discovered, most cancers have already invaded the surrounding tissue or have spread beyond the breast (metastasized).

The most common malignacies of the breast are ductal cancer (which originates in the gland ducts), lobular cancer (which originates in the glandular cells), and Paget's disease. Ductal and lobular cancer take many forms, and each is diagnosed histologically by cell type and growth pattern.

There are numerous benign conditions that must be differentiated from cancer before definitive treatment is instituted. The most common of these are fibrocystic disease, fibroadenoma, intraductal papilloma, and mammary duct ectasia.

Diagnosis of breast abnormalities may be accomplished through a number of techniques, including mammography, xerography, and thermography. The first step, following the patient's complaint, is usually clinical examination. This examination includes inspection and palpation of both breasts and palpation of the areas under the arms and above the shoulder blades. The latter is designed to reveal metastasis of the original cancer through the lymphatic system.

Clinical examination is inconclusive in diagnosing a breast abnormality. Hence a more accurate diagnostic tool, such as mammography or histopathologic examination by aspiration or biopsy, is necessary. The courts have recognized in numerous cases that a physician faced with a patient complaining of a breast abnormality must take active steps to arrive at a conclusive and accurate diagnosis. The physician can neither assume the condition is benign after a cursory clinical examination nor prescribe a "waiting period" for the patient.

CASE ILLUSTRATION

In January or February the patient noticed a change in the size and firmness of her left breast. She initially attributed this to a breast implant that had been inserted 12 years earlier. Her breast continued to increase in size and firmness, the nipple became discolored, and she experienced pain on pressing it. In March, while being examined for a stomach disorder by the physician who had taken charge of her gynecological care, she brought the condition to his attention. The physician made no significant comment about her breast and performed no examination at that time. Thereafter, the patient noticed continuing change in her left breast. In May, she again complained to her physician. Using the palpation method, he confirmed an increase in the size of the breast and made a "differential" diagnosis that the patient's complaints were caused by reaction to a foreign body, mastitis, carcinoma, benign tumor, or fibrocystic disease. The physician did not communicate this "differential" diagnosis to the patient, nor did he mention the possibility of cancer to her. The physician advised the patient to observe the breast for a change of symptoms and return on June 3.

On the morning of June 3, the patient called her physician's office to report no change in symptoms during the observation period and to ask whether she should keep the appointment. She was told that her message would be given to her physician, but no one from the physician's office returned her call. Later in June, the patient noted that her symptoms were becoming more acute. She again called her physician. He was at a medical convention. She was consequently given an appointment for July 8. The patient also scheduled an appointment with a plastic surgeon for July 10. During the examination on July 8, the patient's regular physician noted the swollen and tender left breast in his records but performed no tests since the patient had an appointment with a specialist in two days. On July 10, the plastic surgeon admitted the patient to a hospital, where a mammogram and biopsy confirmed the presence of a malignant mass. On July 18, a radical mastectomy was performed. The surgeon removed a cancerous mass that measured 3.5 to 4.5 centimeters in diameter. Of 40 lymph nodes examined, 24 revealed metastasis from the original cancer. The patient subsequently underwent radiation therapy and chemotherapy, had a therapeutic hysterectomy, and underwent a pericardiectomy.

The patient sued her regular physician. The appeals court upheld a trial court judgment in favor of the patient-plaintiff. The appeals court held that, on the basis of expert and other testimony at trial, the jury could reasonably find that the physician-defendant was negligent in (1) failing to take action in March to determine the cause of the patient's complaints; (2) failing to detect the breast mass in March and May; and (3) failing to adequately follow his patient after instituting an observation period in May. In this regard, the court noted that the physician-defendant made no effort to insure that the patient-plaintiff returned for re-evaluation at the end of the observation period. Therefore, the jury was justified in finding that the physician-defendant was negligent in diagnosing the patient-plaintiff's condition (*Truan v. Smith*, 1979).[2]

A similar situation is presented when the physician-defendant discovers or is shown a breast lump but fails to see that further tests are performed to determine its exact character.[3] In such cases, patients have commonly introduced expert testimony that a biopsy of the suspicious breast tissue is necessary for an accurate diagnosis.

Histopathologic diagnosis of breast lesions can take a number of forms. Material removed through a needle can be examined for cancer cells. A common procedure is for a frozen section to be made of a needle or excisional biopsy and then examined by a pathologist, often while the patient remains under anesthesia in the operating room. A finding of malignancy results in an immediate mastectomy. Frozen section analysis is generally recognized as an accurate method of diagnosis; one source puts the risk of error at less than one percent.[4]

In a number of cases the courts have recognized the sufficiency of frozen section analysis as a diagnostic measure by finding no liability when a mistake was made. These cases are in sharp contrast to those in which physicians are found negligent because of a msidiagnosis based only on a clinical examination.

CASE ILLUSTRATION

The patient was scheduled for an excisional biopsy. Her surgeon removed the tumor from her breast and sent the tissue to the pathologist, who prepared a frozen section using a freezing microtome. The pathologist diagnosed cancer (scirrhous carcinoma), and the surgeon performed an immediate radical mastectomy. The next day, the pathologist examined the permanent paraffin section of the breast tissue and determined that it exhibited granular cell myoblastoma, a benign condition. The patient sued the pathologist. The jury verdict dismissed the patient-plaintiff's suit. On appeal, the court affirmed, finding that (1) the pathologist was following a customary and widely accepted method of diagnosis; and (2) the wrong diagnosis was not unreasonable since cirrhous carcinoma and granular cell myoblastoma are similar in appearance; furthermore, the former is a common cancer found in the breast, while the latter condition is rarely found there (*Lauro v. Travelers Insurance Co.*, 1972).[5]

In misdiagnosis cases, patients have also tried to recover by alleging lack of informed consent. However, because the risk of misdiagnosis is so remote when frozen section analysis is used, the courts have not held disclosure of the risk to be part of the surgeon's duty of informed consent.

CASE ILLUSTRATION

As part of a surgical exploration of a breast lump, the surgeon removed tissue from the patient's breast and sent it to the pathologist, who diagnosed it as cancerous. The surgeon immediately performed a radical mastectomy. The pathologist examined the permanent section the following day and made a new diagnosis of sclerosing adenosis, a benign condition. The patient sued, among others, the surgeon, alleging that he had breached his duty to obtain informed consent by failing to disclose the risk of misdiagnosis by the pathologist. The jury verdict had been in favor of the surgeon-defendant. The court affirmed on appeal. The court held that the risk of misdiagnosis of the frozen tissue section by the pathologist was so rare or remote that it could not have been reasonably anticipated by the surgeon-defendant (*Hanks v. Ranson, Swan, and Burch, Ltd.*, 1978).[6]

Where the procedures used to separate and identify tissue samples in the course of the histopathologic diagnosis deviate from standard practice or otherwise hinder an accurate diagnosis, such procedures may be found to constitute negligence.

CASE ILLUSTRATION

The surgeon removed a cyst from each of the patient's breasts, placed them in a single container, and sent them to the pathology department of the hospital. At this point, one cyst was larger than the other, and each could have been identified with the correct breast. The pathologist dissected the specimens and destroyed their identity. Only one specimen displayed malignancy, but, because its source could no longer be identified, it was necessary to remove both the patient's breasts. The patient sued the surgeon and the hospital. The jury rendered a verdict finding the surgeon-defendant and the hospital-defendant jointly and severally liable to the patient-plaintiff. The lower court entered judgment on the verdict, and the higher court affirmed on appeal, finding that there was evidence that each defendant had violated the applicable standard of care (*Variety Children's Hospital v. Osle*, 1974).[7]

The issue of informed consent is particularly acute in the context of breast cancer. This is due primarily to the wide variety of approaches available to the patient and physician in both the diagnosis and treatment of malignancy of the breast. Also important is the realization that medical treatment of breast cancer usually has a profound physical and emotional impact on the patient.

The courts have found negligence in the use of invasive diagnostic techniques not adequately explained to the patient or consented to by her.

CASE ILLUSTRATION

After a mammogram of the patient's right breast revealed a suspicious lesion, her gynecologist referred her to a surgeon. The surgeon was unable to locate a discrete, palpable lump and therefore recommended a biopsy in order to ascertain whether the lesion was cancerous. During surgery, the surgeon essentially performed a quadrant resection (partial mastectomy), removing three segments of tissue, each measuring 6 or 7 centimeters in diameter. None of the tissue was found to be malignant. The patient stated that, after the surgery, "The top of my breast was gone." She had been told that "They are going to just take a snip out of this lump, and then they will send it to the lab to be examined to see if I do have cancer or not." The patient sued the surgeon, alleging that she was told that only a small sample of tissue would be removed and that she had neither been advised of nor had she consented to a quadrant resection. The court held that the patient-plaintiff had established that the physician-defendant had breached his duty to inform her of the nature of the surgery and that the breach had caused her damage. The court held that a new trial should be held to determine only the damages to be assessed against the physician-defendant (*Dries v. Greger,* 1980).[8]

Because a diagnosis of cancer is such a frightening prospect, some patients will delay or postpone diagnostic tests and treatment. Where such delay exacerbates the patient's condition, the physician may assert this as a defense in a subsequent lawsuit[9] (see §§ 3.20, Contributory Negligence, 3.30, Comparative Negligence).

The treatment of breast cancer can take many forms. It is therefore especially important that the physician who is to treat the cancer disclose to and discuss with the patient alternatives. The following methods are used independently or in combination in the treatment of breast cancer:[10]

   I. Surgery
      1. Tylectomy (partial mastectomy)
      2. Simple mastectomy
      3. Extended simple mastectomy
      4. Modified radical mastectomy
      5. Radical mastectomy
      6. Superradical mastectomy
  II. Radiotherapy
      1. Preoperative radiotherapy
      2. Postoperative radiotherapy
      3. Radiotherapeutic management
 III. Endocrine therapy
      1. Hormone therapy
         a. Androgens
         b. Estrogens
         c. Progestogens
         d. Corticosteroids
      2. Removal of organs
         a. Ovaries
         b. Adrenal glands
         c. Pituitary gland
         d. Testes
  IV. Chemotherapy (many drugs)

The surgical procedures are listed in order of increasing invasiveness. Choice of procedure depends primarily on the size of the tumor and upon the likelihood that it has metastasized. It may also depend on aesthetic considerations of the patient. Sometimes simple removal of the tumor (tylectomy) or breast (simple mastectomy) may be sufficient. More frequently, suspected involvement of one or both pectoral muscles; the axillary, supraclavicular, internal mammary, or mediastinal lymph nodes; or some other local structure will demand a more radical procedure. The radical mastectomy is a common approach. It features removal of the breast, removal of both pectoral muscles, and dissection of axillary lymph nodes.

Radiotherapy can be used to render an inoperable tumor operable (preoperative), to treat local and regional recurrences of cancer after surgery (postoperative), or to treat patients with inoperable cancer (total management). Radiotherapy can also be useful in treating subsequent distant metastases.

Endocrine therapy may proceed through either the administration of hormones or the surgical removal of endocrine organs. This therapy is helpful only to some patients. The physician who considers it must first establish tumor-hormone dependence. Choice of specific procedure is often perplexing. One common procedure is oophorectomy (removal of the ovaries) following radical mastectomy in premenopausal women.

Many drugs have been used in the treatment of breast cancer. The results have been disappointing.[11]

In addition to the duty to disclose alternatives, the duty to disclose risks of treatment applies to breast cancer as well (see § 1.33, Consent and Informed Consent).

CASE ILLUSTRATION

The patient underwent a radical left mastectomy for treatment of breast cancer. The surgeon then engaged a radiologist to administer postoperative radiation therapy. The radiologist prescribed a dose of 4,400 roentgens of cobalt radiation to be administered to the area above the patient's clavicle over a period of 16 days. The patient suffered necrosis of the skin and muscles beneath her left arm and the ribs of the left chest as a result of the treatment. The patient sued the radiologist and the hospital, alleging damage from negligent administration of the cobalt radiation therapy and alleging that the radiologist failed to warn her that the course of treatment he proposed involved the risk of bodily injury or death. At trial, it was revealed through testimony that, although the radiologist recognized that the proposed therapy posed certain risks, he failed to so inform the patient. The jury returned a verdict for the defendants, and the lower court entered judgment on the verdict. On appeal, the court reversed and ordered a new trial. In the course of outlining the duty of the radiologist to disclose the inherent risks and hazards of the radiation therapy proposed, the court emphasized that (1) at the time the patient-plaintiff first saw the radiologist-defendant there was no immediate emergency that would preclude disclo-

CASE ILLUSTRATION

In 1963 the patient contacted a family physician engaged in a general medical practice in connection with her second pregnancy. For the next six years, the physician acted as the primary physician for the patient and her two children. During this period, the physician never performed a Pap smear on the patient. The physician suggested to the patient on many occasions that she undergo a smear, but in each case the patient refused, in one instance saying that she could not afford the cost of the test. The physician offered to defer payment, but the patient wanted to pay cash. The physician did not inform the patient of the risks involved in refusing the test, since he believed that such risks were widely known. In 1969 the patient consulted a urologist regarding a urinary tract infection. While examining the patient, the urologist noted heavy vaginal discharge and a rough cervix. The urologist referred the patient to a gynecologist, who found a large, inoperable tumor. The patient died shortly thereafter.

The patient's two children sued the family physician for failing to perform a Pap smear on their mother. The jury returned a verdict for the physician-defendant. On appeal, the court reversed. The court noted that the evidence showed that the physician-defendant had suggested to the patient that she undergo a Pap smear. Therefore, there could be no contention that the physician-defendant was liable because he had failed to recommend the test. However, the evidence also showed that the physician-defendant had failed to inform the patient of the risks entailed in refusing to undergo the test. The court concluded that it was the duty of the physician-defendant to disclose to the patient all relevant information to enable the patient to make a decision regarding the submission to or refusal of a diagnostic test. The court ordered a new trial to determine whether the physician-defendant had breached this duty of disclosure (*Truman v. Thomas,* 1980).[22]

When the physician's treatment of the patient is not concerned with the patient's reproductive organs, the courts have upheld a finding of no negligence in failing to perform a Pap smear.

CASE ILLUSTRATION

From 1972 to 1975, the physician treated the patient for a number of acute problems. In March 1974, the patient entered the hospital complaining of coughing, shortness of breath, and fever. The physician examined and treated the patient for these complaints. The patient subsequently entered the hospital three additional times, complaining of diarrhea and abdominal pain. On each occasion, the physician treated the patient for these com-

§ 14.10

Cervical Cancer: Recent cases dealing with alleged negligence in the diagnosis of cervical cancer have focused on the use of the Pap (Papanicolaou) smear; the cases indicate that both the physician and the patient have specific responsibilities in the use of the Pap smear as a diagnostic tool. The courts have recognized that cervical cancer can be managed in a variety of ways, hence they have emphasized the physician's duty to disclose and discuss alternatives.

The overwhelming majority of cervical malignancies are squamous cell carcinomas. One source divides these into four types: large cell, nonkeratinizing, keratinizing, and small cell.[17] Much less frequent are adenocarcinomas. Sarcomas of the cervix occur, but they are rare.

Squamous cell carcinoma originates from precursors that form a continuum of intraepithelial disease. This continuum is called cervical intraepithelial neoplasia (CIN) and can be divided into three grades: grade 1, mild dysplasia; grade 2, moderate dysplasia; grade 3, severe dysplasia to carcinoma in situ.[18]

The presence of CIN can be detected by the Pap smear.[19] After examining cells from the smear, the cytopathologist reports his findings using either the Papanicolaou classification scheme or some other system. The former has five classes: Class I, only normal cells; Class II, some atypical cells, none suggestive of malignancy; Class III, abnormal cells suggestive of, but not definite for, malignancy; Class IV, malignant cells; Class V, malignant cells more bizarre than those in Class IV. Richart[20] has suggested the following classification system:

I. Findings inadequate for diagnosis
II. Findings essentially normal
III. Atypical cells present, suggestive of: (specify)
IV. Cytologic findings consistent with:
   1. Cervical intraepithelial neoplasia
      a. Grade 1 (mild dysplasia)
      b. Grade 2 (moderate dysplasia)
      c. Grade 3 (severe dysplasia to carcinoma in situ)
   2. Invasive squamous cell carcinoma
   3. Endometrial carcinoma
   4. Other cancer: (specify)

Use of the Pap smear permits identification of women who are suffering from cervical dysplasia and carcinoma in situ and who are consequently at risk of progressing to invasive cancer. Identification at the earlier stages permits more effective and simpler treatment. The reliability of the test in detecting CIN has recently been put by one source at 90 to 95 percent.[21]

The courts have recognized that the Pap smear is a simple and effective way of diagnosing premalignant and malignant conditions of the cervix. Thus, the courts have stated that a physician undertaking the gynecological care of a patient must inform the patient of the nature of the test, including the risks of not having it performed.

this fact to the first physician, nor did he include it in his written pathology report. The pathologist did not inform the first physician that some other pathologists viewed such immature tissue as malignant or potentially malignant. Hence, the first physician informed the patient that her condition was benign. Subsequently, the patient developed pain in her back, hip, and thigh. X rays revealed a large, retroperitoneal tumor adjacent to the right side of the patient's spinal column and three pulmonary lesions. The patient underwent chemotherapy, radiation therapy, and surgery in an effort to treat the malignancy.

The patient sued both the first physician and the pathologist for their failure to reveal that her teratoma contained immature tissue. The jury returned a verdict for the defendants, and the lower court rendered judgment on the verdict. On appeal, the higher court stated that it is the duty of a physician to disclose to a patient all relevant information in order to enable the patient to make an informed decision on whether to seek additional treatment following surgery. The court then noted that the patient-plaintiff had failed to pursue this theory of recovery. The court stated that the patient-plaintiff's theory thus came under ordinary negligence standards and was essentially that the physician-defendants had been negligent in failing to advise her to pursue a potentially necessary course of treatment. But the court found substantial evidence to support the jury's special verdict that neither of the defendants had been negligent. The court noted that the pathologist could reasonably believe that immature tissue in a teratoma is not malignant since other pathologists shared this belief. The court also noted that the first physician was not aware that the teratoma contained immature tissue nor that some pathologists believed such tissue to be malignant or potentially malignant. Therefore the court upheld the lower court's judgment (*Jamison v. Lindsay,* 1980).[14]

Ovarian cancer is treated with the same variety of methods as are breast and cervical cancer. Surgical methods include unilateral and bilateral oophorectomy and hysterectomy (see § 13.20, Hysterectomy). The choice of surgical procedure will depend on the type of tumor and on whether the patient desires to maintain fertility, among other factors. Radiotherapy may be either preoperative or postoperative and may take the form of either external or intracavitary (from within the uterus) irradiation. Chemotherapy is also used in the management of ovarian tumors.

One characteristic of ovarian tumors is that they rarely cause symptoms in their early stages.[15] As a result, they are sometimes discovered inadvertently and in a relatively advanced stage of growth. In the face of an informed consent argument, one court has recognized that removal of the ovarian tumor is justified, since without laboratory study it is impossible to determine whether it is malignant or benign.[16]

sure and (2) pathological examination of tissue had given no indication of metastatic spread of the original tumor; hence, the patient-plaintiff might have refused further treatment, and that possibility should have been provided for (*Natanson v. Kline,* 1960).[12]

Treatment following the mastectomy may take a variety of forms. A physician who chooses to observe the patient rather than prescribe a regimen of chemotherapy or radiation therapy may not be held liable for this conservative treatment approach if it can be proven that it does not violate the applicable standard of care.[13]

Ovarian Cancer: Many conditions can cause enlargement of the ovary. Some enlargements are true neoplasms, either benign or malignant, and these require surgical removal. The majority are physiologic cysts, which will disappear without treatment.

The ovarian tumors most often encountered include the following:

I. Physiologic cysts (usually less than 5 centimenters in diameter)
   1. Follicle
   2. Corpus luteum
II. Neoplasms (usually more than 5 centimeters in diameter)
   1. Epithelial
      a. Serous cystadenoma, benign or malignant
      b. Mucinous cystadenoma, benign or malignant
   2. Germ cell
      a. Teratoma, benign or malignant
      b. Germinoma
   3. Gonadal stromal
      a. Granulosa-theca cell
      b. Sertoli-Leydig cell
   4. Miscellaneous and unusual, benign or malignant.

Although an enlargment of the ovary can usually be detected by pelvic examination, the specific type of tumor cannot be determined without histologic examination. The courts have recognized both the difficulty of diagnosis and the importance to the patient of accurate information regarding her condition.

CASE ILLUSTRATION

The patient consulted the first physician, an obstetrician and gynecologist, for an abnormal pelvic mass. This physician surgically removed the patient's right ovary and the mass and sent the tissue to the second physician, a pathologist, who diagnosed the mass as a benign teratoma. The teratoma contained some immature tissue, but the pathologist did not communicate

§ *14.10*   *Cancer*

plaints and then released her. Following the patient's last contact with the physician in 1975, she began to hemorrhage from her vagina. A gynecologist diagnosed her condition as stage III carcinoma of the cervix, and she subsequently died. The patient's husband sued the original physician for his failure to perform a Pap smear or pelvic examination. The court upheld the jury verdict in favor of the physician-defendant on the basis of expert testimony by community practitioners that, when a patient presents herself with, or is hospitalized for, a complaint unrelated to her reproductive organs, they do not perform Pap smears or pelvic examinations (*Lambert v. Michel*, 1979).[23]

When a physician has performed a Pap smear and the results indicate that the patient is suffering from an abnormal condition of the cervix, he or she must take reasonable steps to inform the patient of the results. The patient, however, is responsible for providing the physician with enough information to enable communication to take place (see § 3.20, Contributory Negligence).

CASE ILLUSTRATION

The patient first visited the physician for the purpose of obtaining a contraceptive device. As a routine matter, the physician performed a Pap smear on the patient. The report on the smear indicated cells "suspicious for malignancy." Thereafter, the physician attempted to contact the patient on numerous occasions. He was unsuccessful until she paid her bill five months later. At this time, another Pap smear was performed, which again indicated possible malignancy. A biopsy revealed cancer, and the patient was treated with cobalt and radium therapy, which destroyed her ovaries, rendered her sterile, and precipitated symptoms of menopause.

    The patient sued the physician, alleging that he had negligently failed to inform her promptly of the results of the first test. The court of appeals upheld a jury verdict in favor of the physician-defendant, pointing to evidence that the patient-plaintiff gave misleading information about her employment status, failed to inform the doctor of a change of address, had no telephone where she actually lived, and failed to inquire about the results of the test herself (*Ray v. Wagner*, 1970).[24]

The treatment for cancer of the cervix depends largely on the stage of the disease. The International Federation of Gynecology and Obstetrics has developed the following means of describing carcinoma of the cervix:[25]

    I. Preinvasive carcinoma
        1. Stage 0—Carcinoma in situ, intraepithelial carcinoma; cases of stage 0 should not be included in any therapeutic statistics for invasive carcinoma

II. Invasive carcinoma
   1. Stage I—Carcinoma strictly confined to the cervix (extension to the corpus should be disregarded)
      a. Stage Ia—Microinvasive carcinoma (early stromal invasion)
      b. Stage Ib—All other cases of stage I; occult cancer should be marked "occ"
   2. Stage II—The carcinoma extends beyond the cervix, but has not extended on to the pelvic wall; the carcinoma involves the vagina, but not the lower third
      a. Stage IIa—No obvious parametrial involvement
      b. Stage IIb—Obvious parametrial involvement
   3. Stage III—The carcinoma has extended on to the pelvic wall on rectal examination there is no cancer-free space between the tumor and the pelvic wall; the tumor involves the lower third of the vagina; all cases with hydronephrosis or a nonfunctioning kidney
      a. Stage IIIa—No extension on to the pelvic wall
      b. Stage IIIb—Extension on to the pelvic wall, hydronephrosis or nonfunctioning kidney, or both
   4. Stage IV—The carcinoma has extended beyond the true pelvis or has clinically involved the mucosa of the bladder or rectum; a bullous edema as such does not permit a case to be allotted to stage IV
      a. Stage IVa—Spread of the growth to adjacent organs
      b. Stage IVb—Spread to distant organs

Treatment alternatives are available for each stage. The choice of treatment will depend on a number of factors, including the extent of the tumor, whether a surgical or radiotherapeutic approach is preferable for a particular patient, and whether the patient desires to maintain her reproductive capacity. Guidelines for treatment can be sketched, however.[26]

The treatment for stage 0 carcinoma is usually a hysterectomy. However, a patient with carcinoma in situ who desires to bear children may be treated with cervical conization or cryotherapy. Stage Ia microinvasive carcinoma is usually treated by a modified radical hysterectomy without pelvic lymphadenectomy. Treatment of carcinoma in stage Ib can be surgery, radiation therapy, or a combination of these. The usual surgical procedure is radical hysterectomy with bilateral pelvic lymphadenectomy. Radiation therapy consists of both external radiation of the whole pelvis and intracavitary therapy. In the latter, radium or cesium is packed directly against the tumor. Stages IIb through IIIb are commonly treated with a combination of external and intracavitary radiation therapy. Stage IVa is treated with external radiation of the whole pelvis and, when possible, pelvic exenteration (removal of the organs and adjacent structures of the pelvis). Stage IVb calls for palliative radiation and chemotherapy.

The courts have recognized that the choices available in the treatment of

§ 14.10   Cancer   537

cancer of the cervix impose on the physician a duty to disclose and discuss alternatives. Failure to do so may constitute a lack of informed consent, giving rise to liability.

CASE ILLUSTRATION

In 1972 the patient was in the care of a physician specializing in obstetrics and gynecology. The physician took a Pap smear of the patient which indicated the presence of either dysplasia or carcinoma in situ. The physician performed a dilation and curettage and a cervical conization for the purpose of diagnosis and therapy. The permanent paraffin section indicated the presence of foci of carcinoma in situ. The physician believed he had removed all of the cancerous cells and told the patient to return in three months for another Pap smear. About three months later, in March 1973, the follow-up smear was taken and showed no abnormalities. The patient submitted to another smear in October; it displayed no abnormalities.

The patient subsequently began seeing a new specialist in obstetrics and gynecology. On April 29, 1974, the patient related her medical history to this new physician, who took a Pap smear and expressed the opinion that a hysterectomy would be necessary to prevent a recurrence of her cancer. Three weeks later, the physician performed a total abdominal hysterectomy. The tissue removed showed no cancer. The patient sued the physician, alleging a breach of the duty to obtain informed consent. The lower court entered judgment for the physician-defendant. On appeal, the court reversed and entered judgment for the patient-plaintiff. The court concluded that the physician-defendant had breached his duty to obtain informed consent by failing (1) to disclose to the patient-plaintiff that the Pap smear taken by him on April 29 showed no abnormalities; and (2) to instruct the patient-plaintiff that other physicians believe that the treatment procedure followed by the patient's original physician is effective for eliminating carcinoma in situ. The court found that the breach caused the patient-plaintiff to undergo a hysterectomy she would not otherwise have undergone and that therefore she was entitled to damages (*Steele v. St. Paul Fire and Marine Insurance Co.*, 1979).[27]

The issue of informed consent can also arise when a first physician refers the patient to a second physician for additional treatment. The courts have emphasized that the second physician must obtain the patient's informed consent to the additional treatment. Consent to the original treatment is not enough.

CASE ILLUSTRATION

The patient underwent conization of her cervix following a Pap smear. The conization revealed early squamous cell carcinoma of the cervix. The patient's first physician advised her to undergo a radium implant (intracavitary radiation therapy); the physician made an appointment for the patient with a second physician, who would perform the implant. At the time of the implant, the patient executed a standard consent form but was not informed about the nature or risks of her proposed surgery. After being released from the hospital, the patient experienced a number of uncomfortable symptoms and eventually began to pass fecal material through her vagina. A large fistula between her uterus and colon was discovered. The patient subsequently underwent a number of surgical procedures to correct this situation, including a radical hysterectomy and bowel resection. The patient sued her second physician. The court entered judgment for the patient-plaintiff, relying on expert testimony that it was standard medical practice to inform potential implant patients of alternative procedures and of risks, including the possibility of radium burns and fistulas. The court held that the physician-defendant breached applicable medical standards when he "assumed" that consent to the implant procedure had been obtained by the first physician and failed to obtain it for himself (*Peagram v. Sisco,* 1976).[28]

§ 14.20 ENDOMETRIOSIS

Liability may be imposed on a physician in connection with the treatment of endometriosis when: (1) he or she fails to recognize or diagnose the patient's endometriosis; or (2) he or she performs an operation for the treatment of the patient's endometriosis in a negligent manner.

Basic Standard of Care: The American College of Obstetricians and Gynecologists has not published guidelines for the diagnosis and treatment of endometriosis.

Interpretation and Customary Practice: Endometriosis is the abnormal occurrence of endometrial tissue outside the body of the uterus. It occurs most frequently in the pelvis, the ovaries, or the peritoneum covering the bladder. The disease may result from any of the following:

1. Temporary occlusion of the cervix, causing menstrual flow to pass through the tubes into the abdominal cavity, where the material may implant;
2. Peritoneal (coelomic) metaplasia;
3. Vascular and lymphatic dissemination;
4. Embryonic rests; or
5. Surgical implantation.[29]

Endometriosis can be recognized by various characteristics, depending on the severity of the disease. The lesions of early endometriosis are small, rounded, bluish red spots surrounded by a zone of puckered scar tissue and are scattered over the pelvic surfaces. The implants may have the appearance of powder burns. As the disease advances, dense, fibrous vascular tissue restricts the involved structures. The lesions obliterate the cul-de-sac and immobilize the uterus. Endometrial tissue commonly implants on the ovary. Endometriotic cysts in the ovary (endometriomas) may measure up to 10 centimeters in diameter. The large cysts contain the thick, dark residue of old blood and are known as "chocolate cysts."[30]

The most common symptom of endometriosis is pelvic or lower abdominal pain.[31] The endometrium responds to cyclic hormonal change and will bleed during menstruation. The blood flows into the surrounding tissue space and causes an irritative reaction.[32] Acquired (secondary) dysmenorrhea is another common symptom of endometriosis. Secondary dysmenorrhea begins a few days before the menses and continues throughout the entire period. The pain is often constant and severe, in contrast to the cramplike pain of primary dysmenorrhea. There is no correlation between the amount of pain and the extent of the disease. Advanced endometriosis may exist without a single symptom, while minimal endometriosis may be accompanied by severe pain.[33] Complications of endometriosis include infertility, rupture of the endometrium, and intestinal obstruction.[34]

Endometriosis may be diagnosed by direct examination. Laparoscopy is generally preferred over hysterosalpingography as a diagnostic technique. A biopsy may be required to confirm the diagnosis. A suspected case of endometriosis must be differentiated from the following conditions:

1. Pelvic infection—endometriosis may be confused with lesions resulting from salpingo-oophoritis. The two conditions exhibit similar symptoms, with the tubes and ovaries adhering to the posterior leaves of the broad ligaments and the rectosigmoid. In contrast to the endometriotic implants, the lesions caused by infection are relatively smooth.

2. Ovarian carcinoma—ovarian carcinoma may be distinguished from endometriosis by a lack of pain and tenderness until far advanced. A laparotomy or laparoscopy may be necessary to distinguish between the two conditions.

3. Urinary tract lesions—women with cyclic or intermittent hematuria may be suffering from urinary tract endometriosis. Pyelography can be used to demonstrate ureteral involvement. Kidney function may cease as a result of hydronephrosis caused by compression of the ureter.[35]

Allegedly improper diagnosis and treatment of endometriosis has given rise to litigation.[36] Physicians may treat endometriosis by either hormonal therapy or surgery.

Hormonal therapy is indicated for women who are not contemplating pregnancy in the near future and whose endometriosis is minimal or recurs after conservative operations.[37] Hormonal therapy may be used as a temporary treatment after conservative surgery to prevent recurrence of the disease until the women wishes to become pregnant. Women who desire children should be urged to conceive soon after diagnosis.[38] Pregnancy or pseudopregnancy, a state produced by the administration of estrogen or progestogens, or both, can stop the spread of endometriosis.

Surgical treatment is indicated where the following conditions exist:

1. Significant enlargement of one or both ovaries
2. Tubes and ovaries that are bound down in women who cannot conceive
3. Extensive involvement of the pelvic structure, with resultant severe pain and infertility
4. Suspected bowel obstruction accompanied by acute pain

Hysterectomy is often indicated when conservative surgery or hormonal treatment cannot control the symptoms[39] (see § 13.20, Hysterectomy). One surgical procedure that has given rise to a malpractice suit is the presacral neurectomy, performed to alleviate the patient's pain.

CASE ILLUSTRATION

The patient suffered from chronic pelvic pain, which her physicians believed was caused either by endometriosis or inflammation of the pelvis. When drug treatment failed to remedy the problem, the physician recommended a presacral neurectomy. The physician informed the patient that the only other available technique to relieve her pain was a hysterectomy. Because the patient wished to retain her childbearing capabilities, she chose the neurectomy. Following this operation, the patient developed an abscess in the presacral area which was treated with antibiotics. After X rays revealed a blockage of the small intestine, the physician performed a colostomy and successfully removed the blockage. The patient continued to experience abdominal problems. The patient sued, alleging that the physicians were negligent in failing to obtain an erythrocyte sedimentation rate before the presacral neurectomy and in failing to do a biopsy during the operation. The patient-plaintiff also alleged that the antibiotic therapy administered between the two operations was improper. Further, the patient-plaintiff claimed that the defendants (who were obstetrician-gynecologists) were not competent to perform the colostomy.

The court rejected each of the patient's arguments and affirmed a judgment for the physicians. Although expert testimony established that an erythrocyte sedimentation rate is "usually" obtained prior to a neurectomy, the court found there was no evidence that the physicians' failure to obtain one constituted negligence. The failure to take a biopsy was not found to be negligence, because such a procedure would have both prolonged the operation and increased the loss of blood. The court also noted that the patient did not show that a biopsy would necessarily have been of value in the later treatment of her condition. The antiobiotic treatment administered by the physicians, while admittedly ineffective, could not be construed as negligence, because there was no expert testimony to support such an inference. The patient's allegation that the colostomy was beyond the physicians' competence also foundered on her failure to provide supporting expert testimony. The testimony of a general practitioner that he would like to have a general surgeon with him were he to perform a colostomy was held insufficient to establish negligence on the part of the physician-defendants. The court noted that the defendants had greater expertise in gynecological surgery than did the general practitioner. The court concluded that "simply because one doctor testifies he does a procedure in one way, the court is in no position to infer that another doctor who does it in a different manner is negligent" (*Cable v. Cazayou*, 1977).[40]

Endometriosis may be discovered during surgery for the treatment of pelvic or abdominal problems such as a bowel obstruction. At this point, the operating physician must exercise his or her judgment in determining whether or not to treat the endometriosis surgically. Surgical treatment in this context has given rise to litigation; however, where the decision to treat has been proved to be medically proper, liability has not been imposed.

CASE ILLUSTRATION

The physicians operated on the patient for lysis of bowel adhesions and relief of bowel obstruction. They freed adhesions between the bowels and the uterus, as well as other adhesions that were binding down the small bowel in both the right and left quadrants in the cul-de-sac. They also found small areas of endometriosis on the left side of the abdomen; these were attached to the sigmoid, the abdominal wall, the bowels, and the uterus. In the cul-de-sac, they found a tremendous endometriotic mass, approximately the size of a hand and half-an-inch or more thick. The physicians freed all of these masses and attempted to take a sample for laboratory analysis to check for possible malignancy. As they took a small sample, profuse bleeding ensued. It was necessary to act quickly to prevent further hemorrhaging. The physicians felt it was inadvisable to clamp or put a tie on the endometriosis, because the tie would cut through it. Instead, they packed the bleeding area enough to apply a suture and put a tie in that position, which immediately stopped the bleeding.

The patient received treatments for small bowel obstruction during the next few weeks. Then a different physician operated on her. During the operation, this physician discovered that the patient's right ureter had become involved with a chromic catgut suture and was blocked. This had caused a leakage of urine from that ureter, and the leakage had formed a large cystic mass containing urine. The physician removed the cyst and repaired the ureter.

The patient sued the original physicians, alleging that it is not standard practice to suture the ureter in such operations and that the physicians were therefore negligent. The physicians offered expert testimony that the existence of the mass of endometriosis, particularly in an area where previous surgery had been performed, could displace organs or structures such as the ureter from their normal positions; also, where structures are obscured by bleeding, it would constitute unsound medical practice to dissect the mass further (in order to identify hidden structures) because additional bleeding would occur. Testimony offered by the patient established that the ureter was not the subject of operations undergone by the patient and that it was therefore not standard practice to suture the ureter. The court determined that the issue to be resolved was "whether the action of the [physicians], confronted with the endometriosis and hemorrhaging condition, obliterated landmarks, and [the] need for quick stopping of bleeding by placing stitches deep into the endometriosis [sic] mass, conformed to standards of good practice in the community." The court held that, because of the life-threatening situation that the bleeding presented and the fact that organs were thereby displaced and obscured from their normal positions, the conduct of the physicians did not constitute negligence. No liability was imposed (*Lince v. Monson*, 1961).[41]

§ 14.30 INFECTIONS OF THE PELVIS

Liability may be imposed on a physician for the negligent failure to diagnose, appropriately treat, and monitor an infection of the pelvis or for its negligent treatment resulting in sterility or some other permanent injury.

Basic Standard of Care: The American College of Obstetricians and Gynecologists has published the following guidelines for the diagnosis and treatment of the sexually transmitted diseases specified.

1. *Gonorrhea:* The diagnosis of gonorrhea can be established only by bacterial culture. Material to be cultured may be obtained from several sources, including endocervical, anorectal, pharyngeal, blood, or synovial fluid, depending on symptomatology. Gonorrhea may be asymptomatic, and routine culturing for *N. gonorrhea* has been advocated by some physicians. The low yield of positive cultures in practice has led to the belief that discretion in determining the indications for culture is allowed in asymptomatic women. Given the high probability of crossover infection with syphilis, current recommendations are that gonococcal culture should be done in all women with syphilis and that

screening for syphilis should be done prior to treating culture-proven gonorrhea. Recommendations for specific antibiotic therapy of gonorrhea may change depending on the sensitivities of individual strains. The best source for current guidelines is the veneral disease control division of the Centers for Disease Control.[42]

2. *Syphilis*: The diagnosis of syphilis is usually made by serologic testing. There is no satisfactory method for culturing *T. pallidum,* although the spirochete can occasionally be identified by dark field microscopic examination of material from primary or secondary lesions. The nonspecific or reagin tests (VDRL, RPR) are most frequently used for screening. The treponemal tests (FTA-ABS, MHA-TP), which are technically more difficult to perform are most often used to confirm the diagnosis in patients with positive reagin tests. Biologic false-positive tests may occur with either type of serologic testing. Serologic tests may be falsely negative very early in the disease. Special attention is given to assuring that pregnant women do not have or acquire syphilis during pregnancy. A reagin test should be performed at the first prenatal visit and again during the third trimester. A positive test mandates a repeat quantitative reagin test plus a specific treponemal test. Repeating both tests in four weeks is recommended if the treponemal test is negative. If the treponemal test is positive or if the titer rises in the reagin test, treatment is required. Penicillin remains the cornerstone of antibiotic therapy against syphilis. Recommendations for alternative drugs and specific doses may change. The best source for current guidelines is the venereal disease control division of the Centers for Disease Control.[43]

3. *Herpes*: The diagnosis of genital herpes infection is made by recovery of herpesvirus in culture, although suspicion of the diagnosis may be very high if the characteristic lesions are present. There is no completely effective therapy avilable. The high mortality rate in infected newborns has led to the recommendations for elective cesarean section prior to, or within four hours of, rupture of the membranes.[44]

Interpretation and Customary Practice: The female reproductive organs can become infected by any number of pathogens, including gonococci and other anaerobes, streptococci, and staphylococci; they can affect the upper and lower genital tracts. These infections are often generally referred to as pelvic inflammatory disease, but a number of medical authorities have characterized the term as medical jargon that should be discarded in favor of more precise descriptions of the particular acute or chronic infection of the genital tract.[45]

These diseases include the sexually transmitted diseases gonorrhea, syphilis, and herpesvirus. Not all communicable diseases must be reported to the appropriate state agency, however (see § 5.43, Reporting Requirements).

The diagnosis of gonorrhea should be considered in any woman with a vaginal discharge or inflammation of Bartholin's gland. Patients who present with a history of sexual contact with a person in whom gonorrhea has been diagnosed are routinely treated, preferably after a culture has been made. Gonorrhea should also be considered in patients with an unexplained mass or tenderness of the adnexa. Prepubescent female patients who may be the victims of child abuse can also suffer from gonorrhea, and gonorrhea should not be excluded from a differential diagnosis of vulvovaginitis merely because the patient is "too young." Cultures should be obtained from patients in whom any other venereal disease has been diagnosed, such as syphilis, herpes simplex type II, or venereal warts. Gonorrhea is also a part of the differential diagnosis of bacteremia (especially if accompanied by skin lesions), bacterial arthritis, conjunctivitis, endocarditis, and meningitis.

Syphilis can produce many and diverse symptoms. That syphilis is included in the differential diagnosis of many symptom complexes and diseases is reflected in the medical saying that "he who knows syphilis, knows medicine" and the frequent reference to syphilis as "the great imitator." Syphilis may be diagnosed on the basis of the history and physical examination; diagnosis can be confirmed in suspicious cases and made in asymptomatic cases with the use of blood tests. Blood tests for syphilis are more sensitive than are cultures for gonorrhea, but the laboratory tests for syphilis are not completely reliable. There is a significant rate of false negatives, particularly in the first six weeks. Primary syphilis may cause a painless sore or ulcer (chancre). These are commonly found in the genital area or in or around the oral cavity, but chancres can occasionally appear at other sites on the skin. Secondary syphilis may be manifested by lymphadenopathy or a multitude of dermatologic manifestations. Tertiary syphilis results in damage to the central nervous system and to the cardiovascular system. Neonatal syphilis classically produces a number of distinctive physical signs and should be suspected in newborns with hepatosplenomegaly, jaundice, anemia, bone changes, or abnormalities of the eyes or central nervous system.[47]

Genital herpes infections are probably more prevalent than gonorrhea. According to the data reported in the National Disease and Therapeutic Index, the number of consultations for the condition increased from 29,560 in 1966 to 260,980 in 1979.[48] Genital herpes is a recurrent condition responsible for repeated episodes of pain and disability. Individual lesions appear after exposure to an infected sexual partner, and lesions progress through a characteristic sequence of changes. First the involved area itches and burns; small, red, raised papules then appear; these soon blister, rupture, and become infected; the lesions then become crusted and gradually heal. The blisters and the infected lesions are accompanied by intense pain and local swelling. The symptoms subside as the lesions heal. During the active stages of both initial and recurrent infections, virus can be cultured from the genital lesions. Between attacks, when the lesions have healed, the virus is present in the nerve roots that supply the vulva, but none can be recovered from the skin. Between 10 and 15 percent of women who have acute vulvar herpes also have cervical infections that produce no symptoms even though the virus is present. In addition to the pain and discomfort caused by the acute attack, herpesvirus infections have been implicated as a possible precursor of cervical and vulvar cancer. Of even more importance, infants born of mothers with active infections can contract the disease during delivery. At least 50 percent of those infected die of disseminated herpesvirus infection, and others suffer permanent eye and neurologic damage. Diagnosis is made by identifying the herpesvirus in cultures of material from the lesions and from the cervix. Typical cellular changes caused by the virus can be identified in Pap smears of the cervix and the lesions, but this method is less reliable than a culture.[49]

Some kinds of pelvic infection are easier to diagnose than others. In general, those that follow pregnancy are more readily detected, if only because the particular circumstances of the patient's labor, abortion, or delivery will suggest to her physician what complications to anticipate. For example, a serious case of endomyometritis usually follows poorly managed, excessively prolonged labor, and peritonitis is most likely to occur after septic abortion. A pelvic infection is much more difficult to diagnose when it does not follow closely upon pregnancy. It is not easily differentiated from appendicitis, ectopic pregnancy, or inflammatory bowel disease.[50] Consequently, if a plaintiff brings a lawsuit in which she claims that her physician negligently failed to diagnose her actual condition, she may have a hard time trying to establish the physician's deviation from the appropriate standard of care (see § 1.32, Standard of Care).

CASE ILLUSTRATION

On the night of August 10, a 29-year-old woman experiencing severe lower abdominal pains, vomiting, and diarrhea was hospitalized and examined in the emergency room. The physician on duty observed abdominal tenderness, especially in the right lower quadrant, extreme tenderness in the right adnexal area, and a creamy white vaginal discharge. He ordered blood tests, X rays, and cultures to be taken and diagnosed possible "pelvic inflammatory disease" ("PID"), appendicitis, or viral gastroenteritis. Then he contacted the patient's regular doctor, who prescribed Lomotil. The patient left the hospital and took the medication, but her symptoms did not subside. Several hours later, early in the morning of August 11, the patient checked into another hospital, where her regular physician examined her. She exhibited the same symptoms and had no fever. Her physician diagnosed probable "PID" and made a notation to rule out appendicitis, since he considered that a possibility. He prescribed Demerol for the pain and ordered another blood test for a white blood cell count. Later the same morning, the patient felt better and was not suffering from nausea; her physician directed that Demerol be given as needed and that penicillin be administered. On August 12, this physician received an X-ray report from the first hospital indicating a possible fecalith in the appendix, thus suggesting the possibility of appendicitis. He called in a surgeon for consultation. The surgeon found that the patient's cervix was tender when he manipulated it during rectal examination. He had difficulty evaluating her abdomen, however, and concluded that the patient still might have "PID."

During the period from August 11 to August 14, the patient's white blood cell count decreased from 18,900 to 11,700. On August 13, the patient developed nausea and vomiting, which her physician attributed to the changes he had ordered from liquid diet to light food and from injections to oral antibiotic therapy. He doubted bowel obstruction because this would be accompanied by a very distended, firm abdomen, which the patient did not have. Further, she was not experiencing pain consistent with a bowel obstruction and she was having bowel movements. The physician prescribed Tigan to relieve the nausea and vomiting. By August 16, the patient's condition had improved to the point where her physician could conduct a pelvic examination. Her pelvis was still tender, but there were no masses; there was some fullness on the right side, indicating salpingitis. That night and early the following morning, the patient experienced, and was treated for, additional vomiting. On the morning of August 17, the patient was much improved: she was no longer nauseated, her abdomen was soft, and she was without pain. Her physician agreed to discharge her from the hospital, despite the patient's tachycardia and recent episode of vomiting. He prescribed penicillin tablets and told the patient to notify him if her condition worsened and also to report back to his office after a specified time for follow-up examinations and tests.

The patient's pain returned about a week later. She was again hospitalized, and possible "PID" or appendicitis was diagnosed by another team of doctors. Exploratory surgery, performed on August 28, revealed acute appendicitis, marked distension of the small bowel, fecal leakage from a defect in the ileum, and, as a result, extensive contamination of the pelvic area. The necessary corrective surgery proceeded by stages and took ten weeks to complete. The patient was able to return to work in January, and she encountered no further problems.

When the patient-plaintiff sued her physician for malpractice, her expert witness testified that the standard of care at the time of hospitalization was to develop a differential diagnosis of the symptoms and findings that are presented. From the symptoms the plaintiff was exhibiting, the expert witness thought the differential diagnosis would include appendicitis, "pelvic inflammatory disease," disease of the ovary, viral infection of the bowel, and urinary tract infection. He testified that he could not fault the defendant for arriving at a working diagnosis of "PID." On cross-examination, he acknowledged that "pelvic inflammatory disease" can result in an abscess that will surround the appendix and bowel and cause the type of problems the plaintiff had. The district court directed a verdict for the defendant on the negligent diagnosis count, and the Nebraska Supreme Court affirmed, noting that every other physician who made a diagnosis before the surgery made substantially the same diagnosis. The supreme court, however, went on to hold that there was sufficient evidence to allow the jury to determine whether the physician-defendant had negligently and prematurely discharged the patient from the hospital. The district court had directed a verdict for the physician on this issue as well, but the supreme court reversed and ordered that a new trial be held to consider the issue (*Anderson v. Moore*, 1979).[51]

Despite the difficulty of differentiating infections of the pelvis from the conditions they resemble, pelvic infection should always be part of the differential diagnosis of acute lower abdominal pain. It is particularly likely in patients with a history of exposure to multiple sexual partners, patients with a history of prior episodes of venereal disease or salpingo-oophoritis, patients with a history of abortions and patients who use or have used IUDs.

Where gonorrhea is suspected, whether in conjunction with other pathologic organisms or not, an exact diagnosis can be made only by making a culture of gonococci. Making a plate culture—that is, putting material obtained from the patient on a medium in a Petri dish—immediately and putting the plate in a low-oxygen atmosphere maximizes the probability of obtaining a positive culture.[52] Although a physician will not necessarily be guilty of malpractice for using a direct smear or gram stain test for gonorrhea rather than a culture test,[53] a culture test should be used whenever possible. False negative cultures sometimes occur; the physician can guard against them and increase the accuracy of diagnosing gonorrhea to almost 100 percent by taking rectal, and in some instances oropharyngeal, samples as well. In addition to those symptoms that suggest the existence of pelvic infections generally, gonorrhea should be suspected in women with a purulent vaginal discharge, dysuria, or acute infection of Bartholin's gland. In any case, the physician should be certain that an accurate diagnosis has been made before telling the patient she has gonorrhea. Once the patient has been told, however, she should be advised that the infection is contagious and warned specifically of the possibility of transmitting the disease to others.[54]

Antibiotic treatment is indicated for acute pelvic infections. Antibiotic therapy that is begun within the first 24 hours after diagnosis can usually prevent serious damage to the fallopian tubes. Early medical treatment is particularly crucial for the eradication of gonorrhea. Fast-acting penicillin preparations should be used; slow-acting preparations, which release low levels of the drug over long periods of time, reduce the effectiveness of treatment and may contribute to the development of penicillin-resistant strains. In all cases, the patient's condition should be followed carefully. Pelvic infections are frequently mixed; if the antibiotic prescribed has not eliminated all of the organisms, another drug should be used. Normally, appropriate antibiotic therapy should bring acute pelvic infections under control.[55]

CASE ILLUSTRATION

In August 1972, a specialist in obstetrics and gynecology delivered the patient's child by cesarean section. On March 7, 1974, the patient complained to this physician of pain in the lower right side of her abdomen. The physician diagnosed an ovarian cyst and prescribed medication. A week later, he administered an injection to suppress the cyst. On March 22, the patient returned, still complaining of abdominal pain. The physician's examination confirmed that the cyst was still present, and he prescribed penicillin. By April 3, he concluded that the cyst had decreased in size, but he learned that the patient's menstrual period was several weeks overdue. The physician hospitalized the patient and performed a dilation and curettage, from which he learned that she had not ovulated and had not miscarried. In a postoperative examination performed on May 8, he felt no cysts in the patient's ovary, so he released her.

In June, the patient complained again that she had not menstruated, and her physician prescribed medication; this brought on menstruation. In September, the patient experienced pain in her left side but did not come in for examination. In December, she was examined prior to obtaining an IUD and was told to return in six months for her regular checkup. She did so, and the physician found no problems. On July 17, 1975, however, she came back, complaining of a pain in her lower right abdomen. The physician concluded that she had a tender right ovary, and he prescribed ampicillin. The patient returned on July 21; the symptoms had not abated. She had a fever and an elevated white blood cell count. The physician diagnosed appendicitis, as well as the tender right ovary, which he classified as the same thing he had treated in March 1974. He referred the patient to a general surgeon for treatment of the appendicitis, adding that, in his opinion, the patient's symptoms were not a result of any gynecological problems.

On July 24, when the surgeon operated for the appendicitis, he also noted an oozing surface on the right ovary, indicating a ruptured corpus luteum cyst, and he sutured the site of the oozing. At the same time, he examined the patient's reproductive organs and found no evidence of gynecological or ovarian disease. In early August, the patient was treated for an abscess of the surgical incision and was discharged. During the next five months, she experienced various chest and abdominal pains and substantial loss of weight. The surgeon had supervised her postoperative care, and, though he discussed gynecological problems with his associates, he did not consult the patient's gynecologist. The patient herself had not had any menstrual complaints or vaginal bleeding or discharge. In January 1976, though, she began to experience continued bleeding, and her other symptoms intensified. She consulted a new gynecologist, who first removed her IUD, later performed a D&C, and finally, on February 25, after diagnosing a prolapsed uterus, performed a total abdominal hysterectomy, removing her uterus, both fallopian tubes, and the ovaries.

The patient-plaintiff sued both her original gynecologist and the surgeon for malpractice. At trial, the second gynecologist, testifying as an expert witness for the plaintiff, described what he observed during the hysterectomy: the patient's uterus was deeply recessed, the fallopian tubes were grossly abnormal in size, the ovaries were enlarged and very cystic, and both the tubes and ovaries were stuck together and to the side wall of the pelvis. Although he "ventured a guess" that the condition had developed over a two-year period, he admitted that the patient may have had perfectly normal-looking tubes, ovaries, and organs during that time, even though they were causing her pain. Since she did not exhibit any signs or symptoms of gynecological disease, "no one had any jusitification to try to save anything that wasn't giving any problems."

The jury delivered a verdict in favor of the plaintiff's first gynecologist, and the Louisiana Court of Appeals affirmed, noting that no evidence suggested his treatment of the plaintiff in March 1974 was improper. He had testified that 15 percent of his patients each month complain of tender ovaries and that their condition almost always subsides with conservative treatment, as did the plaintiff's. Neither could the court find anything improper in the gynecologist's conduct in July 1975. He began conservative treatment with antibiotics, but when a serious situation with possible appendicitis presented itself four days later, he immediately referred the patient to the proper specialist. The court of appeals also reversed the jury verdict against the surgeon. The plaintiff's evidence, the court held, was insufficient to prove that the surgeon had negligently failed to discover the diseased organs during the July 1975 surgery or that he had negligently failed to seek gynecological consultation during the following period, when he was unable to explain the plaintiff's complaints of abdominal pain (*Baker v. Beebe,* 1979).[56]

Unlike the above case, most instances of acute salpingo-oophoritis will become quiescent without surgical intervention. Therefore, surgery is contraindicated for such infections.[57]

Sometimes the physician cannot differentiate between acute salpingo-oophoritis and conditions for which immediate surgery is essential—appendicitis, for example, or ectopic pregnancy. Often a decision about treatment must be made well before the results of a diagnostic culture are available. Furthermore, even when culture results are available they may not help to eliminate salpingo-oophoritis as a cause of the patient's symptoms: the absence of gonococci does not exclude the diagnosis, because the culture can be negative even in acute gonococcal infections. For all of these reasons, exclusion of pelvic infection may not be possible until surgery is performed. If only infected tubes are found, the abdomen should be closed without disturbing them more than is necessary to make a diagnosis.[58]

Antibiotics may still be prescribed after exploratory surgery has revealed acute pelvic infection, but once the condition has reached the chronic stage, characterized by severe pain, incapacitating dysmenorrhea, or abnormal bleeding, surgery is often necessary. An upper genital tract that has been damaged by gonorrhea is susceptible to exacerbations, and those can be caused by anaerobic streptococci and other organisms, as well as by gonococci. The pelvic structures are damaged further by each new attack, and at some point the patient begins to experience the symptoms continuously, even though the infection is inactive. Since most women who must be operated on are young, the physician should try to preserve ovarian function whenever possible.[59] Litigation has arisen when treatment rendered by the physician results in sterility.

CASE ILLUSTRATION

A 29-year-old woman had experienced acute pelvic infection at ages 17 and 22. She had had three episodes within the previous four months, during which time her condition had not responded to penicillin therapy. Her physician's presurgery diagnosis was recurrent "pelvic inflammatory disease," with appendicitis as a possibility. During the operation, the physician removed the patient's appendix and both fallopian tubes. In his surgical report, he indicated that he found the patient's appendix acutely inflamed and gangrenous and both fallopian tubes afflicted with chronic "pelvic inflammatory disease." He described the tubes as reddened, thickened, covered with adhesions, and filled with pus; the fimbriae of each tube were fused and attached to the ovaries.

The patient-plaintiff brought suit, alleging that the removal of her fallopian tubes had been unnecessary. An expert called by the plaintiff testified that the pathology reports showed that the lumina of the fallopian tubes were patent and lacked evidence of disease of the inner walls. Nevertheless, the jury returned a verdict for the physician-defendant. The plaintiff appealed on the basis of the "uncontroverted physical evidence rule," contending that the jury's verdict cannot stand because the defendant had not challenged the "physical evidence" (that is, the pathology reports)

§ 14.30   *Infections of the Pelvis*   551

introduced by the plaintiff. The Court of Appeals of Washington said this rule was inapplicable: the pathology report was not physical evidence, but merely an expression of the pathologist's opinion, which had been controverted by the clinician's opinion. The verdict was affirmed. The court of appeals also affirmed the jury's verdict that the defendant was not guilty of failing to obtain the patient-plaintiff's informed consent. At trial, the defendant testified that, prior to surgery, he told the patient that he might have to remove her fallopian tubes. The patient had even signed an "informed consent" form for an exploratory laparotomy and for procedures that the physician might consider necessary or advisable during the course of the operation. The court also held, in response to the patient-plaintiff's contention that she had not been informed of feasible alternative methods of treatment, that two of the alternatives she suggested—antibiotic treatment and aspiration of the pus—were alternative treatments for acute, not chronic, stages of the disease, and that the other two she suggested—X-ray tests and consultation with a gynecologist—were diagnostic alternatives, not alternative therapeutic procedures (*Thornton v. Annest,* 1978).[60]

Although it may be desirable to preserve ovarian function, a patient's symptoms are not always relieved by an incomplete operation, and further surgery may become necessary later. In general, a physician should not hesitate to perform hysterectomy and bilateral salpingo-oophorectomy if the damage from repeated pelvic infections is extensive, if there is already a disturbance in ovarian function, or if a more conservative operation has already been performed. Neither should the physician hesitate to perform these operations in patients in their late thirties or forties, regardless of the apparent extent of the damage. If the patient's pelvic infections have become so recurrent and so painful that her physician decides to operate, the surgery should be performed only when her symptoms have subsided from the acute level.[61]

CASE ILLUSTRATION

A physician performed a supracervical hysterectomy on a patient who had experienced recurrent pelvic infections. Following the operation, the patient developed a rectovaginal fistula and a drainage sinus at the lower part of the surgical incision. The abdominal incision was closed relatively soon thereafter, but fecal drainage from the patient's vagina persisted for two years, until surgically corrected by another physician. The patient-plaintiff sued the first physician for malpractice, alleging that his surgery caused the fistula. The patient-plaintiff's expert witness testified that surgery was inadvisable when the patient's pelvic infection was in an acute stage, which would be manifested by a white blood cell count of 20,000 to 25,000. On cross-examination, he stated that the laboratory at his hospital considered as a normal range—in which the surgery may proceed—a white blood cell count of from 5,000 to 10,000. He acknowledged that some laboratories use the outer limits of from 5,000 to 11,000 or 12,000. He agreed that the acute stage would be accompanied by a fever and severe pain. The defendant then testified that at the time he performed surgery on the plaintiff she did not have an acute infection. Her temperature was normal, and her white blood cell count was 10,900—within his hospital's normal limits of 7,000 to 11,000.

The jury returned a verdict for the defendant on the charge of negligence. Both the Illinois Appellate Court and Supreme Court affirmed this verdict, on the grounds that the patient-plaintiff's evidence did not establish a deviation from the standard of care. However, the supreme court over a strong dissenting opinion, reversed both the circuit and appellate courts and held that the evidence was sufficient to send the case back for a jury trial under a res ipsa loquitur instruction. Although it was not clear whether the plaintiff's expert witness meant to testify that fistula formation after hysterectomies is usually a result of negligence or occurs with equal likelihood despite the exercise of due care, the court argued that a reasonable person could conclude the former. If so, the expert's testimony would amount to evidence of something more than merely an unusual surgical result, and from that a jury could infer negligence under res ipsa loquitur. The court's decision was also influenced by evidence of the defendant's statement to the plaintiff's husband that he "went in a little too soon" (*Spidle v. Steward*, 1980).[62]

This case demonstrates that the physician should not be hasty in performing corrective surgery. Acute infections should be allowed to become quiescent and pelvic induration should be allowed to regress as completely as possible, even if it takes up to four to six months, as it sometimes does.[63]

NOTES

1. American College of Obstetricians and Gynecologists, Standards for Obstetric/Gynecologic Services 47–48 (5th ed. 1982).
2. Truan v. Smith, 578 S.W.2d 73 (Tenn. 1979).
3. Fitzmaurice v. Flynn, 167 Conn. 609, 356 A.2d 887 (1975); Wentling v. Jenny, 206 Neb. 335, 293 N.W.2d 76 (1980).
4. Holady & Assor, *Ten Thousand Consecutive Frozen Sections*, 61 Am. J. Clin. Pathol. 769–84 (1974).
5. Lauro v. Travelers Ins. Co., 261 So.2d 261 (La. App. 1972); *cert. denied*, 262 La. 188, 262 So.2d 787 (1972).
6. Hanks v. Ranson, Swan, & Burch, Ltd., 359 So.2d 1089 (La. App. 1978); *cert. denied*, 360 So.2d 1178 (La. 1978).
7. Variety Children's Hosp. v. Osle, 292 So.2d 382 (Fla. App. 1974).
8. Dries v. Gregor, 72 A.D.2d 231, 424 N.Y.S.2d 561 (1980).

9. Goetzman v. Wichern, 327 N.W.2d 742 (Iowa 1982).
10. J. del Regato & H. Spjut, Cancer 846–57 (1977).
11. *Id.* at 857.
12. Natanson v. Kline, 186 Kan. 393, 350 P.2d 1093 (1960); *rehearing denied*, 187 Kan. 186, 354 P.2d 670 (1960).
13. Patelczyk v. Olson, 95 Mich. App. 281, 289 N.W.2d 910 (1980).
14. Jamison v. Lindsay, 108 Cal. App. 3d 223, 166 Cal. Rptr. 443 (1980).
15. J. del Regato & H. Spjut, Cancer 734 (1977).
16. Davidson v. Shirley, 616 F.2d 224 (5th Cir. 1980).
17. Atkin, *Histological Cell Type and DNA Value in the Prognosis of Squamous Cell Cancer of Uterine Cervix*, 28 Brit. J. Cancer 322–31 (1973).
18. Richart, *The Patient with an Abnormal Pap Smear—Screening Techniques and Management*, 302 New Eng. J. Med. 332–34 (1980).
19. G. Papanicolaou, Atlas of Exfoliative Cytology 330 (1954).
20. Richart, *supra* note 18, at 332.
21. C. Haskell, ed., Cancer Treatment 480 (1980).
22. Truman v. Thomas, 27 Cal.3d 285, 165 Cal. Rptr. 308, 611 P.2d 902 (1980).
23. Lambert v. Michel, 364 So.2d 248 (La. App. 1978); *cert. denied*, 366 So.2d 917 (La. 1979).
24. Ray v. Wagner, 286 Minn. 354, 176 N.W.2d 101 (1970).
25. H. Kottmeier, ed., 16th Annual Report on the Results of Treatment of Carcinoma of the Uterus, Vagina, and Ovary 774 (1976).
26. C. Haskell, *supra* note 21, at 484–91.
27. Steele v. St. Paul Fire & Marine Ins. Co., 371 So.2d 843 (La. App. 1979); *cert. denied*, 374 So.2d 658 (La. 1979).
28. Peagram v. Sisco, 406 F. Supp. 776 (1976); *aff'd;* 547 F.2d 1172 (1976).
29. R. Benson, Current Obstetric & Gynecologic Diagnosis & Treatment 323 (2d ed. 1978).
30. R. Benson, Handbook of Obstetrics & Gynecology 580 (6th ed. 1977).
31. R. Willson & E. Carrington, Obstetrics and Gynecology 110 (6th ed. 1979).
32. Ranney, *Endomentriosis: Pathogenesis, Symptoms and Findings*, 23 Clin. Obstet. Gynecol. 865 (Sept. 1980).
33. R. Willson & E. Carrington, *supra* note 31, at 116.
34. R. Benson, *supra* note 29, at 328.
35. R. Willson & E. Carrington, *supra* note 31, at 116.
36. Kleinman v. Armour, 12 Ariz. App. 383, 470 P.2d 703 (1970); *see also* Carmichael v. Reitz, 17 Cal. App. 3d 958, 95 Cal. Rptr. 381 (1971).
37. R. Willson & E. Carrington, *supra* note 31 at 117.
38. R. Benson, *supra* note 29, at 330.
39. R. Willson & E. Carrington, *supra* note 31, at 118, 119.
40. Cable v. Cazayou, 351 So.2d 797 (La. App. 1977).
41. Lince v. Monson, 363 Mich. 135, 108 N.W.2d 845 (1961).
42. American College of Obstetricians and Gynecologists, Technical Bulletin No. 50 (June 1978).
43. *Id.*
44. American College of Obstetricians and Gynecologists, Technical Bulletin No. 51 (July 1978).
45. *See* R. Willson & Carrington, *supra* note 31, at 532–46.
46. R. Benson, *supra* note 29, at 302.
47. *Id.* at 303–6.
48. U.S. Dept of Health & Human Services, Public Health Service, Genital Herpes

Infection—United States, 1966–1979, Morbidity and Mortality Weekly Report 137–39 (1982).
49. Corey, *The Diagnosis and Treatment of Genital Herpes*, 248 J.A.M.A. 1041–49 (1982).
50. R. Willson & E. Carrington, *supra* note 31, at 533–35, 543.
51. Anderson v. Moore, 202 Neb. 452, 275 N.W.2d 842 (1979).
52. R. Willson & E. Carrington, *supra* note 31, at 540–41.
53. *See* Gentry v. Dept. of Prof. & Occupational Regulations, State Bd. of Med. Examiners, 293 So.2d 95 (Fla. App. 1974).
54. R. Willson & E. Carrington, *supra* note 31, at 540–41.
55. *Id.* at 541–44.
56. Baker v. Beebe, 367 So.2d 102 (La. App. 1979).
57. R. Willson & E. Carrington, *supra* note 31, at 543.
58. *Id.*; *compare* Cable v. Cazayou, *supra* note 40.
59. R. Willson & E. Carrington, *supra* note 31, at 543–44.
60. Thornton v. Annest, 19 Wash. App. 174, 574 P.2d 1199 (1978).
61. R. Willson & E. Carrington, *supra* note 31, at 544.
62. Spidle v. Steward, 402 N.E.2d 216 (Ill. 1980).
63. R. Willson & E. Carrington, *supra* note 31, at 544.

Appendix A

Invalid Release Form

TO MY PATIENTS

We have always tried to give you the very best medical care of which we are capable. We will continue to do the same. However, with all medical treatment there is the possibility of permanent disability to you ... or even death. We have no insurance. If you wish to receive injections or treatment under these circumstances, we will be willing to administer them. The above, if accepted, is an assumed risk and is therefore not a matter for litigation. If you don't understand this, consult your attorney before coming in.

DOCTOR-PATIENT CONTRACT

I understand that in seeking medical treatment from either John Doe, M.D. or Associates, who will hereinafter be referred to as "the Doctor," whether speaking of one or more of them, I am not required to use him as my doctor for myself or my family as there are many other doctors in Anytown, Michigan, as well qualified who practice medicine in the specialty of obstetrics and gynecology and that he is willing to refer me to them. As an example he has advised me that two of such doctors are Dr. _____ and Dr. _____ . I understand that if I waive any liability for his care of me or my family, I will help the Doctor keep down the expenses of his practice of medicine due to savings in avoiding malpractice insurance and malpractice lawsuits, the expenses of which would otherwise be passed on to me and his other patients in higher fees. I enter into this contract freely and voluntarily and I understand I am waiving my right to bring a claim against the Doctor for any negligent act or omission he may commit in his treatment of me or for any breach of the contractual obligation to me to render to me that standard of medical care which is rendered in this or similar communities. I understand that this contract applies to all of his medical care to me.

I specifically release the Doctor from any liability to me and I hereby release; discharge and acquit the Doctor from any and all claims for loss, damage or injury of any nature whatsoever to my person, my family, or estate resulting in any way from or in any fashion arising from, connected with or resulting from the Doctor's medical treatment of me or my family whether caused by malpractice or negligent acts of the doctor, his agents, or employees or servants or otherwise. This contract is clearly intended to protect the Doctor against his own negligence and I so understand it.

Further, I specifically release the Doctor from any liability to me and my family which I may claim resulting from a lack of consent or lack of informed consent on my part to the particular treatment he or his agents or employees may render to me or my family, including any effects of that treatment which the Doctor may or may not have discussed with me.

I voluntarily enter into this contract in order to induce the Doctor to render to me medical care at his most reasonable cost.

In witness whereof, I have signed this Contract this _____ day of _____ , 1976.

Witnesses:

_____   _____
                                                    (Patient)

_____   _____

Appendix B

Sample Complaint (Fact Pleading) and Sample Answer

STATE OF MICHIGAN

IN THE CIRCUIT COURT FOR THE COUNTY OF WAYNE

LINDA DINOIR, as Next Friend of
ROBERT DINOIR, a Minor,

        Plaintiff,

—vs—

GEORGE WHITE, D.O., MILL GENERAL
CLINIC, P.C., a Michigan professional
corporation, DONALD R. ROBERTS, D.O.,
GERALD M. MOTT, D.O., JOHN D. DAVID,
D.O., and METRO HOSPITAL, a Michigan
nonprofit corporation, Jointly and Severally,

        Defendants.

No. Case No. 80-143-402-NM

HON. MICHAEL RIGHT

COMPLAINT

NOW COME the above-named Plaintiffs, by and through their attorneys, CHARFOOS, CHRISTENSEN, GILBERT & ARCHER, P.C., and for their complaint against the named defendants state as follows:

1. That the Plaintiffs are residents of the City of Detroit, County of Wayne, and State of Michigan.

2. That the Plaintiff, Linda Dinoir, is the natural mother of Minor Plaintiff, Robert Dinoir.

3. That Linda Dinoir is the duly appointed Next Friend of Robert Dinoir, a minor, and brings this lawsuit in said representative capacity on behalf of said minor.

4. That Defendent Metro Hospital is a nonprofit Michigan corporation, doing business in the City of Detroit, County of Wayne, and State of Michigan; further, that at all times pertinent hereto said Defendant was doing business under the name and style of Metro Hospital.

5. That at all times appropriate to this litigation Defendant George White, D.O., was a licensed and practicing physician, holding himself out as a specialist in obstetrics and gynecology, doing business in the City of Detroit, County of Wayne, and State of Michigan.

6. That the Mill General Clinic, P.C., is a Michigan professional corporation doing business at offices located at 1000 East Jefferson and 700 Virginia Park, City of Detroit, County of Wayne, and State of Michigan.

7. That Gerald M. Mott, D.O., at all times appropriate to this litigation was a licensed and practicing osteopathic physician, specializing in obstetrics and gynecology, doing business in the City of Detroit, County of Wayne, and State of Michigan.

8. That at all times appropriate to this litigation Donald R. Roberts, D.O., was a licensed and practicing osteopathic physician, specializing in obstetrics and gynecology, doing business in the City of Detroit, County of Wayne, and State of Michigan.

9. That at all times appropriate to this litigation John D. David, D.O., was a licensed and practicing osteopathic physician, specializing in obstetrics and gynecology, doing business in the City of Detroit, County of Wayne, and State of Michigan.

10. That Defendants George White, D.O., Donald R. Roberts, D.O., and Gerald M. Mott, D.O., are the agents, employees, and/or servants of Mill General Clinic, P.C., operating through offices located at 1000 East Jefferson and 700 Virginia Park, City of Detroit, County of Wayne, and State of Michigan.

11. That at all times relevant to this lawsuit an arrangement existed between Defendants George White, D.O., Donald R. Roberts, D.O., Gerald M. Mott, D.O., John D. David, D.O., the Mill General Clinic, P.C., and Defendant Metro Hospital, the exact nature of said arrangement being unknown to Plaintiff, but which constituted an arrangement of pecuniary benefit to all parties to the arrangement.

12. That at all times appropriate to this litigation Defendants George White, D.O., Donald R. Roberts, D.O., Gerald M. Mott, D.O., and John D. David, D.O., were licensed and practicing physicians with privileges at Defendant Metro Hospital and that Defendant Hospital did permit said Defendants to practice medicine within that facility as its agents, employees, and/or servants with respect to persons looking to that facility for medical care and treatment.

13. That the amount in controversy in the within cause exceeds Ten Thousand Dollars ($10,000.00).

14. That at all times relevant to this lawsuit the Defendants jointly and severally owed to Plaintiff the duty to provide reasonably competent and proper medical care and assistance to Plaintiff regarding the delivery of the infant Robert Dinoir; and further, that the Plaintiff did look to and rely upon all Defendants to provide said care and assistance to the Minor Plaintiff during said delivery.

15. That on or about May 1974 Linda Dinoir began prenatal care for her first pregnancy at the offices of Defendant Mill General Clinic, P.C., hereinafter referred to as "Defendant Clinic."

16. That Linda Dinoir's estimated date of confinement was January 11, 1975.

17. That between May 1974 and January 1975 Linda Dinoir visited the East

Jefferson office and Virginia Park office of Defendant Clinic on a regular basis, where she received prenatal care from Defendant George White, D.O., and other physician associates of Defendant Clinic.

18. That on or about January 10, 1975, at approximately 11:15 p.m. Linda Dinoir was admitted to Defendant Hospital in early labor as a patient of Defendants Dr. Roberts and Dr. Mott.

19. That on admission Linda Dinoir was 3 centimeters dilated, and her abdomen was noted as astonishingly protuberant.

20. That at 4:00 a.m. January 11, 1975, Linda Dinoir was 4 centimeters dilated, and the fetal presenting part was not engaged.

21. That at 7:15 a.m. January 11, 1975, pelvimetry measurements were ordered, and the results of those measurements interpreted as adequate.

22. That at 8:30 a.m. January 11, 1975, Linda Dinoir was 6 centimeters dilated with no engagement of the fetal presenting part.

23. That between 9:00 a.m. and 12:15 p.m. January 11, 1975, Linda Dinoir was 7 to 8 centimeters dilated, with moderate to strong contractions approximately two minutes apart.

24. That between 9:00 a.m. and 12:15 p.m. January 11, 1975, the station of the Minor Plaintiff was at −3, with a vertex presentation.

25. That at 12:45 p.m. Minor Plaintiff was at a +1 station.

26. That Minor Plaintiff's mother was taken to the delivery room of Defendant Hospital at 1:00 p.m. January 11, 1975.

27. That Minor Plaintiff's mother was attended in the delivery room by Defendants Dr. David, Dr. Mott, and Dr. Roberts.

28. That the birth of Minor Plaintiff was delayed when severe shoulder dystocia was encountered during delivery.

29. That the delivery of Minor Plaintiff was accomplished via low-mid forceps at 1:55 p.m. January 11, 1975.

30. That Minor Plaintiff weighed 11 pounds, 3 ounces at birth.

31. That Minor Plaintiff's Apgar scores were 0 at one minute and 2 at five minutes.

32. That Minor Plaintiff was in cardiopulmonary arrest at the time of delivery and required resuscitation by massage, endotracheal intubation, and the administration of intracardiac adrenalin.

33. That Minor Plaintiff has since been diagnosed as suffering from right Erb's and Klumpke palsy, delayed motor development, and brain damage.

34. That Defendant George White, D.O., was negligent in the following particulars:
    (a) That a reasonable and prudent osteopathic physician would not have undertaken to render prenatal care to Linda Dinoir without adequate preparation to ensure that reasonably competent medical care and treatment would be available for the protection of the Minor Plaintiff at the time of labor and delivery.
        (i) That Defendant George White, D.O., did so, and his doing so was a deviation from the applicable standard of care.
    (b) That a reasonable and prudent osteopathic physician would have referred Linda Dinoir to a specialist in her last trimester when she began complaining of problems with her vision or taken other steps, measures, or tests to determine whether Mrs. Dinoir was diabetic.

(i) That Defendant George White, D.O., failed to do this, and his failure was a deviation from the applicable standard of care.
(c) That a reasonable and prudent, licensed and practicing osteopathic physician, having undertaken to render prenatal care to Linda Dinoir throughout her pregnancy, would have taken appropriate measures to ensure that due care and protection of the Minor Plaintiff would be afforded at the time of labor and delivery.
(i) That Defendant George White, D.O., failed to do this, and his failure was a deviation from the applicable standard of care.
(d) That a reasonable and prudent, licensed and practicing osteopathic physician, having undertaken to render prenatal care to Linda Dinoir, would have been present at the time of labor and delivery in order to adequately monitor the progress of her labor and delivery so as to avoid injury to the Minor Plaintiff.
(i) That Defendant George White, D.O., failed to do this, and his failure was a deviation from the applicable standard of care.

35. That Defendants John D. David, D.O., Gerald M. Mott, D.O., and Donald R. Roberts, D.O., were negligent in the following particulars:
(a) That reasonable and prudent, licensed and practicing osteopathic physicians attending the labor and delivery of Linda Dinoir would have adequately monitored her progress for signs and symptoms of dysfunctional labor.
(i) That these Defendants failed to do this, and their failure was a deviation from the applicable standard of care.
(b) That reasonable and prudent, licensed and practicing osteopathic physicians would have recognized that, notwithstanding 8 centimeters of dilation and moderate to strong contractions, the failure of the Minor Plaintiff's presenting part to descend from a -3 station for a considerable period of time was indicative of a probably obstructed labor, to wit: a large infant and severe shoulder dystocia.
(i) That these Defendants failed to do this, and their failure was a deviation from the applicable standard of care.
(c) That reasonable and prudent, licensed and practicing osteopathic physicians would have recognized that Linda Dinoir was primigravida and that the head of the baby was unengaged and that this is an indicator of cephalopelvic disproportion.
(i) That these Defendants failed to do this, and their failure was a deviation from the applicable standard of care.
(d) That reasonable and prudent, licensed and practicing osteopathic physicians would have sought appropriate consultation regarding the management of the probably obstructed labor before severe shoulder dystocia was encountered in the delivery room.
(i) That these Defendants failed to do this, and their failure was a deviation from the applicable standard of care.
(e) That reasonable and prudent, licensed and practicing osteopathic physicians would not have attempted to deliver Minor Plaintiff when the cervix was 8 centimeters dilated and the station $+1$ by the use of low-mid forceps in the presence of severe shoulder dystocia.

(i) That these Defendants did this, and their doing so was a deviation from the applicable standard of care.
(f) That reasonable and prudent, licensed and practicing osteopathic physicians would have recognized that Linda Dinoir's labor was progressing inadequately prior to 12:45 p.m., January 11, 1975, and would have performed a cesarean section on Linda Dinoir in order to avoid the injuries suffered by the Minor Plaintiff.
(i) That these Defendants failed to do this, and their failure was a deviation from the applicable standard of care.

36. That Defendant Metro Hospital was negligent in the following particulars:
   (a) That a reasonable and prudent, licensed and accredited hospital would have ensured that its obstetrics and gynecology department was staffed by reasonably competent and skillful physicians.
   (b) That a reasonable and prudent, licensed and accredited hospital would have established and enforced policies and procedures for its medical staff regarding the adequate monitoring of a patient's labor progress for signs and symptoms suggestive of dysfunctional labor, such as that encountered in the case of Linda Dinoir, so as to avoid injury to infants such as Minor Plaintiff, Robert Dinoir.
   (c) That a reasonable and prudent, licensed and accredited hospital would have followed a doctor's order (at 2:00 a.m.) indicating that fetal heart tones be taken by Dopptone every half hour so as to identify fetal distress promptly enough to respond.
   (d) That a reasonable and prudent, licensed and accredited hospital would have established and enforced policies and procedures regarding the management of cases of probable dysfunctional labor, such as that encountered in the case of Linda Dinoir, so as to avoid injury to persons such as Minor Plaintiff, Robert Dinoir.
       (i) That Defendant Hospital did none of these things as set forth in paragraphs 36(a)–(d) above, and its failure to do so was a deviation from the acceptable standard of care for a licensed and accredited hospital.

37. That Defendant Hospital and Defendant Physicians either severally or jointly modified certain portions of the records in a negligent fashion, and the effect of such negligence and/or fraud may tend to affect the Plaintiff's ability to make a fair and reasonable recovery.

38. That Defendant Hospital is responsible for the negligent acts of its agents, employees, and/or servants, including Defendant George White, D.O., Defendant Mill General Clinic, P.C., Defendant Donald R. Roberts, D.O., Defendant Gerald M. Mott, D.O., and Defendant John D. David, D.O.

39. That Defendant Clinic is responsible for the negligent acts of its agents, employees, and/or servants, including Defendants George White, D.O., Donald R. Roberts, D.O., and Gerald Mott, D.O.

40. That as a direct and proximate result of the aforementioned negligence of the Defendants, Minor Plaintiff, Robert Dinoir, has suffered the loss of the use of his right arm and suffered arrested motor development on his entire right side. He also suffered brain damage, which affects both his motor and intellectual skills. As a consequence of these injuries, which are permanent in nature, extensive hospital, medical, physical therapy, and prescription expenses have been incurred on behalf of Minor Plaintiff, and such

expenses are likely to continue indefinitely into the future. Furthermore, as a direct and proximate result of the aforementioned negligence of the Defendants, Minor Plaintiff Robert Dinoir has suffered substantial pain, anxiety, humiliation, loss of enjoyment of life, and loss of earning capacity, and these conditions are likely to persist indefinitely into the future.

WHEREFORE, Plaintiff Linda Dinoir, as Next Friend of Minor Plaintiff Robert Dinoir, prays that this Honorable Court enter a judgment in her favor against all Defendants that is just and reasonable and in accord with all the proofs to be presented herein, together with interests, costs, and attorney fees so wrongfully incurred.

> CHARFOOS, CHRISTENSEN,
> GILBERT & ARCHER, P.C.
> Attorneys for Plaintiff(s)
>
> BY:_____
> J. DOUGLAS PETERS (P 25686)
> Penobscot Building, 40th Floor
> Detroit, Michigan 48226
> Telephone: 313/963-8080

DATED: March 7, 1981

DEMAND FOR JURY TRIAL

NOW COME the Plaintiffs, by and through their Attorneys, CHARFOOS, CHRISTENSEN, GILBERT & ARCHER, P.C., and hereby make a demand for a trial by jury of the issues in this cause.

> CHARFOOS, CHRISTENSEN,
> GILBERT & ARCHER, P.C.
> Attorneys for Plaintiff(s)
>
> BY:_____
> J. DOUGLAS PETERS (P 25686)
> Penobscot Building, 40th Floor
> Detroit, Michigan 48226
> Telephone: 313/963-8080

DATED: March 7, 1981

Appendix B

STATE OF MICHIGAN

IN THE CIRCUIT COURT FOR THE COUNTY OF WAYNE

LINDA DINOIR, as Next Friend of
ROBERT DINOIR, a Minor,

    Plaintiff,

—vs—

GEORGE WHITE, D.O., MILL GENERAL
CLINIC, P.C., a Michigan professional
corporation, DONALD R. ROBERTS, D.O.,
GERALD M. MOTT, D.O., JOHN D. DAVID,
D.O., and METRO HOSPITAL, a Michigan
nonprofit corporation, Jointly and Severally,

    Defendants.

No. Case No. 80-143-402-NM

HON. MICHAEL RIGHT

ANSWER OF DEFENDANTS, GEORGE WHITE, D.O., MILL GENERAL CLINIC, P.C., DONALD R. ROBERTS, D.O., AND GERALD M. MOTT, D.O., ONLY TO PLAINTIFF'S COMPLAINT

NOW COME the Defendants, GEORGE WHITE, D.O., MILL GENERAL CLINIC, P.C., DONALD R. ROBERTS, D.O., and GERALD M. MOTT, D.O., only by and through their Attorneys, JONES & FRANK, P.C., answer the Plaintiff's Complaint as follows:

    1. In answer to Paragraph 1 of Plaintiff's Complaint, these Defendants plead no contest.

    2. In answer to Paragraph 2 of Plaintiff's Complaint, these Defendants plead no contest.

    3. In answer to Paragraph 3 of Plaintiff's Complaint, these Defendants neither admit nor deny the allegations contained therein for lack of sufficient knowledge thereof and leaves Plaintiff to his strict proofs.

Appendix B

4. In answer to Paragraph 4 of Plaintiff's Complaint, these Defendants neither admit nor deny the allegations contained therein for the reason that they do not pertain to these Defendants.

5. In answer to Paragraph 5 of Plaintiff's Complaint, these Defendants admit that Dr. White is a duly licensed osteopathic physician, but the remaining allegations pertaining to a holding out and a specialty designation are denied as untrue in the manner and form alleged.

6. In answer to Paragraph 6 of Plaintiff's Complaint, these Defendants admit the allegations contained therein.

7. In answer to Paragraph 7 of Plaintiff's Complaint, these defendants admit that Dr. Mott is a duly licensed osteopathic physician, but the remaining allegations pertaining to a specialty are denied as untrue in the manner and form alleged.

8. In answer to Paragraph 8 of Plaintiff's Complaint, these Defendants admit that Dr. Roberts is a licensed osteopathic physician, but the remaining allegations pertaining to a specialty are denied as untrue in the manner and form alleged.

9. In answer to Paragraph 9 of Plaintiff's Complaint, these Defendants admit that Dr. David is understood to be a specialist in obstetrics and gynecology, but the remaining allegations are neither admitted nor denied in the manner and form alleged, inasmuch as they do not pertain to these Defendants.

10. In answer to Paragraph 10 of Plaintiff's Complaint, these Defendants admit that they are each individually associated with the Mill General Clinic, P.C., and that the professional corporation has offices at various different locations including those set forth in Paragraph 10. The remaining allegations pertaining to agency and employment are neither admitted nor denied in the manner and form alleged, and Plaintiff is left to his strict proofs thereof.

11. In answer to Paragraph 11 of Plaintiff's Complaint, these Defendants admit that Drs. White, Roberts and Mott have staff privileges at Metro Hospital, but any relationship over and above that implied by such staff membership can neither be admitted nor denied at the present, inasmuch as these Defendants lack knowledge as to precisely what "arrangement" is being referred to in Paragraph 11. Further, Drs. Roberts, White and Mott do charge fees for services they render, whether in the Clinic or at a hospital in which they have staff privileges. As to the remaining allegations pertaining to agency and employment, these are denied as untrue.

12. In answer to Paragraph 12 of Plaintiff's Complaint, these Defendants deny that the Plaintiff is entitled to recover any sum of money whatsoever.

13. In answer to Paragraph 13 of Plaintiff's Complaint, these Defendants admit that, to the extent a physician-patient relationship was created at any given time, the law imposed a duty to comply with the standards of practice, but it is denied that at all times relative herein such a physician-patient relationship was created. Any remaining allegations are denied as untrue in the manner and form alleged.

14. These Defendants admit that the Mill General Clinic records reflect that the patient was first seen in July of 1974, at which time a diagnosis of pregnancy was made as to Plaintiff, Linda Dinoir. Any allegations contained to the contrary are denied as untrue.

15. These Defendants admit that the Mill General Clinic records reflect a EDC of 1-11-75.

16. In answer to Paragraph 16 of Plaintiff's Complaint, these Defendants admit

that their records reflect that the patient, Linda Dinoir, was seen on various occasions prenatally by physicians associated with the Mill General Clinic. Any remaining allegations contained therein are denied in the manner and form alleged.

17. In answer to Paragraph 17 of Plaintiff's Complaint, these Defendants admit that the Metro Hospital records reflect that the patient, Linda Dinoir, was admitted to the hospital on the date therein specified, but the remaining allegations are denied as untrue in the manner and form alleged.

18. In answer to Paragraph 18 of Plaintiff's Complaint, these Defendants admit that there is a reference in the Metro Hospital records to a protuberance of the patient's abdomen, and it is also admitted that the records reflect that the first notation of dilation in the labor records refers to 3 centimeters. The remaining allegations are neither admitted nor denied in the manner and form alleged, and Plaintiff is left to her strict proofs thereof.

19. In answer to Paragraph 19 of Plaintiff's Complaint, these Defendants state that based on the labor record at Metro Hospital, these Defendants deny the allegations contained therein as untrue in the manner and form alleged.

20. In answer to Paragraph 20 of Plaintiff's Complaint, these Defendants admit that the labor record at Metro, as well as the radiology reports, reflects that allegations contained therein are correct.

21. In answer to Paragraph 21 of Plaintiff's Complaint, these Defendants admit that notations contained in the labor record at Metro Hospital are consistent with the allegations contained therein.

22. In answer to Paragraph 22 of Plaintiff's Complaint, these Defendants deny that the allegations contained therein accurately depict all of the notations set forth in the Metro Labor record, and therefore said allegations cannot be admitted.

23. In answer to Paragraph 23 of Plaintiff's Complaint, these Defendants admit that the Metro Hospital labor record reflects a notation of -3 station during the time periods referred to therein and that there is also notation of cephalic presentation. Any allegations contained therein to the contrary are denied as untrue in the manner and form alleged.

24. In answer to Paragraph 24 of Plaintiff's Complaint, these Defendants can neither admit nor deny the allegations contained therein inasmuch as the notation of station on the copy of Metro Hospital records supplied to them cannot be sufficiently deciphered to determine the truth or accuracy of the allegation contained therein.

25. In answer to Paragraph 25 of Plaintiff's Complaint, these Defendants admit that the Metro Hospital records reflect that anesthesia was started in the delivery room at approximately 1:00 p.m. on the date therein specified.

26. In answer to Paragraph 26 of Plaintiff's Complaint, these Defendants admit that Dr. Mott is listed as an obstetrician during said delivery: the allegations pertaining to Dr. Roberts are denied as untrue. As for Dr. David, same is neither admitted nor denied, inasmuch as these allegations do not pertain to these Defendants.

27. In answer to Paragraph 27 of Plaintiff's Complaint, these Defendants admit that severe shoulder dystocia was encountered during delivery and that this hampered completion, but the remaining allegations are neither admitted nor denied in the manner and form alleged, and Plaintiff is left to her strict proofs thereof.

28. In answer to Paragraph 28 of Plaintiff's Complaint, these Defendants admit that the Metro Hospital records reflect an approximate delivery time of 1:55 p.m. and the use of low-mid forceps.

Appendix B

29. In answer to Paragraph 29 of Plaintiff's Complaint, these Defendants admit that the Metro Hospital records reflect a birth weight of approximately 11 pounds 3 ounces.

30. In answer to Paragraph 30 of Plaintiff's Complaint, these Defendants admit that the Metro records do reflect at one point Apgar scores as alleged therein.

31. In answer to Paragraph 31 of Plaintiff's Complaint, these Defendants admit that the child's condition required resuscitation and that the methods and implements used were accurately set forth in the records. Any allegations contained therein to the contrary are denied as untrue in the manner and form alleged.

32. In answer to Paragraph 32 of Plaintiff's Complaint, these Defendants admit that their records reflect a reference to Erbs palsy, but the remaining allegations are denied as untrue in the manner and form alleged.

33. In answer to Paragraph 33, subparagraphs (a)–(c) of Plaintiff's Complaint, these Defendants deny the allegations contained therein as untrue.

34. In answer to Paragraph 34, subparagraphs (a)–(e) of Plaintiff's Complaint, these Defendants deny the allegations contained therein as untrue.

35. In answer to Paragraph 35 of Plaintiff's Complaint, these Defendants neither admit nor deny the allegations contained therein as they do not pertain to these Defendants. To the extent any of the allegations contained therein are meant to imply wrongdoing on the part of the Defendants, same are denied as untrue.

36. In answer to Paragraph 36 of Plaintiff's Complaint, these Defendants deny the agency and employment relationship referred to therein as untrue and further deny the implications of wrongdoing as untrue.

37. In answer to Paragraph 37 of Plaintiff's Complaint, these Defendants admit the principle of respondeat superior, but the implication of negligence is denied inasmuch as that allegation is untrue.

38. In answer to Paragraph 38 of Plaintiff's Complaint, these Defendants deny the allegations contained therein as untrue.

WHEREFORE, the Defendants request that this Honorable Court enter a dismissal as to them, Mill General Clinic, P.C., George White, D.O., Donald R. Roberts, D.O., and Gerald M. Mott, D.O., only and further, grant to these defendants costs and attorney fees so wrongfully sustained in defense of this matter.

JONES & FRANK, P.C.

By:_____
DAVID WALLIS (P14902)
Attorneys for Defendants Mill General,
White, Roberts, and Mott
0000 Buhl Building
Detroit, Michigan 48226
963-8000

Dated: March 20, 1981

FURTHER ANSWER

NOW COME the Defendants, GEORGE WHITE, D.O., MILL GENERAL CLINIC, P.C., DONALD R. ROBERTS, D.O., and GERALD M. MOTT, D.O., only, by, and through their Attorneys, JONES & FRANK, P.C., and in further answer to Plaintiff's Complaint state as follows:

1. Further answering Plaintiff's Complaint and each and every section, this Defendant, Mill General Clinic, avers that it was guided by and strictly observed all of its legal duties and obligations imposed by operation of law and otherwise, and that all of the actions of its agents, servants, and employees were careful, prudent, proper, and lawful.

2. Further answering Plaintiff's Complaint and each and every section, these Defendants aver that in their professional relationship with Plaintiff, they were guided by and strictly observed all of their legal duties and obligations imposed by operation of law and otherwise, and that all of their actions were careful, prudent, proper, lawful, and in strict accordance with the standard of practice of their profession as same existed at that time and place in relation to any professional services rendered by them to the Plaintiff.

3. Further answering said Complaint and each and every section, these Defendants aver that the Plaintiff's Complaint on its face is improper in form and not in accordance with the rules set forth in GCR 1963; that it is inadequate, insufficient, and defective in that it pleads only conclusions; that it fails to contain the required allegations necessary to state a cause of action against this Defendant; and that it does not state a cause of action, either as a matter of fact or as a matter of law and accordingly should be stricken. These Defendants give notice that a Motion for Summary Judgment will be brought on for hearing at the time of the final pretrial of this case, before the Judge of this Court duly assigned to conduct such final pretrial hearing, and to be heard and determined by him, or in his discretion and at his direction by him, to be heard and determined at the time of trial in this case, by such Judge of this Court as to whom this case shall be regularly assigned for trial.

JONES & FRANK, P.C.

By:_____
DAVID WALLIS (P14902)
Attorneys for Defendants Mill General
White, Roberts, and Mott
0000 Buhl Building
Detroit, Michigan 48226
963-8000

Dated: March 20, 1981

RELIANCE UPON JURY DEMAND OF PLAINTIFF

NOW COME the above-named Defendants, GEORGE WHITE, D.O., MILL GENERAL CLINIC, P.C., DONALD R. ROBERTS, D.O., and GERALD M. MOTT, D.O., by and through their Attorneys, JONES & FRANK, P.C., and state that they rely upon the fact that the Plaintiff has filed with this Court a Complaint and Jury Demand and that it is assumed that if said Complaint and Jury Demand were served upon the Defendants, same has in fact been filed with the Court with the appropriate fee paid.

JONES & FRANK, P.C.

By:_____
DAVID WALLIS (P14902)
Attorneys for Defendants Mill General
White, Roberts, and Mott
0000 Buhl Building
Detroit, Michigan 48226
963-8000

Dated: March 20, 1981

Appendix C

1983 Joint Commission Utilization Review Requirements

PRINCIPLE

The hospital shall provide for the appropriate allocation of its resources.

Standard I

The hospital shall demonstrate appropriate allocation of its resources through an effective utilization review program.

Interpretation: The utilization review program shall endeavor to assure appropriate allocation of the hospital's resources in striving to provide high-quality patient care in the most cost-effective manner. The utilization review program shall address overutilization, underutilization, and inefficient scheduling of resources.

The hospital shall implement a written plan that describes the utilization review program and governs its operations. The utilization review plan shall be approved by the medical staff, administration, and governing body. The plan shall include at least the following:

- a delineation of the responsibilities and authority of those involved in the performance of utilization review activities, including members of the medical staff, any utilization review committee(s), nonphysician health care professionals, administrative personnel, and, when applicable, any qualified outside organization contracting to perform review activities specified in the plan;
- a conflict-of-interest policy applicable to all involved in utilization review activities;
- a confidentiality policy applicable to all utilization review activities, including any findings and recommendations;
- a description of the method(s) for identifying utilization-related problems, including the appropriateness and medical necessity of admissions, continued stays, and supportive services, as well as delays in the provision of supportive services;
- the procedures for conducting concurrent review, including the time period within which the review is to be initiated following admission and the length-of-stay norms and percentiles to be used in assigning continued stay review dates;
- a mechanism for provision of discharge planning.

To identify utilization problems, the hospital should examine the findings of related quality assurance activities (refer also to the Quality Assurance section of this *Manual*) and other relevant documentation. These may include profile analysis; the results of patient care evaluation studies; the results of surgical case review, antibiotic usage review, blood utilization review, and infection control activities; and reimbursement agency utilization reports that are hospital-specific. To identify problems and document the impact of corrective actions taken, retrospective monitoring of the hospital's utilization of resources shall be ongoing.

Concurrent review shall be focused on those diagnoses, problems, procedures, and/or practitioners with identified or suspected utilization-related problems. The source of payment shall not be the sole determinant in identifying patients for concurrent review. Written measurable criteria and length-of-stay norms that have been approved by the medical staff shall be utilized in performing concurrent review and shall be included in, or appended to, the hospital's utilization review plan. Length-of-stay norms must be specific to diagnoses, problems, and/or procedures. Nonphysician health care professionals may participate in the development of review criteria, particularly as the criteria relate to services they provide.

To facilitate discharge as soon as an acute level of care is no longer required, discharge planning shall be initiated as early as a determination of the need for such activity can be made. Criteria for initiating discharge planning may be developed to identify patients whose diagnoses, problems, or psychosocial circumstances usually require discharge planning. The utilization review plan may specify the situations in which nonphysician health care professionals may initiate preparations for discharge planning. Discharge planning shall not be limited to placement in long term care facilities, but shall include provision for, or referral to, services that may be required to improve or maintain the patient's health status.

The hospital's utilization review program, including the written plan, criteria, and length-of-stay norms, shall be reviewed and evaluated at least annually, and revised as appropriate to reflect the findings of the hospital's utilization review activities. A record shall be maintained of such reviews and evaluations, and appropriate findings shall be reported, through the established mechanisms, to the executive committee of the medical staff and to the governing body.

Appendix D

Sample Obstetrics/Gynecology Department Protocol

CONSTITUTION AND BY-LAWS
GENERAL HOSPITAL

DEPARTMENT
OF
OBSTETRICS AND GYNECOLOGY

ARTICLE I
NAME

The name of this organization shall be: "Department of Obstetrics and Gynecology of General Hospital."

ARTICLE II
PURPOSE

The physicians whose practices include the practice of Obstetrics and Gynecology in the General Hospital hereby organize themselves in conformity with these By-Laws for the purpose of:

1. Insuring that all Obstetrical and Gynecological patients admitted to the hospital or treated in the Outpatient Department receive the best possible care.
2. Providing an educational program and maintaining educational standards.
3. Establishing a set of minimum requirements as to the professional qualifications of the Obstetrical and Gynecological Staff, and regulations for the conduct of the Department.

ARTICLE III
MEMBERSHIP

Section 1:

A. Membership in this Department shall be confined to those members of the hospital staff whose practices include the practice of Obstetrics and Gynecology composed of active and affiliate members.

Appendix D

      1. Active: Those members who specify a desire to be active members and wish voting privileges.
      2. Affiliate: Members not desiring voting privileges.
  B. Application for membership or advancement in the Department shall be made in writing to the Chairman of the Department of Obstetrics and Gynecology. Approval for membership or advancement shall be finally determined by a majority vote of the active membership following suitable recommendation by the evaluating committee.
  C. New members of the Department shall be supervised on all deliveries by the evaluating committee until such time as the committee feels that they can properly classify the individuals.
  D. New members having completed Internship at Lansing General Hospital shall receive Class III privileges upon approval of the Department without supervision.

Section 2: Officers

The officers shall be:

  A. The Chairman's name shall be selected annually by the active members of the Obstetrical Department and passed by the Executive Committee.
  B. The Secretary shall be appointed by the Chairman of the Department.
  C. The Vice-Chairman, who shall be appointed by the Chairman of the Department, if the Department reaches such size that this position seems warranted.

Section 3: Duties

  A. The Chairman of the Department shall call and preside at all meetings; shall be a member, ex-officio, of all committees and shall have general supervision over all the professional work in the Department. He shall further perform all other duties usually pertaining to this office. He is directly responsible to the Chief of Staff of the Hospital.
  B. The Vice-Chairman, in the absence of the Chairman, shall assume all his duties and have all his authority; he shall also be expected to perform such duties of supervision as may be assigned to him by the Chairman.
  C. The Secretary shall keep accurate and complete records of the proceedings of all meetings, shall be custodian of all its records and shall issue all duly authorized notices of meetings. The Secretary shall maintain a record of the attendance of all regular meetings. He shall perform all other duties as ordinarily pertain to this office.

ARTICLE IV
MEETINGS

Section 1: Regular Meetings

Regular meetings shall be held at a place selected by the Chairman of the Department, who shall give due notice of the place selected. Regular meetings shall be held on the third Tuesday in the month at 12:30 PM.

Section 2: Special Meetings
Special meetings may be called by the Chairman of the Department, or in his absence, by the Vice-Chairman, or upon written call signed by one-third of the active membership.

Section 3: Quorum
A quorum for the transaction of business at any regular or special meeting of the Department shall consist of two-thirds of the active membership.

Section 4: Purpose of Meetings
Meetings shall be devoted to the consideration of all Obstetrical and Gynecological complicated cases in the hospital, and all deaths since the previous meeting shall be discussed in detail, and ante- and post-mortem findings compared.

Section 5: Attendance
Active members must attend not less than two-thirds of the scheduled meetings to maintain active status.

ARTICLE V
COMMITTEES

A. Committees shall be appointed from time to time as may be required to carry out properly the duties of the Department. Such committees shall confine their work to the purpose for which they were appointed. These committees shall not have power of action unless such is specifically granted by the motion which created the committee.

B. An evaluating committee shall be appointed by the Chairman of the Department consisting of active members: two holding classification 5 or 6 and two holding classification 4. This committee will receive and review all complaints against members of the Department. The committee will have the power to go over charts of cases involved and will have authority to make recommendations on any infraction of the rules of the Department. This committee shall be empowered to place or remove restrictions on the physician involved.

The evaluating committee will receive and act on all applications for membership and advancement from one group to the next higher group. It shall also be the duty of this committee to grade doctors applying for advancement from one group to another.

ARTICLE VI
CLASSIFICATION OF MEMBERS

Section 1: Privileges

A. Obstetrical privileges shall be as follows:
1. Spontaneous delivery, episiotomy, and outlet forceps on a multiparous patient.

2. Privileges of category one plus outlet forceps on a primigravida.
3. Privileges of categories one and two plus application of low forceps and manual rotations in multiparous patient.
4. Privileges of categories one, two, and three plus multiparous breech deliveries and forceps rotation of a multiparous patient.
5. Privileges of categories one, two, three, and four plus: primipara breech, version and extraction, forceps rotation of a primipara, repair of third-degree laceration or extensions of episiotomies, manual removal of placenta. The only limitation is Cesarean Section.
6. Unlimited privileges, including Cesarean Section.
7. This category is added to the committee's classification due to the fact that many sections will be done by men qualified only in Surgery and not necessarily fitting in Group six. These men are allowed Cesarean Section privileges and surgical repair of lacerations. Cesarean Section privileges are granted to general surgeons. Other obstetrical privileges for these members shall be separately classified.

B. Gynecological privileges shall be outlined as follows:
1. Management of medical gynecological cases.
2. Privileges of category one plus minor gynecological surgery.
3. Privileges of categories one and two plus major gynecological surgery.

Section 2: Consultants

Categories five and six shall be the only groups considered for obstetrical consultants.

Section 3: Advancement

Any member capable of doing a procedure and so checked out in that procedure in the next directly higher classification shall be allowed to carry out said procedure without first completing the full requirements of that classification. He shall not, however, be so classified in the next classification until all the requirements are fulfilled. (Thus in cases of four to five, he shall not be eligible for consulting privileges until all the requirements of five are completed and he has achieved this classification.)

(Explanatory Note) No member shall be denied the right to practice obstetrics as he has been practicing in the past. If he is capable of doing procedures which this change in classification denies him, he is within his rights to so request these privileges and if he has been doing them under his previous classification, they should be granted.

ARTICLE VII
RULES AND REGULATIONS

The Department shall adopt such rules and regulations as may be necessary for the proper conduct of its work.

ARTICLE VIII
AMENDMENTS

Amendments to this Constitution and By-Laws may be adopted according to Robert's Rules of Order. For the purpose of amending this Constitution and By-Laws, a quorum

Appendix D

shall consist of two-thirds of the voting membership. Final approval is dependent upon action by the Board of Trustees of General Hospital.

RULES AND REGULATIONS
GENERAL HOSPITAL

DEPARTMENT
OF
OBSTETRICS AND GYNECOLOGY

1. Each individual practicing obstetrics in General Hospital is to have supervision on all deliveries until such time as he can be properly classified by the Evaluating Committee of the Department upon recommendation by a senior Department member.
2. Consultants in the Department of Obstetrics are those men holding the privileges in Classification five or six as described in the Constitution and are herewith referred to as "Senior O. B. Men" (sic).
3. Consultation by a Senior O. B. Man is advised in the following conditions unless otherwise specified:
    A. Patients in labor longer than 24 hours.
    B. Patients in a state of arrested progress in labor for six hours.
    C. Ante-partum or post-partum hermorrhage.
    D. Induction of labor.
    E. Therapeutic interruption of pregnancy which is contemplated due to one of the following indications:
        1. Decompensated heart disease.
        2. The psychoses.
        3. Uterine neoplasms.
        4. Defective germ plasm resulting in repeated pregnancies with the delivery of monstrosities.
        5. Malignant hypertension.
        6. Severe renal insufficiency.
        7. Any metabolic disturbance sufficiently severe to cause damage to the mother, incompatible with life.
    F. Ligation of Fallopian Tubes:
       This operation may be considered only upon agreement of the Sterilization Committee or if the individual has had three or more Cesarean Sections.
    G. Cesarean Section:
       Indications for Cesarean Sections may be:
        1. Contracted pelvis.
        2. Cephalopelvic disproportion.
        3. Malposition of fetus, i.e. transverse lie breech in elderly primigravida, breech in females with borderline or inadequate pelvic diameters.
        4. Placenta previa.
        5. Abruptio placentae.
        6. Toxemias—pre-eclampsia of fulminating type, controlled eclampsia.
        7. Diabetes.

8. Structural incompatibilities, i.e. bilateral dislocation of hips, fixation of hip joints due to arthritis, etc., preventing abduction of femur in hip.
9. Mechanical obstruction of birth canal, i.e. ovarian tumors, vaginal deformities, bicornuate uterus, etc.
10. Prolapsed cord with un-dilatable cervix.
11. Uterine inertia.
12. Previous Cesarean Sections.
13. Cervical malignancy.
14. Certain selected cases of Rh sensitization with resulting erythroblastosis.
15. Cervical or soft tissue dystocia.
16. Fetal distress, i.e. fetal heart tones below 100, meconium stained fluid, irregular fetal heart tones.
17. Cesarean Section is demanded by the patient.

H. Use of oxytoxics in first and second stage of labor in instances other than when block anesthesia has been given which has interrupted the progress of labor. In this instance, a decision may be reached by the Anesthesiologist and the Obstetrician on the case, if the Obstetrician holds a rating of Class IV or higher, without outside consultation.
I. Malposition or presentation including breech in primipara and elderly primigravidas.
J. Toxemias.
K. Forcep operations above the outlet plane.
L. Version and extraction.
M. Iso-immunization due to Rh factor.
N. Destructive operations on the fetus.
O. Medical complications including hypertension, heart disease, pyelonephritis, etc.

4. Scrub suits and suitable conductive shoes are to be worn at all times in the delivery suite except in instances where a referring man wishes to examine a patient in the labor room. In this instance, the physician must be gowned, however street clothing may be worn. Entry to the labor room is to be made through the North door in this instance and the West door and drapes must be closed to the delivery room suite.
5. Vaginal examinations and amniotomies are to be allowed following at least one periprep and with suitably sterilized gloves, in the labor room, at the discretion of the attending physician. However, when it is deemed necessary, these are to be done in the delivery room under sterile conditions with the examiner suitably garbed.
    A. Other manipulative procedures are to be done in the delivery room under sterile conditions with the examiner suitably garbed.
6. No unauthorized personnel are to be admitted to the delivery room suite.
7. Newborns are to be with the mothers between 10:00 AM and 12:00 noon. For this reason, it is requested that rounds be made before 10:00 AM insofar as possible. If rounds must be made after 10:00 AM, the babies will be returned to the Nursery while the physician is in the mother's room.
8. All examinations of babies are to be made in the examination room adjoining the Nursery.

Appendix D

9. Patients are to be instructed by their physicians to bring at least the following items to the hospital:
   A. Shower cap.
   B. Two brassieres.
   C. Sanitary belt.
10. Initial post-partum orders are, in addition to the physician's usual orders, to include:
    A. Shower order.
    B. Circumcision order.
11. Unless specifically ordered otherwise, routine perineal care will follow the routine established by the Department. Camphorated oil and sitz baths are not considered routine care, and if deemed necessary by the physician in charge, must be specifically ordered.
12. All normal, healthy placentas, free of contamination, are to have the cord removed and discarded and the placentas are to be frozen for use by the Michigan Department of Health for pharmacologic purposes. The value of the placentas lies in the human blood which they contain. Post-partum blood and blood clots are equally valuable, so an effort should be made to salvage as much as possible. Only normal placentas and post-partum blood from apparently healthy women, which are free of urine and fecal contamination, are acceptable. The following types of placentas are to be rejected and disposed of:
    A. Those from toxic pregnancies and eclampsia.
    B. Those in which freezing has been delayed more than one hour.
    C. Placentas which are retained or macerated.
    D. Placentas contaminated with urine or feces.
    E. Those from abortions.
    F. Placentas delivered outside the maternity section.
13. A physician attempting procedures beyond his classification will be held to strict accounting by the Chairman and reprimanded by the O. B. Department. The extent of the reprimand is to be voted by the Department with its recommendations forwarded to the Credentials Committee and the Executive Committee.
14. The Department Chairman will be allowed to act as immediate representative for the Department to make decisions and to step in whenever he deems it wise.
15. Rules and Regulations and major decisions of the Department must be voted on and carried by two-thirds of the active Department members.
16. Rules and Regulations may be amended by two-thirds of the active members.
17. Narcotics, barbiturates and inhalation anesthesia (other than O_2) are not to be used upon women in active labor under thirty-eight (38) weeks gestation.
18. Episiotomies are advised with all premature and breech births, regardless of parity.
19. In cases of Rh negative mothers:
    A. Coombs test shall be done on cord blood.
    B. Type and Rh on infants blood.
    C. Hemoglobin on infant.
    D. Micro-serum bilirubin on infant.

20. Pediatric or Medical consultation will be strongly advised on infants under 3½ pounds, or 34 weeks gestation, and advised on infants under 4½ pounds or 37 weeks gestation.
21. Vaginal examination by the attending physician or anesthesist shall precede all conduction anesthesia on primigravids or abnormal presentations.
22. Post-partum mothers with temperatures of 100.4°F. or above for 48 hours shall be removed from the maternity floor.
23. Infectious (temperature of 100.4°F. or above) obstetrical cases shall not be admitted to the maternity floor.
    A. It is suggested that these cases be delivered in Delivery Room A and that this room then be thoroughly scrubbed down and not used for a period of 24 hours after completion of the delivery.
    B. That these infants be kept in the Isolation Nursery.
    C. That these mothers be placed in a suitable room on the Medical floor and not be attended by the Obstetrical personnel.
24. Visitors to the post-partum floor shall consist of the infant's father and grandparents.
25. An obstetrical patient in the labor room shall be visited by the husband only; or in the event that the husband is not available, the patient's mother. (Only one visitor.)
26. Oxytoxics shall be administered according to the Rules posted in the Obstetrical Department.

Appendix E

Ethical Issues in Surrogate Motherhood*

The American College of Obstetricians and Gynecologists recognizes that there is current interest in the reproductive alternative known as "surrogate motherhood." A surrogate mother may be defined as a woman who conceives and carries a pregnancy for another woman. In the most common example, a couple in which the husband is fertile but the wife is not contracts with a fertile woman for her to be inseminated with the husband's sperm. This woman carries the pregnancy until delivery, and then gives over the child to the contracting couple.

The obstetrician-gynecologist may be requested to participate in surrogate motherhood in a variety of ways, each of which raises ethical issues: (1) the provision of obstetric care to the pregnant surrogate, (2) participation in the process of insemination of the surrogate, (3) recruitment or screening of potential surrogate mothers, (4) counseling or referral of couples who could be candidates for such a procedure and (5) participation directly or indirectly with an organization that provides such services.

One way of examining the ethical issues involved in surrogate motherhood is to compare and contrast it with a procedure that is, in many ways, its logical counterpart: artificial insemination by donor (AID). AID has become a commonly accepted solution for problems of male infertility, although the ethical issues surrounding it are not completely resolved. The ethical issues surrounding surrogate motherhood, however, can and must be considered while its practice is relatively limited.

Issues Shared with Artificial Insemination by Donor

The wide acceptance of AID is based in part on the assumption that couples choosing this course have the same motives and aspirations in seeking to have a child as do fertile couples. Couples who seek surrogate motherhood because of female infertility probably have similar motives, also. Nonetheless, both AID and surrogate motherhood present ethical concerns:

1. Both depersonalize reproduction to some extent. This may affect the particular couple adversely, and with widespread use may lead to a change in the way society views childbearing.

---

*Approved by the American College of Obstetricians and Gynecologists May, 1983.

2. Both procedures may create stress in the relationship of the infertile couple. It is generally believed that this is not a serious problem in successful AID pregnancies; it may or may not be cause for concern in the surrogate mother situation.
3. Both the sperm donor and the surrogate mother risk undergoing psychological stress. Despite the wide experience with AID, this concern has not been investigated in sperm donors. Preliminary evidence suggests that a significant risk may exist for surrogate mothers.
4. Both procedures could be misused in programs for eugenic manipulation. However, both procedures may appropriately involve genetic screening for the purpose of matching surrogate phenotype with the potential parents and preventing the transmission of genetic diseases.
5. Both procedures raise concerns about adverse psychological effects on the children if their situation becomes known to them and others. There are no data that address this issue.
6. Both procedures raise questions regarding the maintenance of donor and surrogate anonymity. Legal questions such as legitimacy of the children also remain unanswered.

Concerns Not Shared with Artificial Insemination by Donor

The surrogate motherhood procedure is clearly distinguished from AID by the extent to which the surrogate herself must be personally involved. This raises several medical and ethical issues:

1. The surrogate mother undertakes two types of risks: physical and psychological. She exposes herself to potential long-term effects on her health and to all of the potential complications of pregnancy, including a remote chance of death. Psychological harm may occur when the child is separated from the surrogate. Although these kinds of risks are easily stated, they perhaps cannot be completely comprehended until experienced. Long-term psychological risks have not yet been evaluated.
2. It is not clear who should receive relevant medical information and participate in decisions affecting the welfare of the fetus and newborn. In general, the biological mother is thought to act in the best interests of the fetus, and so has the authority to make such decisions. In the instance of the surrogate mother, the motivation and the process of decision making raise complex questions. For example, may the surrogate make her own decisions about certain behaviors (such as whether to drink alcohol or smoke), or are these the decisions of the soon-to-be parents? Decisions about prenatal diagnostic and treatment procedures, and the management of the pregnancy, labor, delivery, and complications will also need to be made in concert with the physician, but it must be clarified whether they are to be made by the prospective parents or the surrogate mother.
3. The surrogate mother may change her mind and decide to have an elective abortion or to keep the child after delivery.
4. The surrogate may be confronted with a situation in which, for a variety of reasons, custody of the child returns to her by default.

Additional Concerns Raised by Financial Transactions

Most proposed agreements include financial arrangements that involve payment to the surrogate as well as to the individual or group responsible for the surrogate arrangement. These financial arrangements raise a number of ethical concerns.

1. The selling of infants is both illegal and morally objectionable. It is difficult to differentiate between payment for the service of carrying the child and payment for the child.
2. Payment to surrogates above and beyond reimbursement for expenses creates the potential for exploitation.
3. The physician who receives payment for recruiting or referring potential surrogates or parents is exploiting patients and may be in conflict of interest. The physician who invests in enterprises specializing in surrogate arrangements risks similar wrongdoing.

Special Situations

Beyond the situation of the infertile couple using the surrogate to obtain a desired child, there are other situations in which a surrogate might be employed. For example, the couple might want a child but prefer not to risk interruption of career plans, or may be unwilling to undergo the risks of pregnancy. Using a surrogate for the sake of convenience, rather than for infertility, raises a number of issues:

1. Depersonalization is increased.
2. A risk that could be borne personally is assigned to someone else.
3. The dedication of the couple to parenthood—and thereby their qualifications to rear children—is called into question.

A variety of other situations and combinations of roles in surrogate parenthood can be envisioned, each with a constellation of related problems.

Conclusions and Recommendations

The physician who participates in surrogate motherhood arrangements, provides fertility services or obstetric services for a surrogate, or provides counseling services should carefully examine all relevant issues, including legal, psychological, societal, medical, and ethical aspects. Simple, clear conclusions cannot be anticipated.

Significant ethical concerns exist even in the most uncomplicated situation involving an infertile married couple and no financial transactions. Additional concerns that result from the payment of fees and from special circumstances such as surrogate use for convenience or single parenting magnify the ethical complications.

Thus, while the decision to participate or not in the surrogate motherhood alternative is an individual one for each physician to make, the American College of Obstetricians and Gynecologists has significant reservations about this approach to parenthood and offers the following recommendations for the guidance of Fellows:

I. Initiation of Surrogate Arrangements
   A. When approached by a patient interested in surrogate motherhood, the physician should, as in all other aspects of medical care, be certain there is a full

discussion of ethical and medical risks, benefits and alternatives, many of which have been expressed in this paper.
- B. A physician may justifiably decline to participate in surrogate motherhood arrangements.
- C. If a physician decides to become involved in a surrogate motherhood arrangement, he or she should follow these guidelines:
    1. The physician should be assured that appropriate procedures are utilized to screen the contracting couple and the surrogate. Such screening may include appropriate fertility studies and genetic screening.
    2. The physician should receive only the usual compensation for obstetric and gynecologic services. Referral fees and other arrangements for financial gain beyond the usual fees for medical services are inappropriate.
    3. The physician should not participate in a surrogate program where the financial arrangements are likely to exploit any of the parties.

II. Care of Pregnant Surrogates
- A. When a woman seeks medical care for an established pregnancy, regardless of the method of conception, she should be cared for as any other obstetric patient or referred to a qualified physician who will provide that care.
- B. The surrogate mother should be considered the source of consent with respect to clinical intervention and management of the pregnancy. Confidentiality between the physician and patient should be maintained. If other parties, such as the adoptive parents, are to play a role in decision making, the parameters should be clearly delineated, with the agreement of the patient.

Appendix F

Sample Assault Victim Medical Report Form

Form A
Patient Interview Form

Please type or print all information clearly.
For explanation of each item, see corresponding number in associated protocol.

This report may be completed by any licensed or certified health professional.

1. Date of interview _____ 2. Time of interview _____

3. Patient name _____ 4. Medical file no. _____
   Last   First

5. Patient birth date _____ 6. Patient sex _____ 7. Phone _____

8. Patient address _____ Zip _____

Permission for interview, examination and release of information

Permission is hereby granted to the medical staff of:

9. Hospital/clinic/private doctor name _____

10. Address _____

    ☐ To perform a medical interview and a physical examination as may be necessary
      on the person of _____

    ☐ To release the results of this examination and laboratory specimens and clothing
      to the proper legal authorities.

11. Patient signature _____ 12. Date _____

13. Or parent/guardian signature _____ 14. Relation _____

15. Witness signature _____ 16. Date _____

16. Patient's description of assault (record in patient's words; include all spontaneous utterances):

17. Date of assault _____ 18. Time of assault _____

19. Note indication of pain in patient's own words:

20. Check pain and symptoms mentioned:

    _____ skeletal muscular pain   _____ headache   _____ tenesmus
    _____ abdominal pain   _____ bleeding   _____ dysuria
    _____ pelvic pain   _____ discharge   _____ other

21. Has there been recent treatment of any disorder?

    _____ No   _____ Yes   Describe _____

22. Has there been any cleansing since the assault?

    _____ No   _____ Yes   Describe _____

23. (Vaginal assault only) LNMP _____

24. (Vaginal assault only) Date of last previous coitus before assault _____

25. Additional remarks:

I understand that the law considers the examining licensed or certified health professional as an eyewitness in the body of events surrounding a potential crime. What a patient/victim says to medical staff may be admissible as an exception to the hearsay rule, and these statements may be important in determining the truth before a judge or jury. I agree to preserve these statements as part of this patient's history.

26. Interviewer signature _____

Appendix F

27. Interviewer name _____ 28. Title _____

29. (If known) termination date of this employment _____

30. Interviewer fluent in English _____ Yes _____ No

Form B
Patient Examination Form

Please type or print all information clearly.
For explanation of each item, see corresponding number in associated protocol.
This examination and report may be completed by any licensed or certified health professional. _____

31. Date of examination _____ 32. Time of examination _____

33. Patient name _____ 34. Medical file no. _____
          Last   First

35. Appearance of patient's clothing (check if yes):

   _____ Missing   _____ Soiled or muddy   _____ Leaves, grass embedded
   _____ Torn   _____ Damp or wet   _____ Other as described
   _____ Soiled   _____ Bloodstains   _____

36. Patient changed clothing between assault and arrival at examination?

   _____ Yes   _____ No

37. Itemize clothing placed in containers separately and tagged for evidence:

38. Describe presence of trauma to skin of entire body. Indicate location using chart. Describe exact appearance and size. Indicate possible source such as teeth, cigarette.

       | Patient Frontal View | | Patient Back View |

39. Itemize photos or X-rays of patient:

40. Describe external perineal or genito pelvic trauma:

| Female Anatomical Diagram | Male Anatomical Diagram |

41. Describe internal trauma (speculum and bimanual examination):

　　　　———— Lacerations present, describe:

42. Is there discharge?　　———— No　　———— Yes　　Describe:

43. Checklist of symptoms of <u>extreme</u> mental trauma:

☐ Patient seems extremely quiet, passive, withdrawn, unresponsive—shows little emotion at all.

☐ Patient says little or nothing; seems unable to talk.

☐ Patient cries loudly and continually in a hysterical fashion.

☐ Patient laughs, jokes with those around—incongruously lighthearted.

☐ Patient expresses fear that his/her body was broken, permanently damaged or changed in some way.

☐ Patient exhibits serious breaks with reality, e.g. sensory, auditory or visual hallucinations.

☐ Patient expresses fears of falling apart, going crazy, disappearing.

☐ Patient refuses to leave the facility.

☐ Patient expresses suicidal ideation.

☐ Other _____

44. Immediate laboratory examination of wet mount slide (list source, affected area and check result):

List Source Areas	Sperm Present	Sperm Absent	Sperm Motile	Sperm Nonmotile

45. Signature of legal authority receiving this information, clothing and the following specimens: _____

46. ☐ Air-dried cotton swabs—2 sets from affected area (list body sources)

47. ☐ Dry, unstained slides (list body sources)

48. ☐ Fibers from patient's body

49. ☐ Combing from patient's head

50. ☐ Combing from pubic area

51. ☐ 6–8 hair samples pulled from pubis

52. ☐ 12 strands patient's head hair pulled from different regions of head

53. ☐ Saliva sample: cotton cloth in patient's mouth and air dried

54. ☐ 4 drops of patient's blood dried on cotton cloth

I understand that the law considers the examining licensed or certified health professional as an eyewitness in the body of events surrounding a potential crime, and that I may be called to testify and be cross-examined about my findings in this examination.

55. Examining health professional signature _____

56. Examining health professional printed name _____

Title _____

588　　　　　　　　　　　　　　*Appendix F*

57. Supervising physician name, if any _____

58. (If known) termination date of this employment _____

59. Examiner fluent in English

   _____ Yes   _____ No

Form C
Patient Treatment Record

Please type or print all information clearly.
For explanation of each item, see corresponding number in associated protocol.

60. Date of treatment _____ 61. Time of treatment _____

62. Patient name _____ 63. Medical file no. _____
                       Last   First

64. Statement of patient's rights.

   1. You have the right to considerate and respectful care by doctors and nurses.

   2. You have the right to privacy and confidentiality for yourself and your medical records.

   3. You have the right to full information about treatment.

   4. You have the right to refuse or choose treatment offered, and to leave the location of medical service when you wish.

   5. You have the right to continued care and timely treatment of your future health problems related to this incident.

   Tests given to patient:

65. GC culture ___ Yes   ___ No   66. VDRL   ___ Yes   ___ No

67. Pap smear ___ Yes   ___ No   68. Pregnancy test ___ Yes   ___ No

69. Other information   ___ No   ___ Yes   Describe:

   Treatment given to patient:

70. VD prophylaxis   ___ No   ___ Yes   Describe:

71. Medication given:

72. Medication prescribed:

73. Other treatment given:

Future treatment planned:

74. Transfer to another medical facility. Name _____

75. Appointment in 6 weeks for repeat GC culture, VDRL, and pregnancy test:

Date _____ Time _____ Place _____

76. Referred for counseling, or introduced for follow-up to:

Appendix G

Medical History of the Sexual Assault Victim

1. What happened? What was the nature of the act (cunnilingus, fellatio, sodomy)? What was the frequency of the act (use patient's own words)?
2. When did the act occur—date, time? When and to whom was the first complaint made? What was the reason for any undue delay?
3. Was any clothing removed or disturbed; how and by whom?
4. Was any type of physical force or restraint used on the victim?
5. What positions were adopted during the act?
6. Was any pain experienced and where?
7. Was any injury inflicted upon the assailant (bites, kicks, fingernail scratches)?
8. Did the victim change clothing, wash or bathe any part of the body, urinate, defecate, or douche since the assault?
9. Where did the assault take place?
10. Was the victim a virgin?
11. What is the victim's marital status? Does the victim have children; if so, what are their ages?
12. What is the victim's menstrual history? Date of last period.
13. Date of last coitus before incident and identity of partner. Was a condom used? Did partner have a vasectomy? Did victim douche afterwards?
14. Did the assailant have an orgasm? Did he use a condom?
15. Is the victim using a contraceptive device? If so, what kind?
16. Has the victim had any recent genital disease, operations, or problems?

Appendix H

General Office Procedures

The physician who first sees the alleged rape victim must take the following actions:

1. Secure written consent from the patient, guardian, or next of kin for gynecologic examination; obtain photographs (if they are likely to reveal evidence); and release pertinent information and specimens to the authorities.
2. Notify the police and obtain their permission to examine the patient, or await the arrival of the police physician.
3. Obtain and record the history in the patient's own words. The sequence of events—that is, the time, place, and circumstances—must be included. Note whether the alleged victim is calm or agitated, confused (drugs, alcohol). Record whether the patient came directly to the hospital or whether she bathed or changed her clothing.
4. Obtain appropriate tests (see below).
5. Mark clothing for evidence.
6. Record findings, but do not issue even a tentative diagnosis lest it be erroneous or incomplete.
7. Treat disease and psychic trauma; prevent pregnancy; counsel the patient, especially regarding her legal rights (for example, filing charges); explain subsequent therapy and follow-up, as well as the prognosis.

Appendix I

Sample Patient Care Flow Chart

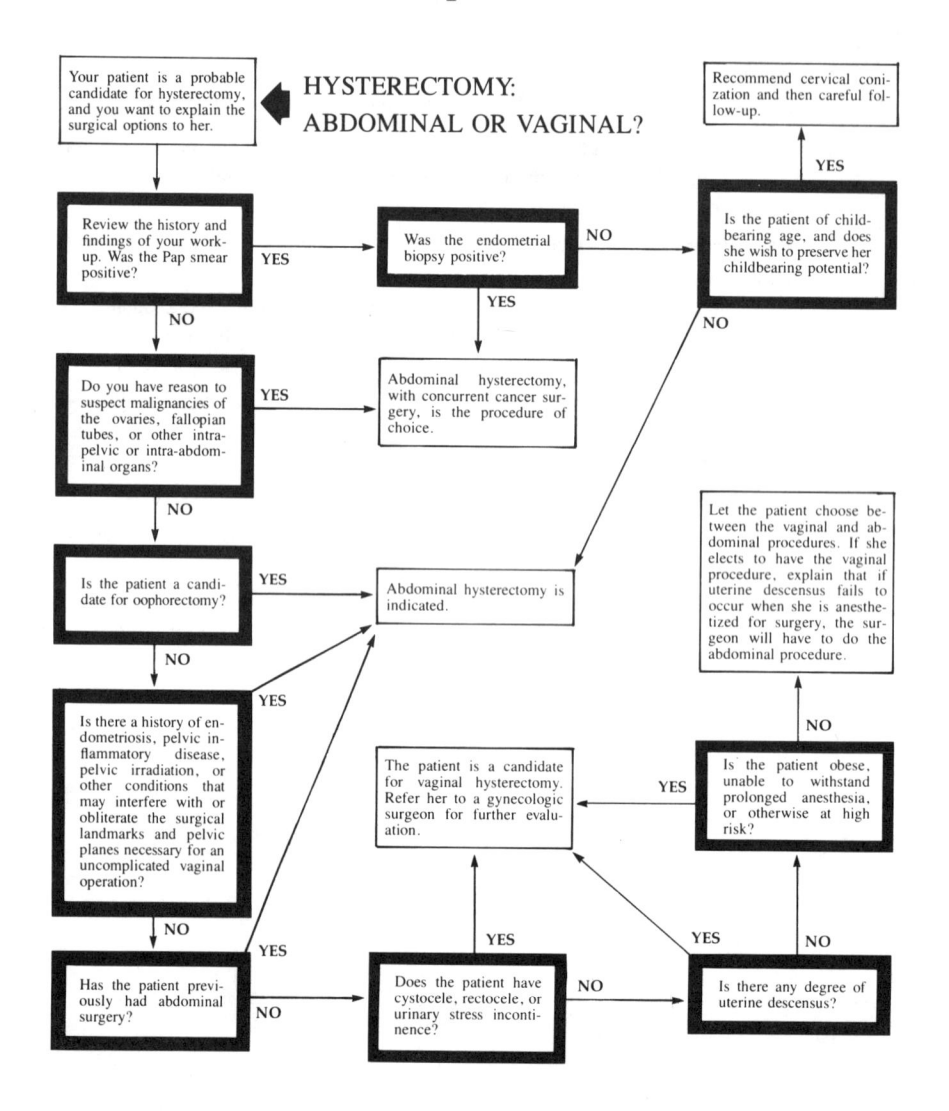

HYSTERECTOMY: ABDOMINAL OR VAGINAL?

- Your patient is a probable candidate for hysterectomy, and you want to explain the surgical options to her.

- Review the history and findings of your workup. Was the Pap smear positive?
  - YES → Was the endometrial biopsy positive?
    - YES → Abdominal hysterectomy, with concurrent cancer surgery, is the procedure of choice.
    - NO → Is the patient of childbearing age, and does she wish to preserve her childbearing potential?
      - YES → Recommend cervical conization and then careful follow-up.
      - NO → (to Abdominal hysterectomy is indicated.)
  - NO → Do you have reason to suspect malignancies of the ovaries, fallopian tubes, or other intra-pelvic or intra-abdominal organs?
    - YES → Is the patient a candidate for oophorectomy?
      - YES → Abdominal hysterectomy is indicated.
      - NO → (continue)
    - NO → Is there a history of endometriosis, pelvic inflammatory disease, pelvic irradiation, or other conditions that may interfere with or obliterate the surgical landmarks and pelvic planes necessary for an uncomplicated vaginal operation?
      - YES → Abdominal hysterectomy is indicated.
      - NO → Has the patient previously had abdominal surgery?
        - YES → Abdominal hysterectomy is indicated.
        - NO → Does the patient have cystocele, rectocele, or urinary stress incontinence?
          - YES → The patient is a candidate for vaginal hysterectomy. Refer her to a gynecologic surgeon for further evaluation.
          - NO → Is there any degree of uterine descensus?
            - YES → Is the patient obese, unable to withstand prolonged anesthesia, or otherwise at high risk?
              - YES → The patient is a candidate for vaginal hysterectomy. Refer her to a gynecologic surgeon for further evaluation.
              - NO → Let the patient choose between the vaginal and abdominal procedures. If she elects to have the vaginal procedure, explain that if uterine descensus fails to occur when she is anesthetized for surgery, the surgeon will have to do the abdominal procedure.

Glossary

ADMISSIBLE. Any evidence that may be properly received and considered in a legal proceeding.

ADMISSION (against interest). A statement made by one person to another in conflict with the interests of the person making the statement.

AFFIDAVIT. A written account of a declaration made under oath.

AGENCY. Any relation in which one person acts for or represents another by the latter's authority. *See* respondeat superior.

ALLOPATHY. A system of therapeutics in which diseases are treated by producing a condition incompatible with or antagonistic to the condition to be cured or alleviated. Licensed practitioners of this system generally hold M.D. degrees. *Compare with* osteopathy.

ANSWER. A defendant's written response to a complaint against him or her.

APPEAL. A petition to a higher court to review and correct or reverse an alleged error committed by a lower court.

APPELLANT. A party who appeals a case or issue from a lower court to a higher court.

APPELLATE COURT. A court to which a party may submit a petition to review the decision of a lower court, usually a trial court. Appellate courts include a court at an intermediate appellate level and a supreme court, the court of last resort in the legal system.

APPELLEE. A party against whom a case or issue is appealed from a lower to a higher court.

ARBITRATION. An alternative to a formal court hearing; the investigation and determination of a dispute between contending parties is made by one or more persons chosen by the parties and called arbitrators or referees.

BATTERY. The unauthorized and offensive touching of a person by another.

BLUE CROSS PLAN. An independently operated, nonprofit plan organized for the prepayment of hospital care.

BLUE SHIELD PLAN. An independently operated, nonprofit plan organized for the prepayment of physicians' services.

BURDEN OF PROOF. The duty or responsibility at trial to present sufficient evidence to establish the truth of a position or set of facts asserted by a party to be true.

CASE. A general term for an action, cause, suit, or controversy.

CASE LAW. Legal principles derived from judicial decisions. Case law differs from statutory law, which is derived from laws written and adopted by legislatures. Case law is sometimes referred to as "common law." *See* common law.

CAUSE OF ACTION. A claim or occurrence that gives rise to litigation.

CAVEAT EMPTOR (literally, "let the buyer beware"). This maxim summarizes the rule that a consumer must examine, judge, or test a potential purchase for himself or herself and take the risk that the quality of the item purchased is acceptable.

CERTIORARI *or* CERT (petition). A request made to an appellate (higher) court asking it to command a lower court to certify and send its records of a case to the higher court for purposes of appellate review.

CHALLENGE FOR CAUSE. A legal right allowing each party to challenge the selection of a juror because of juror bias.

CIRCUMSTANTIAL EVIDENCE. Any evidence of an indirect nature. *Compare with* direct evidence.

CIVIL LIABILITY. Being amenable to a suit or action brought by an individual to enforce a private right. *Compare with* criminal liability.

COMMON LAW. Unwritten law grounded in custom, natural justice, and reason, sanctioned by usage and adopted in judicial decisions. *See* case law.

COMPARATIVE NEGLIGENCE. A legal doctrine that allows the jury to compare the negligence of the alleged wrongdoer with the negligence of the plaintiff. For example, if the plaintiff is found to have contributed 20 percent to his or her injury, the jury's award to the plaintiff will be reduced by 20 percent. *Compare with* contributory negligence.

COMPLAINT. The first or initiatory pleading on the part of the plaintiff in a civil action.

CONFIDENTIAL COMMUNICATION. A statement made in confidence to a lawyer, physician, or clergyman with the implicit understanding that it shall remain a secret. Case law or statutes, or both, in most states recognize privileged or confidential communications.

CONSPIRACY. A combination of two or more persons formed for the purpose of committing, by their joint efforts, some unlawful act or for the purpose of using unlawful means for the commission of an act lawful in itself.

CONSTRUCTIVE NOTICE. Notice to a person not having received actual notice imputed by the occurrence of events that would give notice to a reasonable and prudent person observing those events.

CONTEMPT (of court). A willful disregard or disobedience of the court's orders, as well as conduct tending to bring the authority of the court and the administration of the law into disrepute. The court may issue money or penal penalties to persons found to be in contempt.

CONTRACT. An agreement that is enforceable by law between two or more parties, upon sufficient consideration, to do or not to do a certain thing.

CONTRIBUTION. The sharing of a loss or payment by one or more parties having a common interest of liability. Apart from statute, the general rule is that there can be

Glossary 595

no contribution between tort-feasors, it being against public policy to adjust equities between wrongdoers or to allow a person to base an action on his or her own wrongdoing.

CONTRIBUTORY NEGLIGENCE. Negligence on the part of the plaintiff which results in injury to his or her person or property and precludes the plaintiff from making a recovery against the alleged wrongdoer. *Compare with* comparative negligence.

CONVERSION. A wrongful exercise of dominion over the personal property of another: civil stealing.

COUNTERCLAIM. A cause of action existing in favor of the defendant against the plaintiff.

COURT. An organ of the judicial branch of government whose function is the application of laws to controversies brought before it and the public administration of justice.

CRIMINAL LIABILITY. Being amenable to prosecution for wrongs against a public right or interest. *Compare with* civil liability.

CUSTOM. A usage or practice of the people, which, by common adoption and acquiescence, and by long and unvarying habit, has become compulsory and has acquired the force of a law.

DECREE. A declaration of the court announcing the legal consequences of the facts found.

DEFAMATION. A communication to a third party which tends to diminish the esteem, respect, goodwill, or confidence in which a party is held or which excites adverse, derogatory, or unpleasant feelings or opinions against the party. *See* libel, slander.

DEFAULT JUDGMENT. A judgment entered after the defendant has failed to appear when properly served with a summons and complaint; also, same result but for a variety of additional reasons usually found in the court rules of the various states.

DEFENDANT. The party against whom relief or recovery is sought in a legal action or suit.

DEFENSIVE MEDICINE. The alteration of patterns of medical diagnosis to include more diagnostic tests and procedures than would normally be required for adequate diagnosis of a given condition. The practice of defensive medicine has arisen primarily in response to increased malpractice suits, allowing physicians to document fully the reasons for making a given diagnosis and prescribing a given treatment in the event a lawsuit should arise from the encounter with the patient.

DEMONSTRATIVE EVIDENCE. A type of evidence which consists of things—for example, weapons, photographs, wearing apparel—as distinguished from the assertion of a witness.

DEPOSITION. Sometimes incorrectly used as synonymous with oath, the term is specifically applicable to the testimony of witnesses taken in writing and under oath before some officer in answer to oral and written questions.

DIRECT EVIDENCE. Proof of facts by witnesses who saw acts done or heard words spoken. *Compare with* circumstantial evidence.

DIRECTED VERDICT. When there is no substantial evidence that would support a judgment for the one party, the court may, on motion of the other party, direct the jury to bring in a verdict for that other party. *Compare with* verdict.

DISSENTING OPINION. A minority opinion in the decision of a case.

DUE CARE. The degree of care that would be exercised by the ordinary careful person in the same circumstances.

DUE PROCESS. A provision of the Fourteenth Amendment to the United States Constitution stating that no one may be deprived of life, liberty, or property without "due process"—that is, a notice of a hearing, a hearing, and an opportunity to confront witnesses. Due process concepts also appear in American common law.

DUTY OF CARE. Every person owes a duty to conduct himself or herself as the average, reasonable person would conduct himself or herself in the same or similar circumstances. A professional's duty is to conduct himself or herself as a reasonable professional.

EMANCIPATED MINOR. One who is freed from the custody, control, and service of the parent prior to attaining the age of majority.

EMERGENCY PATIENTS. Acutely ill or injured patients requiring immediate care in a special treatment complex that may include an operating room, X-ray facility, and other services.

ENTRY OF JUDGMENT ON VERDICT. A procedural rule applied where a jury returns a verdict following its deliberations and a trial judge enters an order of judgment certifying the jury's findings.

ESTOPPEL. A state of affairs which arises when a person's own acts preclude him or her from stating anything to the contrary.

ETHICS. A moral-philosophic inquiry into the duties a member of a profession owes to the public, to colleagues, and to his or her patients or clients.

EVIDENCE. Proof presented at trial through witnesses, records, documents, concrete objects, and so on for the purpose of proving or defending an issue or case.

EXECUTOR (of estate). A person designated in a will to administer an estate.

EXEMPLARY DAMAGES. Damages awarded because of the malicious, fraudulent, or wanton character of the acts committed by the wrongdoer.

EXPERT OPINION. The testimony of an expert stating his or her opinion on a question of science, skill, or trade.

EXPRESS CONTRACT. An agreement between parties stated in distinct and explicit language either orally or in writing.

FELONY. A crime considered graver than those designated misdemeanors and that may result in a sentence of death or imprisonment in a penitentiary. *Compare with* misdemeanor.

FIDUCIARY. One holding a position of trust or confidence with respect to the money or property of another.

FRAUD. A general term embracing all the multifarious means that can be devised by human ingenuity and resorted to by one individual to gain an advantage over another by false suggestions or by suppression of the truth.

GARNISHMENT. A court-ordered process by which the plaintiff makes claim to property of the defendant in the hands of a third person for money owed by the third person to the defendant.

GOODWILL. The advantage a business has from its establishment or from the patronage of its customers, over and above the mere value of its property and capital.

GOVERNMENTAL IMMUNITY. An ancient common-law doctrine that a government is protected from suit by private persons unless it waives that immunity. The federal government and a number of states have waived the immunity by statute or court decisions.

GROSS NEGLIGENCE. The intentional failure to perform a manifest duty in reckless disregard of consequences to the life or property of another. *See* negligence.

GUARDIAN AD LITEM. A person appointed by the court to look after the interests of a minor or incompetent in litigation.

HEARSAY EVIDENCE. What the witness says he or she heard another person say. Hearsay evidence is generally inadmissible as evidence, although there are exceptions.

HYPOTHETICAL QUESTION. A combination of assumed or proved facts and circumstances presented as a question upon which the opinion of an expert is asked, to provide evidence in a trial.

IMPEACHMENT. The process of calling in question the veracity of a witness by showing through evidence or process that the witness is unworthy of belief.

INCOMPETENT. The legal status of one who is considered to be unable or unfit to manage his or her own affairs by reason of insanity, imbecility, or feeblemindedness.

INDICTMENT. A formal accusation based on legal testimony of a direct and positive character and the concurring judgment of at least 12 grand jurors that, upon the evidence presented to them, the defendant is guilty of a crime.

INFORMED CONSENT. The duty of a physician to disclose to a patient the risks involved in a proposed course of treatment or surgery as well as the optional or alternative courses of treatment available to the patient.

INJUNCTION. An order issued by a court requiring a person to whom it is directed to do or refrain from doing a particular act.

INSTRUCTION (by the court). The rules or principles of law which are applicable to the entire case or to some phase of it and which the jury is bound to accept and apply.

INTERROGATORIES. A series of written questions drawn up by one party asking an adversary for answers that may be used as evidence in a judicial proceeding.

JUDGMENT. The final word in a judicial controversy. It is entered in the record and is binding on the parties unless overturned or modified by appeal. *Compare with* verdict.

JUDGMENT BY DEFAULT. A judgment rendered against a party because of that party's failure to plead or defend his or her case or issue.

JUDGMENT NOTWITHSTANDING THE VERDICT (N.O.V.). A court reversal of a jury decision on its own motion or on the motion of the aggrieved party.

JUDICIAL NOTICE. Court recognition of facts so well known that the production of evidence would be unnecessary.

JURISDICTION. The authority provided by law to courts that allows them to hear and decide cases.

LIABILITY (in tort). The legal responsibility a wrongdoer assumes for doing a civil or private wrong that causes an injury.

LIBEL. Written or printed accusations against the character of a person which adversely affect that person's reputation. *Compare with* slander.

LIMITED LIABILITY. Owners or shareholders of a corporation are not held personally liable for the obligations of the corporation, except to the extent of their interest in the property of the corporation.

MALPRACTICE (medical). Any deviation from the accepted medical standard of care, due a given patient, which causes an injury.

MANDAMUS, WRIT OF. A command directing an inferior court, officer, corporation, or person to perform a particular duty.

MANSLAUGHTER. The unlawful killing of a human being without malice or intent.

MATERIAL (evidence). Evidence that is relevant to the matters in dispute or that has a legitimate and effective influence or bearing on the decision of the case.

MINOR. A person under the age of legal competency, which is currently 18 years for most purposes.

MISDEMEANOR. A crime that may result in short-term imprisonment or a fine or both. *Compare with* felony.

MOTION. An application made to the court to obtain a rule or order directing some act to be done in favor of the applicant.

NEGLIGENCE. The intentional or unintentional violation of a duty owed to another. *See* gross negligence.

OSTEOPATHY. A system of therapy based on the theory that the body provides its own disease remedies when it is in a normal structural relationship and has favorable environmental conditions and adequate nutrition. It emphasizes the importance of normal body mechanics and manipulative methods of detecting and correcting faulty structure. Licensed practitioners of this system generally hold D.O. degrees. *Compare with* allopathy.

PERJURY. The willful giving, under oath, of false testimony material to the issue in a judicial proceeding.

PLAINTIFF. A person who brings a legal action; the party who complains or sues in a personal action.

POLICE POWER. The power vested in the states and legislatures to make laws for the health, safety, and welfare of the people.

PRECEDENT. A principle of law stated in a case decision that serves as authority for subsequent decision-making in cases involving similar questions of fact or law. *Compare with* stare decisis.

PREPONDERANCE OF EVIDENCE. The greater weight of evidence or evidence that is more credible or convincing to the mind; that which accords best with probability and reason.

PRIMA FACIE CASE. A case established by sufficient evidence that it can be overthrown only by rebutting evidence offered by the other side.

PRIVILEGED COMMUNICATION. Communication between parties to a confidential relation such that the recipient can neither be legally compelled to disclose it as a witness nor voluntarily disclose it without the permission of the person making the disclosure. Privileged communications include communications between attorney and client, husband and wife, physician and patient, and so on.

PROFESSIONAL CORPORATION. An organization established as a corporation pursuant to state law and composed of professionals offering professional services.

PROXIMATE CAUSE. An act or omission which, in a natural sequence, unbroken by any intervening cause, produces an injury and without which the injury would not have occurred.

REGULATIONS. Rules that are promulgated by administrative agencies based on authority conferred in statutory enactments and that have the force of law.

RELEASE. A written contract by which some claim or interest is surrendered to another person, often in exchange for a consideration such as money.

RELEVANT (evidence). Evidence that bears directly on the issue or fact in question and proves or has a tendency to prove the proposition alleged.

RES IPSA LOQUITUR (literally, "the matter speaks for itself"). An evidentiary presumption that a defendant is negligent because the instrumentality causing the plaintiff's injury was in the defendant's exclusive control and the injury was one that does not ordinarily happen in the absence of negligence.

RESPONDEAT SUPERIOR. The legal principle that an employer is vicariously liable for civil wrongs committed by employees within the course and scope of their employment. This is true whether or not the employer has the actual ability to control the employee's conduct.

SLANDER. Oral accusations against the character of a person which adversely affect that person's reputation. *Compare with* libel.

SOCIAL SECURITY ACT. A federal act originally enacted in 1935, it includes authority for Medicaid and Medicare programs, social services programs, and financial assistance to the aged, blind, disabled, and families in need of such assistance. See Titles IV-A, V, VI, XI, XVI, XVIII, XIX, XX of the Social Security Administration.

STARE DECISIS. The principle that the law by which we are governed should be fixed, definite, and known and that, when the law is declared by a court of jurisdiction competent to construe it, such declaration in the absence of palpable mistake or error is itself evidence of the law until changed by competent authority. *Compare with* precedent.

STATUTE. A law enacted by a legislature.

STATUTE OF LIMITATIONS. Legislative statutes and court decisions that define the period of time during which an action must be brought. The failure to bring an action within this period may bar the action.

STIPULATION. Any agreement made by the attorneys engaged on opposite sides of a case regarding any matter related to the case, proceedings, or trial.

STRICT LIABILITY. Liability imposed where certain types of accidents happen, irrespective of whether anyone was at fault. The policy of the law in these cases is that the injured party must be given redress, even though there is nothing legally or morally wrong in what the defendant did.

SUBPOENA. A writ or order directed to a person requiring that person's attendance at a particular time and place to testify. It may also require that the person bring to court any books, documents, or other things under his or her control, in which case it is known as a *subpoena duces tecum*.

SUBSTITUTED JUDGMENT RULE. A rule that authorizes the court to sit in the place of an incompetent in order to make a decision for the incompetent as the court believes the incompetent would if able to do so. *See* incompetent.

SUMMARY JUDGMENT. A procedural rule that allows an attorney to make a motion for a judgment in a case on the pleadings without the necessity of going to trial. If a court issues an order of this type, it is in essence saying that the case has no merit, regardless of what the pleadings say, and should not proceed any further on the trial court level.

SUMMONS. A writ directed to the sheriff or other proper officer requiring him or her to notify the person named that an action has been commenced against him or her in the court and that he or she is required to appear on a day named and answer the complaint.

TESTIMONY. The words heard from a witness under oath in court.

TOLL THE STATUTE. To stop the running of the statute of limitations.

TORT. A private or civil wrong or injury for which one sues for money damages.

TORT-FEASOR. One who commits or is guilty of a tort. To be "joint tort-feasors," the parties must either act together in committing the wrong or, if they act independently of each other, their acts must unite in causing a single injury.

ULTRA VIRES (literally, "beyond the power"). A phrase used to refer to acts that are not within the power of the person or organization committing them. It is used most commonly in reference to unauthorized acts of corporations.

VERDICT. The definitive answer given by the jury to the court concerning the matters of fact presented to the jury for their deliberation and determination. *Compare with* judgment.

VICARIOUS LIABILITY. Civil liability to one for the tortious acts of others.

WAIVER. The voluntary relinquishing of a known right.

WILLFUL AND WANTON MISCONDUCT. The failure to exercise ordinary care to prevent injury to a person who is known to be within the range of one's dangerous act.

WRONGFUL DEATH (statutes). Statutory provisions that override the common-law rule that the death of a human being may not be complained of as an injury in a civil action. The provisions allow beneficiaries to sue for their loss.

Selected Bibliography

BARBER, HUGH R.K. *Manual of Gynecologic Oncology.* Philadelphia, Lippincott, 1980.
BEACHAM, DANIEL WINSTON, AND BEACHAM, WOODARD DAVIS. *Synopsis of Gynecology.* 10th ed. St. Louis, Mosby, 1982.
BENSON, RALPH C. *Handbook of Obstetrics & Gynecology.* 8th ed. Los Altos, California, Lange, 1983. In preparation. Revised triennially.
BENSON, RALPH C., ed. *Current Obstetric & Gynecologic Diagnosis & Treatment.* 4th ed. Los Altos, California, Lange, 1982. Revised biennially.
BURROW, GERARD N., AND FERRIS, THOMAS F. *Medical Complications During Pregnancy.* 2d ed. Philadelphia, Saunders, 1982.
CAVANAGH, DENIS [and others]. *Obstetric Emergencies.* 3d ed. Philadelphia, Harper & Row, 1982.
DANFORTH, DAVID N., ed. *Obstetrics and Gynecology.* 4th ed. Philadelphia, Harper & Row, 1982.
FRIEDMAN, EMANUEL A., ed. *Obstetrical Decision Making.* By the Staff of the Beth Israel Hospital, Boston. St. Louis, Mosby, 1982.
GUSBERG, S.B., AND FRICK, H.C., II. *Corscaden's Gynecologic Cancer.* 5th ed. Baltimore, Williams & Wilkins, 1978.
HUFFMAN, JOHN W. [and others]. *The Gynecology of Childhood and Adolescence.* 2d ed. Philadelphia, Saunders, 1981.
JONES, HOWARD W., AND JONES, GEORGEANNA S. *Novak's Textbook of Gynecology.* 10th ed. Baltimore, Williams & Wilkins, 1981.
MONIF, GILLES R.G. *Infectious Diseases in Obstetrics and Gynecology.* 2d ed. Philadelphia, Harper & Row, 1982.
NOVAK, EDMUND R., AND WOODRUFF, J. D. *Novak's Gynecologic and Obstetric Pathology with Clinical and Endocrine Relations.* 8th ed. Philadelphia, Saunders, 1979.
PRITCHARD, JACK A., AND MACDONALD, PAUL C. *Williams' Obstetrics.* 16th ed. Norwalk, Connecticut, Appleton-Century-Crofts, 1980.
QUILLIGAN, EDWARD J., AND ZUSPAN, FREDERICK. *Douglas-Stromme Operative Obstetrics.* 4th ed. Norwalk, Connecticut, Appleton-Century-Crofts, 1982.
RAYBURN, WILLIAM F., AND ZUSPAN, FREDERICK P., eds. *Drug Therapy in Obstetrics and Gynecology.* Norwalk, Connecticut, Appleton-Century-Crofts, 1982.
RIDLEY, JOHN H. *Gynecologic Surgery: Errors, Safeguards, Salvage.* 2d ed. Baltimore, Williams & Wilkins, 1981.

SANDBERG, EUGENE C. *Synopsis of Obstetrics.* 10th ed. St. Louis, Mosby, 1978. New ed. due 1984.

SPEROFF, LEON [and others]. *Clinical Gynecologic Endocrinology and Infertility.* 3d ed. Baltimore, Williams & Wilkins, 1983. In preparation.

WILLSON, J. ROBERT, AND CARRINGTON, ELSIE REID, *Obstetrics and Gynecology*, 6th ed. St. Louis, Mosby, 1979.

Index to Case Illustrations

Acosta v. City of New York, 380
Alexandridis v. Jewett, 79–80, 448–49
Alleman v. Seventh Ward General Hospital, 510–11
Anderson v. Moore, 545–47
Austin v. Regents of the University of California, 462

Baker v. Beebe, 39–42, 548–49
Baker v. St. Agnes Hospital, 123–24, 385–87
Beck v. Lovell, 89–90, 321–22, 445–46
Becker v. Schwartz, 341
Bergstreser v. Mitchell, 156
Berman v. Allan, 340–41
Berry v. G.D. Searle & Co., 116
Bertrand v. Aetna Casualty & Surety Co., 44–45
Bowers v. Garfield, 35
Brooks v. Serrano, 416–17
Brown v. Colm, 23–24
Bryant v. St. Paul Fire & Marine Insurance Co., 507–8
Buck v. Alton Memorial Hospital, 440–41
Bryne v. Boadle, 48

Cable v. Cazayou, 540–41
Capili v. Shott, 291–92
Carmon v. Dippold, 437–38
Carpenter v. Gauthier, 382–83
Chapman v. Carlson, 468–69
Charley v. Cameron, 436–37
Clapham v. Yanga, 357–58, 488
Coleman v. Garrison, 51
Console v. Nickov, 449–50

Couto v. Oms, 371–72
Cox v. Dela Cruz, 356–57

Davidson v. Shirley, 446–47, 503
Dazet v. Bass, 26–27
Deutsch v. Shein, 355–56
Dick v. Lewis, 422–23
Dickerson v. Hulsey, 518
Downs v. Sawtelle, 325–26
Dries v. Greger, 528–29
Dumer v. St. Michael's Hospital, 368–69

Eckert v. Smith, 429–30

Frantz v. San Luis Medical Clinic, 91–92
Freed v. Priore, 418

Garafola v. Maimonides Hospital of Brooklyn, 472
Gentry v. Department of Professional and Occupational Regulation, 202
Gildiner v. Thomas Jefferson University Hospital, 338–39
Glenn v. Prestegord, 377
Godard v. Ridgway, 315–16
Greenberg v. Bishop Clarkson Memorial Hospital, 478–79
Greenwood v. Harris, 25–26
Gridley v. Johnson, 355

Hall v. Musgrave, 415–16
Hamilton v. Hardy, 309–10

604   *Index to Case Illustrations*

Hanks v. Ranson, Swan and Burch, Ltd., 527
Hardin v. Farris, 155
Haywood v. Allen, 32, 324
Henry v. Bronx Lebanon Medical Center, 28–29, 425–27, 434–35
Hernandez v. United States, 490–91
Hiatt v. Groce, 404–6
Hill v. Ohio County, 15
Hogan v. Almand, 428–29
Hoglin v. Brown, 350–51
Holt v. Nelson, 427–28

Iverson v. Lancaster, 324–25

Jamison v. Lindsay, 531–32
Jarboe v. Harting, 45–46, 354, 382
Johns v. Gauthier, 518–19
Johnson v. Hunt, 384

Kansas Board of Healing Arts v. Seaholtz, 202
Kasper v. Schack, 141–42, 370–72
Katsetos v. Nolan, 469–70
Kauchick v. Williams, 442–43
Killebrew v. Johnson, 46–47, 316
Kleinman v. Armour, 491–92, 353–54
Klinger v. Henderson, 509–10
Klink v. G.D. Searle & Co., 308
Koehler v. Schwartz, 394

Lambert v. Michel, 488–89, 534–35
Lauro v. Travelers Insurance Co., 527
Levett v. Etkind, 147
Lhotka v. Larson, 452–53
Lindsey v. The Clinic for Women, 431–32
Lince v. Monson, 541–42
Lloyd v. Kull, 33–34
Long v. Johnson, 412–13
Longmire v. Hoey, 505
Los Alamos Medical Center v. Coe, 148
Louis v. Parchman, 515–16

Malinowski v. Zalzal, 450
Martineau v. Nelson, 145–46
Mayor v. Dowsett, 458–59
McEwen v. Ortho Pharmaceutical Corp., 114–15

McFadden v. Turner, 84–85
Miller v. Dore, 18–19
Morgan v. Aetna Casualty & Surety Co., 377–78
Murray v. Vandevander, 37

Naccash v. Burger, 98–99
Natanson v. Kline, 530–31
Nelson v. Marrus, 383
Northern Trust Co. v. Skokie Valley Community Hospital, 406–7, 476–77
Norton v. Hamilton, 17

Offut v. Sheehan, 504
O'Grady v. Wickman, 500
Olsen v. Molzen, 160

Park v. Chessin, 331
Parker v. St. Paul Fire & Marine Ins. Co., 36, 88, 409–10
Patrick v. Morin, 157
Patterson v. Van Wiel, 455–56
Peagram v. Sisco, 537–38
Pearson v. Boines, 152–53
Polonsky v. Union Hospital, 273
Poulin v. Zartman, 479–80
Pry v. Jones, 25
Pugh v. Swiontek, 362

Rawlings v. Harris, 154
Ray v. Wagner, 142–43, 535
Reilley v. Straub, 424–25
Renslow v. Mennonite Hospital, 12
Reynier v. Delta Women's Clinic, Inc., 395–96
Rice v. Rizk, 410, 432–33
Richardson v. Holmes, 513–15
Rieck v. Medical Protective Co., 358–59
Rogala v. Silva, 81
Rutherford v. Zearfoss, 439–40

Samii v. Baystate Medical Center, Inc., 90–91
Sanders v. United States, 443–44
Sard v. Hardy, 322–23
Scarf v. Troppi, 94–95
Schlesselman v. Gouge, 381

Index to Case Illustrations

Schreiber v. Cestari, 436
Schuler v. Berger, 473–74
Seeley v. Eaton, 512–13
Sesselman v. Muhlenberg Hospital, 85, 454
Siirila v. Barrios, 22
Sims v. Helms, 506
Slack v. Moorhead, 501–2
Smith v. Knowles, 373–74
Smith v. Shankman, 363
Speck v. Finegold, 398
Spidle v. Steward, 512, 551–52
Sponaugle v. Pre-Term, Inc., 316–17
Stack v. Wapner, 411–12
Steele v. St. Paul Fire & Marine Insurance Co., 489–90, 537
Stephenson v. Kaiser Foundation Hospitals, 352–53
Stewart v. Rudner, 78–79
Stills v. Gratton, 396–97
Stokes v. Haynes, 379
Swanson v. St. John's Lutheran Hospital, 281

Tatro v. Lueken, 53, 507
Teeters v. Currey, 152

Thor v. Boska, 179–80
Thornton v. Annest, 550–51
Tresemer v. Barke, 16–17, 317–18
Truan v. Smith, 525–26
Truman v. Thomas, 534
Turpin v. Sortini, 103–4

Variety Children's Hospital v. Osle,' 528
Vidrine v. Mayes, 14–15

Walker v. Pierce, 326
Wells v. Women's Hospital Foundation, 143–44
White v. Edison, 19–20
Widlitz v. Board of Regents, 204–5
Woodill v. Parke-Davis & Co., 119–20
Wooten v. Curry, 18

Young v. Group Health Cooperative of Puget Sound, 420

Subject Index

Abandonment, 17–21, 396; definition, 17; delayed treatment, 18; hospital liability, 20; physician withdrawal, 18–19; postpartum abandonment, 19–20. *See also* Physician-Patient Relationship, termination

Abortion, 38, 93, 220–28, 316, 357–59, 368, 392–98. *See also* Birth-Related Causes of Action; abandonment, 396; failure to abort, 398; funding restrictions, 227; indications, 393–94; informed consent, 220–21; notification or consent of spouse or parent, 221–23; post-abortion care, 395; regulation of abortion facilities, 224; reporting, 223–24; spontaneous abortion, 378–84, 427. *See also* Spontaneous Abortion; standard of care, 393

Abuse of Process, 181

Academy of Family Physicians, 256

Admission as Standard of Care. *See* Standard of Care

Agent. *See* Vicarious Liability

Alabama Law, 121, 191, 234

Alaska Law, 120, 180

Alcoholism and Pregnancy. *See* Substance Abuse During Pregnancy

Allopathic Standard of Care. *See* Standard of Care

Allopathy, 30

American Board of Medical Specialties, 250, 252

American Board of Obstetrics and Gynecology, 251, 252, 255

American College of Nurse-Midwives, 257, 260–61, 263

American College of Obstetricians and Gynecologists, 31, 254, 256, 301, 357

American College of Obstetricians and Gynecologists Standards: abortion, 393; admission data, 403; amniocentesis, 335; analgesia and anesthesia, 450–51; cancer screening, 524; drug use during pregnancy, 384; eclampsia, 369; extrauterine pregnancy, 359; fetal monitoring, 374; genetic counseling, 329; genetic screening, 333; gynecological evaluation, 485; hemorrhage, 467–71; induction of labor, 408; intrauterine devices, 311–13; oral contraceptives, 31, 305; parturition, 413–14; post-partum care, 475; pregnancy diagnosis, 347; pregnancy management, 363–64; rubella, 365–66; spontaneous abortion, 378; sterilization, 319–20; substance abuse during pregnancy, 388; surrogate parenting, 399; unwanted pregnancy, options of patients with, 393; venereal disease 542–43

American College of Radiologists, 357

American Hospital Association: patient's bill of rights, 34

American Medical Association, 177, 250, 256, 289, 389; guidelines for physician appearing in court. *See* Expert Witness

Amniocentesis, 93, 330, 335–41; consent and consent forms, 338–39; duty to inform of availability, 339–41; fetal risks, 337; indications, 336–37; liability, 338–39; maternal risks, 337; standard of care, 335–36

Amnion Rupture, 430–33

Amnionitis, 431–33

Amniotomy. *See* Induction of Labor

Analgesia. *See* Anesthesia

Anesthesia, 450–60; cerebral depressants, 451; cesarean section, 459; continuous

catheterization, 456; definition, 451; epidural analgesia, 455; general anesthesia, 459; nerve block techniques, 455-57; paracervical blocks, 454; principles of medical ethics, 13; regional analgesics, 454-59; regional anesthesia, 456; spinal anesthesia, 457; standard of care, 450-51
Answer: sample, 563-68. See also Pleadings
Apgar Score, 475-76
Arbitration, 9
Assault and Battery, 31
Assault Victim Medical Report Form: sample, 583
Association of American Medical Colleges, 195
Association of Professors of Gynecology and Obstetrics, 256
Assumption of Risk, 147-48

Battery. See Assault and Battery
Becker v. Schwartz, 341
Bennet v. Hymers, 108
Berman v. Allan, 341
Best Judgment Rule. See Defenses
Bill of Rights, patients', 34
Birth Certificate and Registration, See Reporting Requirements
Birth-Related Causes of Action, 92-105; abortion, 92; benefits rule, 94; emotional suffering, 101; informed consent, 97; warranty theory, 97; wrongful birth, 98-102; wrongful conception, 93-98; wrongful life, 102-5
Blood Banks, 122
Bonbrest v. Kotz, 104
Borrowed Servant Doctrine, 86-87
Breach of Duty. See Duty
Breast Cancer, 321, 524-31; clinical examination, 525-26; diagnostic techniques, 525; histopathologic diagnosis, 526-27; informed consent, 527-28; oral contraceptives and, 305; risks, 530-31; treatment alternatives, 529-30
Breech Presentation, 414-20; attitudes, 415; cesarean delivery, 419-20; definition, 414; diagnosis, 418-19; manipulation and traction, 417; maternal mortality, 415; neonatal death, 415; prolapsed cord presentation, 416; vaginal delivery, 419
Bull v. McCuskey, 181

Burden of Proof. See Evidence
Bureau of Narcotics and Dangerous Drugs, 212

California Law, 62, 109, 120, 165, 216, 231, 289, 318, 333, 340, 489; damages, 57-58; licensure, 191, 194-96, 205; midwife regulation, 261, 263-64; res ipsa loquitur, 508-10; wrongful life, 103, 105
Cancer, 499, 524-38; breast, 524-31; cervical, 533-38; ovarian, 531-32; standard of care, 524. See also specific headings
Cannabis. See Substance Abuse
Carey v. Population Service International, 229
CAT Scanner. See Computerized Axial Tomography (CAT) Scanner
Causation, 9, 42-56; as element of negligence, 9; burden of proof, 44; "but for" formula, 43; cause in fact, 43-46; proof of, 43-46; proximate cause, 43, 46-47; "substantial factor" formula, 43. See also Res Ipsa Loquitur
Centers for Disease Control, 367
Cerebral Depressants. See Anesthesia
Certification: nurse-midwives, 257; obstetricians and gynecologists, 251-54; revocation of diploma or certificate, 253-54; specialty division, 252-53
Cervical Cancer, 489-90, 533-38; consent, 537; International Federation of Gynecology and Obstetrics, 535-36; intraepithelial neoplasia, 533; malignancies, 533; Pap smear, 533-35; Richart's classification system, 533; treatment, 535-38
Cesarean Section, 98, 419, 422, 436, 438-47; anesthesia, 459-60; cesarean hysterectomy, 444-47; classic section, 441; definition, 438; indications for, 419, 422, 428, 439; low cervical section, 441-42; postpartum complications, 442-43; postpartum infections, 443, 471, 474
Collateral Estoppel, 158-59
Colorado Law, 55, 191, 309
Community Standard. See Standard of Care
Comparative Negligence, 145-46. See also Contributory Negligence
Complaint: sample, 557-62. See also Pleadings

Computerized Axial Tomography (CAT) Scanner, 76
Comstock Law, 228
Confidentiality, 5, 110, 177–78
Connecticut Law, 20, 109, 191
Conscience Clause, 280–82
Consent, 30–39, 231, 436; abortion, 38; amniocentesis, 338–39; assault and battery, 31; by minor, 38–39; by parents, 38–39; by spouse, 37; contractual in nature, 30; defined, 31; emergency, 32; form, 32, 34; hysterectomy, 502–04; implied, 31; informed, 37. *See also* Informed Consent; in sterilization procedures, 319–26; therapeutic privilege, 36–37; unplanned procedure, 33
Consortium, 60
Conspiracy of Silence, 22, 48
Constitution, United States, 197, 269–91; due process, 197, 220–21, 269, 270, 280, 288–91; equal protection, 233, 269, 280
Contempt of Court, 168
Continuing Medical Education, 9, 196, 254. *See also* Licensure
Continuing Treatment Doctrine. *See* Statute of Limitations
Contraception, 228–30, 305–28
Contraceptives: intrauterine devices, 311–19; oral contraceptives; 305–11. *See also* specific headings
Contracts, 5–6; 76–82; consent theory, 30; consideration, 80; damages, 78; exclusive contracts, 291–92; express, 77; implied, 77; statute of limitations, 78, 149–52
Contributory Negligence, 140–44; burden, 141; rejected as defense, 144. *See also* Comparative Negligence
Coombs' Test, 287
Coordinating Council on Medical Education, 256
Corporations, 271, 272
Council on Resident Education in Obstetrics and Gynecology, 256
Counseling. *See* Genetic Counseling
Countersuits, 181–82
Court-Appointed Expert. *See* Expert Witness
Cross-Examination. *See* Expert Witness

Dalkon Shield, 317, 318
Dalmane, 273

Damages, 9, 56–63, 100, 102, 105, 181; categories, 56–57; computation, 62; element of negligence, 10; emotional damages 58–59, 101–2; general damages, 56, 57–59; mitigation, 62–63; punitive damages, 17, 57, 61–62; purpose of, 57; special damages, 56, 59–61
Delivery, 413–50; amnion rupture, 430–33; breech presentation, 414–20; cesarean section, 438–47; dystocia, 420–27; episiotomy, 447–50; forceps delivery, 433–38; standard of care, 413–14; placental anomalies, 427–30. *See* Parturition. *See also* specific headings
Deep Pocket, 83
Defamation, 110–11, 181
Defenses, 140–61; assumption of risk, 147–48; best judgment, 29; comparative negligence, 145–46; contributory negligence, 140–44; release from liability agreements, 160–61; res judicata and collateral estoppel, 158–59; statute of limitations, 148–58
Defensive Medicine, 9
Delalutin, 127
Demerol, 363
Department of Health & Human Services (DHHS), 206–9, 213, 227, 231, 250, 281, 389
Department of Justice, 212
Department of the Treasury, 389
Depositions. *See* Discovery
Desoxyn, 204
Detail Men, 307
Diabetes, 307, 309, 321, 371, 394, 408
Diagnosis. *See* specific headings
Diethylstilbestrol (DES), 115, 120–21, 127–29, 387
Dilation and Curettage, 360, 516–19; complications, 517–19; definition, 516; indications, 517
Discharge. *See* Hospitals
Disciplinary Proceedings, 197–205; ex parte actions, 199; grounds, 200–205; hearing, 198; incompetence, 202; judicial review, 199; notice, 197–98; procedural aspects, 197; sanctions, 204–5
Disclosure: duty, 34–37; exclusions and exceptions, 35–36; therapeutic privilege, 36. *See also* Consent
Discovery, 166–69; depositions, 166; limitations under Federal Rules of Civil

Subject Index

Procedure, 167; physical examination, 169; production of documents and things, 168; protective orders, 169; purpose, 166; subpoena, 168; written interrogatories, 168
Discovery Rule. *See* Statute of Limitations
District of Columbia Law, 194, 211
Documents: production of. *See* Discovery
Doe v. Irwin, 230
Doe v. Pickett, 230
Dorlin v. Providence Hospital, 332
Down's Syndrome, 58, 60, 310, 331, 336, 340, 341
Drug Abuse During Pregnancy. *See* Substance Abuse During Pregnancy
Drug Manufacturer's Brochure as Standard of Care. *See* Standard of Care
Drugs, 209–13; Federal Controlled Substances Act, 211–12; generic equivalents, 212–13; license to dispense or prescribe, 210; Uniform Controlled Substance Act, 209–11; Uniform Narcotic Drug Act, 211. *See also* specific headings
Drugs: manufacturer's responsibilities and physician's responsibilities. *See* Products Liability
Due Process. *See* Constitution, United States
Duty: abandonment, 17; breach, 9, 39–42; defined, 10; disclosure, 34–37; as element of negligence, 9; of referral, 392; to fetus, 11; to patient, 12; to continue treatment, 16. *See also* Negligence
Dystocia, 420–27. *See also* Labor

Eclampsia. *See* Preeclampsia and Eclampsia
Ectopic Pregnancy. *See* Extrauterine Pregnancy
Education. *See* Licensure
Education Council for Foreign Medical Graduates, 194
Eisenstadt v. Baird, 228
Eli Lilly, 385
Emergency: consent, 32; defined, 33; duty to render services, 15; informed consent, 36. *See also* Hospitals
Endometriosis, 305, 504, 538–42; characteristics, 538–39; diagnosis, 539; hormonal therapy, 539; surgical treatment, 540–41; symptoms, 539
English Law, 48, 70
Episiotomy, 447–50, 471; complications, 449–50, 474; definition, 447; liability, 449–50

Equipment Manufacturer's Brochure as Standard of Care. *See* Standard of Care
Eugenic Sterilization. *See* Sterilization, nonelective
Evidence, 169–81; adverse witness, 176–77; burden of proof, 44; disciplinary hearings, 198; expert testimony, 11, 23–25, 45–46, 49, 170–74. *See also* Expert Witness; federal rules, 28, 167–76; hearsay, 179; medical records, 178–81; preponderance of, 198; sexual assault, 495–96, 497; textbooks, 27, 176
Exemplary Damages, 61
Expert Witness: American Medical Association guidelines for physician in court, 173; court-appointed, 174; cross-examination, 172; direct examination, 171; fees, 171; hypothetical questions, 172; opinion testimony 175–76; physician-patient privilege, 177–78; preparation for trial, 171; testimony regarding standard of care, 11, 22; qualifications, 23. *See also* Evidence and Witnesses
Extrauterine Pregnancy, 359–63; diagnosis, 360–61; liability, 362–63; incidence, 359; intrauterine device, 319; signs and symptoms, 359–60; simulations, 361; treatment, 361–62

False Imprisonment, 279
Family Planning Services and Population Research Act, 229
Fathers. *See* Natural Childbirth
Federal Comprehensive Drug Abuse Prevention and Control Act of 1970, 200, 201
Federal Controlled Substances Act. *See* Drugs
Federal Rules of Civil Procedure, 164, 165, 167, 172
Federal Rules of Evidence, 28; application to malpractice suits, 28
Federal Trade Commission, 256
Fetal Alcohol Syndrome, 108. *See also* Substance Abuse
Fetal Death, Reporting. *See* Reporting Requirements
Fetal Monitoring, 374–78; fetal death, 376–77; standard of care, 374; tests, 374–76; wrongful death, 378. *See also* Labor
Fetus, 11; condition of. *See* Fetal Monitoring; legal status, 105–8; research on. *See* Human and Fetal Research

Subject Index

Fiduciary Relationship, 275
Fitzgerald v. Porter Memorial Hospital, 462
Florida Law, 191, 196, 222, 225
Food & Drug Administration, 113, 115, 124, 128, 307, 314
Food, Drug & Cosmetic Act, 125
Forceps Delivery, 433–38; battery, 436; classifications, 433; improper use, 434; informed consent, 436–37; lack of consent, 435–37; maternal indication, 433
Foreign Object Rule, 156
Foreign-Trained Physician. *See* Licensure
Fourteenth Amendment, Due Process Clause. *See* Constitution, United States
Friedman Curve, 263
Fuchs, F., 336. *See also* Amniocentesis

Genetic Counseling, 92, 99, 103–4, 329–32; counseling centers, 332, liability, 331, 332; risk categories, 330–31; standard of care, 329
Genetic Screening, 332–35; confidentiality, 335; genetic anomalies, 333–34; liability, 334–35; phenylketonuria, 333–34; sickle-cell anemia, 333–34; standard of care, 332–33
Genital Herpes. *See* Pelvic Infections
Georgia Law, 215, 218, 264, 281, 287, 334
German Measles. *See* Rubella
Gonorrhea. *See* Pelvic Infections
Good Samaritan Law, 15–16; Indiana statute, 16
Griswold v. Connecticut, 228
Gynecological Examination, 309, 485, 497; sexual assault victims, 492–97; standard of care, 485–87
Gynecologist, 8; duties, 8
Gynecology; 8; defined, 8

Hamilton v. Hardy, 310
Health Care Financing Administration (HCFA), 208
Hearsay. *See* Evidence
Hemmorhage, 306, 427, 433, 434, 467–71, 516
Herpesvirus. *See* Pelvic Infections
Hill-Burton Program, 268, 270, 283
Hippocratic Oath, 13
Hirsch, Harold, 7

Hospitals: abortion and sterilization, 280–82; administration, 274–77; administrator; 275–76; admissions, 268, 270, 277; bylaws, 272–73; certificate of need program, 283–84; contracts, 291–92; corporations, 271–72; discharge, 279; due process for physicians, 288–91; emergencies, 277–79; governing board, 274–75; Hill-Burton Program, 268, 270; immunity, 269–71; JCAH. *See* Joint Commission on the Accreditation of Hospitals; liability, 269, 271; licensing of, 283; medical staff, 276–77, 288–90; nonprofit, 271; obstetrics and gynecologic services, 284–88; organization, 274–77; origin and development, 267–68; private hospitals, 269–71; privileges, 288–90; Professional Review Organizations (PRO). *See* Professional Review Organizations; public hospitals, 268–69; records. *See* Medical Records, liability arising from; regulation, 267–92; services and procedures, 277–82; state action, 269; state regulation, 286–88; types, 268–71; ultra vires, 272; utilization review committee, 279–80; vicarious liability. *See* Vicarious Liability
Human and Fetal Research, 213–15; consent, 213–14; National Commission for the Protection of Human Subjects of Biomedical and Behavioral Research, 213
Human Chorionic Gonadotropin (HCG), 349
Hyde Amendment, 227, 228
Hyde, Henry J., 227
Hypothetical Questions. *See* Expert Witness
Hypovolemic Shock, 468–70
Hysterectomy, 316, 320, 395, 497–516, 532, 536, 540, 551; abdominal, 499, 593; complications, 504–16; consent, 502–4; definition, 498; diagnosis, 500–501; fistulas, 504–5, 510; indications, 429, 498–99; res ipsa loquitur, 506–10; unnecessary hysterectomies, 500–501; vaginal, 499, 593

Illinois Law, 96, 110, 119–20, 122, 215, 287, 333; licensure, 191, 196, 197
Implied Consent. *See* Consent
Imputed Liability, *See* Vicarious Liability
Indiana Law, 16, 215, 216, 462

Induction of Labor, 407–13; amniotomy, 409–10; oxytocic agents, 408, 409, 410–13; standard of care, 408
Infections, 431–34, 471–75; amnionitis, 431–33; breast infection, 471; epidemic form, 472–73; pelvic infections. *See* Pelvic Infections; peritonitis, 473–74; postpartum uterine infection, 471; sepsis, 319, 471; surgical wounds, 474; urinary tract infection, 443, 471, 504
Informed Consent, 30, 34–39, 97–98, 307, 322–25, 436–37, 528, 537. *See also* Consent; burden of proof, 37; emergencies, 36; wrongful conception. *See also* Birth-Related Causes of Action
Intentional Tort. *See* Assault and Battery
International Federation of Gynecology and Obstetrics: carcinoma of cervix, 535–36
Interrogatories. *See* Discovery
Intrauterine Device (IUD), 121, 125, 127, 311–19, 547; contraindications, 311; pregnancy, 311–13; problems from use, 313; standard of care, 311–13
Intrauterine Growth Retarded Baby, 375, 417–18
In Vitro Fertilization, 105, 214

Joint Commission on the Accreditation of Hospitals (JCAH): anesthesia care, 285; emergencies, 277–78; hospital administration, 275–76; hospital governing boards, 274; hospital regulation, 270, 271, 272, 282–84; medical staff privileges rules, 269; requirements for affording physician's due process and equal protection, 288; standards for obstetric and gynecologic services, 284–86; utilization review requirements (1983), 569–70
Jones v. T.H., 229
Jury: role in determining damages, 62
Justus v. Atchison, 462–63

Kansas Law, 230
Karyotyping, 336
Kentucky Law, 16, 33, 215
Klink v. G.D. Searle & Co., 309

Labor, 403–7; definition, 403; dystocia, 420–27; fetal monitoring, 404–6; induction of, 407–13. *See also* Induction of Labor; standard of care, 402; stages of, 407–13
Lamaze Method. *See* Natural Childbirth
Lawsuits, Grounds for, 8
Lay Midwives. *See* Midwives
Leboyer Method. *See* Natural Childbirth
Liability: theories of, 6; release from. *See* Release from Liability Forms
Licensure, 190–205, 256; continuing medical education, 196; disciplinary proceedings, 197–205; education and training, 192–93; examinations, 193; foreign-trained physician, 194–95; nurse-midwives, 256–57, 261–63; personal qualifications, 193–94; reciprocity and endorsement, 195; relicensure, 196; requirements, 192–96; state, 190–205
Liaison Committee for Graduate Medical Education, 255
Limitation of Actions. *See* Statute of Limitations
Litigation: incidence of malpractice, 6
Locality Rule, 21
Louisiana Law, 37, 110, 215

Maine Law, 215, 221
Malpractice: countersuits, 181–82; crisis, 6, 9; defenses, 141–61; defined, 5; duty of physician, 10; history, 5–6; legal response, 9; regulation, 189
Marijuana. *See* Substance Abuse
Maryland Law, 191, 194
Massachusetts Law, 21, 191, 215, 224, 333
Maternal and Child Health Programs, 206, 209
Medicaid, 206, 209, 227, 228, 283
Medical Examiners, Board of, 195
Medical History. *See* Obstetrical Care
Medical Procedures, 7; average indemnities, 7; risk indices, 7; unplanned, 33
Medical Records: as evidence. *See* Evidence; hospital policies, 110; liability arising from, 108–11; ownership and possession, 108; patient's right to access, 109; physician's notes, 109; privacy, 110; psychiatric records, 110
Medical Textbook, 27, 176
Medicare, 202, 205, 206, 208, 209, 268, 270, 283
Mentally Deficient Patient, sterilization of, 233
Michigan Law, 6, 27, 78, 82, 94, 120, 168, 178, 182, 223, 226, 279, 289, 332; abortion regulation, 107, 223, 226, 280;

licensure, 191, 194, 196, 200, 203, 205; reporting requirements, 215, 216, 217
Midwives, 256–64; American College of Nurse-Midwives, 257, 260–61, 263; lay midwives, 263–64; nurse-midwife legislation, 261–63; table, 262
Minnesota Law, 28, 63, 231, 281
Minor: capacity to consent. See Consent
Mississippi Law, 109
Missouri Law, 221, 226, 474–75
Mitigating Damages, 62
Model Nonprofit Corporation Act, 271
Model State Administrative Procedures Act, 197
Monitoring. See Fetus
Montana Law, 221, 461
Montezuma, 267
Muscular Dystrophy, 330

Natcher, William, 206
National Association of Insurance Commissioners (NAIC), 6, 7
National Board of Medical Examiners. See Medical Examiners, Board of
National Commission for the Protection of Human Subjects of Biomedical Research. See Human and Fetal Research
National Conference of Commissioners of Uniform State Laws, 209
National Council on Alcoholism, 389
National Disease and Therapeutic Index, 544
National Health Planning and Resource Development Act, 283
National Institute on Drug Abuse, 390
National Sickle-Cell Anemia Control Act, 333
Natural Childbirth: father's participation, 460–61; hospital regulation of, 461–62; Lamaze method, 460–61; Leboyer method, 460–61
Nebraska Law, 215, 221, 473
Negligence: breach of duty, 9, 39–42; causation, 9, 42–47. See also Causation; claims of, 7; comparative negligence, 145–46; contributory negligence, 140–44; damages, 9, 56–63; duty, 9, 10–13; elements, 9–10; reasonable man standard, 10, 35
Nevada Law, 106, 181
New Hampshire Law, 107, 108, 212
New Jersey Law, 95, 109, 218, 263, 290; damages, 60, 62, 341; licensure, 191, 195, 196, 199; obstetrical hospital services, 286, 287; products liability, 120, 121, 122
New York Law, 30, 111, 191, 225, 229, 330, 334, 358, 386, 398; controlled substances, 211, 213; damages, 59, 60, 340, 341; products liability, 121, 124
New York Times, 318
Nonprofit Hospitals. See Hospitals
North Carolina Law, 233
North Dakota Law, 215, 500
Nurse-Midwives. See Midwives

Obstetrical Analgesia. See Anesthesia
Obstetrical Anesthesia. See Anesthesia
Obstetrical Care: physical examination, 364; regulation of hospital services, 284–88
Obstetrician: duties, 8
Obstetrics: defined, 8
Obstetrics and Gynecology, 254
Obstetrics and Gynecologic Services: department protocol, sample, 571–78. See also Hospitals
Office of Management and Budget, 206
Offsetting Damages, 62
Ohio Law, 196, 215, 223
Oklahoma Law, 46
Opinion Testimony. See Expert Witness
Opthalmia Neonatorum, 219
Oral Contraceptives, 121, 305–11, 387; adverse reactions to, 306–7, 310; conditions warranting observation, 309; contraindications, 305; discontinued use to become pregnant, 310; failure to prevent pregnancy, 306; indicated, 305; physician's liability in prescribing, 305; physician's warnings, 307; standard of care, 305
Oregon Law, 114
Ortho-Novum, 125
Osteopathic Standard of Care. See Standard of Care
Osteopathy, 30, 191-95
Ovarian Cancer, 531–32; diagnosis, 531; treatment, 532
Ovulen, 308, 309, 310
Oxytocic Agents: induction of labor, 408–13, 421. See also Induction of Labor; treatment of postpartum hemorrhage, 468–69

Package Insert as Standard of Care. See Standard of Care

Pap Smear, 307, 314, 489, 533-35. *See also* Cervical Cancer
Paracervical Block. *See* Anesthesia
Parturition, 413-50; anesthesia, 450-60; delivery, 413-50; labor, 403-13; natural childbirth, 460-63; standard of care, 413-14. *See also* specific headings for complications
Pelvic Infections, 311, 319, 539, 542-52; antibiotic therapy, 547-49, 550; genital herpes, 544-45; gonorrhea, 543-44, 547; standard of care, 542-43; surgical intervention, 549-52; syphilis, 388, 544; treatment, 547-51
Peritonitis. *See* Infections
Pennsylvania Law, 87, 120, 191
Phenylketonuria (PKU), 218, 333, 334
Physical Examination. *See* Gynecological Examination or Obstetrical Care
Physical Examination for Evidentiary Purposes. *See* Discovery
Physician-Patient Privilege, 177-78
Physician-Patient Relationship, 13; abandonment, 17; continuation of treatment, 16; emergencies, 15; express agreements, 14; formation, 13; mutual assent, 14; rapport, 8; termination, 20; withdrawal, 18. *See also* Abandonment; Good Samaritan Law
Physician's Desk Reference, 122, 307, 386
Pitocin. *See* Oxytocic Agents
Placental Anomalies, 427-30; abruptio placentae, 428; placenta increta, 429; placenta percreta, 429; placenta previa, 427
Planned Parenthood of Central Missouri v. Danforth, 107, 221, 232
Pleadings, 164-66; patient's complaint, 165; physician's answer, 165; sample answer, 563-68; sample complaint, 557-62
Postdelivery Care, 475-80; Apgar score, 475-76; resuscitation, 475-77; retrolental fibroplasia, 477-80; standard of care, 475
Postpartum Care, 19
Postpartum Complications: hemorrhage, 467-70; hypovolemic shock, 468-70; infection, 471-75; postdelivery care, 475-80. *See also* specific headings
Postpartum Infections. *See* Infections
Precis, 254
Preconception Counseling. *See* Genetic Counseling

Preeclampsia and Eclampsia, 369-74; 428; diagnosis, 371; treatment objectives, 373; symptoms, 369-70
Pregnancy: administration of drugs during, 311, 384-87; diagnosis, 347-59. *See also* Pregnancy Diagnosis; extrauterine, 359-63. *See also* extrauterine pregnancy; intrauterine devices in place, 311-13; management, 363-92. *See also* Pregnancy Management
Pregnancy Diagnosis, 311, 347-59; differentiating from other conditions, 351-57; incorrect diagnosis, 99, 354, 491, 501; signs, 348-49; standard of care, 347; symptoms, 347-48; tests, 349-59
Pregnancy Management, 363-92; administration of drugs, 384-87; clinical and laboratory tests, 364; fetal condition, 374-78. *See also* Fetal Condition; preeclampsia and eclampsia, 369-74. *See also* Preeclampsia and Eclampsia; rubella, 364-69. *See also* Rubella; spontaneous abortion, 378-84; standard of care, 363-64; substance abuse during pregnancy, 388-92. *See also* Substance Abuse
Pregnancy Tests. *See* Pregnancy Diagnosis
Principles of Medical Ethics, 13
Privacy: abortion, 220; contraception, 228-30; medical records, 110
Private Hospitals. *See* Hospitals
Production of Documents and Things. *See* Discovery
Products Liability, 111-29; adequacy of warnings, 124; blood banks, 122; defective condition of product, 118, 122; defendant as insurer of product safety, 117; devices, 126; disclaimers, 117; drugs, manufacturer's responsibilities, 123-25; drugs, physician's responsibilities, 125-26; duty to warn, 112-13, 124, 126; negligence as theory of recovery, 112; procedural aspects 127, 128; strict liability in tort, 118; warranty theory of liability, 115
Professional Incompetence, 202
Professional Organizations, 254-56; American Board of Obstetrics and Gynecology, 255; American College of Obstetricians and Gynecologists, 254, 256; Association of Professors of Gynecology and Obstetrics,

256; Coordinating Council of Medical Education, 256; Council on Resident Education in Obstetrics and Gynecology, 256; Residency Review Committee, 255; Structure and Functions of Obstetrics-Gynecology Organizations, 258–59
Professional Regulation. See Regulation
Professional Review Organizations (PRO), 189, 205–9, 284; provisions, 206–8; utilization and quality control peer review, 206
Professional Standards Review Organizations (PSRO) Act, 206, 283
Prolapse of Uterus, 499
Protective Orders, 169
Proximate Cause. See Causation
Psychiatric Records. See Medical Records, liability arising from
Public Health Services Act, 230
Public Hospitals. See Hospitals
Puerperium. See Postpartum Complications
Punitive Damages, 17, 61

Quadrigen, 115
Quality Control Peer Review. See Professional Review Organizations

Rape. See Sexual Assault
Ray v. Wagner, 490
Reasonable Man. See Negligence
Records. See Medical Records
Regulation: governmental, 189–234; hospitals, 286–88; professional review organization, 189; purpose, 189; source of regulations, 189; state licensure, 190–205. See also Licensure
Release from Liability Forms, 160–61; effect, 160; invalid form, example, 555–56; terms, 160; validity, 160
Relicensure, 196. See also Licensure
Reporting Requirements: abortion, 223–24; birth registration, 215–16; fetal death, 216–17; venereal disease, 219–20, 543
Residency Review Committee, 255
Res Ipsa Loquitur 25, 47–56, 506–10; burden of proof, 50; causation, 47–56; damages, 56; elements, 50; expert testimony, 25, 49;

mental and emotional distress, 57–59; multiple defendant cases, 49
Res Judicata, 158
Retrolental Fibroplasia, 477–80
Rights of Patients, 34
Riis, P., 336. See also Amniocentesis
Risk Factors, 7
Roe v. Wade, 92, 100, 106, 107, 222, 398
Royal College of Physicians and Surgeons in Canada, 251
Rubella, 103, 364–69; diagnosis, 365–66; immunization, 367–68; impact on fetus, 100, 366; standard of care, 365–66

Sexual Assault, 492–97; definition, 492–93, 537; examination of minors, 496–97; medical history, 494, 590; office procedures, 591; physical examination, 494; preserving evidence, 495–96; prevention of disease and pregnancy, 496–97; psychological trauma, 496; rape laws, 493
Sherman Antitrust Act, 291
Sickle-Cell Anemia, 333–34
Siverson v. Weber, 508–9
Social Security Act, 206, 228, 230, 283
South Dakota Law, 215
Specialist: See also certification; plaintiff's burden in recovery against, 22
Specialty Certification. See Certification
Specialty Standard. See Standard of Care, specialty standard
Spinal Anesthesia. See Anesthesia
Spontaneous Abortion, 378–84, 427; etiology, 378–79; standard of care, 378
Staff Privileges. See Hospitals
Standard of Care, 11, 21–30, 34–35; allopathy, 30; American College of Obstetricians and Gynecologists. See American College of Obstetricians and Gynecologists Standards; best judgment rule 29; community standard, 21; definition, 21; expert testimony, 22–25; locality rule, 21; manufacturer's brochure or package insert 28; medical textbook, 27; osteopathy, 30; school of medical thought, 30; sources of obstetrical and gynecological standards, 301; specialty standard, 11, 21, 22; statements or admissions, 26

Subject Index

Standard of Obstetric-Gynecologic Services, 254
State Action, 269
State Licensure. *See* Licensure
Statement, as Establishing Standard of Care. *See* Standard of Care
Statute of Limitations, 148–58, 324–25; by jurisdiction, table, 149; continuous treatment doctrine, 154; discovery rule, 152; foreign object rule, 156; fraudulent concealment, 154; in contract. *See* Contract Theory of Liability; legal disability affecting, 155; tolling, 154; wrongful death actions, 157
Sterilization, 93–94, 230–34, 319–26; consent of spouse, 321–22; failure rate, 320; government-funded elective sterilization, 230–31; indications, 320–21; informed consent, 322–24; methods employed, 320; nonelective (eugenic) sterilization, 233–34; standard of care, 319; state regulation of elective sterilization, 231–33; tubal ligation, 95, 319, 320
Strict Liability in Tort. *See* Products Liability
Subpoena. *See* Discovery
Substance Abuse During Pregnancy, 388–92; alcoholism, 108, 389–90; drug abuse, 390–92; duty of referral, 392; heroin addiction, 388, 391; marijuana, 390–91; methadone treatment, 391; negligent diagnosis, 392
Surrogate Parenting, 398–99; ethical issues, 579–82
Synthroid, 381
Syphilis. *See* Pelvic Infections

Tax Equity and Fiscal Responsibility Act, 206
Tay-Sach's Disease, 333, 334, 336, 338, 339
Talwin, 372
Technical Bulletin, of the American College of Obstetricians & Gynecologists, 254
Tennessee Law, 221
Testimony. *See* Evidence
Testing Requirements, 218–20
Texas Controlled Substances Act, 200, 201
Texas Law, 21, 30, 52, 61, 87, 196, 200, 201, 467
Therapeutic Privilege. *See* Disclosure, therapeutic privilege

Tolling. *See* Statute of Limitations
Tort. *See* Negligence
Toxemia. *See* Preeclampsia and Eclampsia
Treatment: duty to continue, 16
Truman v. Thomas, 489
Tubal Ligation. *See* Sterilization
Tubal Pregnancy. *See* Extrauterine Pregnancy

Ultra Vires. *See* Hospitals
Uniform Business Records Act, 179
Uniform Controlled Substances Act. *See* Drugs
Uniform Narcotic Drug Act. *See* Drugs
United States Supreme Court, 393
Unlawful Conduct, 202
Unprofessional Conduct, 200–02
Urinary Tract Infections, 443, 471, 504
Utah Law, 223, 229
Utilization and Quality Control Peer Review Organization, 206

Venereal Disease. *See* Pelvic Infections
Venereal Disease, Reporting. *See* Reporting Requirements
Vermont Law, 106
Vicarious Liability, 83–92; agent, 86; borrowed servant doctrine, 85; captain of the ship doctrine, 86–87; deep pocket, 83; elements, 83; hospitals, 83; liability of obstetrician, 453–54; liability of surgeon, 87

Wale v. Barnes, 435–36
Waltz, Jon R., 334
Warranty Theory of Liability, 97. *See also* Products Liability
Washington Law, 61, 105, 165, 212, 216, 308, 340
West Virginia Law, 120, 230
White, Edward, 7
Wisconsin Law, 27–28, 109, 125, 191, 358
Withdrawal by Physician, 18; *See also* Abandonment
Witnesses: adverse, 176. *See also* Expert Witness

Written Interrogatories. *See* Discovery
Wrongful Birth. *See* Birth-Related Causes of Action
Wrongful Conception. *See* Birth-Related Causes of Action
Wrongful Death, 107, 157; statutory period affecting actions. *See* Statute of Limitations

Wrongful Life. *See* Birth-Related Causes of Action
Wyoming Law, 315

X-ray Pelvimetry, 421–26

Ybarra v. Spangard, 54–55

About the Authors

KEITH S. FINEBERG, J.D., is of counsel to Charfoos, Christensen, Gilbert and Archer P.C., Detroit, Michigan, and is past senior attorney of research at ComLaw, Inc., a computer-assisted legal research service. He is past program director of the Michigan Medical Schools Council of Deans, Medical-Legal Project. Mr. Fineberg has also served as editor at the Lawyers Cooperative Publishing Company, writing legal reference material for attorney use. He has also practiced law as an associate with Sanders, Hester, Holly, Askin and Dye in Georgia and is a member of both the Georgia and Michigan bars. Mr. Fineberg is co-author of *The Law of Medical Practice in Michigan* and *Anesthesiology and the Law*.

J. DOUGLAS PETERS, J.D., is a partner in the law firm of Charfoos, Christensen, Gilbert and Archer, P.C., Detroit, Michigan, and an adjunct assistant professor of law and medicine at the University of Toledo College of Law and the Wayne State University School of Medicine. Mr. Peters has also served as Chairperson of the State Bar of Michigan Committee on Medicolegal Problems and is the author of numerous articles on the subject of law and medicine. He is co-author of *The Law of Medical Practice in Michigan, Anesthesiology and the Law* and the *Social Security Disability Claims Manual* and co-editor of *Legal and Ethical Aspects of Treating Critically and Terminally Ill Patients*.

J. ROBERT WILLSON, M.D., M.S., was graduated from The University of Michigan Medical School in 1937. He served as Professor and Chairman of the Department of Obstetrics and Gynecology at Temple University in Philadelphia from 1946 through 1963, and in 1964 he was appointed Chairman of the Department of Obstetrics and Gynecology at The University of Michigan Medical School. He is now Adjunct Professor of Obstetrics and Gynecology in the University of New Mexico School of Medicine. Dr. Willson is the senior author of *Obstetrics and Gynecology*, now in its seventh edition.

DONALD A. KROLL, M.D., Ph.D., was co-project director and medical director of the Michigan Medical Schools Council of Deans, Medical-Legal Project. He received his M.D. degree from The University of Michigan Medical School, and his doctorate in Pharmacology from The University of Michigan. Dr. Kroll is currently serving as a physician and an assistant professor in the Departments of Anesthesiology and Pharmacology at The University of Michigan Medical School. He is co-author of *The Law of Medical Practice in Michigan* and *Anesthesiology and the Law*.